CW01266507

The Life and Times of Jamyang Khyentse Chökyi Lodrö

The Life and Times of Jamyang Khyentse Chökyi Lodrö

The Great Biography by Dilgo Khyentse Rinpoche
and other stories

TRANSLATED UNDER THE GUIDANCE OF
Dzongsar Khyentse Rinpoche,
Jigme Khyentse Rinpoche, and Orgyen Tobgyal Rinpoche

BY
Drubgyud Tenzin Rinpoche and
Khenpo Sonam Phuntsok

EDITED BY
Janine Schulz

SHAMBHALA
BOULDER
2017

Cover photo: Jamyang Khyentse Chökyi Lodrö in Gangtok, Sikkim, in the late 1950s.
Source: Khyentse Labrang

Shambhala Publications, Inc.
4720 Walnut Street
Boulder, Colorado 80301
www.shambhala.com

English translation © 2017 by Dzongsar Jamyang Khyentse

The photograph on page 119 was originally published in *A Saint in Seattle* by David P. Jackson (Wisdom Publications, 2003).

All rights reserved. No part of this book may be reproduced in any form or by any means, electronic or mechanical, including photocopying, recording, or by any information storage and retrieval system, without permission in writing from the publisher.

9 8 7 6 5 4 3 2 1

First Edition
Printed in the United States of America

⊗This edition is printed on acid-free paper that meets the American National Standards Institute Z39.48 Standard.
♻ This book is printed on 30% postconsumer recycled paper. For more information please visit www.shambhala.com.

Distributed in the United States by Penguin Random House LLC and in Canada by Random House of Canada Ltd

Designed by Gopa & Ted2, Inc.

LIBRARY OF CONGRESS CATALOGING-IN-PUBLICATION DATA
Names: Rab-gsal-zla-ba, Dil-mgo Mkhyen-brtse, 1910–1991.
Title: The life and times of Jamyang Khyentse Chökyi Lodrö: the great biography by Dilgo Khyentse Rinpoche and other stories / Translated by Drubgyud Tenzin Rinpoche and Khenpo Sonam Phuntsok; Edited by Janine Schulz.
Description: First edition. | Boulder, Colorado: Shambhala, 2017. | "Under the guidance of Dzongsar Khyentse Rinpoche, Jigme Khyentse Rinpoche, and Orgyen Tobgyal Rinpoche." | Includes bibliographical references and index.
Identifiers: LCCN 2016029022 | ISBN 9781611803778 (hardback)
Subjects: LCSH: 'Jam-dbyangs Mkhyen-brtse Chos-kyi-blo-gros, 1893–1959. | Sa-skya-pa lamas—China—Tibet Autonomous Region—Biography. | BISAC: RELIGION / Buddhism / Tibetan.
Classification: LCC BQ966.A293 L55 2017 | DDC 294.3923092—dc23
LC record available at https://lccn.loc.gov/2016029022

Contents

Foreword	ix
Translators' Introduction	xvii
Introduction by Dzongsar Jamyang Khyentse Rinpoche	xxiii

Remembering Rinpoche by Orgyen Tobgyal Rinpoche   1

Introduction	3
1. Khyentse Chökyi Lodrö's Early Life	19
2. Katok Monastery	23
3. Dzongsar Monastery	29
4. Regent of Katok Monastery	39
5. The Founding of Khamje Shedra	49
6. The Early Years at Khyentse Labrang	55
7. Summer Camp	75
8. Commanding Spirits	83
9. Masters and Khenpos	91
10. Stories from Dzongsar	135
11. Stories from Khyentse Labrang	145
12. Consorts	157
13. Sacred Hidden Lands	171
14. The King of Yönru	177
15. Pilgrimage from Derge to Sikkim	181
16. Dzongsar after Khyentse Chökyi Lodrö Left for India	223

17. Sikkim   227
18. Pilgrimage to the Holy Places of India   237
19. The Last Months in Sikkim   247
20. Dilgo Khyentse Rinpoche   251

A Wondrous Grove of Wish-Fulfilling Trees:
The Biography of Jamyang Khyentse Chökyi Lodrö
by Kyabje Dilgo Khyentse Rinpoche   261

A BRIEF ACCOUNT OF THE WONDROUS GARLAND
OF REBIRTHS   271

THE GREAT BIOGRAPHY OF
JAMYANG KHYENTSE CHÖKYI LODRÖ   289

Part One: The Ordinary Biography   291

1. How Jamyang Khyentse Chökyi Lodrö manifested as a result of the aspirations and magical displays of his past incarnations and came to be enthroned as a supreme tulku.   292

2. How Jamyang Khyentse Chökyi Lodrö embraced the three trainings (precepts) that are the entrance to the Dharma.   306

3. How Jamyang Khyentse Chökyi Lodrö studied (hearing and contemplation) with supremely learnèd and accomplished teachers, and perfected his education.   313

4. How Jamyang Khyentse Chökyi Lodrö attained the signs of having accomplished the practice of the path by training his mind in the yoga of the two profound stages of meditation (kyerim and dzogrim).   358

5. How Jamyang Khyentse Chökyi Lodrö performed excellent activities for the benefit of the teachings and beings.   387

6. How Jamyang Khyentse Chökyi Lodrö spontaneously accomplished the accumulation of vast merit during the course of his main activities.   414

7. How Jamyang Khyentse Chökyi Lodrö dissolved his body into the dharmadhatu after successfully completing his last activity, plus supplementary explanations.   429

Part Two: The Special Explanation of the Extraordinary Biography 459

The Inner Biography: An Account of Jamyang Khyentse
Chökyi Lodrö's Inner Life 461

   (a) How Jamyang Khyentse Chökyi Lodrö became
a true holder of the teachings of the Nyingma school. 462

   (b) Jamyang Khyentse Chökyi Lodrö's visions and
experiences related to the Kadam lineage. 470

   (c) Concerning the Lamdre, the precious words
that have the four valid factors. 473

   (d) Jamyang Khyentse Chökyi Lodrö's visions and
experiences related to Marpa Kagyü. 478

   (e) Jamyang Khyentse Chökyi Lodrö's visions and
experiences related to the Shangpa Kagyü lineage, the
Golden Dharma of the scholar-siddha Khyungpo Naljor. 483

   (f) Jamyang Khyentse Chökyi Lodrö's visions and
experiences related to Shije and Chö. 484

   (g) Jamyang Khyentse Chökyi Lodrö's experiences
and visions related to the teachings on the six-branch
practice of vajrayoga, the profound meaning of Kalachakra,
the King of Nondual Tantras. 486

   (h) Jamyang Khyentse Chökyi Lodrö's visions
and experiences related to Orgyen Nyendrup. 488

A Brief Explanation of How Jamyang Khyentse Chökyi
Lodrö Received Authorizations for the Profound Terma
Teachings—An Addition to the Main Biography 509

The Secret Biography 523

Dispeller of the Darkness of Ignorance: A Letter to My
Students 529

Notes 541
Bibliography 557
Index 591

Foreword

There is a particularly revealing episode in Dilgo Khyentse Rinpoche's biography of his teacher, Jamyang Khyentse Chökyi Lodrö (1893–1959). It tells of the arrival of Chökyi Lodrö, in his fifteenth year, at Dzongsar Monastery, the home of his previous incarnation, Jamyang Khyentse Wangpo (1820–1892). His future residence, known as "The Garden of Immortality," was not large but had a special sanctity, for it was there that Khyentse Wangpo had remained throughout the latter part of his life, meditating, imparting instructions, and bestowing empowerments. As the young incarnation looked about the room, his teacher, Katok Situ (1880–1925), gestured towards Khyentse Wangpo's seat and then to a cushion he had placed beside it. "It would not be right," Situ told him, "for you to sit in the great Khyentse Wangpo's own seat just yet. That would be like a dog sleeping in the bed of a human being."

The seat itself was unadorned and unassuming, but it was effectively a throne—a symbol of Khyentse Wangpo's enduring presence and imposing authority. Simply to be recognized as his reincarnation, then, would not be sufficient: Chökyi Lodrö would still have to earn the right to occupy such prestigious, sacred space. That he did so—swiftly, and with such resounding success—should not blind us to the enormity of the challenge he first faced.

Jamyang Khyentse Wangpo was a visionary leader who guided and inspired an entire generation of influential followers. Together with Jamgön Kongtrul Lodrö Taye (1813–1899) and other close collaborators, he transformed religious life in the Kham region of eastern Tibet, initiating a nonsectarian, or Rime, movement, which Gene Smith called the "finest flower" of a nineteenth-century renaissance. Recognized as a minor incarnation in the Sakya school—one of its very first, as it was late in adopting the tulku system—Khyentse Wangpo studied with some 150 teachers from all traditions. In his youth, he traveled throughout Tibet, seeking and receiving as many rare, endangered teachings as he possibly could. Later, he arranged and oversaw the compilation of these and other teachings in vast literary collections, helping to ensure their survival. A prolific author in his own right, he is known today for his inspirational prayers, liturgies, and meditation manuals, as well as his encyclopedic commentaries and sweeping surveys of Tibet's religious history, sacred sites, and monastic institutions. His extensive "treasure" (*terma*) revelations, including those discovered in tandem with others, especially Chokgyur Dechen Lingpa (1829–1870), form the basis of popular rituals and led to his inclusion among the five sovereign treasure revealers of Tibet.

By the end of his life, Khyentse Wangpo had amassed scores of senior disciples from all traditions. And, following his parinirvana, no fewer than seven reincarnations were recognized—a clear sign of his immediate impact. This unprecedented number was partly a result of the master's leading students each identifying a tulku of their own. Understandably, the child chosen to remain at Dzongsar, Khyentse Wangpo's principal seat, was accorded special status. But the situation was complicated when, in 1908 (or 1909, according to some sources), the original Dzongsar incarnation, Jamyang Chökyi Wangpo, died suddenly while visiting Dzogchen Monastery.

It was this tragic turn of events that first brought Khyentse Chökyi Lodrö, who had originally been identified as the incarnation associated with the nearby Nyingma monastery of Katok, to Dzongsar. For some, the move would prove controversial, and Katok Situ apparently hesitated before he was eventually persuaded by his own cousin, Kalzang Dorje, who had been Khyentse Wangpo's treasurer. Ailing and close to death, Kalzang Dorje wrote to Katok Situ, expressing his fear that with their tulku gone and his own life almost at an end, the presence of Khyentse Wangpo at Dzongsar would soon be much diminished. By invoking their shared commitment (*samaya*) to their late teacher, he left Katok Situ with little choice but to agree. And so it was that Khyentse Chökyi Lodrö found himself facing the dual challenge of proving himself to be a worthy successor and having to do so as an outsider.

But prove himself he certainly did—and remarkably quickly too. The training that all the Khyentse incarnations received was thorough enough— it had to be—but Khyentse Chökyi Lodrö's was especially effective. The biography charts his remarkable rise to maturity, noting, in particular, the dedication, diligence, and humility with which he served, and later cared for, his aged tutor, Khenchen Thubten Rigdzin Gyatso. Almost as soon as he arrived at Dzongsar, he was ready to fulfill his role, and before too long, he literally took the place of his predecessor.

One of the main themes of Khyentse Chökyi Lodrö's *namtar*—the traditional term for a biography of a realized teacher or enlightened being, in which the focus is on his or her exemplary qualities and route to liberation—is how he followed and contributed to Khyentse Wangpo's original vision and ideals. Dilgo Khyentse tells us how, like his predecessor, Khyentse Chökyi Lodrö sought instruction from teachers of all traditions. And the staggeringly long lists of all that he received (and later passed on) testify to his abiding appreciation and limitless enthusiasm for all aspects of the Dharma. (They are also a valuable reminder of just what it meant to be a teacher in Tibet—all the more pertinent in an age when setting oneself up as a guru requires little more than a website and a flair for self-promotion.) In the accounts of Khyentse Chökyi Lodrö's visionary experiences too, just as with Khyentse Wangpo, we find mention of masters and deities from every form and lineage of Indian and Tibetan Buddhism. And even the lists of his many students testify not only to his great influence but also to how that influence transcended sectarian boundaries and extended even to kings and secular rulers.

The text by Dilgo Khyentse is notably similar to Jamgön Kongtrul's biography of Khyentse Wangpo, especially in its structure. It is divided, first of all, into two major sections, covering both the ordinary and extraordinary aspects of Khyentse Chökyi Lodrö's life. The "ordinary" biography is also referred to as the "outer," while the "extraordinary" section has "inner" and "secret" dimensions. This threefold division—into outer, inner, and secret—is a familiar feature of Tibetan biographical writing; it was explained by Jamgön Kongtrul as follows:

> The outer namtar concerns [actions] carried out in the common perception of ordinary beings to be trained. The inner namtar concerns the unique aspects of the master's own extraordinary spiritual experience. And the secret namtar concerns highly extraordinary aspects entirely beyond the scope of common people.

In Dilgo Khyentse's text, the outer, or ordinary, section is by far the longest. It is further divided into seven subtopics that, broadly speaking, cover

Khyentse Chökyi Lodrö's birth and recognition as a tulku; his taking of various vows and commitments; his study; his practice of meditation; his teaching and granting of transmissions; the accomplishment of various beneficial projects; and finally, his death (or *parinirvana*) and the ritual practices performed in connection with it. Although these might appear to be broadly chronological, they do not result in a straightforward narrative. Nor is it Dilgo Khyentse's aim to offer a dramatic or exhaustive report of events: there is no description of Khyentse Chökyi Lodrö's arduous journey across the Himalayas, for example. Instead, we find a particular life story recounted within a general framework, showing how Khyentse Chökyi Lodrö conformed to a timeless model, or archetype, of what it means to be a student and a teacher while still manifesting in a unique and timely manner appropriate to his situation and circumstances.

The inner section concentrates on Khyentse Chökyi Lodrö's experiences and visions related to the "eight great chariots of the practice lineage"— an important classification for Rime authors, which they borrowed from Trengpo Tertön Sherab Özer (1518–1584). Within this framework, and relying on Khyentse Chökyi Lodrö's own records, Dilgo Khyentse reveals the rich inner life that is more fully documented in the secret biography compiled by Khenpo Kunga Wangchuk (1921–2008). Still, the few examples that Dilgo Khyentse provides show how events and circumstances—even reading a text by a particular author—could trigger a visionary encounter. On a trip to view the dawn from the hills above Darjeeling, for example, Khyentse Chökyi Lodrö recalled that Wu Tai Shan, the famous resting place of the great Dzogchen master Vimalamitra, also lay to the east. And, overcome with intense devotion, he saw the master directly, resplendent in the light of the sun and gliding towards him on its rays.

In the biography's secret section, Dilgo Khyentse focuses on Khyentse Chökyi Lodrö's adoption of the tantric conduct known as the "activity that enhances realization" and his decision, as part of that conduct, to take a spiritual consort. Even though married teachers were relatively common in Tibet, especially in the Nyingma tradition, the fact that Khyentse Chökyi Lodrö was a master of *all* lineages and the principal incarnation of Khyentse Wangpo, who had remained celibate throughout his life, meant that his decision to marry would inevitably meet some resistance. To dispel any doubts or misgivings among his students, he wrote them a letter, which Dilgo Khyentse reproduces in full in the biography. But it would seem that, even after this message, disapproval lingered in some quarters—as Orgyen

Tobgyal Rinpoche makes clear. The majority of Khyentse Chökyi Lodrö's followers, however, celebrated the move in the hope that it would cause his health to improve and prolong his life. And in time, of course, his wife, Tsering Chödrön, was not only accepted but widely revered as a *dakini*, a female embodiment of enlightened wisdom and energy.

Throughout the biography, Dilgo Khyentse quotes Khyentse Chökyi Lodrö's own words, drawing upon his diaries, brief autobiography, and other sources. There are plenty of insights on offer here, as Dilgo Khyentse describes Khyentse Chökyi Lodrö's predilections, concerns, and regular routine, and notes the things of which he disapproved. At times, Dilgo Khyentse adds his own voice to these descriptions, addressing the reader directly, in order to highlight what he considers most important. A recurrent theme, perhaps unsurprisingly, is nonsectarianism.

Dilgo Khyentse makes it clear that the Rime movement did not end with the lives of its founders at the close of the nineteenth century but continued through the activity of Khyentse Chökyi Lodrö and others. Even in the biography's very first chapter, for example, after listing Khyentse Chökyi Lodrö's previous incarnations, he summarizes the lives of Jamgön Kongtrul, Chokgyur Dechen Lingpa, Ju Mipham (1846–1912), and other key figures, as if to set the scene for what follows. Nevertheless, the nature and activity of the nonsectarian movement also evolved as it proceeded from one generation to the next. While the original founders had been great compilers, producing monumental compendia that revitalized Buddhist practice, their successors were charged with transmitting these collections. And, at the same time, many among the second generation also sought to develop and improve monastic education. Of the various projects Khyentse Chökyi Lodrö initiated, for example, the establishment of a new scriptural college, or *shedra*, at Dzongsar was among the most far-reaching in its consequences. Khamje Shedra, as it was known, was completed in 1918, and soon contributed to a dramatic expansion of monastic education throughout eastern Tibet.

The first few decades of the twentieth century witnessed a remarkable proliferation of these colleges at monasteries belonging to the Nyingma, Sakya, and Kagyü orders. Critical in this regard was Shenpen Nangwa, better known as Khenpo Shenga (1871–1927), who founded several shedras and was appointed as the first head teacher at Khamje. A brilliant and influential scholar, he helped to create a nonsectarian curriculum based on the "thirteen major treatises" and his own commentaries upon them. In time, leading graduates of Khamje became celebrated teachers in their own right, many of them going on to found colleges of their own.

While Shenga helped to focus scholarly attention on Indian authors and their major texts, the new colleges also took a keen interest in the writings of Tibetan philosophers. At Nyingma centers, for example, there was an ever-greater reliance upon the commentaries of Jamgön Mipham, several of which had originally been composed at Khyentse Wangpo's behest. For Sakya institutions like Dzongsar, the most authoritative interpretations were those of Gorampa Sonam Senge (1429–1489), whose writings had been banned in Tibet for centuries. It was Jamyang Gyaltsen (1870–1940), one of Shenga's foremost students, who set about gathering and reprinting these works, which were deemed crucial to the revival of Sakya learning.

All this burgeoning activity soon provoked misgivings in some circles within the Gelugpa order, which had come to regard itself as the bastion of scholastic orthodoxy in Tibet. Among the most vocal critics was the charismatic Pabongkapa Dechen Nyingpo (1878–1941), who took exception to the republishing of Gorampa's works on account of their refutations of the views of Tsongkhapa Lobsang Drakpa (1357–1419), the Gelug founder. Pabongkapa even went so far as to dismiss the Rime ideal altogether and discouraged his many followers from studying with teachers from other schools. Staunch conservatism of this kind certainly threatened intersectarian harmony, but it was not the only danger. Even the newfound intellectual confidence that the study colleges helped to instill had the potential to inflame old rivalries and create dissension—and, in some cases, clearly did. The Rime movement had always sought a delicate balance: preserving and nurturing individual traditions while encouraging respect for them all. And this period of Tibetan history shows just how fragile a vision that was.

Khyentse Chökyi Lodrö regarded the establishment of Khamje as one of his greatest achievements and is said to have been especially delighted when he managed to secure Khenpo Shenga as its first head teacher. He was also supportive of efforts to reprint and make available Gorampa's writings, and he sent graduates of Khamje to teach as khenpos in other colleges throughout the region. When a new shrine room was built near his residence in Dzongsar, Khyentse Chökyi Lodrö specified that it should include statues of Mipham, Gorampa, and Tsongkhapa. And among his compositions, we find beautiful praises of the leading scholars of all traditions. In his actions and his writings then, Khyentse Chökyi Lodrö consistently remained above sectarian bias and prejudice. "The spirit of Rime," as Dilgo Khyentse puts it, "pervaded his entire outlook."

But this is not to say that he remained blissfully unaware of sectarian tensions. In fact, even though Khyentse Chökyi Lodrö regarded the persistence of such problems as a feature of the current "degenerate age," they troubled him deeply. On one occasion in particular, in 1955, he expressed "despair" at the state of Buddhism in Tibet. Before a small group of students, he lamented the deceitful character of some contemporary teachers. "Even those who consider themselves to be scholars," he said, "malign the Buddha's teachings and use the power of logic and quotations from sacred texts to support their own prejudices against other teaching traditions." Dilgo Khyentse reproduces this speech before describing Khyentse Chökyi Lodrö's departure from Dzongsar on the pilgrimage that would eventually lead him into exile. The implication is that his frustrations contributed to his decision to leave. By this time, Dilgo Khyentse tells us, Khyentse Chökyi Lodrö had accomplished all that he could and already foresaw the turbulent events that were about to unfold.

The biography of Khyentse Chökyi Lodrö was completed in the early 1960s—shortly after his death in Sikkim in 1959, and a time of upheaval and uncertainty for most Tibetans. For many of the book's earliest readers, adjusting to a new life in exile, it would have been a consoling, inspirational reminder of their beloved teacher and his exceptional qualities. But a namtar is always more than just a faithful record of an individual life, no matter how extraordinary; it conveys something broader too, as it outlines a path to liberation. Most explicitly, then, Dilgo Khyentse's text is about one great master's role, first as a student and then as a teacher, transcending sectarian prejudice and viewing all Buddhist traditions—and all phenomena—with the utmost purity of perception. At the same time, and more subtly, it is a guide for whoever wishes to follow his example.

Our ability to understand and appreciate the biography and its central message is greatly enhanced by Orgyen Tobgyal Rinpoche's wonderful histories, drawn from the rich oral tradition to which he is heir. Told with customary frankness, humor, and relish, these fascinating and colorful vignettes bring to life many of the less familiar characters in Dilgo Khyentse's biography and help to explain much that would otherwise remain unclear. We, the readers, owe him (and his formidable powers of recollection) our deepest gratitude. Above all, however, we must pay homage to Dzongsar Khyentse Rinpoche, who requested Orgyen Tobgyal Rinpoche to share his knowledge and who coordinated the considerable work that has gone into producing this marvelous volume. It is to be hoped that as a result, many more people will be touched by the exemplary life of Jamyang Khyentse Chökyi Lodrö—a truly nonsectarian master who not only lived up to but enhanced the reputation of Jamyang Khyentse Wangpo's hallowed throne and, in so doing, helped to shape Tibetan Buddhism as we know it today.

Adam Pearcey

Translators' Introduction

It's now been more than fifty years since Dilgo Khyentse Rinpoche fulfilled Khandro Tsering Chödrön's request to write the namtar of their belovèd teacher, Jamyang Khyentse Chökyi Lodrö. Since then, Khyentse Chökyi Lodrö's spiritual legacy has spread all over the world, to places he'd probably never even heard of. And so now, Dzongsar Khyentse Rinpoche said over lunch one day at his home in Bir, India, it's time to offer today's students the story of his life in their own languages, starting with English.

Among his many superlative qualities, Dilgo Khyentse Rinpoche was a famous and much admired writer; Khyentse Chökyi Lodrö himself described him as perhaps the greatest Tibetan writer of his generation. Certainly his close students believe that his achingly beautiful and profoundly erudite writing style sprang directly from the perfection of his realization. They all say the same thing: he wrote a great deal but never had to work at it. The words arose spontaneously, then cascaded from his lips or pen like a river in full flood. So the questions facing the translation team were, "How should the first English translation be approached?" and "Is it possible even to attempt to mirror Dilgo Khyentse Rinpoche's exquisite Tibetan in English?"

To help the team focus their efforts effectively, Dzongsar Khyentse Rinpoche asked the advice of two of his greatest friends, both of whom are pioneers in the art of translating Tibetan into modern languages: Jigme Khyentse Rinpoche and Tulku Pema Wangyal Rinpoche.

Concentrate on getting the meaning across, said Jigme Khyentse Rinpoche. Start by making sure that, however rough it looks in English, every single Tibetan word has been translated. Only once you're satisfied that you've fully translated the meaning of each and every word should you then polish the language. Ultimately, the text must sound as though it were originally written in English—don't leave it half-boiled. Use as many literal translations of the Tibetan as you can, but if being literal conveys the wrong meaning or makes the text unreadable or dull, change it. At the same time, try to remove as little as possible. But make sure the end result is good English.

In addition to offering advice about the practical act of translating the text, Pema Wangyal Rinpoche recommended that we pray to Dilgo Khyentse Rinpoche inseparable from Manjushri for inspiration, and then start work. He pointed out that the never-read books gathering dust on umpteen library shelves around the world were often written by scholars who didn't write from the inspiration of bodhichitta. And for this translation to be beneficial and readable, he said, it must be inspiring; to just grind out a text conceptually won't work. "What you need is inspiration, because it's inspiration that opens something up within you. Then you need the guts to dig the translations out of your mouths—to make a real effort, based on genuine renunciation and the courage to attempt to expose the meaning."

Pema Wangyal Rinpoche also recommended that we arouse bodhichitta before we started work, focus our attention as we translated or edited without falling victim to distraction, and then dedicate the merit towards the enlightenment of all sentient beings. In this way, he said, our work would become a spiritual practice, and however long the translation took to finish, ultimately it would help others.

Jigme Khyentse Rinpoche then turned to the issue of how to translate quotations from the tantras. He felt that the words should be set down quite literally, "just as they are," because there's no way of knowing if a "meaning" translation is correct or not. He explained that in Tibetan, tantric language is so wrapped up in poetic devices that even Tibetan readers can't understand it. Literate Tibetans might be able to read the individual words of the namtar, and some may even appreciate the rare grace of the language, but few are able to understand what it truly means—which is why Tibetans usually rely on the commentaries. Whatever the language, poetry by its very nature is enigmatic, so the English translation of a Tibetan verse is likely to be just as obscure as the original. The important thing, both Rinpoches agreed, is that the lyricism—the poetry—should be retained, even if it appears to obfuscate the meaning. If readers really want to know what the verse is about, they should ask their teachers to explain it to them.

Another element of the poetic tradition that Dilgo Khyentse Rinpoche's writing exemplified is the use of honorific and ornamental turns of phrase that elevate an extraordinary quality or event. In Tibetan these phrases are quite beautiful, but when translated word-for-word into English, they can lose their impact. To avoid confusing readers and to move the story along, we decided to simplify many of these more elaborate Tibetan contrivances. Therefore, "when the flower of his major and minor marks blossomed" has been translated as "when he was born." However, the team hasn't applied this method unilaterally; some such phrases have been incorporated as a way of honoring the original text, without, we hope, causing the translation to stagnate.

Based on all the advice we received, we remained as faithful to Khyentse Rinpoche's text as we could. When we came across passages we couldn't make sense of, we asked Dzongsar Khyentse Rinpoche, Orgyen Tobgyal Rinpoche, Jigme Khyentse Rinpoche, Tulku Pema Wangyal, or Khenpo Sonam Tashi for advice and help, and if no definitive solution could be found, Dzongsar Khyentse Rinpoche advised us to leave the text deliberately vague.

But it wasn't all confusion and bafflement; we also enjoyed some wonderfully illuminating moments of clarity. For example, Jigme Khyentse Rinpoche suggested that "an emanation of the boundless display of compassion" (Wyl. *thugs rje yas sprul*) could be translated as "the very manifestation of pure compassion," which not only was a beautiful and brilliant solution, it also encouraged us to allow our imaginations to soar a little.

Early on in the process, Dzongsar Khyentse Rinpoche took the trouble to adjust our rather pedestrian translation of the opening few pages:

> The marvelous and perfect example of your life, as rare as the
>   udumbara flower,
> Pervades throughout Jambudvipa like the light of the sun and
>   the moon.

"'Pervades'? It's more like 'spreads.' Is there a better word for *spread*?" he asked. "It's like this . . ." And he poured the water from his glass onto the table. "The water has 'spread,'" he said, "but the connotation is that it is effortless and unstoppable. Like a flood."

And so the lines have become

> The marvelous and immaculate example of your life, as rare as an
>   udumbara flower,
> Like sun and moon, floods Jambudvipa with a blaze of light.

The modern world is a practical one. To be sure we know exactly who we're talking about, we limit ourselves to using one name for one person. John Smith will always be John Smith, or John, or Mr. Smith. Tibetan literary style, however, is more creative, and great lamas are given dozens, if not hundreds, of names. It's a tradition that has its roots in Indian culture, but it has little to do with identifying characters in a story. For ancient Indians, the more names a person had, the more powerful and influential they were considered to be.

As a passionately dedicated Rime master, Dilgo Khyentse Rinpoche practiced every aspect of the Tibetan Buddhist tradition. This included trying to ensure that masters' lesser-known names were never forgotten by using them in his writings—both the formal names and their colloquial abbreviations. But in these degenerate times, this cultural habit has all but died out. If a friend mentioned having tea with the Duchess of Edinburgh, who among us would know she was talking about Queen Elizabeth II of England? In such a climate, the translation team decided not to use too many different versions of a master's name; and where more than one form of a name appears, we have relied on the context to clarify who's who.

You will not find a glossary at the end of this book; it is an intentional omission. In Tibetan, each term can have a number of different meanings, depending on the context and audience, which makes fixing on one easily digestible definition impossible. On the face of it, naming "five king tertöns" should be simple, but in practice, each lineage has its own version. There are also places where we've been deliberately obscure because the necessary explanation should be given to a student by a teacher, or because the explanation is so long that it would require another book. Your best source of information about Dharma terms and enumerations is, as always, your teacher. And these days many excellent online resources are freely available to which interested readers can turn for initial guidance, such as www.rigpawiki.org and http://rywiki.tsadra.org.

Tibetans don't divide their written texts into paragraphs, use headings, or format lists the way we do in English, so many of the headings and lists in this book are the creation of the English editors to make the text easier to follow.

The titles of books have been italicized throughout the text. As Dilgo Khyentse Rinpoche was writing for well-educated monks and lamas, he often used abbreviations his readers would have been expected to understand. For those of us who haven't received a Tibetan education, it's just confusing, which is why we have generally stuck to one title for each text. However, we weren't always able to establish precisely which book Dilgo Khyentse Rinpoche meant. For example, *Drolö from the Heart Practice* (*Tukdrup Drolö*, Wyl. *thugs sgrub gro lod*) could be one of many heart practices, but we didn't know which. We asked Dzongsar Khyentse Rinpoche to make an informed guess—who better, after all—but even Rinpoche felt it was unwise to commit his speculations to paper.

Also, Dilgo Khyentse Rinpoche often employed a literary device that's generally translated as "and so on." Once again, as he was writing for educated monks and practitioners, he didn't always complete a list or define a term or fully explain a point that his readers would have been expected to know. Instead, he wrote "and so on," which could mean that a fuller explanation exists, or that there are more items in a list, or simply "and so forth," "and others," or "et cetera." After a great deal of discussion and thought, we decided to remain as faithful as we could to Dilgo Khyentse Rinpoche's original text by using "and so on" throughout, which should be read to mean that there's something else to be known.

Without Dzongsar Khyentse Rinpoche's fearless wisdom, single-minded determination, and vivid, unfettered foresight, this translation would never have happened. He brought the team together, created the perfect circumstances in which to work, and made himself available to answer questions throughout the process. He then read every draft, and directed and fully supported us—even when his own life was so busy that he barely had time to take a breath. After ten years with this text, it has become clear to us that Dzongsar Khyentse Rinpoche is truly Jamyang Khyentse Chökyi Lodrö and Dilgo Khyentse in the flesh. No words of thanks for having been invited to participate in this translation could even come close to the depth of our appreciation for the opportunity he has given us to look at what being "buddha" truly means.

Dzongsar Khyentse Rinpoche also inspired other brilliant scholars and devoted students of Buddhadharma, particularly of the Khyentse lineage, to become involved in the translation of Khyentse Chökyi Lodrö's story, most notably Jigme Khyentse Rinpoche, Tulku Pema Wangyal Rinpoche, and Orgyen Tobgyal Rinpoche. We cannot thank these great masters enough for their generosity and patience, and for sharing their unrivaled scholarship and wisdom.

The translation team would also like to thank the many, many willing participants who have offered unstinting help and advice on every aspect of this book and much-needed practical support, including Sogyal Rinpoche, Khenpo Sonam Tashi, Tenzin Dorji, Pema Maya, Jing Rui, Patrick Gaffney, Philip Philippou, Adam Pearcey (Lotsawa House), Andreas Schulz, Rinzin Wangmo, Gyurme Avertin, Heinz Nowotny, Dr. Robert Mayer, Greg Forgues, Raji Ramanan, Prashant Varma, Wulstan Fletcher, Jenny Kane, Florence Koh, Kate Millar, Shechen Archives, Matthieu Ricard, everyone at Dzogchen Beara Retreat Centre, Shambhala Publications, Maggie Westhaver (Khyentse Archive), Pete Fry, Volker Dencks, Milamarpa (Dr. Liu), Lama Ngödrup, Laura Lopez, Tashi Tsering (Dharamsala), Ruth and Sherab Gyaltsen, Pema Wangyal, and Jiga Shenyentsang.

Drubgyud Tenzin Rinpoche
Khenpo Sonam Phuntsok
Janine Schulz
February 2016

Introduction by Dzongsar Jamyang Khyentse Rinpoche

THERE'S A TIBETAN saying that we human beings love to imitate other human beings and that the best imitators are usually the most capable people. It's based on the Tibetan belief that we can attain liberation by learning about and imitating the lives, characters, and manifestations of great beings. What's the reasoning behind this belief? Firstly, one of our great human qualities is that we are easier to influence than any other species—which may be why Buddhist texts emphasize just how precious our human body is. Secondly, for Tibetans, stories that aren't connected with the sublime are described as unbelievable stories (*drung*) or vague stories (*tam*), whereas a story that reveals the life of a great and sublime being is a *namtar*, "one that liberates." And this is why Tibetans believe that simply by learning about and mimicking great beings, we will be liberated.

The namtar you'll find in this book is about one of the greatest of all Tibetan Buddhist masters. He was so exceptional that a little more than fifty years after his death, it's already difficult to believe that such a being ever existed—although "believing" or "not believing" will depend entirely on the stability of our fickle human minds. Imagine, for example, what those living a thousand years from now will think of us and how we live. Our lives may seem ordinary and dull right now, but in a millennium, the stories that survive about our priorities and lifestyles will have passed into the realm of myth.

Of course, it's well known that what seems obvious to one person is entirely incomprehensible to another, and so it's no surprise that what makes perfect sense to a sublime being can be extremely puzzling to the limited minds of deluded beings like us. We are like fireflies, so convinced our own light shines the brightest that the sheer brilliance of the sun is impossible for us to grasp. But if we wish to follow and emulate the Prince of the Shakyas, we have no choice; we must learn to aspire to fathom the unfathomable.

The namtar of the extraordinary being presented in this book was written by another very great being, Kyabje Dilgo Khyentse Rinpoche. There are still many people alive today who met Kyabje Rinpoche and witnessed some of the events in his remarkable life. Yet the stories people tell about him have already become hard to believe. For example, to our ears, what he was able to accomplish in a single day sounds like an extract from a legend.

Have you ever wondered what one buddha might think or say about another? Or how they communicate? Or how one buddha might describe another? Of course, it's impossible for any of us to know what it's like to be a buddha—only a buddha can tell us that. But then again, a buddha wouldn't bother talking about such things. That kind of detail is useful only to people like us, who lack the equipment and power to fathom the unfathomable. And make no mistake: the meaning of *buddha* is completely unfathomable.

Khyentse Chökyi Lodrö and Kyabje Rinpoche were both genuinely sublime beings. This means we can discover a great deal about what one sublime being thinks about another simply by reading this namtar, but in the process we will also discover many, many new questions. For example, why is this so-called life story jam-packed with endless lists of teachings received and teachings given? Who were all these people—this cast of thousands of unknown lamas, deities, and dakinis? Why must the simplest activity be couched in such ornate terms and dressed up with so many superlatives? And why doesn't the story tell us more about Khyentse Chökyi Lodrö the man?

In the Vajrayana we are told we must consider our guru to be a buddha. But as none of us has ever seen a buddha, we don't know what *buddha* looks like, or even what *buddha* means. And while it's true that as we practice, the true meaning of *guru* will eventually become clear, most of us are too impatient to wait that long. So what can we do in the meantime? Read this namtar. It contains a perfect account of how a great master—in this case, Dilgo Khyentse Rinpoche—saw his guru, Khyentse Chökyi Lodrö, as the Buddha. And this aspect of the namtar alone makes each and every superlative and over-the-top construction absolutely priceless.

A traditional namtar lays out the entire path to enlightenment, and as this namtar was written by such an exceptional master, it is actually possible to attain enlightenment merely by reading it. If, though, you find yourself getting bored, if the extraneous details and unwarranted repetitions begin to grate, it's probably because your ability to fathom the unfathomable isn't functioning properly. Yet even something as mundane as a list of teachings received or given shows us exactly where both Khyentse Chökyi Lodrö's and Dilgo Khyentse Rinpoche's priorities lay.

But even if you don't care about liberation, if you are interested in human evolution, you'll find this namtar fascinating because it encapsulates everything that the nineteenth- and twentieth-century Tibetans valued most highly. It also shows us what the Tibetan version of a best seller looked like.

1893 was quite a year. In Scotland, Dundee Football Club was founded; in South Africa, the young Indian lawyer Mohandas Gandhi committed his first acts of civil disobedience; Pyotr Ilich Tchaikovsky died in St. Petersburg; the New York Stock Exchange crashed; and the United States Supreme Court declared the tomato to be a vegetable. It was also the year Khyentse Chökyi Lodrö was born in a tiny village in the far east of a country forbidden to foreigners, which lay concealed behind the most majestic and formidable of all mountain ranges.

1910 was another extraordinary year. The Thirteenth Dalai Lama fled from the Chinese to take refuge in British India; the Portuguese overthrew their monarchy to establish the First Portuguese Republic; Akira Kurosawa, the Japanese filmmaker, was born; Leo Tolstoy, the Russian novelist, died; the earth passed through the tail of Halley's Comet; and Kyabje Dilgo Khyentse Rinpoche was born.

Tibet, the Land of Snows, was the birthplace of both the author and the subject of this book. They both aspired to truly help all suffering beings, and their every action was dedicated towards keeping the blessings of all lineages alive as a way of ensuring the preservation and proliferation of the Buddha's teachings. Decades after they passed away, the fruit of their work continues to be practiced in Dharma centers in Paris, Berlin, New York, and all around the world. And those who previously lacked even a tenuous connection with Lord Buddha are now quite happy to rub shoulders with many of his ideas.

Reading the namtar of such a great being can help on many levels. Not least, it shows us that although our world is home to countless selfish, short-sighted scavengers, great compassionate visionaries continue to manifest, and there is still hope for humankind.

As the narrow-minded are unable even to approach the idea of the infinite, we need to be broad-minded and flexible. Sadly, though, most so-called modern people are lamentably narrow-minded. Lacking the capacity to believe even what's believable, modern minds are so fixed that they're incapable of accepting anything "incredible." For them, trying to grasp the principles of reincarnation and manifestation is like threading the open sky through the eye of a needle.

Even so, there are still a few whose willingness to experiment, store of accumulated merit, and quick wit mean that at the very least they don't reject the inconceivable. For them, the fact that the author of this biography, Dilgo Khyentse Rinpoche, and its subject, Jamyang Khyentse Chökyi Lodrö, were one and the same will be intriguing. But there are also people who, like the owl that grumbles when the sun shines, cannot accept that two people are in fact one. For them, all we can do is practice compassion.

Khyentse Chökyi Lodrö wrote in the commentary to his own guru yoga that the real guru is our own buddha nature; if we accumulate enough merit, he said, the reflection of our buddha nature will manifest as a human guru. If your linear, logical, but rather limited mind can chew on this almost nonsensical idea, you might begin to understand how several manifestations of a buddha can exist at the same time. And as they were essentially the same person, who better to describe the life of Khyentse Chökyi Lodrö than Dilgo Khyentse Rinpoche?

All his life, Orgyen Tobgyal Rinpoche has been collecting stories about Khyentse Chökyi Lodrö. He's never written any of them down, though, just stored them away in his elephant-like memory. So one winter in Bir, I spent several days torturing him for information. In fact, I refused to move from his sofa until he'd spilt every syllable he'd ever heard into my digital recorder. These are the stories that appear at the beginning of this book. And for those of you who prefer a donkey to a Ferrari—who are as interested in the "man" as you are in the "great master"—they may well be your best starting point.

Dzongsar Jamyang Khyentse Rinpoche
November 2015
East Bhutan

Remembering Rinpoche

Orgyen Tobgyal Rinpoche

Jamyang Khyentse Chökyi Lodrö in the Tsuglakhang
at the Palace Monastery in Gangtok, Sikkim, in the late 1950s
Source: Khyentse Labrang

Introduction

One day in the winter of 2010, the present Dzongsar Khyentse Rinpoche, Dzongsar Khyentse Thubten Chökyi Gyatso, burst into my house in Bir like a whirlwind and ordered me to tell him all the stories I'd ever heard about Jamyang Khyentse Chökyi Lodrö.

"We have translated the *Great Biography* into English," he said, "and want to publish it alongside a compilation of all the stories you know about Khyentse Chökyi Lodrö. So tell me *everything* you've ever heard, the good and the bad. And don't leave anything out."

Settling himself comfortably on my sofa, he switched on his recorder. "Now!"

The Sources of These Stories

First of all, I should explain where these stories come from.

I was very young when I first met and made a Dharma connection with Khyentse Chökyi Lodrö. My father, the Third Neten Chokling Pema Gyurme Gyatso, relied on Khyentse Chökyi Lodrö completely. For him, Rinpoche wasn't merely an extremely precious master, he was his main root guru. My mother, Tsewang Paldrön, felt the same, as did Lama Putse, Wangchen Dorje, and our entire household, including myself. Throughout my childhood, I always felt tremendous devotion for Rinpoche, and still do. Over the years, I have also come to admire many of his students, relatives, attendants, and family members. We have all become very close. When we get together, we almost always end up reminiscing about Rinpoche, so it was from his closest friends and companions that I learnt everything I know about Khyentse Chökyi Lodrö.[1] And for us, he was always "Rinpoche."

Dilgo Khyentse told me that Rinpoche once said, "I will be the first to go. As you will be the one who remains behind, it will be your responsibility

The Third Neten Chokling Rinpoche and his wife, Tsewang Paldron
Source: Orgyen Tobgyal Rinpoche

to write my biography." Rinpoche then opened his chest and took out a scroll of papers wrapped in red brocade. He appeared to want to hand it to Dilgo Khyentse, who was still reeling from the shock that Rinpoche might "be the first to go" and wouldn't accept it. Instead, Dilgo Khyentse began to tremble.

"These papers contain what little information there is about my unique life," said Rinpoche, continuing to proffer the scroll. But Dilgo Khyentse simply couldn't summon the courage to reach out and take it—something he regretted deeply in the years to come, as it was never offered again. He included an account of this incident in the *Great Biography*, which, as Rinpoche predicted, Dilgo Khyentse wrote after he passed away.

Much later, when my uncle Orgyen visited Dzongsar Labrang, he found a large bundle of papers written in many different hands, including Rinpoche's. I don't know if *all* Rinpoche's writings were gathered there, but I do know it included lists of dead people for whom Rinpoche had been asked to pray. Initially my family looked after the collection, then Pewar Tulku gave it to Khenpo Kunga Wangchuk, who read it thoroughly and made precise copies. Pewar Tulku then commissioned print blocks of the manuscript and published every word—it has since become known as the *Secret Biography*. We all studied it very carefully and noticed that several years appear to be missing, which must mean that either some events were not recorded, or the records were destroyed when Dzongsar Monastery and the labrang in Tibet were razed during the Chinese occupation.

Nothing I say here could paint a clearer picture of Rinpoche's life than the existing biographies, and frankly, there's no point in trying. From a modern standpoint, some of my stories may seem pointless, but a story is a story. And as the sutras and tantras tell us that remembering and meditating on our guru brings tremendous benefit, so I can't see how talking about all the different aspects of Rinpoche's life that have been preserved in our memories over the past fifty years could ever be described as a mistake.

Dzongsar Khyentse Thubten Chökyi Gyatso told me that I must not exaggerate or lie, but I have no reason to! Lies are usually told for good reasons or to help others. Apart from that, what point is there in lying? None at all. At the same time, I can't be absolutely certain that all my stories are completely exaggeration- and lie-free, just as I can't be absolutely certain that the "truth" recorded in traditional biographies hasn't been embellished in one way or another. Basically, the only person who can verify an eyewitness account is the eyewitness himself. So anything we hear second- or thirdhand always relies entirely on the truthfulness of the narrator. And as people love to retell a good story over and over again, I have no way of knowing if the stories I've heard were colored by the prejudices of those who retold them. But I must insist that it is not and never has been my intention to pass on lies. What would I have to gain by doing so?

Dilgo Khyentse

I first met Dilgo Khyentse in 1964 when I was twelve years old. From then on, I spent a few months with him every year until 1991, the year he passed into nirvana. Shechen Gyaltsab Gyurme Pema Namgyal was his extraordinary root guru, as it was he who introduced Dilgo Khyentse to the display of intrinsic awareness. Dzongsar Khyentse Chökyi Lodrö was his second main root teacher, and Dilgo Khyentse often spoke about him. Over the years, he told us a great deal about how Rinpoche did things and how he behaved. Dilgo Khyentse rarely said anything about Rinpoche unless he was specifically asked, but when someone showed an interest, he was more than willing to talk with them about Rinpoche, no matter who they were. But I don't think Dilgo Khyentse told these stories strictly for our benefit; it was more that he just loved talking about Rinpoche.

Dilgo Khyentse Rinpoche in a Lhasa photo studio
Source: Shechen Archives

The Third Neten Chokling

The same can be said of my father, the Third Neten Chokling. Once he felt comfortable enough with someone to speak candidly, the conversation would always be about Rinpoche. But apart from describing his immense devotion for and pure perception of Rinpoche and their extraordinary teacher-student relationship, I don't think all my father's stories can have been firsthand accounts, because he didn't live at Dzongsar for long enough to have witnessed everything he described.

The Third Neten Chokling Rinpoche
Source: Khyentse Labrang

Chakdzö Tsewang Paljor
Source: Sogyal Rinpoche's
private collection

Chakdzö Tsewang Paljor

As a young man, I went to Sikkim on three occasions. My first visit coincided with the passing of Gyaltön Tulku, and that was when I first met Chakdzö Tsewang Paljor. My father and I stayed in room 4 of the King of Sikkim's state guesthouse, where a man said to have been the private secretary of the previous Khyentse incarnation visited us almost every day. Most people, including former Labrang attendants, seemed a little wary of Tsewang Paljor, but not my father. So I had many opportunities to ask Chakdzö about Rinpoche. And I learnt so much that I met him again during both my subsequent visits.

Khandro Tsering Chödrön

Khandro had a unique personality. She was quite unlike anyone I have ever known, before or since—she was a real dakini. But she never cared much for those who professed immense devotion and respect for her. However purely they perceived her, however much they appeared to deserve her kindness

Khandro Tsering Chödrön
Source: Shechen Archives

and even special treatment, the truth was that they annoyed her, so she barely acknowledged their existence. With others, who to our eyes were far less worthy, she was exceptionally friendly and talked quite openly.

It's well known that she liked me. I could sit wherever I wanted when I was with her. I was even allowed to eat her leftover food, which she gave me herself. And when strangers weren't hanging around, she would share her secrets very generously.

I once stayed at the labrang in Sikkim for about four months and ate with Khandro daily. At ten o'clock every morning, she would bring me homemade sweet bread that she had made herself. The labrang attendants were getting on well back then and Tashi Namgyal was very close to Khandro. Sometimes on a Sunday, Appey Dorje and his sister would come to Gangtok to buy meat and Khandro would spend time with them. Often they were joined by Lama Rinchen Sherab, who was old and bent, and the late Lama Gönpo Tseten, then the five of them would all talk and sing and dance together. At that time I asked Khandro many questions about Rinpoche, and continued to question her during our several visits to Bodh Gaya. (We once spent about a month there together.) And it was from Khandro that I first heard many of these stories.

Appey Dorje (*left*) and Khandro Tsering Chödrön (*center*) with
Sherab Palden at the Palace Monastery in Gangtok, Sikkim
Source: Khyentse Labrang

Tashi Namgyal

Tashi Namgyal was a son of Drumo Tsang and became so intimate with my family that we almost thought of him as one of us. I tried to help him by giving him money, and by speaking up for him whenever necessary. We went to Kham together twice, and to Hong Kong and Taiwan on four or five occasions. He was a slow, relaxed kind of person, and when you gave him a cup of sweet tea to sip, the stories would just pour out of him—so much so that he wouldn't notice where day ended and night began. My attendants used to say that when I was with Tashi Namgyal, I would become so engrossed that I could hear nothing but his voice.

Lama Gönpo Tseten

The late Lama Gönpo Tseten didn't look like a lama, he looked like a liar. But he wasn't. He was a perfect Dharma practitioner. He had tremendous

Tashi Namgyal, attendant to Khyentse
Chökyi Lodrö
Source: Khyentse Labrang

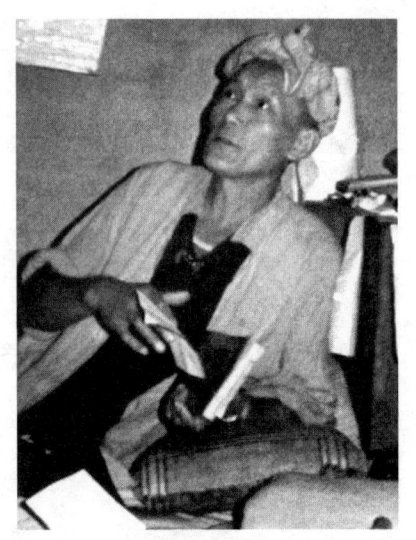

Lama Gönpo Tseten
Source: Sherab Gyaltsen

devotion for both Dezhung Tulku and Khyentse Chökyi Lodrö; it was the kind of devotion that sprang from a full recognition of their exceptional qualities. He was said to be an extremely learnèd student of philosophy, but I don't know how true that was. I can say that he knew *The Words of My Perfect Teacher*, some of the vital points of *Path and Fruition*, and a few Dzogchen pith instructions extremely well. He was also the kind of person who, at least to some extent, always practiced and meditated on every teaching he received.

We stayed with him in Sikkim for three weeks and I found he had a great deal to say about Rinpoche. So when Sherab Gyaltsen, Lama Gönpo Tseten, and I met at Kangyur Rinpoche's monastery in Darjeeling some time later, I asked Lama Gönpo Tseten again about Rinpoche and learnt even more.

Chokden

Chokden was an attendant during the latter part of Rinpoche's life. He talked at length with my father about Rinpoche during a trip we made to Tso Pema. That was when I first heard many of his stories. A few months after the enthronement of Yangsi Rinpoche Thubten Chökyi Gyatso (Dzongsar

Lama Chokden (Jamyang Lodrö Chokden), Khyentse Chökyi Lodrö's attendant and shrine master
Source: Khyentse Labrang

Rakong Sotra in Sikkim in the late 1960s
Source: Khyentse Labrang

Khyentse Rinpoche), Chokden stayed with us in Bir for three months and I was able to ask him about Rinpoche's life in more detail. But he was very proper and a little restrained and would not share stories openly in the way Tashi Namgyal and the others would.

Rakong Sotra

Rakong Sotra was the governor of Hor and worked for Yangsi Rinpoche (Dzongsar Khyentse Rinpoche) for a while. He had a very aristocratic nature and never uttered a single inappropriate word, so he didn't ever comment on Rinpoche's ordinary behavior and everyday activities.

Uncle Orgyen

Tibet opened up to visitors in the late 1980s, and that was when I was first able to visit Dzongsar—in fact, I went several times. It was also when I first met my uncle Orgyen and many other monks who had been close to Rinpoche.

Pewar Tulku

I also spent quite some time with Pewar Tulku, from whom I received numerous empowerments, transmissions, and instructions. During our conversations, Pewar Tulku spoke a great deal about Rinpoche. But although he described his own experiences in some detail, he had little to say about Rinpoche's nature, behavior, or the way he said his prayers and practiced. His narratives were like carvings in rock; every year he would repeat word-for-word what he had said the year before. Even his gestures and tone of voice were identical! I think he must have a perfect and very stable memory.

Khenpo Kunga Wangchuk

As soon as Khenpo Kunga Wangchuk arrived at Dzongsar Institute in Bir, we all went to pay our respects. We immediately felt great devotion for him because of his profound and unwavering devotion for Rinpoche—it was as if he had been blessed with natural devotion. We became extremely fond of him. But although we asked many questions specifically about Rinpoche, he always responded with detailed accounts of life at Khamje Shedra, its rules and regulations, and the vast amount of Sakyapa empowerments, transmissions, and instructions he had received, mainly from the *Compendium of*

Khenpo Kunga Wangchuk in 2004
Source: Philip Philippou

Tarthang Tulku, circa 1958
Source: Tarthang Tulku,
photographer unknown

Sadhanas. He didn't ever say much about Rinpoche's nature, behavior, or unique qualities.

Khenpo Rinchen

The person I was able to talk to most about Khyentse Chökyi Lodrö's life was Khenpo Rinchen, and he always answered with great precision. He also told me what Rinpoche had said to him when he was Rinpoche's attendant during their pilgrimage through Tibet. Khenpo even described how they venerated each and every body, speech, and mind representation they came across along the way. Recently I saw his biography, and it contains all the stories he told us back then.

Tarthang Tulku Gelek

As a young man, Tarthang Tulku had a strong feeling that it was important for him to study in Derge. So he asked Tarthang Choktrul Thubten Chökyi Dawa, his first root teacher, for his permission to go there.

"When I was young, I also visited Derge," replied Tarthang Choktrul. "I received both novice and full monk's ordination from Katok Situ, as well as many empowerments and transmissions. I also received the *Precious Treasury of Terma Teachings* from the previous Penor Rinpoche.

"After I left, I vowed I would return to Derge once more to visit my teachers. My greatest regret this lifetime is that I have been unable to fulfill that vow.

"The masters teaching in Derge today may not be as great as those I met when I was young. It's true that Khyentse and Kongtrul had already passed away, but many of their disciples, like Katok Situ and Shechen Gyaltsab, were still around. Who knows what today's lamas are like? But there must be some who are properly qualified from whom you can receive teachings. Anyway, as you clearly wish to make this journey—and it's a journey you should make at least once in your life—you have my permission to go."

Tarthang Tulku said he visited many teachers in Derge, but not one of them was as magnificent as Khyentse Chökyi Lodrö. He therefore decided to remain at Dzongsar,[2] where he received many empowerments and pith instructions. He and Rinpoche were very close, and he had a great many stories to tell. He told me that he even played games in Rinpoche's presence! He and I are also very close.

Gongna Tulku

Of all the people I spoke to, the person who best described the lives of the lamas, without any bias, prejudice, exaggeration, or denigration, was Gongna Tulku. Even his stories about their daily lives were flavored with Dharma and inspired tremendous devotion in the minds of his listeners. I met him many times. Actually, when you saw him in the flesh, you didn't immediately feel much devotion for him. Nevertheless, we were close friends for many years, and I came to realize that he was a very learnèd scholar. No one can say whether or not he was spiritually accomplished, but he definitely held an extraordinarily pure lineage of empowerments, transmissions, and instructions. And more significantly, he had lived at Dzongsar in the presence of Khyentse Chökyi Lodrö for a very long time.

Those of us who revered Gongna Tulku helped and served him in many ways. He and I spent a lot of time together in Nepal and Sikkim. But I don't think I've remembered everything he told me. If only I'd written down every word that fell from his lips, we would now know far more about Rinpoche's life than can be found in the existing biographies.

From the left: Drayab Lama, Lama Kunga, Lama Chokden, Gonpo Tseten, Gongna Tulku, Khyentse Chökyi Lodrö, Kadro Tulku, Tashi Namgyal, Dosib Thubten, Drungyig Tsering
Source: Khyentse Labrang, photographer Radi Yeshe

Tsejor and Lopön Sonam Zangpo

An old lama called Tsejor from Riwoche, Nangchen, near Chokling Monastery in eastern Tibet, wrote a book about his life with Rinpoche, whom he served from the age of eighteen until he was sixty-four. It's well known in Derge that Tsejor had been Rinpoche's personal assistant for much of his life, right up until Rinpoche left for Lhasa.

I have been to Kham five times, and as Tsejor was still alive each time, I made a point of asking him about Khyentse Chökyi Lodrö's life and activities. Tsejor was a great storyteller, as was Dzongsar Khyentse Rinpoche's grandfather, Lopön Sonam Zangpo. Of all the beings who have walked this earth under the vast expanse of the sheltering sky, no one could tell a story as sweetly as Tsejor or Lopön Sonam Zangpo, or conjure such peace in the minds of their listeners. They could both remember the exact dates of things that happened fifty years ago! So I asked them many questions.

Lama Sonam Zangpo, maternal grandfather of Dzongsar Khyentse Rinpoche
Source: Khyentse Labrang

What Qualifies Me to Speak about Jamyang Khyentse Chökyi Lodrö's Life?

Now I must explain what gives me the confidence to tell you about Khyentse Chökyi Lodrö's life. If I don't, those who think they were closer to him or imagine they know more about him than I do will think me arrogant for suggesting that I can tell them anything they don't already know. As Milarepa said to Rechungpa, "I am more deeply connected to Tiphu Sangak Dongpo than you. Vajrayogini has no better disciple than me." I will therefore start by putting what I have to say into context.

Generally speaking, once a lama has appeared in this world, he is expected to be of benefit to sentient beings. He must therefore teach, practice, and propagate a lineage of empowerments, transmissions, and instructions. By doing so, he will accomplish the three spheres of activity. Later, a biography will be written, describing in detail how he accomplished these three Dharma activities. However high or low the lama, regardless of whether or not he really did exhibit any signs of accomplishment, his traditional biography will always record the same events: his birth, renunciation, and education; the list of practice retreats he undertook in solitary places; having attained a degree of accomplishment, how he nurtured activities for the benefit of sentient beings by building monasteries and establishing study and retreat centers; how he initiated systems for the regular performance of great sadhana practices and sacred ritual dances; and how he propagated his lineage of empowerments and transmissions. As these are the only areas ever covered in a traditional biography, they all tell pretty much the same story.

Other aspects of a lama's life are completely ignored. So of the many biographies written about omniscient Longchenpa, for example, not one includes a description of his physical height and build. These days, everyone knows what contemporary lamas look like. If a lama has a short neck and fat belly, any statues made of him will also have a short neck and fat belly. But traditional biographies are not at all clear about a lama's physical characteristics, nor do they describe his personality or give any hint about how we should picture him. There's no good reason for this lack of detail. And personally, I don't believe that imagining the physical form of a lama is an unnecessary contemplation.

One exception was the manual that omniscient Chökyi Nangwa wrote about how to draw a refuge tree. It includes detailed guidelines about how to represent the physical form of the Drukpa Kagyü lamas, their style of dress, and even the expressions in their eyes. I think it's a very good approach.

In his manual about how to draw the empowerment images for the *General Essentialization of All the Wisdom of the Buddhas*, Minling Lochen included instructions about how all the masters, including Longchen Rabjam, should be drawn. But in those days, writers didn't acknowledge their sources, which means we can't now refer to the original oral instructions and reference texts that Minling Lochen had in mind. What he does do, though, is specify that Sangdak Drophukpa should be dark red and have a large goiter, and that only his head should be depicted. From this we can confidently infer that the manual is based on authentic sources. Apparently superficial, minor details are therefore not unimportant. The present system that dictates some lamas should have bald heads and others beards must have come from somewhere, but we have no idea where. And while we probably should continue to follow traditional guidelines, it would certainly be useful if we could also add more details about the appearance and personality of the masters.

Rabjampa Orgyen Chödrak, a disciple of Minling Terchen, did a tremendous amount of research on the great Fifth Dalai Lama and produced a detailed description of His Holiness's personality and behavior. The publication and distribution of this text was forbidden for many years, but when I read it today, I am struck by just how good it is. Orgyen Chödrak writes that when all the great Fifth Dalai Lama's officials, including his secretary, were away, he would send his attendants to bathe the horses in a pond behind the Potala Palace. And if his attendants weren't around at teatime, he would serve the tea with his own hands, naming each person as he measured their portion, then taking it back if that person was absent. If this is true, these details tell us that the great Fifth Dalai Lama, the sovereign spiritual and temporal leader of Tibet, was a remarkably meticulous person.

The descriptions of historical figures found in modern history books, like the one written by Gedün Chöphel or the recent book by Baba Phuntsok Wangyal, make it possible for readers to picture the faces of people they have never seen. I have long thought that if Tibetan biographers could write in a style that brings a person to life, the biographies of great masters would improve no end. Until now, though, no one has attempted it.

1. Khyentse Chökyi Lodrö's Early Life

His Birthplace

Dilgo Khyentse told me that although we know Jamyang Khyentse Chökyi Lodrö was born in the year of the snake, we cannot be certain of the exact date. I was puzzled by this and asked Dilgo Khyentse why Rinpoche's parents, who were educated people, hadn't kept a note of their son's date of birth. His father, said Dilgo Khyentse, was a very great yogi, but unpredictable; he didn't keep records of any kind. Rinpoche himself mentions in his autobiography in verse that his birthday is unknown:

> Since my parents were carefree,
> They kept no record
> Of planets, stars, ominous dreams, and so on.

What we do know is that he was born in Rekhe,[3] also known as Sa-ngen, the "Badlands." To be born in Rekhe was both a good and a bad thing: good because Rekhe is one of four knots of land in eastern Tibet; and bad because it was home to many thieves, dacoits, and liars. Rinpoche always said that the people of Rekhe were unimaginably stubborn.

The walls of the Rekhe valley were so steep and difficult to negotiate that if a calf was born there, then carried out across the dangerous ravine, once it had grown up it would be unable to find its way back. Strangers, therefore, had absolutely no hope of finding their way in. And from what I've heard, it's an extremely isolated and inhospitable place. Sometimes it's said to be part of Derge, sometimes not, and many stories are told about the attempted invasions and grizzly murders that happened when the nyerpa of Jagö Tsang was young.

Yet it was in Rekhe that Khyentse Chökyi Lodrö was born, and inevitably his habits were influenced by local customs. For example, throughout his life, he loved making tea the way he drank it as a boy and always kept a brick of Rekhe tea by his treasure chest, wrapped in a black, musk deer bag that dated back to the time of Jamyang Khyentse Wangpo. He used to break off a piece of the tea brick, take it to the kitchen, grind it between two stones, mix the fine powder with a little tsampa, butter, and boiling water, churn it into a kind of gruel, then drink it down in one—often three or four cups in quick succession. Sometimes Dilgo Khyentse was invited to join him.

"This is the special tea of Sa-ngen," Rinpoche would say. "Rekhe tea is *so* delicious!"

From this story, it's clear that Rinpoche retained at least one Sa-ngen custom.

Khyentse Chökyi Lodrö's Father

According to Gongna Tulku, Rinpoche used to say, "Masters as learnèd as my father and the Second Neten Chokling, Ngedön Drupe Dorje, who also received vast amounts of empowerments and transmissions, have not emerged among the present generation. These two great masters had similarly wild natures. They never stopped to ask, 'Should I or shouldn't I?'"

I asked Gongna Tulku what Rinpoche had meant by "should I or shouldn't I?" He explained that Rinpoche's father would do things like force his wife to offer her dzi necklaces, coral, and other precious stones to the lama (meaning himself), then sell everything off, including his tents, homes, and belongings so he could live as a homeless ascetic. "From now on," he would say, "I want to be a wanderer without any possessions." But at other times, he would act like a high lama and acquire many tents, a home, and all the usual trappings of wealth and position. He often appeared to crave and be enormously attached to riches and material possessions, and if thieves from Gonjo and Rekhe stole any of his animals, he wouldn't hesitate to destroy them with black magic.

Rinpoche said, "The ultimate deity, the actual yidam of our household, Serpa Tsang, was Dudul Dorje's Vajrakilaya. Our private protector was Zhingkyong. But it was Zhingkyong's attendants who carried out the activities. The power of my father's black magic was unassailable! He must have used it to kill a great many people because the inhabitants of Gonjo and Rekhe were known to live in fear of the sorcery practiced by the Serpa household."

One day, said Rinpoche, his father would wear a long-sleeved robe; the next, a white lower robe and striped shawl; and on the third day, he would wear robes and shawls of the finest cotton. Sometimes he wore his hair long and wrapped it in a blue cloth so his head looked blue; at others, he wore a red cloth and his head looked red. But he always tucked the phurba that had belonged to Dudul Dorje into his waistband in exactly the same way Dudul Dorje had always worn it. Although rituals involving blazing tormas, and so on, are not widely practiced, Rinpoche said his father delighted in performing extremely wrathful rituals and did so repeatedly. He would throw his phurba after each of the blazing tormas he tossed, and if the torma did not turn around he would repeat the ritual the next day.

This man, Gyurme Tsewang Chokdrup, who appears as Gyurme Tsewang Gyatso in the *Great Biography*, son of the old Tertön of Ser and a descendant of Dudul Dorje, was Jamyang Khyentse Chökyi Lodrö's father. Gongna Tulku said he heard all this from Rinpoche's own lips.

I asked Dilgo Khyentse if it was true that of Gyurme Tsewang Chokdrup's two sons, it was Tersey Chime who relished wrathful activities, while Rinpoche practiced them less. He said no, it wasn't true; Rinpoche also engaged in wrathful activity. He was never complacent about any kind of wrongdoing and would always practice a wrathful fire puja to purify even the slightest injury to Buddhadharma or the Khyentse lineage.

KHYENTSE CHÖKYI LODRÖ'S MOTHER

I've heard it said that Rinpoche's mother's family was from Amdo and that she was a descendent of the great master Sergyi Chadral. But women are rarely spoken of in Tibetan culture, and no one I've talked to has been able to confirm who her parents were or even the name of her family. Yet she was a reincarnation of the dakini Shaza Khamoche. Rinpoche told Dilgo Khyentse that in the latter part of his life, long after she had passed away, she sometimes appeared to him in visions and made prophecies. But apart from Dilgo Khyentse mentioning in his *Great Biography* that she was endowed with all the characteristics of a dakini, no one has been able to identify with any certainty into which family she was born.

After his mother passed away, Khyentse Chökyi Lodrö asked Adzom Drukpa and many other lamas to do divinations about her next rebirth. The lamas said it looked as though she had committed a number of minor samaya transgressions and that as many Vajrasattva practices as possible should be done for her. According to Rinpoche, his mother had been a very noble being, but having endured the extreme hardship of living with a man who never ceased to behave in the most peculiar manner, it had been impossible for her to avoid breaking samaya.

Khyentse Chökyi Lodrö's Nephew and Secretary

I asked many people about who had fathered Chakdzö Tsewang Paljor. Tashi Namgyal wasn't sure and said, "Isn't he the son of Rinpoche's sister?" But it turns out that he was the son of Chökyi Lodrö's elder brother Dudul, who was both a layperson and a tantric practitioner. It was Gongna Tulku who gave me a detailed explanation of his family lineage.

2. Katok Monastery

According to Dilgo Khyentse, it was Jamgön Kongtrul Lodrö Taye who recognized all five emanations of Jamyang Khyentse Wangpo, and so it was to Jamgön Kongtrul that Katok Situ Chökyi Gyatso wrote, begging for a Khyentse tulku to be sent to Katok: "A Khyentse tulku would be an indispensable asset to the monastery."

"There aren't any Khyentse tulkus left!" replied Jamgön Kongtrul. "There is one boy who might be of benefit to Katok Monastery... but it's probably not a good idea for me to name him."

Of course, Katok Situ immediately sent many more messages to Jamgön Kongtrul begging him to identify the boy and was eventually summoned to Jamgön Kongtrul's residence.

"You keep asking me to appoint a Khyentse tulku to Katok Monastery," said Jamgön Kongtrul. "Katok Monastery is a very sacred place. Jamyang Khyentse Wangpo is believed to have said that had it been possible for him to live at Katok, it would have been the second best way for him to spend his life. The best would have been for him to live as a homeless wanderer, in which case he would have built a large monastery for several thousand monks somewhere on the border of Ü and Tsang before attaining rainbow body at a place called Tsang Oyuk. But circumstances were against both those options.

"I don't know why Khyentse Wangpo couldn't live at Katok. It may have been an obstacle created by four-faced Mahakala, or perhaps his positive activities outside Katok were so beneficial that it was impossible for him to retire to the monastery.

"Whatever the reason, right now Katok Monastery needs a Khyentse tulku. You must therefore take into your care the grandson of the great Tertön of Ser—he is unquestionably the activity emanation of Khyentse Wangpo. But don't build him a labrang or load him down with the

Katok Situ Chökyi Gyatso, the Third Katok Situ Rinpoche
Source: Shechen Archives

responsibilities of a labrang. And don't make him head of the monastery or impose any of those kinds of duty on him. If he can be left to nurture spontaneity and yogic discipline, he will without doubt become an incomparable mahasiddha in the Land of Snows. So don't ever entrust him with weighty responsibilities! Not before you've really thought about whether it's truly appropriate or even necessary."

Jamgön Kongtrul gave the letter, protection cord, and scarf to Katok Situ and bestowed on Chökyi Lodrö the name Lodrö Gyatso. Katok Situ took it all to Tsewang Chokdrup, the son of the old Tertön of Ser, then returned to Katok with Chökyi Lodrö, who lived there until he was thirteen years old.

Gongna Tulku told me it was snowing the day Khyentse Chökyi Lodrö arrived at Katok. Situ Labrang looked huge from the outside, but inside it was virtually empty, and Rinpoche was given a very shabby room. The following day the snow was so deep that the local villagers were unable to leave their homes, which was very unusual for the region and considered by many to be a good omen. He was quickly enthroned in a simple ceremony.

The following year, Katok Situ traveled with many of his monks to Tsadra Rinchen Drak[4] where Jamgön Kongtrul was to give the great empowerment of the *General Essentialization of All the Wisdom of the Buddhas*. Chökyi

Lodrö longed to go, but Katok Situ wouldn't take him. "You are just a child, there's no need for you to go," he said. Chökyi Lodrö didn't dare argue and later said that missing his only opportunity to meet Jamgön Kongtrul was his greatest regret. This is not mentioned in the *Great Biography*.

Dilgo Khyentse said that Rinpoche never admitted to being a tulku of Khyentse Wangpo. In fact, Rinpoche insisted it wasn't possible. He had been born in the year of the snake and Khyentse Wangpo had passed away only eight months earlier in the first month of the dragon year. He even backed up his assertion with quotations from the *Treasury of Abhidharma* and other texts. This is clearly stated in the *Great Biography*.

Chökyi Lodrö's Childhood

A Vision from a Previous Life

Chökyi Lodrö wrote in his autobiography,

> One evening while memorizing the *Vajra Vidarana Dharani*,[5]
> As I gazed at Katok Monastery[6] bathed in moonlight,
> A great sadness overcame me.
> Again and again, memories of the glorious Sakya Monastery
> appeared in my mind . . .

I asked Dilgo Khyentse what had happened that night, and what Rinpoche had meant when he wrote this verse. He told me that Rinpoche's tutor was practicing in a cave high on the hill behind Katok Monastery, while Rinpoche sat outside on a skin cushion reciting the dharani of Vajra Vidarana. Perhaps it was the blessing of the dharani that coaxed the moon out from behind the clouds to shed its light across the valley, who knows? But at that moment, the outline of Katok Monastery became extremely vivid, and Rinpoche watched, enthralled, as it transformed into a different monastery altogether—a monastery that stood on pale gray sand.

Rinpoche had been wide awake throughout this vision. It wasn't a dream. But once it was over, the memory of having been born as a dungsey of the Khön lineage and of living in a monastery that stood on pale gray sand flooded into his mind. The memory stayed with him throughout the session of accumulation. At the time, he had no idea where that monastery was, and only later discovered it to be Sakya Monastery.

Excellent Memory

Rinpoche must have been a Nyingmapa and a *Heart Essence of the Vast Expanse* practitioner in his previous lives because having read them through just once or twice, he was able to recite from memory the Ekazati, Rahula, and Vajrasadhu practices; the sadhana of the *Gathering of Vidyadharas*; and the invocation of Palchen and other deities from the *Heart Essence of the Vast Expanse* practice texts. He didn't have to make the least effort to memorize them. His excellent memory is clearly described by Dilgo Khyentse in the *Great Biography*.

The Incident with the Quicksilver

As a boy, Chökyi Lodrö was known as Tulku Lodrö. He was a very active child and never stood still for long. One day, Tulku Lodrö was cleaning his tutor's room when he came across an interesting-looking, heavy, blue glass jar. Wondering what it might be, he shook it and found that it made a *throk-thruk, throk-thruk* sound.

"It must be very precious," he thought. "And if it's precious, I should drink it." So he did.

Before long his tutor returned, but as Tulku Lodrö hadn't finished his chores, he continued cleaning. As he filled the offering bowls with water, he noticed his tutor's eyes flickering this way and that. His gaze wandered all over the room, from Tulku Lodrö, to the shrine, to the floor. He was clearly agitated about something, but what? The tutor fiddled rather clumsily with his mala for a while, then abruptly cast it aside, opened a drawer, and lifted out the empty blue jar.

"What's happened to the contents of this jar?" he asked. Tulku Lodrö couldn't lie to his tutor, so he immediately admitted that he had drunk it.

"Argh!" exclaimed the tutor, sinking back onto his cushion. Deep in thought, his eyes continued to dart anxiously around the room, returning again and again to Tulku Lodrö. "Argh!"

Usually Rinpoche's tutor was extremely strict and would slap or beat his charge at the slightest provocation. When I was a boy, we shaved Rinpoche's head, and I saw twenty or thirty scars that still remained from his tutor's most severe beatings. But on this occasion he didn't so much as raise a finger. However, he did report the incident to Katok Situ.

"Tulku Lodrö is a special child," he said. "He swallowed a jar of quicksilver! Then, as he was making offerings, balls of mercury rolled from his body onto the shrine and down to the floor. But the boy himself was entirely unaffected. He truly is a very unusual being."

Tulku Lodrö Examines His Dreams

Katok Situ instructed all the lamas and tulkus of Katok to examine their dreams. Their task was to find out who their predecessors had been. Dutifully, before he went to bed that night, Tulku Lodrö said his prayers and aspired for his previous incarnations to appear before him as he slept. At dawn, he dreamt of an elderly Tibetan man wearing a blue silk brocade robe and turquoise ornaments.

The following day, the tulkus assembled, and Katok Situ asked each of them who they thought they had been. Some of the tulkus said they were the incarnations of lamas who had worn pandita hats, others that they had had horns on their heads, and a few spoke of visions of various gurus and yidam deities. Katok Situ merely responded to each report with, "Ya, ya," without questioning the tulkus any further.

But when he heard Tulku Lodrö's dream, he exclaimed, "A-ley!" He then asked the boy several times if he was sure that the elderly man had been a layman. When Tulku Lodrö said yes, he was definitely a layman, Situ Rinpoche muttered over and over again, "Tulku Lodrö is the incarnation of a *layman*!" And soon all the tulkus were saying it.

Later, at Dzongsar, someone noticed a thangka that had been painted according to the instructions of the previous Khyentse. In it, the Dharma King Trisong Deutsen was depicted wearing that very same blue robe.

I have only this much to say about Khyentse Chökyi Lodrö's early life at Katok.

3. Dzongsar Monastery

Tulku Lodrö Is Given to Dzongsar

I WILL NOW tell you a few of the stories I heard from Dilgo Khyentse, exactly as he told them to me.

The First Khyentse Tulku was receiving the transmission of *Precious Treasury of Terma Teachings* from the Fifth Dzogchen Rinpoche, Thubten Chökyi Dorje, at Dzogchen Monastery, when suddenly, just as the Guru section was drawing to a close, he fell violently ill. As the tulku had a high fever, they all thought it was a flu virus, but it soon became obvious that his illness was rather more serious. His attendants called Dzogchen Rinpoche to his bedside.

"The reincarnation of my root guru is dying," whispered Dzogchen Rinpoche, as he laid the young tulku's head in his lap and wept. Not long after, Dzogchen Rinpoche announced that the tulku had passed away.

The First Khyentse Tulku had been the body emanation of Khyentse Wangpo, but his subsequent incarnation was never recognized. Many suspected it was Dilgo Khyentse, but when I asked him directly, he denied it.

Kalzang Dorje was Khyentse Wangpo's nephew and became the regent of Dzongsar Monastery after Khyentse Wangpo passed away, so it was his job to care for the First Khyentse Tulku. After the tulku died, Kalzang Dorje wrote to Katok Situ: "My Dzongsar Khyentse Tulku has passed away quite suddenly, like a brilliant sun eclipsed by the moon. I am ill and close to death. Please, come what may, give me the grandson of the great Tertön of Ser, the boy you have at Katok. If you care about the samaya between us brothers, and the samaya between you and your uncle, Khyentse Wangpo, you have no choice but to do as I ask. Send the tulku to Dzongsar Monastery.[7] These are my dying words."

Regent Kalzang Dorje passed away the day after he wrote this letter. Nevertheless, it was dispatched to Katok and delivered by hand to Katok Situ.

At first Katok Situ said nothing. Then he summoned Chökyi Lodrö into his presence.

"Jamgön Kongtrul instructed me not to entrust you with any kind of responsibility—not for the monastery, the labrang, or any other institution. But today I received a letter from Kalzang Dorje instructing me to give you to Dzongsar Monastery. If he were still alive, we could discuss the situation, but he is dead, and the only way I can maintain a pure samaya connection with both him and Khyentse Wangpo is to do as he asks. In fact, I have no choice, because this is the one samaya I lack the courage to ignore. So, as I can't think of an alternative, I'm afraid you will have to go to Dzongsar."

Chökyi Lodrö replied that although he felt no great desire to go to Dzongsar, neither was he completely unmoved by the prospect. So, shortly after they spoke, Katok Situ and Chökyi Lodrö, accompanied by six or seven attendants, made the journey to Dzongsar.

Khyentse Labrang was in possession of all of Jamyang Khyentse Wangpo's wealth and belongings but did not display its riches ostentatiously.

When Chökyi Lodrö first arrived at Dzongsar, the residents of the monastery didn't go out of their way to welcome him. But later, on an auspicious day, the officials and attendants of the labrang stacked a few thick cushions on a throne in the empowerment hall, and Katok Situ presided over Chökyi Lodrö's enthronement.

Only a few monks and lamas were present, but the ceremony itself was performed elaborately and included a long speech on the five perfections, and so on. Katok Situ wore a monk's ceremonial robe with 108 patches and a pandita hat, and sat on a thick cushion in front of the throne as butter tea, saffron rice, and tiny buttered sweet roots (a great delicacy) were served. Katok Situ then gave a detailed teaching on the five auspiciousnesses, and the symbolic offerings made by Dzongsar Labrang, Gongna Labrang, and other adjoining labrangs were appropriately arranged. Katok Situ did not explicitly state that the monastery had now been entrusted to Khyentse Chökyi Lodrö, but he did allude to it in his talk.

As he had a great deal to do, Katok Situ left Dzongsar soon after the ceremony. His parting words to the young tulku were, "Tonight you must stay here."

Khyentse Wangpo's Bed

That night, Chökyi Lodrö wandered through the labrang until he found a bedroom with a monk's bed in it. It wasn't until much later that he discovered the bedroom he had chosen was Khyentse Wangpo's and therefore the most important room in the labrang. At the time there didn't seem to be anywhere else for him to sleep, so he moved in. And none of the labrang staff said a word about whose room it had been.

The following year, Katok Situ visited Dzongsar for the second time. When Chökyi Lodrö invited him to sit on his bed, he was shocked.

"Ah?" he exclaimed.

Surprised, Chökyi Lodrö politely asked him to sit down once more. And again Katok Situ refused.

"I could not possibly sit on that bed," said Katok Situ, and instead accepted a thick cushion.

"Where do you sleep?" asked Katok Situ.

"The only bed I could find when I first arrived was this one, and I've slept here ever since," replied Chökyi Lodrö.

"Adzi!" exclaimed Katok Situ. "They say 'a dog sleeps on a man's bed,' and it's true!"

Chökyi Lodrö said nothing.

"Adzi!" cried Katok Situ a moment later. "The saying 'a dog sleeping on a man's bed' is true!"

He repeated the adage several times, until eventually Chökyi Lodrö asked him why he kept saying it.

"This is the bed of Jamyang Khyentse Wangpo, the Sovereign Lord of all the teachings of the Buddha. And *you* sleep in it!" said Katok Situ.

Chökyi Lodrö said he suddenly felt very uncomfortable. Although he had already slept in that bed for many nights, he asked Katok Situ if he should find somewhere else to sleep.

"As you are already sleeping here, you should continue to do so," replied Katok Situ. And he couldn't have been that unhappy about it because later he said he felt an auspicious circumstance had been created.

Katok Situ was immensely kind to Khyentse Chökyi Lodrö. He talked with him at length and gave him a great deal of advice and guidance on the outer and inner practices. But Jamgön Kongtrul's prophecy about the most auspicious option for Chökyi Lodrö's life—that he live the life of a wanderer—never came to be.

When Shechen Gyaltsab visited Dzongsar, Chökyi Lodrö invited him to sit on Jamyang Khyentse Wangpo's bed. Shechen Gyaltsab instantly declared that he would do no such thing. Instead he offered three prostrations, placed his forehead against the bed, then gave Chökyi Lodrö an empowerment—I think it was for a sadhana called the *Perfectly Accomplished Guru* from the treasure teachings of Jamyang Khyentse Wangpo. Only then, as he gave the empowerment, did Shechen Gyaltsab acquiesce; and when he was offered the previous Khyentse's hat to wear, he accepted that too.

"Apart from the previous incarnation of Gyaltsab," said Rinpoche much later, "no one dared sit on Jamyang Khyentse Wangpo's bed. Thinking about it now, I lacked all the qualities that would have qualified me to sleep in the bed of such a supremely excellent and unique master. But as I had already slept there for a number of years, what else could I do?"

The Khyentse Tulku Controversy

Background

As I've already mentioned, when Khyentse Wangpo died the prophecies predicted five incarnations, and it was Jamgön Kongtrul who recognized the tulku who was initially taken to Dzongsar Monastery as its throne holder (the body incarnation)—the tulku who died prematurely in the arms of Dzogchen Rinpoche.

While the First Khyentse Tulku was living at Dzongsar, another Khyentse tulku was also taken to live there, and a rumor quickly spread that he had been recognized by Pönlop Loter Wangpo himself. This other tulku was known as Khyen Trukma. *Truk* means "small" and in this context is a little impertinent, but that's what they called him.

In the meantime, Katok Situ's determination to bring a Khyentse incarnation to Katok Monastery had only increased. As I've already said, the activity incarnation of Khyentse Wangpo had yet to be recognized and enthroned when Jamgön Kongtrul recognized Khyentse Chökyi Lodrö, but not before imposing the condition that the young tulku should not be burdened with the responsibilities of running a big labrang or monastery.

After the First Khyentse Tulku passed away, Kalzang Dorje wrote that strong letter demanding that Katok Situ send Khyentse Chökyi Lodrö to Dzongsar. But then Kalzang Dorje died, which made things very difficult for Katok Situ. Had Kalzang Dorje lived, Katok Situ would have been able to tell him about Jamgön Kongtrul's condition, and together they would have come up with a solution that worked for both monasteries. But as he was dead, Katok Situ's only option was to comply with Kalzang Dorje's final wish.

Yangsi Rinpoche Thubten Chökyi Gyatso said that from what he'd heard,

Khyen Trukma was never fully accepted as the monastery's throne holder by all the Dzongsar monks. This is true. Dzongsar is a Sakya monastery, and the monks who accepted Khyen Trukma only did so because he was a Sakyapa. But the all-powerful Khyentse Labrang, which was entirely separate from Dzongsar Monastery, emphatically did not. (Khyentse Wangpo never had much to do with Dzongsar Monastery.) This was why Kalzang Dorje, who was Khyentse Wangpo's nephew, regent, and the interim head of Khyentse Labrang, demanded that Katok Situ send Khyentse Chökyi Lodrö to Dzongsar. And this is how two incarnations of Khyentse Wangpo ended up living at the same monastery at the same time. Khyentse Labrang and Regent Kalzang Dorje looked after Chökyi Lodrö, and Dzongsar Monastery looked after Khyen Trukma.

I don't know if there were any clashes between those close to the tulkus, but as the rumor that Khyen Trukma had been recognized by Loter Wangpo was never verified, a dispute arose between Dzongsar Monastery and Khyentse Labrang, so serious that many of the monks armed themselves with daggers.

At the height of the hostilities, Katok Situ arrived at Dzongsar to speak with Chökyi Lodrö.

"Jamgön Kongtrul made a prophecy about you," said Katok Situ, over a cup of tea. "But it seems this monastery doesn't want you. They tell me there are even people here who actively dislike you. So if you want to, you can come back to Katok with me, because I really need you."

Chökyi Lodrö, who had grown up a bit by then, thought deeply before he replied.

"I can only ever agree to anything Rinpoche asks me to do," he said. "But first, I would like to say something."

"Ah!" said Katok Situ. "What is it?"

"Rinpoche, you've asked me to go back to Katok with you. Had I not already been given to Dzongsar, that would be a very reasonable course of action. But I have been given to this monastery and I've settled here. It's true, there are problems. But if I leave without resolving them, worldly people won't hesitate to criticize me. On top of which, my dreams indicate that if I do stay, I will be able, in some small way, to benefit the Buddhadharma. As far as Katok is concerned, I could never do more than you, Rinpoche, while you live, as you do everything so much better than I do. But should there be a time when you are no longer at Katok, I promise I will serve the monastery for a full fifteen years."

Katok Situ remained silent long after Chökyi Lodrö finished speaking. He rested his gaze in the sky, and tears flowed down his cheeks.

"We human beings always fall into the same trap!" he said finally. "I thought that being older and more experienced than you, I was somehow greater and more far-sighted. But you have exceeded me both spiritually and temporally. I see now that you should not leave Dzongsar. You must remain here."

So Chökyi Lodrö stayed at Dzongsar.

Yangsi Rinpoche Thubten Chökyi Gyatso said he'd heard that when Chökyi Lodrö was first sent to Dzongsar, Katok Situ had not agreed to give the tulku outright, only to lend him to Dzongsar for fifteen years. But I've not found a single account to corroborate this detail. All I've ever been told is that Khyentse Chökyi Lodrö pledged to serve Katok Monastery for fifteen years—which is also mentioned in the *Great Biography*.

Jagö Tobden Gets Involved

According to Tashi Namgyal, Jagö Tobden visited Dzongsar some time after Chökyi Lodrö gave the *Precious Treasury of Terma Teachings* transmission and just before political turmoil seriously disrupted life in Tibet. He told Chakdzö Tsewang Paljor that the Derge court had ruled that the dispute about which of the two tulkus should be running Dzongsar Monastery must be settled, and that he had been appointed to facilitate the process.

Once it became known that Tobden was involved, Tsewang Paljor and Khyentse Chökyi Lodrö's other attendants made many attempts to present their case. But every time he saw them coming, even if it was only to bring him a cup of tea, Tobden would get angry and send them away. Yet with the supporters of Khyen Trukma he was unfailingly polite and gentle. This went on for ten days, throughout which Tsewang Paljor and the other attendants became more and more enraged. How could Tsewang Dudul of Derge have appointed Jagö Tobden to sit in judgment on *them*! But there was nothing they could do.

Before long, a meeting of the Dzongsar monks was convened. Many speeches were made about the uniqueness of Pönlop Loter Wangpo, "the unequaled life-force and backbone of the glorious Sakya and Ngor lineages" who, it was pointed out, was one of Chökyi Lodrö's own teachers. As Dzongsar was a branch monastery of Ngor, it would be utterly inappropriate to go against Loter Wangpo's wishes by ousting Khyen Trukma. All

Jagö Tobden
Source: Cheme Dorjee Chagotsang

of which convinced Tsewang Paljor that the dispute would not be settled in Khyentse Chökyi Lodrö's favor.

That evening, as Tsewang Paljor stepped out of the labrang kitchen, he saw Jagö Tobden standing motionless and alone in front of Rinpoche's door. Tobden appeared to be weighing something up in his mind. Suddenly he threw open the door and strode in.

"What's going on?" wondered Tsewang Paljor. No more than fifteen minutes later, Tobden reemerged.

Eager to discover what had been said, Tsewang Paljor hurried into Rinpoche's presence. Yes, Tobden had visited him. But that was all Rinpoche would say. And it wasn't until many years later that Tsewang Paljor learnt from Jagö Tobden himself what had really happened.

"Neither of the Khyentse tulkus can be blamed for the current impasse," Jagö Tobden had said to Chökyi Lodrö. "However, it isn't appropriate for you both to live here in the same place, because inevitably, conflicts will continue to arise. I therefore respectfully ask, Rinpoche, would it be better for you to stay at Dzongsar Monastery, or to leave?"

"It doesn't really matter which one of us remains here," replied Rinpoche. "And honestly, I would be far happier if I didn't have to live in a monastery. But if I do stay, Buddhadharma in general and the Derge kingdom in particular will benefit in every respect."

Jagö Tobden then requested that Rinpoche tell no one of what had passed between them and changed the subject.

Soon after Jagö Tobden left Rinpoche's presence, he sat down and wrote his verdict.

"The precious Khyentse Tulku of Dzongsar Monastery (Khyen Trukma) cannot remain at the monastery owing to the Sangha's lack of merit. I will therefore take him to Galing Monastery in Yilung and settle him there."

Tobden's plan was to persuade the highland nomads and the lowland farmers to support the tulku. To that end, he took Khyen Trukma away with him, as well as all the material wealth of the monastery and labrang, including an entire herd of cattle, many horses, gold, silver, and so forth. Tashi Namgyal heard all these details from Chakdzö Tsewang Paljor.

Jagö Tobden admitted to Chakdzö that he had always felt an intense devotion for Chökyi Lodrö, and that his main purpose in taking Khyen Trukma away was to clean up the mess made by the dispute. He said he was worried that worse problems would arise as a result of broken samaya if the dispute were allowed to continue. Although he himself didn't feel the slightest devotion for Khyen Trukma—who was now known as Galing Khyentse—or the remotest connection with him, as the tulku had already been given the title "Khyentse," it was necessary to find him somewhere to live. All of which led him to acquire the land in Galing, build a monastery, and install the tulku. As he had no doubt that Khyentse Labrang would never be destitute, he took its material wealth to support Galing Khyentse. (It's also possible that Chökyi Lodrö didn't have the merit to own absolutely all of Khyentse Labrang's riches.) But Jagö Tobden fastidiously avoided removing even the tiniest sacred body, speech, and mind representation that had once belonged to Jamyang Khyentse Wangpo. Galing Khyentse's supporters, he said, had only been interested in the material wealth. Not one of them had mentioned or even thought of taking a single Dharma book or sacred object.

There's a Tibetan saying, "When a duplicitous person tells you the sun rises in the west, it's obvious he is trying to fool you," which in this case means that although Jagö Tobden had appeared to be pro-Khyen Trukma, he was actually skillfully resolving a very difficult situation. It wasn't until more than two decades later that the people of Dzongsar began to realize what a great service Tobden had done for Khyentse Chökyi Lodrö.

"What really puzzles me," said Yangsi Rinpoche Thubten Chökyi Gyatso, "is why Khyentse Chökyi Lodrö—who never wanted to run a monastery or a labrang, let alone such vast and illustrious institutions as Dzongsar Monastery and Khyentse Labrang—wasn't thrilled and delighted when Khyen Trukma wanted to chase him out. Wouldn't it have been the perfect solution? Why didn't he seize the opportunity to be a wanderer, which was the life he'd always longed for? Why didn't he choose to leave when he had the chance?"

I replied that for Chökyi Lodrö to be able to wander freely may well have been the best tendrel for his life, but that tendrel was never realized. And after a great deal of contemplation, he realized that, given the choice between Khyentse Trukma and himself, it would be better for all concerned if he were to remain in the monastery. Yangsi Rinpoche Thubten Chökyi Gyatso said he could see my point. For Khyentse Chökyi Lodrö to remain at Dzongsar Monastery, he said, was itself an inconceivably wonderful Dharma activity. And in all probability, sentient beings lacked the merit for anything more.

So Jamgön Kongtrul's wish that Khyentse Chökyi Lodrö remain free, and his prediction about the benefit his freedom would bring, were never fulfilled. Towards the end of his life, though, it became obvious that Chökyi Lodrö still longed to become a wanderer. He even made himself a monk's staff and prepared everything necessary to embark on his new life. But although Jamgön Kongtrul's prophecy about Chökyi Lodrö's need to practice the inner yogic discipline was almost effortlessly realized a number of times, he was never to become a wanderer.

Once the dispute was settled, Chökyi Lodrö went on a pilgrimage to Lhasa, and from there to Ngor and Mindrolling, where he received bhikshu ordination. A beautiful notebook written in Rinpoche's own hand includes descriptions of how he was ordained, who assisted during the ceremony, and how intensely he aspired to observe all the precepts perfectly.

He then traveled to Chamdo. An old monk called Drupa Rigyal, a neighbor of ours in Bir who originally came from Chamdo, told me all about his visit. A few years earlier, the previous incarnation of Chamdo Phagpa Lha, a Gelugpa teacher and clairvoyant mahasiddha—and probably the only Phagpa Lha ever to have taken a consort—had placed a visiting lama called Katok Situ on a throne. He then asked Katok Situ, a Nyingmapa, to give the transmission of the *Magical Net of Manjushri* to all the Gelugpa monks of Chamdo Monastery, then compelled his monks to receive it. Years later, a young lama called Dzongsar Jamyang Khyentse Chökyi Lodrö visited Chamdo. Phagpa Lha also placed him on a throne, then sat on a thick cushion in front of him wearing a dark red brocade chuba, and requested the long-life empowerment of Thangtong Gyalpo for himself, the monks, and the lay community of Chamdo Monastery. The more elderly Chamdo monks were so upset by this that they wept openly, complaining bitterly that "Phagchen Gyalwa'i Wangpo has become such a miserable man!"

From Chamdo, Chökyi Lodrö traveled to Neten Monastery, then Kela Monastery. On the way back to Dzongsar, he received many empowerments and transmissions from Kela Chokling (the other incarnation of Chokgyur Lingpa) and Neten Chokling Ngedön Drupe Dorje. It was then that Neten Chokling offered Rinpoche the boy called Tsejor, who was little more than a child at the time but also a kind of monk.

When Chökyi Lodrö reached Chamdo, he received the news that Katok Situ had passed away. He immediately returned to Dzongsar and went into retreat. Having completed his retreat, he wrote to Shechen Gyaltsab. Sadly, though, all his messenger brought back was firsthand knowledge of Shechen Gyaltsab's death. Around that time, Karmapa Khakhyab Dorje and many of Jamyang Khyentse Wangpo's and Jamgön Kongtrul's disciples also passed away.

Katok Situ died after performing ceremonies to remove obstacles for a Tibetan government official, who had fallen seriously ill. As the ceremonies hadn't been completed, Chökyi Lodrö was asked to take over. He did some obstacle-removing rituals, but they had no effect and the official became even more seriously ill.

I have heard that while Chökyi Lodrö was preparing the ritual to repel attack, one of the three protectors[8] asked him whether they should wage war against the enemy inside or the enemy outside, which I think suggests that the government officials of that time were not necessarily acting in the best interests of the country. In fact, there were so many breakages of samaya that Tashi Namgyal always cautioned Yangsi Rinpoche never to perform ceremonies for the politicians in Dharamsala.

4. Regent of Katok Monastery

After Katok Situ passed away, Khyentse Chökyi Lodrö accepted responsibility for Katok Monastery, just as he had promised. As its regent, Rinpoche traveled to Katok quite regularly, always taking the same route over the mountain pass. According to Tsejor, as soon as they reached the Katok side, Rinpoche would become extremely wrathful and wild. In a voice like thunder, he would roar criticisms at his attendants about every aspect of their behavior, from their social manners to their inner practices. But the moment he set foot on the Dzongsar side, he instantly became even-tempered and amiable.

The Expulsion of Women from Katok Monastery

During Katok Situ's time, the Katok Monastery monks were little more than laymen in monks' clothing and their quarters teemed with women. Katok Situ had wanted to forbid all women from living within the monastery walls but was thwarted by those who insisted that doing so would enrage the monastery's main protectress, Lhamo. After Chökyi Lodrö took over, an old lama who lived in Gophuk cave urgently petitioned him to make and enforce a rule barring women from Katok altogether—the old lama turned out to be Khenpo Kunpal. But although he spoke eloquently about the importance and necessity of this expulsion, he was unwilling to help implement it. So it was Khenpo Nüden, Khenpo Jorden, Chökyi Lodrö, and the previous incarnation of Getse (Getse Mahapandita[9]) who met to discuss how such a rule could be enforced. To his dismay, Chökyi Lodrö quickly realized that none of the other three were prepared to do anything more than ask *him* to banish the women. Tsejor was not at all happy.

"All will be well if these so-called monks obey Rinpoche's command," he said at the time. "But Horpo people are so hard-headed, we can't be sure what they'll do. If they flout Rinpoche's authority altogether by openly disobeying him, things will only go from bad to worse. Lhamo herself could turn on Rinpoche! She might make him ill or even threaten his very life!"

A few days later, the monastery's ordained monks and lay practitioners were summoned to a meeting in the courtyard. Three chairs had been set out: Chökyi Lodrö sat in the middle, Khenpo Jorden sat on his right, and Katok Getse Tulku sat on his left. Khenpo Jorden spoke first, but so obscurely that his audience could barely understand a word. Next came Getse Tulku, but he was equally abstruse. Finally, Chökyi Lodrö addressed the gathering.

"Katok Situ enthroned me as a lineage holder of Katok Monastery," he said. "As he is no longer alive, I am his regent. I therefore own Katok Monastery and everything in it, from the golden throne to the stone slabs and pots and pans in the kitchen. I have absolute authority here.

"Tomorrow at sunrise, there will be a thorough inspection of every inch of the monastery. If any women are found, even if they are themselves high lamas or leaders of the community, we will have no option but to flog them. So today, all the women must leave this monastery—for good!"

No one had the power or authority to contradict him, and so the meeting broke up with the unspoken understanding that Chökyi Lodrö must be obeyed.

That night Tsejor could not sleep. "If they leave, all will be well," he kept repeating to himself. "But if they don't, what can Rinpoche do about it? There are so many of them! Rinpoche's position would be weakened, he would be embarrassed—and Lhamo might even strike him down!"

Before sunrise the next morning, Tsejor rose as usual to circumambulate the monastery. To his enormous relief, he saw a long line of women filing out of the monastery gates. Some were wearing yellow hats, and the wealthy were leading long caravans of oxen, dzos, horses, and mules piled high with their belongings.

As the sun edged above the horizon, Chökyi Lodrö, Getse Tulku, and Khenpo Jorden inspected every inch of the monastery, including the inner passages and the monks' quarters; they didn't find a single woman anywhere. Tsejor was amazed. He felt that Rinpoche's accomplishment was nothing less than heroic. And in the process, Rinpoche hadn't even caught cold—which proved just how wrong it had been to imagine that kicking the women out would enrage Lhamo Gönlek.

Katok Monastery's Fear of Khyentse Chökyi Lodrö

For many years, Drupa Rigyal was manager and treasurer of Katok Monastery. When we meet, we often reminisce about the past. According to him, the people of Katok experienced Khyentse Chökyi Lodrö's arrival as something of a tsunami. They said he was like an "invading force" (they used the same Tibetan word to describe the advance of the Communist Chinese) because his sovereignty over them was absolute and indisputable. Monks were punished ten at a time. When a flogging was called for, Rinpoche insisted on four or five hundred lashes, never a mere hundred, and he always watched from the window of his residence as the punishment was meted out. In all honesty, this was probably the only way to deal with the people of Katok, who were extremely tough and uncompromising. They simply didn't respond to more peaceful methods.

Chökyi Lodrö also kept a strict eye on the money that was set aside to make offerings during the ceremonies the monastery performed routinely, as well as those established by Katok Situ, and he imposed fines and demoted officials if even one penny went missing. The monks of Katok Monastery were said to be shocked by just how strict a lama Chökyi Lodrö turned out to be.

Khenpo Tsultrim Nyima was one of the good Katok lamas. He had been serving as the Great Abbot of Tantra for six years when Chökyi Lodrö wrote to ask him to accept the position of abbot at Neten Monastery. Everyone at Katok, from the golden throne-holders to the water bearers, wept when he left, they loved him so much. But they were also well aware that no one—not human beings or even formless gods or demons—could choose whether or not to obey Chökyi Lodrö's command. So Khenpo had to go to Neten Monastery, where he remained until his death.

Drupa Rigyal thought it was strange that when Chökyi Lodrö was at Dzongsar, he didn't seem to give Katok a second thought. In the latter part of his life, Chökyi Lodrö didn't get involved in the affairs of Katok Monastery. He visited very occasionally, but while his body was obviously at Katok, his mind was somewhere else entirely.

Khyentse Chökyi Lodrö's Contribution to Katok Monastery

Gongna Tulku told me many of the stories he had heard directly from Chökyi Lodrö's own lips during their private conversations.

The previous incarnation of Katok Situ always longed to be of benefit, and this longing inspired in him a tremendous respect for the traditional practice of building representations of the Buddha. In the latter part of his life, he had commissioned an enormous number of thangkas, and when Chökyi Lodrö arrived at Katok, he found more than three hundred of them were still unfinished. He also noticed that the outer shell and inner form representations of the Copper-Colored Mountain and Shakyamuni Temple were being put together rather roughly. He therefore personally oversaw the completion of all the thangkas and the temple, and gilded all the statues.

Gongna Tulku visited a large summer house at Katok called Nyenchenpo, which also served as the monastery's treasury. He said that since the time of Katok Dampa Deshek, all the monastery's riches had been stored there, and that everything was beautifully displayed and cared for—like a museum. For example, on one of the pillars hung a headdress sprinkled with turquoise stones, the kind worn in Ladakh, with a label attached saying it had belonged to Drugmo, the wife of Gesar of Ling. Merely to compile a list of all that Nyenchenpo contained had taken many months. And Rinpoche said it had taken him another three months to do a proper inventory before handing responsibility for the collection over to the new managers.

Rinpoche also did a tremendous amount to safeguard and propagate the teachings, for example, by establishing the Tantric College with Khenpo Ngakchung.

In short, he served Katok Monastery faithfully for fifteen years.

Between Katok and Dzongsar

I asked Tsejor if he had ever traveled with Rinpoche on his regular visits to Katok Monastery. Yes, he said, he had been there on a number of occasions. Rinpoche usually traveled to Katok from Dzongsar in early summer and would stay there until the beginning of the rainy season.

A beautiful hand-span-high bronze statue of Gur Mahakala stood in Rinpoche's Dzongsar home. Rinpoche said it was the only thing he had taken with him from Katok. He later offered it to the Yangsi of Katok Situ.

"I was only able to bring it out of Katok by deceiving Katok Situ," he explained, "and as I don't need it anymore, I want to offer it back."

What had happened was that Rinpoche had said to Katok Situ's people,

"You are Nyingmapas, so you won't need this Mahakala statue. But as I am a Sakyapa, I definitely will! Please lend it to me." Then, having kept it for a very long time, he returned it to Katok Situ's attendants because, "even though you are Nyingmapas, you will still need Mahakala."

At Dzongsar, Chökyi Lodrö commissioned many thangkas of the Khyentse Kabab—they must be the thangkas that still exist today—but the only paint his artists could find in the labrang storeroom was old and dried out. Without fresh new paint, they told Rinpoche, it wouldn't be possible to create the luminous radiance necessary for such thangkas. At that time, there was no paint for sale in or around Dzongsar, but Katok Monastery was known to have a large supply. So Chökyi Lodrö wrote and asked them to send him specific quantities of various colors. In fact, he wrote twice, because for reasons unknown to me, Katok Monastery did not dispatch the paint immediately—as Tsejor discovered one day as he sat drinking tea with the artists.

"Rinpoche hasn't provided us with the new paint," they complained. "We are still using the old stuff, and the thangkas look so dull and lifeless. All the splendor is being lost. They don't look good at all."

Tsejor was concerned and resolved to inform Rinpoche.

"You are a lineage holder of Katok Monastery," he said. "You served Katok tirelessly for fifteen years, yet they won't even send you a few tins of paint when you ask for it! What can we do?"

Rinpoche looked annoyed. "Yes, you're right. What do you suggest?"

"Write another *very* strong letter!" said Tsejor firmly.

Which Rinpoche did in his own hand and sent the next morning. Within a couple of days, both the treasurer and the manager of Katok Monastery arrived at Dzongsar with Katok's entire stock of new paint. Although they begged for an immediate audience with Rinpoche, they were left waiting in the anteroom for ages. Everyone at Katok Monastery was terrified of Khyentse Chökyi Lodrö.

A Katok Khenpo

Tsejor also told me about a khenpo at Katok who was asked by Rinpoche to talk about the five auspiciousnesses at the enthronement of the Yangsi of Katok Situ. Although this khenpo went on to become quite famous, at that time he was new to the monastery. As Rinpoche's attendant, Tsejor was sent to inform the khenpo of Rinpoche's instructions and to present him with a brocade shawl embroidered with swastikas to wear at the ceremony.

"Tell him that he must speak as elaborately as possible on the auspiciousness of Dharma in the context of the three turnings of the wheel of Dharma," said Rinpoche. "And he should also give a general explanation of the auspiciousness of Dharma."

Tsejor went to the khenpo's room and recited Rinpoche's instructions word-for-word. The khenpo's face instantly drained of color. He didn't seem to know what to do with himself.

"How many days before the ceremony takes place?" he whispered.

"Three days," said Tsejor, at which the khenpo's face, already ashen, became virtually transparent, as if he were about to vanish into space.

He quickly pulled himself together, served tea, and offered Tsejor something to eat. After drinking his tea, Tsejor returned to Rinpoche, while the khenpo went to ask the treasurer if Rinpoche would attend the enthronement ceremony himself.

"Of course!" replied the treasurer. "Rinpoche is definitely coming."

The khenpo was shaken to his very core.

"Hai!" he wailed, sinking deeper and deeper into despair. "That's the last thing I wanted to hear. Rinpoche is the one person I can't tell that I don't want the job! What shall I do? Adzi! Adzi! Perhaps I should just run away?"

Eventually he calmed down. "Who cares?" he thought. "Whatever happens, happens!" And went about his business with renewed courage.

For the ceremony, the front row of cushions were replaced by thrones for Chökyi Lodrö and the high lamas of Katok Monastery. Katok Situ's throne was placed in front of them. Huge platters of cooked meat and wheat biscuits (a Derge speciality) were arranged on tables in front of the masters and monks, and the khenpo sat at the end of a row of monks, clutching the brocade shawl to his chest.

When Rinpoche indicated it was time for the khenpo to speak, he stood up. Knowing he would become completely tongue-tied if he saw Rinpoche looking at him, he shut his eyes and began to recite every detail he could remember about the three turnings of the wheel of the Dharma of the *Perfection of Wisdom Sutra in Eight Thousand Lines*, barely pausing for breath. Some time later, he felt someone tug his robes.

"Rinpoche wants you to stop here," said Solpön Jamtra, placing a silk scarf around Khenpo's neck. "He says that's enough."

Khenpo blinked once or twice and only then realized that night had fallen. In fact, it was so dark that he could see stars twinkling through the skylight.

Rinpoche, the tulku of Katok Situ, and Khenpo Ngakchung later agreed that the *Perfection of Wisdom Sutra in Eight Thousand Lines* teaching had been extraordinary—a clear sign that all the work they had done for Katok Monastery had been successful. Unfortunately, Tsejor didn't hear the khenpo's talk because he had been too busy receiving and entertaining guests in Rinpoche's home.

Although Katok Monastery doesn't count this khenpo among its exceptionally learnèd scholars, he went on to become well known for his great knowledge of Buddhist philosophy.

Katok Öntrul

Khandro Tsering Chödrön told me a story about Katok Öntrul.

One day, as Khandro made her way to Rinpoche's private rooms, she overheard him castigating someone vehemently. Peering through a crack in the doors, she saw Katok Öntrul sitting silently on a thick cushion in the corner of the room, while Rinpoche strode up and down, shouting and gesticulating furiously.

"Khorey!" Rinpoche cried. "You people have been named and enthroned as holders of the Katok lineage, but I hear nothing good about any of you! Drime Zhingkyong, they tell me, has now gone on *holiday* to Kongpo! And for reasons known only to himself, he's taken the Marnak Chu Nyi reliquary with him. As for you, all you ever do is hang around here in Dzongsar. It's about time you went back to Katok and started behaving like a real lineage holder!

"And you can tell Drime Zhingkyong from me that I know every single thread contained in that reliquary. I don't care if he is the lineage holder of Katok: if even a mote of dust is missing, I'll string him up by his ankles and have him whipped!"

Rinpoche swore without restraint, then continued, "It's true you've given me your long-life vase, and I can't say I don't need it, so I'll keep it here. But you lineage holders of Katok seem incapable of growing up!"

Katok Öntrul didn't dare say a word. But the moment Rinpoche finished his tirade, Katok Öntrul left for Katok.

Khandro said that even when they'd settled in Sikkim, Rinpoche was always worrying about Katok Monastery. In fact, Tsejor told me that Rinpoche always took a great interest in every aspect of the Buddhadharma. If he heard of any kind of trouble brewing in a monastery, no matter what its lineage or tradition, he would worry about it for days. This was why peace rarely dawned in Rinpoche's mind.

Just before Rinpoche left for Lhasa, Drime Zhingkyong (the present Zhingkyong incarnation, not the previous one) returned to Katok from Kongpo, bringing the Marnak Chu Nyi reliquary with him.

"I know exactly what should be in that box," repeated Rinpoche. "I'll check it tomorrow, and if anything is missing I'll have him thrashed!"

Chökyi Lodrö's Last Visit to Katok Monastery

After Kyala Zhingkyong, the previous incarnation of Drime Zhingkyong, passed away, his brother and treasurer left for China, taking with them a great many precious things. The Trepa family was outraged. They were convinced that the brother and treasurer had stolen it all from Katok Monastery, and so they ambushed the Kyala Zhingkyong Tsang party and seized their luggage. The two families instantly became bitter enemies, and the dispute over who owned what became so deadlocked that no one was able to resolve it.

Eventually, when Chökyi Lodrö gave the *Precious Treasury of Terma Teachings* transmissions, Shechen Rabjam agreed to judge the case. For fifteen days, he heard petitions from both sides and spoke at length with each family. Everyone had plenty of opportunities to present their arguments, but none of them were allowed to appeal directly to Khyentse Rinpoche. Finally, a verdict was reached, and Trepa Tsang not only had to return everything they had plundered, they had to pay compensation to atone for assaulting Kyala Zhingkyong Tsang. The only comfort allowed Trepa Tsang was that they could remain at Katok Monastery. After all that had happened, though, the two families never got on.

Much later, when Katok Situ's yangsi was young and Katok Monastery in decline, a new Trepa Tsang bride, her mother, and their entourage, all decked out in their finest clothes and jewelry, attended the ritual dances at the Tsechu Festival. During the Ging dance, the clowns filled their bone trumpets with white earth and purposely blew it all over the beautiful girls and magnificently turned out Trepa Tsang party, which so infuriated their servants that they cut off one of the clowns' ears.

Both Katok Situ Yangsi and Chökyi Lodrö were outraged when they heard. It was at this point that Chökyi Lodrö stopped visiting Katok and no longer looked after the monastery as he had done. Until then, he had been immensely kind to Katok Monastery.

5. The Founding of Khamje Shedra

I've heard it said that Khyentse Chökyi Lodrö made regular tours to collect alms, but it's not true. After completing his studies at the age of thirteen, he was sent by Katok Situ to gather funds in Horkhok and Dzachukha, and Rinpoche mentions in his autobiography in verse that he also went to the kingdom of Ling. But apart from these two tours, I know of only one other, which he undertook at the age of twenty-three (1916) in order to build Khamje Shedra at Dzongsar.

By the light of the full moon, on the fifteenth night of the new year, Rinpoche drew up a detailed plan for the new shedra's construction. At the time it was considered a very ambitious undertaking, but by today's standards it was rather small. Rinpoche visited the proposed site to settle the dimensions of each building with the late Nyerpa of the Khyentse Labrang, then opened up the labrang's storeroom to assess the resources available to finance the project. All he found were two boxes of tea, seven or eight hide bags of barley, and a little butter.

"The storeroom is almost empty," observed the old Nyerpa. "How can Rinpoche even contemplate such an enormous project?"

"I will go on an alms-collecting tour," replied Rinpoche. "There won't be a problem."

He personally explained to his carpenter Tsewang Palden and his team what the shedra should look like, delegated the supervision of the work to Solpön Jamtra, then set out along the Yilung valley to Dargye Monastery to apply for a permit to gather alms. Once permission had been granted, he began his tour with a visit to Adzom Gar and from there went on to gather such a mountain of offerings that by the time he was twenty-four years old, work on the shedra had begun.

Adzom Drukpa

Adzom Drukpa was so delighted to receive Rinpoche's letter announcing his visit that he wrote back immediately, begging Rinpoche to come the very next day.

Rinpoche's party was received by all the lamas, monks, nuns, and lay practitioners of the monastery. They lined the path leading up to Adzom Gar and, at Adzom Drukpa's request, sang Jigme Lingpa's Tsok Lu from the *Heart Essence of the Vast Expanse* for auspiciousness. Adzom Drukpa wore a magnificent brocade robe woven in a golden coin pattern with very long sleeves. Around his head, he wrapped a long silk scarf in the style of a Punjabi turban, and several strings of dzi stones garlanded his neck. As he stepped forward to receive Rinpoche, he performed a lotus mudra and jumped down the steps—to many, it looked as though he was flying. He then seized the reins of Chökyi Lodrö's horse and personally led it to the Gar, where Rinpoche was invited to sit on a very high throne as Adzom Drukpa addressed the assembly.

"Here is the most extraordinary of my root master's tulkus. The wealthy among you must each offer Rinpoche a horse; those who are poor should offer a goat. I myself will offer everything I own: my entire fortune, authority, cattle, sheep, and Dharma lineage."

Later, Chökyi Lodrö described the offering to Dilgo Khyentse.

"It was an immensely generous gift," he said. "And I accepted everything Adzom Drukpa offered me so that Khamje Shedra could be built. He was a delightful master! And in addition to that astonishing offering, I also received the empowerments of *Embodiment of the Three Jewels* and Lhatsün Namkha Jigme's *Accomplishing the Life-Force of the Vidyadharas*."

The Third Dodrupchen, Jigme Tenpe Nyima

Rinpoche then traveled to Dodrup Gar to meet the predecessor of the present Dodrupchen for the first time. Although the Third Dodrupchen was not very old, he suffered from chronic ill health and couldn't walk unaided. Nevertheless, when Rinpoche arrived at his door, Dodrupchen greeted him personally, walking like a toddler and supported by two attendants.

As a rule, during the latter part of his life, the Third Dodrupchen only gave empowerments and teachings; he almost never spoke with anyone privately. But for Rinpoche he made a special effort and was very polite.

In spite of his frailty, Dodrupchen could read empowerment texts effortlessly. He gave Rinpoche the empowerments of *Gathering of Vidyadharas*, *Gathering of the Glorious Ones*, and *Three Roots of Nyingtik*, and it was during the empowerment of *Gathering of Vidyadharas* that Dodrupchen gave him the name Pema Yeshe Dorje.

Dodrupchen suffered from a disease of the mouth known in Tibetan as *bam* and *dre*. A characteristic of the illness is that the sufferer's gums swell and lesions appear between the teeth, and so Dodrupchen's lips and tongue were cracked and swollen, his teeth were black, and blood and pus oozed from his gums. He wrote, "When I was young, I met a sectarian teacher and accumulated a small amount of negative karma by discarding the Dharma. But as the effect of this negative karma is being purified in this life through my physical illnesses, I suffer no mental anguish or pain."

The teacher with "sectarian views" was a Gelugpa khenpo who had taught philosophy at Dodrupchen Monastery. When the khenpo passed away, the monks asked Dodrupchen where his memorial stupa should be built.

"Khenpo is the guru from whom I received teachings on all five volumes of the *Great Treatises*," replied Dodrupchen. "But his stupa should not be built inside this enclosure. It must go outside." Dodrupchen Monastery must have been influenced by the Gelugpas in the early days.

I have no idea how much material wealth Dodrupchen Monastery offered Rinpoche.

The Appointment of Khamje Shedra's Abbot

By the time Chökyi Lodrö returned to Khamje, the shedra had been completed without anyone suffering a shortage of resources. The first twenty-five students were admitted and were sponsored by Rinpoche, who had arranged a new system that would provide them with annual stipends.

Around the time Rinpoche intended to open the shedra, the prince of Derge, Tsewang Dudul, celebrated his wedding at Gönchen Monastery. All the teachers associated with the royal family were invited, including Khenpo Shenga, who traveled up from Palpung, where he was teaching. It was common knowledge that Khenpo wasn't on good terms with Palpung Monastery's authorities, and the wedding celebrations provided Rinpoche with the perfect opportunity to make him an offer.

"I am trying to establish a shedra," explained Rinpoche. "Would you consider coming to Dzongsar to be its abbot?"

Khenpo Shenga, the first
Khenpo of Khamje Shedra
Source: Shechen Archives

Khenpo Öntö Khyenrab, the second
Khenpo of Khamje Shedra
Source: Shechen Archives

Khenpo Jamyang Gyaltsen, the
third Khenpo of Khamje Shedra
Source: Shechen Archives

Khenpo Shenga immediately accepted Rinpoche's offer. "I must leave Dzongsar for now," he said, "but as Rinpoche's vision is so far-sighted, I will definitely return next year."

"The saying, 'if beggars fight, it's a boon for the dogs' is quite true!" said Rinpoche to his close attendants. "Khenpo Shenga has agreed to come back next year!"

"If beggars fight, it's a boon for the dogs" is a Tibetan saying. When beggars fight among themselves, they use their tsampa bags to beat their opponents, which is "a boon" for the dogs because ground barley is scattered all over the floor and easy for them to lap up.

Khenpo Shenga kept his promise and Khamje Shedra was inaugurated when he returned the following year. Gongna Tulku heard all this from Chökyi Lodrö himself.

The Management of Resources

Yangsi Rinpoche Thubten Chökyi Gyatso asked me, "Was Sotra sent to supervise the managers of the monastery's produce?"

No, he wasn't. Khamje Shedra, Dzongsar Monastery, and Karmo Tak Tsang Retreat Centre each had separate managers who were supervised by a senior official. Jagö Lama, who had been the revenue officer (*dzongpön*) for Dzongsar Monastery for many years, was appointed as the Derge government representative (*hodra*); it was his job to check that the barley and wheat were collected appropriately.

In those days, Tibet still followed the ancient tradition under which an institution like Khyentse Labrang didn't own any land itself. The king and queen of Derge owned most of the vast arable lands scattered all over Kham and offered a number of fields to Khyentse Labrang, the shedra, and two retreat centers. A few other landowners in Derge also offered fields and provided the labor to plant, tend, and gather the crops. All the labrang had to do was provide the seeds and send a member of staff to oversee the harvest to ensure the correct amount of produce was collected and distributed to each institution. The administrator of Khamje Shedra would then distribute six months' worth of grain, butter, and salt to each of the shedra monks and staff. The labrang staff were given food and somewhere to sleep but no wage of any kind.

The labrang used a great deal of butter for light offerings and owned large herds of dris specifically to produce the milk that was churned into butter to fill the lamps. (Shops that sold ready-made butter didn't exist in those days.)

These herds were leased out to various nomadic families, who looked after the animals and sent a percentage of the milk and butter they produced to the labrang. Butter was also offered to the labrang by devotees, as were grain, meat, and so on. All the offerings were then locked away in the storeroom of Rinpoche's residence, and the only people allowed to touch them were the two solpöns who made the butter lamps. Money was rarely offered.

Once he had established Khamje Shedra, Rinpoche provided the seed money to fund regular supplies of grain and butter, and so on, for Khamje Shedra, the Karmo Tak Tsang Retreat Centre, and another Sakya retreat center, Dragön, at Derge Rinchen Monastery.

Religious activities at Dzongsar Monastery were usually sponsored by local villagers, and the monastery allocated a separate budget for each of the routine offering ceremonies. It was only when Rinpoche chose to do more elaborate rituals that the labrang had to make up the shortfall—for example, for the annual Vajrakilaya drupchö. The labrang also financed new initiatives. For example, Rinpoche did away with the old tradition of sacred dance at Dzongsar and encouraged the monks to learn new dances from Sakya Monastery, then put on a sacred dance festival. Apart from that, it wasn't necessary for Rinpoche to support the monastery financially or for him to make any kind of offering to Tharpatse.[10]

Nose-Rope

"Jamyang Khyentse Wangpo was a very clever man," said Rinpoche to Dilgo Khyentse one day. "He never lost a nose-rope to others."

Rinpoche was paraphrasing a line from one of the aspiration prayers: "Binding the nose-rope around my own head, may I persevere in the holy Dharma."[11] It means Khyentse Wangpo could never be manipulated or controlled by others.

When Ngor Monastery recognized him as one of their shabdrung and sent a large offering of tents, camping equipment, and horses, Rinpoche managed to head off the caravan and send everything back before it reached him. He would not need any of the equipment, he said, because he intended to become a wanderer. This was a move worthy of Khyentse Wangpo, because had Chökyi Lodrö accepted the recognition and gifts sent by the Ngorpas, from then on he would have been obliged to make substantial annual offerings to Ngor, and if he ever failed in that obligation, he would have been disqualified from being a Ngor abbot. So, in retrospect, Rinpoche turned out to be just as clever as Khyentse Wangpo.

6. The Early Years at Khyentse Labrang

When Khyentse Wangpo was at Dzongsar, he lived in houses offered by the Somo and Dumo families. When Khyentse Chökyi Lodrö first moved to Dzongsar, he lived in a house that had originally belonged to the Dilgo family, where an old monk and relative of Khyentse Wangpo had once lived, and from time to time, Khyentse Wangpo must have visited him there. I think there's still a stone fixed above the door with "Chime Drupe Gatsal" carved into it, like mani mantras are carved into rock. All these buildings were made of bamboo mats and stood side by side. Once Khyentse Chökyi Lodrö had settled permanently at Dzongsar, doorways were cut through the walls to make one large structure, which was then known as Khyentse Labrang. Here are some of the stories I've heard about life in the labrang.

Initially Rinpoche didn't have many attendants, just a cook, a solpön, and Tsejor. He didn't like having laypeople in the labrang. If he heard that a layperson was staying there, he would say, "What is *he* doing here, eating my food and misusing offerings? Tell him to go away!"

In those days, Derge Tsang did not send important emissaries to Dzongsar, and generally life was far less busy than it would later become. Tsejor said that Rinpoche's mind seemed perfectly at peace and very clear, and that he was able to guide a multitude of activities, both large and small. He would practice from early morning until midday in complete silence, relax a little after lunch, then practice again in the late afternoon. His attendants also lived pleasant, leisurely lives.

"That was when I was truly happy," said Rinpoche to Tsejor one day.

"You were happy, even though you had so few attendants and no wealth?" exclaimed Tsejor, a little surprised.

"However much wealth I now own," replied Rinpoche, "I never experience the kind of peace and happiness I enjoyed in those early days."

The Regular Rituals Performed at the Labrang

The *Gathering of the Dakini's Secrets* ritual was performed at the labrang on Khyentse Wangpo's anniversary, but it was usually a drupchö, rarely a drupchen. Mandalas, ornaments,[12] and empowerment substances were set out on a shrine that stood against a wall, with tormas and offering substances arranged in front of it. Although many practitioners who did not live at the labrang gathered to take part in the practice, by and large, it was performed by lamas and monks.

The most expensive celebration at the labrang was the anniversary of the birth of Guru Rinpoche, which falls on the tenth day of the fifth or sixth Tibetan lunar month, and for which an elaborate feast offering based on the *Gathering of the Guru's Secrets* was performed. The Sakya dharmapala practices for Gur Mahakala, Zhal Zhipa, and Makzor Gyalmo, and the dharmapala prayers from Ngödrup Roltso—the nine protectors of the Mindrolling tradition—were performed alternately on the twenty-ninth day of each lunar month. (During the Ngödrup Roltso, it was forbidden to do prayers for the protectors' attendants, so they were not performed.) The *Gathering of Vidyadharas* and *Consort Practice: The Queen of Great Bliss* sadhanas were performed on the tenth and twenty-fifth days, respectively, beginning early in the morning and finishing before dusk.

Every year without fail throughout Rinpoche's life, on the third day of the new year, the Somo family offered him a large square of sweet cheese. This famous annual gift was always placed in Rinpoche's own storeroom alongside his meat and butter. The labrang's treasurer would cut the cheese into twelve equal pieces and offer a portion to every tenth-day tsok that year. The cheese would be added to some tsampa, then one large and one small vajra-headed tsok torma were made from the mixture. These two tormas, some meat, and a little roasted barley were the only substances offered, and the smaller torma was always offered to Rinpoche.

Rinpoche told Dilgo Khyentse that the Somo family "has been giving me cheese ever since I arrived at this monastery and I have always offered it to the tenth-day feast practices. I think they get it from the Copper-Colored Mountain."

For tsoks, Rinpoche would take his bald leopard skin from its cloth bag and spread it out on the shrine. He also took out five cheap plates, a stand, and a knife. The plates (including the "liberation" plate) were arranged from the head to the tail of the leopard skin, and Rinpoche's monks had to make sure a good chunk of torma was placed in the first plate, because if they didn't, an old man who grunted and coughed all the time wouldn't get his share, and Rinpoche would be seriously displeased.

Tsok wine was drawn from a small wooden barrel that had been used for the same purpose since the time of Khyentse Wangpo. The monks were under strict orders to pour the wine directly into a skull cup; they could never pour it first into a kettle or pot, then transfer it into the kapala. And, Rinpoche said, they must never allow the barrel to run even slightly low. If they did, he would scold them furiously.

The old man would shuffle after Tashi Namgyal when he went to fetch the tsok wine. "Azhang! Azhang!" he'd grunt as he held out a large wooden cup. "Give me a cupful!" Tashi Namgyal would fill his cup, and the old man always drank it down in one, making slurping and gurgling sounds as he swallowed. He'd then disappear until the next time Tashi Namgyal went for wine—he never once failed to turn up.

Sometimes, when Rinpoche couldn't sleep or his blood pressure was high, he would fetch some ara from the old barrel himself, mix it with agar 35 (a Tibetan herbal medicine for pacifying the wind element in the body), then drink it down.

At the end of each tsok, the old woman who fetched water for the labrang would appear at the door and, as Rinpoche looked on, was given the leftovers to take home with her.

The tsok tormas for the tenth-day tsoks were vajra-headed, and those for the twenty-fifth-day tsok were always round. Rinpoche never offered any Somo cheese to the twenty-fifth-day feast.

The labrang had a ram's skull complete with horns that was always used during Losar celebrations. For the rest of the year, it was stored in the room where the reliquaries were kept. Rinpoche considered this ram's skull to be very auspicious as it had belonged to the labrang since the time of Khyentse Wangpo. When it was needed, he would go to the storeroom himself to fetch it. In fact, no one was allowed into that storeroom apart from Rinpoche. (I don't know for sure, but Chakdzö might have gone down there once or twice.) On the thirtieth day of the twelfth month of each year, Rinpoche would give the ram's skull to his attendants and ask them to use it to create a beautiful ram's-head torma. The attendants would repair the skull with colored butter, give it eyes and a mouth, anoint its horns with oil, then offer it to Rinpoche on a large platter.

Rinpoche always personally ordered what was necessary for the Losar

Jamyang Khyentse Chökyi Lodrö wearing a Sakya hat
in Jamyang Khyentse Wangpo's room at Dzongsar in the late 1930s
Source: Khyentse Labrang

celebrations with great care and well in advance, including a great deal of fruit like oranges and apples. The fruit sometimes arrived fifteen or twenty days ahead of time and, because he couldn't trust anyone else to do it properly, Rinpoche would pour ten bags of barley into a box and position each piece of fruit individually so that no two pieces touched, then cover it all with a thin layer of grain. In spite of his care, though, there were times when the fruit began to rot. On the thirtieth day of the last month of the year, the offerings were set out on the shrine, and tormas were made. Those invited to attend, including all the residents of the labrang, would paste their names to spots on the shrine room floor to ensure that everyone had a place to sit.

On the first day of the new year, everyone rose at 3 A.M. and did the *Activity Practice: A Garland of Jewels* and the practices of Tseringma and Zhal Zhipa from the Mindrolling tradition. Khampa trumpets were sounded during the practice, and when a really good chant master was present, Rinpoche would let him play Khyentse Wangpo's cymbals; if the chant leader wasn't so good, he would be given a different pair to use. They started early because the practice had to be over by daybreak, when fermented rice, butter tea, and saffron rice were served. After that, apart from the long-life wine and ritual pills that remained on the table in front of Rinpoche, the tsok and tormas were cleared away and the room cleaned, ready for the Dzongsar Monastery monks' New Year's Day audience.

Not many other people would see Rinpoche that day. After the audience, food was prepared for Rinpoche's close family, Shechen Rabjam, Dilgo Khyentse, and Katok Situ, and seats were arranged. Lunch was served on the labrang's best porcelain at around 10 A.M., directed personally by Rinpoche, then for the rest of the day, Rinpoche and the lamas would relax. Dinner was served at 3 P.M., and for supper they all ate noodles.

In those days in Tibet, people usually ate four meals a day. They would have tea and tsampa early in the morning (it was called *den ja*), lunch at 10 A.M., dinner at 3 or 4 P.M., and just a little something before they went to bed.

Khyentse Chökyi Lodrö's Attendants

Solpön Jamtra

I heard this story from Tsejor, but part of it is mentioned in the *Great Biography*.

Rinpoche was no more than eighteen years old when he took a young boy called Jamtra into his care. When he was old enough, Jamtra became one of Rinpoche's attendants and remained with him for ten or twenty years. I asked Tsejor what Jamtra was like.

"Jamtra had great devotion for Rinpoche," he said. "I don't know if it was the kind of devotion described in the sacred texts, but it was obvious that he liked Rinpoche very much. He was a typical Khampa, very full of himself and extremely volatile."

When the shabdrung of Ngochok Tsang visited Dzongsar, Jamtra said, "I don't think Rinpoche will be able to resist going to greet Ngochok Tsang tomorrow with a white scarf." The other attendants agreed that Rinpoche, always polite and deferential, would without doubt take the more submissive position. But the thought of Rinpoche humbling himself in that way infuriated Jamtra.

"Dzongsar Jamyang Chökyi Lodrö is also a shabdrung!" argued Jamtra. "Why should one shabdrung humble himself before another?"

The next day, as predicted, Rinpoche visited Ngochok Tsang Shabdrung and offered him a white scarf. Jamtra was livid and spent the day prowling around the labrang like an angry tiger, growling at everything Rinpoche said to him.

A few days later, Rinpoche asked Tsejor if Jamtra had said anything about traveling to the Ngorpa center in Lhasa.

"Yes," replied Tsejor. "He's said he is planning to go."

"Tell him not to," said Rinpoche. "Do everything in your power to stop him. I have a strong feeling that if he does go, he won't have much success. But don't tell him I said so, he'll just get cross. You must tell him yourself."

So Tsejor told Jamtra not to go to Lhasa.

"Yeh? And why shouldn't I go? Everyone else goes!" yelled Jamtra. "Oh, I get it now. It's not you, it's Rinpoche who thinks I shouldn't go! Well, whatever Rinpoche says, I can't afford to cancel the trip now, so I'll have to go!"

When he heard how Jamtra had responded to his advice, Rinpoche gave Tsejor fifty coins.

"Give this money to Jamtra," he said, "and tell him from me that if he really wants to go to Lhasa, he should take it with him."

But when Tsejor gave Jamtra the coins—which included some of the ancient Chinese coins still circulating in Derge in those days—he instantly lost his temper.

"I have money! My family is rich! I don't need Rinpoche's money!" he snapped.

"Khorey!" said Tsejor. "Bite your tongue! It's a gift from Rinpoche, so you should take it."

Jamtra calmed down and considered his situation. On reflection, he realized he needed at least some of Rinpoche's money, so he pocketed half the coins and asked Tsejor to return the rest to Rinpoche. He then started to plan his trip. Actually, in the end, Rinpoche arranged everything for him. He even provided Jamtra with a good dzo to carry his luggage, which could be sold once Jamtra got to Lhasa. And throughout all these preparations, Rinpoche said again and again that he didn't think Jamtra would be able to look after himself on this trip.

In those days, most people didn't go directly from Dzongsar to Lhasa; they followed a more circuitous route, and the journey usually took between three and four months. Once in Lhasa, Jamtra received all the empowerments, transmissions, and instructions he had gone for. Then, as winter began to bite, he set out for Dzongsar. One night, just south of Tsang, he made camp with some fellow travelers. As they slept, a gang of dacoits collapsed their tent and hacked the six or seven people trapped beneath it to death. News traveled slowly in that part of the world, so no one heard about the atrocity until the following summer. Not much was said publicly, but privately everyone agreed it was a terrible tragedy.

Jamtra's Liberation

I asked Tashi Namgyal if he knew anything about Solpön Jamtra's death, but he didn't. What he had heard, though, was that as a consequence of Jamtra's uncontrollable anger, he had been reborn as a snake and that Rinpoche had then liberated him. So I asked Pewar Tulku if he knew anything about it. He wept as he told me the details.

During lunch one day, Rinpoche said he wanted to visit a mountain slope behind Dzongsar Monastery, not far from Zariju. That afternoon, as Rinpoche and his attendants walked up from the spring, a black snake making a *khyuk-khyuk* sound, slithered from a hole in the rock. Rinpoche approached the snake, but it reacted aggressively and reared up, flickering its forked tongue.

"Khorey, Jamtra! Don't you recognize me?" asked Rinpoche several times.

Eventually, the snake dropped to the ground and appeared to weep. Rinpoche took it back to the labrang in a bamboo basket and his monks fed it milk, but within a few days, the snake was dead. Rinpoche then performed all the usual rites for the dead, including recitations from the *Great Liberation through Hearing in the Bardo*, the liberation sadhanas, and various purification rituals.

I asked Chakdzö Tsewang Paljor if Rinpoche ever said anything about Jamtra's rebirth. Yes, he said, Rinpoche told them that the snake had been reborn as a monk somewhere in Tsang, near Sakya Monastery. I also asked Tashi Namgyal if the stories about Jamtra were true, and he said they were.

"I have never said anything before now," he said, "because we were not supposed to talk about it. It was kept secret in case ordinary people were shocked to learn that a close attendant of Khyentse Rinpoche had been reborn as a snake."

I heard this story from Tsejor, Tashi Namgyal, and Pewar Tulku, and they all told it the same way.

Jamtra's rebirth was the result of his own behavior, but Rinpoche's blessings and Jamtra's accumulated good karma meant that, even as a snake, he lived near Rinpoche's home and that Rinpoche found him, took him to the labrang, and liberated him after he died.

Chokden

Soon after Solpön Jamtra's death, a Dzongsar monk who was a good torma maker and had served as both shrine master and close attendant to the previous incarnation, also passed away. Although several of Rinpoche's monks could make tormas and look after his shrines, none of them knew how to make the Nyingmapa tormas that he needed at that time.

Chokden was a well-educated Drukpa Kagyü monk from Adeu Rinpoche's Tsechu Monastery in Nangchen. He had completed a retreat at the Drukpa Kagyü Ladzo Monastery Retreat Centre, had mastered all the traditional chants, and had a good understanding of the teachings. More to the point, he had an unrivaled expertise in torma-making and first-class knowledge and experience of all shrine activities. He was also a close relative of Dilgo Khyentse, who often employed him when he performed rituals for families like Phuma Tsang. When Dilgo Khyentse realized that an attendant with Chokden's skills was needed at the labrang, he told Rinpoche all about him. So it was thanks to Dilgo Khyentse that Chokden became one of Rinpoche's attendants.

Tashi Namgyal

Tashi Namgyal's elder brother was the dünkor of Drumo Tsang, but as so many of their family had died when Tashi Namgyal was very young, Rinpoche decided to bring him up in the labrang and train him to be the attendant responsible for serving Rinpoche his tea and food, and so on. But as Tashi Namgyal was barely twelve years old, he was still too young to take up all his duties. So he was given to Chakdzö, who was still a monk at the time, to be his attendant. One moment, said Tashi Namgyal, he was a son of the aristocratic Drumo family and wore rich and formal dünkor robes, then suddenly he was a poorly dressed servant and the attendant of a monk.

Just before Rinpoche made his escape to India, the attendant who served Rinpoche's food and drink passed away. It was then that Dilgo Khyentse told Tashi Namgyal that his life might be short and that he could die if he did not immediately become a monk. Rinpoche performed the first haircutting ceremony, and a little later Tashi Namgyal and two others—possibly Dhongthog Tulku and Pewar Tulku—received full bhikshu ordination from Dezhung Tulku Ajam and started wearing zens and monks' robes.

Yangsi Rinpoche Thubten Chökyi Gyatso asked me, "Was Rinpoche good to Tashi Namgyal?" Yes, I think he was. Tashi Namgyal was an aristocrat, and Rinpoche loved him dearly. He served Rinpoche in a number of ways for a very long time. Yet he remained completely uneducated; Rinpoche never once asked him to study. Although I'm quite sure that Tashi Namgyal received many, many teachings on the introduction to the nature of mind. From the moment Tulku Salga told him that his life span was exhausted, he recited sadhanas with great diligence. But, he said, the only instruction Rinpoche ever gave him, which he repeated several times, was that he should try his best to accomplish the practice. On one such occasion, Rinpoche came across Tashi Namgyal as he was practicing near Chakdzö's room. (I think Tashi Namgyal must have been staying in the room through which Rinpoche had to pass to get to the toilet.) "Practice sincerely," Rinpoche said. "Dying is not easy." And he continued on his way, laughing.

Drumo Wangchen
Most of the male children in Tashi Namgyal's family suffered violent and unnatural deaths as a result of ancient family feuds and enmities, but his elder brother, Drumo Wangchen, died at the hands of the Chinese. Drumo Wangchen was known to have enthusiastically embraced bad behavior from a very young age and, throughout his life, demonstrated a voracious appetite for trouble. He was also quite devoted to Rinpoche.

Tashi Namgyal and Drumo Wangchen knew all there was to know about how things worked at the labrang. Before Rinpoche left on his summer camping expeditions, they would know exactly how little dried meat was left for Rinpoche to take with him. The slaughter of animals for meat was absolutely prohibited at the labrang, and meat of any kind was difficult to come by locally. But Rinpoche liked meat and would hardly touch his food if none was available. In fact, of all the different foods he was offered, meat momos were his favorite. He didn't like fancy food at all. Dilgo Khyentse said that Rinpoche used to eat a lot. At lunch he would eat until his stomach was full, but by 3 or 4 P.M. he was hungry again and often called for meat and Tibetan biscuits. So his attendants had to make sure there was always something to offer him.

Bearing all this in mind, Wangchen regularly declared in the middle of a camping expedition that he was missing his mother and had to return home. And Rinpoche always let him go. Then, once Wangchen was sure Rinpoche had left for Dophu, he'd commission a butcher to kill a healthy, nonsuckling dri (if the animal had a calf, its meat would not be good), then camouflage it by wrapping it up and load it onto a horse. He and his brother would then take it secretly to Dophu. The meat would be stored in the white oven in the black, yak-hair kitchen tent that was always pitched near Rinpoche's, and Wangchen would prepare and cook the dri's intestines for Rinpoche to eat.

Drungyig Tsering

Drungyig Tsering was a very intelligent and accomplished pandita. He knew the teachings well and had studied poetry, grammar, vocabulary, and philosophy. Like Khenpo Appey, he came from Kutse. As each family was compelled to send one of their sons to a monastery as a kind of "monk tax," he was sent, at a very young age, to the Nyingma monastery at Mugsang. Later though, his brothers sent him to Palpung, because that was the monastery to which they were particularly devoted. From then on, Drungyig Tsering maintained a close connection with Palpung.

It was when Khyentse Rinpoche decided to make print blocks for the collected works of his predecessor (which still exist today) that Drungyig Tsering was brought to Dzongsar to copy out the texts. He did a good job and was kept on as Khyentse Labrang's resident copyist. I've been told he got drunk quite regularly, and in his cups he easily lost his temper—particularly with Chakdzö Tsewang Paljor. They say he'd pick fights with Chakdzö and once charged straight at him, brandishing a knife! But apart from his weakness for drink and craving for material wealth, he wasn't a bad man.

One day, Rinpoche announced he would do a very strict two-month retreat somewhere outside the labrang. Although Rinpoche usually answered all his letters immediately, throughout this retreat, he said, Drungyig Tsering and Chakdzö should reply on his behalf, and under no circumstance should they forward anything to him.

Many, many letters arrived, including three with official seals from Derge Tsang, each brought by a separate messenger who was instructed to stay at Dzongsar until Rinpoche replied.

The day after his retreat ended, as Rinpoche sat in the sun having his head shaved, Drungyig Tsering brought him a large package.

"What's this?" asked Rinpoche. Drungyig Tsering explained it was a packet of the letters Rinpoche had received while in retreat.

"Get them out, I want to look at them," said Rinpoche.

Drungyig Tsering opened the package and handed Rinpoche a letter. "Letters about divinations aren't important," he said.

So Drungyig Tsering gave him the first letter from Derge Tsang.

"This is a very important letter!" exclaimed Rinpoche. "When did you receive it?"

"Quite a while ago," replied Drungyig Tsering.

"It was extremely improper of me not to have replied before now. Akhi! Who brought it?"

Drungyig Tsering told him about the messenger who was waiting for his reply. Rinpoche put the letter aside and asked for the next. Drungyig Tsering handed him the second letter from Derge Tsang.

"What's this?" asked Rinpoche. "Akhi! Where did I get the courage to ignore these letters? And that one there? Is that also a letter from Derge Tsang?"

"Yes," replied Drungyig Tsering. "It arrived after the second one."

By now Rinpoche was quite annoyed.

"Why didn't you tell me about these letters?" he snapped.

"Rinpoche instructed us not to forward anything at all to his retreat," wailed Drungyig Tsering, but Rinpoche was too angry to listen.

"Khorey! You are nothing but a mouse, yet you try to act like a lion! I can't believe you kept them from me!" And he stood up and slapped Drungyig Tsering's face three times with all his strength. Although he felt irritated and the first slap had hurt a little, Drungyig Tsering said that the second and third caused him no pain at all. In fact, they made him want to burst out laughing.

Rubbing his hands together, Rinpoche sat down and softened visibly.

"My friend, did I really say that? I did? Then I shouldn't have. And I shouldn't have ignored these letters. Get me a sheet of paper, I must reply immediately."

In those days, Rinpoche used to roll up the more commonplace letters he wrote and send them wrapped in a white scarf. Envelopes were reserved for important letters, like those to Derge Tsang, which he always secured with his official seal.

Another time Rinpoche summoned Drungyig Tsering and told him to write a letter to Palpung Monastery.

"Write the letter exactly as I've instructed," he said. "Seal it and send it to Palpung at dawn tomorrow."

"La so," replied Drungyig Tsering, then forgot all about it.

In the middle of the night, he awoke with a start and remembered the letter he was supposed to have written. He leapt out of bed and, as luck would have it, realized he had neither a butter lamp nor even a sliver of moon to see by. He felt around for his inkpot, pen, and paper, and even though it was pitch black, spent the rest of the night writing precisely what Rinpoche had dictated. The messenger turned up far too early, but by then Drungyig Tsering could see well enough to be sure that although an expert might notice the odd mistake here and there, the script was at least legible.

Drungyig Tsering admitted that Rinpoche had lost his temper with him more than once. One of his jobs was to keep a list of the names of the dead that was needed for the liberation rituals and to look after the money offered. For Rinpoche, the most heinous crime anyone could commit was to lose that offering money, and when Tsering did just that, Rinpoche was furious.

Drungyig Tsering served as a personal attendant until Rinpoche left Tibet for India. He then traveled to Shechen Monastery to copy texts for Shechen Rabjam and went on to accompany him on his year-long alms-collecting tour around Dzachukha. After traveling on his own for a while, Drungyig Tsering eventually joined Khyentse Rinpoche in Sikkim, arriving just in time to take part in his pilgrimage to the holy sites of India. He remained in Sikkim until long after Rinpoche's mind had dissolved into primordial space, then moved to Kalimpong, where he worked as Dudjom Jigdral Yeshe Dorje's secretary for a few years. It was when Chatral Sangye Dorje borrowed him to copy out the treasure teachings of Sera Khandro that Tsering's thumb became paralyzed, making it impossible for him to hold a pen. He said he'd always doubted the wisdom of taking on that project, and had even asked if he were really qualified to work on such profound teachings without having received any empowerments, transmissions, or instructions. But Chatral Sangye Dorje had told him not to worry.

Drungyig Tsering stayed with Palpung Situ until he moved to Rumtek. Then, as Drungyig Tsering neither liked the Karmapa nor had much devotion for him, he decided to go to Bir instead. We were living in Rajpur at the time and he stayed with us for a while, then we all traveled up to Bir together. He later passed away in the hospital at Dharamsala.

The texts he copied are extraordinarily well executed. I overheard Dilgo Khyentse say to Butse that Rinpoche must have had a great deal of merit, because without it, he would never have been able to find such an excellent copyist and secretary. It is widely believed that the effectiveness and benefit of a guru's activity is dependent on the extent of his authority and the qualities of his secretary. Most of the texts held by Khyentse Labrang were copied by Drungyig Tsering, which means he must have written out all of Khyentse Wangpo's treasure teachings.

Tsering Tashi: Secretary to Jamyang Khyentse Wangpo
Tsering Tashi was Jamyang Khyentse Wangpo's secretary and lived with him for most of his life. Dilgo Khyentse told me that in Khyentse Wangpo's final year, he had offered Tsering Tashi a choice. "Drungyig, there's an obstacle to your life that I have the power to dispel, but if I do, we will not meet again in our next lives. So you must choose: shall I dispel the obstacle, or would you rather we meet again?"

"In this life I've spent as much time with Rinpoche as I possibly could," said Tashi Tsering. "And as I can't avoid dying, I don't much care whether it happens sooner or later. All I want to be sure of is that I will meet Rinpoche in my next life. So there's no need to dispel the obstacle."

After that, Khyentse Wangpo passed into the realm of peace.

When the print blocks for Khyentse Wangpo's collected writings were made, Tsering Tashi was sent to Derge Gönchen to edit the texts. He chose not to sleep at the monastery and instead spent his nights in a small tent that he pitched by a stream—the one that flowed from Ngulchu Phuk. Then one night, torrential rain swept his tent away, and Tsering Tashi was drowned.

Yangsi Rinpoche Thubten Chökyi Gyatso asked me if Chökyi Lodrö's secretary had been the incarnation of Khyentse Wangpo's secretary. I don't think he was. I asked Dilgo Khyentse a few times to identify Tashi Tsering's incarnation, but he said he didn't know.

Jampal

Now I'll tell you another kind of story. It's one of those stories that almost everyone already knows about, but Tashi Namgyal and I heard it from Jampal himself.

Jampal (Tsangpon Jampal) and his wife, Pema Tsekye, outside
the Tsuglakhang at the Palace Monastery in Gangtok, Sikkim, in 1984
Source: Jiga Shenyentsang

At Khyentse Labrang, Jampal was one of Rinpoche's men of business. He was responsible for doing much of the labrang's shopping, which in those days was a vitally important job. It involved making the perilous journey to China on foot at least once a year—there and back could take six months—and then spending the rest of his time traveling all over Tibet.

One day, Rinpoche sent for Jampal just as he was about to set out on one of his long trips.

"Khorey! What kind of protection do you have?" asked Rinpoche.

Jampal had a statue of Gur Mahakala, but he didn't want to tell Rinpoche about it because he was afraid Rinpoche would take it from him. He was especially nervous because not long before, he'd almost lost that very statue to Sakya Gongma. So he told Rinpoche that his uncle had given him one of Khyentse Wangpo's teeth. Rinpoche asked to see it and said, predictably, "I need that tooth!"

Rinpoche took the tooth and replaced it with a statue of the Medicine

Buddha and a piece of his own clothing, saying it would protect Jampal from deadly weapons.

"You must wear it!" said Rinpoche. "And you will need to be extra careful on this trip. If you aren't, you will attract obstacles. Recite as many Seven-Line Prayers as possible." Rinpoche then placed both his hands on Jampal's head and prayed for a long time.

Nothing happened on the outward journey, but on his way back from Hor, as he crossed a high pass, the group of traders he was traveling with was ambushed by a band of Nyakrong natives. The traders fought back, and from early morning until midday both sides exchanged fire. Fortunately Jampal wasn't hit, even though a couple of bullets ricocheted from rocks close by, but two of his party were killed. The rest of them escaped before nightfall, afraid that if they stayed to fight they'd be overrun in the dark. Jampal said that he had wondered about killing the mule carrying the four bags of black tobacco he intended to sell in Lhasa. He said he could see it quite clearly, grazing among the labrang's mules, which were also heavily laden with valuables. But as it was his own mule, he couldn't bring himself to put it to death. And anyway, as most of the labrang's wealth was tied up in black tobacco, Jampal was very aware that the only way he'd be able get it all to Calcutta and Kalimpong through Lhasa was by mule.

When I asked Tashi Namgyal what he knew about the ambush, he said he'd heard that after fierce fighting, Jampal's group had run away. He wasn't sure if any of the Nyakrong plunderers had been injured or killed, but he was absolutely certain that they had stolen all the labrang's mules and their valuable loads.

Eventually, Jampal made it back to the labrang and reported to Chakdzö, who was so infuriated that he instantly informed Rinpoche. They should perform powerful magic to destroy the thieves, said Rinpoche, which made Chakdzö very happy.

"Rinpoche will make his rage felt!" said Chakdzö, with some relish. "He won't let those marauders get away with it. Something really terrible is going to happen to them!"

The next day, he asked Rinpoche what kind of sorcery he would perform.

"The reason this happened in the first place is that previously accumulated bad karmic debt has not been purified. Are you going against my advice in your business dealings? If you want to use some really powerful sorcery to purify your karmic debts, recite the *Prayer of Excellent Conduct* three hundred thousand times."

Rinpoche's words so angered Chakdzö that by the time he reached the kitchen, his face had turned black. When asked what Rinpoche had said, he replied, "Rinpoche is behaving like a madman! I don't understand him. He says that all we have to do is recite the *Prayer of Excellent Conduct* three hundred thousand times and make offerings!"

Regardless of Rinpoche's advice, Chakdzö insisted it was necessary to destroy the raiders. So he invited Rinpoche's younger brother, Tersey Chime, and three lamas from Rekong to perform the rituals. At noon some days later, Tersey Chime declared, a little testily, "We must make a decision. We can't wait any longer." And everyone held their breath as he swept into Rinpoche's house.

"Arekha! Rinpoche!" yelled Tersey Chime. "You must either stop doing ceremonies for removing obstacles or stop granting protection to the obstacle makers. My practice is getting nowhere! It's certainly not destroying our enemies. I swear I will not complete the ceremony if you continue to protect them!"

"Chime! What's happened?" asked Rinpoche pacifically.

"Chakdzö instructed us to perform these rituals, yet you yourself are protecting your enemies!" snapped Tersey Chime.

"I have done nothing," replied Rinpoche innocently. "I am merely reciting the refuge prayer. Are you suggesting that the Nyakrong bandits are being summoned at the same moment I chant 'all sentient beings as vast as space'? Because apart from that, I have done nothing special for them. All I ever do is chant the refuge prayer."

"No!" insisted Tersey Chime. "You *are* protecting them! As I start to summon the enemies of Buddhadharma from Nyakrong, you take them away with your zen, like this."

The upshot was that, try as they might, Tersey Chime and the Rekong lamas were unable to do anything against the Nyakrong raiders.

As the labrang had lost more than thirty heavily laden mules to the raiders, Chakdzö filed a lawsuit with the Derge court to try to recover them. The court duly notified the Nyakrong people but was unable to resolve the situation.

Chakdzö refused to give up. He traveled to Hor and told the people of Nyakrong that everything they had plundered belonged to Jamyang Khyentse and not the round-eyed lama of Derge, who had been the real target of their revenge. Before long the Chinese turned up, and Chakdzö talked the situation over with them. The Chinese official's interpreter must have liked

Lakar Tsang because he advised Chakdzö not to pursue the case, pointing out that the fact that Khyentse Labrang traded in tobacco was sure to backfire on him. So Chakdzö ran out of options and had to give up.

Had the Chinese not become involved, Tashi Namgyal and the people of Derge would without doubt have combined forces to mount an attack on Nyakrong. Tashi Namgyal wouldn't have thought twice about it and could easily have mobilized at least a thousand fighters. The situation became even more tense when fighting broke out nearby as Shenyen Tsang attempted to avenge the murder of his son, Tsewang Norbu, in Kongpo. But again the Chinese intervened, this time by occupying Shenyen Tsang's land.

Actually, the people of Nyakrong weren't really vicious dacoits. The problem was that so many of them had been killed by people from Derge that their hearts were filled with hatred for everyone and everything that came from that region. So when Jampal was ambushed by the Nyakong raiders, he had simply become caught up in an age-old feud between the two regions.

It must also be said that by trading in black tobacco, the labrang's men of business were playing into the hands of the Chinese, who always claimed that tobacco and bullets were only sold by the monasteries, not ordinary Tibetans. But that was the only kind of business Jampal ever engaged in. These days, if it became known that a monastery acquired its main source of income through the sale of tobacco, the scandal would be devastating.

The Labrang's Messengers

Telephones hadn't yet come to Tibet, so Rinpoche and members of the labrang maintained regular contact with people in faraway places through a team of messengers who spent their lives taking letters and packages all over the country. Having spent many weeks on the road, it was quite common for a messenger to return to the labrang in the morning only to be sent on another errand so quickly that he'd be gone again before sunset.

MEDICINE

Chökyi Lodrö had a large, gray hide bag that he used to store Loter Wangpo's leather hat wrapped in a dark green cloth, and various other health-giving substances. Tsejor said that if he ever caught a cold that provoked a sinusitis attack, Rinpoche would call for Loter Wangpo's leather hat, flick it until a couple of strands of hair fell out, then burn the hair and inhale the smoke. Rinpoche also had the unwashed woolen handkerchief that Adzom Drukpa always used after he inhaled snuff, and when he was ill, Rinpoche would sometimes eat one or two pieces of the dried mucous, without showing any signs of disgust, then hit his body with the hanky. Or he'd hit himself lightly with one of Katok Situ's long belts. But he only ever engaged in such practices as a last resort.

A Cure for Rinpoche's Laryngitis

Tashi Namgyal said that once, as a result of broken samayas, Rinpoche suffered from a bout of laryngitis so severe that he was unable to speak. Shechen Rabjam, Dilgo Khyentse, and his brother, Sangye Nyenpa, were staying at Dzongsar at the time and immediately started doing a Tara puja in the presence of Drolma Lungtenma (the Tara statue that made prophecies). When they didn't come down for lunch, Tashi Namgyal took up some Tibetan biscuits, bread, and tea, and he listened to their conversation as he served their refreshments. Rinpoche's sickness might have been far more serious, they said, but it wouldn't get any worse now, because as a result of their puja, the Tara statue had become even more majestic. They should therefore look out for more signs of accomplishment.

Curious to see if what they said about the Tara statue was true, Tashi Namgyal examined her carefully. Sure enough, he said, she was not only more august but seemed to glisten, as if she had been dipped in a pool of golden oil. After that Rinpoche recovered very quickly and suffered no aftereffects at all.

This Tara statue can still be seen at Dzongsar Monastery in Tibet, but Tashi Namgyal said it looks so different now that it's hard to believe it's the same statue.

SITU RINPOCHE'S RED BELT

Gongna Tulku told me that Trepa Tsang had given him a long red belt that was said to have belonged to Katok Situ. Trepa Tsang had acquired it when the family was still on friendly terms with Katok Monastery. Excited by his new acquisition, Gongna Tulku couldn't resist showing it off and rushed over to Rinpoche's residence.

"Where is it?" asked Rinpoche. "Show me! Let me see if it really is Situ Rinpoche's belt."

Gongna Tulku handed Rinpoche the belt, and Rinpoche examined it closely. He even smelt it.

"Ah! That is definitely Rinpoche's smell. I need this belt. It's not something you'll ever need."

Rinpoche kept statues in some wooden chests behind the headboard of his bed. He instructed Gongna Tulku to open one of the chests and place the belt next to a picture of Katok Situ. It fitted perfectly. Then Rinpoche locked the chest.

"And there was nothing I could do," said Gongna Tulku regretfully.

The Joker

A year after the new house at the labrang was finished, one of the local villagers died. As usual, his body was taken to the charnel ground, and almost immediately rumors began to spread of a corpse that was about to stand up; it was said that even birds would not eat its flesh. Everyone was terrified, and for days and days all anyone talked about was the corpse that had been possessed by a malicious spirit.

The rumor must have unsettled Rinpoche because when he went out to urinate at night, he made sure an attendant accompanied him with a lamp, maintaining his privacy by instructing the attendant to turn away as he did his business.

To distract Rinpoche from his fear, Chokling Rinpoche decided to make him laugh. He grabbed a round, palm-size stone from the threshold of his house and called to Rinpoche, "You need not be afraid, Rinpoche. Look, I have a stone!"

"Ah!" replied Rinpoche. "And what do you intend to do with that stone?"

"I'll hold it ready just in case a malicious spirit attacks us!" explained Chokling Rinpoche.

Rinpoche laughed and laughed. He was so delighted with Chokling Rinpoche's jest that he told everyone about it, chuckling as he retold the story again and again. "Have you heard? Chokling Tulku is always fully prepared to ward off evil spirits . . . with a *stone*! Ha, ha!"

7. Summer Camp

As the new grass brightened the valleys around Dzongsar, Rinpoche and his attendants would begin to look forward to their annual camping expedition. Rinpoche loved camping. He usually pitched his tent beneath Dzongsar Tashi Lhatse, near the forest on the other side of Buyo, and would remain there peacefully for about fifteen days. Even if it snowed and his tent was flattened, nothing would induce him to return to the monastery.

From Tashi Lhatse, Rinpoche would travel to Phuma mountain and then to Dophu, where so many people joined his party that a much larger tent had to be erected. From Dophu, Rinpoche would cross the pass to Sengur Yutso, then another pass to Pema Shelphuk, where he would stay, making tormas, and so on, for about twenty days. Sometimes he would spend a month in a cave there, while his attendants lived in the kitchen below, and as the water at Pema Shelphuk disagreed with Rinpoche's constitution, his attendants had to carry bucketsful up from the stream at the foot of the hill.

The Teeley

Surprisingly perhaps, Chökyi Lodrö was easily frightened, and often reacted strongly to the weird and wonderful stories that were constantly circulating. Like the one about an old woman who, as she slept, had her nose bitten off by a kind of weasel known in Derge as a *teeley*.

In his tent at Dophu, Rinpoche noticed a cloth blind was missing. He asked the attendant serving his tea what had happened to it. It had probably been blown away by the wind, came the reply. Rinpoche instantly demanded that the blind be mended, and Chakdzö quickly stuck a piece of heavy fabric to the window with wheat-flour porridge and gum. An hour or so later, Rinpoche prodded the makeshift patch. It was still damp.

"Will it be dry by nightfall?" he asked.

"The gum dries slowly, so it may take a little longer," replied Dilgo Khyentse. "A day or two, perhaps? It may not dry at all. Does it matter?"

Horrified, Rinpoche replied, "But a teeley might get in and snatch away my nose while I'm sleeping. Just yesterday I saw hundreds of them running around all over the place. What would I do if one of those creatures stole my nose?" He seemed very frightened.

"Tulku Salga says the patch may not dry on its own!" he said to his attendants. "Make a fire and be absolutely certain that the cloth is dry before bedtime!"

At such times, Rinpoche almost appeared to be weak-minded.

Revenge

During one summer camping expedition, a tulku called Markham Gyalse Tulku and the previous Neten Chokling went for a stroll. Quite suddenly all the other tulkus appeared and surrounded them. They seemed disturbed.

"Do you see that small tent in the forest?" they asked, pointing through the trees. "Someone's inside it, shouting and making *brrrrr* noises! We just peeped in and think it might be Khenpo Drayab Lodrö from Dzongsar Monastery. When he loses it, he goes completely crazy! Of course, it might be some other madman. But whoever it is, he has been tied up and imprisoned because he *argued* with Rinpoche *and* beat someone up. He's making such a racket! It sounds as if he's about to escape. And it could happen *any minute now*!"

Neten Chokling and Markham Gyalse Tulku listened wide-eyed. They quickly decided to cut short their walk and instead kept watch with the other tulkus. After a while, a deranged-looking monk with his hat askew, burst out of the tent and ran straight towards the huddle of tulkus. They all screamed and fled, with Neten Chokling and Gyalse Tulku following close behind.

Then something strange happened. One by one the tulkus fell to the ground, each clutching his belly. Neten Chokling was baffled. Were they ill? He looked again, and only then realized that his friends were doubled up with laughter—including the mad monk, who suddenly didn't look crazy at all. Of course! The tulkus had played a trick on him. A trick so successful that Neten Chokling was now honor-bound to take his revenge. And it didn't take long for him to come up with a plan.

"Tonight," he instructed Yenchokma, who was manager of the labrang at that time. "Run up and down by that rock on the other side of Dophu. And make sure you're completely naked. I have a very good reason for making this peculiar request, so don't worry, all will become clear."

"La so," agreed Yenchokma.

Neten Chokling also decided to let Rinpoche in on his scheme, because if he didn't, the shock might be bad for Rinpoche's health.

"Very well!" said Rinpoche. "And I want to help."

That day Chakdzö and the others had been practicing their shooting skills. As darkness fell, they lit a fire, opened the front of Rinpoche's tent, and everyone gathered around—Rinpoche loved to sit by a campfire at night. Before long, Yenchokma began to run around, completely naked, looking crazed and deranged—sometimes on two legs and sometimes crawling on all fours.

Realizing that suspicions would be aroused if he were the first to notice the madman, Neten Chokling pretended to see nothing. Fortunately, it wasn't long before one of the other tulkus said, "Is there something going on over there? Isn't that a female devil?"

"No, it can't be. They don't appear at night," said another.

Rinpoche wasn't slow to join in. "Where is it?" he asked. Someone pointed to Yenchokma, and Rinpoche gazed in wonder.

"We shot in that direction today, didn't we? Perhaps one of us hit a treasure guardian. That wouldn't be good! We should make a run for it. . . . 'I take refuge in the Guru, the Buddha, and the Dharma . . .'"

He leapt up, frantically reciting a refuge prayer, and dashed out of the tent, followed by all the tulkus and attendants. Everyone scrambled for somewhere to hide: some dived into their own tents, others squeezed themselves under Rinpoche's bed, while those left in the tent froze with fear as they clung to the main support pole.

Dilgo Khyentse was present but wasn't in on the joke. He also left the tent but walked out in a dignified manner and kept looking behind him, trying to work out what was really going on. A disgruntled treasure guardian would have been no match for Rinpoche, and Dilgo Khyentse admitted later that he had been quite shocked when Rinpoche ran away.

Dancing

Rinpoche loved to play games like tug-of-war. He also loved to watch people dance and, during the latter part of his life in Tibet, would ask Ani

Ani Pelu (*third from left*) and Ani Rilu (*far right*)
Source: Khyentse Labrang

Tsering Wangmo (Tselu) and Khandro Tsering Chödrön
Source: Khyentse Labrang

Rilu and Ani Pelu (the two nuns of Lakar Tsang), Khandro, and Tselu to dance for him. Khandro danced the Ling dance very well indeed. Rinpoche would sometimes engage dancers to entertain him as he sat around a huge campfire, often until midnight. At such times his attendants had to collect enormous quantities of firewood, and if they ran out, they were severely reprimanded and punished.

Once Rinpoche left Tibet, he no longer made merry in this way, and he never asked anyone to dance for him.

The Thermos Flask

When thermos flasks were first introduced into Tibet, Bu Truk Tsang from Derge offered a pair to Rinpoche, who was very impressed to hear that they would keep tea hot for twenty-four hours.

"If that's really true," he said, "thermoses will be immensely useful to practitioners in retreat because they will be able to drink tea after midnight! Thermoses might be one of the few modern inventions that are actually worthwhile!" And he kept his pair safe in his residence.

Before he left for Dophu that summer, Rinpoche ordered his tailor to make a woolen cover for one of the flasks, with a drawstring opening at the top and a long strap. It was presented to Rinpoche on the morning of their departure. He immediately put a flask of hot tea into the new cover and took it outside.

"This is a little fragile," he said. "So I need someone reliable to carry it for me. Who would be best? Drungyig, you carry it."

Drungyig Tsering slung the flask over his back in the same way people carry guns. From what he'd heard, the thermos would only break if it were hit very hard, so he hung his reliquary and some other things next to it and mounted up.

On the way to Dophu, he could hear his reliquary banging against the thermos, especially when he galloped, but didn't think anything of it. As they passed through the fields below Buyo, he saw black water trickling down his saddlecloth. Where had it come from? Then he felt a burning sensation on his back and realized that the flask had broken! What should he do? If he said anything, he'd be in big trouble!

When they arrived at Dophu, Drungyig Tsering hung the flask on a willow tree. Rinpoche's attendants pitched his tent, put up the fence that always surrounded it, made up Rinpoche's bed, and set out a small table.

"Now," said Rinpoche, "bring me my flask while we wait for fresh tea to be brewed. Where is Drungyig? Bring me my tea!"

Drungyig Tsering handed Rinpoche the thermos and admitted it was broken.

"How did it break?" asked Rinpoche.

Tsering opened the flask and poured out the smithereens of glass. Rinpoche scooped some up and examined them.

"Ya! This glass is thinner than eggshell. How could it not break! Nothing foreign is of any use whatsoever. It's all made to deceive people!" And he threw the broken flask away without a word of reproach.

Murder at Karmo Tak Tsang

In the early days, Rinpoche would travel to Karmo Tak Tsang from Pema Shelphuk and usually stay there for about ten days.

One year, an old and wealthy monk, who had retired from the retreat center to live alone in a private room, suddenly disappeared. Rinpoche was immediately informed and said that the old man was still somewhere in Karmo Tak Tsang. Everyone searched high and low but couldn't find him, yet Rinpoche continued to insist that he wasn't far away. So the Derge government sent one of their representatives to investigate. When even he couldn't solve the mystery, people began to wonder if the monk had simply run away—but as all his belongings were still in his room, it wasn't likely. Convinced that the old monk was somewhere in the area, Rinpoche asked everyone to look again while he performed some dharmapala pujas.

Eventually the body of the old monk was found, and it was discovered that the retreat assistant had killed him, then buried the body. Rinpoche was asked exactly how the monk had died. He replied that although he was not clairvoyant, he had experienced repeated visions of a crane with its neck stuck in the fork of a tree, unable to release itself. He said that as the old monk's birth sign was a rooster, he must have died in the same way.

One of the results of the broken samayas caused by the murder was that Rinpoche became seriously ill and suffered excruciating experiences whenever he stayed at Karmo Tak Tsang Retreat Centre. The retreatants continued to beg him to visit them, so he went a few more times but invariably fell ill. In the end, he stopped going altogether.

Rinpoche was responsible for renovating the retreat cave at Karmo Tak Tsang, and he also commissioned all of its statues. One of the last times he went there, accompanied by Chokden and Tashi Namgyal, was to conduct the consecration ceremony.

On the eve of the consecration, after everything had been set up and a dharani-cord vajra placed in front of the statue of Minling Durtrö Lhamo, someone noticed that the vajra was no longer on the table in front of the statue but in her hand. The only possible explanation for this was that the statue had picked the vajra up herself, because by no stretch of the imagination could it have accidentally dropped upwards into her hand.

"Leave the dharani-cord vajra where it is," said Rinpoche. "We will do the consecration ritual tomorrow as planned, and repeat it again and again until Durtrö Lhamo releases the vajra."

They performed the ritual for three days. When they arrived at the cave on the morning of the fourth day, the dharani-cord vajra had been released, and everyone present was confident that no human hand had removed it from the hand of the deity.

"The consecration has been accomplished," said Rinpoche.

Although Rinpoche renovated the inside of the retreat cave and installed a symbolic palace to revitalize the power of that sacred place, he only visited Karmo Tak Tsang once more—just before the turmoil in Tibet began in earnest—to consecrate the newly made statues.

8. Commanding Spirits

The Death of the Black Horse

One day, Chökyi Lodrö summoned Gongna Tulku and gave him four Chinese coins, a small portion of barley, and a scroll covered with bold characters, all wrapped in an ordinary scarf.

"Aey!" he said. "Take this letter and hang it on the upper wall of Shugden Gyalkhang."

"La so!" replied Gongna Tulku.

On his way to the Gyalkhang, Gongna Tulku stopped off at Gongna Labrang, where he noticed that the knot in the scarf was not secure. With very little effort he read the scroll, which was sealed with Rinpoche's personal seal of command. "The Dungsey of Mindrolling is visiting the monastery," he read. "Malicious spirit, *do not harm him!*"

Gongna Tulku gently replaced the scroll in the scarf without disturbing the knot and made his way to the Gyalkhang. The caretaker let him in, and as he fixed the scarf to the wall, Gongna Tulku noticed six or seven identical scarves already hanging there. "So," he thought to himself, "every time the monastery receives a high-ranking master, Rinpoche sends a similar command and offering."

A few weeks later, Dzogchen Rinpoche and his entourage—which included Lama Yishin Norbu and Khenpo Gönri—made their first-ever visit to Dzongsar. As soon he arrived, Dzogchen Rinpoche went to the labrang to greet Chökyi Lodrö, and Drungyig Tsering served them tea and saffron rice. Once Dzogchen Rinpoche had retired to Lhasar's house, Drungyig Tsering went to see Zöpa, who was the Chakdzö of Dzogchen Monastery. Drungyig Tsering was in charge of hospitality and, to make sure there was enough food, needed to know exactly how many people were in Dzogchen Rinpoche's party. So he and Zöpa made a list.

While Zöpa was dictating names, Drungyig Tsering noticed a very odd-looking man wander into the courtyard. He looked like a nomad from the lowlands, with messy, matted hair and a black cloth wrapped around his lower body. His lips moved constantly as if he were speaking, but he was gibbering nonsense. Suddenly, anxious voices rang out, calling for frankincense and torches. Had someone been taken ill? Drungyig Tsering hurried to see what was going on and found a handsome black horse from Zilling lying dead on the stable floor, its legs stiff with rigor mortis. "Someone should tell Rinpoche," thought Drungyig Tsering, and ran into the residence.

"Akha!" exclaimed Rinpoche, as soon as he heard. "I forgot to send him a letter. Akha! Akha!"

Discord Sown by the Gyalpo

After the *Precious Treasury of Terma Teachings* transmissions had been completed in Derge, Rinpoche presided over a Mindrolling Vajrasattva drupchen assisted by Dilgo Khyentse, who sat next to Rinpoche on a lower throne. Rinpoche was vajra master, but when necessary, Dilgo Khyentse would fill in for him.

One day, about a hundred people from Pangkhar Tsang and Jagö Tsang pitched their tents in the field opposite Buyo, below Phuma. The news turned Rinpoche's face red with anger. After that, apart from reciting his daily practice, he refused to say a word to anyone—which was odd, because when angry, Rinpoche usually said more rather than less, and his vocabulary often became quite colorful. Dilgo Khyentse followed Rinpoche's example and also remained silent.

Without warning, the newcomers rushed into the monastery led by Lama Pangkhar Gönpo, who was wearing layman's clothing that day, and tried to force their way into the assembly hall. Pangkhar Gönpo was held back by a monk wielding a whip, which so enraged him that he stabbed the monk with his dagger. Fortunately the monk was wearing his best robes in four layers, and the thick wad of fabric prevented the dagger from doing more than nick his skin. Even so, the attack provoked such rage in the monk that he threw down his whip and loudly accused Pangkhar Gönpo of stabbing Dzongsar Khyentse Chökyi Lodrö. Instantly, all the other Dzongsar monks fell on Pangkhar Gönpo and beat him viciously.

Although no one inside the temple could hear what was going on, they could all see Rinpoche was furious about something. At the end of the first session, he was heard to mutter, "Why does he always have to go so completely over the top?"

Dilgo Khyentse was puzzling over Rinpoche's anger, when suddenly Rinpoche stood up and said, "Tulku, bring me that vajra!" Dilgo Khyentse timidly did as Rinpoche asked.

Rinpoche usually headed towards the kitchen at the beginning of a break, because it was the only way he could get through to the toilet in the labrang. That day, though, he turned in the opposite direction and climbed up to the Gyalkhang. Dilgo Khyentse attended him but was so obviously terrified that Rinpoche told him to wait at the foot of the stairs. Rinpoche then entered the Gyalkhang alone and shut the door behind him. Dilgo Khyentse said that even from where he stood, he could hear the *kak-kak-kak* of the blows Rinpoche rained down with some force behind the closed doors.

"What is Rinpoche hitting?" wondered Dilgo Khyentse. "One of the masks, perhaps?"

"Enough of your mischief!" shouted Rinpoche several times, followed by three heavy thwacks. A moment later the door flew open to reveal Rinpoche, smiling broadly and looking surprisingly relaxed.

"If I hadn't done that, we would never have been able to control him," he said simply.

This was how Chökyi Lodrö punished the gyalpo Shugden.

I asked Pangkhar Gönpo if he had really stabbed a monk. Oh yes, he said, but he had only intended to threaten the monk, not draw blood. He added that when fighting broke out, he had escaped the worst of it by hiding in a tent.

Jagö Namgyal Dorje and Jagö Tobden arrived a few days later, their faces black with anger.

"We've heard that a nephew of Jagö Tsang *stabbed* the disciplinarian of Dzongsar Monastery. Who was it?" they demanded.

Pangkhar Gönpo, who was Namgyal Dorje's and Tobden's nephew, pretended to know nothing about it. So it was decided that Gesar must have been the culprit. He was tied hand and foot and whipped—but given the circumstances, they didn't punish him particularly severely. However, Namgyal Dorje was determined to find a way of punishing Pangkhar Gönpo. As his servants were too afraid of Pangkhar Gönpo even to try to restrain him, the job fell to Namgyal Dorje's wife, Karma Tsetso. She alone had the courage to bind Pangkhar Gönpo securely so that the rest of them could surround and accuse him.

Jagö Namgyal Dorje
Source: Cheme Dorjee Chagotsang

"You started a fight! You committed a heinous crime at a sacred site while empowerments and teachings were being given! And you did all this in the presence of a supremely great master!"

Tobden and Namgyal Dorje tied scarves and a gun to one of Pangkhar Tsang's best horses—the one Gönpo used to ride—and offered it to Rinpoche, begging him to forgive them. According to Tashi Namgyal, it wasn't Rinpoche who was angry, it was Chakdzö—but then, Tashi Namgyal was very fond of Jagö Tsang. According to Dilgo Khyentse, the anger was all Rinpoche's. In any case, one of them must have been upset, because the next day Chakdzö announced that Rinpoche wouldn't give a public initiation after all. They were afraid, he said, that if fighting broke out again someone would get killed. Eventually, though, after a great deal of discussion, Rinpoche agreed to give the public initiation.

Pangkhar Gönpo was punished by being forced to walk handcuffed all the way from Dzongsar to Derge Gönchen. Yet however bad this story might make him out to be, Pangkhar Gönpo always had immense devotion for Rinpoche.

Later, after Rinpoche had left for India, Drungyig Tsering went to

Yidlhung Lhaga. By then Jagö Tobden had calmed down, and Drungyig Tsering went to see him to discuss the local situation. When he got there, he discovered that the Chinese Communists were very active in the area and suspicious of anyone from the other side of the Gönchen valley, so Drungyig Tsering quickly fled to the home of a villager he knew in the lower valley, and even there the streets were empty. A few days later he heard that Tobden had been arrested by the Communists and taken to Zilling.

An Invitation from Yidlhung Lhari Ga

Rinpoche sent for Dilgo Khyentse. "I have been invited to Yidlhung Lhari Ga to perform a ritual for removing obstacles. I don't like going there, but it would be improper for me not to send someone, so please go in my place."

"La so," replied Dilgo Khyentse, with a heavy heart. Lhari Ga propitiated the gyalpo Shugden. Although Dilgo Khyentse was immediately apprehensive about his visit, he chose not to share his misgivings with Rinpoche. But he did ask Rinpoche if he himself might be harmed by the gyalpo.

"I don't know," replied Rinpoche. "Probably not." He then told Dilgo Khyentse the following story.

Chokgyur Lingpa and Jamgön Kongtrul were both still alive when Jamyang Khyentse Wangpo visited Gönchen Monastery. At Gönchen he found and read a copy of the *Ornament of Clear Realization* with a commentary by Panchen Sodak. It was only then that he realized what a great scholar Sodak had been. At the very moment that thought occurred to him, Shugden appeared before him.

"Do you consider Sodak to be learnèd?" asked the gyalpo.

Khyentse Wangpo replied with a question of his own. "Why were you reborn as a malicious spirit even though you were once such an accomplished scholar?"

"Although I learnt many, many words by heart," replied the gyalpo, "I didn't contemplate their meaning. That's why I have now taken the form of a malicious spirit." He then added, "Please find a way to include me tomorrow in the assembly of those who will receive the empowerment of *General Essentialization of All the Wisdom of the Buddhas*."

"As you hate the Nyingma lineage so much that you constantly put obstacles in the way of the teachings and lineage holders," replied Khyentse Wangpo, "you can only attend if you promise not to make trouble. If you don't make that promise, you can't come."

At these words, the gyalpo shed many tears and vowed to behave.

Shugden was also present when Khyentse Wangpo taught the *Perfection of Wisdom Sutra in Eight Thousand Lines* to nonhumans. Jamyang Khyentse even asked him to teach the revision class, which he did without any difficulty whatsoever.

"That gyalpo might be able to explain texts easily," said Chökyi Lodrö to Dilgo Khyentse, "but he is still a samaya breaker and the same malicious wretch who does everything he can to harm Nyingmapa lamas and tulkus. He has no shred of respect for any of the vows he took. Perhaps I should have a word with him."

Dilgo Khyentse left for Lhari Ga accompanied by the resident Dzongsar monks and all the visiting monks. He took with him Rinpoche's ritual objects, including his damaru, bell, and even his summoning cloth.

A few days later, Chakdzö Tsewang Paljor called Shedrup into his room. He was very upset.

"Tulku Salga is in a critical condition," he said. "Rinpoche summoned me into his practice session this morning. He was so surprised and shocked by the news that he couldn't sit still. He was pacing up and down, up and down.... I think we should ask for a divination about which rituals must be done to remove obstacles to Tulku Salga's health. If we don't act now, no good will come of it."

Shedrup was shocked—even more so because Rinpoche himself was so troubled. "Surely," he thought, "this must be a sign that my brother is about to die."

"We should send for Dilgo Khyentse straightaway," he said. "If he has to die, he should die here at Dzongsar, in Rinpoche's presence. It doesn't look as though we can do anything to save him. And ultimately none of us can escape death."

Chakdzö agreed, and Shedrup requested an audience with Rinpoche to ask his advice. "Just go straight in," said Chakdzö. "This is no time for formalities!"

Shedrup was a courageous man when he had to be and went straight to Rinpoche's room.

"Oh, it's you!" exclaimed Rinpoche as Shedrup prostrated, looking very distressed. "You've been talking with Tsewang Paljor."

"Yes, Chakdzö told me the news," replied Shedrup. "I'd like to send someone right away to bring Dilgo Khyentse back to Dzongsar. If he's here

The Ninth Sangye Nyenpa Rinpoche,
Dilgo Khyentse Rinpoche's brother, Shedrup
Source: Shechen Archives

in your presence, I won't have any regrets about what happens to him. Anyway, what else can we do?"

Rinpoche comforted Shedrup, saying, "Tulku Salga has some big obstacles ahead of him, but I have done my best to remove them. Nothing awful will happen in the near future, so there's really no need to bring him back. Just send a message reminding him to take care."

Dilgo Khyentse Rinpoche, who told me this story himself, said that Shedrup did as Rinpoche asked and sent the message.

Shedrup passed away in Tsurphu just before the worst of the violence erupted in Tibet. He was very devoted to Rinpoche, but his greatest devotion was for Mipham, closely followed by Shechen Gyaltsab and Dilgo Khyentse.

9. Masters and Khenpos

During Khyentse Chökyi Lodrö's time at Dzongsar, many high lamas traveled from all over Tibet to meet him. Of the Nyingma masters, Shechen Rabjam visited often, as did Katok Situ Orgyen Chökyi Gyatso and his reincarnation. Both the previous incarnations of Shechen Gyaltsab and his tulku visited several times, but the Dungsey of Mindrolling, who was killed by the Chinese Communists, only went once. The last Nyingma master to visit was the Sixth Dzogchen Rinpoche.

Zimwog Tulku

Among the great Sakya masters to visit Chökyi Lodrö were Sakya Gongma of Phuntsok Phodrang, the previous Zimwog Tulku (Gongna Tulku's son's predecessor) and Ngochok Shabdrung of Ngor.

Gongna Tulku told me that Zimwog Tulku arrived at Dzongsar during one of Rinpoche's strict retreats, which Rinpoche immediately left in order to exchange empowerments and transmissions with him.

"The all-pervasive master of the Tripitaka has arrived in Dzongsar," said Rinpoche. "He is such a great Sakya master, rich in empowerments, transmissions, and teachings. He told me several times in my dreams that he would be coming, and although strictly speaking I shouldn't leave my retreat before it's finished, I will make an exception to see him."

The Eleventh Palpung Situ, Pema Wangchok Gyalpo

The Eleventh Palpung Situ visited Dzongsar several times. Derge Tsang had complete confidence in Palpung Situ, and Khyentse Rinpoche had tremendous respect for him. Palpung Situ was one of the lamas who strongly

The Eleventh Palpung Situ, Pema Wangchok Gyalpo
Source: Shechen Archives

encouraged Rinpoche to take a consort, and after Rinpoche married Khandro Tsering Chödrön, he traveled to Dzongsar to visit them.

During his stay, the two great masters exchanged numerous empowerments. After Chökyi Lodrö had given the empowerment of Hevajra, Palpung Situ asked Dilgo Khyentse, who was sitting next to him, "What did you see today? Did you see Hevajra?"

Dilgo Khyentse replied that he had seen nothing.

"Oh? I saw the actual form of the glorious Hevajra," said Palpung Situ.

Dilgo Khyentse said that until then he hadn't felt much devotion for Palpung Situ, who was known to play cards and dice, own guns and horses, and be extremely authoritarian. But from then on, he considered Palpung Situ to be an extraordinary being and developed immense devotion for him.

Just before he passed into nirvana, Palpung Situ visited Dzongsar for the last time. My father was there. He said that the procession to receive Palpung Situ began at Juring Ju and that Rinpoche himself traveled to the crossroads to receive him, followed by Gongna Tulku, Neten Chokling, and all the other tulkus. Palpung Situ arrived on a Chinese mule led by two horsemen. He wore a thick woolen robe, dark crystal glasses, a golden sunshade, and had wrapped himself up against the cold so thoroughly that his entire face was covered. Chökyi Lodrö gestured respectfully to him as he approached.

"Adzi!" exclaimed Pema Wangchok Gyalpo. "Is this Tulku Tsang[13] here to receive me? Help me down. Slowly!"

Palpung Situ dismounted and touched Rinpoche's forehead with his own, then the two masters politely inquired after each other's health.

"Apart from death itself, I have suffered all the illnesses it is possible for a human body to experience," said Palpung Situ. "This will be my final visit to Dzongsar and our last meeting."

At the gates of the monastery they were met by monks carrying fragrant incense. The monks wanted to lead Palpung Situ into the monastery, but he was too old to keep up and told them to go on ahead.

"And stop making that dreadful racket!" he snapped. "It hurts my ears. Stop blowing those shawms!"

The monks fell silent and walked a long way ahead of the two Rinpoches, who supported each other as they made their way into the monastery.

At the labrang, Rinpoche instructed Tashi Namgyal to set up a comfortable but very high throne with a backrest next to the previous Khyentse's monk's throne that stood by Rinpoche's bed. He then asked Palpung Situ to sit there, but the old man refused.

"Rinpoche's throne is so high, and I am too old to climb all the way up there," he said. "Let's sit here." And he made himself comfortable on Rinpoche's bed.

Palpung Situ stayed at Dzongsar for three or four days but spent his nights at Nera Tsang, not the labrang.

Later, when Palpung Situ fell ill, Chökyi Lodrö sent Dilgo Khyentse to offer him a tenshuk. He also asked him to write a long-life prayer for Palpung Situ, using as his reference the prayer Khyentse Wangpo had written for the previous Palpung Situ. Dilgo Khyentse searched for the prayer in the labrang's small volume of long-life prayers, written in Khyentse Wangpo's own hand, but couldn't find it. So he composed a new one from scratch and offered it to Palpung Situ. He said not being able to find Khyentse Wangpo's prayer must have been a sign that Palpung Situ's passing was imminent.

Palpung Situ's Last Illness

Among the many stories Gongna Tulku told me, the most important was about Palpung Situ's last illness. He was suffering from acute diarrhea and had become so ill that he begged Khyentse Rinpoche to visit him at Palpung.

"Palpung and Dzongsar stand on hills opposite each other," said Chökyi Lodrö. "We are also emotionally very close. So it would be entirely inappropriate for me to do anything other than accept his invitation. But I am not convinced that I will be able to accomplish the service Palpung Situ is about to ask of me."

Nevertheless, Rinpoche went to Palpung and took Gongna Tulku and about fourteen assistants with him. During the practice of *Yamantaka, Destroyer of Enemies* in the great shrine room of Palpung Situ's residence, they sat facing each other in two rows.

"Khorey!" said Chökyi Lodrö to Gongna Tulku one day. "Glorious Dzongsar Monastery plays the cymbals so badly! You're barely rubbing them together! Get a better sound from them!"

Although Palpung Situ was extremely ill by then, he occasionally joined them in the afternoons, wearing a bright yellow, raw silk coat over a chuba made of glossy yellow brocade. His head was so snugly bound that only his eyes could be seen. He'd either sit on a chair, or walk from one end of a row of monks up to Rinpoche, touch Rinpoche's forehead with his own, exchange a few words, and then leave. The only time he dressed was when he intended to go to the shrine room, and afterwards he immediately returned to his room to sleep.

Rinpoche went to Palpung Situ's room daily to offer him a ritual purification bath involving a mirror, but just a few drops of vase water sprinkled on Palpung Situ's body would make him tremble violently.

After five days of practice, Rinpoche ritually cast away the wrathful torma. Originally, he had planned to throw it onto a female goatskin in the shrine room, but as the monks began to chant, "Today, manifest signs showing how to avert death," he saw an unmistakable sign indicating that he would only be able to ransom death effectively by throwing the torma outside. So Rinpoche went out onto the roof terrace to cast the torma away as he performed the ritual dance. Unfortunately, the torma did not land with its head pointing towards the obstacle makers. Visibly irritated, Rinpoche retrieved the torma and threw it a second time, but again it landed inauspiciously. Rinpoche threw it a third time, and although it didn't turn upside down, it landed with only one side facing in the auspicious direction. During the first and second attempts, storms threatened to break when the torma fell badly, but the atmosphere calmed considerably after the third casting. Everyone then gathered by the open door to do the covenant and tenma rituals, and after performing the usual Hayagriva dance and long-life rituals, they returned to the shrine room to conclude the practice.

"Today, the face of the wrathful torma did not turn as it should," said Rinpoche to Gongna Tulku as they walked back to his room. "And Venerable Palpung Situ is still critically ill. He may not live much longer. I really don't know what's going to happen."

To Lama Choga and other senior Palpung Monastery monks, Rinpoche said that although he couldn't make an accurate prediction, if they performed all the important obstacle-removing long-life ceremonies, over the next three years "things wouldn't be too bad." After that, the situation would become extremely difficult. This was all he said.

Palpung Situ's attendants asked Rinpoche to remain near Palpung Situ for a few more days, which he did. Just before he left, Palpung Situ, accompanied by many attendants, personally offered him eight or nine statues; a set of silver-gilt ritual objects; and so many brocades, carpets, and precious things that Rinpoche's room overflowed with gifts.

"I am extremely grateful to Rinpoche for visiting this old man just before he dies," said Palpung Situ. "Palpung Monastery may be a huge building, but it's completely empty, so I don't have much to offer—nothing to truly delight Rinpoche. But of all the lamas who walk this earth, only one has a place in my heart. I have always believed that no lama is greater or better than you. Please accept these gifts. I make this offering knowing that when I die, all these things will dissolve anyway, but if you have them, at least they will belong to someone noble and virtuous. Please don't refuse anything! Please don't disappoint me! If I am let down in that way, I won't be able to fulfill my wishes at the moment of death—and that would be very bad."

"La so! La so!" was Rinpoche's only response.

"Everything I offer is valuable, and I hope my offering pleases Rinpoche," continued Situ Rinpoche. "Chakdzö and Choga say that horses, yaks, and various animals are tethered nearby, but I doubt any of them will be useful to you as many are sick or lame. Nevertheless, I have told them to select the best. And although Rinpoche can't go down there, do please look at them from the window and take them with you when you leave."

Rinpoche gazed out the window and saw a shed full of animals, all of which he took with him when he and his party finally left for Dzongsar. On their way back, they rested for a while by the river that ran next to the ridge on which Palpung Monastery stood. Rinpoche asked his attendants to collect some stones. He then chose a few bird-head- and dog-head-shaped pebbles and tossed them into the water. Gongna Tulku said it looked as though he was doing a visualization to suppress obstacles. Rinpoche said that if they had performed another suppression ritual at Palpung, it would definitely have averted the other potential obstacle the monastery faced, but he wasn't sure it would have helped Palpung Situ. He didn't tell anyone, he said, because they might have suspected him of fishing for more offerings. Palpung Situ died not long after.

Karse Kongtrul[14] passed away the following year. Gongna Tulku thought he might have lived a little longer had Rinpoche been able to accomplish that final suppression ritual.

The Death of Palpung Situ

Pewar Tulku told me about what happened after Palpung Situ passed away.

When Pewar Tulku lived at Khamje Shedra, he would go to Khyentse Chökyi Lodrö's residence early each morning to ask if Rinpoche would give any empowerments, transmissions, or teachings that day. If, when Pewar Tulku drew back the curtain to his room, Rinpoche's mind was clear and he was in a good mood, he would invite Pewar Tulku to join him. But if Rinpoche said nothing, Pewar Tulku would let the curtain fall and leave without disturbing him.

One day, Rinpoche invited Pewar Tulku in and told him that Palpung Situ had died the previous night.

"So I want to go to Palpung," said Rinpoche. "Will you come with me as my assistant?"

"La so!" replied Pewar Tulku, and ran to Khamje to tell his tutor.

"Alay!" exclaimed his tutor. "What is Rinpoche thinking? Dzongsar Monastery has so many lamas, why is he taking someone like *you* as his backup? But he's giving you a wonderful opportunity, so you must go."

Pewar Tulku always stayed with the same monk at Dzongsar Monastery, who said that although Pewar Tulku's thin woolen robe was entirely appropriate for his trip to Palpung, his tatty zen wouldn't do at all. So the monk lent Pewar Tulku his nephew's long "dancing" zen made of soft Indian wool.

At the lower end of the valley, near the stretch of river where everyone did their washing, Rinpoche and his party were met by ten or fifteen Palpung monks. Rinpoche couldn't see who they all were, so he asked Pewar Tulku if Palpung Öngen was among them.

"If he is," whispered Rinpoche, "I will need a special silk scarf to offer him. If he isn't, the usual kind will do." As Palpung Öngen wasn't there, Rinpoche exchanged ordinary scarves with the monks, and they all made their way to Palpung.

Palpung Situ had passed away in the east room of his residence, so Derge Tsang was given a room nearby, as was Rinpoche. Not long after Rinpoche had settled in, news of the arrival of Gyalwa Rinpoche spread like wildfire throughout the monastery. Pewar Tulku and the other monks wondered who the skinny old lama was, with his bony cheeks and a zen that wrapped up most of his head. He looked as though he was hiding behind his attendants. At first Pewar Tulku thought he might be Karma Norbu, but as the lama drew closer, he saw it was Drupwang Gyatrul.[15] He and Rinpoche exchanged scarves, touched foreheads, and then settled down for a good talk that went on until dusk. No one had any idea what they talked about.

The following day, Rinpoche entered the room where Palpung Situ had died. He had passed away facing west and wearing his monk's ceremonial robe, with his right hand in the mudra of Guru Nangsi Zilnön. Rinpoche spent quite some time with the kudung and, according to Pewar Tulku, said many prayers of aspiration.

It was necessary on the third day to bring Palpung Situ out of meditation, and the monastery asked Rinpoche if he would do it. Rinpoche entered the room just as he had the day before, while Pewar Tulku and the attendants stood by the door. After a while, Rinpoche summoned Pewar Tulku to ask him to bring the bell and damaru that were standing on the table in front of the throne. As the kudung itself sat on the throne, there was only just enough space for Pewar Tulku to squeeze through and reach them. Rinpoche said they should chant some prayers together and began with the invocation prayer from the Hevajra sadhana. He played the bell and damaru for a long time and then chanted the vajra song from the same text. As he began to ring the bell and beat the damaru once more, the head of the kudung fell forward, which, Rinpoche said, was the sign that Palpung Situ had come out of meditation.

After they left Palpung Situ's house, Rinpoche asked Pewar Tulku, the late solpön, and other attendants to say prayers of aspiration because, he said, at the moment a master comes out of meditation, his blessings are exceptionally powerful. Pewar Tulku didn't tell me much about the kinds of aspiration he made, only that he made them despite having no idea about how to generate devotion. But back in their room, Pewar Tulku asked the late solpön what his aspirations had been. The solpön replied that he had aspired to be able to practice in solitary retreat, without relatives to sustain or enemies to subjugate, and for the opportunity to remain in seclusion with firm resolve. Pewar Tulku said that people like the solpön, who spend a considerable amount of time with sublime masters, are able to develop the most extraordinary qualities. The solpön's aspiration had really impressed him. But, he said, he didn't know how to aspire that way himself.

Benchen Sangye Nyenpa (Dilgo Khyentse's brother) said that one of the symptoms of Palpung Situ's illness was that his body shivered and shook. He wept as he spoke. But there were also times when he could talk about Palpung Situ without getting emotional.

After a while, Sangye Nyenpa asked for some new soap, rolled up his sleeves, and washed his hands. It was time to prepare the kudung. Rinpoche, Sangye Nyenpa, and some senior Palpung lamas entered Palpung Situ's room, closed the door behind them, and proceeded to adorn the sacred body with sambhogakaya ornaments. Pewar Tulku was not invited to join them and told me he had had no interest in doing so.

Later, as he walked back to his room with Pewar Tulku and the attendants, Rinpoche said, "Alah! Today I've done something quite barbaric." After wiping the kudung with a white Chinese cloth called a *luklon*, Rinpoche had secretly hidden it in his robes. As it was still wet and blood-stained, he asked Pewar Tulku to put it in a cool place to dry.

The late solpön brought them some of the water used to wash the kudung, and everyone drank a little. Pewar Tulku was also offered some, but he didn't drink his share, saying he would add it to some pills he intended to make and eat.

Khyentse Rinpoche, his attendants, and the whole of Dzongsar Monastery practiced Mindrolling Vajrasattva; Palpung Monastery practiced the long sadhana of the *Ocean of the Victorious Ones* by Karma Kamtsang; and offerings were made to the kudung.

Two days later, the old lama Doko Chulu asked Rinpoche to say prayers for and bless the two horses that would be sent to Tsurphu as offerings to Gyalwang Karmapa, with the request that he say dedication prayers for Palpung Situ. Doko Chulu wanted Rinpoche to ensure that the gifts would reach their destination safely. Rinpoche could see the two fat horses from his window and blessed them by throwing some rice in their direction.

The Ninth Sangye Nyenpa Rinpoche

The predecessor of the present Tenth Sangye Nyenpa Rinpoche regularly attended transmissions at Dzongsar Monastery and would stay with his younger brother, Dilgo Khyentse, at Dilgo Tsang. He always circumambulated the outer walls enclosing Khamje Shedra, not just the buildings themselves, and offered a hundred prostrations from the east and west doors as he prayed fervently that he might study at such a shedra in his future life. But in spite of his great devotion to Rinpoche, Dilgo Khyentse said that Sangye Nyenpa was more devoted and committed to Palpung Monastery than he was to Dzongsar.

The Ninth Sangye Nyenpa was a tulku of the Kamtsang Kagyü lineage. He was an extraordinary teacher and an exceptionally diligent and sincere practitioner. He built a great many body, speech, and mind representations, including one thousand buddha statues. It was as he was gathering holy substances to fill these buddhas that Sangye Nyenpa discovered his brother had in his possession a large, two-inch splinter of wood from Chökyi Lodrö's bed—the one that could be transformed into a throne when a plank was added as a backrest.

"As this is part of the throne that belongs to Jamyang Khyentse and his incarnation," he said, "there is no representation more precious! I would like to offer it as a consecration substance to the one thousand buddha statues I am making." He then cut the splinter into one thousand pieces and put a piece into each statue as an inner support.

The Eighth Khamtrul

The Eighth Khamtrul, Dongyü Nyima, was a great lama who held a very high position, but I don't know how much real authority he had or how genuinely respected he was. As a high lama, tradition dictated that he should only visit monasteries when formally invited. For some reason, Dzongsar never extended such an invitation, but as Khamtrul Dongyü Nyima very much wanted to meet Chökyi Lodrö, he decided to flout convention and just turn up.

Plans for his journey to Dzongsar were made with great care, but at

Dilgo Khyentse Rinpoche, Khamtrul Rinpoche,
and Neten Chokling Rinpoche in Benuri, Kangra Valley, in 1964
Source: Shechen Archives

the last moment an obstacle prevented his entire entourage from leaving Khampa Gar. Undeterred, Khamtrul Dongyü Nyima left his people behind and with just four attendants—Drongpa Lama, Tokden Ajam, A-long, and a monk called Ngakten—secretly slipped away on horseback disguised as laymen. They traveled incognito because if they hadn't, Khamtrul Dongyü Nyima would have had to visit all the monasteries on the way to offer gifts and receive offerings himself—a custom that could, and often did, attract an ocean of difficulties.

Khamtrul Dongyü Nyima and his tiny party rode fast so they would arrive at Dzongsar before dusk. They set up camp on the gray grassland of a hilly valley on the mountain opposite the monastery. The next morning at daybreak, A-long, who had once been a monk at Dzongsar, and a lay companion were sent to ask Chokden to come at once. But on no account, commanded Khamtrul Dongyü Nyima, was A-long to reveal the identity of his master to anyone at Dzongsar.

A-long and Chokden had been monks together at Tsechu Monastery and knew each other well. So although A-long followed Khamtrul Dongyü Nyima's instructions faithfully, Chokden recognized his boots and robes (the golden-head boots that monks of Khampa Gar Monastery always wore with their traditional dark robes with light red borders) and immediately guessed that the mysterious visitor must be Khamtrul Dongyü Nyima. He hurried to the campsite and, finding the tent door wide open, strode in.

"Ah! Isn't this Khamtrul Dongyü Nyima?" cried Chokden, and immediately prostrated to him.

"I would like to see Rinpoche. Can you arrange it for me?" asked Khamtrul. "I have come as an ordinary person because I want to receive teachings from Rinpoche to forge a spiritual connection between us."

"I'll inform Rinpoche right away," said Chokden. "These days Rinpoche rarely gives empowerments outside his usual schedule, but there are other lamas here right now, so it's possible that empowerments will be given quite soon."

Chokden returned to the monastery, and before long, a dark-skinned man wearing a thick, black woolen shawl arrived at Khamtrul Dongyü Nyima's tent accompanied by two or three assistants carrying tea, scarves, and cups. This must have been Tsewang Paljor.

The first time the Eighth Khamtrul Dongyü Nyima visited Dzongsar Monastery, Rinpoche went to the door of the main temple to receive him personally. He didn't have time to arrange a really elaborate welcome, but shawms were sounded, incense burnt and scarves offered as Khamtrul Dongyü Nyima and his party entered the monastery in procession.

According to Drongpa Lama, for the first time ever, Rinpoche introduced each member of his household individually: Tsewang Paljor, "my treasurer"; Khandro Tsering Chödrön, who was very young and still had short hair, "my wisdom companion"; Drungyig Tsering, "my secretary"; and so on.

Khamtrul Dongyü Nyima then asked Chökyi Lodrö to grant him empowerments, transmissions, and teachings.

"I've almost given up offering empowerments," replied Chökyi Lodrö. "And anyway, why do you want to receive such things from someone like me?"

Before Khamtrul Dongyü Nyima arrived, Chökyi Lodrö had been preparing to give Trungpa Gar the great empowerment of Kalachakra from the Butön tradition. A tall monk with long, black hair and a dark complexion was rearranging misplaced pages in the Kalachakra text for Rinpoche—back then no one knew him as Dilgo Khyentse Rinpoche, only as Tulku Salga. And a young, skinny, rather good-looking lama was also there. His name was Chögyam Trungpa. Although the preparations had

Chögyam Trungpa Rinpoche
Source: Khyentse Labrang

gone well, for some reason Rinpoche kept postponing the empowerment itself. In retrospect, many suspected that Rinpoche had foreseen Khamtrul Dongyü Nyima's arrival, because just three days after Khamtrul Dongyü Nyima turned up, Rinpoche gave the empowerment.

After the Kalachakra empowerment, Rinpoche, who also wanted to make a spiritual connection between himself and Khamtrul Dongyü Nyima, received the long-life empowerment of the *Embodiment of the Three Jewels* from him. He then presented Khamtrul Dongyü Nyima with a letter reminding him not to neglect all the different Gesar teachings he held. Khamtrul Dongyü Nyima then begged Rinpoche to visit Ga Nyak to give the transmission of the *Precious Treasury of Terma Teachings*. Rinpoche responded to his request in a letter, one of two he wrote that have been preserved at Khamtrul Dongyü Nyima's monastery:

> An old man like me, plagued by chronic illness, is unable to give many empowerments and teachings. Since Tulku Salga is an extraordinary master whose mind is inseparable from my own, you should receive these empowerments and teachings from him.

Once everything had been completed, on the next dakini's day, Surmang Trungpa, Dilgo Khyentse, Khamtrul Dongyü Nyima, and Khenpo

Gangshar offered a ganachakra feast (the *Gathering of Vidyadharas*). At the appropriate point in the tsok, Khandro Tsering Chödrön sang a Tsok Lu so beautifully that the lamas and monks of Khampa Gar Monastery dissolved into tears. They said that when she sang, they thought they were in Zangdokpalri (the Copper-Colored Mountain where Guru Rinpoche now dwells). Surmang Trungpa responded by singing a different Tsok Lu.[16] I don't understand the logic, but on this occasion, it seems they took turns singing Tsok Lus. Khamtrul Dongyü Nyima then told his monks to learn the Tsok Lu Khandro had sung, and so she taught it to them.

On his way back to Khampa Gar, Khamtrul Dongyü Nyima visited the printing press at Derge Gönchen. Although he was still dressed as an ordinary Tibetan, many of the Khampa Gar engravers recognized him. Ignoring his attendants' urgent requests to keep their visit secret, the engravers invited Khamtrul Dongyü Nyima to Derge Tsang, where people like Jamkhar Gön-nam came to see him. The next morning, Rinpoche and his party rose early to make their escape across Chutok to Gangtok Drukha.

Late that summer, just before the escalation of Communist aggression in Tibet, Dilgo Khyentse was preparing to visit Chutok when Khamtrul Dongyü Nyima, following Khyentse Chökyi Lodrö's advice, invited him to Khampa Gar to give various transmissions, including those for his own treasure teachings. Dilgo Khyentse changed his plans and made his way to Khampa Gar. But his time there didn't turn out well. Having received the transmissions they requested, the lamas and monks borrowed two volumes of treasure teachings—*Yamantaka: Lord of Life* and the orally transmitted *Vajrakilaya of Nyak Lotsawa*, both termas that Dilgo Khyentse had revealed himself—because they wanted to copy them. Unfortunately, they hadn't completed the copies by the time Dilgo Khyentse was ready to return to Dzongsar, so he had to find someone to pick them up for him.

At that time, although Yudrön[17] was married to Drugu Tulku, she was absolutely determined to meet Chökyi Lodrö. As Chökyi Lodrö had already left for central Tibet, she decided to travel to Lhasa to see him there. When Dilgo Khyentse heard about her trip, he asked her to stop off at Khampa Gar to collect his texts, which she did. But the monks still hadn't finished copying the Shinje text (by far the more profound of the two) and only gave her the Vajrakilaya.

Not long after Yudrön's visit, Khamtrul Dongyü Nyima and his party left Khampa Gar, and one night, as so often happened in Kham, a thief crept into their camp. Imagining that the heaviest load he could find would

Yudrön, mother of Khenpo Phuntso Tobjor
Source: Khyentse Labrang

contain gold, silver, and valuables, the thief grabbed a box of extremely precious Dharma texts, including Dilgo Khyentse's Shinje, and made off with it. The loss was discovered the next morning. Certain that once he realized his mistake the thief would dump the books, Khamtrul Dongyü Nyima sent his people out to search for them, but they found nothing. That was how the Shinje text was lost. But we still have the Vajrakilaya text.

Tertön Sogyal

Of Chökyi Lodrö's many gurus, one of the most important was Tertön Sogyal.

After Patrul Rinpoche passed away, Tertön Sogyal became a student of Khyentse Wangpo, from whom he received many empowerments, reading transmissions, and pith instructions. Khyentse Wangpo teased and scolded Tertön Sogyal a great deal; he hardly ever praised him. After the great tertön had moved to Nyakrong, where he established his monastery, Khyentse Wangpo started calling him Nyakrong Nakrama—"dreadlocked black man from Nyakrong." (I think he called him Nakrama because Tertön Sogyal had such a dark complexion.)

For the majority of his life, Tertön Sogyal traveled freely around the country as a wandering ascetic. Khyentse Wangpo, by contrast, directed a

Tertön Sogyal
Source: Tertön Sogyal Foundation

vast number of activities and held a position that brought with it enormous merit, power, and wealth. Yet he too signed many of his writings "Manjugosha, the Wanderer." Tertön Sogyal couldn't understand it at all. Eventually he asked Khyentse Wangpo directly how he, of all people, could truly describe himself as a wanderer.

"It's not something you will understand right now," replied Khyentse Wangpo. "Go to central Tibet towards the end of your life. Then you'll understand."

As things turned out, Tertön Sogyal did eventually go to Lhasa. It was there that he became the guru of many of Tibet's highest lamas, including His Holiness Thubten Gyatso, the Thirteenth Dalai Lama and preceptor of the Tibetan government. As Khyentse Wangpo had predicted, in the midst of his new and very busy schedule, the great tertön came to realize how Khyentse Wangpo had truthfully been able to describe himself as a lifelong wanderer and ascetic. In spite of all his responsibilities, Khyentse

Wangpo had always practiced the Dharma and never indulged in the games worldly people play. For example, he never even attempted to be tactful or politically shrewd, yet he was held in the highest esteem by great masters, scholars, members of the aristocracy, politicians, and the rich. As a result of this realization, Tertön Sogyal developed even greater confidence in him.

I don't know the details or fully understand why, but at one of Khyentse Wangpo's seats, broken samaya caused Tertön Sogyal to become so ill that he could barely move. Chökyi Lodrö immediately visited him and offered him empowerments and many purifications. He instructed Dzongsar Monastery to recite Samayavajra and many hundred thousand Vajrasattva mantras, promising offerings for the recitations from the donations he collected. He made more offerings to the very best Dzongsar monks, asking them to accumulate one hundred thousand Vajrasattva mantras each, and even recited a large number himself. As a result, Tertön Sogyal recovered completely and is known to have declared that he owed Chökyi Lodrö a tremendous debt of gratitude.

Chökyi Lodrö always said that Tertön Sogyal was one of his root gurus. They were very close.

Drikung Tertön Ösel Dorje

I learnt the following during conversations I had with Gongna Tulku.

Drikung Tertön Ösel Dorje often visited Dzongsar. He was reputed to be both a habitual liar and exceedingly stubborn, as Chökyi Lodrö mentions in his autobiography in verse:

> Drikung Tertön Ösel Dorje granted me a long-life empowerment and dispelled obstacles to my life. Although he was an authentic treasure discoverer, his activity did not flourish because of his stubborn nature.

Mipham's wooden house stood below Dzongsar Monastery with a notice nailed to its door saying no one should go beyond that point without good reason. The only person ever to visit Mipham there was Adzom Drukpa, who, having announced that he had important things to discuss, simply turned up on the doorstep. But apart from Adzom Drukpa, no one else dared go there.

One day, Drikung Tertön Ösel Dorje told Chökyi Lodrö that, having

Drikung Tertön Ösel Dorje
Source: Drikung Tertön Ösel Dorje Facebook page

examined his dreams, he realized it was crucial to subjugate Chökyi Lodrö's enemies, various evil spirits, and some ruinous obstacles with a standard suppression ritual that should be performed inside Mipham's house. There were also negative forces that needed suppressing lower down the valley, beyond Khamje, at Dranen Gak.

Gongna Tulku watched as the tertön, assisted by about nine monks, performed the suppression ritual. They enclosed a space in which the objects for suppression were set out behind a black curtain, then they began. In the middle of the summoning ritual, a mouse with a red nose and crooked tail suddenly ran up and down the middle of the enclosure. Nevertheless, the monks continued to practice until the relevant signs were accomplished. But tertöns will always be tertöns, and after consecrating the suppression substances, Drikung Tertön Ösel Dorje drank a barrel of chang and proceeded to brag loudly and at great length about what he'd just accomplished. He also wrote a letter to Chökyi Lodrö, which in Tibetan reads like a warlord's call to arms:

Rinpoche must ride to Dranen Gak to where negative forces must be suppressed. I will ride there too, and all the tulkus, monks, and laypeople must come with us. If all goes well, it'll take one day to accomplish. If conditions prove a little more difficult, it will take a month. At worst, the ritual will take three months. But however long it takes, it's vital that there's enough food and drink for every member of our party.

Almost everyone then decamped to Dranen Gak, and the suppression ritual was completed. According to the tertön, it was thanks to Rinpoche's blessings that everything was accomplished so easily and so well. On the way back to Dzongsar, the tertön drank a drong's horn of home brew, became extremely drunk, and started making prophecies, one of which was, "Thirteen enemy demons will arise from Dranen Gak." The party spent that night at Somo Palace, where Rinpoche was heard to say, "We should probably write down what the tertön said today, but I can't find anything to write with. Anyway, everything he foretold was terrible! He performed the suppression well enough, but who knows whether or not the prophecies will come true—when a tertön's prophecies don't work out, it can ruin his reputation. He really shouldn't talk so much."

Later, the Khampas of Derge mounted a fierce resistance to the Chinese Communist invasion, and many were killed at Dranen Gak. Dilgo Khyentse heard about it during his visit to the Chime Yungdrung Centre in London. Tenga Tulku and a few of us were with him during that trip. He pointed out that, in this case, the tertön's prophecy had been quite accurate.

Pewar Tulku's account of the story was almost the same as Gongna Tulku's, but he added that the monks had buried the red-nosed mouse with a crooked tail in the suppression pit. Apparently the mouse had appeared at the point when Rinpoche and Tertön Ösel Dorje threw the symbolic dungeon into the pit, and they both insisted that the mouse should not escape. So a few monks waved their zens and drove it into the pit, while others shoveled earth and stones to bury it alive. The tertön cried, "Victory to the Celestial Beings (*Lha gyal lo*)!" and announced that perfectly auspicious circumstances had been established.

Dilgo Khyentse told me another story from that time. Each evening Rinpoche would sit alone in his room facing north to practice the suppression ritual of Vajrakilaya, while the tertön would sit in his room facing south to practice the suppression ritual of Yamantaka of Drikung. They practiced like this for many days, the tertön preferring to practice in the most elaborate and splendiferous way possible, with much beating of drums and clashing of cymbals, and so on. It was then arranged that the two suppression ceremonies would happen at the same time in the same pit.

After processing into the suppression pit, chanting, "OM AH HUM, the golden drink becomes the great ocean of amrita of undefiled wisdom . . . ," the tertön asked for a ceremonial hat.

Chokden took some hats from a skin bag and asked, "Which would you like?"

The tertön chose the *rigdzin chok zha* (the vidyadhara's hat), put it on, and stood facing south; Rinpoche took the *zhanak trokzhu* (the black, helmet-shaped hat) and stood facing north. The other tulkus and monks sat in a circle a little way away, and the laypeople sat behind them. As they chanted the summoning verses, the tertön jumped up and threw the suppression symbol into the air. But as he did so, his hat fell off and landed on top of the symbol.

"Ya ya," grumbled the tertön. "That didn't go well. Pick up that hat."

Chokden's face turned black, and he picked up the hat. They then buried the suppression symbol in the pit under a great weight of earth and stones. Dilgo Khyentse, Gongna Tulku, and Pewar Tulku all told this story in virtually the same way.

Years later, the stupa built over that suppression pit started falling to pieces. As the suppression symbol was still believed to be there, Dilgo Khyentse told me again and again that the stupa should be renovated. He said the same to the lamas and monks at Dzongsar Monastery. So Tulku Pema and a few Dzongsar monks decided to do a Sidok retreat as a way of restoring the stupa and asked me to give them the Sidok empowerment, which I did when I visited Dzongsar Monastery in Tibet. While I was there, I asked Tsejor about the tertön.

"Ösel Dorje must have been a very precious tertön," he said. "But he told lies all the time, and I neither had any devotion for him, nor did I like him. It was only because Rinpoche thought he was special that I served him.

"The tertön did obstacle-removing rituals every few days, and we had to make a great many tormas for him with meticulous care. But it was a real nuisance to have to soak our hands in water from morning to night. So one day, I didn't go. Instead I went to Khamje and Nera Tsang and didn't return to the labrang until dusk. I was sure the tertön would yell at me, but when I showed my face, he just asked where I had been and pretended not to mind. Anger must have been raging inside him, but he chose not to show it."

The next day, the tertön ate with Rinpoche.

"If I have to do rituals for Rinpoche's long life, I need someone to make the tormas," said the tertön, then he pointed at Tsejor. "But *he* isn't willing to help, and yesterday he disappeared for the entire day!"

Tsejor wondered how Rinpoche would respond, but he just asked where Tsejor had been and what he'd done. He didn't scold him at all.

I heard this next story from Khandro. The tertön was staying in Mipham's wooden house, and Chakdzö Tsewang Paljor went there to see him. On the table by the tertön lay a tooth that must have just fallen out.

"Chakdzö, there you are!" said the tertön. "You are very fortunate, you possess great merit. One of my teeth has fallen out, and I am going to give it to you."

"La so," replied Tsewang Paljor, accepting the gift so as not to cause offense, but somewhat reluctantly. He wrapped the tooth in paper, tucked it into his front pocket, then forgot all about it. About a year later, he came across the package, and when he looked inside, he discovered that eight or nine relics had sprouted from the tooth, each a different color. Chakdzö treasured that tooth from then on. Khandro said she had seen it herself, and that Chakdzö had shown it to Rinpoche. Tashi Namgyal said he had seen it too.

Pönlop Loter Wangpo

Gongna Tulku didn't ever meet Pönlop Loter Wangpo himself but said he had a reputation for being unusually short-tempered and for lambasting people brutally and often for no apparent reason. So I asked Tsejor, who had met him on a number of occasions, "Was Loter Wangpo really that volatile?"

"Oh yes!" said Tsejor. "He would scream as if his bones were on fire!"

Tsejor told me that after Khyentse Wangpo died, his nephew, Gyaltsab Kalzang Dorje, followed the tradition of offering his belongings to other lamas. He had acted quite properly, but Loter Wangpo was furious with him. According to Tsejor, Kalzang Dorje had given Tharpatse Labrang[18] an enormous brocade curtain that had originally been offered to Khyentse

Wangpo by Nyenchen Tangla, which was said to have been woven by nonhuman beings. It was a very special piece, but for some reason only Khyentse Wangpo had known of its uniqueness—it hadn't been listed in any of the labrang's records. Tharpatse was one of the four great Sakya labrangs of the Ngorpa tradition and the richest, and as Loter Wangpo was a Tharpatse, he knew all about the distribution of Khyentse Wangpo's possessions. What so infuriated him was that the people at Tharpatse Labrang, who knew nothing of the brocade curtain's history, had merely stuffed it into a box and forgotten all about it.

During a retreat at Karma Tak Tsang, Tsejor witnessed firsthand how Loter Wangpo felt about that brocade curtain. Loter Wangpo had to give an empowerment and asked Chökyi Lodrö for Jamyang Khyentse Wangpo's golden migthur. When it was handed to him, he was so moved to see it again that he pressed it to his eyes as a blessing. "This belonged to Dorje Chang, my root teacher. He really was the Vajradhara!"

A second later, his mood changed, and staring intently at the migthur, he growled, "But where is the red ribbon?"[19]

Khyentse Chökyi Lodrö was barely out of his teens at the time, certainly no more than twenty years old, and knew nothing of the history of Khyentse Wangpo's belongings. So when he said he didn't know anything about a red ribbon, Loter Wangpo exploded, castigating Chökyi Lodrö mercilessly while hurling insults at Kalzang Dorje's memory.

"That eater of his own father's flesh," yelled Loter Wangpo, using the strongest profanities in the Tsangpa dialect—he tended to slip into pure Tsangpa when he was really livid. "That ribbon was of great significance and should never have been lost! As my representative, you're supposed to look after the monastery, not destroy it! Adzi! Adzi! Kalzang Dorje lost all the Lord Guru's representations of body, speech, and mind, and all his wealth! He even offered a brand-new brocade to Tharpatse Labrang, which is now being devoured by moths in a moldy old box. Adzi! Adzi!"

Khyentse Chökyi Lodrö didn't know what to do.

"Find that ribbon!" yelled Loter Wangpo. "It's of great significance. You must not lose it!"

Having fully vented his spleen, Loter Wangpo calmed down. Chökyi Lodrö asked Tsejor to look for the ribbon, but they didn't ever find it. Tsejor often wondered who had taken it.

Another time, Loter Wangpo instructed Tsejor to bring him the jewel ornaments of the five buddha families, which Tsejor did, offering them to him individually and explaining carefully what each one was.

"I won't steal them," snarled Loter Wangpo. "Leave them here. Stop acting like this is some grand official ceremony!"

Tsejor gathered the jewel ornaments together and offered them all to Loter Wangpo, who said nothing more.

"Loter Wangpo was extremely fat," continued Tsejor. "He looked as though all he ever did was eat!"

So I asked Tsejor to describe his eating habits. He said that although Loter Wangpo only ate once a day—lunch at midday—he ate voraciously, as if stuffing his body with as much food as it would take.

According to Gongna Tulku, everyone believed Pönlop Loter Wangpo to be Mahakala in human form, even though he was very, very short and not a single hair grew on his head. When giving empowerments, at the point where he was supposed to cross a vajra and bell over his heart, he couldn't because his arms were too short. His legs were short too, and he couldn't sit cross-legged, so he sat with both heels pressed together and covered his legs with his robe. He looked like a bald dwarf.

When Chökyi Lodrö commissioned a clay statue of Loter Wangpo, he quoted a text to the sculptor that states statues should not reproduce any of the ugly aspects of a lama's form. The statue therefore presented Loter Wangpo with limbs of a normal length and his head painted gold. Chökyi Lodrö really treasured that statue and said it looked exactly like Loter Wangpo. It was later smashed by the Chinese.

Neither Mipham nor Loter Wangpo would allow photographs to be taken of themselves. They said cameras were evil inventions made of chemicals and all kinds of dreadful things that sucked the life force, merit, activity, and power from their subjects. Katok Situ had no such qualms and allowed several pictures of himself to be taken. But when Loter Wangpo was asked to consecrate a photo of Katok Situ (taken when he was in a peaceful mood—it looked as though it had been washed with varnish), he became very anxious, then almost mad with rage about it.

Shechen Gyaltsab, who was a student of Mipham, also refused to have his photo taken. And initially Dilgo Khyentse, who was a great admirer of Mipham, felt he had a point. So the first time Dilgo Khyentse faced a camera in Lhasa, he felt very nervous. Later, though, having been photographed so often throughout his life and come to no harm, he realized that cameras weren't dangerous after all.

Pönlop Loter Wangpo's Students

Whenever a student of Pönlop Loter Wangpo visited Rinpoche, he would always invite that student to sit next to him, but he never treated his other teachers' students with as much respect. One day, Dilgo Khyentse asked him why he considered Loter Wangpo's students to be so special.

"Ah!" said Rinpoche. "Of all my many teachers' students, the Guru Vajradhara's are unique. Each one is better than the last! Adzom Drukpa has quite a number of students, all of whom are good, but they're so dull. Katok Situ shouldered the great responsibility of upholding and spreading the teachings, but not many can truly be said to be his students. And although Dodrup Tsang (the Third Dodrupchen) is a very holy master, he has hardly any students at all."

Dilgo Khyentse felt that Rinpoche spoke the truth.

THE DEATH OF KARSE KONGTRUL

This is one of the more unfortunate stories Yangsi Rinpoche Thubten Chökyi Gyatso said I should include. I heard it from Tashi Namgyal.

The year after Palpung Situ died, Karse Kongtrul passed into nirvana. The Chakdzö and Yönten Phuntsok of Tsadra immediately traveled to Dzongsar and, shedding many tears, begged Rinpoche to visit Tsadra Rinchen Drak. Their minds would not find peace, they declared, until Rinpoche had visited the center, however briefly. Rinpoche agreed, and Karse Kongtrul's people sent horses to take him and his party to Tsadra.

On the morning of their departure, in the labrang enclosure, Tashi Namgyal tried to saddle a usually very timid horse, but it reared violently, then broke away from him and galloped towards the mountain, spinning round and round in frenzied circles. It took a long time to retrieve, and by the time Tashi Namgyal finally mounted up, his heart was uneasy. What had frightened the horse so much that it bolted?

As Rinpoche's party crossed the Hala Pass, Tashi Namgyal caught sight of a doubled-up weasel with a dead mouse in its mouth. Tsejor, Chokden, and Khenpo Namzang (a khenpo from our monastery at Nangchen) were Rinpoche's attendants at the time, and it was Khenpo Namzang who shouted "Shud!" at the animal. The weasel immediately dropped the dead mouse and scampered off, which everyone in the party agreed was a very bad omen indeed. They dismounted to rest while Khenpo Namzang, an expert astrologer, consulted his star charts and drew some symbols and figures on a large flat stone. After lengthy, anxious discussions with his companions, a hole was dug and the mouse's body laid in it with some water and fire. It was then covered with the flat stone and sealed in place with mud.

Tashi Namgyal was deeply disturbed by the events of the morning and sent an urgent message to Khandro and Tsewang Paljor.

"Khenpo Namzang and the other attendants are worried about a horse that bolted this morning, and a weasel just abandoned a dead mouse on our path. Please ask for a divination and perform ceremonies to remove obstacles."

The whole party then rode directly to Karse Kongtrul's home at Tsadra Rinchen Drak and began to prepare his kudung. But the Dzongsar monks, who were very superstitious, continued to worry. They decided to chant a Tara sadhana and do some other rituals, but while they were practicing, a black musk deer ran down from Gyagen in broad daylight, wandered through the monastery, and tried to break into the labrang enclosure. When it couldn't, it climbed over the cliff and down into Khamje Shedra, finally escaping along a footpath. So now both the upper and the lower monasteries were worried. The monks performed rituals in the monastery itself, and the khenpo and main monks of Khamje Shedra went to the labrang to do pujas on the top floor. (They made large cauldrons of tea and soup, which they set on the small labrang stoves, to sustain themselves during the rituals.)

Before long, the entire village of Menshö and everyone at Dzongsar Monastery were in a state of panic. The monastery sent a seemingly endless stream of messengers to Tsadra to beg Rinpoche to return immediately. All they managed to do, though, was disturb Rinpoche's mind, as did the news about the musk deer.

"Calm down and don't rush me," he snapped at one of the messengers. "I'm here now. Going straight back to Dzongsar won't do any good at all." And he had a cup of tea. He then went to the Tara Hall with his attendants and, in the presence of the "speaking" Tara statue, chanted a Tara sadhana three times. He then returned to his room, where he wrote the following letter:

> It's true that all these signs are usually considered to be bad omens and may well foretell all kinds of difficulties for the Buddhadharma and beings. But nothing alarming will happen to any of us. I have arrived at Tsadra and have been asked to stay for a

week. After that, I'll return to Dzongsar. There is no need for you to worry. Doing rituals can only be good. Nothing bad will come of it.

After he'd written this letter, the monastery's Chakdzö and Yönten Phuntsok assured Rinpoche that as he had already so graciously favored Tsadra with his presence, there was no reason why he shouldn't return to Dzongsar that very day—meaning they felt that if he left immediately, the predicted obstacles wouldn't affect him. Nevertheless, Rinpoche stayed.

Then, on the sixth night of Rinpoche's visit, a messenger arrived with a note from Khandro begging Rinpoche to return to Dzongsar without delay. He left the next morning.

I don't know what they were so worried about, but the moment Rinpoche arrived back at Dzongsar, all the old people broke down, weeping uncontrollably. Rinpoche went straight to the top floor of the monastery and remained there while the monks continued to accumulate hundreds of thousands of Tara prayers. Khyenrab Singye said that hearing Rinpoche cough during the practice had instantly made him feel peaceful and relaxed. But apart from that, everything seemed empty and dry.

Khandro and Tashi Namgyal told me all this as we sat together under the willow trees near the bell at the Palace Monastery in Sikkim. Khandro said they thought it very strange that no disasters struck in the wake of such dreadful omens. I certainly never heard of anything specific happening, apart from the widespread injury to the teachings and beings that was being perpetrated throughout Tibet at that time. Perhaps the omens were signs that the monastery would soon be empty?

Dezhung Tulku Ajam

Gongna Tulku told me that Dezhung Tulku Ajam always presented himself as a Sakyapa. Whenever he gave an empowerment or authorization blessing, however short, he always related it to the Sakya view of the nonduality of samsara and nirvana and went into great detail about why that view is so special. Secretly, though, there's no doubt that he practiced the Nyingma teachings, which made him very popular. Gongna Tulku confirmed this to be true during one of Dezhung Tulku's visits to Dzongsar, when he hid behind a curtain in Rinpoche's room after serving tea and eavesdropped on their conversation.

"And then?" said Rinpoche, when he thought they were alone.

Immediately, Dezhung Tulku recited from memory a portion of the root text and commentary on the *Treasury of Dharmadhatu* and the *Wish-Fulfilling Treasury*.

"Apho!" he said. "This is what is written in the *Treasury of Dharmadhatu*."

As he was particularly knowledgeable about the *Treasury of the Supreme Vehicle*, Rinpoche encouraged Dezhung Tulku to recite some more, so he did. Eventually Rinpoche said, "Akhi! Many years ago I read all these texts, but I've forgotten them now. You, though, seem to have them engraved on your heart."

Dezhung Tulku replied that he had studied them with great diligence and had taken their meaning to heart because he believed they proved that he had at some point practiced the teachings of Longchen Rabjam. He added that their conversation must remain secret and should never be made known to the Sakyapas.

Gongna Tulku secretly listened to Rinpoche's conversations on a number of occasions and heard many such things.

Chatral Sangye Dorje

Orgyen and the old monks I met when I visited Kham asked me, "Does Chatral Sangye Dorje live in India?"

"Yes, he does," I replied.

"He must be a very great scholar!"

"Why do you think that?" I asked.

They told me that Chatral Sangye Dorje had spent many months at Dzongsar, but Rinpoche always closed his door when they were together, so no one ever knew whether he was giving teachings or receiving them. Chatral Sangye Dorje had free access to Rinpoche's home and was allowed to borrow an unlimited number of books from the labrang library. He was also known to have a huge library of his own. It was said that his house was full of books and that he read all the time. Everyone was convinced that he was very learnèd, particularly after Rinpoche said as much to old Tsejor.

Sometimes, while he was waiting to receive transmissions and teachings from Rinpoche, Chatral Sangye Dorje would sit in the woodshed with three mud walls above the labrang. He'd make a fire from any wood chips he could find and boil up a thick brew of tea. If there was a yak's leg hanging from the beam, he would roast some in the fire and eat it.

Later, I asked Chatral Sangye Dorje which empowerments and trans-

Chatral Sangye Dorje
Source: Shechen Archives

missions he had received from Rinpoche and whether he'd ever offered Rinpoche anything himself. Chatral Sangye Dorje said he received and offered countless empowerments and transmissions. The most important oral transmissions, he said, were of the biographies of Jigme Gyalwe Nyugu and Gyalse Shenphen Taye, copies of which he had found in the labrang library. As Rinpoche had never received them before, Chatral Sangye Dorje gave them to him to ensure that the lineages wouldn't die out. He asked me many times to get him copies of those texts, but I couldn't find them anywhere. Tulku Pema Wangyal came across the biography of Jigme Gyalwe Nyugu some time later, but we have yet to locate the biography of Gyalse Shenphen Taye.

Tertön Tsewang Drakpa and Shardzapa Tashi Gyaltsen

Of the Bonpö masters, Rinpoche was closest to Tertön Tsewang Drakpa, from whom he received many empowerments and transmissions. Tertön Tsewang Drakpa had offered a large quantity of Bön treasure substances to the previous Khyentse, Jamyang Khyentse Wangpo, and later also offered many such things to Rinpoche.

The biography of a master called Shardzapa Tashi Gyaltsen, who attained rainbow body, states that he met Chökyi Lodrö and received many empowerments, transmissions, and Dzogchen pith instructions from him. But none of Khyentse Chökyi Lodrö's students have ever breathed a word about him. The number of treasure substances Bönter Tsewang Drakpa gave Khyentse Wangpo must have been huge, because Khyentse Chökyi Lodrö had to ask Shardzapa to sort them out for him. This was how those substances came to be of such immense benefit to the Buddhadharma.

Lithang Shokdruk Kyabgön

Lithang Shokdruk Kyabgön from the Gelug school wrote to say he wanted to visit Khamje Shedra to debate with the khenpo and monks. He also wanted to visit Khyentse Labrang, he said, to debate with Khyentse Rinpoche. It was Khenpo Rinchen who told me about his visit to Dzongsar.

Lithang Shokdruk Kyabgön was the kind of lama who maintained a private army and always traveled with two or three hundred bodyguards and a large entourage, so his encampment was invariably enormous. One day, as the khenpo of Khamje Shedra was about to start the monk's revision class, scores of horses and mules were heard entering the courtyard. A man in a yellow brocade chuba and ho tuk tuk hat burst into the room and swaggered to the front of the hall through the front row of monks.

"Khor sum," yelled the intimidating newcomer, as he launched some well-aimed dialectic arguments at the khenpo, who had just seated himself on the throne.

Tashi Namgyal must have been present because according to him, although it was customary to remove your hat, the lama had purposefully left his hat on his head, proclaiming that it had been conferred on him by the Tibetan government (it might have been the Chinese) and under no circumstance could he take it off.

In those days, Khamje Shedra was not politically strong and had yet to establish its scholastic reputation. This blustering Gelugpa lama and politician had therefore seized the opportunity to increase his own standing by traveling from Tolung specifically to terrorize the shedra's khenpo and monks in debate. I've been told that although he made a donation and some offerings to Khamje Shedra, he wasn't liked. It's true, he deigned to sip the tea they served, but the overwhelming impression was that he had a very disagreeable personality. Rinpoche was believed to have said that he was "somewhat learnèd," but when he heard that the lama intended to visit the labrang, he left for Karmo Tak Tsang to avoid him.

Gatön Ngawang Lekpa

Tsejor told me that Gatön Ngawang Lekpa stayed at Dzongsar for about three months. On the morning of his departure for Ga, he and Rinpoche exchanged scarves, touched foreheads, and bade each other farewell. A few minutes after Ngawang Lekpa had returned to his room, Rinpoche cried out, "Ai, Ai! I've forgotten something. I wanted to ask Ngawang Lekpa to swap bowls with me!" And he sent Tsejor to offer his bowl to Ngawang Lekpa with the request that he send his back to Rinpoche.

Tsejor found Ngawang Lekpa at the door of his room, his zen already knotted and ready to leave. Tsejor gave him Rinpoche's begging bowl and passed on Rinpoche's request.

Gatön Ngawang Lekpa in Minyak in 1928
Source: Mingyur Rinpoche

"Well, I would never say no to the Vajradhara," said Gatön Ngawang Lekpa. "But the only bowl I have is a Tsang bowl." And he directed his nephew to give it to Tsejor, who took it to Rinpoche.

"What did Ngawang Lekpa say?" asked Rinpoche. Tsejor described how Ngawang Lekpa had paced up and down, saying it was completely unnecessary it to swap bowls and that his was very poor compared to Rinpoche's Chinese bowl. Rinpoche then explained that as Ngawang Lekpa was such a saintly being, his bowl was extremely blessed regardless of its material value. And from then until just before he took his consort, that was the bowl Rinpoche always ate from. After that, he offered it to Khamje Shedra.

Later, during the Cultural Revolution, it was entrusted to my uncle Orgyen. I noticed it when we visited Nangchen and asked him about its history.

"It was Gab Balma's begging bowl," said Uncle Orgyen.

"Who was Gab Balma?" I asked.

"While Gatön Ngawang Lekpa was staying with Khyentse Wangpo, he was given the nickname Gab Balma. He had visited Dzongsar because he wanted to receive the *Path and Fruition* teachings, but although Khyentse Wangpo gave *Path and Fruition* three times during his stay, on each occasion Khyentse Wangpo personally kicked Ngawang Lekpa out of the empowerment hall and pelted him with stones to drive him away."

After that Ngawang Lekpa became very poor and had to beg for food. He was so poor that his robe became unusually shabby, and the Dzongsar monks gave him the rather derogatory nickname of Gab Balma, or "wearer of frayed robes." Even after he had become famous, people often used his old nickname when they spoke of him.

After Uncle Orgyen passed away, I offered Ngawang Lekpa's ordinary-looking bowl to Khyentse Labrang and told them of its remarkable history.

OTHER MASTERS

Many other masters traveled to Dzongsar to visit Khyentse Chökyi Lodrö. For example, of the less well-known teachers, there was Shar Lama, Nub Lama, Gyaltsen Lama of Dzongsar Monastery, and others of their caliber, and from Gönchen Monastery many masters of the same stature as Pewar Tulku and Dhongthog Tulku. Tarthang Tulku traveled from Golok and spent the best part of two years at Dzongsar, only leaving to gather offerings. Both Kela Chokling and Neten Chokling visited; Khyentse Chökyi

Lodrö gave each of them the complete transmission of the *New Treasures* (I don't know who else was present). But Dudjom Jikdral Yeshe Dorje never visited Dzongsar.

I asked Tsejor who Chökyi Lodrö was referring to when he said, "Rinpoche," "Dorje Chang," "Lama Tsang," "Drukpa Tsang," and "Gyaltsab Rinpoche." He said that "Rinpoche" only ever meant Katok Situ, no one else; "Dorje Chang" was Loter Wangpo; "Lama Tsang" was Dodrup Tenpe Nyima; "Drukpa Tsang" was Adzom Drukpa; and "Gyaltsab Rinpoche" was Shechen Gyaltsab.

Khenpo Ngakchung

One day, I asked Tsejor, "What kind of person was Khenpo Ngakchung? Did you ever meet him?"

"Yes," he replied, "I met him. He was a stout man with a dark complexion. And he had a ferocious look about him, as if his tendons had been singed."

"How did he behave?" I asked.

Khenpo Ngakchung
Source: Shechen Archives

"He always mumbled so quietly that you couldn't hear what he was saying. But if you asked him to repeat himself he'd lose his temper. 'Flesh-eating foe! Can't one human being understand another when he speaks?' Whenever he visited Rinpoche, they would meet behind closed doors, and none of us ever knew what they talked about."

Tsejor had no idea what Khenpo Ngakchung taught. He said, "Most people considered Khenpo to be Vimalamitra in the flesh." Then he added, "But I didn't like him."

Khenpo Nüden

One day, Rinpoche told Dilgo Khyentse that he wanted to receive the empowerment of the *Heart Essence of Vimalamitra* or the *Innermost Heart Drop of Profundity* (from the *Four Parts of Nyingtik*) from Khenpo Nüden and asked if he was interested in receiving it too. Dilgo Khyentse said he was. So Rinpoche instructed Chokden to set up the mandala shrine in front of the statue of Khyentse Wangpo in his private room. Dilgo Khyentse sat on a thick square cushion beside Rinpoche, and Khenpo Nüden sat on a throne of three stacked cushions facing them.

To confer the empowerment, Khenpo Nüden wore a brocade ceremonial shawl decorated with swastikas. He looked magnificent, but he had no idea what he was supposed to do, so Rinpoche had to guide him through the empowerment process from beginning to end.

"The vajracharya must wear the ceremonial hat," read Khenpo, then asked Rinpoche what he should do, and Rinpoche told him to put on the pandita hat. Khenpo put it on and also perched a pair of dark crystal glasses on his nose.

"I told you, I don't know how to give empowerments," sighed Khenpo Nüden. "You will have to show me how to do everything as we go along."

Next Khenpo read, "holding the vajra and bell," and asked Rinpoche how. Rinpoche showed him. Khenpo continued reading. The vajra master is supposed to "unite vajra and bell," and again Rinpoche showed Khenpo how to cross the vajra and bell at his heart. When Khenpo read, "the acharya must stand up," he asked Rinpoche if he should, and Rinpoche explained that during an elaborately performed ritual he definitely should stand and that during a simpler one to stand would not be a mistake. So Khenpo stood up because, he said, he thought it might be necessary.

"The manual says I should touch my eyes with my fingers," said Khenpo.

So Rinpoche showed him how, and Khenpo copied Rinpoche exactly, asking anxiously if he'd done it correctly. Khenpo even admitted that he didn't know how to turn the pages of the text, so Rinpoche showed him.

This was the manner in which Khenpo Nüden granted an empowerment to Khyentse Chökyi Lodrö and Dilgo Khyentse. Dilgo Khyentse later said how amazed he had been that such a great scholar—and Khenpo Nüden was a highly accomplished Dzogchen master—had such difficulties giving an empowerment, but that watching him struggle through it had increased his own devotion for him.

Khenpo Nüden's Retreat

Tsejor told me that Rinpoche once instructed Tashi Namgyal to assist Khenpo Nüden during one of his retreats. So I asked Tashi Namgyal, "Did you go?"

"Yes, I went," he replied. "Rinpoche told me to prepare a cave at Lha Chok Ding, and I took two assistants from Dzongsar Monastery to help me clean it, repair the stone wall at the entrance, and weave a bamboo mat to use as a door. The ladder up to the cave was so long and thin that we were worried Khenpo might fall off, so we replaced it with a new cypress wood ladder. I then sent word to Khenpo that everything was ready."

A couple of days later, Khenpo and Tashi Namgyal arrived on horseback, leading a mule laden with the meat, tsampa, butter, and cheese that Chakdzö had provided. As soon as he saw the cave, Khenpo nodded his head in approval, saying, "Peaceful! So peaceful! It's absolutely peaceful here. Ha! Ha! Ha!" They wove some tree branches into a wicker carpet and laid it on the floor inside the cave. Khenpo spread his monk's mat over the wickerwork, then sat down to meditate.

Tashi Namgyal and Khenpo's other assistants opened the tsampa and cheese bags, unpacked two bowls of butter and a leg of meat, and arranged everything so that Khenpo could reach each item easily. Once they had finished, Khenpo dismissed them, saying, "I don't need anything else. You can go."

After less than a week, Rinpoche told Tashi Namgyal to go and see if Khenpo needed anything. Tashi Namgyal rode to Lha Chok Ding, tethered his horse, and approached the mouth of the cave. Khenpo was sitting bolt upright. Tashi Namgyal raised his head so Khenpo could see him.

"Khenpo Tsang!" he called.

"Ah!" exclaimed Khenpo. "That sounds like the Vajradhara's attendant. Adzi!"

Tashi Namgyal entered the cave and saw immediately that the tsampa, meat, and butter were untouched. Khenpo had not eaten for five or six days! Was he sick? Did he need anything?

"I don't need anything at all," replied Khenpo. "It's so peaceful here. Adzi! So peaceful!"

Khenpo Nüden spent about two months in retreat at Lha Chok Ding.

Katok Monastery and Tashi Namgyal's family had enjoyed a close spiritual connection spanning many generations, and Tashi Namgyal said it was thanks to this relationship that he had had so many opportunities to spend time in Khenpo's presence. Tashi Namgyal always felt tremendous devotion for Khenpo Nüden.

Khenpo Kunpal

It was from Khenpo Kunpal, who had been a student of Mipham, that Rinpoche received many teachings on Buddhist philosophy. He cherished Khenpo as a great jewel in his crown of gurus. But Tsejor, who'd lived for quite some time at Katok, knew little about him. In fact, as Khenpo rarely left his room, Tsejor only saw him once or twice. During the latter part of his life, Khenpo didn't teach much, only to high lamas and tulkus. Yet everyone held him in the very highest esteem and had great devotion for him.

The Debate between Khangmar Rinchen and Khenpo Appey

Khenpo Rinchen told me about a debate between Khangmar Rinchen and Khenpo Appey that took place before Appey had been enthroned as a khenpo.[20]

Khenpo Pedam was the khenpo of Neten Monastery in Nangchen and an exceptional Nyingma scholar. Appey was a Sakyapa. They studied together at Khamje Shedra and often clashed in philosophical debate. Pedam would sometimes take their disputes to Rinpoche, especially when Appey appeared to refute Mipham's philosophical viewpoint successfully. Rinpoche held Mipham in very high regard and didn't consider the refutation of his arguments to be at all beneficial, so he decided to ask Khangmar Rinchen to enter into a debate with Appey. He was certain Khangmar

Khenpo Appey holding the mandala
Source: Khyentse Labrang

Rinchen would win, and felt that a resounding defeat was just what Appey needed to help him appreciate Mipham's position more fully.

The circumstances necessary to hold such a debate arose one Losar when all the monks, including Appey and Khangmar Rinchen, had gathered at Rinpoche's residence. Rinpoche instructed Appey to take the role of "defender" and Khangmar Rinchen that of "advocate." Later, said Rinpoche, they could swap.

As Appey and Pedam had debated so often, Appey was well versed in Mipham's interpretation of whether or not shravakas and pratyekabuddhas realize the selflessness of phenomena. He therefore decided to deflect the focus of the debate by telling jokes. As a result, the debate proper never really got started, because Khangmar Rinchen couldn't make head or tail of what Appey was saying. Unfortunately, those listening didn't realize what Appey was doing and interpreted Khangmar Rinchen's confusion as a failure to defend his position. They then lionized Appey, declaring he was such an exceptional scholar that even the great Khangmar Rinchen was unable to defeat him. The reality, as both Appey and Khangmar Rinchen told Khenpo Rinchen, was that the debate had not been carried out as Rinpoche had originally wished.

Sakya Gongma of Phuntsok Phodrang

Sakya Gongma's First Visit to Dzongsar

When Sakya Gongma of Phuntsok Phodrang (Sakya Dagchen) accepted a formal invitation to visit Dzongsar Monastery for the first time, Khyentse Labrang, Dzongsar Monastery, and Dzongsar village were thrown into a state of chaos and confusion.

Preparations began immediately, with Khyentse Chökyi Lodrö himself making lists of the lamas who would ride in the procession sent to greet Sakya Gongma, those who would then attend the formal reception ceremony, and so on. Only wealthy Dzongsar monks made it onto Rinpoche's lists because only they already owned the splendid clothes and horses necessary for such an occasion—Rinpoche wouldn't have to provide them with anything. None of the poorer Khamje Shedra monks were chosen. The labrang staff were another matter. Rinpoche had to order about twenty new monk's vests, as well as clothes and silk bags for those carrying anything Dagchen Rinpoche might need for the empowerments, plus hats and matching saddle blankets for everyone. It took the labrang's tailors three months to finish everything. Gongna Tulku added that the tailors had to make Khampa-style, long-sleeved coats because they didn't know how to make traditional central Tibetan monk's vests.

A little more than a week before Dagchen Rinpoche's arrival, Rinpoche asked Dilgo Khyentse what he was planning to wear to the reception. Dilgo Khyentse described his clothes, and Rinpoche immediately told him they were entirely inappropriate.

"Rinpoche, it's all I have. What should I do?" asked Dilgo Khyentse.

"Don't worry, I'll find you something," said Rinpoche.

The next day, Tsewang Paljor brought Dilgo Khyentse one of Rinpoche's own robes, a zen, and a gold brocade monk's vest, but he was so tall that nothing was long enough. The best he could do was drape Rinpoche's rare and expensive shawl of finely woven wool over his own best shawl. Rinpoche also said that he should wear special ceremonial boots and sent him many pairs to choose from. But again, none of them fit, and Dilgo Khyentse was forced to wear his old ones.

Gongna Tulku said that although Rinpoche had instructed everyone to follow central Tibetan traditions throughout Sakya Gongma's visit, it quickly became clear that the labrang staff had no idea what that meant. Rinpoche

Sakya Gongma of Phuntsok Phodrang in Tibet
Source: H.H. Jigdal Dagchen Sakya's family photo album

had to show them how to do everything, from arranging plates of Tibetan biscuits, to serving droma and saffron rice, and so on, in the right order.

The day of Dagchen Rinpoche's arrival finally dawned, and everyone gathered to greet him. According to Dilgo Khyentse, the reception procession was a truly magnificent spectacle. Even though Rinpoche had not specifically instructed the entire community to turn out, a line of monks wearing ceremonial robes and shawls from both the upper and lower monasteries of Dzongsar began below Khamje and ran right up to the hill above Juring Ju. Of course, they may genuinely have wanted to greet Sakya Gongma, but as Dilgo Khyentse said, it was just as likely that they'd turned out because they'd heard Rinpoche would be granting empowerments and transmissions.

"Such a procession is unimaginable to us today," said Dilgo Khyentse. "There were so many monks, and each one of them had at least some idea about Buddhist philosophy—these days we'd call them all khenpos. And I'm sure they were all genuine Dharma practitioners."

Pewar Tulku said Rinpoche wore a shawl sewn with silken thread and a robe of the best-quality wool over a gold brocade monk's vest and glistening yellow brocade. He also wore a golden hat, ceremonial boots, and a reliquary on his back. His horse, led by two ponies, was adorned with all kinds of precious ornaments, and the finest white silk scarves hung from its bridle. Tashi Namgyal said that Dhongthog Tulku wore the most resplendent robes and rode the most majestically ornamented horse, and Dilgo Khyentse was the worst dressed and by far the worst mounted! The lamas and tulkus in the procession were instructed by Rinpoche to follow him in a disciplined line; they were to neither run on ahead nor lag behind. Once the procession had passed by, the monks who lined the path fell in behind. Everyone was so sumptuously turned out that their radiance rivaled the brilliance of the sunrise.

Sakya Gongma arrived in a palanquin borne by four men and wore a ceremonial Sakyapa hat. Rinpoche greeted him with the greatest possible courtesy, removed his hat with both hands, and rode around him at a respectful distance. The lamas and tulkus followed his example, removing their hats with the traditional flourish to the right. Sakya Gongma then took his place in the middle of the procession, and they took the long, formal route to Dzongsar.

At Tashi Darthang, they stopped for refreshments. As was customary among central Tibetans, after Rinpoche removed his hat, he stretched out his tongue and scratched behind his ears. He politely asked Sakya Gongma how he was after his long journey, and they exchanged white ceremonial scarves.

But Khampas will be Khampas, and as Sakya Gongma walked to the tea tent, the crowd pressed in on him, each person straining for a better look. Rinpoche himself had to shoo them away with his zen, shouting, "Go away! Go away!"

Once inside the tent, Sakya Gongma and Dagmo Kusho, his wife, were shown to their thrones and served tea. The traditional exposition of Dharma was then given, and everything was arranged in such a way that from where he sat, Sakya Gongma could see the three-deities dancers whirling around the monastery.

Tashi Namgyal told me that the tea server, a labrang attendant monk, had been chosen for the job because he had been to central Tibet and was therefore thought to have the best chance of doing it properly. At the rehearsal, Rinpoche asked the monk to demonstrate how he would pour

Sakya Gongma of Phuntsok Phodrang, his wife, and their children
Source: H.H. Jigdal Dagchen Sakya's family photo album

tea into Sakya Gongma's cup. The monk lifted the vase-shaped, silver-plated kettle with a ceremonial tea leaf and paper flower in its lip and swung it as if he were pouring tea. He then repeated the process, and did it surprisingly well. Rinpoche said he should pour tea exactly like that on the day, but frankly wasn't convinced the monk was up to it.

The next day, once Sakya Gongma had taken his place on the throne, the tea server approached him, looking very nervous. As he swung the kettle, two things happened simultaneously: he realized he'd forgotten to remove the paper flower from the kettle's spout, and its lid fell into Sakya Gongma's cup. Fortunately the cup didn't break, but the incident proved extremely embarrassing for Rinpoche and for Dzongsar Monastery. Rinpoche was heard to say, "I told you he was incapable of doing it properly! You should have asked one of Sakya Gongma's attendants to serve the tea. Azhang! You were far too quick!"

After tea, everyone processed into the monastery, escorted by monks who played all the songs and dances they knew on every single cymbal, horn, trumpet, conch shell, and gong that Dzongsar Monastery possessed. People wearing white-bearded masks stood next to the group of musicians by the statue of Thangtong Gyalpo to recite verses of auspiciousness, then as the procession passed, they all joined in behind. Fish skin, a fan, and a pair of boots hung on either side of the palanquin as offerings, which Pewar Tulku thought represented the seven semiprecious gems that are traditionally offered to a great being.

At one point, Sakya Gongma disappeared. Anxiously, those closest to the palanquin scanned the procession. Eventually he was spotted standing next to a bush by the side of the road with his splendid robes bunched up around his waist so he could relieve himself.

In the Tse palace, Sakya Gongma sat on a throne, and Dagmo Kusho sat on a throne next to him, wearing a large jeweled headdress and a yellow tsang hat. To the astonishment of all the great lamas and aristocrats of Kham, as Rinpoche prostrated to them, Dagmo sat in heroic posture without moving a muscle.

"Adzi!" they exclaimed. "What shall we do with this woman? She stays seated in heroic posture while Khyentse Dorje Chang prostrates!"

That evening, Rinpoche was told of her behavior, but he said it wasn't a problem, because Sakya Gongma and his consort were both so highly respected. Sakya Gongma then spent a year at Dzongsar.

The Eldest Dungsey's Birthday
During Sakya Gongma's time at Dzongsar, his eldest son had a birthday, and Rinpoche decided he wanted to celebrate as magnificently as possible.

"I would have liked to celebrate just as they do at Sakya Monastery," said Rinpoche. "But that would mean arranging a procession flanked by rows of one hundred young women on the right, one hundred mantrikas holding phurbas on the left, and one hundred monks and one hundred young men in the procession itself, which we can't afford. But we should try to assemble at least twenty-five of each." Which they did, and the elaborate procession that circumambulated the monastery included young women, monks, mantrikas, and young men, with monks in Sakya dharmapala masks darting in and out.

A great feast followed, during which some of Sakya Gongma's attendants chanted the central Tibetan-style namtar. Rinpoche himself shaved the head of the eldest dungsey, and I have seen with my own eyes a packet containing a six-inch hank of hair labeled "the plaited hair of Sakya Dungsey Manju."

Once the birthday celebrations had been concluded, Rinpoche wanted to do an elaborate Vajrakilaya practice. Dzongsar Monastery must have practiced a Vajrakilaya ritual at some point in its past, but Rinpoche wasn't convinced that the dances known in Kham were the authentic ones. It was his wish that the dances be performed exactly as Sakya Gongma had last seen them at Sakya Gongma Tsang in the main Sakya monastery. "Because," he said, "when a large nugget of gold happens to roll onto your doorstep, you should take as much advantage of your good fortune as you can." Meaning, as Sakya Gongma was there with them at Dzongsar, they should take the opportunity to learn as much from him as they could. Rinpoche therefore instructed the monks to enlist the help of one of the Gongma Tsang dance masters, who then oversaw their practice for several months.

At that time, Dzongsar Monastery possessed an old dog-head mask that had been presented to it by the main Sakya monastery, and Sakya Gongma had also brought a dog-head mask with him. Yet Rinpoche decided to make an exquisite new mask, into which Sakya Gongma himself wove seven layers of thread. After the mask had been covered with powdered medicines[21] and other sacred substances, it was returned to Sakya Gongma, who painted it with his own hand, then gave it to the artists to finish off. Dzongsar Monastery still has both the new and the old masks.

Sakya Gongma's Dance
During the sacred dances, all the lamas followed Dzongsar Monastery tradition and sat on thrones inside the Ber Kang (where the masks and dance costumes were stored). Just before Sakya Gongma appeared in the new dog-head mask, Rinpoche asked everyone to stand up and pray to him as he danced. Thigh-bone trumpets were sounded to summon negativity with a proclamation of the truth as Sakya Gongma entered the field under a parasol. Dilgo Khyentse said that at that moment he felt a sudden tremor, but no one else mentioned it. Rinpoche is believed to have remained standing throughout Sakya Gongma's dance, only regaining his seat once the dance was over. (Gongna Tulku told me that at that dance, Sakya Gongma offered golden drinks.)

Before the blazing torma for repelling negativity was tossed away, Sakya Gongma had to change into an extremely elaborate ceremonial costume, and only the shrine master of the main Sakya monastery had the skill necessary to help him put it on. The sleeves of his warrior's robe were raised high on his shoulders and pinned back. Underneath the robe, he wore a white cloth. And under his black hat, he wore a lock of hair with lice eggs stuck to it, which was believed to have belonged to one of the early Sakya Gongmas.

Sakya Gongma sprang forward like a hero going into battle, then tossed the torma of the four Shona mothers, followed by the torma for the four Dagni mothers. They both landed pointing towards the obstacles, which was a very good sign. But when he tossed the torma for the four Sadak mothers, it landed pointing towards him, which was a bad sign, and he had to do it again. Then came the tormas for the four Kyebu Ging and the wrathful-faced torma for the main deity, Vajrakumara. But they did not land auspiciously either.

The next evening, Zhappey, an aristocratic old man from Sakya Tsang who always wore a long turquoise stone, suddenly died. His unexpected death convinced everyone that the final torma's inauspicious landing had been a very bad sign. So Gongna Tulku went to see Sakya Gongma, taking with him a token of condolence from Dzongsar Monastery.

"Ah! Yesterday, when the torma for the four Dagni mothers reversed itself, I was worried!" said Sakya Gongma. "I thought to myself, I haven't done a good job here; this could cause an obstacle to Dorje Chang's life. But it turned out all right because the torma hit Zhappey's head, and as he's now dead, nothing else will be affected."

The Empowerments Rinpoche Bestowed on Sakya Gongma

Gongma Tsang was always offered rooms that were reserved exclusively for high-ranking visiting lamas. In those days, his attendants were all villains who would steal anything that wasn't nailed down, even stale Tibetan biscuits. Not one of them was worthy of being an attendant to Gongma Tsang. Even a few Khampas who, in those difficult times, had been stranded at Sakya Monastery, became attendants, and they were all extremely accomplished thieves. But it didn't matter much. Khyentse Labrang was far too rich to miss any of the things they took.

Rinpoche bestowed a number of empowerments and reading transmissions on Gongma Tsang, and although he couldn't give the *Treasury of Precious Instructions*, he did give the *Path and Fruition: The Explanation for Private Disciples*; the *Compendium of Sadhanas*; a few great empowerments, including the Seven Mandalas from the Ngor tradition; and some mandalas from the Tsar tradition.

Pewar Tulku told me about the labrang's three small thangkas of the Three Red Deities, which were believed to have been made either by Rinpoche or his predecessor. They were displayed when Rinpoche, wearing a magnificent coat of red silk, gave Sakya Gongma the extraordinary empowerments for the Three Red Deities. Gongna Tulku also received them.

The following day, Rinpoche seemed unwell, so Sakya Gongma visited him in his private room. Later that day, Rinpoche asked his attendants to offer Sakya Gongma the thangkas, red coat, and hat he had worn the previous day. Mandala flowers offered to Sakya Gongma Phuntsok Phodrang at that time still exist in reliquaries stored in the labrang in Bir.

Rinpoche also gave Sakya Gongma the authorization blessing of Gur Mahakala. According to tradition, having received the blessing, a student should, at best, accumulate ten million Mahakala mantras. If that's not possible, the student should do at least one hundred thousand recitations of each syllable. If he doesn't, the teacher usually won't grant the empowerments and instructions for the secret practice. But on this occasion, Rinpoche gave the authorization blessing *and* the secret empowerment at the same time, saying he could not follow tradition because Sakya Gongma was in such a hurry. He also gave transmissions for the two volumes of Zhal, the four-armed Mahakala, and a volume of Durdak (Lord of the Cemetery) that other traditions did not have.

Gongna Tulku had detailed knowledge of all the empowerments, transmissions, and instructions that Chökyi Lodrö gave at that time, as did Dezhung Tulku.

The Empowerment of Great Yellow Vaishravana
The day Rinpoche offered Phuntsok Phodrang the empowerment of the *Great Yellow Vaishravana*, an amazing thing happened. He received an offering from Yab Tsang of Chamdo of the first print run of the entire Kangyur, made from print blocks Rinpoche himself had commissioned. Rinpoche was overcome with delight.

"Once, during the transmission of the *Compendium of Sadhanas*, when I gave the empowerment of the *Great Yellow Vaishravana*, a shower of gold dust was said to have fallen from the sky. It may well have happened—many people not only saw it, they gathered up the gold and took it away with them. But actually, a shower of gold is a very ordinary kind of siddhi. Today something far more wonderful has happened, and it's an unbelievably good sign: we have experienced a shower of Dharma!"

He immediately gathered all the monks who lived at Dzongsar but were not supported by the monastery and asked them to recite the Kangyur from beginning to end.

At the End of Sakya Gongma's Second Visit to Dzongsar

Sakya Gongma's second visit to Dzongsar was a very long one, but eventually he and his party had to return to Sakya. For days before they left, Dagmo Kusho wept continuously, but no one knew why. And her tears must have disturbed Sakya Gongma, because he wept too. On the morning of their departure, they rose early, intending to leave promptly. But Dagmo Kusho became so distressed at being parted from Rinpoche that she collapsed and was unable to walk.

As usual, Rinpoche was entirely unmoved by her wretched state—he would never make a fuss, even if the universe turned upside down! The labrang staff were similarly indifferent and went about their daily business as usual.

Dilgo Khyentse Rinpoche said that after Sakya Gongma left Dzongsar, Khandro Tsering Chödrön would stride up and down wearing a Sakyapa hat, imitating the way Sakya Gongma said, "So, Ani, what then?" It was her way of having fun.

10. Stories from Dzongsar

Khenpo Kunga Wangchuk's Stories

THIS STORY was told to me by Khenpo Kunga Wangchuk.

While Khenpo was a revision teacher at Khamje Shedra, a huge brocade thangka of the Dharma Lord Sakya Pandita was made, and on his anniversary it was displayed in the shedra's willow grove. Offerings were made and rituals performed, but Rinpoche wouldn't go down to the grove himself to consecrate the thangka. Instead, he said, he'd do it from his residence at Tashi Lhatse. Towards evening that day, grains of rice and wheat were seen to rain down on the image. Then a second shower appeared, leaving piles of grain all over the grass in the courtyard. Khenpo Kunga Wangchuk said he saw it with his own eyes. Only later was it confirmed that Rinpoche had in fact thrown grain from his window twice to bless the thangka.

There's no need for me to tell you about how Rinpoche scattered the consecration grain in a similar way for two other monasteries, because the stories appear in the *Great Biography*.

Two Bronze Cauldrons

During Rinpoche's time, two bronze cauldrons were cast at Dzongsar Monastery. The first was finished while he was away, so messages were sent asking Rinpoche to say prayers and to consecrate it. Although he was so far away, everyone in Dzongsar saw the rainbow that appeared on the surface of the cauldron at the same moment Rinpoche was saying the consecration prayers. Since then it has been known as the "rainbow cauldron."

Before they cast the second cauldron, another message was sent to Rinpoche to request his blessings. Again Rinpoche blessed the cauldron from afar, and in Dzongsar three kernels of grain suddenly appeared in the bottom of the cauldron that could neither be removed nor burnt. Even after the Cultural Revolution one grain remained, and although it's since been dislodged, you can still see its imprint in the bronze. Khenpo Kunga Wangchuk confirmed that Dzongsar Monastery still has these two cauldrons. They are called Jazukma, the "rainbow cauldron," and Nejarma, the "cauldron with wheat grains stuck to it."

Khenpo Receives the Compendium of Sadhanas

Having served as a revision teacher at Khamje Shedra for some time, Khenpo Kunga Wangchuk became a khenpo at Wara Monastery. At that point, although Khenpo had studied Buddhist philosophy, he had received very few empowerments or oral transmissions. When he finally decided he wanted to received such things, he asked Rinpoche for the necessary empowerments. Rinpoche said he was too busy, but that he'd send for Khenpo next time an empowerment happened.

Eventually, it became known that Rinpoche would give the transmission for the *Compendium of Sadhanas* in the empowerment hall of Chime Drupe Gatsal. It turned out to be the only time Rinpoche ever gave that transmission there.

"The first and second times I gave the *Compendium of Sadhanas*," said Rinpoche, "the transmissions took place in the assembly hall of Dzongsar Monastery, and many people received them. But come what may, this time the transmission will be given in the labrang's empowerment hall to as many people as can be squeezed in. I want to do it there because it's where my predecessor gave so many empowerments that his vase wore out! Khyentse Wangpo did everything in that empowerment hall. He didn't have to wander all over the place to give transmissions."

Khenpo Kunga Wangchuk immediately begged Rinpoche to consider finding a space for him. "Come tomorrow," said Rinpoche. "I'll see if it's possible." But he avoided making a firm promise.

The next day, as everyone waited outside the hall for the transmission to begin, Khenpo Kunga Wangchuk peered in through a window. He saw Rinpoche seat various lamas and tulkus, then lead Khyenrab Singye to a thick cushion at the end of a long row of Rinpoches. To Khenpo's delight, Rinpoche then called his name and sat him next to Khyenrab Singye.

Once Rinpoche had personally seated everyone and the hall was full, he said, "Now, close the doors!" The room was so packed with bodies that it was only just possible to swing the doors shut.

Jamyang Khyentse Chökyi Lodrö in Jamyang Khyentse Wangpo's
empowerment room, Chime Drupe Gatsel, at Dzongsar Monastery
Source: Sogyal Rinpoche's private collection

"The hall is full! However tightly we huddle together, not even one more person could squeeze in. Giving the empowerments and transmissions of the entire *Compendium of Sadhanas* again will create auspicious circumstances," said Rinpoche, and he began the transmission.

Both Khenpo Kunga Wangchuk and Khyenrab Singye made notes, and Khenpo Kunga Wangchuk went on to write a catalog of the lineages of the empowerments and transmissions that are contained in the *Compendium of Sadhanas*. Unfortunately it was destroyed, but Khenpo said that Rinpoche spoke about the transmission lineages of each empowerment in detail and that some had six or seven different lineages. Although Khenpo didn't catch everything Rinpoche said, he did remember Rinpoche saying during the authorization blessing for White Simhamukha that he had once received that transmission from Simhamukha herself.

The Great Maitreya Statue at Khamje Shedra

Khyentse Chökyi Lodrö wanted to restore Khamje Shedra's great Maitreya Hall, which had originally been built by Jamyang Khyentse Wangpo, and cast a new Maitreya statue. Khenpo Kunga Wangchuk was living at Dzongsar at that time and was able to describe how it happened in great detail. Much of what he knew came directly from his close friend Negema (Nera Geshen), who had overseen the project.

Negema's knowledge of proportion was unrivaled. Had he been asked, there is no doubt that he could have built perfect temples at both Palpung and Dzongsar monasteries. He once told Palpung Situ, "If you were to build a temple that had a door the height of Sela mountain, it would measure fifteen stories. A complete blueprint of how to install staircases and separation walls has appeared vividly in my heart." Both Rinpoche and Palpung Situ explained that he was able to calculate the proportions of buildings so accurately because he had perfected creation meditation (*kyerim*) in his previous life. He was, they said, a unique human being.

"Rinpoche was in retreat," said Negema. "But on the fifteenth of the month, he asked me to bring him a measuring stick. So I gave him one that was two arm-spans long. We discussed the proportions of the statue, and Rinpoche said he wanted the face to be ten fingers high. When I told him that would be too big, he insisted that I should do exactly as he asked. But Rinpoche was a very tall man. He'd also been in retreat for several months, and his fingernails hadn't been cut. So when he measured his ten fingers on the stick, the result was far longer than the ten fingers of an average-size man. Far too long, in fact, and I was seriously worried about whether the statue would even fit into the temple! But I couldn't argue. Rinpoche was adamant that I follow his orders precisely."

Tashi Namgyal told me that the best sculptor available at the time was Uchen Phurbu Tsering of Chamdo, who was old, had a pronounced squint, and chewed constantly for no reason. Nevertheless, he and his students were engaged to cast the statue. Negema made sure they followed Rinpoche's instructions to the letter, and as he expected, once the body had been assembled, it was obvious that the statue would be much too big to get into the temple.

When Rinpoche saw the immense statue, he immediately announced that he would build a new, much bigger temple to put it in. So everything had to be taken out of the old temple, and Rinpoche personally performed the traditional rituals that accompanied the removal of the clay statues. The great Maitreya statue was wrapped in dozens of old tents tied in place with jute ropes and the frescoes were shaved from the walls, then carefully wrapped and labeled. There were about a hundred packages in all. The walls were then knocked down and the entire structure rebuilt. Two years later, the new temple was finished, and Rinpoche led an elaborate consecration ceremony.

Khenpo said that although he hadn't seen it done with his own eyes, the shaved frescoes must have been mixed with clay, because once they had been transferred to the walls of the new temple, they looked quite different.

A monk from Gönchen Monastery called Lama Dzola was invited to prepare the consecration dharanis and offering substances that were to be placed inside the statues. Everyone believed him to be extremely disciplined because he only ate before midday and never ate meat—his lunch was usually yogurt, if there was any, or tsampa mixed with plain water. He never rode to Dzongsar from Gönchen Monastery—he always walked, invariably traveling alone, without any kind of escort, carrying an umbrella. Nor did he ever light a fire because, he said, it would incinerate insects.

Lama Dzola was a strict, meticulous character who had a very short temper, and he permitted only two Dzongsar monks, Bhugay and his assistant, to help him. Every day before they started work, the two monks had to wash their mouths, faces, and hands and then recite the dharani of Vajra Vidarana. After the recitation, they had to wash again in the water they had blessed with the dharani, light incense, and chant, just as they would if they were about to take part in a puja. A white sheet would be spread on the grass in the courtyard, and the three monks would sit in a row with Lama Dzola at its head. They'd cover their mouths, unroll the dharanis, and smear them with saffron. Lama Dzola personally checked each dharani, joined the sheets of paper together, rolled them up, and labeled them.

For more than twenty days, the three men worked in this way, while another group of monks printed the dharanis, which were checked and corrected by monks personally appointed by Lama Dzola. Once all the dharanis had been completed, it was Lama Dzola's responsibility to consecrate the statues.

Lama Dzola continued to do this kind of work at Khamje for many years. A large number of statues owned by Khyentse Labrang were made by Lama Dzola.

Tashi Namgyal said that the carpenter and blacksmith were so skilled and worked together so well that not only did all the different parts of the statue fit together perfectly, the offering substances slotted into place with extraordinary precision. He said he had never seen such excellent craftsmanship.

In a room in Rinpoche's house, Lama Dzola and the most important lamas and tulkus, including Gongna Tulku, laid out all the relics and sacred substances that had been gathered, including a triangular piece of bone that was believed to have been part of Dharma King Trisong Deutsen's skull, wrapped in red and yellow scarves and anointed with saffron. The wrapped bone was the shape of a wheel, and as turquoise, coral, and sapphire had been sewn to its back, it looked like a piece of jewelry.

Rinpoche himself chose everything that was to be put into the statue and thought long and hard about whether or not a pair of empowerment vases should go in the statue's neck. At the time, no one dared offer an opinion, so he did a divination.

"It's better not to include the vases," said Rinpoche. "Even though I have given many empowerments and transmissions, I still haven't completed the *Compendium of Tantras*, so I might need them. Put them aside for now."

Gongna Tulku said an egg-size pouch containing relics and a kutsab were also put in the statue, but the kutsab was neither beautiful nor elegant. A piece of Khedrup Je's skull and five ritual bells belonging to five great lamas, including Gatön Ngawang Lekpa, were also offered. Details of the consecration ceremony are clearly described in the *Great Biography*.

Tashi Thongmon

Khenpo Kunga Wangchuk was abbot of Wara Monastery when he heard that Rinpoche would pass through Lhasa on his way to the pilgrimage sites of India. Knowing Rinpoche, Khenpo thought it unlikely that he would accept an invitation to visit Wara from an individual, so the monastery itself extended a formal invitation. At the very least, Khenpo thought, they should strongly request that Rinpoche make camp nearby. A large tent was pitched in readiness, but as there was no time to adorn it with black cloth and silk brocade, a mixture of ground indigo and goat's milk was used to paint auspicious symbols all over it. Then they waited.

The moment Rinpoche arrived in Lhasa, all the old lamas and monks of the Wara Monastery rushed to greet him and fervently requested that he visit their monastery. Rinpoche declined, explaining that he wasn't accepting any invitations at all. But he did agree to consecrate the newly built temple from the tent they'd erected. In fact, he liked the tent so much that he named it "Tashi Thongmon" and gave many teachings and empowerments there—which was extremely auspicious for Wara Monastery and the surrounding village. That was the last time Khenpo saw Rinpoche.

Horses and Forced Labor

Before Khyentse Wangpo's time, it was customary for local villagers to lend visitors the horses they needed to carry their luggage up to Dzongsar Monastery. But towards the end of Khyentse Wangpo's life, the great lamas and lords of China, Tibet, and Hor who flocked to Dzongsar to see him, used to demand that the villagers give them horses as their right. This caused so much hardship for the people of Menshö that they were even heard to say, "Why won't that old monk die?"

Once Khyentse Chökyi Lodrö had established himself at Dzongsar, he appealed to the teachers of the royal family of Derge Tsang and all the high lamas of Kham—like Shechen Rabjam and Dzogchen Rinpoche—to stop forcing the locals to give them horses when they visited him.

"I am happy to have you here," he said, "but compelling the villagers to help you in this way makes things very difficult for them."

After Chökyi Lodrö made his appeal, whenever Shechen Rabjam, Dzogchen Rinpoche, and Situ Rinpoche visited, they always traveled as ordinary Tibetans, brought their own horses, were never high-handed, and never browbeat the locals into helping them.

The Year the Dzongsar Monastery Lhachen Fell Over

Uncle Orgyen said that Dzongsar Monastery had two large, hollow hide statues of Vajrabhairava and Yamantaka, which were used whenever the Guchen dance was performed. They were known as the "Lhachen" and were hollow so that monks could easily slip into them to take part in the procession to the courtyard, then get out, leaving the statues to preside over the dancing.

One year, Rinpoche was in his residence when the Guchen dance took place. Suddenly, he exclaimed, "Oh! The Lhachen has fallen over. Ha, ha!" As Rinpoche couldn't see into the courtyard from where he was, his attendants rushed outside to see what had happened. And there, on its side on the ground, lay one of the Lhachen.

Uncle Orgyen said that everyone knew about this demonstration of Rinpoche's clairvoyance, and that the incident was always spoken of as "the year the Dzongsar Monastery Lhachen fell over."

The Consecration of Dzing Namgyal Gönkhang

The Dzing Namgyal Gönkhang had been built during the era of Chögyal Phakpa, so by the time Khyentse Chökyi Lodrö was living at Dzongsar, it needed renovating. Dilgo Khyentse heard about the renovation and reconsecration from the shrine master of Dzongsar Monastery in Tibet. When I visited Tibet, the shrine master had passed away, so I asked his nephew, Tikgay, what he knew about it. He said the renovation had been necessary after a water leak had badly damaged the hall and that once it had been restored and new frescoes painted, Rinpoche had personally led an elaborate reconsecration ceremony.

During the ceremony, having dispelled obstacles with a clash of cymbals in the style of the Sakyapas, the shrine master swung a censer of burning frankincense in front of the statue of Gur Mahakala. Rinpoche must have been focusing his mind extremely intently on the statue, because at that very moment, the statue shook so violently that the earth trembled, and the shrine master heard a *tsak-tsak, khob-khob* sound. Mistaking the tremors for an earthquake, the shrine master instantly dropped his censer and jumped out of the nearest window.

In the *Great Biography*, Dilgo Khyentse writes, "It is widely known that during the ceremony to drive away obstacles, [Khyentse Chökyi Lodrö] stared with one-pointed concentration so wrathfully that the statues shook violently, and the shrine master, who was standing nearby burning frankincense, was so terrified that he fled."

Tashi Tsering's Protection Cord

Tashi Tsering was a servant in the Trepa Tsang household and escaped with them to Sikkim, where he ended up serving Khandro Tsering Chödrön and Tashi Namgyal. He told me this story.

In Tibet, the entire Trepa Tsang family and many of their servants visited Rinpoche in Dzongsar on two occasions. During their first visit, Tashi Tsering asked Rinpoche for a blessing cord to protect him from deadly weapons. Slowly, Rinpoche tied various knots into a cord, rubbed it thoroughly between his hands, and gave it to Tashi Tsering with the assurance that it would protect him from all kinds of weapons.

On their way home, the Trepa Tsang party stopped for a tea break, and some of the men took the opportunity to practice their marksmanship.

"Khorey, Tashi Tsering!" shouted Trepa Tsewang. "Hold up your cup, and I will try to hit it. If I succeed, it's your loss. But if I miss, I'll give you ten white-silver coins."

As there was no guarantee Trepa Tsewang would hit the cup and a useful profit to be made if he missed, Tashi Tsering did as he asked. He lodged his cup in the fork of one of the trees on their makeshift shooting range, slipped a snippet of his protection cord between the cup and its holder, and prayed to Rinpoche. Trepa Tsewang fired three times but each bullet landed a long way from the cup, and the amazed and delighted Tashi Tsering won ten coins. Rinpoche's protection was clearly very effective.

Later, during their second visit, Trepa Tsang told Rinpoche that they wanted to flee Tibet with most of their household, including Tashi Tsering. Again, Tashi Tsering begged Rinpoche for his prayers and protection, this time from being shot by the Communist Chinese. Rinpoche thought for a while, then agreed to give him an especially reliable protection. He pulled a fine red silk vest from behind his bedstead, spread it out on his table, and wrote in ink, "I, Jamyang Chökyi Lodrö, have worn this garment." As he gave it to Tashi Tsering, he said, "If you roll it up and wear it on your body, no weapon will have the power to harm you."

On their way to the Indian border, the Trepa Tsang household fought many battles, but not a single bullet landed anywhere near Tashi Tsering. Even those who stood next to him were so well protected that they couldn't hear the gunfire, yet if they moved away from him, it was deafening.

After a while, Trepa Pegyal asked Tashi Tsering what was protecting him. "Nothing much," he replied. "Just this bundle of silk." He later lent the vest to Trepa Pegyal, who never gave it back, and that was the only time Tashi Tsering came close to being hit.

11. Stories from Khyentse Labrang

Rinpoche's Porcelain Cups

Rinpoche was working in the labrang when Neten Chokling offered him a cup of tea. Rinpoche was very fond of antique cups and before he sipped his tea, he raised the lid of his cup to admire it.

"This is an extremely special cup," he said. But when he tried to return it to the silver salver in Neten Chokling's hands, it slipped and fell to the floor, shattering into tiny pieces.

"My best cup has broken! Akhi, Akhi!" wailed Rinpoche. "What shall I do? You mustn't tell Tsewang Paljor; he'll scold us! Clean up the broken pieces immediately and throw them somewhere no one will find them."

Chokling Rinpoche obeyed, while Rinpoche found one of his other Chinese cups, poured himself some more tea, and sitting rather awkwardly, drank it.

Tashi Namgyal told me about another very fine porcelain cup that Rinpoche loved, which had been accidentally broken by the king of Yönru, Yönru Lhasey Jamyang Sonam. At the time Rinpoche said, "It's a shame the king broke my cup, but clearly such a magnificent object couldn't continue to exist in this world."

Rinpoche took the loss quite well, but the king was beside himself with remorse. That very same night he ran all the way to his home in Lithang to fetch a similar round, squat, Chinese porcelain cup decorated with the eight auspicious symbols, then ran straight back to Dzongsar. And from the moment the king offered him the cup, Rinpoche used it constantly. Rinpoche loved that kind of porcelain cup.

The king's cup was used during Sakya Gongma's stay at Khamje to offer him some yogurt. Sakya Gongma received many, many visitors in his tent that day, and a great mountain of kataks eventually buried the cup completely. Later, as Tashi Namgyal tidied up, he accidentally knocked the cup onto a rock, smashing it to pieces. Rinpoche was extremely distressed by its loss—so much so that Tashi Namgyal felt his precious human birth would be utterly wasted if he didn't find an equally beautiful cup to replace it, even if it cost him his entire box of silver coins. After all, he reflected, the king had undergone tremendous hardship to replace the cup he had broken.

The next time Tashi Namgyal visited Lhasa, he took all his silver coins with him. If he couldn't find a beautiful cup in Lhasa, he thought, he wouldn't find one anywhere. He contacted all the Derge businessmen he knew to ask for their help but was bitterly disappointed. Not a single cup of that pattern was available for sale anywhere in Lhasa. So Tashi Namgyal approached the drönyer[22] of Phalha Drönyer Chenmo.

Who was the drönyer of Phalha Drönyer Chenmo? Well, at one point he claimed to be a Nyingmapa and became one of Rinpoche's students. He was often of service to Rinpoche, and Rinpoche responded by telling him how to build the Guru Rinpoche temple. I think it was he who facilitated a connection between Rinpoche and Phalha Drönyer Chenmo, the chief of protocol to Gyalwa Rinpoche (Dalai Lama). Apart from that, he wasn't particularly close to Rinpoche, although Tashi Namgyal and the other attendants often talked about him and visited him whenever they could.

Anyway, when Tashi Namgyal asked the drönyer about how to find the right cup, he said, "Solpön-la! Such cups are rare. Your only hope is for Rinpoche's merit and majesty to inspire an aristocrat to offer him one. This kind of porcelain is very popular in Lhasa, but those who own it don't use it much; they just hide it away in their treasure chests. They certainly never sell it."

So Tashi Namgyal couldn't replace the cup, and he always felt he had accumulated a huge amount of negative karma for having smashed something that Rinpoche loved so much.

A Quarrel between Chakdzö and Tsejor

One day, Chakdzö and Tsejor were arguing loudly in Chakdzö's room. But Tashi Namgyal, who told me this story, said he didn't know why.

"I don't care who you are," screamed Tsejor, showing his little finger to Chakdzö. "I'm only here for Rinpoche, and I don't have to show you even this much respect! How can Serpa Tsang have spawned such an evil man?"

"You're one to talk," countered Chakdzö. "You! Who is neither layperson nor monk."

Tashi Namgyal and the others stood silently outside the door as Chakdzö spat out a long string of expletives and some very harsh observations, before finally insisting, "One of us will have to go!"

Chakdzö stormed out of the room, and the attendants melted away to avoid him. From afar they watched as he marched, fuming, into Rinpoche's house, then they crept closer to eavesdrop.

"Tsejor talks such rubbish," roared Chakdzö. "Rinpoche, do you really need that long-haired brute? He's neither a monk nor a layperson and completely bereft of vows or samaya! We can't both remain here. If he won't go, I'll resign! It's either him or me!"

Rinpoche continued silently counting his mala beads while Chakdzö continued ranting for a while, and eventually, Chakdzö stormed out.

"Tell Tsejor to come here," commanded Rinpoche. Tashi Namgyal hurried away, a little anxious that Tsejor might be in for a scolding. He found him in his room, trimming his moustache. Without showing an ounce of fear, Tsejor immediately responded to Rinpoche's summons and ran to his room.

"Tsejor," said Rinpoche, "I've been having some disturbing dreams recently. Please do the *Heart Essence of Deathless Arya Tara* for two months in the central chamber of the residence. I believe you have pure samaya, and it's always better that a good-natured person does this practice. Do it alone."

Tsejor asked when he should start, and Rinpoche replied, "This evening."

"Wo! La so!" said Tsejor.

Tashi Namgyal followed Tsejor to the room in the hall where the Nyenchen Thanglha prayers were chanted, which doubled as a guest room. Tsejor found a cloth (it wasn't gray) and a huge woven zen. He took them both to the room where he would practice, along with his tsampa bag and two cups. He also tried to take a mattress stuffed with musk deer fur to sleep on, but Tashi Namgyal felt it was inappropriate to move it into the central chamber because it had been used by other guests. In the end, Tsejor didn't need it, as there were already many mattresses there for him to choose from.

Tsejor put two cushions in the corner of his retreat room and covered them with a carpet. This was to be his bed. He put his pillow and layman's clothing at the head of the bed and his tsampa bag and two cups at its foot, then he sat in the middle and began to practice. He remained there for two months. In all that time, Chakdzö did not move one inch from the labrang.

Rinpoche was very fond of Tsejor; they were very close. Rinpoche often promised that he would return from the buddhafields the moment Tsejor stopped breathing and personally lead him to the pure realms.

When I could, I asked Tsejor himself about his quarrel with Chakdzö. He just laughed. All he would say was that Chakdzö could be a bit short-tempered and that at such times they tended to rub each other the wrong way.

Burning Meat and Milk in the Labrang

Meat was roasted very carefully in the labrang, but if it burnt, it wasn't a serious problem. Letting the milk boil over was another matter entirely. Although both the white (milk) and the red (burnt meat) contaminations are pollutions of the hearth, the red is not nearly as serious as the white. If milk boiled over or was burnt in any way, Rinpoche would immediately summon the retreat masters of Karmo Tak Tsang and ask all the retreatants to say one hundred thousand prayers to appease Tseringma. (They practiced Tseringma the same way we do here.)

Rinpoche Sees Düsolma

One day, Rinpoche said to Dilgo Khyentse, "I am experiencing a sign that the goddess Düsolma is present! We should chant a prayer . . . but I can't, so you must do it." He gave Dilgo Khyentse the prayer to appease Düsolma from the *Luminous Heart Essence*, and Dilgo Khyentse recited it every evening in the labrang's protectors' hall. After about a month, Rinpoche told him to stop. "Last night, I clearly saw a blue Düsolma," he said. "Whatever needed to be done must have been accomplished, so you don't have to chant the prayer anymore."

Swords and Guns

The Throthung Sword

Rinpoche was invited to Gongna Tsang for dinner—he was still young at the time, not even twenty. As he walked through a storeroom towards a staircase, he saw a long, crooked sword sticking out of what looked like a pile of junk. Rinpoche asked an old monk about the sword, but the man knew nothing. So Rinpoche examined it himself and said he thought it must have once belonged to Tagrong Tsang. Later they discovered he was right.

The Mongolian Gun at Palpung Monastery

Gongna Tulku attended Rinpoche when he visited Palpung Monastery and was there when, in the corner of a large gallery—the one with a long staircase leading up to the floor above—Rinpoche caught sight of a gun propped up against the wall. He stared at it intently as he climbed the stairs, then again on his way back down.

"That is a very nice long, thin Mongolian gun," said Rinpoche to Choga, the stone carver. "Where did Situ Rinpoche get it?"

"It's said that Palpung Monastery doesn't have a better gun than this one," replied the stone carver. "But it doesn't work anymore. When it was new, it was the best model you could buy and very popular." He added, "Adzi! Rinpoche knows about so many different things. He even knows about guns!"

The gun, which was of medium length, appeared to be made of iron decorated with gold and silver, most of which had rubbed off. It was certainly very old. Rinpoche did not touch it. He was looking for a good gun, he said, but so far had been unable to find one.

When Gongna Tulku told me this story, he said he didn't think Rinpoche ever found a gun that truly delighted his heart because he never saw him hold one. Generally, Rinpoche didn't touch the guns he was offered but sent them straight to Chakdzö, who could do as he liked with them.

Both Tashi Namgyal and Gongna Tulku spoke of these things in the same way.

The Third Neten Chokling Rinpoche's Stories

Khyentse Chökyi Lodrö's Clairvoyance

During his time at Dzongsar, the previous Neten Chokling became fond of playing a bamboo flute. One day, after playing it in a field for a while, he went to see Rinpoche.

"Aley! Neten Tulku likes to play a bamboo flute," said Rinpoche. "And you play very sweetly."

A little shocked, Neten Chokling just said, "La so," but had no idea what to do or say. He said he felt very odd because Rinpoche seemed to know about everything he did, even when he was outside the labrang. Then suddenly he realized that for Rinpoche there was no difference between "inside" and "outside."

Until then, Neten Chokling hadn't always told Rinpoche the truth because he was afraid of his reaction. But from that moment on he stopped telling made-up stories altogether. Rinpoche already knew everything anyway, so what was the point? That was when Neten Chokling's inhibitions vanished entirely and he became completely fearless.

Grave Robber

Neten Chokling shared his room at Dzongsar with a monk called Azhang Butse Lhaje. Gongna Tulku was also staying at Dzongsar, but in a room in the monk's quarters at Gongna Tsang.

One day, Gongna Tulku called out to Neten Chokling, "Tulku, I think we should go somewhere."

"Where?" asked Neten Chokling.

"Let's just go," replied Gongna Tulku.

Neten Chokling suggested that Gongna Tulku come to his room so they could make a proper plan, but the tulku insisted they meet at his place immediately. So Neten Chokling wrapped himself in his zen and made his way to Gongna Tulku's labrang.

The moment he arrived, Gongna Tulku said, "Let's go now!"

"But *where* are we going?" demanded Neten Chokling.

Gongna Tulku looked over his shoulder to see if anyone was listening, then said in a hushed tone, "We are going to the cemetery to get some human skulls and thighbones to make kapalas and trumpets. Someone's wife died recently, and someone else died last year. Their corpses are buried in the cemetery, and you and I are going to dig them up."

They arrived at the cemetery at dusk, and Neten Chokling immediately dug up a fleshless, bare-boned corpse. He removed the skull from the open grave, threw away all the facial bones and kept the cranium. He loaded it and the corpse's leg bones onto his horse, and as it wouldn't have been appropriate to take the bones into the monastery that day, he hid them nearby. The following day, he returned to wash the bones in the river below Dzongsar Monastery. While he was arranging them on a rock to dry, a small-time hunter turned up.

"Isn't that a human thighbone?" exclaimed the hunter. He turned the bone over to get a better look, and to their amazement, the bone made a cracking sound.

Neten Chokling returned to his rooms with one of the thighbones and the skull, but as his roommate was very superstitious, he hid them under the bed. There was only one bed in Neten Chokling's room. Azhang would sleep on it when Neten Chokling was away, but whenever Neten Chokling was at Dzongsar, Azhang slept on the floor on a mattress.

That night, after midnight, they were awoken by the sound of something falling to the floor, followed by a smacking sound.

"Aro! What's that?" asked Azhang. "What's making that *gob-gob-gob, tak-tak-tak* noise?"

Neten Chokling muttered drowsily that he didn't know, and they went back to sleep.

Again they were awoken by the *gob-gob-gob, tak-tak-tak* sound, and again Azhang asked Neten Chokling Rinpoche, "What is it? What have you brought into this room?"

This time Chokling Rinpoche told him about the skull under the bed. "But surely a skull can't have anything to do with these strange noises, can it?"

Azhang Butse was immediately curious and pulled the skull out to examine it. As he lifted a burning ember above his head to get a better look, the skull suddenly scuttled across the floor. Startled, Azhang Butse tried to smother it with one of his own shoes.

"We must cover it. If we don't, we won't be able to control it!" he screamed. Then he changed his mind. "Better use one of your shoes." He snatched up one of Neten Chokling's shoes and slammed it over the skull. It instantly fell silent.

Azhang was a doctor and usually had many visitors, so the next morning he asked his nephew—who was also his attendant—to say he was too busy to see anyone. Instead, he and Neten Chokling lit a fire under a brass cauldron of water and boiled the skull and thighbones with a little baking powder. Once the bones were cooked, Azhang took them back to his room to cut them properly, then hid the pieces in the wheat store.

Neten Chokling did not see Rinpoche until two days later.

"Aro! Tulku!" said Rinpoche.

"La so," replied Neten Chokling.

"Have you been to the cemetery recently? Did you dig up a skull?" asked Rinpoche.

Imagining Gongna Tulku or Azhang had said something to Rinpoche about what they'd been up to, Neten Chokling replied truthfully, "Yes, I found a skull."

"I need that skull!" cried Rinpoche. "Bring it to me!"

"Wo, la so," said Neten Chokling anxiously. What would Azhang have to say about giving up their skull?

"How did Rinpoche know about the skull in the first place?" asked Azhang. "Did you tell him?"

"No, no, I didn't. I thought you did!" insisted Neten Chokling. But there was no denying it, Rinpoche had specifically asked for the skull.

"Perhaps you and I lack the merit to keep this skull," said Azhang. "And if Rinpoche says he needs it, we must offer it to him."

Azhang filled the skull with grain, and Neten Chokling took it to Rinpoche. Having accepted the skull, Rinpoche poured the grain onto his folded shawl and examined it carefully.

"This is something I will need," he said, and he took it to his room.

Revelation of Spiritual Treasure

Rinpoche called Neten Chokling to his private rooms to tell him about an Ekazati life-stone treasure that he wanted him to reveal. It was somewhere on Phuma mountain, on the way to Sengur Yutso, said Rinpoche, and Neten Chokling must fetch it immediately. Neten Chokling asked precisely where the treasure could be found, and Rinpoche directed him to a cliff, describing clearly the landmarks he should look out for.

"If *you* don't go, we won't be able to get this life-stone," said Rinpoche. "By the way, nothing will happen before you find it, but it might get a little chaotic once you've picked it up. So be careful and be vigilant!"

Neten Chokling immediately saddled up and set off. It was dark by the time he reached the mountain, and, as he hadn't brought any camping equipment with him, he took shelter with a nomad family.

"Lama, where have you come from? What are you doing?" they asked. Neten Chokling avoided answering by telling them bits of gossip about this and that, and they settled into a conversation about quite ordinary things. His hosts had no spare blankets, just a raw fiber mattress, so he used it to cover himself as he slept. Early next morning, he set off to find the stone, telling his hosts that he had work to do.

By following Rinpoche's instructions carefully, Neten Chokling found the cliff. He peered over the cliff's edge and into a cave, where he could see a square black stone lying on the floor. He instantly knew that this stone was the treasure he had been sent to find. To get into the cave, he had to climb down about ten feet of sheer rock, which he managed quite easily. But once inside, he discovered that what he'd expected to be a pocket-size stone was a great deal larger and not at all easy to lift. How would he get it back up the cliff?

He thought for a moment, then removed his raw silk coat, wrapped the stone in it, and slung it across his back, tying it firmly in place with a knot at his chest. As he climbed out of the cave and onto the rock face, a gust of swirling wind blew so strongly that he had to steady himself by grabbing hold of a small shrub. Then the skirt of his robe billowed up over his face. As he could neither see nor move, he just clung on for dear life and prayed desperately to his guru. After a while the wind died down, and he was able to scramble up the cliff. By now there wasn't time for him to get back to the monastery before nightfall. So he hid the stone in a marmot's hole near his hosts' tent, marking it so he would be able to find it again, and went back to the nomad family's tent to beg for shelter.

The old woman asked Neten Chokling again and again, "Lama, what's happened to your silk coat?" He told her it was outside somewhere, but she wasn't satisfied and continued to badger him mercilessly, even asking, "What are you taking away from here?" Neten Chokling had to make something up, and eventually they all went to bed.

Early the next day, he set off for Dzongsar with the stone tied to his back. Although he didn't realize it at the time, he arrived at the labrang just as Rinpoche invoked the dharmapalas. He sent word to Rinpoche through an attendant that he had something for him, and Rinpoche immediately asked that he bring the "something" into his presence.

"It's very big!" observed Rinpoche, then placed the stone in the large drawer by the pillow of his bed.

When I visited Dzongsar, I saw a big square stone with images of Ekazati and her brothers and sisters etched into its surface, so this treasure still exists.

Bloodletting

Neten Chokling's body was tingling from the top of his head to the tips of his toes, and he felt as if every hair on his body was standing on end. So he asked Azhang Butse Lhaje what was wrong with him. Azhang checked his pulses and declared, as he reached for his suction cups, "Unless the toxic blood is drained out immediately, your health will suffer serious complications."

"But I don't want my blood sucked out!" cried Neten Chokling, and he ran from the room with Azhang in hot pursuit.

Neten Chokling went straight to Rinpoche and told him about Azhang's diagnosis and recommended treatment. Rinpoche asked him to sit down, grabbed a leather sandal wrapped in a furry cloth, and hit Neten Chokling three times on the head so hard that he almost knocked him unconscious. Rinpoche then directed Neten Chokling to sleep in the labrang's hall, stressing that he should go straight there and not stop anywhere on the way. "If you do as I have instructed, your illness will disappear." Neten Chokling followed his instructions to the letter.

Before long, Azhang turned up at Rinpoche's door.

"Is Chokling Tulku in here?" he shouted. "His blood pressure is dangerously high. He really must be bled."

Rinpoche told Azhang that he had performed a protection blessing, and as a result, the illness would not harm the tulku. Neten Chokling confirmed later that he recovered completely without being bled.

A Wealth Vase

One day, Rinpoche consecrated a number of wealth protection vases[23] (Lama Norlha) and gave one to each of the people who were with him. When Neten Chokling asked for one, Rinpoche said it would be better to make his wealth vase inside his body. So he gave Neten Chokling a Palchen pill (a wealth substance), small quantities of all the other necessary substances to eat, and a Langpo Tobchen chakra (a symbol of great strength[24]) printed on thick paper. He placed one hand on Neten Chokling's head and held a long-life arrow in the other as he chanted Lama Norlha's *Gathering of Wealth*. Once he'd finished the ritual, he told Neten Chokling that he had just planted the wealth protection vase in his stomach.

A Boiling Skull Cup

One day, Neten Chokling went to see Rinpoche in his private rooms and found him consecrating empowerment substances. As he entered Rinpoche's room, Neten Chokling heard a skull cup on the shrine make exactly the same sound tea does just before it boils. Within seconds, the contents of the skull cup were bubbling vigorously. Rinpoche asked Neten Chokling to bring it over to him. Neten Chokling carefully carried the boiling skull cup over to Rinpoche, and received the four empowerments and a drop of amrita. Rinpoche then asked him to return the skull cup to the shrine, and as soon as it had been replaced, the amrita stopped bubbling and fell silent.

Neten Chokling told many such stories, but all in all, he did not spend that much time with Rinpoche.

12. Consorts

Chökyi Lodrö's Illness

DILGO KHYENTSE often visited Khyentse Chökyi Lodrö at Dzongsar and on one occasion was asked to say prayers to avert an illness Rinpoche suffered from that was similar to what modern medicine calls epilepsy.[25] Frightened and worried, Dilgo Khyentse racked his brains for a way of averting the illness, but could think of nothing. He asked Rinpoche himself what should be done, but he didn't know either. Neither of them had a clue what to do. Eventually, it occurred to Dilgo Khyentse that the sadhana of *Vajrapani Holding a Vajra Cudgel* might help. So he took the handwritten text of *Wish-Fulfilling Jewel Essence Manual of Oral Instruction* to Rinpoche's residence, sat on the floor in Tsejor's room, and recited the mantra for a whole day. At dusk, much to his own and everyone else's astonishment, Rinpoche announced he had fully recovered.

The Dakini's Hair

My father told me about the first time he witnessed one of Rinpoche's fits. Rinpoche was practicing in his private rooms when suddenly his body began to shake uncontrollably. His eyes rolled upwards and stretched open so wide that Neten Chokling thought they'd pop out of his head! Worse still, Rinpoche began whimpering as if he were about to die, which terrified Neten Chokling, who had no idea what was happening or what he should do.

As he debated with himself about whether or not to scream for help, Rinpoche waved his hand in the air. Neten Chokling watched carefully for a moment. Rinpoche appeared to be pointing at a drawer in a chest. Neten Chokling pulled opened the drawer and found a heavy plait of what looked like a woman's hair. Rinpoche continued gesticulating. Neten Chokling thought he was telling him to burn the hair, so he threw a large handful into the fire. The stench of singed hair quickly wafted towards Rinpoche, up his nose, and into his body. Suddenly he bent double as if to vomit (but didn't), then straightened himself up, and instantly began chastising Chokling Rinpoche for his reckless extravagance.

"That hair is incredibly precious! It is the only medicine capable of stabilizing my life when the fits overcome me, and *look at how much you just wasted*!"

Chokling Rinpoche discovered later that the hair had belonged to a consort from Golok whom Rinpoche had spurned. Rinpoche must have been about twenty-five years old when she traveled to Dzongsar to tell him that she wanted to be his consort. At that time, Rinpoche was a very strict monk and wouldn't admit the girl into his presence. In spite of his rejection, she hung around in Dzongsar for several months, and whenever his attendants prepared tsok offerings at the labrang, she always managed to find the portion intended for the guru. Eventually she got fed up with waiting, cut off her hair, and offered it to Rinpoche through his attendants. "It will help Rinpoche regain consciousness," she said. She died not long after she left Dzongsar, and so their auspicious connection was never realized.

Around the time the girl died, Rinpoche had the first of his fits—which are generally believed to be a sign the dakinis are angry—and was instantly cured by smoke from the girl from Golok's burning hair.

Khyentse Chökyi Lodrö and the Lakar Family

When Chökyi Lodrö was about forty years old, he visited the home of Adhuk Lakar Tsang. Khandro Tsering Chödrön was still a baby—she had just started to crawl—and Tselu was a fat, round-headed toddler. Drikung Tertön Ösel Dorje was also staying with the family, as he often did, but no one called him Tertön in those days. He used to perform various rituals for the household and on this occasion was there to read the Kangyur aloud in one of their many shrine rooms.

One evening, after Rinpoche had bestowed a long-life empowerment on Drikung Tertön and the family, the tertön said, "Today, having received the long-life initiation of the *Heart Essence of Deathless Arya Tara* from the incarnation of Jamyang Khyentse Wangpo, exceptionally auspicious circumstances have been created. When he becomes a great vajradhara and starts to practice the discipline of inner yoga, these girls will become his vajra consorts." And he caressed Khandro Tsering Chödrön and Tselu's heads.

Appalled, Chökyi Lodrö exploded more wrathfully than ever before. Dilgo Khyentse Rinpoche said the tertön must have foreseen Khyentse Chökyi Lodrö's future, because his prediction turned out to be quite accurate. It was widely believed that the Lakar family made a particularly generous offering to Chökyi Lodrö at that time.

Khandro Tsering Chödrön

Six or seven years before Chökyi Lodrö took Khandro Tsering Chödrön as his spiritual wife, Drikung Tertön warned Rinpoche that if auspicious circumstances were not properly established he might not live. He offered Rinpoche a statue of Yishin Khorlo (White Tara) and performed many rituals for his long life. The procession that escorted the statue to Khyentse Labrang was long and stretched way beyond Dzongsar Monastery. But it did not enter through the usual gate, because Rinpoche said it should come in through a tiny door near where the firewood was kept. The door was hurriedly unlocked, and all the pendants, victory banners, multicolored decorative hangings, and canopy and pillar ornaments that were part of the procession had to be squeezed through—some barely made it. Then everyone congregated outside the labrang while Drikung Tertön went in to offer Rinpoche the statue.

When she was very young, a Gelugpa lama had asked Tsering Chödrön if she would like to be a nun when she grew up. No, replied Khandro, she would not be a nun. What she really wanted was to go to Dzongsar to be Khyentse Chökyi Lodrö's consort.

Some years later, when she was about thirteen years old, the entire Lakar family visited Dzongsar to pay their respects to Rinpoche and make offerings. Khandro told me that for some reason, the same small door the White Tara had used, which led straight to the labrang, had been left unlocked (no one knew who had opened it). So the first time Khandro entered the monastery, it was through that tiny door.

Khandro's head was always shaved when she was young, and once it had been decided that she should go to Dzongsar, there wasn't time for her hair to grow back before she left. So when she entered the monastery, her head looked like a smooth, round, shiny stone—the kind Tibetans call an *a-go*. And as she was also wearing the traditional sleeveless robe favored by Horpas, the monks of Dzongsar Monastery couldn't tell whether she was a consort or a nun.

If you are interested in the detailed prophecy about Chökyi Lodrö's consort, read the *Great Biography*. It's all there.

Pewar Tulku thought Khandro Tsering Chödrön was the incarnation of Zurza Metok Drön, but that doesn't seem right to me. Most people believe she's an emanation of Shelkar Dorje Tso.

Yangsi Rinpoche Thubten Chökyi Gyatso commanded me to tell him everything that happened or was said at that time, the good and the bad, including the criticism Khyentse Chökyi Lodrö attracted for taking a consort.

I don't know exactly how widespread the criticism was, but the late Drungyig Tsering told me of a conversation he had with the solpön. After the chaos of the wedding celebrations had died down and the stream of those seeking an audience with Rinpoche finally dried up, the solpön exclaimed, "Arok! I should have died last year."

"Khorey!" replied Drungyig Tsering. "What are you talking about?"

"I should have died last year," he repeated. "Things are so much worse now there's a *married couple* living here."

Drungyig Tsering said that as he himself was just a layman, he had never indulged in wrong views about Rinpoche taking a consort. I don't know exactly how many Khamje Shedra monks were critical of Rinpoche, but according to Tashi Namgyal, there were plenty. Their disapproval was so widespread that it even reached the ears of Dezhung Ajam Rinpoche. He became so concerned that he traveled to Khamje, where he set up camp below the shedra and challenged the monks to substantiate their condemnation of Rinpoche's actions. They would follow tradition, he said, and debate using valid quotations and logical arguments to support their points of view. And he would, he promised, utterly refute all their objections. He told them, for example, that the "male and female vajradhara" described in the sacred texts, refers to the "master" and the "consort," which are expressions of upaya and prajna, shunyata and compassion, and so on. He talked of such things with the monks for a long time. He said he wasn't surprised by what the monks of Dzogchen Monastery were saying, but if Dzongsar Monastery monks criticized and denigrated Rinpoche, the resulting broken samaya could shorten his life. It was for this reason, he said, that he had made the journey to Khamje.

Tashi Namgyal said that the monks of Dzogchen and Shechen monasteries were scathing in their condemnation of Rinpoche for having taken up with the "old woman" of the Lakar family, but I don't think the lamas were. Dzogchen Rinpoche, for example, received empowerments and oral transmissions from Rinpoche *after* he had taken his consort, and Shechen Rabjam was one of the main masters to encourage Rinpoche to take a consort in the first place. Perhaps the Shechen and Dzogchen monks were trying to alienate Rinpoche by emphasizing his Sakya affiliations? Perhaps they didn't have much devotion for him? I don't know. Neither do I know precisely how many Dzongsar monks disapproved. But Dzongsar Monastery was never particularly connected with Khyentse Labrang, and Rinpoche rarely gave empowerments, oral transmissions, or instructions to the Dzongsar monks.

After the *Precious Treasury of Terma Teachings* transmissions, Rinpoche insisted that, regardless of cost, they should hold a celebration to honor Khen Lop Chö Sum (Khenpo Bodhisattva, Guru Padmasambhava, and King Trisong Deutsen). A tent was pitched at Khamje. Dilgo Khyentse wore the robes of Guru Rinpoche and rang a bell, while Khyentse Rinpoche wore King Trisong Deutsen's yellow brocade chuba and played the monastery's famous cymbals. (I forgot to ask who dressed as the great abbot Shantarakshita.) The procession began at the far end of the hill on which Dzongsar Monastery stands. By the time they reached the lower slopes, it was obvious that playing the cymbals had somehow disturbed Rinpoche's mind. He felt dizzy, he said, and asked Dilgo Khyentse to swap instruments with him. (That particular pair of cymbals would disturb the blood of anyone who wasn't able to play the entire invocation!)

Dilgo Khyentse Rinpoche's brother, Shedrup, was standing among a crowd of Dzongsar monks at the time and overheard them say, "Hey! Rinpoche and Tulku Salga are swapping cymbals and bell. Who knows? Maybe next they'll swap their old women!"

That night Shedrup spoke with his brother.

"What were you and Rinpoche up to?" he asked. "People in the crowd started wondering if you'd swap your consorts next!"

As for Derge Gönchen Monastery, I really don't know what they thought of it all. Rinpoche must have visited them at some point in his early life, but he never went there later on—such a visit would have been as rare as stars in daylight. In fact, I would say that the habit today's incarnations of Khyentse Wangpo and Khyentse Chökyi Lodrö have adopted of traveling so much it's as if they're riding a tornado is a direct result of their predecessors' habit of staying in one place for far too long.

Khyentse Chökyi Lodrö Chooses Tsering Chödrön

I don't know exactly how Khandro Tsering Chödrön was chosen, but I do know there were authentic prophecies clearly stating that Khyentse Chökyi Lodrö would take a consort. Khyentse Wangpo, for example, wrote the following verse, which also appears in Khyentse Chökyi Lodrö's *Secret Biography*:

> Cuckoo in the bamboo grove of Mon in the south,
> Singing the vina's melody from the east where dakinis linger,
> Come, be my partner in sorrow, help me extract the summer shoot.
> There is wonder in the blossoming lotus of joyful experience.

At the time this prophecy was made, no one knew what it meant. Khyentse Wangpo himself never took a consort, even though he was meant to have had one. According to Dilgo Khyentse, Khyentse Chökyi Lodrö didn't take a consort until he was fifty-five years old.

Dilgo Khyentse's visits to Dzongsar usually lasted for several months, during which he always received many empowerments, transmissions, and instructions. Rinpoche always treated Dilgo Khyentse with immeasurable kindness, and each time he left, Rinpoche would shower him with gifts. At the end of one such visit, Rinpoche and Dilgo Khyentse sat together late into the night, as they so often did. Eventually, when Dilgo Khyentse said it was time for bed, Rinpoche replied, "You are leaving tomorrow, so let's sit a little longer."

They continued their conversation, and once again Rinpoche brought up Dilgo Khyentse's departure. Dilgo Khyentse explained that various responsibilities obliged him to leave, and Rinpoche began to weep. His tears unsettled Dilgo Khyentse profoundly. Could this be a sign that Rinpoche would die before they could meet again?

Finally Dilgo Khyentse rose to go to bed, and Rinpoche presented him with a white scarf.

"Once I've finished my retreat next year," he said, "you must come again. Come at all costs! I will offer you some empowerments ... and there will be a great deal of work for us to do."

Dilgo Khyentse replied that of course he would come.

"I have examined all the outer, inner, and secret aspects of my life a number of times," Rinpoche continued, "and have seen that I may not survive if I do not become like you.²⁶ So we must do something to make that happen. This is why I need your help. For me not to live would be no great loss, but for now there is more benefit in living than in dying. And I haven't yet finished giving the transmissions for the *Compendium of Tantras*. So we must meet again next year, joyfully and in good health."

Rinpoche's words were a great relief to Dilgo Khyentse. He instantly felt peaceful and experienced a calm certainty that Rinpoche would live as long as Thangtong Gyalpo. Actually, he should have pressed Rinpoche for more details about what they would do next time they met, but Rinpoche's majesty and radiance were so great that Dilgo Khyentse became tongue-tied. All he managed to say before he left was, "La so, Rinpoche."

Most people believe it was Dilgo Khyentse who created the circumstances for Rinpoche to take a consort, but Dilgo Khyentse himself always insisted that he had lacked the courage even to hint at such a thing. And despite the many long-life practices and practices for turning back the summons of the dakinis that were performed at the time, Rinpoche continued to be plagued by violent fits.

A year later at Shechen, Dilgo Khyentse received a letter from Rinpoche saying he had done a divination to determine which of a selection of girls would make a suitable consort. The best choice, he said, appeared to be Tsering Chödrön, daughter of Lakar Tsang. Situ Rinpoche's divination concurred. Not long after that, Dilgo Khyentse learnt that Rinpoche had taken a consort. He immediately set out for Dzongsar, and by the time he arrived, Chakdzö and the other labrang attendants had already sent emissaries to escort Tsering Chödrön to Dzongar—emissaries who could be trusted to ensure that she arrived on an auspicious day. In the meantime, Rinpoche instructed Dilgo Khyentse to accumulate long-life mantras, so he undertook a month-long retreat.

The day before the marriage ceremony, Rinpoche asked Dilgo Khyentse to do a Mahadeva fire puja in the empowerment hall, but I don't know why. Dilgo Khyentse practiced the Mahadeva sadhana all day and did the fire puja that evening, while Rinpoche sat quietly in his residence saying his daily prayers. But the rest of the labrang was in a state of uproar as everyone frantically prepared for the following day's celebrations.

The next morning, the traditional ceremony for the inauguration of a dakini took place. Khandro Tsering Chödrön sat on a high throne, and Dilgo Khyentse offered her a mandala, followed by the body, speech, and mind supports. He also did the "summoning the life force"[27] ritual and offered her long-life pills and dütsi. It was not an elaborate celebration.

The news of Khyentse Chökyi Lodrö's spiritual marriage spread like wildfire, and many well-wishers turned up at the labrang to pay their respects.

Reactions to Rinpoche Taking a Consort

The king and ministers of Derge were all aware that Rinpoche had taken a consort. The queen herself had urged him to do so.

Rinpoche had written the *Bright Torch of the Innermost Essence* for the queen of Nangchen when she was still Princess Yudrön and a daughter of Derge Tsang. She had had a connection with Rinpoche long before she married the king of Nangchen and was very devoted to him. In fact, she was in his presence so often that many speculated Rinpoche would take her as his consort. Before she married the king of Nangchen, she had been with Khunu Lama Tenzin Gyaltsen. At that time, Khunu Lama was teaching Tsewang Dudul (the prince of Derge Tsang) Tibetan grammar and poetry. Yudrön and Khunu Lama had had a son together, but I believe the boy passed away.

The princess of Ling Tsang, who these days is a consort of Dodrupchen Rinpoche, was also said to have aspired to be Khyentse Chökyi Lodrö's consort. There must have been others, but I don't know who they were.

Before all this happened, though, Rinpoche and Chakdzö fell out. For some reason, Rinpoche didn't travel from Hor to Dzogchen Monastery with Chakdzö and the Lakar family, he went straight to Dzongsar. Something must have happened between them, but I don't know what exactly.

"Khorey!" cried Rinpoche. "What are you doing? You try to tame two black mares and then throw all your frustration and hatred on me. What do you want me to do?"

Perhaps Chakdzö had tried to bed both Khandro and Tselu on the way to Dzogchen Monastery? I don't know. But after the scolding, a very chastened-looking Chakdzö was seen backing slowly out of the residence saying, "La so, Rinpoche! La so!"

Everything seemed to return to normal the next day, though, when Chakdzö, who was the labrang's main administrator, went back to work.

Katok Monastery's Offering

News of Rinpoche's spiritual marriage did not reach Katok Monastery for some time. Eventually a group of about fifty people led by Katok Situ and Moktsa Tulku, flooded into the reception room at Dzongsar. Before Khyentse Chökyi Lodrö could utter a syllable, the big, famous Katok Umze began to chant a mandala offering. Many, many gifts were offered, but nothing valuable or useful, just a houseload of worthless objects, including a saddle.
"I don't need all this!" exclaimed Rinpoche.

More Reactions to Rinpoche's Marriage

Khenpo Jorden

Before long, reports reached the labrang that Khenpo Jorden had denounced Chökyi Lodrö for having married. "This is terrible news! Dzongsar Khyentse is a disgrace to his previous lineage masters. It would have been better for him to die than to relinquish his monk's vows and take up with that old woman!"[28]

Rinpoche's attendants repeated everything Khenpo Jorden was supposed to have said several times, but Rinpoche didn't believe a word.

"I don't think he means it," he said. "We are close, we like each other, and he is well aware of all my reasons for taking a consort. Whatever he is supposed to have said, none of us can guess why he is saying it."

A decade later, just before the eruption of political unrest in Tibet, Khenpo Jorden visited Rinpoche in Dzongsar. Khenpo was very old by then and coming to the end of his life. Curious to know if the reports of Khenpo's criticism of Rinpoche had had any truth to them, Tsejor hid himself behind a door to eavesdrop on their conversation.

Khenpo entered Rinpoche's presence and prostrated to him while chanting the prayer of confession that begins:

> OM,
> The supreme wisdom body, the self-existing mandala,
> Is like the full moon and has no elaboration . . .

"Khenpo, what are you doing?" said Rinpoche. "Sit down and be quiet." Khenpo sat on a thick cushion and began to speak.

"Rinpoche, I don't have much to say, but as I am approaching death, there is one thing I must tell you.

"When you took a consort, I knew it was for a greater purpose. I also knew that having a consort is very important for you, that it will help you progress along the path and increase your experience and realization. However, if a jackal jumps where a tiger leaps, it will break its spine, and I was worried that the news might have a bad effect on the tulkus of Situ, Drime Zhingkyong, and Onpo. This is why I spoke out against you.

"Today, I have come to confess. The teachings tell me that if my lama is alive, I must make my confession in person, so here I am, to confess my faults to my living lama. This is all I have to say because I am sure Rinpoche already knows everything that's in my mind."

"Yes, of course I know!" replied Rinpoche. "How could I not know? There is no need for you to worry."

Khenpo Jorden was one of the two greatest Katok khenpos of his generation (the other was Khenpo Nüden) and a student of Khenpo Kunpal. After overhearing this conversation, Tsejor was of the opinion that Khenpo had no faults whatsoever.

I asked Tsejor what Khenpo Jorden looked like. He said he was a short, fat monk with a bald head and that he looked very manly.

Khenpo Nüden

I then asked Tsejor what Khenpo Nüden looked like.

"He was a skinny old monk with dark skin, who wore a thick woolen zen and a visor that he almost never took off."

Rinpoche loved to tease Khenpo Nüden. Khenpo was a Nyingmapa, so Rinpoche would set himself up as a Sakyapa and provoke Khenpo mercilessly with contentious philosophical arguments. Khenpo never failed to take the bait. He would raise his hands in horror, scramble to his knees, and insist passionately, "It's not like that. It's not like that at all." Delighted, Rinpoche would continue goading him in the hope that eventually he would abandon logic altogether. Khenpo usually responded by removing his visor, cloak, and zen, then pacing to and fro, he would shoot carefully aimed arrows of logic directly at Rinpoche. This could go on for some time. In the end, Khenpo would plead exhaustion, often saying, "Nothing beneficial has come of this debate." He would then replace his visor and robes and quietly sit down.

When Khenpo was in retreat at Lha Chok Ding, which is opposite Karmo Tak Tsang, he wrote to Rinpoche every two or three days. Tsejor asked Rinpoche what Khenpo was writing about. Rinpoche showed him the letters, and Tsejor saw for himself how Khenpo had urged Rinpoche again and again to take a consort, often using the words, "For you, a consort is indispensable. You really must take one!"

"How should I respond?" asked Rinpoche.

Tsejor thought for a moment, then said, "Why not tell Khenpo that he too should take a consort."

So Rinpoche wrote, "You should also take a consort as there is immense benefit to be gained from relying on one."

Khenpo calmed down after that, and Rinpoche heard nothing more from him. Tsejor said that Khenpo Nüden must have been aware of the obstacles to Rinpoche's life, which was probably why he kept urging Rinpoche to take a consort. Unlike Khenpo Jorden, Khenpo Nüden had great devotion for Rinpoche, but Tsejor said he couldn't tell how learnèd he was. Rinpoche used to say that from the Sakya tradition there was no scholar more learnèd or greater than Dezhung Tulku, and from the Nyingma tradition, none could rival Khenpo Nüden.

Another Consort

I don't know if Khyentse Chökyi Lodrö took any consorts other than Khandro Tsering Chödrön. There was a lot of gossip in Nangchen suggesting he might have been the father of the Third Neten Chokling, but that's impossible because Rinpoche continued to ordain bhikshus long after Neten Chokling was born. And I've never heard even a whisper about him taking consorts in his youth.

Chakdzö was drunk when he told Chokling Rinpoche that after Khandro Tsering Chödrön was found, Chakdzö had been convinced that Rinpoche's life would finally be perfectly auspicious. But then Rinpoche had fallen seriously ill, and Chakdzö wondered if perhaps he had met the wrong consort. So he offered Rinpoche his wife (Tselu). Not long after that, Rinpoche's health improved and his mind became very clear, which, Chakdzö concluded, must have meant that Rinpoche had "had" Tselu.

Many of the labrang's most precious antiquities were kept on an upper floor, and when I went through them, I found about a meter of spindled female hair labeled in Rinpoche's own hand: "The brahma-thread made

Tsering Wangmo (Tselu)
Source: Sogyal Rinpoche's private collection

from the hair of two dakinis, consecrated in the usual way during the Chakrasamvara empowerment in Nepal." I think the two dakinis must have been Khandro Tsering Chödrön and Tselu.

According to Khenpo Ngakchung, Tselu is the emanation of Ushnishavijaya and Khandro the manifestation of White Tara (Yishin Khorlo). Khenpo was always extremely kind to both of them. He would pat their heads and insist that they sit next to him. He called them "my girls."

When Nyoshul Khenpo was in France, I asked, "Abu! What shall we do? Is Tselu a dakini or not?"

"What is there to do or not to do?" he replied. "I wear some of Lakar Tselu's hair around my neck. She is a very special dakini."

At first I had my doubts, but Nyoshul Khenpo was a truly authentic master, so maybe it's true, maybe she is special. Until I spoke with Khen Rinpoche, though, I never thought of Lakar Tselu as being anything out of the ordinary. When I went to Tibet, I asked Tsejor what he thought, and he said, "Hu! She is a great dakini. What more is there to say?"

I've been told that when Tsewang Paljor first met Tselu, Rinpoche told him that unless he accumulated one hundred million Vajrakilaya mantras, his merit and power would not be sufficient to control her intense energy. Tsewang Paljor believed Rinpoche and diligently recited the Vajrakilaya mantra day and night. People say he accumulated one hundred million mantras. He, himself, said he didn't know exactly how many because when his mala broke, he lost one of his counters. I asked Tashi Namgyal if Rinpoche really had told Tsewang Paljor that he wouldn't be able to control Tselu unless he accumulated mantras, and Tashi Namgyal confirmed that he had.

RINPOCHE AND KHANDRO

I asked Tashi Namgyal how Rinpoche and Khandro related to each other in Tibet. He said that at Dzongsar they had separate rooms. Nothing was known about when they visited each other privately. During the afternoons when Rinpoche received visitors, Khandro tended to stay in her room, and after dinner, they retired separately to their respective rooms. Sometimes Khandro went into Rinpoche's private rooms or the central empowerment hall, where entry was generally restricted, to draw, string malas, and play—she was still very young and often distracted herself with childish pastimes. She even asked Rinpoche for permission to play and draw during the transmission of the Kangyur.

When they traveled, their bed was made up near one of two central tent poles. Chokden and Tashi Namgyal usually slept by Rinpoche's pillow. At first, they said, they were in such awe of him that it was impossible to sleep, but after a while they got used to it. They slept in Rinpoche's tent quite a few times when he went camping to enjoy the scenery. At night, they always saw Rinpoche lie down to sleep, but whenever they awoke, he would be sitting upright and wide awake. They said they couldn't hear exactly what Rinpoche was reciting, but they always remembered the *click-click-click* of his mala beads. I am quite sure that Tashi Namgyal always slept very peacefully, as he tossed and turned and farted his way through the night!

Rinpoche always rose before daybreak, and Tashi Namgyal would get up with him. Having dressed, Rinpoche and Khandro would sit on two cushions placed somewhere open and peaceful, perhaps under a tree or by a rock, and do their practice. They never did any exercise.

While they practiced, Tashi Namgyal and Chokden would dismantle the tent and pack everything away. Breakfast was then served, and Khandro often ate it sitting next to the folded tent. Tashi Namgyal and Chokden then had their breakfast, finished packing, and saddled Rinpoche's horse, ready to set out for the next campsite.

Chakdzö would be up by then, but Karma Gyaltsen always had to wait until Tselu had put on her makeup before he started packing; under no circumstances was he permitted even to open the tent flap until she had finished. Tselu spent quite some time each morning applying the cosmetics she always bought from China—white powder, red lipstick, and various kinds of paint. She never emerged until her face was perfect.

Jamyang Khyentse Chökyi Lodrö and Khandro Tsering Chödrön
Source: Khyentse Labrang

13. Sacred Hidden Lands

Opening the Sacred Land of Tso Ziltrom

Just before political mayhem erupted in Tibet, Khyentse Chökyi Lodrö went into retreat. In a letter to Dilgo Khyentse, he wrote, "It is now time to open the gateway to the sacred hidden land of Tso Ziltrom. So don't overlook any of the experiences or pure visions you have. Make sure you write them all down. Please come soon!"

Tremendously inspired by this letter, Dilgo Khyentse was unable to control his desire to write and quickly produced a forty-page guide to the sacred hidden land of Tso Ziltrom. He also wrote down something that had appeared in his mind long before he received Chökyi Lodrö's letter, which included instructions about how to find that hidden land.

On his way to Dzongsar with the freshly written texts, Dilgo Khyentse stopped off at the place where Tso Ziltrom was believed to be hidden. I've never been there myself and don't even know its name, but I've been told that it lies under a high cliff called Dark Go, near some juniper trees growing above a stream said to flow directly from the hidden land. As Dilgo Khyentse and his party rested, they gazed up in wonder at the towering rock face. Suddenly an old monk exclaimed, "Rinpoche! Look up there. Who can have hung anything up so high?" To Dilgo Khyentse's amazement, an unusually long, fine silk scarf was hanging between two juniper bushes high on a cliff so rugged that even the rakshasas could not climb it. He said nothing.

As soon as Dilgo Khyentse arrived in Dzongsar, he went to see Rinpoche.

"It's time to decipher the guide to the sacred place of Tso Ziltrom," said Rinpoche. "We must go there and open up the sacred hidden land."

"Rinpoche, I have already deciphered the guide," replied Dilgo Khyentse, as he offered him both texts. "The instruction manual for opening the sacred place appeared in a vision in my mind, so I wrote that down too."

Rinpoche was always talking about Tso Ziltrom.

"Yesterday I looked at the stream that flows beneath the rocks and feel it must have its source in the sacred land. The current had swept a yak's nose ring downstream, as well as a turquoise earring, a ladle, a bowl, and many other things. The land beyond the cliff is definitely sacred. We must open it up! But before we do, I want to accomplish two things. Firstly, I want to gather monks from both the upper and lower monasteries and accomplish one million recitations of *The King of Aspiration Prayers: Samantabhadra's "Aspiration to Good Actions."* If one million isn't possible, we must do seven hundred thousand, or at the very least three hundred thousand, recitations. And secondly, I want to finish gilding the more than fifty statues that are kept in the top floor temple. Once I've accomplished these two tasks, there will be nothing left for me to do. I'll be able to wrap up my activities and fly to Tso Ziltrom."

Rinpoche seemed constantly to be turning over in his mind whether or not he would be able to create the right circumstances to open that sacred land. As there was little more for him to do at the monastery, some people believed that opening the sacred land would be his last project. He never did it though. Perhaps the circumstances were never auspicious. But a sacred land must have been hidden somewhere in that region. If it hadn't been, Rinpoche would not have spoken about it so much. As it was, he returned to the subject again and again—so much so that his close attendants sometimes felt he had nothing else to talk about. He was very serious about going there and often worried over which route to take, and so on. I heard all this from Dilgo Khyentse.

Rinpoche also spoke to Gongna Tulku about Tso Ziltrom. When Gongna Tulku arrived in Sikkim, Rinpoche said, "You should go back to Dzongsar. I'll join you later. On my way here I wasn't able to visit Ngor Monastery, and as Jamyang Khyentse Wangpo, sovereign holder of all the teachings of the Buddha, lived at the Ngorpa monastery of Dzongsar, Ngorpa Tsang might have been offended. There's a saying that when human beings are unhappy, the gods are disappointed. These days I'm always ill and my body hurts, but on my way back to Dzongsar, I want to visit Ngor once more. If I make a big enough effort, maybe I'll be able to offer the transmission of the entire *Compendium of Tantras*. If I can't, I'll try to offer the transmission of the twenty-five mandalas of the purification tantra[29] or some similar mandalas. Even though there's not much left for me to do in Dzongsar, I want to return to my homeland. I want to gather the monks to recite *The King of Aspiration*

Prayers: Samantabhadra's "Aspiration to Good Actions," and I want to gild a few statues. Then I'll open the sacred land of Tso Ziltrom. I've heard that Katok Öntrul is telling everyone he'll stop eating tsampa if he can't visit Kongpo to open the sacred land of Pemakö. But opening Tso Ziltrom is a far more difficult proposition. It'll be quite unlike opening any other sacred place. We really must work out the best way to get there."

With these words, Rinpoche sent Gongna Tulku to Dzongsar. However, as it was obvious to Gongna Tulku that he wouldn't be able to open Tso Ziltrom, he returned to Sikkim through Lhasa, Assam, and Kalimpong.

Opening Sacred Lands and Other Miracles

I heard this story from Dilgo Khyentse Rinpoche. It's really part of Dilgo Khyentse's own biography, but it's also about Khyentse Chökyi Lodrö.

There are sacred lands, and there are places that act as substitutes for sacred lands. For example, Lhado Burmo in Derge is the substitute for the sacred land of Pemakö and was cared for as such by Jamgön Kongtrul. Rinpoche used to say that those who wanted to visit Pemakö could reduce the obstacles to their journey and make the whole enterprise far more fruitful by first visiting Lhado Burmo to make one hundred thousand—or at least one hundred—tsok offerings.

Opening the Sacred Site of Gyagen Khyungtak

The substitute for the sacred site of Maratika is Gyagen Khyungtak. Khyentse Wangpo and Jamgön Kongtrul were the first to open it, then later, it was reopened by Khyentse Chökyi Lodrö and Gyarong Khandro.

After Gyarong Namtrul broke samaya with Rinpoche, he laid many curses on him, which his sister, Gyarong Khandro, then removed. One evening at Dzongsar, she dug out a curse and threw it into the river. That night, a violent storm raged as tremendous claps of thunder and brilliant flashes of lightning filled the sky. The following morning, Dilgo Khyentse went to see Rinpoche.

"What visions did you have last night?" asked Rinpoche.

"I had none," replied Dilgo Khyentse. "But I heard a thunderstorm."

"Last night," said Rinpoche, "a suppressed curse must have been released by the spiritual power of Gyarong Khandro. Today I feel light, as if I'd been set free."

Khandro Tsering Chödrön told me how the sacred site of Gyagen Khyungtak was reopened. Gyurdrak[30] often told this story. He wasn't someone Khandro liked much because he always spoke of her and Gyarong Khandro as the "two dakinis," which she felt was a bit sycophantic. According to Gyurdrak, during the opening of Gyagen Khyungtak, it was if a tentlike canopy had been pitched over the sun. He also said that when Rinpoche and his party entered Khyungtak, the smoke from their sang offering swirled like a dragon flying around a mountain peak. These were both signs of accomplishment, he said, and he attributed them to the "two dakinis." Khandro Tsering Chödrön, who was there to assist Gyarong Khandro, said it wasn't like that at all.

"So," I asked, "what really happened?"

"I will tell you," she replied. "And as you know, I always speak the truth. I *never* lie."

Rinpoche and his party pitched their tents in a meadow opposite the Khyungtak practice cave and performed the feast offering from the *Consort Practice: The Queen of Great Bliss*. After receiving the siddhi, Rinpoche declared, "It's now time to discover the treasure."

"Yes! It's time!" cried Gyarong Khandro. "Let's go now. Come! Tsering Chödrön, please come with me!"

Rinpoche asked Khandro to accompany Gyarong Khandro, while he stayed at the camp with the others. The two women set out together, Khandro following as closely behind Gyarong Khandro as she could. Gyarong Khandro was wearing a thick, silk robe with a drab-colored lambskin on top; Khandro said the overall effect was that she looked very gray. When Gyurdrak told the story, he said that the two Khandros followed a path, but according to Khandro Tsering Chödrön, there was no path. They climbed the mountain until, quite high up, they found a large, flat rock with what looked like a swastika in one corner. It stood next to another rock that looked as though it were crouching to hide from something. The two Khandros stood between the two rocks.

"We didn't bring anything to dig with," said Gyarong Khandro. "What to do?"

She picked up a stone and showed it to Khandro Tsering Chödrön.

"Look at this!" she said.

Khandro examined the stone but couldn't see anything special about it. Gyarong Khandro hit it twice against one of the rocks, chipping off eggshell-size pieces and igniting sparks of fire. The third time she hit the rock with the stone, a hole appeared into which she inserted her hand and said, "Come on! Give it to me!"

Suddenly, to Khandro Tsering Chödrön's horror, Gyarong Khandro fell heavily to the ground. Khandro thought she was dead. Terrified, she turned to run away, but Gyarong Khandro, who had only fainted, grabbed her hand and wouldn't let it go. Still stupefied, she whispered, "Don't leave, and don't worry! Nothing bad's going to happen."

Recovering quickly, she told Khandro about the two extremely hot stones that she had pulled from the hole, each the size of a small egg.

"He only has enough merit to have one of them," she said. "So go and ask him if he wants the right one or the left. Take them from me without looking, and don't show them to anyone at all!"

She passed the two hot stones to Khandro Tsering Chödrön under the cover of her long Tibetan sleeves to ensure they remained unseen, then Khandro took the stones down to Rinpoche, who was sitting with Dilgo Khyentse.

"Gyarong Khandro says you only have enough merit to have one stone," she explained. "Do you want the right one or the left one?"

Rinpoche thought for a moment, then chose the right one, which Khandro gave him. She took the other stone back to Gyarong Khandro, returning it to her under cover of their long sleeves as before. With a flourish, Gyarong Khandro replaced the stone in the hole, and the rock instantly turned to mud. Khandro was amazed. As she was wondering what would happen next, Gyarong Khandro picked up a cup-size stone and pushed it into the hole. It sank into the mud-like rock, and she smoothed the surface as if she were plastering a wall. They then returned to camp.

The right-hand stone turned out to be the treasure known as *The Razor-Flame Vajrakilaya of Tsogyal from the Profound Treasure of the Two Dakinis*,[31] which Dilgo Khyentse deciphered and wrote down.

Dilgo Khyentse Rinpoche's Footprint

Rinpoche and his party made their way to the foot of the mountain and pitched their tents. Thick cushions were unpacked; Rinpoche sat on one, and Dilgo Khyentse sat next to him.

"Tulku Salga! Leave a footprint in that big rock down there," commanded Rinpoche.

Dilgo Khyentse put down his teacup and stamped on the rock. His foot left a clear indentation. As his consort, Khandro Lhamo, was not with them, Khandro Tsering Chödrön and Tashi Namgyal gathered some rocks and built a stone mandala in front of the footprint. They also left a sign, "The footprint of Tulku Salga." Dilgo Khyentse's shoe must have been patched, because when, sometime later, Khandro, Tashi Namgyal, and Lhamo went to see its imprint, it was so distinct that they could see where the shoe had been mended. I asked Dr. Lodrö Phuntsok whether he had seen such a footprint near Dzongsar. He said he had. Later, I asked Dilgo Khyentse if it was true that he had left a footprint in solid rock. He said that as Rinpoche had asked him to, he had stamped on a rock, and yes, he believed his foot had left an impression.

14. The King of Yönru

Yönru in Lithang was home to a large community of nomads. Their much-loved king was quite an eccentric character. He had a very large, flat nose, and everyone knew he could make his horse dance in the air like a lion. When his son was fifteen years old, the king ran away from his people and headed straight to Dzongsar because, he said, he wanted to become a student of Khyentse Chökyi Lodrö and practice the Dharma. A few days later, a party of forty or so of his subjects, led by his son, came looking for him, and they wouldn't leave without him.

To avert a crisis, Rinpoche suggested that the king agree to look after the affairs of the Yönru community for three more years. His son would then be eighteen and old enough to take on all the responsibilities of a king. Once he had formally transferred his powers to his son, the people of Yönru must then release the king so he could do what he wanted. It was a good solution that satisfied everyone, and the king went home with his son and subjects.

Three years later, the king returned to Dzongsar alone as a true ascetic. I've been told that the day he left Lithang none of his people would leave their tents to bid him farewell because they couldn't bear to see their beloved king carry his own luggage. And the women wept and wept.

The first period of the king's life at Dzongsar was full of incident, much of which has become legendary, like the time he broke Khyentse Chökyi Lodrö's cup. Later on, he traveled to Lhasa and Pomda, where many Lithangpas lived, but soon returned to Dzongsar to practice.

His son, the new king, was a brutal man—brave, but very stupid. When the Communists invaded Tibet, a large platoon of heavily armed soldiers ran him to ground by the great statue of Buddha Shakyamuni at Lithang. There was no escape. He cast aside all his protection cords and gaos, fired his gun into the air, and swore that unless the soldiers killed him then and there, they would never get him. The solders shot him dead. He probably threw away all his protections because had he kept them, the Communist bullets could not have penetrated his body, and if he had lived, he would have been tortured to death. The Communist soldiers then razed all the ex-king's property to the ground. News of these tragedies and many others reached the king, but he remained entirely untroubled by what he was told and always maintained the attitude of a perfectly pure Dharma practitioner.

Khenpo Rinchen got to know the king quite well in Dzongsar. They also spent a lot of time together in Sikkim and talked a great deal. According to Khenpo, as he had worn silk and soft brocades throughout his life, the king didn't like to wear cheap, rough fabrics. But he had no attachment at all to the kind of food he ate.

Rinpoche was on pilgrimage when the king first arrived in India. After Rinpoche passed into nirvana, the king traveled to Sikkim to make offerings for the fulfillment of Rinpoche's aspirations. After the cremation of Rinpoche's kudung and the completion of his stupa, the king went on pilgrimage to Bodh Gaya accompanied by Khenpo Rinchen (it was Khenpo's first visit). They also visited the site of the first Buddhist council and stayed in a cave above Rajgir.

"I might die soon," said the king, "but the thought of death brings me no pain at all. Rinpoche has already passed away, and we have heard nothing about his yangsi. We certainly don't know yet if he will be as great as Rinpoche was. But as far as I am concerned, Dilgo Tulku is Rinpoche's regent. He has to be! So I am going to offer him my *Heart Essence of Vimalamitra* text and would like you to find someone to take it to him for me."

He also offered Khenpo Rinchen his kerosene stove and an aluminum pot, saying they were now useless to him. Khenpo said he didn't need the cooking gear but gladly accepted the task of delivering the *Heart Essence of Vimalamitra* text to Dilgo Khyentse.

After a short stay in Sikkim, the king moved into a cave in the hills above Tso Pema, near Guru Padmasambhava's meditation cave, and locked himself in to meditate. One evening, as thoughts of Rinpoche filled his mind, there also arose a series of extremely unwelcome speculations. One was that Rinpoche would not have passed away if Chakdzö Tsewang Paljor and others had let him return to Tibet; another was that the royal family of Sikkim had caused great harm by keeping Rinpoche in Gangtok. If Rinpoche had gone to India, thought the king, his health would have been good, and he might not have passed into nirvana. These impressions erupted into a volcano of turbulent thoughts, and the king wept bitterly in the face of their onslaught.

He was quite alone in the cave, yet even as he struggled and wept, he noticed an unfamiliar smell. Sitting bolt upright, he saw a vision of Rinpoche in the sky before him, just as radiant as he had been in life.

"Khorey, King of Yönru! You don't know how to keep faith with your guru!" said Rinpoche, with a hand gesture. "Your guru and your mind are inseparable. All this weeping and whining is not devotion! You really don't know how to keep faith, do you?"

That was all he said, nothing more. But as soon as Rinpoche had finished admonishing the king, something quite unexpected happened. The king leapt up and ran out of the cave. To emulate the great yogis of the past, he had chosen to be naked as he meditated and was still naked as he ran down the mountainside and circumambulated the lake.

When he eventually became conscious of his surroundings, the king was surprised to find himself behind bars in the local jail. He had no memory of what had just happened, and as he spoke no Indian languages, he couldn't ask his jailers. But he knew a girl who was married to a Ladakhi who ran a restaurant below the lake, so he called her name aloud several times. Before long, she was brought to him.

"What's happened?" she asked.

"Nothing," he replied.

"Lama!" she said. "You've been behaving like a madman. You ran naked around the lake, and no one could catch you! That's why the police picked you up and brought you here. Are you hurt?"

The king assured her that however overexcited he may have been, he felt no physical pain. And as he had now regained his senses, could she please persuade the police to release him? Soon he was free and immediately returned to his cave. It was only when he arrived there and found the door locked that he realized just how strange the experience had been; he had to break the door down to get back into the cave.

The king stayed in the cave until it was time for him to die. He then traveled to Manali, where he took shelter in the house of Sunder, a doctor from Kinnaur, whose old, wooden, two-story house sat on a ridge overlooking the town. Doctor Sunder offered the lama-who-had-once-been-a-king a room, but the old man refused. Even though he was ill and had a swelling in his belly, he preferred to sleep on the veranda. The doctor offered him medicine, and out of politeness, the lama took one dose but no more. Dr. Sunder felt his pulses. They were far from normal, and he feared that the lama's death was fast approaching.

Then one day, the lama simply disappeared. As he had been a good practitioner, it occurred to Dr. Sunder that he had gone away to die. He went in search of the old lama, and it didn't take long to find him, dead under a deodar tree in the woods on the other side of the Manali bridge. With the help of a few Khampas, the doctor cremated his body in the cemetery nearby.

I knew Dr. Sunder personally, and he told me about the death of the king of Yönru himself, as did Khenpo Rinchen.

In the year the Communists "liberated" Tibet, His Holiness the Dalai Lama was teaching in Dharamsala when three men from Yönru Tsang arrived in India to make enquiries about their king.

"Dzongsar Khyentse is no longer alive," they said. "But a lama called Dilgo Khyentse is still living. Since Dzongsar Khyentse and Dilgo Khyentse are as one, he might have news of our king. That's why we want to see him."

I was with Dilgo Khyentse at that time. He said he vaguely remembered receiving a *Heart Essence of Vimalamitra* text but didn't know that the king had died in Manali. So I met the three men from Yönru myself and told them what I knew of their king's life and death in India. They seemed satisfied with what they heard and returned to Kham.

15. Pilgrimage from Derge to Sikkim

Departure from Dzongsar

ONE DAY, Pewar Tulku came across a sheet of paper that was lying in front of the Kutsab Ngödrup Palbar in the empowerment hall at Dzongsar. On it was written the verse, "I want to enter the presence of Shakyamuni..."

"I wonder if Rinpoche is thinking of traveling to Lhasa to see the Jowo statue," he thought. "If he does go, I want to go with him."

At that time, Rinpoche was believed to be facing a major obstacle to his life. He therefore did a divination in the presence of Kutsab Ngödrup Palbar and the "Looks like Me" statue to find out whether it would be better for him to go on pilgrimage or remain in strict retreat. Pilgrimage turned out to be the best option, but not the pilgrimage of a great lama with a large entourage. He should travel simply, with as little fuss as possible. So Rinpoche decided to go on a pilgrimage.

The news that Rinpoche would soon be leaving Dzongsar spread quickly. For a whole month, people swarmed into the labrang to offer gifts and to entrust Rinpoche with packages to deliver en route. Gelek, one of the attendants, said the crowds were dense and extremely determined. One day, as he was packing away the labrang's precious objects, the monks of Khamje Shedra elbowed their way into the empowerment hall, filling it so completely that only the tiniest of spaces was left for Rinpoche to sit down in. It was then that Rinpoche gave them the following advice:

"Lamas of the past were able to bless holy places with their meditative experience, realization, and spiritual power. By comparison, lamas today are absolutely useless. Far from giving blessings, all we can do is receive blessings to safeguard and prolong our own lives. We no longer have the power to bless a place and make it sacred.

"A divination I did in the presence of Kutsab Rinpoche Ngödrup Palbar and the "Looks like Me" statue suggests that by going on pilgrimage, I may be able to extend the length of my life. I have therefore planned an extensive pilgrimage tour. But I'll return to Dzongsar in two or three years—one year at the earliest. While I'm away, Khamje Shedra must not, under any circumstance, fall apart. However violently the storms rage in the skies above you, however deep the rising floods, however fierce the conflict, whatever happens, Khamje Shedra must continue to function as it does now. Its discipline and code of conduct must not degenerate or become corrupt: you must observe them faithfully!

"Do not be lax in your studies," commanded Rinpoche, pointing at Khyenrab Singye, who appeared to want to respond. But Rinpoche silenced him. "You are not to say one word. I will not listen! I am busy now, so go!"

The monks couldn't show any emotion while they were in Rinpoche's presence, but as soon as he had sent them away, they began to weep.

Dzongsar to Sikkim

Rinpoche left Dzongsar early one morning accompanied by eight attendants. They first traveled to Menshö, where Rinpoche performed a *Combined Practice of the Three Roots* tsok offering. They spent the night there, then went to the foot of Pawo Wangchen Drak. The next day, just as Rinpoche was about to leave for Kamthok Drukha, Goma Rinam and two attendants from Derge Tsang arrived with a request that he visit Gönchen—we never discovered who it was who leaked Rinpoche's travel plans.

"I have pledged not to walk even one inch towards a monastery during my pilgrimage," said Rinpoche to Goma Rinam. "Be sure to tell the queen not to come here; it would be too exhausting for her. Say I will be back either next year or the year after and that we'll meet again, happily and in good health." After a moment, he added, "And don't let them bring a huge crowd down here. It would be too chaotic!"

Turning away, Rinpoche left Goma Rinam deep in thought. A few minutes later, he hailed Tashi Namgyal. "Where will Rinpoche make camp tonight?" he asked.

"Sengchen Namdrak," replied Tashi Namgyal.

At Sengchen Namdrak, Rinpoche was met by fifty-five masters and attendants from Derge Tsang, led by the queen and Prince Oga. The labrang attendants had packed rich, thick cushions and two ornate tables for just such an occasion, but when they were set out for the royal guests Rinpoche became irritable and cross.

"What are you doing? Where did you get that table?" he snapped. The attendants replied they had brought it from the labrang. "Pilgrims don't bring gilded tables on pilgrimage! Send everything back immediately!"

By contrast, Rinpoche was delighted to see that Tashi Namgyal had rolled up his monks' robes and tied them to his saddle.

"Loads and saddles are auspicious! They are pure and good! It would be excellent if each and every one of you had a saddle for this journey."[32]

Derge Tsang remained at Sengchen Namdrak for a day, and Rinpoche granted them a long-life empowerment. They also visited the holy places of Sengchen Namdrak together. The queen of Derge offered Rinpoche fifty-five bolts of yellow and orange brocade and also brought with her a great deal of Chinese bread and milk. But Rinpoche refused it all.

A wealthy merchant, Tromge Bu Truk Truk, who was a generous benefactor of the labrang, asked Tashi Namgyal what Rinpoche would be taking with him on his journey.

"What would a pilgrim and a wanderer take with him?" replied Tashi Namgyal.

"Adzi!" exclaimed Bu Truk Truk. "How can a great master travel in such a manner!"

Tashi Namgyal pointed out that there was a limit to how much they could carry. So Bu Truk Truk offered not only two tong boxes but the mule they'd need to carry them. Once again, Rinpoche refused it all, and Bu Truk Truk could see that if he mentioned the other mule he wanted to offer, the one laden with rice, Rinpoche would refuse that too. Instead, he asked Tashi Namgyal privately to take the mule, saying that if he did, he would be able to serve Rinpoche rice porridge on the journey. So Tashi Namgyal agreed.

As Rinpoche left Sengchen Namdrak, the queen of Derge watched from the crest of the hill. She was so moved and sad that she fainted. (She later distributed the bolts of brocade among nearby monasteries.)

After two or three days, Rinpoche's party arrived in unfamiliar territory, a long way from Derge, but not quite as far as Nangchen. Rice porridge was served, and Rinpoche instantly asked where the rice had come from. It was only then that he was told of Tromge Bu Truk Truk's gift.

"Bu Truk Truk knew we would need rice," said Rinpoche, "and this porridge really is delicious! We must all have some."

And that was all he said.

A Dzo for Rinpoche

Tenzin Phuntsok was an old lama who had spent most of his life in retreat. He had received the *Path and Fruition* teachings from Rinpoche many times, so when he heard that Rinpoche's party was camping below Sumda Monastery, he abruptly left his retreat to pay his respects. Rinpoche was very pleased to see him, and they talked for a long time.

"Why, Rinpoche, are you traveling with so few attendants and living so simply?" asked Tenzin Phuntsok.

"A pilgrim is a pilgrim," explained Rinpoche. "It is better to travel on foot like an ordinary pilgrim than to ride horses or mules. But I must admit, my old bones would be more comfortable on a well-trained dzo."

None of Rinpoche's party overheard this conversation and couldn't understand why the old lama almost ran from Rinpoche's tent. He hurried to a nearby nomad camp with such haste that he didn't notice his zen trailing behind him in the dust. A couple of hours later, six or seven saddled dzo suddenly appeared, as if from nowhere, next to Rinpoche's tent.

Eventually, it was discovered that Tenzin Phuntsok had been talking to the local nomads.

"Rinpoche needs a dzo to ride, and I'm looking for a good one to offer him. In exchange, I'll give you my fine horse, Lung Nagma."

When they heard who the dzo was for, rather than trade with the lama, several of the nomads decided to offer dzos themselves. Which was how so many animals appeared, as if by magic, at Rinpoche's door.

"It was such a mistake to confide in that lama!" lamented Rinpoche.

In the end, though, Rinpoche didn't take any of the dzos with him when he left Sumda for Nangchen.

Nangchen Gak

From Nangchen, Rinpoche went to Gechak Monastery, where five hundred nuns received him in an elaborate procession. Traditionally, the monks of all the Nangchen monasteries, including Neten Monastery, wore pandita hats, whereas the nuns didn't—all except the nuns at Gechak Monastery.

"Ha, ha!" said Rinpoche. "How strange that the nuns wear pandita hats!"

I asked Tashi Namgyal to tell me about Rinpoche's visit to Nangchen Gak. He said that since Nangchen Tsang only learnt of Rinpoche's visit minutes before he arrived, they barely had time to arrange smoke offerings and blow a few trumpets. They certainly weren't able to organize an elaborate reception. In fact, Rinpoche was already crossing the threshold of the palace as Prince Achen, in full royal regalia, rushed down the steps to escort him to the reception.

According to Adeu Rinpoche, while Rinpoche was at Nangchen Gak, nothing he wore or did marked him out as a high-ranking lama. He dressed simply—just a ceremonial hat[33] and a monk's vest with yellow stripes—and he circumambulated the bonfire and monastery accompanied by very few attendants.

During the visit, Deshek Kundü and the monks of Nangchen Monastery led an elaborate ritual based on the sadhana of the *Great Compassionate Avalokiteshvara*, over which Rinpoche presided. This was how Rinpoche consecrated Queen Yudrön's twenty-one Taras statues in the Tsechu Hall, thereby fulfilling a request she had made many years before. During the ceremony, Rinpoche seized the opportunity to offer Deshek Kundu some advice.

"Your monastery really knows how to practice this sadhana, you do it very accurately. If you continue to practice like this and to consecrate representations each year, all outer and inner obstacles will be dispelled, everything will be auspicious, and all your good wishes will be fulfilled."

Rinpoche loved sorting through reliquaries and in the process tended to help himself to any of the precious contents he felt he needed. So when he arrived at Nangchen Tsang, he asked who had what and broke open each reliquary to see what he could find. Tsoknyi Monastery had a round, thumb-size golden earring that looked like crystal threaded on a string that was said to have belonged to Yeshe Tsogyal. Rinpoche insisted that they give it to him and took it away when he left, but I haven't seen it in the Bir archive and wonder what happened to it.

At Yarchen Kyasu, the birthplace of Chokgyur Lingpa, Rinpoche was offered a tong box by someone who then received from Rinpoche the reading transmission of the *Profound Path in Seven Chapters*. Rinpoche gave a wonderful teaching that day, a teaching that seemed to spring from a supremely clear and exalted mind. Rinpoche spent about fifteen days at Yarchen Kyasu.

Neten Monastery

After leaving Yarchen Kyasu, Rinpoche traveled to Neten Monastery. By then, Tsejor had retired and was dividing his time between Neten Monastery and Khyentse Labrang. This is his version of Rinpoche's visit.

Neten Chokling was in the jungle at Khyungthang Gak, gathering timber to build a new temple, when his attendant, Sophel, brought him some good news and some bad news. Which, he asked, did Neten Chokling want to hear first?

"Khorey!" exclaimed Neten Chokling. "Give me the bad news first."

"The bad news is that the daughter of Yab Tsangma, Tsering Dolkar, has died in childbirth," said Sophel.

"And the good news?" asked Neten Chokling.

"Jamyang Khyentse Chökyi Lodrö has arrived at Nangchen Gak."

At first Neten Chokling wouldn't believe him, because when Rinpoche traveled, it was almost always in great style and an immensely complex operation—something like moving a mountain! However Sophel assured him it was true, explaining they had received the news through a messenger who had seen Rinpoche lead the consecration of the queen's Tara statues with his own eyes. Neten Chokling was extremely surprised and instructed his attendants to saddle up and return to Neten Monastery immediately. He, Tsejor, and a few others then sped to Nangchen Gak to beg Rinpoche to visit their monastery, however briefly. Rinpoche refused but added that he would visit the holy site of Tsegyal Drak, where Chokgyur Lingpa had discovered the *Long-Life Practice: A Garland of Vajras* sadhana, because he wanted to do a ganachakra practice at Yegyal Namkha Dzö. And Yegyal Namkha Dzö was just half a mile from Neten Monastery.

When Rinpoche arrived at Tsegyal Drak, the monks began to play every single musical instrument owned by Neten Monastery. In his autobiography (which he kept in a travel guide with Mao's picture on the cover), Rinpoche wrote that more than three hundred horsemen received him. But that must have been how many he saw in a pure vision, because there can only have been about fifty men on horseback that day. Anyway, however many there were, they received him with all the splendor and majesty befitting such a high lama.

Worried that as Rinpoche was traveling incognito, he might be irritated if too much fuss was made, Tsejor put on his very best clothes and went to inform Rinpoche about what Neten Chokling had planned. He found Rinpoche in very good spirits. When Tsejor asked if it was acceptable for Neten Monastery to play *sirna dora* music—reed instruments and drums played at the same time—to celebrate the auspicious occasion of his visit, Rinpoche said, "Do whatever has been arranged. You have my permission."

As it seemed to be just the right moment for the music to begin, Tsejor ran down past the mani stones at Nangchen Gak to tell the monks to prepare themselves. Tsering Sangye, an old monk from our monastery who passed away in 2008, was one of the sirna dora players. The idea was that Sophel and two laymen would ride ahead of Rinpoche with incense pots of burning juniper leaves tied to their horses (the smoke offering), followed by a procession of people carrying banners, parasols, and so on. The sirna dora music was to begin the moment Rinpoche appeared.

The king and ministers of Nangchen arrived with their attendants and servants, and just as they were about to mount up, Rinpoche emerged on horseback in his saffron-colored robes. Instantly the monks began to play music and make smoke offerings as they processed clockwise through the palace and behind the mani stones. The queen of Nangchen was thrilled when she saw how the monks escorted Rinpoche through Mangyo Gak. She said that even though they were from such a small monastery, they had performed beautifully. But there were also those who felt Neten Monastery had shown off a bit too much. It was not the custom to play sirna dora music in the palace—in fact, it was prohibited past the palace gate. And low-profile lamas were usually expected to dismount before they got there.

As Rinpoche rode, the wind blew in great gusts, which Tsejor felt was an antidote to negative elemental spirits. At one point, Rinpoche paused at the top of a hill to rest. While he was taking tea, the sirna player, Tsering Sangye, lost the reed to his instrument, then miraculously found it again soon after Rinpoche had learnt of its loss. The sirna dora music started up again after tea, and Rinpoche went straight to Tsegyal Drak, where they set up camp. The following day, he offered a tsok in front of Yegyal Namkha Dzö, and an account of the enormous quantity of experiences and pure visions he had during that time can be found in the *Great Biography*. Rinpoche then gave instructions about how the new temple at Neten Monastery should be built, then presided as everyone made the bodhisattva vows of both the profound view and vast conduct.

The White Dragon Cup

The journey to Lhasa took them through Sedor and Sang Zhung. Throughout this time, Rinpoche had been using a teacup that was said to have belonged to Khyentse Wangpo, and Chakdzö Tsewang Paljor had been using a plain white cup with a dragon etched into the porcelain that was only visible when held up to the light. Chakdzö's cup intrigued Rinpoche, and he asked to see it. Chakdzö immediately threw away his tea, wiped the cup clean, and offered it to Rinpoche. Rinpoche examined it from every angle, inside and out, and said it was lovely, "much more worthwhile than a dri." So Chakdzö offered Rinpoche his cup. When I was in Sikkim, I saw it in a treasure chest, full of melted butter.

Averting Sorcery

At Neten Monastery, Rinpoche's tent was pitched on snow. He invited Neten Chokling to visit him there and asked about the traveling conditions between Lhasa and Pemakö. Neten Chokling advised Rinpoche to visit Pemakö only if he intended to open the sacred hidden land, because it wasn't safe to travel in that area. Rinpoche agreed that it was a perilous place, adding that to open the hidden land would be difficult.

"Wo, la so," said Neten Chokling.

Rinpoche paused, then said, "Tulku!"

"La so," responded Neten Chokling.

"Everyone says Gyarong Namtrul is casting black spells and that he is directing them at me. I don't know if it's true—after all, we are Dharma brothers—but I keep having dreams in which I'm attacked by strong black magic. I need the help of a spiritually powerful person to avert whatever that black magic may be; an ordinary person wouldn't have a chance. So after I leave here, do the wrathful practice to avert negativity through *Yamantaka, Destroyer of Enemies* until you achieve clear signs of accomplishment. But do it in quite a relaxed way. For this service, Chakdzö will offer you gifts and provide you with money to buy offerings. But remember, the ritual should be just strong enough to repel the magic. Don't be excessive or risk physically harming my enemies. If you overdo it, the consequences could be quite serious."

Neten Chokling was so surprised by the request that he only managed to reply by saying "la so" before leaving Rinpoche's presence. He went straight to see Chakdzö, who offered him a female mule loaded with a crate of tea and advised Neten Chokling to offer as much on his own behalf as he could afford. Neten Chokling accepted the mule and the tea and, as he had already heard about the attacks, decided to begin the ritual as soon as he could.

Winter was little more than a month away when Rinpoche and his entourage left Nangchen. Almost as soon as he had gone, Neten Chokling began a month-long retreat in the cave at Tsegyal Drak. As Rinpoche had instructed, Neten Chokling performed a long-life sadhana, and we all chanted the long-life prayer that Rinpoche had composed for himself. My mother and Wangchen Dorje told me about the signs of accomplishment that appeared, but everyone who was there at the time knew about them.

On the ninth day, Neten Chokling asked his monks to make a special kind of wrathful torma for averting negativity. They produced a huge one and stood it on a large platter with smaller blazing tormas arranged very precisely around it. After a week of practice, Neten Chokling asked the monks to take the tormas to a massive rock nearby and leave them there. The next day, the monks returned to the rock and found that both the tormas and the plate they had been standing on had disappeared—no one knew what had happened to them. But there were no other signs at that time.

On the nineteenth day, Neten Chokling asked the monks to make another torma, which they stood on a large stone slab. They practiced the ritual for three days and left all the tormas on the rock as before. When they returned some days later, the stone slab and all the tormas had disappeared without a trace.

It was very calm and quiet when, on the twenty-ninth day, Neten Chokling once again asked the monks to make a wrathful torma, which this time was placed in a small bowl bristling with sharp-pointed sticks. Neten Chokling began to chant the sadhana of the activity Yamaraja. Before long, a thunderous boom echoed throughout the cave, and the earth shook. Calmly, Neten Chokling continued to chant and beat a drum. He then indicated that the torma should be removed. As it was carried out, three sparks of fire shot upwards, one after another, as if the first gave birth to the second, which gave birth to the third. They flew so high that they could no longer be seen. Then suddenly, one spark grew bigger and bigger until it was the size of a large wooden house and hurtled across the lower part of the valley, bellowing like a bull. I was standing in the cave with my mother and the attendants, but we were too afraid to stay where we were and ran out as fast as we could. I can still remember how tightly I clung to my mother's hand.

Later I asked Neten Chokling to tell me what he remembered about the ritual. He said that he had followed Rinpoche's instructions and performed the wrathful ritual on the ninth day of the month, but as there were no signs of accomplishment, he had repeated it on the nineteenth day. Again nothing happened, so on the twenty-ninth day he did it again, determined to keep practicing until he achieved a sign. At one point, he said, he heard what sounded like someone blowing a long horn—which must have been the bellowing sound we heard. The earth had also shaken a little, he said, but bearing in mind that he couldn't allow himself to get distracted, he had continued chanting the invocation and beating a drum until he had a vision of two or three doglike animals running around, barking and wagging their tails. A spotty dog lay down beside him and vomited a beating, blood-stained heart into his lap. Neten Chokling then performed a liberation ritual outside the cave. The next day the bowl had disappeared, but not before spilling what looked like a cupful of blood onto the rock. These were the signs Neten Chokling accomplished. Soon after, Gyarong Namtrul passed away.

Neten Chokling visited Sikkim some time later to see Rinpoche.

"You are such a fool!" snapped Rinpoche. "You have created an impossibly difficult situation! The first ritual was quite enough to avert the magic, so the other two were entirely unnecessary! You are a tulku of Chokgyur Lingpa! For you to repeat such rituals over and over again is nothing less than barbaric! You're such a brute! And now you'll have to face serious consequences."

Yang-gön Phakchok

The highest-ranking lamas in our region were Neten Chokling and the previous incarnation of the present Phakchok Tulku, Yang-gön Phakchok of Riwoche[34] (one of four Gon Tsang monasteries). Yang-gön Phakchok also held a high political position in the Tibetan government and was considered to be of the same rank as Chamdo Phakpa Lha and Drakyab Kyabgön. I don't know how holy a master he was, but he was very popular among the politicians.

While Rinpoche was camping at Tso Kha in Serdor, Yang-gön Phakchok asked if they might meet. When the meeting became known, most people assumed that Rinpoche would demonstrate great respect for Yang-gön Phakchok, who himself expected a lavish ceremonial reception. But Rinpoche's only reaction to the request was to say that Yang-gön Phakchok could come around anytime he liked. Phakchok tried asking again, hoping for a more formal response, but again Rinpoche simply said he would be in whenever Phakchok chose to pop by.

So one day, Yang-gön Phakchok, supported by two attendants, entered Rinpoche's tent holding a katak. Rinpoche politely stood up to receive him but didn't prostrate as many people thought he would. His lack of fear of such a high-ranking lama astonished everyone.

Later, the gossips reported that when Phakchok asked after Rinpoche's health, Rinpoche's reply was almost curt, and for the rest of the audience he said very little. The previous Neten Chokling said, with wonder in his voice, Rinpoche wasn't afraid of anyone, no matter how highly placed they were. The khenpo of our monastery added that people were generally very afraid of Yang-gön Phakchok.

Drak Yerpa

On the way to Lhasa, Khyentse Chökyi Lodrö visited Drak Yerpa to do a month-long retreat in a cave there. But soon after they arrived, it became clear that Chakdzö didn't want to stay. The point of their trip, he declared, wasn't to get stuck in the wilderness or on a barren mountain. And in a matter of days, he left for Lhasa.

Having obtained the permit necessary to use the retreat cave, Rinpoche and Khandro settled in, while Tashi Namgyal, Chokden, and the other attendants moved into a room in a house below the cave's entrance. Rinpoche and Khandro began their practice very early each morning and were served breakfast in the cave after their first session. Lunch and dinner were also served in the cave, and at midday, they took a break to circumambulate the hill.

Meanwhile, Chakdzö found conditions in Lhasa very difficult. He wrote to Rinpoche saying that although water was free, firewood was expensive and almost unavailable. He was particularly worried that the horses might not survive. Rinpoche should come to Lhasa very soon, wrote Chakdzö, so they could continue their journey to Mindrolling or Sakya as soon as possible. Lhasa was not the place to settle. But Rinpoche showed no sign of wanting to leave Drak Yerpa, not even to visit local landmarks. This presented his attendants with a dilemma: Chakdzö was adamant that Rinpoche should go to Lhasa immediately, but Rinpoche himself was relaxed and very happy at Drak Yerpa.

One afternoon as the whole party circumambulated the cave, Tashi Namgyal picked up a large, dry pat of cow dung. "They say there is no firewood in Lhasa, yet there are so many cow pats here that all we have to do is bend down and pick them up! I want to send some to Chakdzö."

Rinpoche, Khandro, and the two Lakar nuns immediately began to gather cow pats, which were then loaded onto seven mules and dispatched to Lhasa with Tsering Wangpo and his friends. Having dung to burn helped Chakdzö a great deal. He quickly returned the mules and asked for another load as soon as possible. After that, he stopped pressing Rinpoche to leave for Lhasa.

Lhasa

Eventually Rinpoche finished his retreat, offered a tsok, and relaxed for two days before riding to Lhasa, where he accepted the hospitality of Samdrup Phodrang. From then on, the whole party was extremely well taken care of. All they had to do each day was eat, drink, and gather offerings. And as there was no longer any lack of funds or resources, Chakdzö calmed down and stopped his nagging.

Rinpoche was determined not to give the impression that he considered himself to be a high-ranking lama. He therefore wouldn't allow his attendants to turn anyone away, so a continuous stream of visitors flowed through his rooms, all of whom wanted to ask questions, request blessings, and make offerings. As none were refused, Rinpoche was busy all day, every day. The only time he wasn't surrounded by visitors was during his afternoon circumambulation of holy sites and images.

Tashi Namgyal and Chokden were also kept busy distributing blessed cords and pills, with never a moment to sit down. They even had to drink their tea standing up. Their legs became so numb that they might as well have been someone else's! The only time the attendants could rest a little was when Rinpoche performed rituals, like the ritual for securing wealth that he did at the home of Phalha Drönyer Chenmo following the death of the bride of Pomda Tsang, and the ritual at Ngagpoi Tsang with Dudjom Jigdral Yeshe Dorje. Apart from that, they were on the go all day, every day, and often had to work until midnight to make sure there were always enough protection cords. By contrast, Chakdzö lost himself in his horse- and gun-trading business.

The Right-Swirling Conch Shell

Each day, Rinpoche practiced at the Jokhang then, accompanied by Tashi Namgyal and Chokden, circumambulated the temple again and again along the outer and middle paths. These paths were lined with shops, and Rinpoche really enjoyed looking at their displays as he circumambulated.

Jamyang Khyentse Chökyi Lodrö at Samdrup Phodrang, Lhasa, in 1956
Source: Khyentse Labrang

One day, he wandered into the shop of Zhamo Karpo, who was a Nepali and a benefactor of the Karmapa. His shop, which is still there today, used to be the most popular in Lhasa. It was there that Rinpoche found a conch shell that swirled to the right.

"How much does this conch cost?" asked Rinpoche.

"Seven hundred silver coins," said one of his attendants.

"I need to buy it," said Rinpoche. "A conch with a swirl to the right is very precious and very holy. If we buy it, we'll be able to add some powdered conch to the treasure vases we bury."

But even though Rinpoche asked three times, Chakdzö refused to buy the conch. "It's far too expensive," he said. "We're bound to find a much cheaper one in India."

Usually all the money offered to Rinpoche was given to Chakdzö for safekeeping. However, when it became clear that he had no intention of buying the conch, Rinpoche told the attendants not to give him anything for three days. Instead, Tashi Namgyal collected all the money that was offered and kept it safe in a drawstring bag. After three days, Rinpoche asked how much had been collected.

"Enough for the conch shell," replied Tashi Namgyal.

"Wo ya!" exclaimed Rinpoche. He stood up and adjusted his zen. "Bring the money with you, I must do my circumambulations." And he strode out of his room, making a beeline for Zhamo Karpo's shop.

"Ya! I don't care whether I have money or not, but no one else can have that shell!" he said firmly. "You two, pay the man." And he continued his circumambulations, taking the conch with him.

As Tashi Namgyal and Gönpo Tseten were counting out the money, Chakdzö turned up. When he heard how much Rinpoche had paid for the conch, he complained vehemently about its exorbitant price. "But by then it was too late to do anything about it," he said later.

They returned to their lodgings and found the conch standing on Rinpoche's table.

"Tsewang Paljor is trying to protect my finances by being tightfisted!" said Rinpoche. "He refused to buy me this conch, even though I asked him many times. But I can afford it!" And he caressed the conch shell for several days.

Later, it was found to be a fake. I think it's still kept at Khyentse Labrang because I once saw a very lumpy-looking conch there. It was the only thing Rinpoche ever bought with any enthusiasm. He rarely bought or sold anything at all.

This was all Tashi Namgyal had to say about Rinpoche's trip to Lhasa.

A Case of Mistaken Identity

Lama Godi said that of all the lamas who have walked this earth, the master he felt the greatest devotion for was Khyentse Chökyi Lodrö. He felt that way, he said, even before they met in person. But when he heard that Rinpoche was visiting Lhasa, his longing to gaze on Rinpoche with his own eyes became so strong that he dug out the few ounces of silver he had saved and set off for Samdrup Phodrang.

As Lama Godi entered a top-floor room at Samdrup Phodrang, he saw Rinpoche for the first time, sitting next to a young girl with long hair. She

Lama Godi and family
Source: Nyima Lhamo, Lama Godi's daughter

was dressed in gray and sat very close to Rinpoche, but on a higher throne on two thick cushions. Of course, at that very moment, Lama Godi had to concentrate on seeing Rinpoche as Jamyang Khyentse Wangpo in the flesh as he offered prostrations, so he had no time to examine the girl. It wasn't until after Rinpoche had blessed him that he could take a really good look at her. She puzzled him. Could this be Khandro Tsering Chödrön? Surely Khandro would never agree to sit on such a high throne. Who, then, wondered Lama Godi, could she possibly be? In the meantime, he prostrated to her, and she gently placed her hands on his head to bless him before he left the room.

Out in the reception area, Lama Godi asked one of the attendants to request a teaching from Rinpoche on his behalf. A few days later, he was invited to an empowerment that Rinpoche was to give at Samdrup Phodrang. (It was probably the *Heart Essence of Samantabhadra*. And as Rinpoche played the damaru and bell and chanted, "Jamyang Khyentse Wangpo OM AH HUM, Jamgön Lodrö Taye OM AH HUM, Terchen Chokgyur Lingpa

OM AH HUM," it must have been the empowerment of the display of awareness of tögal.) Once again, the same girl was present, sitting on a high throne, just as before. Rinpoche addressed her with the greatest respect and humility, and she seemed to be the main recipient of the empowerment. But Lama Godi still didn't know who she was. So he asked an attendant.

"That's Dudjom Tulku from Pemakö," came the reply. Lama Godi was extremely surprised. He had, of course, heard about Dudjom Tulku, but he had never seen him and was quite taken aback to hear that the "girl" was not only a man but a great tulku!

Kalon Tripa Samdhong Rinpoche
In his youth, Kalon Tripa Samdhong Rinpoche had studied with Trijang Rinpoche (Trijang Lobsang Yeshe) in Lhasa. He told me that he was one

Dudjom Rinpoche with the late Prince Paljor Namgyal and
Maharani Kunzang Dechen Tshomo Namgyal, the elder daughter of
Rakashar Depon Tenzing Namgyal, a general in the Tibetan army
Source: Private collection of Semo Tinley Ongmo,
Namgyal Institute of Tibetology, Sikkim

of about twenty tulkus who used to cram themselves into Trijang Lobsang Yeshe's tiny room every day to receive teachings. Although the room was small, it overlooked the courtyard and provided an excellent vantage point from which to keep an eye on the comings and goings of the household.

One day, Trijang Lobsang Yeshe suddenly broke off in the middle of a sentence.

"Ah! Khyentse Rinpoche is coming!" he cried. "Quickly! Get up! Go and wait in the other room. Go right now!"

All the tulkus scurried into the adjoining room to watch as a very tall lama wearing a flat lotus Guru Rinpoche hat arrived, bringing with him a beautiful consort and several attendants. Trijang Lobsang Yeshe received Khyentse Rinpoche on the sun terrace at the top of his house, and after Khyentse Rinpoche had prostrated, they touched foreheads. Then Trijang Lobsang Yeshe invited Khyentse Rinpoche into his room, and they talked for more than two hours. As there was obviously not going to be any more teaching that day, Samdhong and the other tulkus were told to go home.

"I only saw Khyentse Chökyi Lodrö once during all that time," said Samdhong Rinpoche.

Trulshik Ngawang Chökyi Lodrö
At Ngagpoi Tsang in Lhasa, Dudjom Rinpoche said to Trulshik Rinpoche, "Tomorrow I will seek an audience with Dzongsar Jamyang Khyentse Chökyi Lodrö. We have corresponded many times, but I have never met him in person."

A book written in Minling Lochen's own hand lay on Dudjom Rinpoche's table and was either the *Heart Essence of Vimalamitra* or the *Innermost Heart Drop of Profundity*.

"This is the heart jewel of all my wealth," said Dudjom Rinpoche. "There is nothing more precious to me than this book, and tomorrow I will present it to Khyentse Rinpoche as a mandala offering."

Eagerly, Trulshik Rinpoche said that he too would like to meet Khyentse Chökyi Lodrö.

"I cannot take you to see him myself," replied Dudjom Rinpoche, "because I have too many questions to ask him. It would be better if you went alone at some other time."

Dudjom Rinpoche went on to describe Khyentse Rinpoche as the most highly realized master alive. Yet he steadfastly refused to take Trulshik Rinpoche to see him.

Trulshik Rinpoche
Source: Shechen Archives

Later, Trulshik Rinpoche went to Samdrup Phodrang alone to meet Khyentse Rinpoche and to request a teaching so they would make a spiritual connection. Rinpoche agreed to the teaching but added, "I will not be giving any empowerments because I have made a vow."

Phalha Drönyer Chenmo had been an acquaintance and benefactor of Trulshik Rinpoche for some time. He said he wanted to ask Khyentse Chökyi Lodrö to perform a wealth protection ritual for him, and he suggested that Trulshik Rinpoche join him when he made his request.

Rinpoche agreed to do the ritual, and at the appointed time, Trulshik Rinpoche found himself sitting at the head of a row of monks, and Rinpoche sat opposite on a low throne with his attendant monks on either side. Rinpoche was the chant master and also played the cymbals, while a monk with a wispy beard (probably Chokden) beat the drum. By midday, they had performed the sadhana for summoning life-force and wealth three times. As they were about to start a fourth repetition, Rinpoche received a respectful summons from Pomda Tsang: his mother had fallen seriously ill.

"I must go. I know the family well, and it would be entirely inappropriate for me not to respond to their request. They are generous benefactors," he said. "I will return tonight to close the practice. In the meantime, accumulate the ritual."

Rinpoche returned just before dusk and said that although he had given an empowerment, commanded the spirits and the illness to leave the woman's body, driven away obstacles, summoned longevity, and done everything he possibly could, nothing had helped. Two days later, she passed away.

Once the wealth-summoning ritual had been completed, Rinpoche told Trulshik Rinpoche to leave one of his "gho" with the family, as they were an important connection for him.

"La so," replied Trulshik Rinpoche, but he had no idea know what a gho was.

"I myself will leave my shirt here," said Rinpoche. He removed his thick woolen jacket, then took off the silk Khampa shirt he was wearing, folded it neatly, and placed it in the family's treasure chest. Only then did Trulshik Rinpoche realize that a gho was an article of clothing.

During the entrustment of wealth ceremony, Rinpoche gave a long-life empowerment to members of Phalha Tsang and Drönyer Tsang. Surprised, Trulshik Rinpoche reminded Rinpoche that he had vowed not to give any empowerments.

"A vow is a compounded phenomenon," replied Rinpoche, "and, like all compounded phenomena, eventually disintegrates."

The Statue of Guru Rinpoche in Lhasa

When Chökyi Lodrö visited His Holiness the Dalai Lama in Lhasa, he was asked to do a divination to determine the future security of Tibet. The outcome was that above the mandala palace in the Tsuglakhang temple, a one-story-high statue of Guru Nangsi Zilnön should be built facing China, and it should be surrounded by four stupas, one at each corner of the circumambulation path. His Holiness the Dalai Lama immediately commanded the Tibetan government, through Phalha Donyer Chenmo, to build the image and stupas exactly as Chökyi Lodrö had instructed. Tragically, as each member of the government was biased towards a different Dharma tradition, they ignored Khyentse Rinpoche's instructions. Instead, they built a small Indian-style statue of Guru Rinpoche facing India and didn't bother to add the four stupas—they said there was nowhere to put them. Rinpoche heard what they'd done on the eve of his departure for India.

"Ceremonies to avert misfortune do not help if they are not accomplished at the right time," he said. "As they have chosen to build a small, Indian-style Guru Rinpoche facing India instead of a wrathful Guru Rinpoche facing China, Gyalwa Rinpoche and a few lower-ranking lamas might be able to escape to India. Apart from that, such a statue will be of no help to Tibet whatsoever."

According to Tashi Namgyal, Rinpoche's prediction was even written down, yet the Tibetan government still failed to follow his instructions. Their behavior, Rinpoche declared, was not only improper but catastrophically ill-judged.

I have also heard that after some time, a small lotus petal was added to the front of Guru Rinpoche's hat, paid for by Phalha Tsang, as well as a few patches of gold. But that's all I know. I never saw it myself.

His Holiness was very young at the time, and although he was certainly curious about the implications of the prediction, he was unable to take responsibility for ensuring Rinpoche's instructions were carried out. Those who held that responsibility, he said later, had made a very poor job of it, and he deeply regretted their failure. It is believed that this was why the statue of Guru Rinpoche in Zahor clothing at Thekchen Chöling Tsuglakhang in Dharamsala was built and why it faces Tibet. But it was built too late to have any effect.

In the seventies, after Gyalwa Rinpoche had settled in Dharamsala, he often spoke about Rinpoche's prediction and told the Tibetan people publicly on a number of occasions about the gray-haired old lama from Kham who had made it.

Durtö Lhamo
Trulshik Rinpoche visited Rinpoche again and again, and on one occasion asked Rinpoche to consecrate a thangka depicting Durtrö Lhamo in a running posture. On the back of the thangka was written, "Painted by the father, Jigme Dorje, as an object of devotion for his son, Yizhin Ledrup."

"This is incredibly special!" said Rinpoche, as he blessed the thangka. "You must give it to me! I must have it at all costs!"

Khyentse Rinpoche asked Trulshik Rinpoche for the thangka twice, but as Trulshik Rinpoche neither offered it nor uttered a single syllable, Rinpoche returned it to him. Trulshik Tsang still has that thangka.

Trulshik Rinpoche said Chökyi Lodrö never behaved like a high-ranking, high-profile lama and that he circumambulated the Tsuglakhang temple every day, just like all the other pilgrims.

His Holiness the Fourteenth Dalai Lama

Both Pewar Tulku and Tashi Namgyal told me about Rinpoche's pilgrimages, but their versions of some of the stories were slightly different.

Rinpoche requested a meeting with His Holiness the Dalai Lama in Lhasa through Phalha Tsang. The audience took place at the Norbulingka Palace, and Tashi Namgyal, who told me this story, said that he and Rinpoche's other attendants were also allowed into His Holiness's presence. Unfortunately, none of them had expected such an honor, so they hadn't brought any offerings with them. As they waited outside the audience chamber, one of His Holiness's monks gathered up some silver pieces wrapped in a small silk katak. Tashi Namgyal ran over and asked His Holiness's head of protocol if they could borrow three of the silver pieces so that he, Chakdzö, and Chokden didn't have to go in empty-handed.

It was on this occasion that Rinpoche first introduced Khandro to His Holiness as his wisdom consort. His Holiness blessed them all and asked Rinpoche where he was going. Rinpoche replied that he intended to do an elaborate circumambulation of Uru Barkor and to make offerings at Samye and Tradruk. His Holiness said he would command the Kashag to send an attendant to accompany Rinpoche to Tawu—either a tsedrung or a drungkhor.

"No need," replied Rinpoche politely. "I don't want anyone to take me. There's really no need for you to provide me with any kind of assistance."

"Well," said His Holiness, "if you find you need any help, please let me know."

At that time, only Phalha Drönyer Chenmo was allowed to enter His Holiness's residence; his secretary had to wait outside. And it wasn't until they had returned home that Phalha Drönyer Chenmo expressed his amazement and shock at what had just happened.

"This Khampa really is a Khampa, and a stupid one! He is the only person in the world ever to refuse help from His Holiness! He should never have said, 'No need...' He should just have said 'La so,' whether he needed help or not! If he really didn't want any help, he should have let His Holiness know through his lower-ranking officials. As it is, he's effectively *disobeyed* Gyalwa Rinpoche!"

Pewar Tulku spent a great deal of time with Rinpoche in Lhasa. The day Rinpoche left, Pewar Tulku went to see him off, and although he arrived early, he found Rinpoche wrapped in his zen and ready to go.

"Before I leave," said Rinpoche, "I first want to circumambulate the inner pathway of the Jokhang temple."

Rinpoche blessed Pewar Tulku, then rode to the stupa on the other side of Potala Palace. Pewar Tulku said that one of the two government officials attending Rinpoche led his horse. But this is a little difficult to believe because a government official would never stoop to accepting such a task. It was probably someone known to Phalha or the servant of a local official.

"There's no need for you to leave Lhasa too. You should stay here," said Rinpoche. When they reached the stupa, Rinpoche placed his hands on Pewar Tulku's head once more to bless him, then said twice, "Leave your mind at ease! Don't think too much!"

Pewar Tulku said he overheard Rinpoche tell the drungkhor that he was one of the better-educated of Rinpoche's many students. As he spoke, Pewar Tulku began to weep because this was the last time he ever saw Rinpoche.

Sangphu

From Lhasa, Rinpoche's pilgrimage took him to the great Dharma center of Sangphu. Tashi Namgyal said it sat on top of a plateau surrounded by many villages, but when I visited Sangphu, I found it at the upper end of the valley and didn't see any villages.

"Sangphu is the source of many great panditas," said Rinpoche. "No other Dharma center in the Land of Snows has ever produced such distinguished or learnèd scholars. Therefore, today the auspicious circumstances are considerable. We should hold a debate. I will be the defender!"

He looked around for a worthy opponent. His eye settled on Gönpo Tseten, who, unlike most of the other attendants, had at least studied a little philosophy. Rinpoche sat on a thick cushion, then, as stipulated by the Tibetan rules of debate, Gönpo Tseten advanced towards him as he put forward various dialectic questions. Rinpoche answered faultlessly, then proceeded to point out the flaws in Gönpo Tseten's original argument. Delighted, Gönpo Tseten took this as a sign that Rinpoche was unable to refute his premise. He jumped up and down with his zen wrapped around his waist, shouting that Rinpoche had fallen into the "three spheres of self-contradiction" and had therefore been defeated. Rinpoche laughed and laughed, clapping his hands and encouraging Gönpo Tseten by saying, "And then?" and "You are becoming such a great scholar!" until his knees buckled under him, and he fell to the ground.

Mindrolling Monastery

Khochen Rinpoche told me that having agreed to visit Mindrolling Monastery, Rinpoche was received in the most elaborate style possible by all the lamas and monks, including the Eighth Minling Khenchen and Minling Chung Rinpoche. From the great stupa, Rinpoche was escorted to the main temple, placed on the throne, and offered a mandala and the representations of body, speech, and mind. He was then invited to the empowerment hall, where he granted the complete transmission of the *Four Parts of Nyingtik*. Trulshik Rinpoche said Khyentse Rinpoche didn't give the transmission of the *Heart Essence of the Dakinis* at that time, but Khochen Rinpoche has always insisted that he gave the entire *Four Parts of Nyingtik*.

The Eighth Minling Khenchen and Chung Rinpoche
Source: Shechen Archives

(Khochen Rinpoche said Trulshik Rinpoche didn't get the *Heart Essence of the Dakinis* because he left early.) Rinpoche also gave Dungsey Rinpoche of Mindrolling, Khenchen Rinpoche, Chung Rinpoche, and a few tulkus the empowerments, reading transmissions and instructions for the *Heart Essence of Chetsün* and Jamgön Kongtrul's *The Drop that Embodies All Secrets*, using Minling Khenchen's commentary. He stayed at Mindrolling for a long time.

One day, Mindrolling Monastery offered Rinpoche a tenshuk. About forty senior monks at Mindrolling Tsang were qualified to wear the six red and saffron ornaments of a disciplinarian. These were the monks who practiced the long-life sadhana of *Gathering of the Innermost Essence: A Long-Life Practice* in the empowerment hall at Chökhor Lhünpo. The hall had once been the labrang of Terdak Lingpa, and during the tenshuk, Rinpoche was invited to sit on Terdak Lingpa's actual empowerment throne.

Although Chokden and Tashi Namgyal sat inconspicuously in a corner of the hall, their chanting was unmistakable. Not only were they out of tune with the extremely disciplined and well-trained Mindrolling monks, they couldn't even keep up. And when tea was served, their vulgar guzzling and slurping reverberated throughout the hall.

After lunch, as they walked back to the residence, Rinpoche said to Chokden, "I expected more of you."

I asked Tashi Namgyal what the monastery had offered Rinpoche. "Nothing useful," he said, but he didn't know any details. At that time, most of Rinpoche's wealth and belongings were stored in the residence of Minling Khenchen. Mindrolling Monastery had tremendous devotion for Rinpoche because both he and Jamyang Khyentse Wangpo had received their full monk's ordination there. The Khyentse tulkus have a very strong historical connection with Mindrolling Monastery.

Dorje Drak Monastery

The reception that greeted Rinpoche when he visited Dorje Drak Monastery was very grand. During his time there, Rinpoche gave empowerments, visited sacred sites, and paid his respects to all the representations of body, speech, and mind in all the temples. He also visited the retreat cave of Dordrak Rigdzin Chenpo Ngagi Wangpo on the hill above the monastery. At the center of a fenced-in courtyard inside one of the temples, he found a dark red statue of Chemchok Heruka with twenty-one heads and forty-two arms in union with a nine-headed consort. When he asked what it was, Dordrak Rigdzin Chenpo said it was the elaborate Kagye mandala that Nyang Rinpoche had revealed. Rinpoche was amazed and not a little shocked by it.

"This is truly extraordinary!" he said. "Lakar Tsang used to own a similar mandala—they gave it to Dzogchen Monastery. But this one is even more incredible."

He immediately sat down on the bare ground in front of the statue and chanted a prayer, but no one could hear well enough to say which one.

Rinpoche spent two days at Dorje Drak. As he was about to leave, Dordrak Rigdzin Chenpo brought the Kagye statue wrapped in a katak (a monk brought its lotus seat), saying that the monastery wanted to offer it to him.

"Is that appropriate?" asked Rinpoche. "Adzi! Is it really a good idea to give me such a precious image?"

Dordrak Rigdzin told Rinpoche that the labrang of Dorje Drak and all the chant masters and disciplinarians of the monastery had had a meeting the previous night, during which it was decided that, as the vajradhara had been so gracious as to visit their monastery in person, their greatest wish was to offer what had delighted him the most. Rinpoche was stunned.

"Adzi, adzi, adzi!" he exclaimed. "This is so very precious. It's really quite unbelievable!" And as he spoke, those present say the wings of the statue quivered.

The eight devas, eight nagas, and eight main animals were removed from the lotus seat and wrapped in woolen cloth offered by Mindrolling and Tsethang, and the mandala was packed in two loads. It was then added to Rinpoche's luggage, which was made up of the purchases he had made in Lhasa and things of his that had been sent from the main Sakya monastery. A total of about 125 loads of material goods was then left in the care of Minling Khenchen. Rinpoche must have felt very close to him, and Khenchen must also have had great devotion for Rinpoche.

Tsurphu Monastery

Meeting the Sixteenth Karmapa

This is Tulku Urgyen's account of Chökyi Lodrö's visit to Tsurphu Monastery, where he met the Sixteenth Karmapa.

Rinpoche arrived at Tsurphu to a rather ordinary reception. Every day throughout his stay, he visited each and every temple and residence in the monastery, and the Karmapa sent one of his own teachers, Tulku Urgyen,

The Sixteenth Karmapa in the 1960s
Source: Khyentse Labrang

to help and guide him. But the Karmapa himself did not once accompany Rinpoche as he toured the monastery, not even to the temple closest to his home.

"This family!" said Rinpoche to Tulku Urgyen. "The power and wealth of the Karmapa is inconceivable."

One day, as he roamed around the monastery, Rinpoche caught sight of an old bamboo basket covered with a tiger skin so worn and rotten that it was virtually unrecognizable. The basket contained a pair of cymbals, which Rinpoche asked to see. Tulku Urgyen said that if the basket opened easily, then of course Rinpoche could look immediately, but if it was secured in any way, it would be better to check with Yishin Norbu before opening it. As the basket had been nailed shut, the Karmapa was consulted. He said, "Do whatever you want. Open the basket, by all means." So the basket was opened the next day.

"Katok Monastery has some cymbals like these," said Rinpoche, the moment he set eyes on them. "Otherwise I don't think another such pair can be found in the whole of Kham!" And he placed the cymbals on his head as he chanted supplication and aspiration prayers. As Rinpoche had recognized extraordinary qualities in these cymbals, the monks looked into their history and discovered that they had once belonged to Karmapa Chödrak Gyatso.

Directing Blessings Properly

The Karmapa invited Chökyi Lodrö to lunch one day, but they talked only of ordinary things, not the Dharma. Karmapa asked Rinpoche about the gao he was wearing, and Rinpoche explained that it contained Kutsab Ngödrup Palbar and various Chokling relics. The Karmapa asked for a blessing, so Rinpoche placed the gao on his head and chanted something—most likely the Seven-Line Prayer.

"Ah! No! Not like that! Blessing me like that won't help at all. You are not directing your mind. Please, bless me by directing your mind towards me properly, with good intentions. And make good aspirations!"

"What do you want from me?" exclaimed Rinpoche. Then he raised the gao, circled it once, and placed it on the Karmapa's head.

"Wo!" said the Karmapa, feeling the difference immediately. "You are a realized lama with great meditative experience. Just as a lama should be! Now I am satisfied."

Tulku Urgyen said nothing more about the empowerments and transmissions Rinpoche offered the Karmapa.

Receiving an Empowerment from a Woman

During Rinpoche's stay at Tsurphu, he received empowerments from the Karmapa, but the Karmapa did not receive any teachings from Rinpoche. Instead, he invited Rinpoche to watch birds with him, or sports, or to go on picnics.

One day, Rinpoche received a visit from Khandro Chenmo (Khandro Orgyen Tsomo[35]), consort of the Fifteenth Karmapa Khakyab Dorje. Rinpoche instantly prostrated to her, and she prostrated to him. Rinpoche instructed Tashi Namgyal and his other attendants to prostrate to her too. Rinpoche told Khandro Chenmo that more than anything he wanted to receive the empowerment for one of Jamgön Khakhyab Dorje's treasure teachings. Would she give it to him? Khandro said she had never given an empowerment before. But Rinpoche insisted.

"There's no escape! I didn't ever meet Khakhyab Dorje in person, but I have now met you, and for me there is no difference," he said.

Khandro said that Rinpoche should ask for the present Karmapa's permission. If he agreed, she would do it. When Tulku Urgyen told the Karmapa about Rinpoche's enthusiastic request to receive an empowerment from Khandro, he was shocked.

"Ha! A lama who receives empowerments from a *woman*!"

Tulku Urgyen explained that Rinpoche was so eager to receive this particular empowerment that yes, he was even prepared to receive it from a woman. So Karmapa granted his permission, and Rinpoche received the empowerment. Tulku Urgyen must have received it too, but the Karmapa himself appeared to deplore the idea. Rinpoche believed Khandro Chenmo to be a very special, very spiritual person.

I asked Tashi Namgyal if he knew whether or not Tulku Urgyen's story was true. He said yes, it was perfectly true. To his knowledge, there were only three women to whom Rinpoche had prostrated. At Nenang Monastery, he prostrated to the old consort of the previous incarnation of Nenang Pawo. He probably didn't receive any empowerments from her, but he did receive a teaching as a way of making a strong spiritual connection between them. Samten Dorje Phagmo[36] was another—Tashi Namgyal and Rinpoche's other attendants also received the empowerment. And Khandro Chenmo, as I've already mentioned.

Drongsar Draknam and Tulku Urgyen

At Tsurphu, Tulku Urgyen quickly realized that Rinpoche was an extraordinary master and made a special effort to receive empowerments from him. Unfortunately, although he very much wanted to, he was unable to receive teachings or pith instructions or to ask for clarification about his own meditation and practice. He particularly wanted to clarify his understanding of the Dzogchen teachings with Rinpoche, but Drongsar Draknam had prevented him from doing so.

Drongsar Draknam had been given a room by the staircase that led up to Rinpoche's rooms. Tulku Urgyen's room was a little farther away, and whenever he went to see Rinpoche, he had no choice but to walk past Drongsar Draknam's door. But each time he walked by, Drongsar Draknam would dart out of his room and pester Tulku Urgyen with provocative questions. Is Avalokiteshvara a male or female deity? What kind of being is Manjushri? That kind of question. All of which prevented Tulku Urgyen from going into Rinpoche's room to clarify his Dzogchen practice. Tulku

Tulku Urgyen in the 1950s
Source: Erik Pema Kunsang

Urgyen said that Drongsar Draknam had caused him unimaginable harm by obstructing him in this way—more harm than any other human being in this world had ever caused another.

Tulku Urgyen remained at Tsurphu because Karmapa commanded it, but nothing much happened, just a black hat ceremony, picnics, parties, and performances of Tibetan opera. The Karmapa never once mentioned anything about empowerments or teachings.

Later, when Tulku Urgyen first arrived in Sikkim, he found a room in Banyak village where, quite by chance, Rinpoche was also staying. So Tulku Urgyen was finally able to present Rinpoche with all his meditative experiences and realizations. Rinpoche, he said, had then given him all the necessary instructions and clarifications, including the pith instructions for the essential teaching of Samantabhadra[37] based on the root terma and a word-for-word explanation of the text. And once he had received these instructions, he said, his mind was at peace. "If I had not seen Rinpoche at that time, I would never have received the pith instructions."

Drakmar Drinzang

Tashi Namgyal told me that at Drakmar Drinzang, Rinpoche visited a pit in which the dried-out roots of a dead tree marked the spot where Trisong Deutsen was believed to have been born. As he sat near the stump chanting prayers, he said, more than once, "This tree would live again if only its roots were watered. Where can I get some water?"

The caretaker of the temple, who was a woman, brought a bucket of water, and Rinpoche himself watered the tree's roots while making fervent aspirations. Unable to control his unruly tongue, Tashi Namgyal muttered, "How can a tree grow from dead roots?" Rinpoche's eyes flashed instant displeasure, but he said nothing. Tashi Namgyal knew he'd gone too far.

After Rinpoche settled in Sikkim, Tashi Namgyal went back to Khamje to release stipends for the monks of Khamje Shedra. By this time, his brother had been killed by the Communist Chinese and had left Tashi Namgyal all his money, which he used to go on a pilgrimage, just as Rinpoche had. This was how, about a year after Rinpoche's visit to Drakmar Drinzang, Tashi Namgyal found himself there once more, and he was astounded to see that not only was the tree alive, it had grown quite tall and was covered in green leaves.

"Ah! It's always a mistake to doubt Rinpoche. That tree only started growing again because of his aspirations!"

Yarlung Zorthang

After Rinpoche left Drakmar Drinzang, he traveled to Yarlung Zorthang, where the first-ever field had been cultivated, banishing famine from Tibet for good. The moment they arrived, Rinpoche commanded Tashi Namgyal to "fill a sack full of earth and bring it to me." He then scrutinized Tashi Namgyal's every move as he emptied one of the sacks he was carrying and filled it with earth. Rinpoche left the earth in the care of Minling Khenchen at Mindrolling.

The Kudung of Yarje Orgyen Lingpa

From Yarlung Zorthang, Rinpoche visited Lhodrak Phenzang and other nearby sacred sites to make offerings. At Lhodrak Phenzang, Rinpoche discovered he was running out of dütsi and said he wanted to perform a drupchen and mendrup near the sacred body of Yarje Orgyen Lingpa. He had bought all the necessary substances in Lhasa, he said, and if he didn't seize this opportunity to make some more dütsi now, visiting and viewing the sacred body of Orgyen Lingpa might prove difficult. Officially, no one was permitted to see the kudung, but Rinpoche was determined.

Dilgo Khyentse told me that a letter of command written in verse by the great Thirteenth Dalai Lama, Thubten Gyatso, had been pasted to a wall near the kudung. I tried to find out what was in that letter for a long time but only succeeded quite recently, when I finally managed to visit Phenzang myself. The letter is still there, exactly as Dilgo Khyentse described it:

> A lama from Kham called Jamyang Khyentse (Wangpo) took a large chunk of flesh from the body of Orgyen Lingpa, which he claimed as a blessing. Later, another lama also removed a lump of flesh and took it away with him. Since then, no one has been allowed to see the kudung, because the sudden and unexpected removal of its flesh is harmful to the well-being of Tibet.

At Orgyen Lingpa's monastery, Rinpoche was offered a room on the top floor. He then performed the drupchen and mendrup based on the *Ocean of Dharma That Combines All Teachings* in the monastery's assembly hall. There were only about thirty monks in the monastery at that time and many small children. Chokden was the official chant master, although Rinpoche took over from time to time. The nuns of Lakar Tsang also took part, and Tsewang Paljor joined in every so often.

One evening, as they mixed the dütsi ingredients in preparation for the mendrup ritual, Rinpoche asked the elderly caretaker, who was also one of the most senior monks, where they kept the kudung.

"I want to see the sacred kudung," he said, "and I want to receive blessings from it."

"If the Tibetan government finds out you've been allowed to see it, our hands will be chopped off!" exclaimed the monk. But he lacked the courage to beg Rinpoche not to remove flesh from the kudung. Instead, he suggested that Rinpoche read the Thirteenth Dalai Lama's letter, which he did.

"Don't worry, nothing terrible will happen if you show me the kudung," said Rinpoche. "I am more than willing to risk the wrath of the Tibetan government."

The monks took him to the room where the kudung was kept. The base of the reliquary was made of clay, and the wooden dome and upper part were shaped like a milk can. White, yellow, red, and green silk threads had been woven together over the whole thing, each sealed with an official stamp. Rinpoche directed his attendants to open the reliquary. Tsewang Paljor removed the seals and pulled aside the threads. As he was about to take down the dome, Rinpoche said, "No need! No need!" So first they removed the Dharma wheel and only then lifted the dome to reveal the sacred body.

The kudung was wrapped in cloth. Rinpoche felt a thigh. "Khyentse Wangpo must have cut his chunk of flesh from here," he said. "It's been patched up." He then cut himself a chunk of flesh from the other thigh, ate a thumb-size piece, and gave some to each of his attendants. He also added some to the dütsi he had just made, then rewrapped the kudung and returned it to its reliquary. He didn't say much after that, but people say that rainbow-colored lights were seen to dissolve into the copper urn that contained the dütsi.

The Thirteenth Dalai Lama Thubten Gyatso's letter was preserved when the monastery was renovated, but the kudung is no longer there. Accounts of the pure vision of Orgyen Lingpa experienced by Rinpoche at this time, and the prophecies he received, are mentioned in the *Secret Biography*.

Namkhai Nyingpo

Next, Rinpoche traveled to Lhodrak with the intention of visiting Kharchu Phukring. When he heard Rinpoche was in the area, the previous Namkhai Nyingpo immediately sent an invitation asking Rinpoche to spend two or three days at his labrang in Palgyi Phukring—"to relax," he said. I don't know if Rinpoche and Namkhai Nyingpo had a close friendship before that visit, but they must at least have heard about each other. Rinpoche accepted the invitation but stayed for only one day. And far from relaxing, he ended up presiding with Namkhai Nyingpo over the ganachakra of the *Sadhana of the Lineage of Awareness Holders* from the *Northern Treasures*, according to the practice tradition of the great Fifth Dalai Lama. Just before receiving the siddhi, Rinpoche said that as it was such an auspicious day, a Tsok Lu should be sung, and so he sang one; although Namkhai Nyingpo's singing voice wasn't up to much, he also sang the *Lemön Tendrel* very loudly. Namkhai Nyingpo offered Rinpoche everything he could afford.

The Bones of Sangye Lingpa

Rinpoche continued his travels accompanied by Yongdzin Chöying Rangdrol, an attendant of the present Namkhai Nyingpo Yangsi of Lhodrak.

Rinpoche said he wanted to visit a particular monastery, but when they arrived, it looked more like a ngagpa's house than a monastery. Inside the house stood a wooden stupa, which Rinpoche examined carefully.

"What is in this stupa?" he asked.

"The reliquary of a great treasure revealer from Kongpo called Sangye Lingpa," came the reply.

"Does the reliquary contain his kudung or other relics?" asked Rinpoche.

"No one knows exactly, but most people think it contains the kudung."

Rinpoche circumambulated the stupa, saying how very holy it was. He pressed the crown of his head against it and made prayers of aspiration.

Rinpoche slept that night in a monastery at the lower end of the valley. The following morning, he told Yongdzin that he wanted to return to the stupa of Sangye Lingpa.

"I have something to say to you," said Rinpoche to the owner of the monastery. "I want you to agree to remove the kudung from your home and to build a stupa for it over there. I'll give you the money and do all the necessary rituals for subjugating, acquiring, and blessing the land. But please, take the kudung out of your house."

As none of the family said anything at all, Rinpoche instructed his attendants to dig the kudung out, whether the owner agreed or not. As the stupa was falling apart, the stone slabs that represented the thirteen Dharma wheels were easy to remove and revealed a large wooden barrel containing the complete set of bones of a cremated body. Although the bones must originally have been clothed, the material had rotted away, and only a few threads remained; on top of the bones lay an extremely fat plait of hair. Rinpoche confirmed that the bones and hair had been Sangye Lingpa's and took them into his care for safekeeping. He then promised to return the next day to perform rituals and bless the land, and he asked the family to bring something to represent a golden drink—which they did, but it stank.

During the ritual, Rinpoche cast the phurba he usually kept at his waist into the middle of the new site and instructed the family to build the stupa precisely on that spot. He offered them many silver coins to pay for its construction and then left.

In his travel journal, the one with Mao's picture in it, Rinpoche wrote,

> I saw the sacred body of Sangye Lingpa and had a vision of him. That night I went to the lower end of the valley, then returned the next day to receive a small share of siddhi from the bones and hair[38] that had not been consumed by the cremation fire. I performed the ritual for blessing the land and offered money to pay for the construction of a new stupa.

Tashi Namgyal and Yongdzin, Namkhai Nyingpo's attendant, both told me this story.

Khyentse Labrang still has a large quantity of bones that are said to be those of Sangye Lingpa. Yongdzin gave a few to the present Neten Chokling Tulku, because the previous Neten Chokling had been one of his special friends.

Nyenchen Thanglha

Rinpoche then traveled to Damzhung for three days' rest. He had a good view of Nyenchen Thanglha from his room and asked his attendants to make elaborate tormas for a smoke-offering ritual to the local deities—"and buy two white yaks."

Acquiring the yaks was far from easy, but eventually they managed it. Chakdzö, Tselu, and Khandro plaited white, yellow, red, and green silk threads into the animals' coats to make them look stripy, and the following day, Rinpoche performed an elaborate smoke offering to the local deities. (It must have been from the *Heart Practice for Dispelling All Obstacles*, because that's the only text that includes such an offering.) As they offered tormas, Rinpoche shot a gun into the air several times, shouting, "Ki ki so so lha gyal lo!" and the yaks cantered up the mountain.

A nomad couple who lived near Damchok Tsela visited Sikkim some time later, and Tashi Namgyal was able to ask them about the yaks. They told him that yes, two white yaks had joined their herd for a while but had suddenly returned to the mountain. This couple were still alive when the People's Liberation Army invaded Tibet but said they didn't know what the Chinese Communists had done with the yaks.

PILGRIMAGE FROM DERGE TO SIKKIM — 215

Sakya Gongma of Dolma Phodrang, His Holiness Sakya Trizin, at age eleven, returning from a pilgrimage to India. Tromo, southern Tibet, 1956.
Photograph by Jetsun Sakya Kushola, reprinted courtesy of Sakya Dolma Phodrang

Sakya Monastery

While Rinpoche was in Lhasa, Sakya Gongma of Phuntsok Phodrang (Sakya Dagchen Rinpoche) asked Rinpoche to visit his home first when he next came to Sakya.

"As I have received empowerments from Sakya Gongma of Phuntsok Phodrang," Rinpoche explained, "it would be improper for me not to do as he asks. So I'll visit Phuntsok Phodrang Tsang first, then I'll go on to Drolma Phodrang Tsang (His Holiness Sakya Trizin)."

Just as Rinpoche was about to leave Lhasa, he discovered that Sakya Gongma of Phuntsok Phodrang hadn't yet left for Sakya. Sensing a potential conflict in protocol, the day before Rinpoche reached Phuntsok Phodrang

Tsang, Drolma Phodrang (and the young Sakya Trizin) left for a hot spring near Khau Drak Dzong.

As Sakya Gongma was still in Lhasa, there were only four senior attendants in residence when Rinpoche arrived. Nevertheless, they slaughtered a yak to ensure there was plenty of meat for Rinpoche, and also gave some to Tashi Namgyal and the other attendants. Rinpoche remained there for about a week with nothing to do.

As the throne holder of the Sakya lineage, Sakya Gongma of Drolma Phodrang (His Holiness Sakya Trizin) returned to Sakya Gong in a palanquin with a parasol. Rinpoche knew of Drolma Phodrang's arrival but was careful not to visit until he received a formal invitation. Drolma Phodrang Tsang is close to Lhasa, and although Sakya Gongma of Phuntsok Phodrang was staying nearby, he did not go there to meet Rinpoche. It's been suggested that he stayed away to avoid receiving empowerments alongside Sakya Gongma of Drolma Phodrang. Whatever the reason, Rinpoche did not meet Sakya Gongma of Phuntsok Phodrang at Sakya Gong.

At Drolma Phodrang, Rinpoche bumped into Khenpo Rinchen as he was hurrying to an appointment.

"What are you doing here?" asked Rinpoche.

"Serving as the ritual monk at Drolma Phodrang," explained Khenpo. "It is my job to recite the *Prajnaparamita Sutra* and Tara prayers."

Rinpoche was appalled and remonstrated with him vigorously.

"What will you achieve by performing family rituals? Dagchen Rinpoche (the present Sakya Trizin) is growing up. It's high time he began his studies. You should be offering him teachings. Why aren't you?"

"La so!" sighed Khenpo Rinchen, scratching his head. "No one's asked me to. Until they ask, I can do nothing."

"I'll talk to them," said Rinpoche firmly. "You should be teaching Dagchen Rinpoche philosophy, not wasting your time like this."

Rinpoche left Khenpo to circumambulate the great Trulpe Lhakhang. Then he went to see Dagchen Rinpoche's mother. Although I have no firsthand reports of their conversation—Tashi Namgyal and his other attendants were not with him—Rinpoche must have spoken to her about Dagchen Rinpoche's education, because the next day, Khenpo Rinchen visited Rinpoche wearing a magnificent new wool coat. Rinpoche asked him why he was wearing such a splendid outfit. Dagmo Kusho had given it to him, said Khenpo, and Rinpoche felt sure she must have accompanied the gift with instructions about teaching Dagchen Rinpoche philosophy. By then Khenpo had already spent quite some time in Sakya and would remain there for a further seven years.

Butter Lamp Offerings

For twenty days after Rinpoche's arrival at Sakya, people flocked to see him. They made many offerings, including an enormous quantity of butter, which the monks melted and used to fuel the butter lamps that burnt day and night. Yet, however much butter was poured into the lamps, they never managed to use up all that had been offered. Not wanting to waste any, the monks poured the leftovers into large leather sacks, but a little carelessly, and great pools of butter appeared all over the place. Determined not to waste a drop, the monks inserted wicks into the butter ponds and lit them to make even more light offerings. The butter lamps burnt so intensely that they fully heated the inner chamber of Lhakhang Chenmo (the great Sakya Temple). Khenpo Rinchen said he had been moved to tears by the merit and splendor of this extraordinary lama, Khyentse Chökyi Lodrö.

When Rinpoche had first arrived, the butter lamps, incense holders, and water offering bowls in Trulpe Lhakhang and the upper and lower temples had been so filthy that he instructed the monks to wash and clean them all. He even went into the temples himself to help, taking his attendants with him. I heard all about it from Khenpo Rinchen.

Gyado Pills and Statues

Tashi Namgyal told me that during his visit to Sakya Gongma Drolma Phodrang, Rinpoche blessed the place with substances that he kept in a three-layered offering container,[39] and that he visited each of the temples to pay his respects to all the holy representations.

In one of the temples, Rinpoche came across a large bookcase draped with a dark red brocade curtain. Pulling the brocade aside, he found a mask wrapped in scarves of various colors and filled with pills. Rinpoche asked what the pills were for, and the monks replied that they were the basis for the gyado pills used in rituals.

"If they remain in the mask like this, they will go soft," said Rinpoche. "May I have a few?" And he helped himself to half a dozen.

On the other side of the room stood a great many shining statues of Gur Mahakala, Zhal, and Palden Lhamo, as well as the molds from which they had been cast. Rinpoche pointed out a few of the statues, saying he wanted to receive them as blessings. He must have taken fifty or sixty away with him.

The Heretic's Hair

Next, Rinpoche spotted a long-haired human head hanging upside down above the wooden ornaments over the door of Trulpe Lhakhang.

"What's that?" he asked.

"The head of the Hindu heretic Trokje Gawo," replied the monks.

"Ha!" exclaimed Rinpoche. "I need a few strands of his hair. Let me have some as a blessing."

The monks had a terrible time trying to scale the wall to reach the head, but having finally secured it, Rinpoche pulled out three or four strands of hair. Tsewang Paljor couldn't imagine what Rinpoche needed the hair for, so he asked him.

"Ha!" exclaimed Rinpoche. "Did you just ask why I need a heretic's hair?"

"La so," replied Tsewang Paljor.

"Heretic's hair is used for averting heretic sorcery. None of the heretics alive today can fly, but Trokje Gawo could! He flew high into the sky. And his hair is the supreme protection."

Nyakrong and Sernya

Rinpoche visited all the protectors' halls at Sakya Gongma Drolma Phodrang, where he made money offerings and scattered blessed rice as he recited aspiration prayers and requested that the protectors secure the lives of the great masters and safeguard the teachings of Buddha.

In a gallery adjoining the protectors' hall dedicated to Tsimara were two pillars. On one hung the figure of a man in a large, fringed, Derge-style turban adorned with a circular coral design, striped trousers, and a red brocade chuba. He looked like a scarecrow, except that from his waist hung a sword in a gilded sheath.

"Who is this?" asked Rinpoche.

"The protector of the teachings from Nyakrong," came the reply.

"Who exactly is the Nyakrong protector?" asked Rinpoche.

"Nyakrong Dorje Gönpo," said the monks.

"Ah ha! Is this Bu Sharma?" exclaimed Rinpoche.

"Yes," they replied.

"So the main Sakya monastery was propitiating malevolent spirits and demons, was it?" muttered Rinpoche, and he threw some rice at the protector.

On the other pillar hung the figure of a majestic-looking monk in robes, wearing his hat the wrong way around. Rinpoche asked who it was.

"Sernya," replied the monks.

Rinpoche tossed rice at it, saying, "Isn't that the demon of a dead person?" Then he turned south and walked away. He made no offerings to either figure, nor did he entrust them with any activities.

Some years later, I spoke with the monks about the two figures, and they said Nyakrong and Sernya had been given to Pomda Tsang as their protectors. Pomda had been a high-ranking government official and prominent businessman, and although he was born in Markham, he settled in Lhasa. At the height of Pomda Tsang's wealth, elaborate figures of those two protectors were made and displayed in the gallery. Nyakrong and Sernya were bound by oath by one of the Sakya Gongmas, and it looks as though back then, subjugated demons were given to Sakya monasteries and the nobility as protectors.

Rinpoche sat by the Dharma throne on which Sakya Pandita had composed his commentary on the *Ascertainment of the Three Types of Vow* and chanted some prayers. He then dug a chunk of mud out of the wall of the monastery and went to Khau Drak Dzong, where he appeased the Dharma protectors. I think he also visited some standing rocks and trees nearby that he believed to be sacred; and he took a number of stones away with him, some of which are now in the Bir labrang.

Offerings Made to Rinpoche

Sakya Monastery offered Rinpoche a phurba and many other objects, but nothing very valuable and not much gold or silver. In Tibet, according to Tsejor, Queen Yudrön probably offered Rinpoche a great deal personally, but apart from that, Nangchen Tsang didn't make unusually large offerings or give Rinpoche anything of exceptional quality. Kings and high-ranking lamas seem to fare badly when it comes to the quality and quantity of offerings they make to great masters.

Lhodrak Kharchu

By the time Rinpoche visited Lhodrak Kharchu, His Holiness the Dalai Lama had already recognized Thuksey Rinpoche as the reincarnation of Peling Thuksey of Lhalung. However, Lhalung Monastery had been reluctant to enthrone him because the divination they requested from Mindrolling had predicted that the authentic reincarnation would be born near the monastery. Rinpoche surprised and shocked everyone when he pointed at one of six monks walking down a flight of stairs and said that he was, without doubt, the tulku of Lhalung Thuksey.

"Who was that young monk?" I asked.

"Lopön Tseten," replied Tashi Namgyal. Lopön Tseten is the present abbot of Tamshing Monastery in Bumthang, Bhutan. Tashi Namgyal told me this story during a walk we took with the Lopön, who immediately said that we should not talk of such things.

Longchenpa's Skull

Rinpoche visited all the holy places in Lhodrak Kharchu. At Lhalung, Rinpoche asked to be shown the skull of Gyalwa Longchen Rabjam because, he said, he wanted to receive a blessing from it. He then borrowed Tsewang Paljor's knife, sliced off a large chunk of bone, and took it away with him. Later, Lopön Tseten told me that the monks hadn't shown Rinpoche the real skull because they were afraid he'd confiscate the whole thing.

Tsang

Once he arrived in Tsang, Rinpoche insisted on visiting a very poor village, even though his attendants assured him that there was nothing holy there at all, just a pack of stray dogs. The attendants were mystified. Why was Rinpoche so determined to go to such a place?

Once they'd arrived, Rinpoche purposefully avoided the only relatively rich households in the area and instead walked into an extremely old and dilapidated house. On the top floor, he found an elderly woman and her daughter—the rest of the family were probably working—and asked to be shown the family's holy images. "I long to see them!" he said. His request dumbfounded the elderly woman, but eventually she admitted that the family did indeed own a few statues. Rinpoche asked to see a statue of Guru Padma, if they had one, and she brought him a Guru Rinpoche that was about an arm's length in height. Did she know the history of this image? No, she didn't. All she knew was that it was very precious.

"I know its story," said Rinpoche. He went on to explain its background in some detail, but Tashi Namgyal couldn't remember a single word. Rinpoche used the statue to give Chakdzö and the other attendants an empowerment, then recited prayers of aspiration for a long time. The village where this happened turned out to be the home of the mother of Kangyur Tsang.

Benpa Chakdor

Next, Rinpoche traveled to Benpa Chakdor. In a monastery on the mountain above Drul Tso Pema Ling, he found two statues of Vajrapani, one large and one small. Rinpoche did not comment on the larger statue but, pointing to a hole beneath the foot of the smaller one, said, "A yellow scroll has been taken from this hole. This is an exceptional image! Wherever it is kept, it will prevent nagas and kshetrapalas from inflicting harm." Rinpoche sniffed the statue, then blessed everyone with it.

I bought a statue in Lhasa when I went to Tibet with Tashi Namgyal, and he confirmed it was the very same Vajrapani that Rinpoche had gone to Benpa Chakdor to see.

During Rinpoche's visit to Sekhar Guthok,[40] he offered tea to the old women and nuns who were living there. Then, with the help of Khyentse Wangpo's pilgrimage guide, he traveled to Lingbu Monastery. From there, the whole party turned around and made for Sikkim. This is all I have to say about Rinpoche's pilgrimage in Tibet.

16. Dzongsar after Khyentse Chökyi Lodrö Left for India

The Execution

Rinpoche took all the labrang attendants to India with him, including Tashi Namgyal, Gelu Chime, and Tsering Wangpo. Yenchokma, who like me was born in Nangchen, was appointed as the new manager of Dzongsar Monastery and remained in that job until the Cultural Revolution in Tibet. An old lama from Tsang called Sakya Lama was given the job of taking care of Rinpoche's residence and labrang. He had come to Dzongsar from the main Sakya monastery to receive the *Path and Fruition* transmissions and many other teachings from Rinpoche, then spent the rest of his life at Karmo Tak Tsang and Pema Shelphuk. He had tremendous devotion for Rinpoche. My uncle Orgyen was appointed as their secretary, just in case they needed help writing up lists or notes.

After Rinpoche and his party set out for India, the first thing Drungyig Tsering did was travel to Shechen Monastery, where he offered his services to Shechen Rabjam. He took novice ordination not long after, because he quickly realized that if he was wearing robes as he accompanied Shechen Rabjam on his travels, he would not want for offerings. This, I've been told, was his main reason for taking ordination; in every other respect, he was definitely not an authentic monk. Three months later, he returned to Dzongsar.

Drungyig Tsering and my uncle Orgyen were not just neighbors, they also liked each other very much. After Rinpoche left, Drungyig Tsering heard about the Chinese suppression of Tibetans at Derge Gönchen on the other side of the river. Then one evening, as he and Uncle Orgyen enjoyed a cup of ara, he said, "Tomorrow I will follow Rinpoche to India. I must warn you, *don't* go to the labrang anymore or claim any responsibility for it. If you do, there's only one place you'll end up! But if you never go there again, you won't come to any harm. You're not the heroic type, are you?"

Uncle Orgyen took his warning seriously and stopped going to the labrang. From then on, Yenchokma and Sakya Lama took sole responsibility for it, which is why they were both arrested and imprisoned by the Chinese Communists. As Gongna Tulku and Ngari Tulku had also left Dzongsar, the Communists decided to convict the main nyerpa of Gongna Tulku's labrang and Yenchokma for committing offenses against the Chinese. The two men were brutally beaten, and the Menshö community in Derge was herded into Khamje Shedra's courtyard to watch as long wooden signs detailing their crimes were hung across their shoulders. They were then led away at gunpoint to be executed.

On the way to the execution site, the Nyerpa whispered to Yenchokma, "Ya! Khorey! Now's the time to say your prayers! If you don't, today's the day they'll finish us off."

"Oh ya," replied Yenchokma.

At the river, the soldiers ordered the two men to kneel down. They both obeyed and closed their eyes. The Nyerpa heard a shot ring out. Knowing he was next, he braced himself for the bullet. But nothing happened. Suddenly he was kicked very hard. "Go! Go!" shouted one of the Communists. The Nyerpa opened his eyes and saw Yenchokma's body lying in a lifeless heap on the ground beside him, and to his amazement, the corpse was radiating white light.[41] Looking around, he could see that he wasn't the only one to see the light, and he learnt later that the Chinese soldiers and everyone gathered on the opposite side of the river to witness the killings had all seen the light enter Yenchokma's body at exactly the same moment as the bullet.

Sakya Lama

Sakya Lama, the nyerpa of Gongna Tulku's labrang, and Shechen Rabjam were all imprisoned by the Chinese Communists. Throughout his time in prison, Sakya Lama only ate as much food as he could hold in one hand. The rest he threw away.

"I don't want to eat," he said. "But to die of hunger is not auspicious as it breaks the samayas of the secret mantrayana."

The Communists were eager to discover where the wealth of Dzongsar Monastery and Khyentse Labrang was hidden, but however viciously they tortured him, Sakya Lama would tell them nothing. He was like a rock.

When he called on his master, Dorje Chang, the beatings became more savage. And although he was specifically ordered never to speak that name, he kept repeating it over and over again: "Dorje Chang. Dorje Chang. Dorje Chang." He revealed nothing. "Dorje Chang instructed me to make water and butter lamp offerings, that was all. He didn't tell me the whereabouts of his possessions or money. So I don't know."

But he did know. He had hidden as much of Rinpoche's wealth as he could by tirelessly seeking out people he trusted and asking them to conceal Rinpoche's possessions and keep them safe. All those things have now been given to Yangsi Rinpoche.

"I have had a sign that if my body falls apart, I will immediately meet Rinpoche," he once said. "Which means that wherever Rinpoche is, I'll be able to join him. And so, if my body would just disappear, my mind could be at peace."

Sakya Lama died in prison.

Robert Godet and Jamyang Khyentse Chökyi Lodrö
Source: Shechen Archives

17. Sikkim

Recording Rinpoche's Voice

Gerard Godet[42] had an elder brother, Robert, who was a student of Khyentse Chökyi Lodrö in Sikkim in the 1950s. I believe he invited Rinpoche to visit France but have never heard anything to suggest that Rinpoche intended to accept his invitation. Most of those I have spoken with say Rinpoche had no desire whatsoever to visit foreign lands.

Robert had a tape recorder and asked Rinpoche if he could record his voice. Rinpoche called my mother and a few others into his room and asked them to sing and chant some prayers with him, including the Tsok Lu beginning "The pure realm Khechara . . ." When I visited Kham much later, I asked about that tape and even managed to get hold of a copy. But when I listened to it, I could hear only my mother's voice; not one syllable of Rinpoche's voice comes through. It's not that it wasn't possible to record Rinpoche's voice, because we know he taught a Tsok Lu and some other texts on All India Radio in Delhi—I've been told Rinpoche read the texts very slowly rather than explaining them—and that they broadcast a recording of that teaching at least once in the 1970s. They don't seem to play it anymore. There was even a film made of Rinpoche outside the Tsuglakhang in Gangtok, but no one knows where it is now.

Rinpoche's Personal Retreats and His Writings

Rinpoche usually remained in retreat during the winter, probably because of the cold, and taught in the summer. He organized his personal retreats in a variety of ways. Sometimes he allowed himself some freedom and one or two regular visitors, and other times he was far stricter and conducted his retreat in complete solitude.

It is widely believed that Rinpoche was introduced to the nature of mind by the great Sakyapa master Pönlop Loter Wangpo (this is what Dilgo Khyentse writes in the *Great Biography*). Yet Rinpoche only ever wrote about the nature of mind based on the Dzogchen view, never on the Sakya view of the nonduality of samsara and nirvana. I don't know why.

> I have written seven crucial instructions on the nature of mind,
> But I myself have only glimpsed it.

As such comments and accounts of his inner experiences can be found in his *Secret Biography*, I won't say anything here about the many lamas who introduced him to his true nature and looked after him spiritually.

Tashi Namgyal's Return to Kham

Soon after Rinpoche arrived in Sikkim, he said it was time to release the stipends for the monks of Khamje Shedra. News had reached Sikkim that Adrung Phuntsok had recently been killed during fierce fighting in Derge. The situation in Tibet was desperate. So Rinpoche wanted to send an especially capable person to Dzongsar to ensure that the job was done properly. Chakdzö suggested Tashi Namgyal, who was keen to go, but Rinpoche really wanted to send Chakdzö himself. Tashi Namgyal said he overheard them arguing about it.

Chakdzö didn't want to go because he was afraid of being arrested the moment he set foot in Kham. Rinpoche argued that Tashi Namgyal's family had also attracted the enmity of the Chinese and that there was no guarantee he would return either. After all, Rinpoche pointed out, his brother had already been arrested by the Communists. Eventually, though, Chakdzö wore Rinpoche down.

"There's no alternative," Rinpoche told Tashi Namgyal. "You're the one I'll have to send to Kham. I've already done a divination about the trip. It confirms that you will be able to accomplish the task, and of course, I will pray for you."

Rinpoche paused for a moment, then continued, "You have a strong desire for wealth, but you must not try to bring back any representations of body, speech, and mind or anything valuable. Just distribute the six-month stipends. Nothing else! Tell the land managers that the shedra will fall apart if the stipends are not provided on time. Gather what grain is available and make up any shortfall from the labrang granary. I will write in detail to the khenpos of Khamje Shedra about how all this should happen."

Just before he left for Kham, Rinpoche asked Tashi Namgyal to bring him a piece of a robe his father had worn (when burnt, its smoke could be inhaled as a medicine), which was stored in the labrang's treasury. Rinpoche warned him again and again, even after he had blessed him, not to try to bring anything valuable back with him.

Tashi Namgyal left for Kham and accomplished his task exactly as Rinpoche had wished. He did wonder if he shouldn't give each monk enough grain for a year, but as Rinpoche had clearly told him only to give them six months' worth, that's what he did. Later he felt it was a mistake, because eighteen days after he returned to Sikkim, the Communist Chinese demanded that Gongna Tulku hand over six thousand bags of Dzongsar Monastery's barley. So Gongna Tulku had to find the keys to the labrang and give them the monastery and labrang's entire store of barley.

While at the labrang, Tashi Namgyal noticed how spotlessly clean it was being kept and that all the butter lamps burnt continuously. The monastery's horns and trumpets were still intact and neatly packed in their cases, and work on the wooden carvings in the coral temple that would house the statues of the eighty mahasiddhas in Rinpoche's new residence was going well.

For three nights, Tashi Namgyal slept in his old room. On the wooden shelf behind his pillow stood the bell Rinpoche had given him, and more than once he thought about taking it back to Sikkim with him. But when he remembered just how much wealth and how many holy images Khyentse Labrang had had to leave behind, he decided the bell should stay where it was. After all, everyone at the labrang was certain that one day, Rinpoche would return.

Having completed his task, Tashi Namgyal left Tibet empty-handed, just as Rinpoche had advised. He stopped off in Drumo to pick up the forty or fifty statues that had not been sent to Mindrolling, then went straight to Sikkim. The moment he arrived, he went to see Rinpoche to give him all the news.

"What have you brought back with you?" asked Rinpoche.

"I followed Rinpoche's advice and brought nothing," he replied.

"Where's my father's robe?" asked Rinpoche. Tashi Namgyal handed him a small square of black brocade.

"This is not my father's robe," said Rinpoche. "It belonged to Terchen Chokling. Anyway, it doesn't matter."

They talked a little, then Rinpoche asked if he had brought anything else with him. Tashi Namgyal said no, he hadn't.

"I thought that at the very least you would have brought the horns and trumpets, because you know how much we need them for the tenth- and twenty-fifth-day tsok feasts. But if you didn't, it's also fine."

Apparently Rinpoche had mentioned to Chakdzö and Khandro several times how much they needed horns and trumpets and that he thought Tashi Namgyal would probably bring some back with him. But Tashi Namgyal said he hadn't dared disobey Rinpoche's original instructions.

The Destruction of Khamje Shedra

Not long after that, a monk, who I think was a Ladakhi, visited Rinpoche in Sikkim. He brought devastating news. Khamje Shedra had been destroyed, the statue of Maitreya desecrated, and all the khenpos driven from the monastery. Rinpoche was extremely saddened by everything he heard. The Ladakhi monk told me later that informing Rinpoche about the ruination of the shedra had been a big mistake, one that he bitterly regretted. But by then it was too late. And Rinpoche himself had asked for all the news, so what else could he do?

Prophecies

I don't have much to say about Rinpoche's life in Sikkim because I've heard very little about it. There don't seem to be any really good stories from that time, just bits and pieces about disagreements and Rinpoche's general dissatisfaction with his life there. Rinpoche didn't want to live in Sikkim. If he really couldn't return to Tibet, he would have preferred to live in India, but Chakdzö Tsewang Paljor constantly spoke out against both options. He said that if Rinpoche went back to Tibet, he would be thrown into prison by the Communists and die there; and if he went to India, they would be separated from their rich Sikkimese benefactors. Without financial support, he said, as they owned neither houses nor land outside Tibet, they would all die of starvation.

The Old Woman from Mon

Prophecies made by Pönlop Loter Wangpo stated that Rinpoche would face tremendous obstacles in his fifties or sixties. He said the main obstacle-maker would be an old woman from Mon, who would invite Rinpoche to her home, and he advised Rinpoche not to accept that invitation. Rinpoche, Khandro, and most Tibetans at that time thought that Mon was Bhutan, and that was why Rinpoche didn't accept either of the two invitations extended by Queen Mother Phuntsho Choden of Bhutan.

Later, it was realized that Sikkim was also part of Mon, so perhaps the old woman referred to was the Queen Mother of Sikkim? I know Dilgo Khyentse always thought she was. Certainly, the Queen Mother of Sikkim developed tremendous devotion for Rinpoche and received many empowerments and teachings from him. But amid all that activity, Rinpoche became so overpowered by obstacles that he was unable to take even one step out of Sikkim. As a result, he didn't live out his full life span. I didn't hear this from Dilgo Khyentse himself; Tashi Namgyal told me. He said that Dilgo Khyentse mentioned it to him privately. If Khandro Tsering Chödrön had heard even a whisper that Rinpoche's attendants and students believed her kind and loving royal friends were samaya-transgressing demons, the HUNG syllable in her heart would have turned upside down!

Some of the older people say that although the Sikkimese royal family hadn't been on bad terms with Lhatsün Namkha Jigme, they'd definitely not been on good terms with most of his incarnations, including Lhatsün Jigme Pawo. Therefore, none of the royal family was allowed to touch any part of Lhatsün Namkha Jigme's wealth or belongings, which were stored at Dolung in Sikkim. If they had, Rahula would have struck them down with violent convulsions, making death inevitable.

Khyentse Chökyi Lodrö was an incarnation of Lhatsün Namkha Jigme and suffered from an illness that looked very like the kind that's stirred up by samaya-breaking demons.

Bad Temper

Rinpoche did not like Sikkim and, when he felt ill, would scold and beat the people around him. One day, the bones of Ratri Lama, who had passed away in Tibet (the reliquary is now at the labrang), a statue of Amitayus, and many silver coins were sent to Rinpoche with a request that he perform a liberation ritual. Once he had completed the ritual, Rinpoche asked Chokden to add some powdered gemstones to Ratri Lama's bones and make some tsa tsas.

While Chokden was pounding earth by a curtained door, Rinpoche circumambulated the temple, followed by Tashi Namgyal and Khandro. When

Rinpoche reached Chokden, he asked if he'd mixed the powdered gemstones into the earth. Chokden admitted it had slipped his mind, and Rinpoche exploded with an anger so fierce that he nearly fell over! He hurried to his room, grabbed Ani Rilu's walking stick, and strode back to Chokden, shouting, "Are you my attendant, or am I yours? Why don't you listen to my instructions?" And he beat Chokden three times across his back. Laughing with surprise, Chokden ran as fast as his legs would carry him to find the powdered gems.

Rinpoche then returned to his room. His attendants served tea, and after a while, he asked them what one old man beating another had looked like.

The Lakar Family Dzi Stones

Once Rinpoche and Khandro had settled in Sikkim, Lakar relatives in Tibet sent Khandro a string of dzi stones. Tselu was infuriated. "I am also a daughter of Lakar Tsang," she snapped, and tore the stones from Khandro's neck to keep for herself.

Ani Rilu and Ani Pelu were Khandro's father's older sisters and were also daughters of the Lakar family, but they chose to live with Khandro rather than at Lakar Tsang. In Tibet, they too had been given strings of dzis, and although Ani Pelu's had been lost before she left Kham, Ani Rilu still had hers. Tashi Namgyal told me that after Tselu had taken Khandro's dzis, Ani Rilu offered to share hers with her niece. Khandro accepted her aunt's gift, then asked Gönpo Tseten to sell a twelve-eyed, twelve-inch-long dzi and with the proceeds buy her two complete sets of the Kangyur. He was responsible for making sure the texts were bought, she said, regardless of how much the dzi fetched. Lama Gönpo Tseten asked for Dilgo Khyentse's help, and in the end, Dilgo Khyentse himself bought the texts for Khandro. I believe that twelve-eyed dzi now belongs to Dilgo Khyentse's labrang.

In Sikkim, Khandro wore a nine-eyed dzi until just after her stomach surgery. As she washed her face in the bathroom not long after she had been discharged from the hospital, she heard a loud splitting sound and immediately thought, "That's my dzi breaking!" When she returned to her room, she found that the dzi had indeed split in two.

"What kind of sign is this?" she wondered.

That night, she felt a burning sensation where her stomach had been cut open and heard the sound of thunder and lightning. When she awoke the next morning, the wound in her stomach had dried up. Later, when she went to the hospital for a checkup, the doctors said she had completely recovered from the operation.

Khandro herself told me that the dzi had averted obstacles to her life by taking them upon itself. She also showed me the two halves of the broken stone. She never wore it again, though, because back then no one thought of gluing it together.

Drupchens and Mendrups

Accomplishing the Life-Force of the Vidyadharas

At the request of the Queen Mother of Sikkim, Rinpoche performed the drupchen and mendrup of *Accomplishing the Life-Force of the Vidyadharas* at the Tsuglakhang in Gangtok, with Kachu Tulku, Thuksay Yangtrul, and all the monks of Pema Yangtse Monastery.

By the end of the first day, it was clear that Rinpoche was not at all happy with the Pema Yangtse monks' performance. The following day, he told them that as they obviously didn't know how to chant, that evening, the best of them should come to his room, and he would show them how to do it properly. They all gathered at the appointed time, and Rinpoche demonstrated how to chant and play the cymbals. But he only went through everything once, then asked if they'd got it, but none of them dared say a word.

"Tomorrow, you must chant as I've taught you," he told them. "You are monks of Sangchen Pema Yangtse, a highly respected and important monastery. You are also practitioners of the treasure teachings of Lhatsün Namkha Jigme. But the way you do this ritual is nothing less than embarrassing! Particularly for your monastery."

The following day, the monks quickly reverted to their habitual way of practicing. At one point, they played the cymbals for so long that the practice fell apart completely. Rinpoche was furious. He glared at the monks again and again, his eyes red-hot with anger. By the time they took a break, he was incandescent.

"You eaters of your fathers' and mothers' flesh!" he yelled. "Why don't you listen to me? You bear the name of Sangchen Pema Yangtse, and yet *this* is how you perform rituals!"

He continued admonishing them for almost an hour. Then suddenly, his attitude changed.

"I, an old man, have gone mad," he muttered sadly. "How can a wanderer like me criticize the monks of Sangchen Pema Yangtse. You, who are the teachers of the king of Sikkim! I am sorry. You are right. I have nothing more to say." And not another syllable passed his lips throughout the entire drupchen.

Later, Kachu Tulku said Rinpoche had so terrified him that day that he'd wished the earth would open and swallow him up.

The Last Drupchen

Lhatsün Namkha Jigme's *Accomplishing the Life-force of the Vidyadharas* was the last of the many drupchens Rinpoche performed during his life. It took place in the Tsuglakhang in Gangtok under the patronage of the royal family of Sikkim. Some rather pale amrita pills were made and blessed during that drupchen. But from what I've heard, even after five days of practice, the amrita failed to emit any kind of fragrance. Those responsible for making it tried desperately to work out what had gone wrong. Had they forgotten to add the yeast? The least charitable among them laid the blame firmly on Chokden's incompetence.

Eventually they consulted Trulshik, the lama who built the Do-Drul Chorten Stupa in Gangtok, about how they might save the situation. At first he looked as though he were about to lose his temper. But eventually he said, "Don't worry about forgetting the yeast. It doesn't matter. The amrita can be fermented with ritual dancing."

Instantly, Rinpoche began to dance around the mandala, playing his damaru and bell, and went on to circumambulate it twenty times. Trulshik followed behind him but didn't dance himself. After about ten circuits, a wonderful fragrance began to rise from the amrita that filled the entire assembly hall.

The Sikkimese royal family still have some of that amrita. I saw it once, stored in metal containers on the upper floor of the palace monastery. It was believed to be very sacred. But I don't know where it is now.

RINPOCHE'S FALL

One day, because he knew that Khandro was sitting with Rinpoche in his room, Tashi Namgyal took the opportunity to sit and chat with the two old women of Lakar Tsang in their kitchen. While he was still there, Khandro left Rinpoche to circumambulate the temple. Rinpoche was alone when he fainted, probably as a result of a lung disturbance. He fell out of his thinmattressed bed and banged his nose on the spittoon that stood nearby. Dazed and groaning, he lay on the floor, unable to pull himself upright. Jampal's wife was circumambulating the temple at the time and alerted his attendants.

"Someone's groaning!" she told them. "Has Rinpoche fallen?"

The attendants rushed into Rinpoche's room and found him writhing with pain. As they pulled him upright, he slapped Tashi Namgyal's face three times, saying he'd fallen because of his attendant's neglect. Tashi Namgyal said the slaps caused him no pain or irritation.

I haven't heard that Rinpoche ever hit Khandro, but people don't tend to talk about such things.

Jagö Namgyal Dorje

Jagö Namgyal Dorje visited Rinpoche several times in Sikkim. On his last visit, he found Rinpoche bedridden and seriously ill. He touched the foot of Rinpoche's bed with his forehead and wept with despair as he told Rinpoche the news from Tibet, most of which was extremely discouraging and very upsetting.

"The Chuzhi Gangdruk army has been defeated, and the Communists rule Tibet. Surely the teachings of Buddha will now degenerate and disappear. And although Rinpoche has escaped to India, soon even he might pass into nirvana. What can we do?"

Rinpoche sat bolt upright.

"Abu!" he said. "A man of your station should not whine and mope like this. I may not live, but the teachings of Buddha will not be affected. Yesterday, I heard that Tulku Salga has arrived at the Bhutan-Tibet border. He is an excellent teacher! So the teachings will not disappear."

Later, Jagö Namgyal Dorje[43] told Dilgo Khyentse what Rinpoche had said. He added that after hearing Rinpoche praise Dilgo Khyentse, his own confidence in him had grown. It was obvious, said Jagö Namgyal Dorje, that Dilgo Khyentse would be extraordinarily beneficial to the teachings. Dilgo Khyentse told me himself that Namgyal Dorje had spoken to him in this way.

Restoration of the Buddhadharma

I spent a great deal of time with Tashi Namgyal of Ngochok Tsang during my long stay in Sikkim. This is something he told me during that time.

Ajam of Ngochok Tsang spoke to Rinpoche about the deep concerns he and everyone at Ngochok Tsang had about the degeneration of the Buddhadharma. Rinpoche responded by telling him that there were methods available that could restore it. As the teachings were still in good shape, Rinpoche said, if ceremonies for the longevity of the Buddha's Dharma were performed wholeheartedly, even though its decline was likely to continue, it would happen slowly over six decades or, at the very least, over several twelve-year cycles. According to Ngochok Ajam, Rinpoche said the same thing to Gongna Tulku.

Rinpoche always insisted that it would be possible to revive the Buddhadharma in Tibet. There was no hope of doing so during the Communist takeover, but today the Buddhadharma is flourishing once again in the Land of Snows, which itself is proof that Rinpoche spoke the truth.

Rinpoche's Prediction about the Site of His Cremation Pyre

While Rinpoche was staying in a guesthouse at Yab Ling in Sikkim, as he gazed towards Tashiding, Khandro, Chokden, and others heard him say, "I often dream of a ruined, pale green monastery that was built on the foundations of my cremation pyre. I think this is it. This is where I'll be cremated."

And he pointed in the direction of Drakar Tashiding. I think this is mentioned briefly in the *Great Biography*.

18. Pilgrimage to the Holy Places of India

The *Great Biography* records many stories about Rinpoche's life after he left Tibet, but not this one.

The Ganachakra Feast Offering at Siliguri Train Station

In Sikkim, Rinpoche and his attendants began talking incessantly about his wish to go on pilgrimage to India. The prospect of such a pilgrimage sent the entire labrang into a state of anxious confusion. One of the problems was that the attendants were convinced that fire didn't exist in India, and without fire, they said, they wouldn't be able to boil water to make tea. Rinpoche asked how Indian people made their tea. They had black stones called "coal," said the attendants, which they soaked in water then lit. But there wasn't any coal in Tibet, and anyway, the whole procedure always took at least half a day. Rinpoche then asked how food and drink could be prepared without fire and was told the only solution was to eat in restaurants.

"Restaurants are expensive," said Rinpoche. "And what if they don't serve the kind of food we like?"

Eventually, though, in spite of all their concerns, Rinpoche and his party set out for Siliguri to catch the night train to Bodh Gaya, in two jeeps hired for them by the Sikkimese royal family. But as Lakar Tselu gave birth to a baby girl that very night, they missed their train.

The following evening, Rinpoche summoned his attendants.

"Ha, ha!" he declared, looking both shocked and amazed. "Our activities are heading in the wrong direction. *Today* is the beginning of our pilgrimage! We must offer a ganachakra feast here, in Siliguri, because Siliguri is our gateway to the holy places of India. We really can't afford *not* to offer a tsok here!"

His attendants were disconcerted. How, they asked Rinpoche, could they do a ganachakra feast when all they had to offer was tsampa? Rinpoche produced a fifty-rupee note and gave it to Tashi Namgyal.

"Go and buy offerings," he commanded.

But it wasn't that simple because Tashi Namgyal didn't speak Hindi. As he stood by the roadside wondering what to do, Tashi Namgyal saw a man throw an empty biscuit packet to the ground. It gave him an idea. He picked up the packet, showed it to a rickshaw driver, then gestured to him to get moving. Soon Tashi Namgyal found himself at a grocery shop. By pointing at everything that caught his eye, he quickly accumulated a large pile of biscuits, ladoos, and sweets, which he loaded onto the rickshaw and took back to the railway station. Rinpoche was very pleased with everything Tashi Namgyal presented to him and said he had accomplished his task well. Preparations were then made to do a ganachakra feast offering from the sadhana of *Consort Practice: The Queen of Great Bliss*.

Even though she had given birth the night before, Rinpoche insisted that Tselu attend the ritual. Chakdzö Tsewang Paljor tried to reason with Rinpoche, saying she had no strength and couldn't stand up. But Rinpoche was adamant that she should be there, whatever the cost!

"No, no! Tell her to come!" he commanded. "This is the gateway to our pilgrimage. It would be wrong for her to miss this tsok. Everyone must gather. Tell everyone to come!"

So Tselu attended, settling herself as best she could near the offerings. A monk beat a drum, and Rinpoche led the practice as chant master. As they recited the fulfillment and confession prayer, *The Spontaneous Vajra Song*, Tselu suddenly jumped up and started spinning right and left. She shrieked, "Aek, Aek, Ai!" then jumped up and down, chanting, "TA PA TRA, TA PA TRA, TRA TRA TRA" and many other things. Her body shivered, and she shook her head, twisting it this way and that, her arms flailing wildly. Yet throughout her extraordinary display, Rinpoche continued to chant without faltering once. His attendants looked on in wonder.

After a while, Tselu calmed down. "Aag! Aag!" she muttered, gazing into the sky with wide-open eyes. Then she sat down. Even back then, there were people who believed her to be quite a special being. Tashi Namgyal said that at that moment, he felt they might be right.

Before Tselu met Tsewang Paljor, she had had another man, Tulku

Sogyal's father, but they didn't marry. He was a close relative of Lingtsang Gyalgenma, who was himself related to Dilgo Khyentse.

How Rinpoche and his entourage traveled to Bodh Gaya from Siliguri is described in the *Great Biography*.

Bodh Gaya

It was Gönpo Tseten who told me about Rinpoche's time in Bodh Gaya.

After they arrived, the whole party went straight to the Burmese Guesthouse. For some reason, the residents of the guesthouse were unwilling to open their doors, so Rinpoche sat outside, while his attendants searched frantically for accommodation and somewhere to make tea. Rinpoche didn't seem at all bothered by the commotion around him. He was far more interested in planning his visit to the Mahabodhi Temple.

Khandro Tsering Chödrön offers Khyentse Chökyi Lodrö
a katak under the Bodhi tree in 1956
Source: Khyentse Labrang, photographer Radi Yeshe

"Where is the Bodhi tree?" he asked. "Where is the Great Stupa? Where is the great Mahabodhi Buddha statue? That's where I want to go!"

Finally, the attendants found somewhere to make tea and offered Rinpoche a cup, which he drank very quickly.

"Now, let's go to see the Great Mahabodhi Stupa and the Bodhi tree!"

In those days, Bodh Gaya was very run-down, and Rinpoche was able to walk freely around the stupa. As he gazed at all the holy representations in their niches, Chokden read to him from Gendün Chöphel's *Guide to Holy Places*.

Circumambulating Bodh Gaya on the Back of an Elephant

One day, Chakdzö Tsewang Paljor told Rinpoche that he had seen people riding elephants nearby. "And if we pay the mahoot," he said, "We can ride an elephant too!"

"Ah! That's right!" cried Rinpoche. "It's said that even dreaming about

Jamyang Khyentse Chökyi Lodrö, Chakdzö, probably Tashi Namgyal, and an Indian man riding an elephant. On the ground next to the mahoot are Khandro Tsering Chödrön and Tulku Sogyal
Source: Khyentse Labrang, photographer Radi Yeshe

riding elephants, tigers, lions, and eagles greatly increases your good fortune. So let's actually ride an elephant while we have the chance. Let's go! Pay the man whatever he wants!"

The elephant knelt down, and Rinpoche, Chakdzö, and an attendant mounted up. As there were no fences or walls in those days, Rinpoche was able to circumambulate the stupa on the back of an elephant.

Later, Rinpoche prostrated to a Hindu sadhu called Mahabodhiraja, explaining to his attendants that the sadhu was a very holy guardian of the sacred site of Bodh Gaya.

Circumambulating the Stupa

One evening, Rinpoche announced his intention to offer full-length prostrations at Bodh Gaya. He rose well before dawn the following day and immediately started prostrating around the stupa. The sun hadn't yet begun to rise as he reached its western face, but he'd used up all his strength and

Sogyal Tulku, Khyentse Chökyi Lodrö, and Lama Chokden
Source: Khyentse Labrang, photographer Radi Yeshe

could no longer stand upright. Tashi Namgyal, Chokden, and Khandro all helped him, but in spite of their support, he was so weak that after taking just three more steps, he fell over. Again, they lifted him up, and again he fell after three steps. But he didn't give up and managed to complete the circuit by the time the sun began to rise.

Scattering Hair and Nails

Rinpoche said that as Bodh Gaya was such a holy place, they should all scatter their hair and nails there. He sat next to the Bodhi tree, cut off a clump of his own hair, and sent Tashi Namgyal to sprinkle some at the foot of each of the stupas. Tashi Namgyal told me that he did as Rinpoche asked, but after releasing just a few strands, he put the rest in his gao.

Namgyal Dorje's Confession

Namgyal Dorje accompanied Rinpoche on his final pilgrimage. At that time, he said, they all still assumed they would eventually return to Tibet.

As a photograph of Dzogchen Pönlop, the Sixteenth Karmapa, and Khyentse Rinpoche sitting under the Bodhi tree was being taken, Namgyal

Kadro Tulku, Gongna Tulku, and Khyentse Chökyi Lodrö
under the Bodhi tree in 1956
Source: Sogyal Rinpoche's private collection, photographer Radi Yeshe

Dorje decided this was the perfect opportunity for him to approach these great masters. He offered each of them three prostrations, then began to speak.

"You already know how much negative karma I have accumulated and how many people I have killed, so there's no need for me to tell you all that. You masters always say that negative karma can be purified through confession. So today, in your presence, I will confess my negative actions, offer prostrations, and recite the *Confession of Downfalls* three times. Please pray that I successfully purify my karma. And please confirm that I will be able to purify my negative karma and prevent myself from falling into the lower realms in my next life."

Karmapa told him that all he had to do was confess and everything would be taken care of—but the Karmapa often said such things, and Namgyal Dorje didn't feel at all reassured. So he called for a response from Khyentse Chökyi Lodrö.

"The Wish-Fulfilling Jewel has spoken," said Rinpoche. "And as the two of us will do our best for you, let's abide by Yishin Norbu's advice. Now you must recite the *Confession of Downfalls*."

Namgyal Dorje recited the prayer three times and prostrated again to the three Rinpoches.

Khyentse Chökyi Lodrö, the Sixteenth Karmapa,
and the Sixth Dzogchen Pönlop at Bodh Gaya in 1956
Source: Khyentse Labrang, photographer Radi Yeshe

Yangsi Rinpoche Thubten Chökyi Gyatso asked me if it was true that his father, Dungsey Thinley Norbu, had offered Rinpoche a golden ring at Bodh Gaya. I think it must be true, but I've heard nothing about it.

The experiences and pure visions Rinpoche had while at Bodh Gaya are described in his *Secret Biography*. I know nothing else about this visit.

Sankasya

The Suppression Ritual

After Bodh Gaya, Rinpoche's party traveled to Sankasya, where Lord Buddha descended from the god realm. The *Great Biography* only mentions the suppression ritual and the prophecies Rinpoche received in pure visions, but I know a few other stories from that time.

Rinpoche boarded a train at Sankasya for the next stage of his pilgrimage. But after two stops, he announced he had had a pure vision and they must immediately return to Sankasya to perform a suppression ritual. Everyone disembarked at the next station and took the first train back, which turned out to be rather small and very slow.

At Sankasya train station, Rinpoche, Chokden, and the other attendants drew a linga[44] and consecrated it. During the suppression ritual, as Rinpoche rang his bell and sipped his tea, an Indian acharya carrying a packet of ink drawings of snakes, scorpions, crabs, and so on, wandered among them, muttering gibberish. Rinpoche said nothing but stared at him a few times. At the end of the ceremony, they dug a pit near the station, buried the suppression effigies, and performed subjugation dances over them.

There were no trains that night, so everyone, including Rinpoche, slept on the station platform. Just after midnight, a tremendous thunderstorm woke them up. As the lightning flashed, everyone saw Rinpoche sit bolt upright and make a summoning mudra in the sky. What they didn't know was that Rinpoche was experiencing a vision of the glorious protector Vajrakumara, smiling joyfully and speaking to him in Sanskrit.

Later, Rinpoche is believed to have said that if a monastery could be built at Sankasya, it would be of immense benefit to both the teachings and beings. When it became possible to buy land at Sankasya, I felt we should do as Rinpoche had suggested and build a monastery. So I asked Tashi Namgyal if he could identify precisely where Rinpoche had suppressed the obstacle-maker. But he couldn't. All he could tell me was it was probably somewhere behind the train station (which today is still exactly as it was in Rinpoche's time). These days, Sankasya is filling up with monasteries and temples because land there is so cheap, but as we haven't been able to pinpoint the site of the suppression ritual, the monastery Rinpoche spoke of has yet to be built.

Rinpoche's Vision of Shavaripa

One of the most famous stories from the *Great Biography* is of Rinpoche's visit to the Sitavana charnel ground where he saw Shavaripa in a pure vision. Shavaripa, wearing a crown of flowers, walked towards Rinpoche carrying a bow, an arrow, and the carcass of a deer. He threw the carcass down in front of Rinpoche, and Rinpoche immediately performed phowa[45] for it and said prayers of aspiration. According to the *Great Biography*, the vision invoked such clarity in Rinpoche's mind that he experienced the splendor of many blessings, and his body trembled.

Gönpo Tseten was there when it all happened, so I asked him to describe exactly what he saw. He said that he had been with Rinpoche in the meditation cave while Chokden and the other attendants were outside making tormas for a tsok. Rinpoche was gazing into the sky, holding a monk's staff[46] and a kutsab, when suddenly his whole body began to shake. And he was still trembling violently when he started jumping up and down, shouting, "Hik hik hik!" and "Phat!" At the time, Gönpo Tseten wondered if the lack of ventilation in the cave combined with smoke from the incense had aggravated Rinpoche's illness. These thoughts made him restless, and he began to worry about how they would be able to help Rinpoche without a doctor to advise them. He did not see Shavaripa.

KANGRA

Rinpoche and his party continued their journey to Kangra. At Pathankot, they changed to the narrow-gauge line run by the Kangra Valley Railway. At dawn, Rinpoche had a vision of many of the Indian mahasiddhas—including Saraha and Dombi Heruka—in the sky before him, all singing songs of realization. This vision intensified Rinpoche's own realization, and he too burst into song. The train they were traveling in must have been one of the ordinary ones, because the benches weren't wide enough or long enough for Rinpoche to lie down. So he stood on the edge of a bench, naked to the waist, singing spontaneous songs of realization. Tashi Namgyal was there but said he wasn't aware that Saraha and Virupa were also present. In fact, none of the labrang attendants noticed any of the important things that happened during that part of the journey. Chokden would probably have had more idea, but there was never an opportunity to ask him about it. Apparently Rinpoche said afterwards that the old Indians they were traveling with must have thought him quite mad.

It was almost dawn by the time they reached Kangra, which Tashi Namgyal said looked pretty much the same then as it does today.

19. The Last Months in Sikkim

Last Conversations with Dilgo Khyentse

Before Dilgo Khyentse left Tibet, he spoke with Khyentse Chökyi Lodrö twice. Rinpoche was in Sikkim by then and walked all the way down the hill to the wireless station just so he could talk with Tulku Salga. In those days, the wireless was far clearer than many of today's telephone lines. As Dilgo Khyentse sat in front of an open metal box in the Lhasa wireless station, he could hear everything that was going on in Gangtok: Rinpoche's footsteps as he walked into the station, what Rinpoche said to his attendants, and even the sound of chairs being arranged.

Khyentse Chökyi Lodrö
Source: Khyentse Labrang

"Ya, Tulku Salga!" said Rinpoche.

"La so, Rinpoche!" replied Dilgo Khyentse.

At first they talked about how much they both wanted to return home. Towards the end of their conversation, Rinpoche said, "I have just given the empowerments and instructions for the *Three Categories of Dzogchen*, but it didn't go well. There were too many distractions—it was all too quick. So you must try to give detailed and complete empowerments and instructions for those teachings. Don't forget!"

Rinpoche also mentioned a lama with an average reading speed.

"I have received a few reading transmissions from him," said Rinpoche, "but couldn't receive everything because there were too many people around, and I couldn't stay long enough. Try to visit him when you're next in his area. Request the transmissions for the pure vision teachings of Lhodrakpa Namkha Gyaltsen, teacher of Je Rinpoche Tsongkhapa. It's important because this lineage is disappearing. If you can, receive both the empowerments *and* the reading transmissions. But if you can't manage both, make sure you get the reading transmission for the entire cycle because that's the lineage that no longer exists."

Dilgo Khyentse went on to compile all the texts for this set of teachings. In fact, it was when I asked him about them that he mentioned Rinpoche's two wireless calls. He told me that after they spoke, he bought the *Three Categories of Dzogchen* text, just as Rinpoche had asked him to. And that conversation, he said, turned out to be the last time he ever spoke with Rinpoche.

The Paranirvana of Khyentse Chökyi Lodrö

Now I will tell you about how Rinpoche passed into nirvana.

Rinpoche ate very little for two days—just some milk, porridge, and hot water—and on his last evening admitted that he might not manage to survive the night. Everyone was very anxious and very worried.

It was late when Khandro went to her room to rest, leaving Tashi Namgyal to sit with Rinpoche. Suddenly Rinpoche sat bolt upright, made a summoning mudra in the direction of the summit of Namtong La, then lay down again. Tashi Namgyal moved towards the bed to rearrange Rinpoche's blankets, but even before he got there, Rinpoche had taken a final deep breath and passed away. It all happened very quickly.

Tashi Namgyal immediately told Chokden, who studied the body and

The Fourth Dodrupchen Rinpoche,
Jigme Trinle Palbar, in Sikkim in the 1960s
Source: Khyentse Labrang

said it looked as though Rinpoche had passed away. Then Chakdzö was told, and when he saw the body, he agreed that Rinpoche's mind had indeed dissolved into primordial space and asked Tashi Namgyal to fetch Dodrupchen Thubten Trinle Pal Zangpo. Tashi Namgyal jumped into the labrang's worn-out old jeep and drove through the night to find him. When he heard what had happened, Dodrupchen didn't hesitate for one moment to return with Tashi Namgyal to the labrang.

Dodrupchen entered Rinpoche's room, offered three prostrations to Rinpoche's body, and with his forehead pressed to Rinpoche's feet, recited prayers for about fifteen minutes. He then sat on a thick cushion at the foot of Rinpoche's bed and began to weep, quietly at first, then gradually louder and louder. Finally his tears stopped flowing, and he sat for two whole hours without uttering a word. No one knew what he was doing. Just before daybreak, he said, "Now, let's go! Get up! Let's go!" And he left.

Rinpoche's death was kept secret for three days. On the morning of the fourth day, as Rinpoche didn't seem to be in meditation, Chakdzö went to his room to remove the blankets. As a striped yellow blanket was pulled from his body, white and red bodhichitta flowed from Rinpoche's nose onto the white vest he was wearing. After they'd finished preparing the kudung, Chakdzö Tsewang Paljor took possession of that vest.

How they cremated the kudung and built the memorial stupa and reliquary is explained in detail in the *Great Biography*, so there's no need for me to say anything about it here. But I must add that I have not heard a single report that even suggests Rinpoche remained in meditation after he passed away.

Khandro's Reaction to Chökyi Lodrö's Death

Yangsi Rinpoche Thubten Chökyi Gyatso instructed me to tell him everything I know about Khyentse Chökyi Lodrö's life, the good and the bad. This is something Tashi Namgyal mentioned that doesn't appear in the *Great Biography*.

Khandro wasn't immediately told about Rinpoche's death. It was only when she looked into his room the next morning that she realized what had happened. Distraught, she ran back to the house, where she found Ani Rilu. She threw herself into her aunt's arms and wept uncontrollably for about twenty minutes. The attendants didn't dare say anything. So it must have been her aunts, Ani Rilu and Ani Pelu, who gently explained that her behavior might be considered inappropriate, because she soon calmed down.

Khandro went upstairs while the kudung was being prepared. She noticed something rolling around on one of the cloths they had used and asked what it was. "Whatever it is, I need it!" she declared. And before anyone could reply, she snatched the "something" up and found it to be a tooth that had fallen from Rinpoche's mouth. From then on, she kept the tooth with her, and over the years, the syllable AH is said to have arisen naturally from its surface.

20. Dilgo Khyentse Rinpoche

Enthronement

Khyentse Chökyi Lodrö and Dilgo Khyentse were very close. Dilgo Khyentse told me they often continued talking long after they had finished their evening meal, sometimes until midnight.

Khyentse Chökyi Lodrö wasn't present when Shechen Gyaltsab enthroned the very young Dilgo Khyentse at Shechen Monastery (he was teaching somewhere else), and by the time he returned to Shechen, Dilgo Khyentse had learnt to read. As Shechen Gyaltsab had already started teaching the young tulku the *Treasury of Precious Instructions*, Rinpoche and Dilgo Khyentse used to read the text together.

Over tea one day, Chökyi Lodrö said to Shechen Gyaltsab, "You have accomplished a great many things while I've been away."

"You could say that," said Shechen Gyaltsab. "The year I visited the Dilgo family, I slept in the room where the torma box Önpo Tenzin Namgyal made for a statue of Nyingtik Tseringma was kept, and in the middle of the night, the statue transformed into her true form. I was left with the impression that the family's son was an emanation of Jamyang Khyentse Wangpo. And after careful and repeated examination of the vision, I bestowed the title Khyentse on the boy, because I believe it will be of benefit."

"The year I first met him," said Chökyi Lodrö, "I felt certain that he was an emanation of Khyentse Wangpo, and Pönlop Loter Wangpo agreed. You've done well, and I very much appreciate what you have accomplished."

Chökyi Lodrö then presented Dilgo Khyentse with the traditional representations of body, speech, and mind and a list of all the other offerings that had been made. Then he said to Shechen Gyaltsab, "You must bestow all the empowerments, transmissions, and instructions on him while you are still alive. But as you are getting older and your health isn't good, it might be difficult for you to give him the *Precious Treasury of Terma Teachings*. So I will pledge to offer those teachings to him myself."

Shechen Gyaltsab immediately folded his hands and said, "Adzi, you show such great kindness! What more is there to say? Hey! Did you hear that? That is such a pure pledge!" And he touched Chökyi Lodrö's forehead with his own again and again.

Every day at noon, Dilgo Khyentse would set out for the dining room. And every day as he descended the stairs, he would be intercepted by Rinpoche, who was staying in the room directly underneath Shechen Gyaltsab's.

"The weather's so bad today! Why don't you stay here and have lunch with me?" With his own hands, he would serve all the food Dilgo Khyentse liked best, including meat. This, said Dilgo Khyentse, was the dawning of Chökyi Lodrö's extraordinary kindness to him. And it so affected him that he almost wept.

It wasn't until after Shechen Gyaltsab had passed away that Dilgo Khyentse first traveled to Dzongsar.

"Last night in my dream, I had a vision of Jamyang Khyentse Wangpo in his actual form," said Chökyi Lodrö, the night after Dilgo Khyentse arrived. "All the circumstances are very auspicious! We must have made many pure aspirations and commitments in our previous lives."

Playing Games

Rinpoche loved to play games, but Dilgo Khyentse never did. Even as a child, he always sat quietly and watched as the others played. But during summer camp in Dophu one year, Rinpoche so enjoyed taking part in Ling dances and various other games that he repeatedly asked Dilgo Khyentse to join in.

"Come! Let's play!" he'd say, and out of respect for Rinpoche, Dilgo Khyentse would make an effort to participate, but his heart wasn't in it. He sometimes took part in hide-and-seek, but other than that, he rarely played games.

Shechen Rabjam and Chökyi Lodrö's Blunt Knife

"Arok!" said Shechen Rabjam. "Have you ever had any thoughts in Rinpoche's presence that were not quite pure?"

"I must have had some," replied Dilgo Khyentse.

The Sixth Shechen Rabjam Rinpoche
Source: Khyentse Labrang

"I really feel we shouldn't have such thoughts," said Shechen Rabjam.

"La so," agreed Dilgo Khyentse.

Shechen Rabjam then told Dilgo Khyentse that one afternoon Rinpoche had said he was hungry and wanted some meat. He removed a large basket of meat from a cupboard, took a piece for himself, and offered a piece to Shechen Rabjam. As they ate, Shechen Rabjam noticed the old, horn-handled knife Rinpoche was using. Its blade had almost worn away with sharpening. Shechen Rabjam didn't have to use it himself because he had his own knife, but a thought about how strange it was that such a great lama should use such a worn-out knife passed through his mind. At that very moment, Rinpoche stared at him with wide-open eyes.

"Do you see this?" he asked, pointing at his bowl. "This is Jamyang

Khyentse Wangpo's bowl. Do you see this? This knife also belonged to Khyentse Wangpo. These things were in the labrang when I first came. This is what they looked like when I first saw them, and I have changed nothing."

"Since then," said Shechen Rabjam, "I feel I should never entertain any critical thoughts about Rinpoche *at all.*"

Dilgo Khyentse and the Black Scarf

Dilgo Khyentse was going to Phuma Tsang to perform a ritual for removing obstacles and an exorcism. Before he left, he asked Rinpoche to lend him a black scarf. Rinpoche immediately responded by giving him the one tied to a vajra that happened to be on his table.

While Dilgo Khyentse was away, Rinpoche gave a few empowerments. Dilgo Khyentse's older brother was at those empowerments and said that during an empowerment for wrathful activity, Rinpoche had asked for the black scarf. The shrine master looked everywhere but couldn't find it. Then Rinpoche remembered that he had lent it to Tulku Salga, who hadn't yet returned it.

"But as a zen is the supreme kind of black scarf," said Rinpoche, "it's probably all right for me to use my zen instead." And he flicked it seven times as he chanted the verses for summoning obstacles.

The moment Dilgo Khyentse returned, he was set upon by Shedrup, his brother.

"Why couldn't you find your own piece of black cloth?" scolded Shedrup. "Why did you have to take Rinpoche's? He had to do without black cloth altogether when he gave the empowerment today, did you know that? Only you would do such a thing!"

Nak Ralma

The monks of Dzongsar Monastery used to call Dilgo Khyentse "Nak Ralma" ("one with long, black hair") because when he visited Rinpoche, he would sit by the window and all they could see of him was a cascade of long, black hair. The monks knew that if that particular window was curtained with Dilgo Khyentse's hair, no one else would be admitted into Rinpoche's presence. But Nak Ralma is not a respectful name.

In Lhasa, Nyoshul Khenpo Rinpoche's attendant, Tsultim Namgyal, told Dosib Thubten, the abbot of Dzongsar Khamje Shedra, that he wanted to meet Khyentse Rinpoche.

"Ah!" exclaimed Khenpo Dosib Thubten, "I think you mean Nak Ralma. He doesn't have a Khyentse title!"

I don't know whether the khenpo, who also escaped to Gangtok, held sectarian prejudices or not, but at Dzongsar, he always called Dilgo Khyentse "Nak Ralma."

One of Gongna Tulku's attendants was from Riwoche. He had heard such negative gossip about Dilgo Khyentse that even though he'd been living in Kalimpong for several months, he neglected to pay his respects because he wasn't sure what kind of lama Dilgo Khyentse really was.

Dilgo Khyentse and the Khenpos

In the early 1960s, Dilgo Khyentse traveled from Bhutan to Kalimpong to receive teachings from Dudjom Rinpoche. Khenpo Dazer, Khenpo Thubten Nyendrak of Pangaon Monastery, Khenpo Mewa Thubten, tutor of the present Dzogchen Rinpoche, and Rahor Thubten made the same journey. In fact, they followed behind Dilgo Khyentse during the day and pitched their tent a little above his at night. But they never so much as looked in his direction for the entire journey.

A building made of zinc panels had been built to accommodate all the lamas and monks attending Dudjom Rinpoche's teachings. Dilgo Khyentse and his family and attendants stayed in one room, and the four khenpos were given the room opposite.

From their room, the khenpos could hear that Dilgo Khyentse Rinpoche was teaching the *Guhyagarbha Tantra* but pretended not to listen. Until one day, when the late Khenpo Thubten suddenly leapt up from the dinner table and started eavesdropping at Dilgo Khyentse's door. After two days of covert listening, he made an oath that from the next day onwards he would "receive the *Guhyagarbha* teachings from Nak Ralma. He is giving the most extraordinary explanations! They are similar to those given by teachers from the Shechen and Dzogchen monasteries, yet unlike anything I've ever heard before."

"Why on earth would you want to receive teachings from *him*?" scoffed his fellow khenpos. "Stay here!"

But Khenpo Thubten was adamant. "When such auspicious circumstances arise," he said, "come what may, one should make the most of them!"

The next day, he went to the teaching carrying a white katak. Before long, Mewa Thubten decided that he, too, wanted to attend. And two days later, Pöpa Tulku joined them.

"His explanations surpass even Rinpoche's!" he said. "I will receive these teachings from tomorrow onwards."

By the end of the teaching, all four khenpos were present. And they all ended up receiving everything, because Dilgo Khyentse Rinpoche was so kindhearted that every time a khenpo joined in, he would start all over again. None of the khenpos missed a syllable.

Khenpo Rinchen

Khenpo Rinchen said he met Dilgo Khyentse in Lhasa. Khenpo was staying with Khyentse Chökyi Lodrö and Sangye Nyenpa, and one day Chökyi Lodrö asked him to take part in a debate. Khenpo should present the view of a scholar from Khamje Shedra, said Rinpoche, and defend that position against Dilgo Khyentse. At that time, Khenpo wasn't sure whether Dilgo Khyentse was a Shentongpa or not, so he assumed he was and made many inflammatory and derogatory remarks about them, like "There is no difference between Shentongpas and heretics, except that Shentongpas are far worse than heretics!" He said this in Rinpoche's presence. Dilgo Khyentse, who was completely nonsectarian and entirely unmoved by such accusations, sat like Mount Meru and said nothing.

Later, when Dilgo Khyentse taught Adzom Drukpa's commentary on the *Guhyagarbha Tantra* in Kalimpong, Khenpo Rinchen requested permission to receive the teachings.

"Yes, of course you can," Dilgo Khyentse said. "Anyone can come to me for teachings."

Within a few days, they had become very close, and when Khenpo sought clarification on certain points, Dilgo Khyentse observed, "You seem to know philosophy quite well. I thought you were more biased, but you are not. You know, if you cannot accept the Shentong view, you won't be able to accept or understand the *Guhayagarbha Tantra*."

Dilgo Khyentse's Journey to Sikkim

Below the Thimphu valley stands a stupa surrounded by trees. In 1959, Dilgo Khyentse was traveling past the stupa on his way from Paro to Thimphu, when suddenly he knew beyond a shadow of doubt that Rinpoche had just died. In Thimphu, he received the news officially and immediately prepared to leave Bhutan for Sikkim. It wasn't easy to arrange, as he first had to travel

Dilgo Khyentse Rinpoche
Source: Shechen Archives

to Kalimpong to apply for a travel permit, which took several days to come through. As soon as he had it, he set off by bus for Gangtok, taking very little with him—just a few Bhutanese yathra, some thick woolen textiles that his wife wanted to offer as condolence gifts, and a change of clothes.

Physically, he wasn't at all well. When he first arrived in Bhutan, he had fallen ill with severe diarrhea and continued to suffer from it for several months. It had weakened him considerably. And on top of his physical exhaustion, he was emotionally devastated by the tremendous grief he felt at Rinpoche's passing. Such a catastrophic loss felt like the end of everything,

Khandro Tsering Chödrön at Khyentse Chökyi Lodrö's stupa
at Tashiding, Sikkim
Source: Khyentse Labrang

and Dilgo Khyentse had almost convinced himself that he too would die within days.

On the bus, he was so frail and sleepy that he couldn't keep track of the stops, so he asked the young Sherpa attendant to let him know when they arrived in Gangtok. Eventually the boy woke him, and Dilgo Khyentse asked him to unload his luggage. It was nowhere to be found, and none of the passengers had seen who had taken it. So Dilgo Khyentse made his way to the labrang empty-handed, where he told Chakdzö and the other attendants about his loss and lack of offerings. As he sat quietly and sadly among them, they assured him that all they really needed was his gracious presence.

Dilgo Khyentse arrived just before Rinpoche's forty-ninth day.

Dilgo Khyentse's Vision at Tashiding

When Dilgo Khyentse was in Sikkim, I think in 1963, he felt a sudden strong urge to visit Tashiding. As he climbed the hill, his body became heavy and his mind agitated, so he leaned against a large rock for a moment's rest. Suddenly his weariness and sadness disappeared. As he gazed into the immaculate sky, he thought alternately of Rinpoche and Lhatsün Namkha Jigme as he recited a prayer of supplication. All at once, Lhatsün Namkha Jigme,

Dilgo Khyentse Rinpoche
Source: Shechen Archives

naked, with plaited hair, wearing bone ornaments and holding a bone trumpet in his right hand, appeared before him. Lhatsün Namkha Jigme blew his trumpet so loudly that Dilgo Khyentse felt each blast as sixty-four hundred thousand dakinis were summoned, and he experienced Rinpoche's vivid presence. He then received blessings from the inseparable form of Rinpoche and Lhatsün Namkha Jigme. It was as a result of this vision, he said, that he wrote the Guru Yoga of Lhatsün Namkha Jigme and included an account of his experience in the colophon.

A Wondrous Grove of Wish-Fulfilling Trees

The Biography of Jamyang Khyentse Chökyi Lodrö

Kyabje Dilgo Khyentse Rinpoche

The statue of White Manjushri called Jamyang Zer Barwa (Blazing Light Manjushri), in the Manjushri Hall at Deer Park Institute, Bir, India
Source: Deer Park

A Wondrous Grove of Wish-Fulfilling Trees

A glimpse of the life and liberation of our beloved Guru,
All-Pervasive Lord of the ocean of buddha families and mandalas,
Manjushri Chökyi Lodrö,
Upholder of all the teachings of the Buddha,
Supreme Illuminator of the Tripitaka through words and reasoning,
Fearless Lion of Speech,
Glorious and Most Excellent One,
known as the
Wondrous Grove of Wish-Fulfilling Trees.

───

The Biography of Jamyang Khyentse Chökyi Lodrö Rime Tenpa'i Gyaltsen Tsuklak Lungrik Nyima Mrawa'i Senge Pel Zangpo

by Kyabje Dilgo Khyentse Rinpoche

All-pervasive dharmadhatu, Manjushri's wisdom *body*,
Wellspring of infinite teachings, mellifluous Brahma *speech*,
Filling the whole of space, immaculate, indestructible vajra *mind*,
May the Guru, ocean of fearless wisdom, be victorious!
As you watch over those born in this degenerate time,
Your compassionate smile of unceasing grace
Blossoms like a white lotus[1] in the garden of the enlightened mind.
Replete with the nectar of the two accumulations
And having perfected completion, maturation, and purification,
You appear with infinite kayas and wisdom as the fourth
  Perfect Guide,[2]

The illuminator of this dark age:
Field of merit for the three worlds,
Teacher of gods and humans,
Lion of the Shakyas, at your feet I bow.
Lord of the buddha families
Imbued with the inexhaustible secret qualities of infinite buddhas,
Wondrous activity of wisdom, compassion, and power,
You manifest as the fearless vidyadhara for those difficult to tame.

Sole source of teachings in the Land of Snows,
Protector, whose every undertaking contributes untold help and
    happiness,
Magical cloud-like display of adamantine wisdom:
To you, the Sovereign Lord Padmasambhava, I bow.
Custodians of the sublime celestial stream of Buddhadharma—
The seven patriarchs, six ornaments, and two supreme ones,
Nine vidyadharas, eighty-four mahasiddhas,
The ancestral Dharma Kings and their ministers,
Learnèd and accomplished translators and panditas of the
    eight great chariots—
Complete with all the qualities of liberation,[3]
Overflowing with devotion and the deepest respect,
We are drawn to your ocean of prodigious activity,
Like bees to a garden of udumbara flowers.

Gentle protector, from the immense cloud-like display of your
    wisdom,
Gracefully arranged throughout infinite realms,
May the precious, gentle rain of unfettered activity,
Amass in my mind throughout all my future lives.

Waves of impartial activity,
Enriched with the priceless treasure of your noble inherent nature,
And your resplendent majesty, beyond imagining;
To you, teacher of all the buddhas, I offer praise.

Your vajra speech is, likewise, perfect—
Even the sweet lyricism offered by Brahma's heavenly flute is pitiful
    by comparison.

If sublime beings cannot conceive all the qualities of complete
   liberation
How could *I* ever understand or express them?

Infinite phenomena—the knower and all that is knowable—
United as one within the mirror of wisdom,
Has the power to pervade and go beyond both samsara and
   nirvana;
Fount of all teaching, vast and profound,
Lord of the learnèd and accomplished ones,
Jewel in the crown of those who uphold the teachings,
Great pioneer from whom the Buddha's teachings spring;
The marvelous and immaculate example of your life, as rare as an
   udumbara flower,
Like sun and moon, floods Jambudvipa with a blaze of light.

In the depths of your mind's ocean-like renunciation,
The four continents of the excellent path[4] overflow with the wealth
   of the two accumulations.
From the luminous sun and moon of the great secret tantra,
The effulgence of maturation and liberation lights up the whole
   of space,
And countless dharani clouds embellish the citadel of the devas,
   the wisdom mind.

Only father of the buddhas of all directions and times,
You are the sole companion of beings to be tamed in the three
   realms.
Just as a flawless jewel suffuses the ocean with its brilliance,
Ordinary people can fathom very little of your many-faceted life,
Yet throughout all the infinite buddhafields,
You are renowned for being truly authentic—
As you should be, since those with such profound realization
Appear but rarely in this world.

Therefore, even this paltry evocation of your exemplary life,
This sliver hewn from a precious gem,
When read or heard by the intolerant and narrow-minded,[5]
Has the potential, by its very nature, to liberate.

Just how it was possible for my limited mind[6] to grasp any part of the life of Jamyang Khyentse Chökyi Lodrö will now be clearly explained.

> Our glorious and sublime Guru,
> Treasury of all the noble teachings of the buddhas,
> Lord of Dharma,
> Praised and honored for your glorious, inexhaustible knowledge and wisdom,
> Great Dharma King,
> Supreme Sovereign of Dharma,
> Refuge of gods and all beings,
> Lord of the ocean of buddha families and mandalas,
> To dare to speak your name is to limit
> The infinite abundance of your exceptional qualities.
> Yet it is for ordinary people that I teach,
> And by uttering the words
> "Jamyang Chökyi Lodrö Rime Tenpa'i Gyaltsen Palzangpo"[7]
> I hoist the banner of that illustrious name
> High above samsara and nirvana.
>
> You bestow temporary and ultimate benefit and happiness on all sentient beings
> Through the radiance of your enlightened mind and activity, filling the dharmadhatu;
> As the Jinas proclaimed, you are
> The magical display of the hero Manjushri,
> The jnanasattva of all the buddhas.
> Even bodhisattvas dwelling on the highest bhumis
> Cannot fully comprehend the manifestation of such a supreme being,
> Or the immensity of your sphere of activity.

From the *Magical Net of Manjushri*:

> First of the supreme kayas, holder of the three kayas,
> Embodiment of the five buddha kayas,
> All-Pervasive Lord, possessor of the five wisdoms,
> Adorned with the crown of the Lord of the five buddha families,
> Holder of five eyes, free from attachment,[8]

> Bringer-forth of all the buddhas,
> Offspring of the buddhas, supreme among the excellent ones.

And,

> The great heart[9] of all the buddhas,
> With various wheels of emanations.

Such things have been said many times. And from the *Flower Garland Sutra*:

> Having fully attained an ocean of enlightenment,
> To perfectly mature an ocean filled with multitudinous beings,
> You manifest an ocean-like mind filled with bodhichitta,
> And continuously display an ocean of unobstructed activity.[10]
> Such is the emanation of the sugatas.

Similarly,

> Known as the primordial Buddha Bhagavat Manjushri Jnanasattva,
>   omnipresent Lord,
> Your glory is renowned throughout samsara and nirvana.
> Having complete control over the three kaya buddhafields,
> How you appear (your different forms and names[11]),
> And your enlightened activity, and so on,
> Are all by nature inconceivable, unceasing, all-pervasive, and
>   spontaneously present.

Your manifestation as either "one who tames" or "one to be tamed" knows no limit, and your unimaginable magical display brings benefit to sentient beings to whom you appear, each according to their needs.

From the *Magical Net of Manjushri*:

> Possessor of the continuum of the nirmanakaya buddhas,
> Sending emanations, many and various, throughout the ten
>   directions.

And also,

> One who knows the minds of all beings,
> Who is present in the minds of all beings,
> Whose activities are fitted to the minds of all beings,
> Who brings contentment to the minds of all beings.

And also,

> Going beyond conceptual mind to dharmata,
> Embodying the nondual nature of wisdom,
> Free from concept and spontaneously accomplished,
> Performing the activities of the buddhas of the three times.

As it is said in the *Sutra of the Torch of the Triple Gem*,

> They could be princes among poets, composers of verse,
> Performers, drummers, strong men, and musicians,
> Dancers moving in elegant circles, flourishing ornamental garlands,
> Conjurers performing magic tricks,
> Cities, governors of cities, and charioteers.
> They could be sea captains, merchants, or householders,
> Kings, ministers, counselors, and messengers,
> Physicians, laymen, scholars, observers of ritual;
> Or they could manifest as great trees in solitary places,
> Medicine, inexhaustible treasure of incalculable worth,
> A wish-fulfilling jewel, a wish-granting tree,
> A guide for travelers who have gone astray.

Appearing with various names and in different forms in innumerable worlds throughout all of space and with the characteristics of buddhas, bodhisattvas, shravakas, pratyekabuddhas, panditas, siddhas, spiritual friends, deities, rishis, chakravartin kings, feudal lords, ministers, subjects, householders, birds, and animals; appearing as arts, crafts, and all beneficial, skillful activities; as the sun, the moon, jewels, the excellent vase, potent medicines, trees, ships, bridges, food, clothing, and shelter, to name but a few. Everything cherished by sentient beings is none other than the magical display of Manjushri himself.

I will now say a little about Manjushri, based on what can be found in the sutras and tantras.

A Short Biography of Manjushri

Long ago, Manjushri became fully enlightened as the Tathagata Nagadhiraja[12] and Bhagavan Manjuketu. And it is said that in the future, he will demonstrate the attainment of enlightenment as the Tathagata Sarvarakshaka.[13] Presently, in a buddhafield north of the world of Saha, having attained enlightenment as the Tathagata Ratnaparvatadhiraja,[14] he is undertaking the buddha activities that help sentient beings who need to be tamed. In this same realm, King Shuddhodana, the father of our Guide,[15] is also said, ultimately, to be an emanation of Manjushri.

When Buddha attained complete enlightenment, Manjushri assumed the form of a tenth bhumi bodhisattva and spoke with him about all the vast and profound approaches to Dharma. By manifesting various magical displays, Manjushri subdued beings to be tamed and matured countless others by articulating that which is beyond the reach of ordinary minds—for example, the preeminence of the Buddha. In China, on Mount Wutai Shan, the five-peaked mountain, Manjushri was born miraculously as an eight-year-old child. From the knot of a tree, he immediately revealed the Chinese astrological sciences. In Shambhala, having appeared as the king of humans, Manjushrikirti,[16] he essentialized the primordial Buddha's excellent twelve thousand root tantras into the five chapters of the *Abridged Kalachakra Tantra* and liberated beings to be tamed into a single vajra family. It is said that in the future, Manjushrikirti will arise again as Raudra Chakrin, subdue all the barbarians of Jambudvipa, and bring about the next golden age.

There are numerous examples of how Manjushri miraculously took on the different forms that made it possible for him to accept into his care most of the panditas and siddhas of India and Tibet. Even the buddhas of the three times continually offered garlands of praise to the vast ocean of his infinite great qualities.

Therefore, from the *Magical Net*:

> By the blessings of great compassion,
> The activities of buddhas on worlds in all ten directions
> As numerous as the atoms they contain are beyond imagination.
> Through the body, speech, mind, qualities, and
> Spontaneously accomplished activities of the buddhas,
> The potential of tamable beings is not wasted,

Those in the lower realms are purified and enlightened,
And the perfection of the accumulation of wisdom manifests unceasingly.

That being said, there follows a brief account in three parts of how our Lord Guru, Manjushri, appeared in person to those with limited perception as the vajra master and engaged in innumerable activities to tame sentient beings by manifesting in various different forms.

Good in the Beginning[17]
A Brief Account of the Wondrous Garland of Rebirths

Good in the Middle
The *Great Biography* of Jamyang Khyentse Chökyi Lodrö

Good at the End
Conclusion: An Account of the Continuation of His Extraordinary Activities in the Future

A Brief Account of the Wondrous Garland of Rebirths

Jamyang Khyentse Chökyi Lodrö's previous incarnations in India and Tibet, both the successive and simultaneous magical displays, brought great benefit to sentient beings and to the teachings. Those mentioned in the *Succession of Lives* and in the *Great Biography* are well known. Others, however, are not listed in either volume, although they are referred to in the expanded and abridged versions of the *Prayer to the Garland of Rebirths* by Khyentse Chökyi Lodrö himself. Here is a list of a few of those great masters.

Vimalakirti the Licchavi,[18] the "human vidyadhara," was honored by our guide, Buddha Shakyamuni, as a great and fearless bodhisattva with prodigious intelligence. He was one of the five outstanding individuals who became Vajrapani's first students after Vajrapani first brought the Vajrayana teachings to the continent of Jampudvipa and, on the peak of Mount Malaya in the land of Lanka, opened the secret treasury of tantra. Drime Drakpa applied each and every one of the ocean-like activities of a true Mahayana bodhisattva and led the Dharma King Lungten Dorje (King Ja the Fortunate) and others to enlightenment.

Mahapandita Smritijnana, whom the pandita Danashila praised for his great learning and realization, was unrivaled throughout India, from east to west. When he visited China and Tibet, he demonstrated countless miracles and Dharma activities.

Bhikshu Namkhai Nyingpo was born into the Nub clan and became the authorized holder of the four rivers of transmission of the secret mantra and the Vishuddhi mandala. He attained the supreme accomplishment equal to that of the Great Heruka.[19]

Könchok Jungne, also known as Langdro Könchok Jungne and Langdro Lotsawa, was one of Guru Padmasambhava's heart-sons and endowed with wisdom, compassion, and power.

Mila Shepa Dorje (Milarepa) was king of siddhas in the Land of Snows, principal heart-son of the great translator Hevajra Marpa, and celebrated illuminator of the practice lineage.

Yutok Yönten Gönpo,[20] the buddha of medicine in the form of a vidyadhara, possessed immeasurable wondrous qualities and extraordinary compassion and blessings. He helped beings in countless ways, but mainly through healing.

Drikung Kyobpa Rinchen Pal was an emanation of the great pioneer Nagarjuna and was endowed with sublime qualities. His appearance on this earth was predicted by the Buddha, and his activities were so prodigious that they filled the whole of space.

Lotsawa Sherab Rinchen, the translator from Mustang, was a great scholar and siddha and was nurtured by Manjushri himself.

The glorious Lama Dampa Sonam Gyaltsen[21] appeared as the seventh holder of the glorious Sakya lineage. A great treasury of wisdom, compassion, and power, he was Lord of all the learnèd and accomplished ones.

Muchen Könchok Gyaltsen was heart-son of omniscient Ewampa (Ngorchen Kunga Zangpo) and Chakrasamvara in the form of a vajradhara.

Gö Lotsawa Yezang Tsepa[22] was educated and supported by numerous Indian and Tibetan scholars and siddhas, and he actively upheld, safeguarded, and spread the Buddha's teachings in every direction. He was universally renowned as an authentic master.

Vidyadhara Tsewang Drakpa was the body, speech, and mind son[23] of the Dharma King Ratna Lingpa, illuminator of the teachings of the Nyingma school. He lived to the age of 110 years, and his every action was wholeheartedly directed towards benefiting all beings.

Sakya Lotsawa Jampe Dorje, learnèd in the five areas of knowledge and described in a prophecy as an emanation of the great translator Vairochana, acknowledged that he himself was a manifestation of the Dharma Lord Sakya Pandita.

Jamgön Amnye Zhab Kunga Sonam[24] was born into the luminous Khön lineage and embodied the excellent qualities of scholarship and realization.

Pema Gyurme Gyatso[25] was sovereign master of the Kama and Terma teachings, one of Orgyen Terdak Lingpa's sons, and an emanation of Hayagriva. He was both extremely learnèd and highly realized.

Lobsang Tsangyang Gyatso (the Sixth Dalai Lama) was Padmapani in human form, the sole source of peace and happiness in the Land of Snows.

Rigdzin Longsal Nyingpo Pema Do-ngak Lingpa (Longsal Nyingpo) was an emanation of Langdro Lotsawa, who subdued the samaya breakers and malevolent spirits of this dark age through the power of Pema Drakpo.

Drubwang Mingyur Namkhai Dorje, the fourth Dzogchen Rinpoche[26] and Vimalamitra in person, perfected the four visions of clear light and brought great benefit to everyone with whom he made a spiritual connection.

These names also appear in Jamyang Khyentse Chökyi Lodrö's autobiography. For example:

> One evening, while memorizing the *Vajra Vidarana Dharani*,[27]
> As I gazed at Katok Monastery[28] bathed in moonlight,
> A great sadness overcame me.
> Again and again, memories of the glorious Sakya Monastery
>   appeared in my mind,
> As well as vague impressions of my previous incarnations in the
>   Khön lineage.
> Other of my rebirths also surfaced from time to time,
> For example, Ngari Panchen, the great Lhatsün, Ngawang Lobsang
>   Gyatso (the great Fifth Dalai Lama), Tsangyang Gyatso (the Sixth
>   Dalai Lama), Pal Khyen, and the rest.

This is how some names appear explicitly, and those that are not specifically mentioned are included in "and the rest."

KING TRISONG DEUTSEN

Khyentse Chökyi Lodrö had a very clear memory of having been Dharma King Trisong Deutsen. While he was still very young and living at Katok, he and a group of young tulkus were asked to recount, without making anything up, any memories they had of who they had been in previous lives. Tulku Lodrö reported that he remembered being a layperson who wore gold earrings and a blue silk brocade robe. Laughing, the other tulkus teased him, saying, "Tulku Lodrö was a *layperson* in a previous life!"

Later, at Dzongsar, someone noticed a thangka that had been painted according to the instructions of the previous Khyentse, in which the Dharma King Trisong Deutsen was wearing the very same blue robe. Although this seems to clarify the context of his dream, like a splinter of stone returning to its place on a damaged rock, Chökyi Lodrö's only comment was, "How can a child's prattling be taken seriously?"

However, the vivid image of a layman in blue Tibetan-style clothing and wearing long golden earrings[29] was often on his mind, and I overheard him say, "How could *he* be a Dharma King? It's far more likely that he was just an ordinary Tibetan."

Jetsün Milarepa

While at Dzongsar, Chökyi Lodrö mentioned some memories he had of having been Jetsün Milarepa. One day, after washing his hands in the sunny courtyard, he gazed up at the snow-capped, mist-shrouded peaks of the Dza mountains in the south and asked me, "When you look up at such mountains, what goes through your mind?"

Lost for words, I said nothing, so he continued, "When I look at these mountains, feelings of both joy and sorrow well up inside me, and I long to sing songs of realization. Perhaps this happens because in the past I was a Kagyüpa. And you are not being candid with me! When you were in retreat, you wore nothing but a white shawl and were never separate from a statue of Milarepa. Isn't that so?" Then he laughed.

This clearly confirms that he remembered being Milarepa.

Do Khyentse Yeshe Dorje

In the longer version of the *Prayer to the Garland of Rebirths*, he wrote,

> I pray to the emanations of Yeshe Dorje's body,
> Kunga's speech, Wangchok's mind, Losal's quality,
> And the great activity of Khyentse Wangpo,
> Manjushri in person.

This verse confirms that Khyentse Chökyi Lodrö was also the body manifestation of Do Khyentse Yeshe Dorje,[30] a true heruka, who was himself the incarnation of omniscient Jigme Lingpa.[31] The glorious heruka Do Khyentse Yeshe Dorje had the power to tame beings. By appearing in different forms and engaging in various activities, like killing then restoring to life, he subdued those hostile to the lineage holders, the teachings of the *Indestructible Essence of Clear Light*, and particularly nonhuman spirits.

Rigdzin Jigme Lingpa

Do Khyentse Yeshe Dorje and the omniscient Lord Guru, Jamyang Khyentse Wangpo, the great illuminator of all the teachings in the Land of Snows, were both incarnations of Rigdzin Jigme Lingpa and lived at the same time. It is widely known that they were of one mind, and as Khyentse Wangpo himself confirmed, when Do Khyentse entered parinirvana, he dissolved into Khyentse Wangpo. As Patrul Rinpoche wrote,

> Your excellent body, imbued with the first of the ten powers,[32]
> Is supreme among the five buddha families
> And those prophecied by the "lotus of nonattachment."[33]
> May the remaining auspicious circumstances from your previous life
> Land in the palm of your hand in this life,
> And may the truth of this prophecy be realized.

Patrul Rinpoche offered a prayer of longevity along with thirteen statues of Amitayus to Khyentse Wangpo to create auspicious circumstances for him to live for eighty-five years, which was how long the prophecies had predicted Jigme Lingpa would live.[34]

Omniscient Dodrupchen Jigme Tenpe Nyima (1865–1926), the emanation of Jigme Thinley Öser and heart-son of Jamyang Khyentse Wangpo, empowered Khyentse Chökyi Lodrö through the ritual of abhisheka as the great king of the four kayas[35] in the mandala of the *Gathering of Vidyadharas* of the *Heart Essence of the Vast Expanse*. At that time, he offered Chökyi Lodrö the secret name Pema Yeshe Dorje.[36] This made it clear that the reason the incomparable mahasiddha Dodrupchen Rinpoche took such great compassionate care of Khyentse Chökyi Lodrö was because he knew the secrets of our Lord Guru's past lives.[37]

During the empowerment and transmission of *Self-Liberation from Grasping* bestowed on Khyentse Chökyi Lodrö by Dzogchen Khen Rinpoche Sonam Chöphel, Khenpo spread out a leopard skin mat and confirmed that the mind of the supreme lama, Chökyi Lodrö, was inseparable from that of Do Khyentse Yeshe Dorje. Khyentse Chökyi Lodrö, who was a monk at that time, felt a little uncomfortable about this,[38] but later realized it was a sign[39] that foretold his future.

Not only that, Khyentse Chökyi Lodrö widely propagated the teachings of the *Luminous Heart Essence* and was able to maintain the discipline of the Mantrayana precisely. He even admitted that he had understood and realized the profound meaning of the ground, path, and fruition of Dzogpachenpo, which is beyond the comprehension of most people.

Vajradhara Ngorchen Kunga Zangpo

Although Kunga's speech has already been mentioned, it was not clear to which Kunga it referred: Kunga Nyingpo, Kunga Gyaltsen, or Kunga Zangpo. However, I heard Khyentse Chökyi Lodrö say that he had been blessed with many visions of the vajradhara Ngorchen Kunga Zangpo. It is therefore logical to infer that he was most likely the speech emanation of omniscient Ewampa, Buddha's representative in the north.[40]

(Why Khyentse Chökyi Lodrö stated explicitly that he had been blessed by Sakya Pandita directly and in meditative experiences will be explained later in this text.)

As a result of the pure motivation and kindness of our Lord Guru, the centers for the study and practice of the secret philosophical texts on sutras and tantras by Sachen Kunga Nyingpo, Sakya Pandita, Chögyal Pakpa, and their followers flourished in all directions. Logically, this proves that he was the emanation of the combined speech activity of all these masters.

Gyurme Tsewang Drakpa

According to prophecy, Terchen Chokgyur Lingpa's three sons were the emanations of the three bodhisattvas Manjushri, Avalokiteshvara, and Vajrapani. It seems that Chökyi Lodrö had vivid recollections of having been an emanation of Manjushri, who was both a scholar of unrivaled ability and a highly realized master. His name was Gyurme Tsewang Drakpa, and his secret name was Wangchok Dorje. We know this because one evening my Lord Guru presented me with the finest of gifts and asked me to investigate his previous life. As I know myself all too well, I was painfully aware that an investigation carried out by such an insignificant being would be unreliable at best. But as I lacked the courage to find a good reason for not responding to a direct request from my own guru, I quickly acquiesced and began to examine my dreams.

One night, I saw Jetsün Rinpoche Drakpa Gyaltsen, the great Sakya Pandita, and Chögyal Pakpa sitting together on one of the previous Khyentse's thrones in the empowerment hall at Dzongsar. When I told Khyentse Chökyi Lodrö about my dream, he instructed me to examine it further.

I told him that in the dream I had heard a voice declaring itself to be Nub Namkhai Nyingpo. Khyentse Chökyi Lodrö responded by suggesting that as the emanations of Namkhai Nyingpo are said in the treasure teachings of Khyentse, Kongtrul, and Chokling to be Tersey[41] Tsewang Drakpa and Tsawa Rinchen Namgyal, it could well have been the voice of Tersey. It seemed to me that later he discreetly acknowledged he was indeed the mind incarnation of Tersey, because he completed all of Tersey's unfinished Dharma work and both put into practice and transmitted the treasure teachings of Chokling.

Khyentse Chökyi Lodrö wrote many texts clarifying the teachings, including those about how to teach tantras with restriction seals. He also established new study and retreat centers at both of Chokgyur Lingpa's monasteries, which without doubt benefited the continuity of the Buddhist teachings. He recognized eminent tulkus, made a point of giving them extensive transmissions and teachings, enthroned them on the seat of Dharma, and so on. Therefore, directly and indirectly, the teachings of this lineage and the holders of the teachings have all rested in the shade of our Lord Guru's monumental compassion.

Shalu Losal Tenkyong

As for Khyentse Chökyi Lodrö being the quality emanation of Losal, I heard our Lord Guru say that he felt unceasing devotion for the supreme emanation, omniscient Shalu Losal Tenkyong. He also said he believed it was Shalu Losal Tenkyong's face that sometimes flashed into his mind—a clear sign he was the quality emanation of that great master.

The style in which Khyentse Chökyi Lodrö taught the profound meaning of the great secret tantra was quite distinctive. A specific example of this is that when he received special authorization[42] for the *Kalachakra Tantra*, he propagated it widely by giving the empowerments, instructions, and clarifications.

Twenty-Fifth King of Shambhala

He also promised to manifest in the future as the Twenty-Fifth King of Shambhala.

Tsarchen Losal Gyatso

It was believed that Khyentse Chökyi Lodrö truly loved the tradition of the Dharma King Tsarchen (Losal Gyatso), and he said himself that he had been blessed by Tsarchen's wisdom body. He spread the teachings of the oral tradition of Lamdre still further by encouraging the serious practice and propagation of the profound instructions of the *Path and Fruition: The Explanation for Private Disciples* in the meditation centers he established for its practice. Consequently, it was clear to everyone that Chökyi Lodrö possessed all the qualities of Tsarchen Losal Gyatso.

He was unquestionably the great emanation of Jamyang Khyentse Wangpo's infinite ocean of activity, because in the spirit of Rime, he championed and propagated all existing teachings and worked tirelessly for the benefit of all sentient beings. That he actually manifested Jamyang Khyentse Wangpo's qualities was something even Chökyi Lodrö himself admitted, as you will see.

The Supreme Guru Jamyang Khyentse Wangpo

As a result of their regular discussions on meditative experience and realization, omniscient Lodrö Taye praised Khyentse Wangpo highly, describing him as a great pioneer of the teachings whose extraordinary qualities were beyond compare. Manjushri Mipham (Mipham Rinpoche) also expressed admiration for him in his writings, as did his heart-son, omniscient Dodrup Tenpe Nyima (the Third Dodrupchen Rinpoche).

For many centuries, the precious teachings on sutra, tantra, and the arts and sciences had been firmly established in the Land of Snows. They came to Tibet thanks to the visionary activities of the three ancestral Dharma Kings and the kindness of the enlightened panditas and translators. During the centuries since their introduction, innumerable beings had studied and practiced them and, as a result, had become learnèd and realized lineage holders. However, by Jamyang Khyentse Wangpo's time, many of the surviving lineages were on the verge of extinction. So much so that even though teachers continued to proclaim themselves to be intellectually learnèd, they were rarely able to identify the true essence of the Buddha's teachings.

The opportune ripening of aspirations Khyentse Wangpo had made during his previous lives meant that, with great confidence and determination, he was able to travel as a wanderer far and wide throughout central and greater Tibet with his mind focused solely on one goal: to benefit the precious teachings of the Buddha.

Over a period of more than thirteen years, he endeavored to serve more than 150 teachers of the Nyingma and Sarma schools through the three ways of pleasing the master. Consequently, he received all the teachings on the sutras, tantras, and arts and sciences from all the study lineages that existed in Tibet at that time. He assiduously received empowerments, instructions, and oral transmissions—from the well known to the extremely rare—from the Nyingma and Sarma lineages and published all the related instruction texts to ensure their preservation.

At various times throughout his life, he practiced the sadhanas of an enormous variety of deities, as well as completion meditation. He remained in his room for the latter part of his life, where he practiced continuously, never once crossing the threshold. This was how he achieved all the relevant signs of accomplishment as described in the respective texts. He also attained the wisdom of the inseparability of shunyata endowed with all sublime aspects[43] and supreme, unchanging great bliss—he even admitted to being a fully accomplished, sky-like yogin. He dissolved the gathering of nadi, prana, and bindu into the expanse of his central channel, and the clear inner vajra signs that he had accomplished the bhumis and path matured fully.

The buddhas and bodhisattvas, as well as the scholars and siddhas who were the illuminators of the Buddha's teachings in the sacred lands of India and Tibet, cared for and blessed him repeatedly, each bestowing their own secret treasury of instructions. Jamyang Khyentse Wangpo was therefore able to receive directly in pure visions all the profound teachings of the Nyingma and Sarma lineages and reveal numerous profound new and rediscovered treasures. The treasury of the great expanse of his realization (the innermost essence of his mind) burst out, and he continuously experienced visions of the innumerable deities of the three roots and gained mastery over the limitless teachings he had received in pure visions and as oral transmissions.

He mastered the samadhis of the stream of Dharma and, by remembering the secrets of his past lives, fully understood the crucial points of the teachings. As a result, he was able to truly live up to his name and reputation for being a great pioneer of all the Buddha's teachings.

It would be impossible for ordinary people to fully understand even a fraction of the extraordinary qualities of Khyentse Wangpo's three secrets, which bring benefit to the teachings and happiness to all beings. To be more precise, for the benefit of the holders of the teachings of the Nyingma and Sarma schools, regardless of whether they were high or low or just ordinary people, by actively guaranteeing the gift of Dharma through its continuous propagation in ways that suited each individual's capacity, he breathed new life into the teachings of the Buddha and ensured that all lineages would remain unbroken and continue to spread in the future.

Jamyang Khyentse Wangpo's flawless, clairvoyant wisdom led him to empower Jamgön Lodrö Taye, the great translator Vairotsana himself, as the transmission holder of the *Five Great Treasuries*.

Citing the authentic words of the omniscient Buddha and predictions made by Padmakara in his treasure teachings, and by virtue of Jamgön Lodrö Taye's extensive teaching and writing activities, the King of the Victorious Ones, Jamyang Khyentse Wangpo, honored Jamgön Rinpoche as a great Rime master and illuminator of the teachings of the Buddha. He then bestowed many rare empowerments and transmissions on Jamgön Kongtrul and gave him a list of the uncommon treasure teachings he intended to assemble and some volumes of those that had already been compiled.

Jamgön Kongtrul went on to receive some of the rare empowerments and instructions from the Nyingma and Sarma schools that Lord Khyentse had received during his life, the essence of which were put together in a collection of twenty volumes called the *Infinite Profound Instructions*. Although he had already received some of the teachings, he took them again from Khyentse Wangpo, who had received them directly in pure visions; others he had not received before.

As a result, thanks to the positive auspicious circumstances created by Jamgön Kongtrul Lodrö Taye and Terchen Chokling's repeated requests that Khyentse Wangpo reveal teachings, and as the three of them were of one mind, the vast treasure teachings of the *Secret Treasury of the Seven Great Transmissions* were revealed, not one of which had been seen or heard before. The essential instructions from the Nyingma tradition's ocean of profound treasure teachings, distinguished by the six transmissions, were then compiled by these great masters, creating the *Precious Treasury of Terma Teachings*.

Jamyang Khyentse Wangpo revealed the tradition of the chariot of the *Treasury of Precious Instructions*, the innermost essence of the essential teachings of the Buddha in the Land of Snows (the experiential practice lineage of which exists to this day) that were then gathered into one complete cycle distinguished by the power of its blessings. The noble Jamgön Lodrö Taye then wrote whatever clarifications were necessary and propagated this cycle by teaching it again and again, reinvigorating the teachings and ensuring the continuity of the lineages for future generations. The remaining three treasuries also came into existence because Lord Khyentse requested and inspired Jamgön Lodrö Taye to put them together and was both personally and indirectly involved in the process.

Lord Khyentse laid the initial foundation for a series of teachings to be given on these great treasuries of Dharma, and at the end of the teaching, by making vast mandala offerings of thanksgiving, he paid tribute to both the teachings and the teacher, declaring they were both absolutely authentic. He went on to explain why they were so crucially important and made powerful aspiration prayers to create positive circumstances for the proliferation and longevity of these teachings and for their ever-increasing benefit to beings.

Again and again, Jamyang Khyentse Wangpo gave Jamgön Kongtrul Lodrö Taye every support to accomplish his extraordinarily beneficial activities, thereby fulfilling the true meaning behind the prophecies of the ominscient Buddha and Padmakara. These two great masters were both student and teacher to one another. Their minds merged inseparably, and their aspirations and activities were as one.

The noble Jamgön Lodrö Taye honored Jamyang Khyentse Wangpo, saying he was an unrivaled scholar, a great siddha, and a pioneer of all the teachings of the Buddha in the Land of Snows. He praised Jamyang Khyentse Wangpo repeatedly and acknowledged all his exceptional qualities and compassion, saying that it was solely owing to the grace and kindness of his Lord Guru that he had not incurred the karma of abandoning the Dharma[44] this lifetime. He also declared that Jamyang Khyentse Wangpo was his main root guru.

Jamyang Khyentse Wangpo recognized Orgyen Chokgyur Lingpa as the incomparable and preeminent treasure revealer of his time. He removed obstacles and increased Chokgyur Lingpa's realization by bestowing on him the initiations of Vajrakilaya and Vishuddha Heruka. Through the blessings of Jamyang Khyentse Wangpo's enlightened mind, Chokgyur Lingpa's throat chakra was liberated,[45] and the two wisdoms matured in his mind.

When Chokgyur Lingpa first met Jamyang Khyentse Wangpo, the auspicious connection they had made during their lives as King Trisong Deutsen and his son was reawakened and any degenerate condition restored.

This enabled Chokgyur Lingpa to discover an extraordinary secret repository of treasure teachings that had never before been revealed. Also, both personally and indirectly, Chokgyur Lingpa was responsible for identifying hundreds of locations where treasures were hidden, and his activities for the benefit of beings spread in all directions.

This cooperation between Jamyang Khyentse Wangpo and Chokgyur Lingpa led to most of their treasure teachings being attributed to them both, especially the four cycles of guru sadhanas, the cycle of the *Seven Heart Essences* teachings, and most significantly, the *Three Categories of Dzogchen*. Together they also revealed and deciphered many other treasure teachings.

It's well known that the continuity of blessings from the *Heart Essence of Manjushri* called the *Seventh Lamp*—one of Lord Khyentse's profound mind treasures—is included in the *Heart Essence of the Three Bodhisattvas*, which is part of the *Three Categories of Dzogchen*.

On many occasions, Terchen Chokgyur Lingpa perceived Lord Khyentse in the form of the main deity of the mandala of whichever empowerment he was receiving—for example, as Vimalamitra, Yangdak Heruka, or White Tara, the noble wish-fulfilling wheel. He also said that Padma Ösal Dongak Lingpa (Jamyang Khyentse) was his ultimate root guru and looked upon him as Lord of the enlightened families, the sole object of refuge upon whom he could rely. As it is said, "The five king tertöns are surrounded by a hundred servants."

Jamyang Khyentse Wangpo was empowered as the fifth king of tertöns and representative of Guru Rinpoche as a result of vajra prophecy. All the major and minor tertöns who appeared at various times were his students, whether they met him or not—for example, Terchen Lerab Lingpa, Drime Pema Lingpa, Khamtrul Tenpe Nyima, and Sangwa Kundrol Tsal (a Bön tertön). As they were his students, Khyentse Wangpo cleared away all their obstacles and supported them as necessary by, for example, giving them advice about how to fulfill the prophecy that they would benefit the teachings and beings. They, in turn, relied exclusively on Jamyang Khyentse Wangpo as the authoritative clarifier of any doubts they may have had about the treasure teachings they revealed.

For example, Jamyang Khyentse Wangpo and Jamgön Lodrö Taye were supposed to decipher one of Jamgön Kongtrul's treasure teachings, the *Embodied Realization of the Three Roots*, but as they were unable to do it together, it was left unfinished. Later, after Jamyang Khyentse passed away, even though Jamgön Lodrö Taye was perfectly capable of translating the symbolic script, he didn't do it because he was unable to clarify his queries with Jamyang Khyentse.⁴⁶

Jamyang Khyentse Wangpo cared for the mahapandita Mipham Jamyang Namgyal (Mipham Rinpoche) by bestowing on him an ocean of vast and profound instructions and opening the door to the wisdom of perfect knowledge. Khyentse Wangpo made Mipham Rinpoche the ritual offering of body, speech, and mind representations and gave him his own pandita hat and other articles. He then named him Mipham Jamyang Namgyal Gyatso to create auspicious circumstances for his future activities. In this way, Khyentse Wangpo empowered Mipham Rinpoche as the propagator of the Buddha's teaching with the three skills of a scholar, which gave Mipham Rinpoche the authority to write many commentaries clarifying the sutras and tantras.

As a result of Khyentse Wangpo's aspirations and the auspicious circumstances he created, Mipham Rinpoche was able to manifest according to Jamyang Khyentse Wangpo's wishes and become a great scholar whose fame spread in all directions.⁴⁷ An unrivaled pioneer of the Nyingma school, Mipham Rinpoche taught widely and promoted the teachings and practice of a vast number of philosophical sacred texts, especially those on the three inner yoga tantras (mahayoga, anuyoga, and atiyoga), which became his unique legacy.

Both Lord Khyentse Wangpo and Terchen Chokling urged Palyul Gyatrul Dongak Tenzin to compile the Kama teachings of the Nyingmas, and by way of encouragement, Lord Khyentse conferred on him the entire transmission (both the empowerments and the oral transmissions). And during "commanding the spirits" at the end of the Kasung Legden empowerment, the image of Legden shook so terrifyingly, it was as if Legden himself had entered and possessed it. Khyentse Wangpo then entrusted the protector with activities over and over again.

Khyentse Wangpo gave Palyul Gyatrul Dongak Tenzin detailed teachings about how to be a ritual master, including all the necessary advice about ritual objects. This led to Palyul Gyatrul Dongak Tenzin establishing an annual drupchö of the twenty-seven great mandalas of Kama at the illustrious monastery of Palyul Namgyal Changchub Ling.

After that, Khyentse Wangpo collected all the original texts belonging to the Kama tradition, including those for which the oral transmission lineages were still intact, and had them brought to the monastery, where he oversaw the carving of new woodblocks for the entire collection. This was how he laid the foundations for gradually increasing the number of Kama texts kept at Katok, Shechen, and Dzogchen monasteries. At Terchen Chokling's two monasteries, the auspicious door to the establishment of Kama drupchös was also opened. In this and many other ways, the continuity of the teachings of the Kama lineage was ensured and widely propagated, thanks solely to Jamyang Khyentse Wangpo's astonishingly prolific activity, of which this is just one small example.

When the vajradhara in human form Sangdak Jamyang Loter Wangpo decided he wanted to compile the tantras, he was convinced that the *only* way to accomplish his task was first to take refuge in Jamyang Khyentse Wangpo. So Loter Wangpo approached Khyentse Wangpo, much to Khyentse Wangpo's delight.

"At one point, I also thought about compiling the tantras," said Khyentse Wangpo, "but couldn't because so many other activities required my attention. But if *you* were to do it, the benefit would be enormous."

He promised to provide Loter Wangpo with whatever support he needed and conferred on him a vast number of empowerments, oral transmissions, and profound instructions on completion meditation, as well as explanations of the major and minor tantras transmitted through many different traditions, particularly the Sakya, Ngor, and Shalu. He advised Loter Wangpo of the authentic sources he needed to consult to establish an order for the *Compendium of Tantras* and which rituals to include. He also gave him guidance about how to elaborate and abbreviate the structure, as well as methods for adapting rituals and the details of ritual practices from different traditions of the outer and inner tantras. He also took full responsibility for correcting and editing the collections and for doing any research necessary, and so on.

Jamyang Khyentse Wangpo urged Jamyang Loter Wangpo to receive the transmission of tantras belonging to the Marpa, Ngok, and Jonang traditions from Jamgön Kongtrul Lodrö Taye, as he would need them to accomplish his task. Khyentse Wangpo instructed his own student, Drakyab Dongkam Tripa Ngawang Lobsang Damchö Gyatso, to catalog all these tantras and assigned Mangthö Norbu Tenzin and others to support and help Loter Wangpo. Consequently, before long, the profound compilation of the great ocean of secret tantras was complete. And Khyentse Wangpo promised to sponsor the initial teaching event.

One outcome of having gathered the tantras together in this way was that all the public and restricted Lamdre texts were also effortlessly and naturally compiled within the collection, as was Mipham Rinpoche's extensive commentary on the *Kalachakra Tantra* (although it could not be included in the principal section).

At the heart of these great Dharma treasuries lie almost all Jamyang Khyentse Wangpo's extraordinary secret writings—particularly in the *Compendium of Sadhanas*, which is a compilation of the countless sadhanas and instructions related to the four classes of tantra that had been bestowed on learnèd and accomplished acharyas in the Land of Sublime Beings (India) by Buddha Vajradhara himself and by many individual yidam deities. These teachings were translated into Tibetan, taught by the lotsawas, and held and propagated by authentic scholars and siddhas—the lineage holders—who kept them alive.

Khyentse Wangpo included in the *Compendium of Sadhanas*

- all the individual tantric teachings with unbroken instruction lineages—for example, authorization blessings, and so on—the origins of which could be authenticated;
- some texts concerning the extraordinary sadhana practices that originated in the Kama and Terma traditions of the Nyingma;
- teachings taken from the *One Hundred Sadhanas of Bari Lotsawa*;
- the *Ocean of Sadhanas*;
- *One Hundred Sadhanas from the Narthang Tradition*; and
- *Two Kinds of Blessings of the Eighty Mahasiddhas*.

These teachings were based on the original manuscripts, sadhanas, and written instructions produced by the authentic early masters, and those that needed clarification were embellished with Jamyang Khyentse Wangpo's own unique explanations. Eventually, the exhaustive compilation of this great Dharma treasury was completed, brimful with many, many wonderful qualities, like that of describing the correct and absolutely reliable method for perfecting the two accomplishments, free from the extremes of being too elaborate or too abbreviated.

Khyentse Wangpo also composed numerous miscellaneous writings that were not included in the great treasuries, like the collection of praises, the songs of realization, writings on the major and minor sciences, and numerous notes. There also exist many profound treasure teachings that were not included in the main body of the *Precious Treasury of Terma Teachings*, like the mind treasure *Luminous Heart Essence of the Three Roots*.

The teachings mentioned above represent a mere fraction of Jamyang

Khyentse Wangpo's contribution to the Dharma. In short, the great Dharma treasuries, which alone brought about the revitalization of the Buddha's teachings in the Land of Snows, were compiled by the power of Jamyang Khyentse Wangpo's inconceivable enlightened mind and skillful activity. There is no doubt the intention behind these collections was to ensure that the teachings survived these degenerate times. Even now, as teachings continue to disappear, we owe the fact that we still have a huge variety of the most crucial Dharma teachings to choose from entirely to the graciousness of the Lord Guru, Jamyang Khyentse Wangpo. And it is imperative that the holders of the teachings persevere in their service of the Dharma by studying, propagating, and practicing these teachings in remembrance of the kindness of our revered guru, Jamyang Khyentse Wangpo.

In the words of the noble Jamgön Lodrö Taye,

> Within the Buddhist tradition of Tibet,
> He is Lord of the Gathering, the Lord of All;
> For this reason alone, in this world
> He embodies the qualities of the second Buddha.

And,

> Elements, like the earth, are powerful,
> Yet cannot equal the power of the all-encompassing sky;
> Likewise, the example of his extraordinary life is unique
> Among the holders of the teachings in the Land of Snows.

Mipham Jampal Gyepe Dorje (Mipham Rinpoche) also praised him highly, saying,

> Nowadays in the Land of Snows,
> Those acknowledged to be siddhas are neither scholars nor are they disciplined,[48]
> And to discern the result of practice among those who are learnèd is hard,
> Which makes finding anyone with all these perfect qualities[49] extremely difficult.
> But in your case, the qualities of knowledge, discipline, and realization multiply,
> As if vying with one another for supremacy.

Wondrous as these qualities may be, to recognize them isn't easy, Consequently, they are rarely perceived.

Many masters have praised Jamyang Khyentse Wangpo's exemplary life in the highest possible terms. For details we can consult

- his *Great Biography*;
- the biography of Jamgön Kongtrul Lodrö Taye;
- the biography of Chokling's treasure teachings that were given in response to questions;
- the list of transmission lineages and catalog for the *Five Great Treasuries*, the *Compendium of Tantras*, and the *Compendium of Sadhanas*;
- and so on.

This brings to a conclusion a brief explanation of the wondrous succession of the previous lives of Jamyang Khyentse Chökyi Lodrö.

Some of these learnèd and accomplished masters lived at the same time, others appeared towards the end of another master's life, but most appeared consecutively. Khyentse Wangpo himself confirmed that he had been an emanation of all the most renowned, learnèd, and accomplished masters in India and Tibet.

It is beyond the capacity of ordinary, short-sighted beings to understand how one master can be the emanation of many others. Unlike the consciousness of an ordinary being, which is blown into the womb of its future mother by karmic winds, the consciousness of a great being is not reborn in the three realms by the power of karma. The power of the aspirations and compassion of those who dwell in the bhumi of realized beings is what causes them to appear in many different forms (the magical display of wisdom beyond one and many). In the same way the sun's reflection will appear in multiple containers of water and fit each one according to its shape and size, each master is adapted to meet the needs of countless types of beings to be tamed.

As it is said in the *Treatise on the Sublime Continuum*,

> Just as Brahma, without moving from his dwelling place,
> Effortlessly appears in all the realms of the gods,
> The dharmakaya Buddha, without moving from his true nature,
> Effortlessly manifests to fortunate beings in all the worlds.

How emanations appear for the benefit of others is described in the *Ornament of the Mahayana Sutras*:

> Although that is how it is, by this power,
> And the relative fate of beings,
> Throughout samsara's existence
> Their activity will never cease.[50]

Second:

The Great Biography of Jamyang Khyentse Chökyi Lodrö

In two parts:

Part 1: Mostly the general explanation of the ordinary biography
Part 2: The special explanation of the extraordinary biography

Part One: The Ordinary Biography

The ordinary biography is a general explanation written from the point of view of ordinary beings who have similar karma and aspirations. It is in seven parts:

1. How Jamyang Khyentse Chökyi Lodrö manifested as a result of the aspirations and magical displays of his past incarnations and came to be enthroned as a supreme tulku.
2. How Jamyang Khyentse Chökyi Lodrö embraced the three trainings (precepts) that are the entrance to the Dharma.
3. How Jamyang Khyentse Chökyi Lodrö studied (hearing and contemplation) with supremely learnèd and accomplished teachers, and perfected his education.
4. How Jamyang Khyentse Chökyi Lodrö attained the signs of having accomplished the practice of the path by training his mind in the yoga of the two profound stages of meditation (kyerim and dzogrim).
5. How Jamyang Khyentse Chökyi Lodrö performed excellent activities for the benefit of the teachings and beings.
6. How Jamyang Khyentse Chökyi Lodrö spontaneously accomplished the accumulation of vast merit during the course of his main activities.
7. How Jamyang Khyentse Chökyi Lodrö dissolved his body into the dharmadhatu after successfully completing his last activity, plus supplementary explanations.

1. How Jamyang Khyentse Chökyi Lodrö manifested as a result of the aspirations and magical displays of his past incarnations and came to be enthroned as a supreme tulku.

Since the enlightened aspiration and activity of noble beings never waver for a moment from helping those to be tamed, the great bodhisattvas do not linger in the bliss of nirvana but take birth in samsara to master the beings of this degenerate time.

From the *Verse Summary of the Prajnaparamita Sutra*:

> Wherever the hero (bodhisattva) dwells *is* transcendent wisdom:
> He has gone beyond the three realms of samsara yet has not entered nirvana;
> All emotion has been extinguished, yet he appears to be reborn;
> He is beyond aging, sickness, and death yet appears to die.

And,

> Just as a powerless maidservant is controlled by her master,
> A hero is controlled by the needs of all sentient beings.

The nature of the sublime ones is, therefore, to work ceaselessly through their limitless manifestions for the benefit of beings to be tamed.

The vajra words of the second Buddha, Guru Padmasambhava, repeatedly predicted that the three protector bodhisattvas Manjushri, Vajrapani, and Avalokiteshvara would frequently manifest emanations—particularly King Trisong Deutsen, the emanation of Manjushri, whose kindness and compassion for his Tibetan subjects were immense. Therefore, one way or another, these great beings have continued to appear in this world.

Jamyang Khyentse Chökyi Lodrö displayed the unmistakable signs—detailed in the *Embodiment of the Guru's Realization*—of an emanation predicted by prophecy. If we examine his writings and activities, we are left in no doubt that the innate karmic connections he had had with profound treasure teachings dated back to early childhood. However, in his great wisdom, his root teacher, Katok Situ Rinpoche, felt that at that time and in that place it would be entirely inappropriate for Chökyi Lodrö to reveal treasure teachings and make prophecies, especially given the state of the Dharma in those days, and repeatedly scolded Khyentse Chökyi

Lodrö if he did so. His tutor felt the same way, which reinforced Khyentse Chökyi Lodrö's resolve to keep his extraordinary qualities hidden. He even went so far as to give the impression that he felt such things were unimportant.

Lord Guru Khyentse Wangpo writes in the part of his autobiography where he talks about his future lives,

> In the future, I will die while practicing the *Guru Yoga of*
> *Vimalamitra*,
> And immediately dissolve into the heart of Mahapandita
> Vimalamitra—the basis of my emanations—
> Who dwells on the five-peaked mountain.
> By the power of my aspiration to manifest in five different forms,
> I will benefit all lineages of the Buddha's teachings.

And so the omniscient Dharma King Khyentse, having completed his activity in the form of Jamyang Khyentse Wangpo, dissolved into the heart of Vimalamitra, and the five inexhaustible hidden qualities of body, speech, mind, quality, and activity manifested once more to benefit all teachings and all beings. How he fulfilled his own prophecy will now be explained.

Jamgön Vajradhara Lodrö Taye, in his letter of prophecy, wrote about where the supreme tulku would be found:

> A river of nectar flows to the right,
> A river of gold flows to the left,
> From the confluence of these two,
> One league up a hill,
> Three emanations have been born,
> In the years of the snake, the horse, and the sheep.

The precious supreme emanation (Jamyang Chökyi Wangpo, 1894–1908/9) was born in the year of the horse at the confluence of the Zil and Dri[51] rivers. He was recognized and named by the Fifteenth Gyalwang Karmapa, Khakyab Dorje, and enthroned at Dzongsar, the main seat of Jamyang Khyentse Wangpo.

The speech emanation, the First Beru Khyentse Rinpoche, Karma Jamyang Khyentse Özer (1896–1945), was given his name and robes by Jamgön Lama Kongtrul Rinpoche and enthroned at Palpung Monastery by

Khenchen Tashi Öser. Born to the king of Beri in Treshöd, he received the *Three Precepts* from Khenchen Tashi Öser.

From the Fifteenth Gyalwang Karmapa, Khakhyab Dorje, he received

- the oral transmission of the precious *Kangyur* and the most detailed empowerments of the mandalas of the great *Treasury of Kagyü Tantras*, preceded by a seven-day drupchö; and the effective instructions and oral transmission;
- explanations of the *Profound Inner Meaning*;
- *Two Sections of the Hevajra Root Tantra*;
- the *Treatise on the Sublime Continuum*;
- two minor treatises, the *Tilopa Zhung Chung* and the *Naropa Zhung Chung*;
- detailed effective instructions on the profound path of the *Six Yogas of Naropa*;
- the cycle of Mahamudra teachings;
- *One Hundred Jewel Sources* from the Jonang tradition;
- empowerments, authorization blessings, and explanations of the tantra of *Tarayogini* according to the Anuttarayoga;
- the empowerment, pith instructions, and profound teachings of the special Dharma protector Mahakala from the Kamtsang tradition;
- all the empowerments and authorization blessings for the five retinues of Mahakala and their followers; and
- the oral transmission for the writings of all red and black hat Karmapa incarnations.

From the Dharma Kings of glorious Dzamthang, he received

- the empowerments and oral transmission for Chakrasamvara from the Jonang tradition;
- the *Infinite Lord of Death* cycle of teachings;
- all the empowerments and oral transmissions of the collected writings of Jetsün Taranatha;
- the great empowerment of Kalachakra according to the Jonang tradition; and
- guidance on the completion meditation of the six-branch practice of vajrayoga[52] (Kalachakra).

From the great scholar Lama Tashi Chöphel, he received detailed explanations of the ten branches of science and numerous important empowerments and oral transmissions.

From the Tenth Surmang Trungpa Rinpoche, he received the *Treasury of Vast Teachings* and the *Treasury of Precious Instructions*.

From Gyalse Jamgön Choktrul, he received the entire transmission of the *Precious Treasury of Terma Teachings*.

The First Beru Khyentse Rinpoche studied extensively and went on pilgrimage to the holy places in India, China, central Tibet, and Bhutan. He established a retreat center for practicing Künrig at Palpung Monastery and made new print blocks for the collected writings of his guru, the Fifteenth Gyalwang Karmapa, Khakhyab Dorje. All his Dharma activities, study, and meditation were quite marvelous.

The mind emanation, Phakchok Dorje (1893–1943), was the body, speech, and mind[53] son of Mahasiddha Shakya Shri. He perfected the three ways of pleasing his father, the mahasiddha, with unwavering devotion and perceived his every action purely. His main activity was to practice the essence of the teachings, through which he mastered the royal seat of realization.[54] He followed in his father's footsteps by completing the remainder of the mahasiddha's activities and liberated various beings into the joyous grove of definitive meaning[55] by giving them the effective instructions.

During a conversation with Phakchok Dorje about his experience and realization, Chökyi Lodrö praised him, saying that he had complete power over his realization of the view of the supreme vehicle. He then received from Phakchok Dorje the empowerments and instructions from Shakya Shri's mind treasures, and so on.

Phakchok Dorje was gifted with the ability to benefit the teachings on the profound meditative practices; for example, he made the ultimate object of offering, the dharmakaya, accessible to ordinary people by publishing the exact words of his father's extraordinary direct instructions on Mahamudra and Dzogchen.

The activity emanations were the master Khyentse Chökyi Lodrö, who was born in the year of the water snake (1893), and the supreme tulku, Dzogchen Khyentse Rinpoche, who was born in the year of the sheep (1895) and recognized and enthroned by the Fifth Dzogchen Rinpoche, Thubten Chökyi Dorje,[56] at Rudam Dzogchen Monastery. His knowledge and realization were peerless.

The most reliable source of information about all this is Jamyang Khyentse Wangpo himself, who said that one of his emanations would appear in the Sakya family. Dagchen Ngawang Thutop Wangchuk then confirmed himself to be that Khyentse emanation and was later renowned as such, having manifested many extraordinary signs of accomplishment. For example, immediately after his father passed away, he visited the country of Shambhala and brought back a bouquet of Shambhalan flowers that everyone could see.

The omniscient guru Manjushri[57] worked tirelessly to keep the bodhisattva vow of upholding, preserving, and propagating all the teachings of the Victorious Ones. Since his activities were propitiously timed, he had many close students throughout Amdo, central Tibet, and Kham[58]—as many as there are specks of dust on this great land. Some were renowned teachers, while others were hidden yogis, and their devotion and pure perception enabled them to recognize many of Khyentse Wangpo's tulkus.

After the Fifteenth Gyalwang Karmapa had formally recognized him, Khakhyab Dorje Jamgön Situ Padma Wangchok Gyalpo of Palpung[59] traveled to Palpung Monastery through Menshö Dzongsar.[60] At that time, Jamyang Khyentse Wangpo said to his messenger, "When Palpung Situ Choktrul passes by on his way to Palpung, he doesn't need to come up here to see me. Instead, when he sees my house, tell him that the person living there is Khyentse."

When the house came into view, the message was duly delivered. At that very moment, Khyentse Rinpoche, holding a bundle of long incense tied with a white scarf, appeared on the veranda and looked down at Palpung Situ Tulku. He then turned to Dzogchen Khen Rinpoche Padma Dorje, who was with him, and said, "Gyalwa Karmapa, Kongtrul Rinpoche and I named and enthroned that boy with one intention in mind. You and I must bless and entrust him with the wisdom mind transmission so that he becomes inseparable from us." This was how Palpung Situ Tulku was specially blessed by Khyentse Rinpoche.

When Katok Situ gave empowerments and teachings, the sound of his voice and style of teaching were very similar to those of Khyentse Wangpo. Shechen Gyaltsab Rinpoche Pema Namgyal and Terchen Lerab Lingpa said they felt he was a magical display of Jamyang Khyentse's wisdom mind.

Other emanations were also recognized by Jamyang Khyentse Wangpo's heart-sons (both scholars and siddhas) after he passed away.

There was a great and remarkably knowledgeable khenpo named Lobsang Tenzin Gyatso at Sido Monastery in the region of Dome Rekong, from whom I received the empowerments and explanations of the *Guhyasamaja Tantra* and the *Chakrasamvara Tantra*. During a private conversation, his students asked me to write a prayer based on the garland of his lives. So first I examined my dreams. I saw the khenpo as Rechung Dorje Drakpa and

Jamyang Khyentse Wangpo, and when I told Khenpo what I'd seen, he read the detailed biographies of both those masters.

"As a follower of the Gelug tradition," he said, "when I first began my studies, my attitude was sectarian. Now, having heard teachings from all traditions and having understood the essential points, I realize there is no fault greater than having prejudices about different traditions, imagining some are good and others bad. I now follow the example of the early Kadampa masters and consider that no teaching contradicts any other. I will now receive Nyingma teachings from you in order to make a connection with them. I'll then do the approach and accomplishment practices, buy the text of the *Precious Treasury of Terma Teachings*, read the teachings of all lineages in detail, and pray that I will hear and teach the *Precious Treasury of Terma Teachings* in my next life."

He wrote all this in the letter to Dzongsar Khyentse Chökyi Lodrö that I took with me when I returned to Dzongsar Monastery, along with his offerings and requests for prayers of protection. Khenpo asked me to say prayers for the fulfillment of his wishes and received from me the empowerment of the *Gathering of the Sugatas of the Three Roots*. He even accomplished the sadhana practice.

When I told the Lord Guru Chökyi Lodrö about Khenpo Lobsang Tenzin Gyatso buying the Terdzö texts, and so on, he said, "Jamyang Khyentse Wangpo is believed to have made the promise that one of his own emanations would appear in each of the four Buddhist schools of Tibet, including Yungdrung Bön. This khenpo may well be the Khyentse emanation of the Gelug school."

Although I lack the knowledge and realization of all the other Khyentses, I have also included myself in this list of Khyentse emanations, because when Sangdak Loter Wangpo visited our house less than a month after my birth and my mother showed me to him, he said, "In my dreams, I have seen Jamyang Khyentse Wangpo very clearly for three nights in a row, and each time he looked extremely happy. Surely this boy must be an emanation of Khyentse!"

He then gave me a single mala bead and an authentic blessing cord, both of which had belonged to the previous Khyentse, and put a beautiful white scarf around my neck.

When I was three, Shechen Gyaltsab Rinpoche, Pema Namgyal, came to our house and said to my father, "Give me this child!" He went on to say that I was an extraordinary tulku.

Later, at sixteen, when I was pronounced a Khyentse emanation, I was offered the extraordinary representations of body, speech, and mind[61] and Mipham Rinpoche's letter. Jamgön Chökyi Lodrö was also present and said, "Jamgön Loter Wangpo and Kyabje Gyaltsab Rinpoche have gazed on this boy with their wisdom eyes and seen him to be the mind emanation of Jamyang Khyentse. In my own mind, too, I have no doubt that he is the mind emanation of Khyentse."

He offered me the representations of body, speech, and mind and recited many prayers to invoke auspiciousness. Later on, when I met him during my first visit to Dzongsar, he said, "Last night I saw Jamyang Khyentse Wangpo very clearly in a dream. It must have been a sign that you would be coming."

Such things exist in the pure perception of noble beings, but I myself know nothing of them. It was not my intention to write about myself here, but it came up in the process of describing Jamyang Khyentse Wangpo's emanations. It is clearly stated in the biographies of mahasiddhas of the past, like Thangtong Gyalpo and Gyalwang Karmapa Mikyö Dorje, that great beings who have attained the level of a sublime bodhisattva are able to manifest many pure and impure emanations simultaneously to benefit sentient beings. Maybe I am one of the impure emanations?

The Detailed Biography of Jamyang Khyentse Chökyi Lodrö

I will now write the detailed biography of the illustrious Jetsün Lama, the most exalted of incarnations, the crown that tops their victory banner. He embodied all the same qualities and engaged in the same activities as the Dharma King Jamyang Khyentse Wangpo and was therefore the manifestation of activity that embodied the three secrets and quality. By the power of both his compassion for beings and their merit, he was reborn in the form of an ordinary human being.

From the *Treatise on the Sublime Continuum*:

> Just as the image of Indra's body
> Is reflected in the immaculate lapis lazuli floor,
> In the pure ground of the mind of ordinary beings,
> Appears a reflection of the form of the Muni[62] king.

Our teacher, Jamyang Khyentse Chökyi Lodrö, the sun-like embodiment of the wisdom of all the buddhas, was born in the land of four rivers and six mountain ranges known as Dokham in the region of Zalmogang. Here, through four counties known as the four knots of land, flows the golden Drichu (Yangtze) River, and in the county called the knot of the land of Rekhe, the great tertöns Dudul Dorje and Longsal Nyingpo revealed their profound treasures. Pema Dechen Lingpa and Katok Rigdzin Tsewang Norbu described it as the "sacred vajra land."

The district of Rekhe was the responsibility of a great local guardian called Yönten Ritra, known as Iron Man, who is also the protector of the Vajrakilaya teachings. It was here that Jamyang Khyentse Chökyi Lodrö was born—or to be more precise, in Ajam, in the district of Sa-ngen Rekhe.

His paternal forebears included many outstanding vidyadharas. Gyalse Pema Namgyal was a descendent of Dudul Nüden Dorje, who had attained the tenth bhumi and was one of twenty-five powerful vidyadhara representatives of Guru Padmasambhava. He settled in the Ser Thar region of Kham and, given the time and place, must have been Katok Gyalse Pema Namgyal, the great master who could clearly see past, present, and future, and who was mentioned in the colophon of the Vajrakilaya practice by Jamgön Rinpoche from the Khön lineage.

Gyalse Pema Namgyal's son was the old tertön of the Ser valley, Dudul Rolpatsal Nüden Namkhai Naljor. His qualities of wisdom, compassion, and power were unrivaled, and he revealed numerous profound treasure teachings. Renowned as the manifestation of Dudul Dorje and cared for and blessed by the wisdom body of Dudul, he gained control over his life span and lived for 180 years. His activities were vast, and during the latter part of his life, he visited the districts of Drak Yab and Sa-ngen, where he eliminated and subdued all human and nonhuman enemies of the teachings with the power of his wrathful activity.[63] When Katok Monastery appointed him as their göndak, he settled in the district of Sa-ngen.

After he passed away, his consort went to see Jamyang Khyentse Wangpo, who received from her the lineage of all the treasure teachings of Dudul Rolpatsal in the form of the dakinis' seal of entrustment.[64] The texts of these treasure teachings were kept in the library at Dzongsar Monastery.

A son was born to this accomplished mahasiddha in the latter part of his life and was blessed by his body, speech, and mind. This boy was named Serpa Tersey Gyurme Tsewang Gyatso and was to become the father of our excellent Lord Guru Khyentse Chökyi Lodrö. Dudul Rolpatsal bestowed on his son all the empowerments of his own treasure teachings, as well as those revealed by Dudul. He spent a long time at Mindrolling Monastery, where he studied extensively and also received Kama and Terma empowerments, teachings, and ritual practices from Trichen Yizhin Wangyal, Jetsün Dechen Yeshe Chödrön, Dorzin Döndrup, and others.

Khyentse Wangpo cared for Gyurme Tsewang Gyatso with tremendous love, bestowing on him many profound teachings in their entirety, most notably the empowerments and teachings of the *Ocean of Dharma That Combines All Teachings,* which took more than half a day.[65] He showed him a small volume that was the original manuscript of the *Ocean of Dharma That Combines All Teachings,* written in dakini script and Tibetan; the yellow scroll of the *Magical Net of the Three Roots;* and a chakra in the form of a text that liberates when worn.

He also gave him the empowerments of

- *Avalokiteshvara Resting in the Nature of Mind;*
- *Yamantaka,* one of the *Seven Profound Cycles of Chokling;*
- the rediscovered treasure, the *Gathering of the Dakini's Secrets;* and
- the *Heart Essence of Deathless Arya Tara.*

During the empowerment of the *Heart Essence of Deathless Arya Tara,* Jamyang Khyentse Wangpo conferred on Gyurme Tsewang Gyatso the secret name Chime Nangze Dorje[66] and empowered him to be the holder of all of these teachings. Jamyang Khyentse Wangpo also gave him the extensive empowerments, explanations, and oral transmissions of the two volumes of the *Heart Essence of the Vast Expanse,* saying, "You will need this when you go to central Tibet."

When Gyurme Tsewang Gyatso offered Jamyang Khyentse Wangpo the tantric costume of the old Tertön of Ser, Khyentse Wangpo gave it back to him, saying, "A time will come when you'll need it," thus confirming Jamyang Khyentse Wangpo's prophecy that his next incarnation would be reborn as the son of this authentic vidyadhara.

Jamgön Lodrö Taye also very kindly took care of Gyurme Tsewang Gyatso. As they were both emanations of one master,[67] Jamgön Rinpoche considered Tsewang Gyatso worthy to be lineage holder of the treasure teachings from the *Embodied Realization of the Three Roots* and recognized him as the lineage holder of the *Secret Essence* and *Seven Verses* cycles. He bestowed all the empowerments and explanations on him in detail.

Gyurme Tsewang Gyatso also received the extensive transmissions of the *Precious Treasury of Terma Teachings,* including the supplementary texts and all the treasure teachings of Chokling, from Palyul Kuchen, Katok

Situ, and many other noble masters. He perfectly accomplished the recitation practices and the creation and completion meditations for numerous yidam deities, and bound the Dharma protectors to be his servants. He eliminated the negative forces that harm the Dharma and beings through wrathful practices. On numerous occasions, the signs of his power were plainly apparent, even to those who harmed others.

At Khochen Monastery in Gonjo, the main object of reverence was the Pehar spear in the protectors' hall, which had once been incorporated into the straw statue of Gyalpo Ku Nga at Samye Monastery. It was first concealed[68] by Guru Rinpoche, then later rediscovered by Minling Terchen.[69] One day, looking rather drunk, Gyurme Tsewang Gyatso threw the spear from the roof of the main temple. It hung in midair for several seconds before falling harmlessly to the ground. This is one example of how Gyurme Tsewang Gyatso became renowned for being extremely powerful while outwardly maintaining the appearance of a carefree yogi.

He transmitted numerous profound teachings, and his great Dharma legacy was that he gave our Lord Guru many profound Kama and Terma teachings, such as the *Sutra which Gathers All Intentions* and the *Magical Net*, the entire transmission of the *Precious Treasury of Terma Teachings*, and the treasure teachings of Chokling.

Khyentse Chökyi Lodrö was the son of this great vidyadhara, who possessed peerless qualities of wisdom, compassion, and power, and Tsultrim Tso, who possessed all the characteristics of a dakini, like gentle behavior and immense compassion for others, and who had been born into a family of mahasiddhas known as Amdo Sergyi Chadral of the Achak Dru clan.

Chökyi Lodrö was born[70] in the fifteenth rabjung in the female water snake year called *namgyal*, during the celebration of the harvest of the three autumns. He said no detailed record existed of the exact position of the planets and stars and their transits at the moment he entered his mother's womb or of when he was born. Although his parents would undoubtedly have had auspicious dreams around the time of his conception, and wonderful signs must have appeared at the time of his birth, his father, a realized yogi who had completely dismantled illusion, kept no records, and no other reliable accounts of these events are known.

Jamyang Khyentse was brought up in the customary way, like any other child, and was fully supported by his family at every stage of his development. It was his father who gave him the name Jamyang Chökyi Lodrö.

How our Lord Guru was recognized as the supreme emanation of Manjushri Guru.

When the nephew of the previous Lord, Kalzang Dorje, wrote to Jamgön Kongtrul to inquire about the supreme tulku of Jamyang Khyentse Wangpo, Kongtrul Rinpoche replied by describing what he had seen with his irreproachable wisdom eyes. In a detailed letter written in his own hand, he said he was fully confident that Shakya Shri's son, Phakchok Dorje, was the mind emanation of Jamyang Khyentse Wangpo, and that Jamyang Khyentse Chökyi Lodrö was the activity emanation. In response to repeated requests from omniscient Situ Rinpoche of Katok (a nephew of Jamyang Khyentse Wangpo) for him to recognize an emanation of Khyentse at Katok Monastery, Jamgön Kongtrul said, "Omniscient Khyentse Wangpo is said to be the combined emanations of King Trisong Deutsen's body, Guru Rinpoche's speech, Namkhai Nyingpo's mind, Vimalamitra's qualities, and Langdro Könchok Jungne's activity. Of the twenty-five sacred places in Dokham, Katok Monastery is hailed as the place where beings are tamed. It is where the vidyadhara Longsal Nyingpo, an emanation of Langdro Könchok Jungne, established the teachings. And since that auspicious connection already exists, it would be of immense benefit for all teachings and beings, and especially Katok Monastery, if the activity emanation of Khyentse were taken to live there. However, since one of the Khyentse emanations will, according to prophecy, be a lay tantric practitioner, and since the emanation in question is a descendant of vidyadharas, he may well embrace the way of life of a tantrika and wander freely throughout the sacred lands."

Kongtrul Rinpoche then advised Katok Situ to raise the young tulku in his own household, not the monastery, and not to enthrone him or entrust him with any monastic responsibilities.

Following Jamgön Kongtrul's advice, when Jamyang Khyentse was seven years old, on an auspicious winter's day during a waxing moon, he was taken to the incomparable great seat of Katok Dorje Den Monastery, source of the study and practice of the Kama and Terma traditions and the oldest Nyingma monastery in Dokham. Snow fell heavily the day he arrived, turning the mountains white, a clear and auspicious sign that the radiance of his enlightened mind and activity would spread in all directions.

The extraordinary and auspicious circumstances for the gentle Dharma rain of study and practice to fall at glorious Katok—the unceasing, pervasive, spontaneous activity manifesting effortlessly in the three worlds—was created naturally, and Khyentse Chökyi Lodrö took up residence at Katok, in Dzong-go Tashi Khang Sar, the home of the great vidyadhara Longsal Nyingpo.

On an excellent, auspicious day, before the statue of the Muni king (Lhachen Palbar) in the main temple of Katok Monastery, Maitreya, the fifth supreme guide of this fortunate aeon manifesting as the omniscient mahapandita, supreme Lord of the teachings of the Nyingma tradition, Tai Situ Orgyen Chökyi Gyatso (Katok Situ Rinpoche), performed the haircutting ceremony and enthroned the tulku, giving him the name Jamyang Lodrö Gyatso Thubten Shedrup Gyaltsen Palzangpo. It is said that, in accordance with Jamgön Rinpoche's advice, no other special enthronement ceremony was performed.

While Khyentse Chökyi Lodrö was fully occupied with an extensive program of study at Katok Monastery, the supreme Khyentse Tulku at Dzongsar Monastery, the main seat of Jamyang Khyentse Wangpo, suddenly died.[71]

As Chökyi Lodrö had been recognized by Jamgön Rinpoche and from childhood had possessed all the excellent qualities of a realized being, the nephew and treasurer of the previous incarnation, Kalzang Dorje, insisted that Katok Situ Rinpoche send him to Dzongsar Monastery. If he did not, Kalzang Dorje said, the bond of samaya between Katok Situ and Khyentse Wangpo would be irrevocably broken![72]

So at fifteen years of age, Jamyang Khyentse moved to the second Shri Nalanda Dzongsar Tashi Lhatse, seat of the illustrious Sakya and Ngor lineages, blessed by the glorious protector of the beings of the three worlds, the Dharma King Phakpa Rinpoche, and took up residence at Tashi Chime Drupe Gatsel. The sun of auspicious circumstances dawned when Khyentse Chökyi Lodrö ascended the seat of Dzongsar as holder of all the teachings of the Buddha. By so doing, auspicious circumstances were created for the fortunate aeon of the sun-like activity of the previous Khyentse to radiate the light of his unceasing, pervasive, and spontaneous qualities throughout the Land of Snows once more.

From the *Ornament of the Mahayana Sutras*:

> Before engaging in practice, beings have
> Compassion, faith, patience, and
> Behave virtuously.
> These must be understood as the signs of buddha nature.

As it is said, since the power of sublime beings' buddha nature is unsurpassable and always perfect—unchanging, like the inherent majesty of a precious diamond—Chökyi Lodrö continued to be a perfect example. He was both physically disciplined and a mature and deep thinker, even though he had no personal tutor at that time to guide him. He inspired tremendous devotion by performing virtuous activities of such magnitude that they failed to penetrate the minds of ordinary people. For example, he continued the studies he had begun earlier with his noble teachers, received profound teachings from all lineages, taught them to devoted students, created holy images of the Buddha, and accumulated merit by making offerings.

For some ignorant beings whose minds had been overpowered by demons, such remarkable activities stung their hearts, causing them personally and through others to create many obstacles for him. However, our Lord Guru's mind, like Mount Meru, remained unwaveringly focused on loving-kindness and the discipline of humility, and he transformed the obstacles he faced into causes for the refinement of his noble qualities, which then blazed even more brightly—like wood thrown on a fire. Those who thought badly of him gradually realized how wrong they were, and as their respect and devotion for him grew, they bowed before his lotus feet.

This shows that noble beings who have yet to attain maturity and perfect their practice still have to face many obstacles. But as their minds are so great, they are not crushed by difficult circumstances and instead use obstacles to enhance their bodhisattva activities.[73]

How this works is explained in the *Verse Summary of the Prajnaparamita Sutra*:

> A prince who aspires to give away his wealth and help others
> Is much sought after as the leader of all, and
> Even now, as a prince, makes many happy.
> How much more happiness will he bring
> By accepting the crown and sustaining the monarchy.
> What more is there to say?
> Likewise, the bodhisattva who is wise,
> Makes gods and humans happy
> With the gift of amrita (the Dharma) and
> Even now, diligently benefits many.
> How much more benefit will he bring
> Once he has attained the state of Dharma King.

What more is there to say?
At that time, the hearts of demons will throb with pain,
Tormented by anguish, misery, suffering, mental illness, and weakness.
They will ask, "How can we make this bodhisattva depressed?"
To terrify him, they will set fire to the world, and stars will fall from the sky.
When demons cause such obstacles, wise beings with perfect intentions
Will contemplate the name and meaning of Prajnaparamita,
And like birds, their bodies and minds will soar into the sky.
What chance, then, will negative forces have to harm them.

Our precious Lord Guru's supreme father was a yogi who had transcended confusion, but from a worldly perspective, he didn't take much care of his son. The supreme protector Katok Situ's activity was so vast that he, too, had little time to devote exclusively to Chökyi Lodrö, whose personal tutor passed away when he was very young. So it seems he did not receive much special training or nurturing in his youth. Nevertheless, he kept alive all the major and minor activities that benefit both the teachings and beings with his own inherent power—like mercury scattered on the ground. No other master could rival him, nor could ordinary beings understand him. The magnificent, noble qualities of his activities were supreme and manifest from his compassion. Thus, his unsurpassable life story is wonderfully inspiring.

2. How Jamyang Khyentse Chökyi Lodrö embraced the three trainings (precepts) that are the entrance to the Dharma.

The second Buddha, Vasubandhu, said,

> With perfect discipline train in hearing and contemplation,
> And perfectly apply them to meditation.

This is how Khyentse Chökyi Lodrö, like Nagarjuna before him, enriched his mind with the adornment of the three vows by embracing the training in the *Three Precepts*, one after another. In this way, he entered into the precious teachings of our Peerless Guide, the incomparable Shakya Singha. It is also how he adorned himself with the discipline of unstained wisdom, which is like an ornament of pure gold, through the perfection of his training in the three disciplines.

In the *Sutra Completely Dear to Monks*:

> An extremely well-disciplined person is
> Beautiful to look at,
> Abides by the Vinaya,
> Trusts the practice of discipline,
> Accumulates in a single day
> Inexhaustible mountains of merit;
> And thus will attain enlightenment.

And Arya Nagarjuna said,

> "Discipline is the ground of all qualities," said the Buddha.
> "Just as the earth is the ground that supports animate and inanimate phenomena."

How Khyentse Chökyi Lodrö took the pratimoksha vow, knowing it to be the crowning glory of one who holds, propagates, and safeguards the Buddha's teachings.

At the age of ten, with a Sangha of five bhikshus as witnesses, Chökyi Lodrö took the shramanera pratimoksha vow of the Vinaya lineage from Katok Situ Pandita (to whom it had been transmitted by Jamyang Khyentse

Wangpo). The preceptor was supreme, omniscent Katok Situ Pandita, the Lord who possessed the good qualities of pure discipline and was learnèd in all Vinaya procedures; the activity acharya was our Lord Guru's tutor, Khenpo Thubten Rigdzin Gyatso, who had also been his teacher Katok Situ Rinpoche's tutor; and the rest of the monks were the other acharyas.

Jamyang Khyentse received his ordination name at this ceremony: Jamyang Lodrö Gyatso Tsuklak Lungrig Nyima Mra Wai Senge Thubten Shedrup Gyaltsen Palzangpo. I have heard him say, "The name Lodrö[74] has a special and auspicious significance for me, since no teacher who has given me a name has ever altered it." His father was the first, having named him Chökyi Lodrö when he was born.[75] Katok Situ Pandita named him Jamyang Lodrö Gyatso when he enthroned him as the supreme incarnation of Jamyang Khyentse Wangpo; Gyaltsab Gyurme Pema Namgyal, Shechen Gyaltsab, bestowed the name Jamyang Lodrö Gyatso on him when he took the bodhisattva vow; and Thartse Shabdrung of Wara Monastery named him Jamyang Chökyi Lodrö Rime Tenpe Gyaltsen Pal Zangpo.

At the age of twenty-six, Khyentse Chökyi Lodrö traveled to the great center of Nyingma teachings, Dzogchen Rudam Orgyen Samten Chöling Monastery. In the main meditation hall of the Tsering Jong Retreat Centre, before all the representations of the Triple Gem, he received bhikshu ordination according to the Vinaya lineage of Shantarakshita from omniscient Khenpo Jigme Pema Losal (Könchok Drakpa), assisted by Dzogchen Khenpo Sonam Chöphel as the activity acharya and three other monks who made up the required Sangha of five. This lineage was transmitted through Gyalse Shenphen Taye to Khenpo Pema Dorje to Khenpo Jigme Pema Losal.

In his pilgrimage guidebook to the sacred Ziltrom valley, Terchen Chokgyur Lingpa wrote that Khenpo Pema Losal was an emanation of the great Khenpo Bodhisattva (Shantarakshita) and endowed with all the excellent qualities. For example, he was extremely skilled at training monks in the Vinaya precepts through the practices of abstinence,[76] observance,[77] and authorization.[78] He was immensely compassionate and had the ability to prevent monks from transgressing their vows by connecting them directly with the precious precepts of the Vinaya, and in this way, he became the cause of their eventual liberation.

Later, in the year of the wood ox (1925) when he was thirty-five,[79] during a visit to central Tibet, Khyentse Chökyi Lodrö followed the tradition of his predecessor and once again received both shramanera and bhikshu ordination. He received shramanera ordination from Khenpo Ngawang Thubten Norbu at sunrise on the twelfth day of the third spring month, in the Shakyamuni Buddha temple at the great monastery of Ogmin Mindrolling, the radiant lotus realm in the Land of Snows. And before noon he received the bhikshu ordination, this time from Khenpo Ngawang Norbu Gyatso as preceptor, Gyurme Namdrol Gyatso as the activity acharya, Gyurme Sherab Tenzin as the secret guide, Gyurme Chöphel Tenzin as the timekeeper, and Patrul Gyurme Rigdzin Chöwang as the assistant, plus a few other monks to make up the required Sangha of ten. In this way, he continued to keep the pratimoksha vow of the bhikshu.

As Panchen Lobsang Chogyan wrote,

> In the words of Damchö Yarphel,
> Precious khenpo of the Vinaya lineage,
> "First rely on the lineage of the mahapandita;
> Next, generate supreme devotion and
> Gradually come to know all that is knowable;
> Then, having received the tremendous merit of full ordination,
> Apply what you have learnt appropriately."

How Jamyang Khyentse Chökyi Lodrö took the bodhisattva vow.

From the *Gandavyuha Sutra*:

> Noble son, bodhichitta is like the seed of all the teachings of the Buddha.

And from the *Verse Summary of the Prajnaparamita Sutra*:

> Here too, without bodhichitta,
> How can the wisdom of the sugatas emerge into the world?

From the *Category of the Bodhisattva Teachings*:

> One who wishes swiftly to attain supreme and perfectly complete enlightenment,
> Must practice the pure motivation of bodhichitta.

Although throughout beginningless time, Khyentse Chökyi Lodrö had perfected the practice of the bodhichittas of aspiration and action—the sole cause for becoming a buddha with the perfect qualities of benefiting oneself and others—to inspire his students, he reaffirmed the bodhisattva vows of both traditions. He took the bodhisattva vow of the Madhyamika tradition in the presence of the vajradhara Jamyang Loter Wangpo, omniscient Katok Situ Chökyi Gyatso, and Shechen Gyaltsab Jamyang Lodrö Gyatso'i Drayang, following the instruction manuals by Minling Terchen and Jamgön Kongtrul Lodrö Taye. He used Jamyang Khyentse Wangpo's instruction manual when he took the bodhisattva vow from the Chittamatra tradition. He again took the bodhisattva vows from the Madhyamika tradition in the presence of Venerable Gemang Choktrul Shenphen Chökyi Nangwa using the manual by Minling Terchen.

He took the bodhisattva vow of Patrul Rinpoche's lineage in the presence of Khenchen Kunzang Palden. He also took the bodhisattva vows from both the Madhyamika and Chittamatra traditions in great detail in the presence of the Chöje Jamgön Ngawang Lekpa, using manuals by various scholars and mahasiddhas; and in the presence of Palpung Situ Rinpoche, Pema Wangchok Gyalpo, he took the bodhisattva vows of the Chittamatra lineages. Each time he took these vows, he made vast and elaborate cloudlike offerings and mandala offerings.

Omniscient Katok Situ Rinpoche gave him the bodhisattva name Jamyang Gawe Gocha, and as he had faultlessly taken the vows of conduct appropriate to a son of the Buddha, the strength of the primordially pure potential of the Mahayana was awakened within him. Every second of his profound and vast activities would now help others for oceans of kalpas, and it was clear to everyone that he acted for the benefit of all sentient beings continuously and without interruption.

How Jamyang Khyentse Chökyi Lodrö took the secret mantra vows by entering the great mandalas of the Vajrayana and receiving empowerments.

When students receive the great tantric empowerments of Kama and Terma, the meaning of *empowerment* itself (what is purified and that which purifies) is identified and understood.

At the great temple of Katok Dorje Den, Khyentse Chökyi Lodrö received from his main root teacher, omniscient Katok Situ Rinpoche,

- the powerful and profound outer, inner, and secret empowerments within the *Mandala of the Peaceful and Wrathful Deities of the Magical Net*, which is the root mandala[80] of the eighteen Nyingma mahayoga tantras of the Kama;
- the four streams of outer, inner, secret, and accomplishment empowerments, together with the authorization for all the root and branch mandalas of the *Great Assembly* of the anuyoga;
- the eighteen empowerments for the display of rigpa from the "mind" category of the Dzogchen teachings;
- the meditation methods from the "space" category of Dzogchen teachings called *Guru's Blessings*; and
- the most elaborate, less elaborate, simple, and simplest empowerments from the *Unsurpassable Innermost Secret Mother and Son Heart Essence of Vimalamitra* from the Dzogchen pith instructions.

Of the treasure teachings from the great mandala of the 725 deities of the Kagye, he received

- the outer empowerment based on the ritual substances[81] for taking liberation as the path to tame those who are extremely angry;
- the inner body empowerment of taking the deity as the path to liberate those who are extremely proud;
- the secret mother empowerment of taking union practice as the path to tame those who are extremely passionate; and
- the empowerment based on the wisdom of taking discursive thoughts[82] as the path to liberate those who are extremely ignorant.

At the dawning of the auspicious condition of Khyentse Chökyi Lodrö's enthronement on the guru's Akanishta[83] seat (Tashi Chime Drupe Gatsel) at the second Shri Nalanda (Dzongsar Tashi Lhatse), the sun-like radiance of the unceasing, all-pervasive, spontaneously accomplished activity of Jamyang Khyentse's previous incarnation spread once more throughout the Land of Snows. At that time, since Khyentse Chökyi Lodrö had to practice the glorious Hevajra, the ultimate secret tantra and root practice of Khyentse Wangpo, he received for the first time the cause and path empowerments of the glorious Hevajra pith instructions from the Chöje Bodhibhadra of Dzongsar Monastery. I believe Lord Bodhibhadra received this empowerment from the vajradhara Khyentse Wangpo.

Later, while receiving the Lamdre teachings from the sovereign of the ocean of mandalas, the true vajradhara, Jamyang Loter Wangpo and Jamgön Dorje Chang Ngakgyi Wangchuk Kunga Lekpe Jungne Trinle Kunkhyab Palzangpo, he received the empowerment of the glorious Hevajra based on the sand mandala, which involves eight procedures.

At the great Dharma center of Lhundrup Teng, preceded by the ritual of being accepted as a student and the preparatory initiation, he received from the vajradhara, the supreme guru Khyenrab Taye, all the empowerments of the glorious Kalachakra, king of the nondual tantras, which includes the seven empowerments to guide ordinary beings[84] and the higher[85] and highest[86] empowerments based on the sand mandala. Jamyang Khyentse Wangpo, a great holder of the Kalachakra teachings, was one of the lineage masters of this teaching.

These are just a few of the main empowerments Jamyang Khyentse Chökyi Lodrö received. In addition, he received kriya, upa, yoga, and anuttarayoga tantras from numerous learnèd and accomplished masters, the details of which appear later in this text.

This was how Khyentse Chökyi Lodrö embraced the precepts of a vidyadhara in the ocean of Vajrayana tantras. Then, without wavering from the stream of yoga—the nature of his perceptions and actions were thoroughly immersed in the great purity of the display of the three vajras—he disciplined his ordinary discursive thoughts into the wisdom of the great seal of inseparable bliss and emptiness. Thus, he became the sovereign of all the sutra and tantra teachings of Buddha, the great vajradhara of the triple vow.

Since his naturally disciplined mind maintained all the major and minor areas of training related to the *Three Precepts*, by practicing awareness and vigilance without hypocrisy, he became completely faultless. All his actions, body, speech, and mind were an inspiring example for everyone and were not contradictory, being neither wild and heedless nor narrow-minded and uptight. Basically, his body, speech, and mind were unstained by wrongdoing, and his mind remained clean and pure. Even his physical appearance and behavior always adhered to those of a perfect monk, and he proved to be an ornament to the infinite ocean of the Buddha's vast teachings. In this degenerate time, the extraordinary hidden qualities that informed his exemplary life were extremely rare, like those of Atisha Dipamkara.

These days, most people place their trust in empty words, essenceless miracles, and temporary, mirage-like visions, believing them to be extraordinary. But I and those who think like me believe there's almost no one who can follow in the footsteps of Jamyang Khyentse Chökyi Lodrö, whose magnificent qualities so enriched and ennobled the teachings.

3. How Jamyang Khyentse Chökyi Lodrö studied (hearing and contemplation) with supremely learnèd and accomplished teachers, and perfected his education.

From the *Sutra Requested by the Noble Narayana*:

> Son of a Noble Family, if you can hear, knowledge will take birth
> in your mind; and if you are knowledgable, conflicting emotions
> will disappear.
> Maras cannot prey upon those whose minds are free from
> conflicting emotions.

From the *Ornament of the Mahayana Sutras*:

> First, hearing the teachings gives birth to right attitude,
> Then right attitude gives birth to the wisdom that realizes the
> ultimate truth.

From the *Verse Summary of the Prajnaparamita Sutra*:

> Therefore, wise people with strong aspirations
> For complete enlightenment subdue their pride;
> In the same way that the sick must rely on doctors to treat their
> illnesses,
> The wise must steadfastly rely on their spiritual companion.
> Bodhisattvas on the path to buddhahood,
> Who practice the paramitas, rely on spiritual friends.

Those who wish to attain the goal of enlightenment should cultivate their knowledge of the path of Buddhadharma. To step onto that path, they should first listen exhaustively to the teachings. In particular, it's essential for those masters who hold, propagate, and safeguard the precious teachings of the Buddha to fill their minds to the brim with the ocean of knowledge that is attained by listening. The extraordinary prerequisite for doing this is to rely on a spiritual friend.

From the *Perfection of Wisdom Sutra in Eight Thousand Lines*:

> A bodhisattva who is fully accepted and cared for by a spiritual friend
> Will attain the unsurpassable enlightenment of buddhahood.

From the *Verse Summary of the Prajnaparamita Sutra*:

> The Buddha of Supreme Knowledge said,
> "The Dharma of buddhahood is dependent upon a spiritual friend."

How Khyentse Chökyi Lodrö learnt to read and write, which is the basis of all knowledge.

At the age of six, while he was still living at his birthplace, Khyentse Chökyi Lodrö practiced reading with his uncle, Lama Gelek, and in the process effortlessly formed the black and white scripts[87] and memorized the seven branch offerings, mandala offerings, and so on, from the text called the *Embodiment of the Guru's Realization*. Later, shortly after his arrival at Katok Monastery, he continued his studies with great diligence. He started with reading and writing, guided by his tutor, Khenchen Thubten Rigdzin Gyatso, who had also been Kyabje Katok Situ Rinpoche's tutor. Khenchen had a million qualities of learning, discipline, and kindness, and he lived at Bartrö Chöling. Chökyi Lodrö said that in the course of little more than a year, he had to memorize all the ritual texts of Katok Monastery (about ten volumes) and then recite them from memory in the presence of Situ Rinpoche—much to Situ Rinpoche's delight.

Chökyi Lodrö's noble tutor advised him always to follow the ritual practices of the Kama and Terma teachings, and whether practicing them, studying, or engaging in everyday activities like sitting or eating a meal, he was always encouraged to model his behavior on the Vinaya teachings. Khyentse Chökyi Lodrö said it was the kindness of his tutor that had made him fit for human society, as Khenchen had taught him both how to practice the Dharma and how to live considerately among others.

Later, Chökyi Lodrö tirelessly and joyfully attended his tutor throughout a three-year-long illness (a phlegm disorder), serving him in every way possible, great and small. For example, he fetched water for his tutor, made tea, and emptied and washed his chamber pot. His sublime tutor was overjoyed and gave him detailed advice on outer discipline and the inner way of thinking, as well as numerous important texts, saying, "You will be the custodian of these books after I die." Jamyang Khyentse always enthusiastically expressed his admiration for his tutor and remembered all his many kindnesses.

Omniscient Kyabje Katok Situ Rinpoche was endowed with the extraordinary qualities of being learnèd, disciplined, and kind, and was a representative of the pioneers of Rime (the two Jamgön lamas, Jamyang Khyentse Wangpo and Jamgön Kongtrul Lodrö Taye). Katok Situ Rinpoche's incomparable enlightened intention, as pure as the most refined gold, was a tremendous inspiration for Khyentse Chökyi Lodrö. Like a skilled craftsman whose artistry transforms gold into something even more beautiful and valuable, Chökyi Lodrö diligently endeavored to completely reawaken his accumulated inherent knowledge.

From the *Category of the Bodhisattva Teachings*:

> Listening and hearing can bring the knowledge of Dharma,
> Turn beings away from unwholesome actions,
> Discard that which is not meaningful,
> And bring about nirvana.

And Lord Maitreya said,

> Adorned with the vast radiance of knowledge acquired through
>   listening and hearing,
> The wise will swiftly enter the sphere of activity of the buddhas.

We need to hear and contemplate all areas of knowledge before we embark on the path to buddhahood because, as Sakya Pandita said,

> If mind is not trained in all areas of knowledge,
> Omniscience is further away than the very edge of space.
> Knowing this, the advice of the Victorious Ones and the
>   bodhisattvas is,
> "Train in all fields of knowledge."

Initially, to establish himself as sovereign of the holders of the teachings, Khyentse Chökyi Lodrö studied the common outer fields of knowledge.[88] At ten, he studied the root texts and commentaries on the two kinds of Tibetan grammar with his tutor, Khenpo Rigdzin Gyatso. At eleven, he received a detailed explanation of the Sarasvata system of Sanskrit grammar[89] that followed the commentary by Katok Getse Pandita. At twelve, he started studying Indian astrology and received instructions on the five collections of astronomical calculations traced in sand. When necessary, he studied the Kalapa system of Sanskrit grammar with Palyul Lama Sherab Özer—who had been a student of Khewang, Jamyang Lekpe Lodrö—using the commentary by Sazang Mati Panchen. He studied poetry with Khewang, Lama Tashi Chöphel, and the four root tantras of the science of medicine and their commentaries with Lamen Atsang, who also guided him as he put those medical theories into practice. And from Khenchen Kunzang Palden Chödrak (Khenpo Kunpal), he received the explanation of the *Commentary on Valid Cognition*, based on the commentary by victorious Manjushri Mipham Rinpoche.

Concerning Jamyang Khyentse Chökyi Lodrö's study of philosophy (the science of inner meaning).

Omniscient Manjuvajra Mipham Jamyang Namgyal (Mipham Rinpoche) instructed Katok Situ Rinpoche to build a great shedra for the study of tantra at Katok Monastery in the heart of the Dome region, because he foresaw that such a shedra would be vital for the revitalization of the life-force of the Nyingma teachings. Katok Situ Rinpoche therefore created the auspicious circumstances that led to the establishment of a shedra, precisely according to Mipham Rinpoche's instructions.

At the shedra, the great omniscient Situ Mahapandita Orgyen Chökyi Gyatso (Katok Situ Rinpoche), who was learnèd in all the spheres of knowledge described in the sutras and tantras, gave detailed teachings based on his remarkable erudition—including how to differentiate logically between the Sarma and Nyingma schools based on each school's interpretation of the great philosophical texts (the root verses and the commentaries produced by the scholars of India and Tibet). Jamgön Mipham Rinpoche's main heart-son, Khenchen Kunzang Palden Chökyi Drakpa, known as Khenchen Kunpal, served as Katok Situ Rinpoche's revision teacher. They were the sun-like abbot and moon-like acharya. The other teachers were the great abbot of Shar Katok, Khenpo Lama Tenzang, whose grasp of the three skills of a scholar was unrivaled; Khenpo Aka Rinpoche, venerated for both his great knowledge of sacred texts and his realization; and Khenpo Kalzang Wangchuk, holder of the Tripitaka. When these masters began teaching at Katok Shedra, they all took Chökyi Lodrö as their main heart-son. To complete the mandala of his profound inherent and cultivated knowledge as an auspicious circumstance for opening the door of knowledge, he received from the two noble masters, Katok Situ Rinpoche and Khenpo Kunpal, firstly,

- *Praise to Venerable Manjushri*;
- *Praise to Glorious Excellent Knowledge*;
- *Praise to the Extraordinary Qualities of Buddha*; and
- *Praise to the One Who Outshines the Gods*.

Then,

- *The Way of the Bodhisattva*;
- the root text and explanation of the *Ascertainment of the Three Types of Vow*;
- the root text and explanation of the *Treasury of Precious Qualities*;
- the root text, explanation, and supplementary texts of the *Precious Wish-Fulfilling Treasure* (*Yishin Rinpoche'i Dzö*);
- the *Five Dharmas of Lord Maitreya*;
- the *Vinaya Sutra*;
- the great commentary on the *Ornament of the Middle Way*; and
- the detailed explanation of the *Guhyagarbha Tantra* from the Zur lineage, based on Minling Lochen Dharmashri's commentary explaining the general meaning, the *Words of Vajrapani*, and the literal commentary called the *Ornament of the Realization of Vajrapani*.

He also received teachings on other *Guhyagarbha Tantra* commentaries:

- the explanation of the general meaning called the *Garland of Jewels* by Minling Rabjampa Orgyen Chödrak;
- the commentary by Katok Gyurme Tsewang Chokdrup;
- the Parkab[90] commentary by Acharya Lilavajra;[91]
- Nyi Ö Senge's detailed commentary;
- the elaborate and simple teachings on the *Gradual Path* by Buddhaguhya;
- the *Jewel Commentary* on the *Guhyagarbha Tantra* by Rongzompa;
- omniscient Longchenpa's commentary;[92] and
- Yungtönpa's commentary.

Chökyi Lodrö also studied all the supplementary texts to these teachings, including the teacher's manuals.

From Sangdak, noble Loter Wangpo, he received

- the detailed explanation of *Two Sections of the Hevajra Root Tantra* according to the Sakya tradition;
- the *General Commentary on the Tantras* by Lopön Sonam Tsemo;
- Jetsün Drakpa Gyaltsen's *Great Wish-Fulfilling Tree*, including the commentary called *Possessing Purity*;
- the *Root Explanation of Ashta* by the Dharma King Sakya Pandita;
- Könchok Lhundrup's *Two Beautiful Ornaments*; and
- the annotated commentary by Khenpo Ngawang Chödrak.

In the process of receiving these teachings, he also received the oral transmissions of the required supplementary texts.

From Khewang Lama Tashi Chöphel, Chökyi Lodrö received

- the lineage of the *Five Dharmas of Lord Maitreya* that Jamyang Khyentse Wangpo had received directly from Arya Asanga;
- the *Commentary on the Root Verses of Vajrakilaya* by Jamgön Guna (Jamgön Kongtrul Lodrö Taye);
- the detailed explanation of the *Root Tantra of Hevajra* from the Ngok tradition, based on the commentary by Ngok Shedang Dorje and the great commentary by Jamgön Kongtrul;
- the root tantra of *Chakrasamvara*, based on Sakya Jetsün Sonam Tsemo's commentary; and
- the teaching transmission of the explanatory *Gur* and *Samputa Tantra* (the lineage Jamyang Khyentse Wangpo received directly in a pure vision).

From omniscient Katok Situ Rinpoche, he received

- the explanation of the tantra of the *Magical Net of Manjushri*, based on the commentary by Lord Gedun Gyatso;[93] and
- the explanatory lineage of Tsawa Lotsawa Rinchen Namgyal's commentary on the *Magical Net of Manjushri* by omniscient Khyentse Wangpo.

From Öntö Khenpo Khyenrab, Chökyi Lodrö received the explanation of the commentary on the abbreviated tantra of Kalachakra called *Immac-*

ulate Light, which was part of the explanatory lineage of Jamgön Kongtrul Rinpoche.

From Khenchen Kunpal, he received the explanation of the tantra of Adi Buddha Shri Kalachakra from the lineage of Lords Khyentse and Kongtrul, based on the great commentary by Jamgön Mipham Rinpoche.

Khenchen Kunpal said that a prophecy made by Terchen Dudjom Dorje foretold of his meeting with an emanation of King Trisong Deutsen,[94] the result of which would be the proliferation of his activities. Khenchen Kunpal then asserted that by going to Katok Monastery to offer teachings on philosophy to Khyentse Chökyi Lodrö, he had been able to fulfill that prophecy. He then expressed his deep faith in Chökyi Lodrö and always cared for him with great kindness, bestowing on him without hesitation the extraordinary profound points on the view, meditation, and action from the Nyingma tradition and the writings of omniscient and victorious Manjushri Mipham (Mipham Rinpoche).

The lotus of Khyentse Chökyi Lodrö's perfect intelligence, both inherent and cultivated, blossomed magnificently, and his nectar-like memory, confidence, and wisdom increased enormously. He considered Khenchen Kunpal to be one of his main root gurus.

Once the door of Khyentse Chökyi Lodrö's perfect knowledge had been opened, and by the blessings of the gurus and supreme deities, the great treasury of eloquence that bursts out as a result of realization was revealed. By merely glancing at texts, he was able to understand the essential meaning of the teachings of the sutras and shastras far more fully than the ordinary beings who had studied them extensively. Through the power of having obtained the four kinds of discriminating knowledge and the eight great treasures of eloquence that are sharp, swift, and unimpeded, he understood all the profound meanings of sutra and tantra. Since his mind was pure, he also had an extraordinary understanding of all the outer and inner areas of knowledge.

From Jamyang Khyentse Wangpo's autobiography:

> At various times over a period of thirteen years, I sought out teachings in the three provinces of Kham, Ü, and Tsang. Relying on 150 crown jewels, including vajradharas and spiritual friends, Vedic scholars, and the rest, I studied the arts; medicine; Sanskrit grammar; epistemology, including the branch sciences; and the

traditional explanations of Vinaya, Abhidharma, Madhyamika, and Prajnaparamita.

I received the empowerments, blessings, authorization blessings, and so on, from the Sarma and Nyingma traditions of the Vajrayana; all the empowerments, authorization blessings, explanations, and oral instructions of the existing ancient lineages of Kama and Terma, Kadampa, Sakyapa, Drikung, Taklung, Tsurphu, Densapa, and Drukpa; and the oral transmissions and explanations of the tantras of Chakrasamvara, Hevajra, Guhyasamaja and Kalachakra, Guhyagarbha, and so on. I also received the oral transmissions of sutras, shastras, and the writings of the great masters. In all, I received more than seven hundred volumes of teachings—basically, most of the teachings in the existing ten chariots of explanatory lineages—and trained a little in and have some partial knowledge of them all. They helped me enormously to accept the philosophical schools of all traditions and were invaluable as I familiarized myself with the Dharma.

Some people feel such pride in their own family's lineage, position, learning, and wealth that they are afraid to accept lamas of lower rank as their gurus in case they lose their standing in society—even when those lamas possess great Dharma qualities. Others are filled with the pride of imagining that they themselves overflow with knowledge, and this pride obscures their pure perception so much that they refuse to bow to anyone, however great the person's qualities. Still others are so attached to their own tradition that they do not consider teachers from other traditions or lineages to be in any way special, even the exceptionally erudite, and take no interest in either them or the Dharma, which they consider somehow unimportant.

I will now show how Khyentse Chökyi Lodrö, unlike these kinds of people, reached the shore of the ocean of great learning by the power of not falling prey to sadness or weariness and by constantly receiving all the authentic transmission lineages of the Buddha's precious teachings that existed at that time in the Land of Snows. He did this without harboring sectarian attitudes or being satisfied with the bare minimum and with the constant exertion of supreme diligence.

From the *Gathering of Precious Qualities*:[95]

> By practicing the path to supreme enlightenment with pure motivation,

Excellent students who respect their gurus
Must always rely on learnèd masters,
Because they are the source of knowledge for those who are wise.

Jamyang Khyentse Chökyi Lodrö had the innate ability to seek out, gather, hold, propagate, and understand the Dharma throughout all his lives. He also aspired to follow the example of Katok Situ Rinpoche, whose great qualities included that of always seeking out Dharma, just like Arya Sadaprarudita and the bodhisattva Sudhana, and whose mind was enriched with the treasure of having heard many teachings, just like the second Buddha, Vasubandhu. Therefore, Khyentse Chökyi Lodrö received the following from his root guru, Orgyen Chökyi Gyatso (Katok Situ Rinpoche).

From the Kama teachings of the Nyingma school:

- the *Mandala of the Peaceful and Wrathful Deities of the Magical Net*;
- the *Two Dongtruks*;
- Vishuddha (Yangdak);
- Vajrakilaya (Phurba);
- the cycle of *Yamantaka* teachings;
- all the root and branch empowerments of the *Great Assembly*;
- most of the Kama teachings, such as the *Mandala of the Eight Great Deities: The Fortress and Precipice*;
- the empowerment of *Wrathful Guru Rinpoche: The Great Gathering of the Sugatas*, a treasure revealed by Nyang Ral Nyima Özer;
- the detailed direct instructions on guru practice (Lama Martri);
- the textual transmission of the *Wrathful Guru and the Great Compassionate One*;
- the empowerment and explanation of Black Vajravarahi; and
- the textual transmission of the sadhanas of Vajravarahi and the *Great Dakini*.

All the empowerments, instructions, and textual transmission of

- Guru Chöwang's *Gathering of the Guru's Secrets*;
- the *Inseparable Union of the Buddhas of the Great Perfection*;
- *Gathering of the Innermost Essence of Great Compassion;*
- the empowerments of the seventeen tantras;
- the essential empowerment of the *Embodiment of the Guru's Realization*, as revealed by Sangye Lingpa;
- the elaborate empowerments and instructions of Karma Lingpa's

Mandala of Peaceful and Wrathful Deities, including the textual transmission;
- the very detailed empowerments and explanations of the *Twenty-Five Teachings with Restriction Seals*, revealed to the omniscient Fifth Dalai Lama in a pure vision;
- the uncommon, profound explanation of the *Four-Faced Treasure Protector* from the Mindrolling tradition;
- all the empowerments, explanations, and oral transmissions for the *Four Parts of Nyingtik*;
- the empowerments of all the treasure teachings revealed by Terchen Longsal Nyingpo and Terchen Dudul Dorje;
- the complete cycle of Mahasiddha Thangtong Gyalpo's *Secret Conduct: The Oral Lineage of the Dakinis*;
- the profound treasure of omniscient Manjushri Pema Ösel Dongak Lingpa, the *Five Cycles of the Essence of Sadhana*, the *Heart Essence of the Mahasiddha's Wisdom Mind*, the *Mandala of the Eight Great Deities: The Siddha*, and so on, which Katok Situ Rinpoche received from both Jamgön lama Rinpoches[96] since he was the holder of these teachings, as predicted in prophecy;
- the three cycles of Lama Tenyi;
- the *Heart Essence of the Immortal Lotus-Born*;
- the oral lineage of Yamantaka;
- the sadhana of the *Combined Practice of Vishuddhi and Kilaya* from the oral lineage;
- the extensive root empowerment of the *Embodiment of All the Buddha Families: Lotus Bud* that Jamyang Khyentse Wangpo received in a pure vision after Chokgyur Lingpa passed away;
- the empowerments and explanations of the *Gathering of the Sugatas of the Three Roots* and the rediscovered treasures, the *Embodiment of the Three Roots* and the *Combined Practice of the Three Roots*.
- the empowerment of the *Heart Essence of Deathless Arya Tara* and the explanation of the visualizations for the daily practice sadhana;
- the root and branch empowerments and oral transmissions for Mahasiddha Maitripa's *White and Red Amitayus* and Trisong Deutsen's Guru Yoga of the teaching, which were revealed in a pure vision to Jamyang Khyentse Wangpo, and the three-kaya guru yoga;[97]
- the empowerment of the Guru Yoga of Karma Chagme, by Jamyang Khyentse Wangpo;

- *Vajrasattva: Liberate into the Pure Realm of Manifest Joy* from the *Heart Essence of the Vast Expanse* tradition;
- all the root and branch empowerments, explanations, and oral transmissions of the teachings received in pure visions that make up the cycle of the *Luminous Heart Essence of the Three Roots*;
- the transmissions for most of the profound essential teachings, such as the empowerment of twenty-one Taras, which is the inner *Consort Practice* from the *Heart Essence of the Vast Expanse*;
- the great empowerment for the sadhana of *Peaceful Manjushri* from the Gyuluk tradition of omniscient Mipham Rinpoche;
- the blessings and explanations of the *Father and Mother Consorts of the Simultaneously Arising Chakrasamvara* from the oral lineage of Rechungpa;
- the oral transmissions for the Chakrasamvara texts by Jamyang Khyentse Wangpo;
- the detailed explanations of *One Hundred Profound Commentaries* by Jonang Jetsün Kunga Drolchok;
- all the treasure teachings revealed by Ling Jedrung Pema Drodul; and
- the oral transmissions of twenty-five volumes of *One Hundred Thousand Precious Tantras of the Nyingma*.

These are just a few examples of the elaborate teachings Chökyi Lodrö received from the essence of the treasury of the profound secret from omniscient Katok Situ Rinpoche, Chökyi Gyatso.

From Drime Zhingkyong Jewön Rinpoche Pema Gyaltsen (Jewön Rinpoche), he received

- the extensive oral transmissions of the Dharma cycles of Longsal Nyingpo and Dudul Dorje;
- the transmission of about two volumes of notes from the Kabum of Khyentse Rinpoche;
- the transmission of the text of *Protector Ganapati*, revealed by Khamtrul;
- the empowerment and oral transmission of the *Ocean of Dharma That Combines All Teachings*;
- the oral transmission of the Mani Kabum;[98]
- the empowerment and oral transmission of *Vajrasattva of Manifest Joy* from the *Heart Essence of the Vast Expanse*;

- all the empowerments and oral transmission for *Accomplishing the Life-Force of the Vidyadharas*;
- the empowerments of Vajravarahi;
- and so on.

I heard Khyentse Chökyi Lodrö say that since Jewön Rinpoche's contemporary knowledge and understanding of the two traditions[99] were unrivaled, and because the way he practiced virtue and abandoned unvirtuous actions greatly benefited our Lord Guru when he was very young, he considered Jewön Rinpoche to be one of the most gracious of his masters.

At seventeen, Khyentse Chökyi Lodrö traveled to the Lasey retreat center to meet a close student of Thartse Khenchen Jampa Kunga Tenpe Gyaltsen, called Manjushri Loter Wangpo, pioneer of the great secret tantra and a glorious ornament adorning the Sakya and Ngor teachings. He possessed extraordinary qualities of great learning, discipline, and kindness, and for about twenty years, he had studied with the sun- and moon-like Jamgön lamas, particularly the noble lama Khyentse Wangpo.

Jamyang Loter Wangpo had received the nectar of all the profound and vast oral instructions from the Sarma and Nyingma traditions in their most complete form from Jamyang Khyentse Wangpo. Having been imbued with the qualities of Khyentse Wangpo's body, speech, and mind—like pouring water from one vase into another and filling it to the brim—he had become Jamyang Khyentse Wangpo's supreme heart-son.

After inviting Chökyi Lodrö to sit on a throne with gold brocade cushions and a backrest, Loter Wangpo entered into a profound conversation with him, during which they spoke intimately with one another, like father and son. Manjushri Loter Wangpo went on to care for Chökyi Lodrö with such extraordinary love and compassion that our supreme Lord Guru effortlessly developed unconditional faith in him and a yearning devotion, which was a wonderful thing.

Gradually, from the noble lama and vajradhara in human form, Loter Wangpo, and Dagra Shabdrung Tashi Gyatso, Chökyi Lodrö received numerous teachings. They began by giving him the *Compendium of Tantras*, which opens with the general mandala of the three families (the root of the kriya tantra). However, having completed the yoga tantra, the transmission was delayed for some time, which was when Khyentse Chökyi Lodrö privately received from Loter Wangpo

- the *Parting from the Four Attachments*;
- numerous root and branch explanations of the *Seven Points of Mind Training*; and
- detailed and in-depth empowerments and instructions from the extraordinary *Path and Fruition: The Explanation for Private Disciples*, the innermost essence of the great secret tantra.

Having received the elaborate introduction to the investigation of the mind—the view of the inseparability of samsara and nirvana based on the causal tantra of the ground of all phenomena—the realization of wisdom that is inseparable awareness and emptiness awakened in Khyentse Chökyi Lodrö's mind. He developed unwavering faith in Loter Wangpo and considered him to be one of his main teachers, praising him highly again and again.

In fact, since Jamgön Loter Wangpo had received the effective instruction of the *Heart Essence of the Pith Instructions of Dzogpachenpo* from Nyoshul Lungtok Tenpe Nyima, heart-son of the Dharma Lord Patrul Rinpoche, and had practiced it diligently, he held the essential lineage of the realization of the *Radiant Pith Instructions*, the stream of which converged with all the other transmissions of teachings he had received.

Even though Khyentse Wangpo's ultimate secret had been that he was truly inseparable from the great and glorious Heruka, the All-Pervasive Lord of the Ocean of Mandalas, ordinary beings only saw him as a master whose root practice was Hevajra. But as a result of Jamyang Khyentse Wangpo's aspiration that Hevajra be the root practice of the Khyentses, Khyentse Chökyi Lodrö fully realized the teachings of *Path and Fruition: The Explanation for Private Disciples* (the oral lineage with four valid factors) so that the teachings would not merely survive as empty words.

In these degenerate times, most oral instructions from all lineages have become empty mouthings because no one practices the teachings and transmissions they receive, and teachings on realization only exist in name. So, recognizing just how extraordinary and wonderful this Sakyapa teaching—of which the two Khyentse Rinpoches are lineage gurus—is, I think the lineage holders should uphold the instruction lineage.

From Shabdrung Rinpoche Tashi Gyatso, Chökyi Lodrö received

- the elaborate empowerments for *One Hundred Transmissions of Mitra*;

- the elaborate empowerments for the Seven Mandalas of Ngor;
- the elaborate empowerments for the nine-deity Yamantaka from the Ra Lotsawa tradition;
- the elaborate empowerments for the mandala of thirteen deities from the Tsarpa tradition; and
- the explanation of the Lamdre based on Khenpo Ngawang Chödrak's commentaries.

After returning to his seat, as the moon waned in the first month of the year of the iron dog (1910), Khyentse Chökyi Lodrö received many empowerments from his father, the learnèd and accomplished great vajra acharya, the vidyadhara Gyurme Tsewang Gyatso. On an auspicious day after Jamyang Khyentse Wangpo's anniversary,[100] he opened the treasury of teachings with

- the great empowerments for the *Great Assembly*;
- the *Peaceful and Wrathful Deities Who Stir the Pits of Hell* from the *Nyingma Kama*; and
- the treasure teaching, the *Mandala of the Eight Great Deities: The Assembly of Sugatas*.

He then bestowed on Khyentse Chökyi Lodrö the complete transmission of the *Precious Treasury of Terma Teachings*, following the structure of tantra and sadhana texts. He also gave all the transmissions for all the great tertön Chokgyur Lingpa's treasure teachings in conjunction with the teachings I've already mentioned.

In short, our Lord Guru received detailed teachings from his father for eight months.

In the year of the iron pig (1911), in response to his supplication for the *Compendium of Sadhanas*, Loter Wangpo gave Chökyi Lodrö his blessings and instructed him to receive the teachings from Khenchen Ngawang Samten Lodrö. And so the great Khenchen Vajradhara of Derge, Lhundrup Teng, bestowed on him the empowerments, explanations, and oral transmissions of the *Compendium of Sadhanas* and the oral transmission for the three volumes of *Collected Teachings on Vajrayogini*.

For more than four months in the year of the water rat (1912), from Thartse Shabdrung Jampa Kunzang Tenpe Nyima of Wara Monastery, he received extensive empowerments, explanations, and oral transmissions of the remaining part of the *Compendium of Tantras*—from the *Highest Yoga*

Tantra onwards. Khyentse Chökyi Lodrö often said that Shabdrung's mind overflowed with a wealth of supreme noble qualities, and that if he had lived longer, he would without doubt have become an ornament of the Sakya and Ngor traditions.

Then, from the Lord of Scholars of Palpung, Lama Tashi Chöphel, at various appropriate times, he received the detailed empowerments, explanations, and oral transmissions of the *Golden Dharmas* of the glorious Shangpa Kagyü tradition and the complete transmission of the glorious Kalachakra of the Jonang tradition, including

- the ritual for formally accepting a student, the preparatory initiation, the beginners' empowerment, the supreme (ordinary and extraordinary) empowerments, and empowerment of the sovereign and great sovereign vajracharya;
- effective instructions from the explanatory text combined with the supplementary text; the oral transmission for the writings of Taranatha, the *Clear Explanation of Kyerim and Dzogrim*, and the *Mandala of Accomplishment*, and so on; and all the teachings associated with Kalachakra;
- the Shije and Chö cycles of teachings, Druptob Orgyenpa's *Approach and Accomplishment Practices of the Three Vajras*, and the empowerment and instructions, including the oral transmission for all these teachings, which are contained in the *Treasury of Precious Instructions*;
- the great empowerment, the entrustment of the vidya mantra, the authorization blessing, the explanation of the tantras, and the instructions of *Tarayogini*;
- the explanatory oral transmission for *One Hundred Profound Commentaries*;
- the oral transmission for Atisha Dipamkara's *One Hundred Minor Dharmas* and the precious texts of the Kadampa tradition;
- the oral transmission of Marpa and Milarepa's biographies and songs of realization, and the collected writings of Dakpo Lhaje (Gampopa);
- the explanations of the *Jewel Ornament of Liberation* and the *Precious Garland of the Supreme Path*;
- the oral transmission for the *Mountain Dharma* by Yang Gönpa; and

- the empowerment, explanation, and oral transmission of Vajrakilaya from the Khön tradition, which carries the direct transmission blessings of omniscient Khyentse Wangpo and is based on Jonang Jetsün Rinpoche's empowerment manual, which was clarified and elaborated by the great Jamgön Kongtrul.

Also,

- the empowerments for supreme enlightenment and the wrathful activity[101] of Vajrakilaya from the Khön tradition, based on Sakya ritual texts;
- the empowerment, explanation, and oral transmission of the mind treasures of Lord Khyentse Wangpo;
- the *Luminous Heart Essence of the Three Roots*;
- all the empowerments and instructions from the *Profound Essence of Vimalamitra* by the great Chetsün Senge Wangchuk;
- the explanation and oral transmission of the root text of the *Treasury of Encyclopedic Knowledge*, along with the commentary that Tashi Chöphel received from Jamgön Kongtrul Rinpoche himself;
- the oral transmission for all the root and branch treasure teachings of the *Wish-Fulfilling Jewel Essence Manual of Oral Instruction* from the *Heart Practice for Dispelling All Obstacles*;
- the explanation and oral transmission of the great commentary on the *Ascertainment of the Three Types of Vow* called the *Fruit of the Wish-Fulfilling Tree*;
- the empowerments for the Guru Yogas of Marpa and Milarepa by Jamgön Guna (Jamgön Kongtrul Lodrö Taye);
- the oral transmission for Jamgön Kongtrul's collected works; and
- the explanation of the root verses and commentary of the *Gradual Path Called the "Essence of Wisdom."*

Lama Tashi Chöphel received these teachings from Khyentse, Kongtrul, and Chokling, which meant that the many rare teachings Khyentse Chökyi Lodrö received from him were from entirely authentic transmission lineages. He honored Lama Tashi Chöphel as his supreme guide with the unwavering devotion of one whose mind was inseparable from his guru's. Lama Tashi Chöphel also praised Khyentse Chökyi Lodrö again and again, saying that of all the supreme emanations of the two Jamgön lamas, his intelligence and activities were unsurpassed.

The backbone[102] of the Nyingma tradition, the great scholar and siddha Shechen Gyaltsab Rinpoche, Gyurme Pema Namgyal, first met Khyentse Chökyi Lodrö at Phukgon Monastery during a summer pilgrimage in the north to collect alms.[103] They met in the temple during a drupchen to bless amrita (mendrup), over which our Lord Guru presided, as the Sangha recited the following verse from the aspiration prayer of the *New Treasures of Chokling*:

> May the glory of the teachings, the precious teachers,
> Spread like space throughout the universe.

The vajradhara Shechen Gyaltsab expressed great delight that their meeting happened at such an auspicious moment.

Chökyi Lodrö received the long-life initiation of the *Gathering of the Innermost Essence of Deathlessness* to create a spiritual connection with Shechen Gyaltsab Rinpoche. From then on, he considered Gyaltsab Rinpoche to be one of his main teachers. Gyaltsab Rinpoche, too, felt an unfailing devotion and love for Khyentse Chökyi Lodrö. He traveled to Chökyi Lodrö's seat, Dzongsar Tashi Lhatse, for an extended visit, during which he gave him empowerments, explanations, and oral transmissions of

- all the *Northern Treasures* received directly by Jamyang Khyentse Wangpo in pure visions;
- Ngari Panchen Rinpoche's *Mandala of the Eight Great Deities: The Complete Gathering of Vidyadharas*;
- the bodhisattva vow based on the writings of Tsele Natsok Rangdrol;
- *Yamantaka* from the Kama tradition;
- *Iron Scorpion Yamantaka* revealed by Dumgya Shangtrom;
- the great empowerment of the *Mandala of the Eight Great Deities* revealed by Dorje Lingpa, the transmission of which Jamyang Khyentse Wangpo received directly in a pure vision;
- the sadhana of the *Innermost Secret Razor-Edge Vajrakilaya* revealed by Guru Chöwang, and the commentary by Lord Shechen Gyaltsab himself;
- omniscient Jigme Lingpa's great empowerment of *Vajrakilaya: The Tradition of the King*;
- the *Combined Practice of Vishuddhi and Vajrakilaya* from the treasure teachings of Lord Khyentse and the wonderful commentary by the supreme Lord Guru Shechen Gyaltsab himself;

- all the empowerments for the *Four Parts of Nyingtik* of Dzogpachenpo;
- the empowerment of awareness display[104] from the *Profound Meaning of Ati* from Chokgyur Lingpa's treasure teaching; and
- the empowerments and explanations of Vajrasattva and Vishuddhi from the *Heart Essence of Garab*, and *Chakrasamvara: The Inseparable Union of Buddha*.

These are just a few examples of the many teachings Chökyi Lodrö received. He went on to receive many more of the old and rare treasure teachings Shechen Gyaltsab Rinpoche had received from the two Jamgön lamas. Later, at the Shechen retreat center, Pema Öling, Khyentse Chökyi Lodrö received the empowerments, explanations, and oral transmissions of all the treasure teachings of Minling Terchen (Terdak Lingpa). But as Gyaltsab Rinpoche was very ill at that time, Chökyi Lodrö performed a long-life ceremony and begged him to live longer. As a result, Gyaltsab Rinpoche recovered completely, and the auspicious circumstances necessary for his long life were established.

In the year of the water rooster (1933), at the Shechen retreat center Dechok Tashi Gephel, Khyentse Chökyi Lodrö received

- the detailed empowerments, instructions, and oral transmission of the *Treasury of Precious Instructions*;
- the empowerments and oral transmission for the three volumes of *Teachings with Restriction Seals from the Treasury of Terma Teachings*;
- the transmission of all the writings by Gyaltsab Rinpoche that he had not received earlier, which were also entrusted to him.

Gyaltsab Rinpoche wanted to receive the *Compendium of Sadhanas*, so Khyentse Chökyi Lodrö began by giving him the authorization blessings for the *Three White Deities*.

Gyaltsab Rinpoche then received

- the great empowerment of *Yamantaka* from the Nub lineage of the *Nyingma Kama*;
- the explanation of *Guhyagarbha Tantra* from the Zur tradition based on the commentary by Minling Lochen Dharmashri, which Khyentse Wangpo received directly in a pure vision;
- the oral transmission of the complete collected works of Tsele Natsok Rangdrol; and

- many other empowerments and instructions from the Kama and Terma.

After Gyaltsab Rinpoche passed away, Khyentse Chökyi Lodrö spent three weeks at Shechen Monastery performing ceremonies for the fulfillment of his wishes, such as making offerings to the kudung, and presiding over the cremation ceremony. Later, through the power of his wisdom mind, Chökyi Lodrö recognized Shechen Gyaltsab Rinpoche's precious, supreme tulku. He then transmitted most of the teachings he had received from the previous Gyaltsab Rinpoche to the tulku and, by so doing, placed him on the Dharma throne of the supreme vehicle. This is how, with great kindness, he was able to help Shechen Monastery.

During their many private conversations, Chökyi Lodrö and Gyaltsab Rinpoche's heart-son, Shechen Kongtrul Rinpoche, Pema Drime Lekpe Lodrö, discovered they enjoyed a special rapport. Chökyi Lodrö went on to give Shechen Kongrul Rinpoche teachings to clarify his meditation practice and detailed advice about how to continue the activities of their guru, Shechen Gyaltsab.

Then, from Shechen Kongtrul Rinpoche, Chökyi Lodrö received

- all the empowerments of the *Great Assembly* from the *Nyingma Kama*, the transmission of which Jamyang Khyentse Wangpo had received directly in a pure vision and Shechen Kongtrul Rinpoche received from Shechen Gyaltsab Rinpoche;
- the great accomplishment empowerment[105] for the *Mandala of the Eight Great Deities: The Assembly of Sugatas*, for which Jamgön Kongtrul Rinpoche had written the empowerment manual;
- all the oral transmissions of Padmasambhava's and Vimalamitra's traditions of the great Nyingtik;
- the oral transmission of the collected works of the Second Shechen Rabjam, Gyurme Künzang Namgyal;
- the oral transmission of Shechen Gyaltsab Rinpoche's most important writings; and
- many other empowerments and teachings.

From the Fifth Shechen Rabjam, Gyurme Künzang Tenpe Nyima (1864–1909), he received

- the abbreviated empowerment for *Krodhikali* revealed by Nyang Nyima Özer;

- the empowerment for *Yamantaka: Destroyer of Demons* from the Mindrolling tradition;
- the *Gathering of the Innermost Essence of Deathlessness*;
- Ling Tsang Tertön's *Chandali, Long-Life Consort*;
- the empowerments and oral transmissions for the complete Dharma cycle of the great tertön Pema Lingpa; and
- other transmissions.

Khyentse Chökyi Lodrö and the Fifth Shechen Rabjam had great devotion for each other and a very strong spiritual bond. Chökyi Lodrö received the oral transmissions for most of the writings of Shechen Gyaltsab Rinpoche from Lama Jamyang Losal, the personal attendant of Vajradhara Shechen Gyaltsab Rinpoche himself.

At the age of twenty-eight, in the year of the iron monkey (1920), Khyentse Chökyi Lodrö traveled to Dodrupchen Monastery in the north to meet omniscient Jigme Tenpe Nyima, from whom he received

- the elaborate root empowerment for the inner sadhana of the *Gathering of Vidyadharas* from the *Heart Essence of the Vast Expanse* of Dzogpachenpo, based on the manual by the First Dodrupchen Rinpoche, Jigme Trinle Özer;
- the empowerment for the *Innermost Secret Guru Yoga Called the "Sealed Quintessence"*;
- instructions for the creation and completion meditations of the *Heart Essence of the Vast Expanse*, and above all, the profound, vast, and very effective instructions for the *Wisdom Guru of the Great Perfection*; and
- the explanation of the commentary on the general meaning of the *Guhyagarbha Tantra* by the omniscient guru, the Third Dodrupchen himself, called the *Key to the Precious Treasury*.

With extraordinary loving-kindness, omniscient Jigme Tenpe Nyima also gave Chökyi Lodrö numerous instructions and a great deal of advice, as a result of which their minds merged as one. He specifically entrusted Chökyi Lodrö with all his own excellent writings and joyfully gave him permission to teach, study, uphold, and propagate them.

Later, from Choktrul Rinpoche, Jigme Thubten Trinle Palzang, Chökyi Lodrö received the empowerment for the *Heart Essence of the Dakinis* and many other empowerments and teachings.

From Dogar Khenpo (Könchok Drönme), he received the cycle of the

Supreme Dharma, the Sublime Path to Great Bliss, one of the first Dodrupchen's (Jigme Trinle Özer) mind treasures.

On his way back to Dzongsar, Chökyi Lodrö went to meet Terchen Lerab Lingpa. Even before he had met the terchen face-to-face, merely hearing his name had aroused a tremendous natural devotion in his mind. His devotion inspired him to travel to visit the terchen on many occasions.

From Lerab Lingpa, Chökyi Lodrö received the empowerment, explanation, and oral transmission of the *Innermost Essence of the Razor-Edged Phurba*, the profound treasure of Jamgön Lodrö Taye that had been revealed by Lerab Lingpa for a specific purpose.

From Lerab Lingpa's treasure teachings, Chökyi Lodrö received

- *Vajrakilaya: The Display of Vajras* and *Vajrakilaya: The Vast Display*;
- the long and medium versions of *Removing Inauspicious Circumstances*;
- the Dharma cycle of Gesar (a mind treasure) and oral instructions and authorization for all Terchen Lerab Lingpa's treasure teachings;
- the empowerment and textual transmission of the *Self-Liberating Realization of the Essence of Liberation* revealed by Trengpo Terchen; and
- the empowerment for the great Chetsün Senge Wangchuk's *Profound Essence of Vimalamitra*, with an explanation based on the authentic commentary given by omniscient Khyentse Wangpo Rinpoche.

Khyentse Chökyi Lodrö received numerous profound teachings from Terchen Lerab Lingpa and said that merely hearing the great tertön's name had caused a yearning devotion to arise spontaneously in his mind. He asked Lerab Lingpa to decipher the short *Removing Inauspicious Circumstances* from a yellow terma scroll and praised the terchen's wonderful qualities of learning and realization.

In the year of the water ox,[106] at the age of thirty-three, during his first pilgrimage to central Tibet, Khyentse Chökyi Lodrö received the *Gathering of the Innermost Essence: A Long-Life Practice* from Minling Trichen Gyurme Döndrup Wangyal.

From Minling Chung Rinpoche Ngawang Chödrak, he received

- the long-life practice and Gönpo Maning revealed by Pema Lingpa;
- *Secret Wisdom* and the long-life empowerment of the *Gathering of the Innermost Essence of Deathlessness* from the Minling tradition;

- the long-life empowerment of the *White Guardian*; and
- Dorje Lingpa's life-force empowerment[107] to Maning and the empowerment for the long-life practice, as well as the authorization blessing for Shang Lön of Tertön Drapa Ngönshe.

He also received

- the empowerment of the four-armed Mahakala from the Nyang tradition from Khenchen Ngawang Khyentse Norbu; and
- the *Heart Essence of the Vidyadharas* and the *Wrathful Red Guru Rinpoche* from Dordzin Rinpoche Namdröl Gyatso.

In order to make a spiritual connection between them, from the supreme Victorious One, the Thirteenth Dalai Lama, Thubten Gyatso, Chökyi Lodrö received the *Lamp for the Path to Enlightenment*.

He entreated Terchen Lerab Lingpa and Avalokiteshvara, the Thirteenth Dalai Lama, who were like father and son to each other, to live for a long time for the benefit of the beings and teachings in the Land of Snows, and put forward many reasons why they should, at which the Dalai Lama expressed his utmost delight.

In the latter part of his life, Khyentse Chökyi Lodrö received the empowerment for *Great Compassionate Avalokiteshvara* from the Mitra tradition (one of Takphuwa's treasure teachings) from Avalokiteshvara, Tenzin Gyatso, the Fourteenth Dalai Lama, whom he visited many times. They met together in the Dalai Lama's private room for profound conversations and cared for each other with extraordinary kindness.

From the Khewang, Amdo Geshe Jampal Rolpe Lodrö, he received

- the great empowerment for the root tantra, the *Guhyasamaja Tantra*;
- the empowerment of *Solitary Hero Vajrabhairava*; and
- many other empowerments.

They had great devotion for each other.

When our Lord Guru was young and living at Katok Monastery, in the Guru Padmasambhava temple, he received from Rigdzin Tsewang Norbu, the son of Chokgyur Lingpa,

- the empowerment for the *Heart Practice That Spontaneously Fulfills All Wishes*;

- the oral transmission of the biography of Padmasambhava known as Pema Kathang;[108] and
- many other transmissions.

From the precious Chokling Tulku of Neten Monastery, Pema Gyurme Tekchok Tenzin, he received

- the root and supplementary teaching cycles of the *Heart Practice for Dispelling All Obstacles*;
- all the transmissions of the *Seven Profound Cycles* of Vishuddhi and Vajrakilaya;
- *Three Cycles of the Secret Essence*;
- *Avalokiteshvara: The Lord of the Dance*;
- *Avalokiteshvara Who Stirs the Depths of Samsara*;
- the *Heart Essence of the Three Bodhisattvas* in detail;
- the explanation of the *Gradual Path Called the "Essence of Wisdom,"* and so on;
- the profound empowerment of completion meditation called the *Self-Liberated Five Poisonous Conflicting Emotions*, from the *Heart Practice That Fulfills All Wishes*;
- the entrustment of life-essence[109] for the *Assembled Realization of Dharma Protectors*; and
- entrustment with the *Life-Force Phurba* of the protectress Shona, including the teachings with restriction seals.

And,

- the transmissions of all of Chokgyur Lingpa's treasure teachings and the empowerments for the six heart practices of Zurza that had just been compiled by the Third Neten Chokling himself;
- the transmission for the short commentary on the *Guhyagarbha Tantra* by Tsawa Lotsawa Rinchen Namgyal, based on the detailed explanation he had received from Jamyang Khyentse, Jamgön Kongtrul, and Chokgyur Lingpa;
- the wisdom blessings for the *Praise and Practice of Manjushri* thirteen times; and
- the empowerment for the *Heart Practice of Vajrasattva* from the Mindrolling tradition, which Neten Chokling, Pema Gyurme Tekchok Tenzin (the Third Neten Chokling), received six times from the omniscient precious guru.

He also received many other essential teachings.

From the supreme tulku of Terchen Lama (Chokgyur Lingpa), Gyurme Tenpe Gyaltsen of Tsikey Mindrol Norbu Ling Monastery (the Second Tsikey Chokling), Chökyi Lodrö received many teachings that had been transmitted through Jamyang Khyentse Wangpo, including

- the empowerment for the *Wish-Fulfilling Jewel That Spontaneously Fulfills All Wishes*;
- the empowerment and instructions for the *Guru Yoga of Vimalamitra* from the mind treasure of Chokgyur Lingpa; and
- the textual transmission of *Accomplishing the Life-Force of the Vidyadharas*.

The Dharma King of Ling, Vidyadhara Pema Shepa Wangchen Tenzin Chögyal, and his consort visited Khyentse Chökyi Lodrö at Katok Monastery when he was ten years old. To make a spiritual connection, Chökyi Lodrö gave, from memory, an explanation of the praise to Manjushri called *Gangloma*, as a result of which the king and his consort felt such overwhelming devotion for him that they wept. Later, the royal couple invited Chökyi Lodrö to lead many drupchens and mendrups at their palace.

From this vidyadhara (the king of Ling), Chökyi Lodrö received

- the empowerment for *Chandali, Long-Life Consort*;
- the life-essence empowerment of *Indestructible Deathless Gesar*, revealed in a pure vision by Lha Rik Dechen Rölpa Tsal and transmitted through Jamgön Mipham Rinpoche's lineage; and
- the empowerment of the *Chandali, Long-Life Consort*, the Dharma King of Ling's own mind treasure.

The king then empowered Khyentse Chökyi Lodrö as the main holder of the *Chandali, Long-Life Consort* and, by so doing, created the auspicious circumstances for overcoming obstacles to the guru's life, and so on. They had complete devotion for each other and a strong spiritual bond.

Khyentse Chökyi Lodrö invited the sovereign of all the holders of the oral transmission lineage, Gatön Dorje Chang Chöje Ngawang Lekpa Rinpoche—who had attained the state of indivisibility in a single lifetime through the practice of *Precious Words*—to visit Dzongsar. Then having established a teacher-student relationship, they met on many different occasions.

Khyentse Chökyi Lodrö received

- the most elaborate transmission of the *Oral Transmission Endowed with the Four Valid Factors* of the *Path and Fruition: The Explanation for Private Disciples*;
- the blessing and explanation of Vajrayogini;
- the empowerment for the thirteen Vajrabairava deities of the Ra Lotsawa and Tsar traditions;
- the direct instructions for the *Oral Transmission Lineage of the Dakinis*;
- the direct instructions from the Tsembu tradition; and
- the explanations of the long-life practice of White Tara.

In short, he received all the crucial empowerments and oral transmissions from the Sakyapa tradition.

Gatön Dorje Chang also admired our Lord Guru immensely and showed him great kindness, declaring that the Jamgön lama, Khyentse Chökyi Lodrö, was his root guru and omniscient Khyentse Wangpo in the flesh.

From Ewam Thartse Khenchen Jamyang Kunzang Tenpe Nyima, Khyentse Chökyi Lodrö received the great empowerment of the *Cause and Path Hevajra*, and the blessings for the outer and inner *Profound Path*.

From Thartse Shabdrung Namkha Kunzang Tenpe Gyaltsen, he received the empowerment for the nine-deity Amitayus, and the authorization blessing and textual transmission for *Tiger Rider*.

From the great vajradhara and abbot of Ngor, Dampa Dönpal, he received the long-life empowerment of Amitayus and Hayagriva in one sadhana. Khenchen Dampa paid tribute to Chökyi Lodrö, saying he was the master who had accomplished the activity of a vajradhara in this degenerate age exactly as described in the sacred texts.

From Luding Gyalse Jampal Chökyi Nyima, he received the authorization blessings for the *Three White Deities*.

From Zimwog Choktrul Rinpoche, he received the *Cause and Path Hevajra* empowerments, blessings for the profound paths, and all the empowerments and explanations of the Protector Zhal.

From Dezhung Choktrul Kunga Tenpe Gyaltsen Rinpoche, Dezhung Tulku Ajam, he received

- the authorization blessing for the *Ocean of Sadhanas*;
- the *Body Mandala of Chakrasamvara* from Drilbupa's tradition;
- the blessing for Vajrayogini;

- the extraordinary authorization blessings for Mahakala and White Tara;
- the Hevajra path empowerment; and
- many other transmissions.

They discussed the extraordinary profound key points of the *Great Secret Esoteric Oral Instructions* from the precious words of Manjushri Gatön, and Chökyi Lodrö implored Dezhung Tulku Ajam to write those instructions down, making him the life-force that inspired the spread of the Lamdre teachings. Over and over again, Khyentse Chökyi Lodrö spoke highly of Dezhung Tulku Ajam. He had great respect for him and said that, at that time, no Sakya master was more learnèd, and that he had perfectly accomplished the three kinds of service that please the guru (Gatön Dorje Chang) and had merged his mind with the mind of his teacher. The supreme Tulku Rinpoche also praised Chökyi Lodrö, saying he was omniscient Manju in the flesh[110] and that he had developed deep faith in him.

From the noble Dezhung Tulku of Gatö Tharlam Monastery, Chökyi Lodrö received a vast number of teachings, including the oral transmissions of the collected works of the five founding masters of the Sakya tradition and those of Ngorchen Dorje Chang (Kunga Zangpo) and Zhuchen Mahapandita (Tsultrim Rinchen). (When he was young, Chökyi Lodrö had received the oral transmissions of the collected works of the five founding masters of the Sakya tradition and the supreme scholar Tsele Pema Lekdrup from Khyentse Wangpo's shrine master, Lama Sherab.)

From Jamyang Gyaltsen, a great spiritual friend whose way of life was in perfect accord with the sublime Dharma, he received

- the *Cause and Path Hevajra* empowerments;
- the empowerment for *Fifteen Dakinis Free of Self*; and
- the explanation and oral transmission of the *Path and Fruition: The Explanation for Private Disciples*.

Jamyang Gyaltsen was appreciated for the immense devotion he had for Chökyi Lodrö and for having accomplished many great services for him.

From the vajra master of Dzongsar Monastery, Bodhibhadra, Chökyi Lodrö received many empowerments and explanations of Akshobhya from the Sakya tradition, Hevajra, and Vajrayogini.

From the hidden yogi Tenphel, who had been blessed by Arya Tara herself, he received

- the empowerment and explanation of the *Secret Conduct: The Oral Lineage of the Dakinis* by Thangtong Gyalpo;
- the empowerment, authorization blessing, and profound instructions for Mahakala (Gönpo Gur);
- the empowerment of Tara related to the four classes of tantra; and
- the blessing and explanations of Vajrayogini.

From Drakyab Tsangsar Tulku, he received

- the great empowerments for complete enlightenment and the wrathful activity of Vajrakilaya from the Khön tradition;
- Vaishravana and Mahakala (Gönpo Gur); and
- many other teachings only transmitted within the Sakya tradition.

From Shar Lama of Derge Lhundrup Teng, Jamyang Khyenrab Taye, he received

- the great empowerment of the glorious Kalachakra from the Butön tradition; and
- the textual transmission of Vajrabhairava and Zhal.

From Dordzin Palden Jamyang, he received

- the great empowerment of Chakrasamvara from the Luipa tradition; and
- all the empowerments and instructions for Zhal.

From Shar Lama, Könchok Tenzin, he received

- all the authorization blessings and in-depth and detailed explanations of Mahakala (Gönpo Gur); and
- the explanation of *White Tara Radiating Six Rays of Light*.

Khyentse Chökyi Lodrö foresaw that the great holder of the Tripitaka, Lama Ngawang Tenpa of Ga Thubten Monastery, was a master from whom he could receive the oral transmission of the *Kangyur*. So, over a period of many years, he urged Lama Ngawang Tenpa to receive, in detail, all the different transmission lineages and provided him with the support he needed to do so. As a result, Lama Ngawang Tenpa received them all and subsequently succeeded in giving the transmission a total of thirteen times. Khyentse Chökyi Lodrö then received the oral transmission of the complete *Kangyur* from him and made vast cloud-like offerings throughout.

Khyentse Chökyi Lodrö said to me, "Having given the oral transmission of the *Kangyur* so many times, Lama Ngawang Tenpa's speech is blessed with truthfulness.[111] Of course, the teachings of our omniscient guide Buddha Shakyamuni are all wonderful, particularly the *Flower Garland Sutra*, which contains the Buddha's inconceivable and secret words imbued with extraordinary vast and profound meanings. But I am so inspired by Lama Ngawang Tenpa's clear, pure, and melodious voice that I have developed a confident and joyful devotion for all the teachings of the Buddha."

From Kyabgön Dagchen Ngawang Kunga Sonam of Sakya Phuntsok Phodrang, he received

- the great empowerments for complete enlightenment and the wrathful activity of Vajrakilaya from the Khön lineage;
- the combined practice of Amitayus and Hayagriva;[112]
- the long-life empowerments of the *Peaceful and Wrathful Gurus*;
- the *Black Garuda* from the *Golden Dharmas*;
- the *Eight Deities of Gur*; and
- the White Zhal who lengthens life.

From the throne holder of Sakya Drolma Phodrang, Ngawang Kunga Thekchen Palbar Trinle Wangyi Gyalpo (Kyabgön Sakya Trizin), he received numerous major empowerments, including Vajrakilaya from the Khön tradition.

From Lhakhang Khenchen, Jampal Zangpo, he received the great empowerment of the *Extremely Wrathful Hayagriva*, based on the Sakya text.

To make a spiritual connection with each of the four heirs of the great Ngor vajradhara (Ngorchen Dorje Chang)—Ngor Thartse Khen Rinpoche, Phenkhang Khenpo, Luding Khenpo, and Khangsar Khenpo—he received teachings at the appropriate time.

From Khenpo Apal, the attendant of Rabjampa Kunzang Sonam, he received the *Great Treatise on the Stages of the Path to Enlightenment* by Je Tsongkhapa.

Although Khyentse Chökyi Lodrö wished to receive the detailed transmission of the collected works of Je Tsongkhapa, his two main students, and so on, from a sublime lama from Amdo Mewa, and had even scheduled the year and month during which the transmission would happen, the turbulent political situation in Tibet at that time prevented his wish from being fulfilled.

From the Fifth Drubwang Dzogchen Rinpoche of Dokham, Thubten Chökyi Dorje, he received

- *Vimalamitra's Guru Yoga Called the "Essence of Blessings"* from the *Heart Essence of Deathless Arya Tara* cycle, a profound treasure teaching revealed by the previous Khyentse;
- *Black Dzambhala* of Balpo Ah Hung Bar;
- the empowerment of the awareness display[113] from the *Wisdom Guru*;
- *Cutting Through: Self-Liberation from Fixation*, the profound treasure teaching revealed by the glorious mahasiddha Heruka Khyentse Yeshe Dorje;
- Jatsön Nyingpo's *Embodiment of the Three Jewels*; and
- other important and profound teachings.

From the sixth incarnation of Dzogchen Rinpoche, the supreme Tulku Jigdral Changchub Dorje, he received

- the long-life empowerment from the *Embodiment of the Three Jewels* and Nyima Drakpa's *Long-Life Practice That Brings Complete Victory Over the Four Maras*;
- *Hayagriva Who Overpowers the Haughty Ones*;
- the authorization blessing for the *Female Holder of Mantra*;
- and so on.

Chökyi Lodrö also gradually received the entire transmission of all Nyima Drakpa and Khyewo Rigdzin Chenpo's teachings.

From Dzogchen Khen Rinpoche, Sonam Chöphel, Khyentse Chökyi Lodrö received empowerments, explanations, and the oral transmission of *Cutting Through: Self-Liberation from Fixation*.

From Nyakrong Tertön, Drime Özer Pema Lingpa, he received the great empowerment of Taksham Samten Lingpa's *Embodied Realization of the Yidam Deities* and numerous empowerments, explanations, and oral transmissions of the profound treasure teachings of the unbroken lineage blessed by the previous Khyentse, including

- *Rediscovered Treasure: Three Cycles of Lama Tennyi*;
- *Great Compassionate Peaceful and Wrathful Pema*;
- *Oral Transmission Lineage of Vishuddhi*;
- *Yamantaka*; and
- *Vajrakilaya*.

Also,

- the empowerments and explanations of the *Innermost Essence of the Dakini* and the *Essence of the Definitive Meaning* received directly by Jamyang Khyentse Wangpo in a pure vision;
- empowerments of the seventeen tantras;
- the empowerment, explanations, and oral transmissions of the Dzogchen teaching *Cutting One Liberates All*;
- the medium and abbreviated empowerments for the *Mandala of the Eight Great Deities: The Assembly of Sugatas*;
- the empowerment for the *Precious Lamp of the Accomplishment of Activity*;
- the empowerment for *Intensely Blazing Wisdom Wrathful Guru*;
- Ratna Lingpa's life-force empowerments for Gönpo Maning, and Mahadeva of the *Northern Treasures*;
- many transmissions from the *Heart Essence of the Vast Expanse* cycle;
- transmissions for the cycle of teachings revealed by Zhikpo Lingpa, which Tertön Drime Pema Lingpa received from Jamgön Kongtrul Rinpoche;
- the elaborate, medium, and abbreviated empowerments for the *Heart Practice That Spontaneously Fulfills All Wishes*, along with the long-life empowerment;
- the combined practice of Amitayus and Hayagriva, revealed by Jamgön Kongtrul Rinpoche;
- the empowerment for *Iron Scorpion Yamantaka*, based on the empowerment manual called the *Garland of Pearls*;
- Tukdor's *Eye-Opener*; and
- the *Spear's-Length Sun Vajrapani*.

He also received extensive empowerments and oral transmissions for the tertön's own treasure teachings, such as the empowerments and oral transmissions for the Yamantaka cycle of teachings. On a number of occasions, Tertön Drime removed obstacles to Khyentse Chökyi Lodrö's life by performing ceremonies to avert adverse circumstances. As a result, they developed a deep love for one another.

From Khenchen Lama Gyaltsen Özer, the brother of Tertön Drime Pema Lingpa, Chökyi Lodrö received

- the empowerment for the *Mandala of the Peaceful and Wrathful Deities of the Magical Net*; and
- the transmissions of the cycles of Nyingtik teachings and the empowerment for *Vajrasattva of Manifest Joy*.

Khyentse Chökyi Lodrö studied all the many wonderful methods for giving empowerments and performing drupchens, and he received the extraordinary stream of the two Jamgöns' empowerments and instructions held by Tertön Drime and his brother, who also had great devotion and affection for him.

From Tertön Drime's son, Pema Tukje Wangchuk, the supreme tulku of Jamgön Kongtrul, he received many empowerments and oral transmissions, such as

- *Avalokiteshvara with a Hundred Lotuses Who Stirs the Depths of Samsara*;
- the Two Dongtruks;
- the cycle of teachings called the *Complete Gathering of Terchen Lerab Lingpa*; and
- comprehensive empowerments and oral transmissions for the *Heart Practice* cycle of teachings.

He received oral transmissions for the complete cycle of Taksham's treasure teachings[114] from the lama of Phel Tsa Wo-phung Monastery.

From the son of Mahasiddha Shakya Shri, Phakchok Dorje, the mind emanation of Jamyang Khyentse Wangpo, he received

- the empowerments, instructions, and oral transmissions for the *Embodiment of the Three Roots*, with which Shakya Shri had been empowered as the lineage holder by the previous Lord (Khyentse Wangpo), from whom he had received the special authorization;
- the empowerment, explanation, and oral transmission of the *Rediscovered Treasure: Guru Chakrasamvara*;
- the empowerment for Gyari Chögyal Dorje's *Wrathful Dark Blue Guru*; and
- the empowerment for Shakya Shri's *Mind Treasure: Guru of Great Bliss*.

From Ratrul Thubten Gyaltsen, Chökyi Lodrö received all the empowerments and oral transmissions for the *Sky Teachings* revealed by Mingyur Dorje and Ratna Lingpa's cycles of treasure teachings.

From Dzigag Choktrul Rinpoche, he received the complete transmission of the *Nyingma Kama*, which had been transmitted to Dzigag Choktrul Rinpoche by Gyatrul Dongak Tenzin, who had received it from Jamyang Khyentse Wangpo.

From the supreme tulku of Katok Monastery, the great scholar and siddha, Gyalse Kunzang Tenzin, he received

- the empowerment of great accomplishment for the *Embodiment of the Guru's Realization*, transmitted to Gyalse Kunzang Tenzin by Gyalwang Karmapa Khakhyab Dorje;
- the oral transmission of all fifteen volumes of the *Embodiment of the Guru's Realization*;
- the explanatory oral transmission of the *General Essentialization of All the Wisdom of the Buddhas*;
- the *Trilogy of Finding Comfort and Ease* and the *Treasury of the Supreme Vehicle*, which Khyentse Wangpo had received directly in a pure vision;
- empowerments from the Dzogchen lineage, including the *Heart Essence of Vimalamitra* and the *Heart Essence of the Dakinis*; and
- many other crucial teachings and empowerments.

When Khyentse Chökyi Lodrö was young and still living at his birthplace, he received a long-life empowerment from Drakmar Choktrul Yizhin Wangyal.

From Katok Khenchen, Ngawang Palzang, he received

- all the empowerments and oral transmissions for both Longsal Nyingpo and Dudul Dorje's cycles of treasure teachings;
- the great empowerment for the profound treasure of Guru Chökyi Wangchuk, the *Mandala of the Eight Great Deities: The Complete Secret*, and the lineage transmission of the accomplishment empowerment that came from Jamgön Kongtrul;
- the empowerment and instructions for the *Innermost Essence of the Dakini*; and
- many other empowerments and teachings.

From Khenpo Lekshe Jorden of Katok, he received oral transmissions for

- all nine volumes of omniscient Jigme Lingpa's writings;
- the six volumes of Jatsön Nyingpo's cycles of treasure teachings;
- nine volumes of the compiled Kama ritual texts printed from Dzogchen Monastery woodblocks; and
- many others.

From Drikung Tertön Ösel Dorje, he received

- the empowerment of Red Tara, the tertön's own profound treasure teaching;
- the great empowerment of the *Obstacle-Averting Yamantaka*;
- the torma empowerment of *Molten Metal Yamantaka*;
- the empowerment of the long-life practice of the *Secret Moon*; and
- the introduction to the Drikung Dharma protectress, Achi Chödrön; the ritual for breaking curses;[115] and the long-life empowerment.

The tertön also offered a tenshuk and performed rituals for protection and to avert obstacles, thereby removing obstacles to Khyentse Chökyi Lodrö's life. Since he and Drikung Tertön Ösel Dorje were connected by the same karmic links and aspirations, as the tertön deciphered the treasure teachings, Khyentse Chökyi Lodrö would transcribe his words. Chökyi Lodrö told me a number of times that Drikung Tertön Ösel Dorje was an authentic tertön.

From the supreme Dudjom Tulku Jigdral Yeshe Dorje, Chökyi Lodrö received all the empowerments and instructions related to Dudjom Rinpoche's own mind treasure, Guru Dorje Drolö, along with the authorization seal for all his profound treasure teachings. Khyentse Chökyi Lodrö praised Dudjom Rinpoche and held him in very high esteem.

From Chatral Sangye Dorje, he received

- some old Kadampa texts;
- all of the great Lhatsün Namkha Jigme's cycles of *Vajra Essence*;
- the supplementary teachings of the *Accomplishing the Life-Force of the Vidyadharas*;
- the *Mountain Dharma: Not Crossing the Threshold* by Karma Chagme;
- a few cycles of the teachings of Dudjom Lingpa and his Dharma sons, including *Purifying Perception*; and

- the empowerments and oral transmissions for the complete cycle of the treasure teachings of Sera Khandro.

From his younger brother, Chime Pema Dorje, Khyentse Chökyi Lodrö received numerous transmissions, such as the long-life practice and Hayagriva from the profound treasures of the old Tertön of Ser.

From Adzom Gyalse Rinpoche, Gyurme Dorje, he received

- a long-life empowerment;
- the elaborate empowerment for the *Heart Essence of the Dakinis*; and
- many oral transmissions.

From Gyalse Pema Wangyal, he received many profound teachings, including explanatory oral transmissions and the yoga from the *Heart Essence of the Vast Expanse*.

From the great Dzogchen yogi Kunga Palden, he received detailed clarification of the profound instructions from the *Innermost Essence of the Guru*.

When the Tenth Surmang Trungpa Rinpoche, Karma Chökyi Nyinje, visited Katok Monastery, Chökyi Lodrö and omniscient Katok Situ Rinpoche received

- the detailed empowerment and instructions for the *Dakini's Oral Transmission Lineage of Chakrasamvara* and the ritual dances;
- Dorje Lingpa's *Vast Expanse of the View*;
- instructions for the *Six Yogas of Naropa*; and
- Mahamudra.

From Gegye Dabzang Choktrul Rinpoche, he received

- the empowerments for the *Ocean of the Victorious Ones* from the Kamtsang tradition;
- the empowerments for the *Five Deities of Vajravarahi*; and
- the oral transmissions and empowerments for Drime Kunga's *Nine Deities of the Ocean of the Victorious Ones*, rediscovered by Jamyang Khyentse Wangpo. (Jamgön Kongtrul Lodrö Taye recognized Dabzang Tulku as the main holder of this treasure teaching.)

When Khyentse Chökyi Lodrö met Drungnam Gyaltrul Rinpoche, he received the empowerment of Chakrasamvara and the extraordinary authorization seal of instructions. They had a detailed discussion about the depth of their realization, and so on, after which Chökyi Lodrö said, "I had thought your teacher was just a yogi, not a scholar, but I now believe this demonstration of his unfettered knowledge of all the profound key points of sutra and tantra to be the wisdom that bursts from the depths of meditative realization."

When, at the age of fifteen, Avalokiteshvara in person, the Sixteenth Karmapa Rangjung Rigpe Dorje displayed the black hat that liberates when seen at the second Akanishta pure realm, Dzongsar Tashi Lhatse, the power of Khyentse Chökyi Lodrö's yearning devotion enabled him to see Karmapa as the Lord of Dharma, Düsum Khyenpa, in person. On other occasions, when Karmapa again wore his black hat, Chökyi Lodrö saw him as Vimalamitra and Karma Pakshi.

Later, when he visited central Tibet, Chökyi Lodrö traveled to the great seat of Tsurphu specifically to visit the Karmapa, and they exchanged long-life empowerments as an auspicious way of increasing the length of each other's lives.

At Drakar Tashiding, at the heart of the hidden land of Sikkim, without having made any formal invitations, Gyalwa Karmapa, Khyentse Chökyi Lodrö, and the Gyalse Lama of Sikkim somehow met up. Gyalwa Karmapa and Chökyi Lodrö performed the ceremonies of invoking blessings to a sacred place, subduing the gods and spirits, and so on. How this meeting led to an extraordinary coincidence is described in the secret biography that follows.

During the pilgrimage they made together, they had profound discussions about their realization and practice, and their minds merged as one. Gyalwang Rinpoche praised Khyentse Chökyi Lodrö, saying, "As all appearance and existence appear to you as the dharmakaya, if all your activities meet with auspicious circumstances, you will become like the Dharma King Ratna Lingpa."

From Jamgön Situ Rinpoche, Pema Wangchen of Palpung Monastery (Palpung Situ Rinpoche), Chökyi Lodrö received

- the bodhisattva vow from the *Lineage of Vast Conduct*;
- the great empowerment of Hevajra from Marpa's tradition;
- the empowerment for *Fifteen Dakinis Free of Self*;
- the empowerment of Hayagriva from the Kyergang tradition;
- the root empowerment for the *Heart Essence of the Immortal Lotus-Born*, the treasure teaching revealed by Khyentse Wangpo;

- the torma empowerment for *Secret Essence Vajrakilaya;*
- the empowerments for *White Manjushri* from the Mati tradition, Saraswati, by Brahmin Phurbu, and Padampa Sangye's *Lion's Roar Manjushri* that had been transmitted through Jamgön Mipham Rinpoche;
- the authorization blessing and explanatory oral transmissions for the Heart Practice of White Tara from the Jonang tradition;
- the long-life empowerment from the *Embodiment of the Three Jewels* cycle;
- the torma empowerment and authorization blessing for six-armed Mahakala; and
- the empowerment of Gönpo Nyingkhug.

Khyentse Chökyi Lodrö told me that once when he was seriously ill, Palpung Situ Rinpoche had turned up uninvited, and in his dreams that night, he had seen signs of the mahasiddha Drombipa dispelling obstacles. They became very close, as if their minds were one, and Chökyi Lodrö offered Palpung Situ Rinpoche a tenshuk. Later, after Palpung Situ had passed away, Chökyi Lodrö graciously performed ceremonies for the fulfillment of his enlightened wishes.

From the supreme Gyalse Jamgön Choktrul, Palden Khyentse Özer (Karse Kongtrul) of Tsadra,[116] he received

- the empowerment for Ratna Lingpa's Vajrakilaya;
- the empowerments for Vishuddhi (Yangdak) and the *Secret Practice of Drolö Called "Taming All Malevolent Spirits,"* the profound treasure revealed by the previous Jamgön Kongtrul Lodrö Taye; and
- the empowerments for four-armed Mahakala from the Ga Lotsawa tradition.

Gyalse Jamgön Choktrul also received from Khyentse Chökyi Lodrö the great empowerments for the *Great Assembly* from the Nyingma tradition, and *Manjushri: Holder of Secrets* from the Ngok tradition.

From the Fifth Supreme Tulku of Terchen Rolpe Dorje, Chökyi Lodrö received all the Tsodrak cycles of the tertön's treasure teachings. As a result, the Fifth Choktrul developed deep confidence in Chökyi Lodrö and received the complete cycle of the *Luminous Heart Essence of the Three Roots*, one of Jamyang Khyentse Wangpo's mind treasures. The Fifth Choktrul then bestowed on Chökyi Lodrö the authorization seal for all the treasure teachings of Terchen Rolpe Dorje. Chökyi Lodrö then offered him a mandala and the representations of body, speech, and mind, before asking him to compose various texts, such as a commentary on the Vajrapani tantra. The Fifth Choktrul immediately complied. The two masters became very close as both teacher and student to each other.

From the Ninth Sangye Nyenpa Tulku,[117] Karma Shedrup Tenpe Nyima, Chökyi Lodrö received many teachings and transmissions, such as the empowerment of White Tara from the Jonang tradition, and *Mahamudra: The Ocean of Definitive Meaning*.

From Traleg Choktrul, he received

- the explanation of *Two Sections of the Hevajra Root Tantra* based on the general commentary by Jamgön Kongtrul Rinpoche;
- the empowerments for Akshobhya and Nine-Deity Amitayus from the Karma Kagyü tradition;
- the essential empowerment for Ratna Lingpa's *Long-Life Practice of the Gathering of Secrets*;
- and so on.

From the Palpung retreat master, Lama Norbu, he received the oral transmission for the great commentary on the *Gradual Path Called the "Essence of Wisdom"* by Khewang Karma Tsepal.

From Khenpo Dosib Thubten, he received oral transmissions for the collected writings of Ngorchen Könchok Lhundrup and most of the *Compendium of Tantras*.

From Tenzin Tulku of Surmang Monastery, he received the empowerment for Rolpe Dorje's *Very Wrathful*.

From Khargo Angkhar Tulku, he received oral transmissions for all the treasure teachings of Chöje Lingpa, and so on.

The teachings listed above are mostly those Khyentse Chökyi Lodrö briefly mentions receiving and studying in his autobiography. A detailed account of all these teachings is said to have been recorded in his *Transmissions Catalogue* (which comprises more than four thick volumes), but as I don't have that text, I am unable to list everything here.

Even I, the worst of our Lord Guru's students, having had the good fortune to meet him for the first time when I was about fifteen, was cared for by him with extraordinary kindness. He taught me both spiritual and worldly traditions, and placed me among the teachers from whom he received profound Dharma teachings. To comply with his instructions and with the strong wish to make cloud-like offerings of profound Dharma to Manjushri Guru throughout all my successive lives, I began by offering him the long-life empowerment of the *Consort Practice* from the *Heart Essence of the Vast Expanse*. I went on to offer him

- the great empowerment of *Vajrakilaya: The Tradition of the King*;
- the empowerments for the *Ocean of Dharma That Combines All Teachings* and *Hayagriva Who Liberates the Haughty Ones*;
- the most profound long-life blessing of the *Heart Essence of Deathless Arya Tara*;
- the empowerments for the *Gathering of the Glorious Ones* and individual practices for the four classes of blood drinker from the *Heart Essence of the Vast Expanse*; and
- oral transmissions for most of the writings of Jamgön Mipham Rinpoche and Shechen Gyaltsab Rinpoche, and for the collected works of Jonang Jetsün Taranatha and the *Treasury of Kagyü Tantras*.

It is said in the sacred texts that the sound of Dharma emerges from the trees and rivers through the blessings of the extraordinary magical display of the wisdom of buddhas and bodhisattvas who have gained mastery over the power of meditation and miracles. Also, that Manjushri transformed an unvirtuous demon into a being endowed with the major and minor marks of a buddha who was able to teach the vast and profound sutras. In the same way, the wisdom eye of Khyentse Chökyi Lodrö could see and confirm that all my writings labeled "mind treasures" were authentic treasure teachings. Having commended these teachings as excellent and having made many offerings of special representations of body, speech, and mind, he instructed me to decipher the treasures, after which he received from me all the empowerments and oral transmissions.

I have none of the qualities that qualify a person to write down these kinds of teaching; however, I firmly believe that they appeared solely through the power of the tiny portion of Jamyang Khyentse Wangpo and Khyentse Chökyi Lodrö's blessings that have entered my mind-stream. For this reason and to fulfill his command, I offered these teachings to our Lord Guru and have only added this information to complete the section.

Chökyi Lodrö took special care to receive all the profound teachings and practices that had been expressly conferred individually[118] on most of the heart-sons of the sun- and moon-like Jamgön Dharma Kings.[119]

As a rule, Khyentse Chökyi Lodrö's desire to hear and receive teachings was insatiable. He was constantly receiving vast and profound empowerments, instructions, and oral transmissions for teachings of all lineages, and encouraged others to do the same. Not content with hearing a teaching just once, even though he already knew the distinctive features of each lineage thoroughly, he continued to receive all the essential teachings over and over again.[120]

During his life, he received teachings from more than eighty contemporary teachers from each of the traditions, all of whom were both learnèd and accomplished, and whose minds overflowed with bodhichitta. Just as, day after day, all rivers flow ceaselessly into the vast ocean without ever satisfying its thirst, Chökyi Lodrö constantly received from those great noble beings all the streams of the nectar-like vast and profound Dharma, and was never content with the secret treasury of comprehensive knowledge he had managed to accumulate.

Khyentse Chökyi Lodrö did not receive teachings from people whose Dharma lineage or teachers had been tainted by broken samayas, or without having properly examined them, or to avoid displeasing others, or with a sectarian attitude, or with the carelessness of being excessively open-minded. Instead, he relied only on spiritual friends who had all the excellent qualities of learning and realization. He did not receive a teaching merely because it was appropriate to a particular occasion, or in pursuit of fame to boost his own reputation, or out of attachment to a particular sect; rather, he received teachings that directly or indirectly brought the most benefit to the precious Buddhadharma and paid special attention to rare teachings that were on the verge of extinction.

He completely understood all the teachings he received. For example, he knew each teaching's origin and its specific interpretation by individual philosophical schools; the final establishment of the view and philosophical tenets of each school; the significance of the pith instructions, which are the profound crucial points of each creation and completion meditation; and even the tiniest detail of each tradition's ritual practices without ever mixing them up. He remembered all this, never forgetting a single detail. And when practicing or teaching, he never confused or made mistakes about the methods employed by different traditions.

Chökyi Lodrö loved the Dharma from the depths of his heart, and as a result, his prodigious knowledge of the individual Nyingma and Sarma teachings—which he also practiced—was far more extensive than that of other more vainglorious teachers who did not hesitate to declare themselves lineage holders.

Always bearing in mind the importance of the continuity of the teachings and to serve as an example for future students, he immediately published all the teachings he received to ensure they were not wasted. He also printed rare texts and made new tsagli images of the various mandalas. He did approach and accomplishment practices and propagated the teachings to such an extent that tangible results were clearly visible, and after empowerments and teachings would make huge thanksgiving offerings. His activities were truly vast in number.

To benefit the continuity of the teachings, Khyentse Chökyi Lodrö would receive necessary teachings from even the humblest practitioner (who often hid their qualities) if that practitioner had authentic knowledge of a specific teaching. He always spoke very highly of such people. Tireless in all his wonderful activities and never easily satisfied, Chökyi Lodrö constantly sought out rare Dharma teachings and was sincerely devoted to the teachers from whom he received them. With him, there was no hint of duplicity, and his reliance on all his spiritual friends was in perfect accord with the teachings of the sutras and tantras.

It is said in the *Verse Summary of the Prajnaparamita Sutra,*

> Therefore wise people with strong aspirations
> For complete enlightenment subdue their pride;
> In the same way as the sick must rely on doctors to treat their illnesses,
> The wise must rely steadfastly on their spiritual companion.
> Bodhisattvas on the path to buddhahood
> Practice the paramitas and rely on their spiritual friends.
> Those who rely on their spiritual guides and practice (the Two Causes)
> Will swiftly attain the bhumi of accomplishment, Buddhahood.

And, from the sutras,

> Those who please their spiritual friend will attain the enlightenment of the buddhas.

Also, Nagarjuna said,

One whose hair is white and face is wrinkled
Should continue to accumulate an abundance of knowledge.
Never can the physical body venture
Where a mind brimful of knowledge roams.

Khyentse Chökyi Lodrö kept all this in mind.

To people with high worldly positions, he merely showed the customary respect. Being very direct, he was not sycophantic nor did he flatter those bloated with pride in their meager spiritual or political knowledge.

He always remained firm in thought and action, and followed the teachings to the letter as described in the sacred texts. And he knew his place; he always behaved entirely appropriately both as a guru and a student and never distorted the auspicious connection between the two. As a result, his actions were worthy ornaments of the teachings. Were these actions to be thoroughly examined through the eyes of pure, unbiased wisdom rather than our ordinary, prejudiced perception, in the words of the previous incarnation, Jamyang Khyentse Wangpo,

> From early childhood, I could never remain in perfect meditation at all times, even in my dreams, and I never aspired to perform village rituals or longed only to lead the life of an ascetic. By renouncing this life, I have completely severed all pretensions with everyone, high and low, as well as the fabrications of hope and fear.

Khyentse Chökyi Lodrö attained the sublime bhumis in the same way. By the power of his inner wisdom, he dissolved the eight worldly preoccupations into one taste and completely dismantled the illusions of hope and fear. As a result, he attained extraordinary secret qualities, inconceivable to the minds of ordinary beings. These days, though, such things are unknown to all but a few.

Nagarjuna said,

> Hearing increases wisdom:
> To one who can *hear* and *contemplate*,
> *Meditation* will arise perfectly.
> Through these three, unsurpassable accomplishment will
>   be attained.

And Dromtonpa[121] said,

> While hearing, I reflect and meditate;
> While contemplating, I hear and meditate;
> While meditating, I hear and reflect.
> Combining all these practices into one,
> I know how to carry the Dharma onto the path.
> I am a Kadampa without prejudice;
> I understand things to be a mere display, like an actor's many masks.[122]
> To embody all that is excellent, this is the Kadampa tradition.

Khyentse Chökyi Lodrö sailed across the great ocean of all the Buddha's teachings, propelled to the other shore by billowing sails of wisdom filled with the winds of intelligence (*prajna*) and diligence. As a result, he fully gathered into his mind the profound and essential ultimate meaning of the teachings—a veritable treasury of precious jewels. He did this by studying extensively, by memorizing the root verses and structural outlines of individual Indian philosophical texts on the sutras and Tibetan texts, and by clarifying any doubts or confusion about difficult points by consulting commentaries and then being examined on his understanding.

The Indian and Tibetan texts consisted of

- the *Flower Garland of the Vinaya* and the *Vinaya Sutra*;
- the *Higher and Lower Abhidharmas*;
- the *Verse Summary of the Prajnaparamita Sutra*;
- the *Five Treatises on the Middle Way*;
- *Four Hundred Verses on Madhyamaka*;
- the *Pratimoksha Sutra*;
- the *Fifty-Verse Getsul Karika* and *Three Hundred-Verse Getsul Karika* (about the Vinaya);
- the root text and the commentary for the *Introduction to the Middle Way*;
- the explanation of *The Way of the Bodhisattva* based on mahasattva Patrul's teachings;
- the *Five Dharmas of Lord Maitreya*;
- the *Ornament of the Middle Way* based on Mipham Rinpoche's detailed explanation, which Lord Khyentse Wangpo received directly in a pure vision;

- the root text, commentary, and all supplementary texts about the *Wish-Fulfilling Treasury*;
- the root text and commentary for the *Ascertainment of the Three Types of Vow*;
- the root text and commentary for the *Treasury of Precious Qualities*; and
- the *Summary of the Gateway to the Perfection of Knowledge*.

In terms of the *Guhyagarbha Tantra*, Khyentse Chökyi Lodrö received and perfected teachings based on many texts, such as the great Indian and Tibetan commentaries that outline the meaning and elucidate the hidden significance. When the tantric shedra at Katok Monastery was first established, he received the extremely elaborate form of these teachings from omniscient Katok Situ Rinpoche.

To be more specific, he received from Rago Choktrul the explanation of the *Guhyagarbha Tantra* that Jamgön Khyentse had received directly in a pure vision, based on Minling Lochen Dharmashri's *Ornament of the Realization of Vajrapani*, and transmitted it to Shechen Gyaltsab Rinpoche, Shechen Kongtrul Rinpoche, and others.

He also received a thorough explanation of the general meaning of the *Guhyagarbha Tantra*, called the *Key to the Precious Treasury*, from omniscient Dodrupchen Jigme Tenpe Nyima and repeatedly sought to clarify its more obscure connotations.

He also received detailed explanations of *Two Sections of the Hevajra Root Tantra* from the Sakya and Ngok traditions.

To comply with his instructions, I also offered, as a mandala offering, the explanations and oral transmissions of the commentary on the *Guhyasamaja Tantra*, the sky-like king of tantras, known as the *Four Combined Commentaries on the Guhyasamaja Tantra*, and the commentary on *Chakrasamvara Called "One Who Illuminates the Hidden Meanings,"* from the authentic transmission lineage I had received from a scholar from Amdo called Sido Khenchen, the student of a student of Sherab Gyatso.

From Gatön Jampalyang, the two Dezhung Choktrul Rinpoches, the great scholar Lama Tashi Chöphel, the Tenth Surmang Trungpa Rinpoche Chökyi Nyinje, Amdo Geshe Jamrol, and other lineage holders from different traditions, Khyentse Chökyi Lodrö received detailed clarifications on the Dharma terminology, philosophical views, and conclusions of each tradition. He also received the lineage transmission of the early masters' oral instructions and maintained them perfectly in the eternal knot of his mind.

Although Gatön Jampalyang had not formally completed his studies at a shedra, as he had practiced and fully perfected the *Precious Words*, the knot of his inner nadi was released, and he understood all the essential points of view and meditation—in particular, the profound meaning of the Lamdre. He was also able to give extraordinary direct instructions that sprang from his own experience. Judging from his vast and profound wisdom and intelligence, and so on, Gatön Jampalyang must have been blessed by either the Dharma Lord Manjushri Sakya Pandita, or one of his emanations.

Inspired by Gatön Jampalyang's extraordinary life, during various informal conversations, Khyentse Chökyi Lodrö repeatedly urged his main students, the two Dezhung Choktrul Rinpoches, to write the biographies—genuine and reliable religious histories—of the early masters and how the signs of accomplishment of having practiced the profound meaning take birth in the minds of practitioners. He said there were so many important oral teachings that to write them down would be very beneficial.

Khyentse Chökyi Lodrö wrote in his autobiography,

> In particular, Khenchen Lama (Khenpo Kunpal), Kunzang Palden Chökyi Drakpa cared for me with great kindness. I received from him various empowerments and oral transmissions, including those for the Nyingma tantras, and a comprehensive explanation of the *Guhyagarbha Tantra*. By receiving teachings many times about difficult points of philosophy, and so on, a glimmer of understanding took birth in my mind.

Before the establishment of the new shedra, mahapandita Manjushri Mipham was invited to Katok, where omniscient Katok Situ Rinpoche and many other sublime masters received numerous teachings and studied with him. Later, once the new shedra had been established, Mipham Rinpoche commanded the shedra's administrators to appoint Khenchen Lama Kunzang Palden Chödrak (Khenpo Kunpal) as its main khenpo, and he gave extensive teachings on philosophy.

During that time, all the masters (like Khenchen Atop, Gyaltsen Öser), who knew of Khenpo Kunpal's qualities, said as if with one voice, "As Khenchen Lama studied with Mipham Rinpoche himself for a long time and holds the oral lineage of the extraordinary key points of the philosophical views and systems of all the tantric texts from the immaculate interpretations[123] of omniscient Rongzompa and Longchenpa, it is important for us, with his guidance, to persevere in the practices of hearing and contemplation."

Following their advice, Khyentse Chökyi Lodrö, diligently and without giving in to distraction, clarified all his questions with Khenchen Lama and developed perfect intelligence. As a result, he understood the philosophical interpretations of the great spiritual pioneers of India and Tibet in their authentic forms. When he focused on discourse, he supported his arguments with relevant quotations and logical reasoning based on the profound key points of those masters' interpretations, as well as the extraordinary profound meaning of the Buddha's words and commentaries. However, although he fully understood the essential points of the distinctive characteristics of each system of view, meditation, and philosophy, he never refuted or established points of view that might upset the minds of others by stabbing them with the thorn of attachment and aversion. When he taught individual texts, by explaining the profound meanings in detail, he made all the philosophical teachings seem as fresh and direct as oral instructions. So his tremendous knowledge and experience of the four reliances was perfectly complete.

As he wrote in his autobiography,

> I developed strong pure perception, unstained by negative thoughts, for all the eight great chariots of Tibet and abandoned sectarian denigration of the different schools. Empowerments, explanations, instructions, and tantric transmissions, all that existed, I, with utmost diligence, received and aspired to receive.

And so Chökyi Lodrö listened, contemplated, and practiced without being affected by bias or sectarian attitudes and became the holder of all teachings.

When he gave empowerments or explained teachings, he did not mix up or dilute the practice methods or essential meanings of pith instructions from different traditions. He taught his students according to their capacities and the conventions of each lineage. Therefore, he was the only teacher able to keep his pledge to maintain the genuine and exemplary qualities that enabled him to ascend the lion throne of the two Jamgön Dharma Kings, Jamgön Kongtrul Lodrö Taye and Jamyang Khyentse Wangpo.

4. How Jamyang Khyentse Chökyi Lodrö attained the signs of having accomplished the practice of the path by training his mind in the yoga of the two profound stages of meditation (kyerim and dzogrim).

Sublime beings persevere to preserve the tradition of progressively hearing, contemplating, and meditating on the precious teachings and to benefit those who long for liberation by bestowing the two wish-fulfilling benefits. Therefore, fundamentally, their sole wish is to gather both the treasury of supreme teachings contained in the sacred texts and those realized through practice. How Khyentse Chökyi Lodrö received and studied the textual teachings has already been roughly described; now, how he accumulated the treasury of realization will be explained.

Although from early childhood the noble Lord Manjushri Guru, Khyentse Wangpo, dwelt in the womb of view and meditation—the great inherent and spontaneously perfect natural meditation—he devoted his life to practice, remaining in strict retreat and never crossing his own threshold from the age of forty until his parinirvana. Similarly, Khyentse Chökyi Lodrö was without doubt an emanation of boundless compassion and had no need to strive to attain the stages of the path like ordinary people. However, he made it look as though he engaged in the two stages of meditation as a skillful means to tame short-sighted beings.

As it says in the *Sutra which Precisely Explains Suchness*,

> Shariputra, those who meditate one-pointedly on the samadhi of suchness for as long as it takes to snap their fingers gain more merit than those who listen to the teachings for more than an aeon. Therefore, Shariputra, advise others again and again to meditate on the samadhi of suchness.

From the *Ornament of the Mahayana Sutras*:

> Thus, meditating on the natural state is not without benefit;
> Likewise, the teachings of the sugatas are not without benefit.
> If it were possible to realize the ultimate meaning merely by hearing the teachings, meditation would be meaningless.
> If it were possible to enter into meditation without hearing the teachings, the teachings would be meaningless.

Bearing this in mind, Khyentse Chökyi Lodrö's advice to others was, "Although these days, the wheel of Dharma activity—building representations, teaching the sacred texts, receiving and giving empowerments, transmissions, and so on—is widespread, more important by far is to emphasize the practices of approach and accomplishment." And even when, in the latter part of his life, his activities had increased exponentially, during the winter and spring of most years, he would apply himself, in strict retreat, to accomplishing approach and accomplishment practices.

He had no interest in the activities of the eight worldly preoccupations, nor did he appreciate pompous behavior or industry for the sake of celebrity. He always behaved with great humility, like an ordinary teacher, and never presented himself as being in any way a "great lama."

Having constantly engaged in the Mahayana practice of training the mind, his great compassion moved him to bless those who were terminally ill or injured in war, and whenever necessary, he performed the ritual for liberating the dead.

One piece of advice that Khyentse Chökyi Lodrö often gave his students was that, if they did not subdue their minds through renunciation and the compassion attained by training in the bodhichitta of helping others, trying to grab hold of the highest view of Mahamudra and Dzogchen would get them nowhere. Training thoroughly in the preliminary practices is crucially important.

As he had fully perfected compassion, the perception of hard-hearted, impervious beings and those born into noble families was completely transformed by the devotion they felt as they merely gazed upon his face. Everyone immediately trusted him wholeheartedly. And when he taught, he never wept or showed any sign of emotion on the pretext of demonstrating his disgust for samsara. This was how Khyentse Chökyi Lodrö brought under control all the beings of the three realms.

At the age of seventeen, during the empowerments for the *Compendium of Tantras*, although he played around a little, he didn't make any mistakes when he placed the empowerment substances on the different centers of his body or while performing various mudras. He was much admired by Shabdrung Rinpoche Tashi Gyatso, who said, "How can this Lord, who is never distracted and completely without fault, be compared to others of this age?"

I often heard Chökyi Lodrö advise students that if they were unable to receive the effective instructions, it was enough instantly to put into practice the profound explanations they received on how to concentrate on the object of their practice, whatever it might be. This is, without doubt, how he practiced himself.

In his record of the transmissions of the *Treasury of Precious Instructions* he received, he mentions the following: "Those of us who receive these teachings and who have texts must read them carefully, try to remember the meaning of the words, and instantly focus on the object of practice, and so on, to avoid our actions bearing no result. We must not merely give the appearance of having heard and received the teachings while allowing our minds to fall under the power of distraction. By making every effort to apply these methods (the best possible for benefiting our minds), the torrent of blessings will be extraordinary." From this it is clear that Chökyi Lodrö would instantly put into practice all the teachings he received.

When he received instructions on the great secret *Path and Fruition: The Explanation for Private Disciples* from the noble vajradhara Loter Wangpo, although he was a fully realized being, he went through the motions of appearing to recognize the ultimate wisdom directly.

Later, from vidyadhara Natsok Rangdrol, Dodrup Jigme Tenpe Nyima, and the Fifth Dzogchen Rinpoche, Thubten Chökyi Dorje, he received many great empowerments from the *Display of Awareness of Dzogpachenpo*. When Kyabje Shechen Gyaltsab Rinpoche gave the introduction for Jangdak Tashi Tobgyal's empowerment of the *Embodiment of the Three Kayas*, he bestowed on Khyentse Chökyi Lodrö the blessings of realization. Chökyi Lodrö said that these blessings enriched his spiritual practice, and through them, the realization of great vajra wisdom had arisen in his mind, pervading everything. Without having to exhaust himself by accomplishing each stage of the path, all his perceptions and actions appeared as the infinite display of wisdom. Therefore, having entered the womb of the view and meditation of inseparable emptiness and luminosity, Khyentse Chökyi Lodrö spontaneously accomplished the two benefits through a combination of practice and study. All this was widely known.

I will now say a little about the particular practices Khyentse Chökyi Lodrö accomplished in retreat.

Firstly, based on the *Heart Essence of the Vast Expanse* of Dzogpachenpo, he followed the practice tradition of his previous incarnation to complete the purification and accumulation practices found in the ordinary and extraordinary preliminaries (Ngöndro). He accomplished the five hundred thousand accumulations perfectly.

He always practiced the appropriate teaching at the appropriate time, but he mainly practiced the profound treasure teachings of Lord Khyentse Wangpo. If there were special visualization instructions for a preliminary practice, he would do both the elaborate and essential accumulation, and the purification stages. Then for countless Sarma and Nyingma yidams, he accomplished innumerable recitations combined with creation meditation. The length of his retreats was determined by the amount of time he had, or the number of mantras to be accumulated, or the signs of accomplishment he achieved. Here is a rough list of those practices:

- the detailed approach practice of Hevajra from the Ngor tradition, complete with preliminary, main, and concluding practices;
- the extremely detailed approach practice of Vajrakilaya from the Khön tradition;
- *Guhyasamaja Manjuvajra*;
- *Vajrabhairava* from the Tsarpa tradition;
- the recitation of Vajrayogini from Naropa's tradition;
- the practice of Dragdzongma, the guardian for protector Gur, three times;
- more than eight million recitations of the seven syllables associated with the inner and secret practices of Mahakala;
- the secret accomplishment practice of the four-faced Mahakala, the related long-life practice of the seven Gurs, and the *White Enhancer of Life*;
- the *Father and Mother Consorts of the Simultaneously Arising Chakrasamvara* from the oral lineage of Rechungpa;
- the *Abbreviated Five Tantric Deities* and the *Combined Practice of the Four Deities* from the teachings of Shangpa Kagyü;
- the *Guru Yoga of the Six-Armed Blue Mahakala*;
- the elaborate approach practice for the kriya tantra's *General Mandala of Three Families* from the *Compendium of Sadhanas*;
- Mitra's *White Amitayus, White Tara Radiating Six Rays of Light* from the Bari Lotsawa tradition, and Samantashri's *White Saraswati*—the *Three White Deities*;
- the king of mahasiddhas Thangtong Gyalpo's *Drubgyal Tsepakme*;
- Bari Lotsawa's *White Ushnishavijaya*;
- the long-life practice of Kurava;
- a guru yoga based on the three long-life deities;[124]
- the *Praise and Practice of Manjushri*;

- Mati's *White Manjushri*;
- *Manjushri: Lion of Speech* from Padampa Sangye's tradition;
- *White Saraswati* from the Phurbu tradition;
- *Red Saraswati* from the Becha Bari tradition;
- *White Varahi* from the Kankadata tradition;
- *White Achala* from the Danashila tradition;
- *White Tara* from the Jonang tradition;
- *Green Tara* from the Nyima Bepa tradition;
- *Black Manjushri*, *Striped Garuda*, and *Kurukulla* from the *Golden Dharmas*;
- *Vajrapani: Tamer of Spirits*;
- *Utsarya*;
- *Vajrapani Dressed in Blue* from the Sutra tradition;
- *Hayagriva* of Kyergang;
- *Vajra Vidharana* from the Bari tradition;
- *Bhurkumkuta* from Atisha's tradition;
- Drapa Ngönshe's *Red Dzambhala*;
- *White Six-Armed Protector* from the *Golden Dharmas* of the Shangpa tradition; and
- the recitation of the Sitatapatra prayer approximately ten thousand times.

These are the practices he did that are, for the most part, from the Sarma tradition:

- the *Heart Practice of Vajrasattva*, the embodiment of all the buddha families, a combined Kama and Terma practice from the Mindrolling tradition;
- the *Combined Practice of the Three Roots*, a rediscovered treasure teaching;
- the elaborate approach practice from Guru Chöwang's *Gathering of the Guru's Secrets*;
- Ratna Lingpa's *Long-Life Practice of the Gathering of Secrets*;
- Guru Yoga from the *Innermost Essence of the Dakini*;
- *Guru Yoga That Pacifies Suffering* from Trengpo Terchen's cycle, *Essence of Liberation*;
- Jatsön Nyingpo's *Embodiment of the Three Jewels*;
- the *Long-Life Practice of Extracting the Pure Essence* from the great Fifth Dalai Lama's *Teachings with Restriction Seals*;

- the guru practice from the *Heart Essence of the Vast Expanse* called *Gathering of Vidyadharas*;
- the *Outer Practice That Removes All Obstacles*; the *Vidyadhara Heir of the Victorious Ones*, one of the individual sadhana practices in the *Heart Practice for Dispelling All Obstacles*; and the *Inner Practice That Spontaneously Fulfills All Wishes*, which can be found in the treasure teachings of both Lord Khyentse and Chokling;
- the *Secret Essence Guru Yoga*, a treasure teaching common to both Jamgön Kongtrul Rinpoche and Jamyang Khyentse Wangpo;
- the *Innermost Secret Guru Yoga Called the "Sealed Quintessence"* from the *Heart Essence of the Vast Expanse*;
- the guru yoga from the *Heart Essence of the Mahasiddha's Wisdom Mind*;
- *Guru Dorje Drolö from the Teachings with Restriction Seals*;
- Karma Guru;
- the *Wrathful Red Guru Rinpoche* from Minling Terchen's treasure teachings;
- *Wrathful Guru Rinpoche with Lower Part as a Phurba* from the Namchö teachings;
- Longsal Nyingpo's *Dark Red Fierce Deity*;
- the *Wrathful Guru of the Assembly of Great and Glorious Herukas* and the *Fierce and Blazing Wrathful Guru, Hayagriva, and Garuda* from the *Heart Essence of the Vast Expanse*;
- *Drolö from the Heart Practice*;
- Jamgön Kongtrul Rinpoche's *Secret Practice of Dorje Drolö*;
- the elaborate approach practice of the *Mandala of the Eight Great Deities: The Assembly of Sugatas*, one of Nyangral Nyima Özer's treasure teachings;
- the approach and accomplishment practice of the *Ocean of Dharma That Combines All Teachings*, along with the elaborate, grand drupchen, and mendrup;
- the *Mandala of the Eight Great Deities: The Assembly of Blood Drinkers* from the heart essence of the mahasiddha;
- *Manjushri: Lion of Speech* from the *Heart Practice*;
- the great approach practice of *Peaceful Manjushri* from the Gyüluk tradition;
- the basic approach practice for Shangtrom's *Yamantaka: Lord of Life*, from the *Northern Treasures*;

- two practice retreats based on the *Oral Transmission Lineage Yamantaka*;
- *Manjushri Who Overpowers the Lord of Death* from the *Luminous Heart Essence*;
- two practice retreats based on *Yamantaka: Destroyer of Enemies* from the *Heart Practice* cycle;
- the *Ultimate Averter from the Essence of Liberation*;
- Rinchen Lingpa's *Nagaraksha*;
- *Long-Life Practice "Iron Tree"* from the *Northern Treasures*;
- *Red Amitayus* from the *Heart Practice* cycle;
- *Avalokiteshvara: The Gathering of the Innermost Essence*;
- *Avalokiteshvara Who Stirs the Depths of Samsara*;
- *Hayagriva Who Liberates the Haughty Ones*, a rediscovered treasure teaching;
- *Fire-Wheel of the Thunderbolt*;
- *Five Antidote Deities*;
- *Hayagriva Who Overpowers the Three Realms* from *Teachings with Restriction Seals*;
- *Supreme Emanation Hayagriva* from the oral lineage;
- *Profound Essence of Vishuddhi* from the oral lineage;
- the *Combined Practice of Vishuddhi and Vajrakilaya*;
- *Blazing Vajra Vajrapani*, a rediscovered treasure teaching;
- *Vajrapani* from the Longsal cycle;
- *Vajrapani Holding a Vajra Cudgel* from the *Tukdrup* cycle;
- the guru yoga from the *Heart Essence of Yutok*;
- *Sambhogakaya Medicine Buddha* from the Zurkhar tradition;
- *Vimalamitra's Guru Yoga Called the "Essence of Blessings"*;
- Guru Chöwang's *Innermost Secret Razor-Edged Vajrakilaya*;
- Ratna Lingpa's *Secret Practice of Vajrakilaya*;
- Dudul Dorje's *Secret Practice of Vajrakilaya*;
- *Vajrakilaya: Overpowering the Forces of Mara* from the *Heart Essence of the Vast Expanse*;
- *Vajrakilaya: The Oral Transmission Lineage*;
- the *Combined Practice of the Assembly of Kilaya Deities* from the *Luminous Heart Essence*;
- *Vajrakilaya from the Seven Profound Cycles*, its *Sharp Point: The Wrathful King in Whom All Power Is Gathered*, and two practice

retreats based on the *Secret Essence Vajrakilaya* from the treasures revealed by Chokgyur Lingpa;
- *Trönak* from the treasure teachings of Nyang Nyima Özer;
- Guru Chöwang's *White Tara*;
- *White Tara: Supreme Wish-Fulfilling Jewel* from *Teachings with Restriction Seals*;
- *Consort Practice: The Queen of Great Bliss* from the *Heart Essence of the Vast Expanse*;
- the combined approach and accomplishment practice based on the entire mandala of the rediscovered treasure teaching *Gathering of the Dakini's Secrets* and just one approach practice based on a daily sadhana; and the practice of the peaceful, increasing, and magnetizing Varahis;
- Shikpo Lingpa's *White Tara*;
- the *Secret Practice Simhamukha* from the *Teachings with Restriction Seals* cycle;
- *White Tara* from the Jonang tradition, with the three transmission lineages transmitted to Jigme Lingpa;
- *Green Tara* from the *Tukdrup* cycle;
- *Simhamukha of Vimalamitra* from the treasure teachings of Chokgyur Lingpa;
- the rediscovered treasure teaching about *Sitatapatra* from the Shije tradition;
- the *Great Peacock*;
- Longsal Nyingpo's *Yellow Dzambhala*;
- three practice retreats on *Chandali, Long-Life Consort*, a teaching that was received in a pure vision;
- the mind treasure *White Varahi Who Kindles Prajna*;
- a rediscovered treasure teaching of Rongzompa's *Padma Dakini*;
- *Red Kingkara* from the *Northern Treasures*;
- *Dispelling the Faults of Samaya Defilements*;
- *Bhurkumkuta* from the *Tukdrup* cycle;
- Mitra's *White and Red Amitayus*, a teaching that was received in a pure vision;
- the rediscovered long-life practice of *Rishi Vimalashanti*;
- three practice retreats on the mind treasure the *Heart Essence of Deathless Arya Tara*;

- *Chandali, Long-Life Consort* from the treasure teaching of Ling Chögyal;
- the long-life practice of the *Peaceful Form of the Mother Who Repels Negative Forces* from the *Teachings with Restriction Seals* cycle; and
- the *White Enhancer of Life* from the treasure teachings of Nyang Nyima Özer.

These were the main practice retreats Khyentse Chökyi Lodrö completed by the age of fifty-six, as they appear in his autobiography. I heard about the unrecorded practices he did later from our Lord Guru himself and other reliable and trustworthy people. I then compiled them all into one list, which I have arranged sequentially.

In addition, following the practice traditions of the early vidyadharas, Chökyi Lodrö performed countless supreme activities, such as mendrup drupchens and drupchös. Whenever he performed either elaborate or simple tsok offerings, or offerings on the two auspicious tenth days[125] (and other special days), he always took every opportunity also to accumulate, purify, and increase merit.

As for the practice of completion meditation with characteristics,[126] I gathered from my daily conversations with him that he practiced the *Precious Words: Path and Fruition*, the completion meditation of *Vajrayogini* practice, the *Six Yogas of Niguma*, and the path of the second and third empowerments from the Nyingtik teachings.

Without doubt, Khyentse Chökyi Lodrö's inherent abilities enabled him to attain, with very little effort, the yoga of nadi, prana, and bindu with characteristics, and the kayas and bindus of the vision of luminosity. In terms of yoga without characteristics, we know that for the most part he practiced the oral instruction traditions of Mahamudra and Dzogchen and especially the teachings of the old and new Nyingtik.

As Khyentse Chökyi Lodrö had completed the process of hearing, contemplating, and meditating on all the teachings of Sarma and Nyingma that are as numerous as the ocean is vast, he taught the details of the path based on his own personal experience, using the relevant contexual language, according to the capacities of those he taught. Unlike other teachers, he never bluffed his way through a teaching if his knowledge of it was only partial; he always fully understood everything he taught.

His mind was extremely profound, yet he diligently hid his extraordinary qualities and rarely revealed anything at all. Occasionally he would say, very modestly, "I have received many teachings, but I have done no practice whatsoever!" However, when giving the effective instructions, having already fully understood and perfected the practice himself, he could teach based on his own experience, which proved extremely beneficial to the minds of his students. By putting these teachings into practice, he was able to hit the vital point and actually experience whatever he taught.

He was especially committed to making sure that his teachings were never at odds with the minds of his students, and so to those who made a great effort to practice one-pointedly, he gave thorough introductions and teachings on how to dispel obstacles, enhance experience, and so on, entirely suited to their level of meditative experience. During the latter part of his life, he concentrated on giving students one-to-one transmissions of the effective instructions.

As all the teachings of the eight great chariots of the practice lineage had been gathered into the excellent vase of his mind over countless successive lifetimes, he not only became renowned as the "holder of an ocean of hidden qualities," he actually was!

Therefore, in the prayer Khyentse Chökyi Lodrö composed in response to a request of mine, he wrote,

> Great repository of the secret treasury of profound instructions,
> Maturation[127] and liberation[128] of the eight great chariots of the
>   practice lineage,
> Endowed with the glorious qualities of wisdom and compassion,
> To Pema Yeshe Dorje, I pray.

In this prayer, by acknowledging the extraordinary nature of his qualities, he reveals the truth about himself.

This is how he could effortlessly perpetuate the activities of the early masters of the practice lineage, without having to do retreats or endure the hardships of mountain retreat to attract attention.

How he attained the signs of having accomplished the perfect qualities of the inner vajra path will now be described.

However vast the ocean-like qualities of sublime beings, they are always hidden because sublime beings practice the discipline of humility; even the wisdom mind of a realized being cannot fully appreciate the profound hidden qualities of the body, speech, and mind of another such being. It is therefore extremely difficult to express even a fraction of their remarkable qualities.

By examining the space enclosed by the eye of a needle, we can get an idea of what space is. Similarly, by merely seeing, hearing, or remembering the tiniest example[129] of the priceless, precious qualities of a sublime being, we will benefit from higher rebirths and liberation, and will effortlessly realize that sublime beings are endowed with inconceivable hidden qualities. Therefore, I am going to state, without exaggeration or understatement, all that I have seen, heard, and inferred about Khyentse Chökyi Lodrö, knowing it will inspire confidence in the minds of those who follow the path of faith and devotion.

Since Khyentse Chökyi Lodrö was the very manifestation of pure compassion,[130] his activities were beyond the comprehension of ordinary beings. From a very young age he taught philosophical texts and flawlessly performed the activities of a vajra master. Like his predecessors, his sole intention was to benefit the teachings and beings, and so during the process of accumulating the treasure of understanding sacred texts through intensive study or attaining realization through intensive meditation practice, he never became bored, nor did these activities either depress or satisfy him.

In all his everyday activities,[131] as his more practical projects created opportunities for everyone, both noble and ordinary, also to practice the Dharma, one of the side effects[132] was that not only did the teachings flourish, but they became even more secure.

He introduced a system for spreading and propagating the authentic teachings by building countless representations of body, speech, and mind, and established numerous exceptional study and practice centers, both as fields of merit and to ensure the continuity of teachings. Since he had realized the illusory nature of phenomena, however difficult his activities to benefit the teachings may have appeared to be, he said nothing, neither complaining nor expressing the slightest sign of weariness or exhaustion.

Khyentse Chökyi Lodrö lived as a hidden yogi throughout his life, but having strengthened his inner wisdom, the fame of his sublime qualities spread throughout the land, and noble masters from all traditions bowed before his lotus feet and spoke of him with great admiration.

Although his visionary experiences were unmistakable signs of realization, he chose not to reveal them. Instead, he steadfastly concealed his secret qualities, always behaving as though there were nothing special about him at all. Although he was held in the highest esteem by all those who governed the country, both high and low, he cared nothing for the eight worldly preoccupations and, for the most part, led the life of one who had renounced worldly pursuits.

Having fully realized the view of emptiness, he sometimes acted spontaneously, and was always able to accomplish, without obstacle, all the wonderful activities, great and small, that were difficult for ordinary beings to comprehend.

With great compassion and perfect timing, in order to plant the seed of enlightenment in the minds of inconceivable numbers of beings, he traveled a great deal, from Kham to India and Nepal, so that as many people as possible had the opportunity to see the mandala of his *body*, born from vast accumulations of merit and wisdom. With nectar-like *speech*, he gave each student the teachings they needed, embracing them all within the expanse of his nonconceptual *mind*. This is how he was able to accomplish all his activities.

In a nutshell, all the pure hidden qualities of his body, speech, and mind were perfectly attuned to the Dharma and worthy of veneration by all sentient beings, including the gods. Even the buddhas and their sons, the bodhisattvas, praised his qualities.

From the *Verse Summary of the Prajnaparamita Sutra*:

> For example, emanations of the buddhas perform the activities of buddhas
> But never feel the slightest pride in their actions.
> Likewise, the bodhisattvas, adept at the practice of prajna,
> Perform all their activities through their magical emanations.
> Images of male and female human beings
> Created by skilled carpenters and craftsmen fulfill a specific purpose;
> Likewise, the bodhisattvas skilled in the practice of prajna,
> Nonconceptual wisdom, continue their activities.
> To those proficient in this kind of practice,
> Innumerable gods prostrate with folded hands, and
> The buddhas of the realms of the ten directions
> Extol these qualities in a continuous stream of praise.

During a private conversation, Khyentse Chökyi Lodrö said, "As malevolent spirits entered me when my mind was already disturbed, there is nothing I have not seen or done." However, in reality he had gained control over nadi, prana, and bindu through the practice of the inner yogas and realized the ultimate truth, having dissolved the wind of his life-force into his central channel.

In the *Abridged Kalachakra Tantra*, it is said,

> The bodhisattvas make offerings to the one who has purified the prana of life-force and gone beyond the paths of the sun and the moon.

This is explained in *Immaculate Light*:

> Here, "purification of the prana of life-force" denotes the stage at which a yogi transcends the paths of the sun and the moon to abide perpetually in the central channel. He is then free from the prana of life-force. Hence, the bodhisattvas make offerings and sing his praises.

So when the prana that moves through the right and left channels enters the central channel of a yogi, his mind is liberated from the chains of grasping and fixation, and the abandonment and realization of the indestructible ten inner bhumis are fully perfected. In this way, he gains mastery over the four kinds of discriminating knowledge, and the treasury of boundless recollection, courage, and clairvoyance bursts forth. As the object of the yogi's wisdom is already pure, his beneficial activities are spontaneously and effortlessly accomplished. This auspicious situation prompts a bodhisattva to make offerings and the buddhas to make prophecies about him. The yogi becomes famous, and because he has created the auspicious circumstance of having conquered his prana, bodhisattvas, and so on, are brought under his control. There is no doubt that Chökyi Lodrö had actualized all the supreme signs of realization that are mentioned here.[133]

At Nedong Bentsang in Yarlung, when Khyentse Chökyi Lodrö was sixty-four years old, as the moon waxed during the fourth month in the year of the fire monkey (1956), he performed the elaborate drupchen of the *Ocean of Dharma That Combines All Teachings*.

On the tenth day of the waning moon of that same month, he performed the consecration combined with the drupchö of the *Ocean of Dharma That Combines All Teachings* at Tradruk temple, based on a mandala drawn on cloth that was placed on a table in the middle of the assembly hall. He offered an enormous, elegant tsok, as well as many other offerings and purification ceremonies, and scattered flowers of consecration throughout all the large and small inner temples and over the stupas that lined the path outside.[134] He also performed the supreme activity of blessing amrita, the common long-life practice, the wrathful ritual for averting obstacles, recitations of the fulfillment offering, confession practices, and the accumulation of more than a hundred tsok offerings. All these individual practices were performed elaborately in a single day. In an expression of great joy, he declared that the day's ceremonies were even more beneficial than the drupchen he had performed earlier at Bentsang. The practice began once the sun had risen, long breaks were taken at various intervals, and it finished early in the evening. To the amazement of everyone who was present, rainbows appeared in the sky.

When Chökyi Lodrö bestowed the empowerments and oral transmissions for the *Compendium of Sadhanas* in the main temple at Dzongsar Monastery, while he was giving the authorization blessing of the *Great Yellow Vaishravana*, students found gold dust scattered between the rows of those assembled. After a thorough search, a great deal of gold dust was discovered—there was even some on the canopy that hung above Chökyi Lodrö's head—so much so that gold, the most precious of all substances, was found to have spread throughout the entire temple, inside and out, and people were able to take some away with them to be objects of their devotion.

At the age of sixty-two, in the year of the horse (1954), Khyentse Chökyi Lodrö gave the same transmission again in the empowerment hall of his residence. As he gave the authorization blessings for the deities who magnetize and increase (Wangye Lha), the Yab family from Chamdo offered the first set of a newly printed edition of the *Kangyur*. Playfully, Chökyi Lodrö observed, "Last time I gave this teaching an exaggerated report circulated about a shower of gold dust raining down. Who knows if it did or not? But even if it did, it was a very commonplace sign. This time is more extraordinary by far because we have received the great Dharma treasury of the precious *Kangyur* in a tangible form." And he immediately asked the Sangha to read the text with all reverence. This is an irrefutable sign that Chökyi Lodrö had attained mastery over the extraordinary treasury of Dharma.

At Katok Monastery, he accidentally swallowed half a cup of mercury, which was then secreted from his body onto a cushion without causing him any harm. Many believed swallowing the mercury was an innocent, childish mistake, saying he was lucky not to have died. However, in reality, it was an indisputable display of his realization.

Not long after Khyentse Chökyi Lodrö first arrived at Dzongsar Monastery, he found a mixture of powdered precious substances. Believing it to be the material used for making *kutsaps* (statues), he made a few, which were put in a box and consecrated for several days. When the box was reopened the statues had been transformed; they were magnificent and beautiful and too hot to touch. Actually, the material hadn't really been for making kutsaps; nevertheless, as stated clearly in the sacred texts and as Khyentse Chökyi Lodrö himself confirmed, practice performed with confident devotion and faith brings about accomplishment.

In the year of the wood sheep (1955), during the waning moon of the fourth month, Chökyi Lodrö performed the drupchen for blessing amrita based on the *Mandala of the Eight Great Deities: The Assembly of Blood Drinkers* from the *Heart Essence of the Mahasiddha's Wisdom Mind*. As the consecration ritual began, rays of rainbow light streamed into the practice hall, and throughout the practice, even though the entire country had been gripped by a terrible drought, countless instances of heavy rainfall were reported, as well as many rainbows and other auspicious signs.

It is widely known that Khyentse Chökyi Lodrö often performed miracles. For example, he transformed long-life amrita into yogurt and vase water[135] into amrita, and he multiplied a handful of long-life pills into enough for more than a hundred students.

On their way to China, the Dharma Lords Sakya Pandita and Chögyal Phakpa, who were also uncle and nephew, built the Dzing Namgyal Gönkhang. The gönkhang was said to have been blessed with Buddha Shakyamuni's staff and other relics, which were the main representations. The monastery had an amazing history, and although at one point monk soldiers from Chatreng wrecked it, it was subsequently restored and reconsecrated by Chökyi Lodrö. It is widely known that during the ceremony to drive away obstacles, he stared with one-pointed concentration so wrathfully that the statues shook violently, and the shrine master, who was standing nearby burning frankincense, was so terrified that he fled.

With perfect timing, Chökyi Lodrö performed the ritual for averting attack based on the sadhana of the *Wrathful Vaishravana Riding a Blue Horse*, who was the guardian of the teachings called the *Heart Practice That Spontaneously Fulfills All Wishes*. He was performing this ritual to ensure the well-being of the teachings and beings, when out of the blue, a huge army of dark forces was seen advancing from the southeast. As a result, the entire army drowned in the river, disappearing without trace—a sign that confirmed the ritual had been accomplished.

Although Chökyi Lodrö had gained confidence in the power of wrathful activity, apart from one or two rituals that he performed spontaneously the instant he foresaw how essential they were for the future welfare of the teachings, he did not generally like wrathful activities and neither performed such rituals himself nor encouraged others to do so.

In terms of ceremonies for the security of the teachings and beings in general, and those performed for specific purposes, Khyentse Chökyi Lodrö approved of and recommended the three gentle activities, saying, "Although ceremonies for the well-being of the teachings and beings are important, in these degenerate times, the lamas who perform them merely crave offerings that they then misuse. They have rarely attained the realization of the view. As patrons with pure samaya are scarce and sentient beings have little merit, the practice of wrathful activities, like guarding, averting, liberating, and suppressing, do more harm than good."

When he conferred the life-essence empowerment of Vaishravana on me, he said playfully, "From the perspective of common accomplishments, praying to protector Gur brings wealth and propitiating Vaishravana brings wrathful power, but nobody knows it!" At the time, I felt this statement was connected with his preference for peaceful activities.

A rat once stole the cloth label of a Mahakala text from among Khyentse Chökyi Lodrö's volumes of practices, so he performed the ritual requesting the Dharma protectors to carry out their activities. The next morning the label had been returned and placed by the text.

For many years, there was an extraordinary stone[136] at Dhongthog's house that was closely associated with Tseringma. It had been left there by Khyentse Wangpo (who was related to Dhongthog) as a support for the *Consort Practice: The Queen of Great Bliss* and the prosperity practice of Tseringma from the *Heart Essence of the Vast Expanse*. Later, during a period of upheaval and unrest, it was lost, until one day, Khyentse Chökyi Lodrö declared he had come across that very stone as he traveled up from Katok to Dzongsar, and that it had been replaced in its original position. This is a clear sign that the samaya-bound protectors fulfilled his commands.

The incarnation of Nyidrak Atsa Togden, Kunzang Namdröl, who lived near Sog Tsenden Monastery, offered Chökyi Lodrö a pair of cymbals. They were, he said, a treasure revealed by Sangye Lingpa. Later, though, Chökyi

Lodrö wondered if a contaminated spirit[137] had been attracted to him, because he felt sure one had appeared during the night and that by giving the command he had subjugated it.

At the time Chökyi Lodrö established the Dragang retreat center, a stuffed statue of Shugden that had been kept near the retreat center for a long time and was thought to be very powerful and easy to displease was moved to the Gyalkhang at Gönchen Monastery. As soon as the statue was out of sight of its original home, it suddenly became extremely heavy. So Chökyi Lodrö went to where the statue had originally stood, recited mantras, then blew on some rice and scattered it over the scraps of offerings and water bowls that had been left behind. Angrily, he gave instructions for all the remaining offerings to be gathered and taken to the statue. That done, the statue gradually became lighter, until eventually it could be carried quite easily. That night, a violent uproar was heard throughout the monastery. It seemed to come from the Gyalkhang. But although cymbals crashed and dogs howled, no one was even slightly hurt. Chökyi Lodrö's part in this extraordinary incident astonished everyone, inspiring even greater confidence in him.

When the previous Khyentse conferred the great accomplishment empowerment of the *Great Assembly* from the *Nyingma Kama* at Lhundrup Teng, reliable sources reveal he experienced an unusual vision. The gyalpo Shugden was among the assembly and was waiting there to receive the empowerment and even accept the words of the sutras.

Although there was a statue of this gyalpo at Dzongsar Monastery and an earlier tradition of propitiating it, on no occasion—not even during elaborate empowerments of Kama and Terma teachings, the many drupchens that were performed, or the rituals of making offerings to gyalpo spirits—did either of the successive Khyentse incarnations intentionally offer it scarves or request it to perform any activities. Yet there were never any signs of the kind of obstacle this gyalpo usually creates. From this it is quite obvious that it had been subjugated and bound by oath by Lord Khyentse Wangpo and his incarnation.

In the year of the water horse (1942), when Khyentse Chökyi Lodrö was fifty years old, a widespread epidemic struck Kham, killing all the cattle. To liberate the beasts, Chökyi Lodrö performed a Buddha Amitabha puja, and in the vision the demon that had caused the epidemic offered him its life essence.[138] Chökyi Lodrö then wrote a brief burnt offering practice for the demon, which was circulated widely, and the spread of disease was checked wherever the practice had been distributed. This incident was well known to everyone.

Many people died during an epidemic in Terlhung and one of the corpses was possessed by a malevolent spirit. Lamas and monks performed various exorcism rituals to try to expel the spirit, but no one was able to get anywhere near the possessed corpse. Just as the corpse was about to stand up, Chökyi Lodrö was spotted some way off, and the villagers ran over to request his blessings. As a result, a stream of blood immediately began flowing from the mouth and nose of the corpse, and the corrupt spirit instantly faded away. Some of those present were said to have exclaimed in astonishment that Khyentse Tulku's compassionate blessing was as swift and powerful as a Chinese gun.

One of the ministers of the mischievous demon of Dragyab took the form of a ngagpa. It wore a black hat and cloak and was said to have sucked the life-force out of many eminent people in Dome. When Khyentse Chökyi Lodrö gave Yönru Lama the empowerment of Black Hayagriva from the Nyang tradition, he had a vision during the liberation empowerment of having liberated this ngagpa.

There were many similar instances of Chökyi Lodrö compassionately granting protection to dead people who were then possessed by powerful demons, and to the sick who were troubled by fierce and malicious spirits. Several people who had been abducted and held for days by nonhuman spirits were summoned back through the power of his protection prayers, and the fascinating stories they told when they returned inspired tremendous confidence in him.

Although there are many stories about how Khyentse Chökyi Lodrö intervened to call a halt to crops being spoilt by hailstorms, animals, and so on, I have not included them in this text because I don't want to overdo it.

Yudrön, the princess of Derge, repeatedly asked Khyentse Chökyi Lodrö to fill, consecrate, and bless the statues of the three long-life deities and twenty-one Taras that stood in the temple she had built at Nangchen. When he agreed, everyone saw both eyes of one of the Tara statues open spontaneously.

Muksang Tulku Kunzang of Derge in Kham went to central Tibet, intending to perform a mendrup drupchen at Gangri Tökar on the tenth day of the third month. He sent a message to Khyentse Chökyi Lodrö requesting his blessings for that day and received a letter granting his request. On the tenth day, the fragrance of amrita pervaded the whole area, from the cave of omniscient Longchenpa to Shugseb Labrang. Yet they discovered later that Muksang Tulku had been unable to perform the ritual that month. Everyone was amazed.

In the year of the water sheep (1955), when Khyentse Chökyi Lodrö was sixty-three years old, he visited central Tibet. On the second day of the seventh month, as he arrived at upper Rimda, he received a request to consecrate the recently completed temple and statues of Dungdo Monastery. He responded by promising to send his blessings on the fifteenth of that month. On that day, the Sangha assembled to perform the prayers for the spread of the teachings and make elaborate offerings. During the morning, as cloud-like offerings of everything necessary were made, including music, and so on, a rainbow appeared in the sky, and consecration flowers (mostly blue) in the form of multicolored rice rained down throughout the outer and inner parts of the temple. I've heard that many witnesses gathered these flowers and kept them as a support for their devotion. Personally and through others, I have investigated this story thoroughly, and when I asked the many local people who saw it happen, they all said the same thing. It was undoubtedly an amazing event, which is why I have included it in this text.

There are also many stories about consecration flowers thrown by Khyentse Chökyi Lodrö while he was at his seat in Dzongsar that were miraculously seen by people several days' journey away.

For a long time, I repeatedly entreated Khyentse Chökyi Lodrö to write his autobiography. Eventually he agreed, saying, "Although I have nothing meaningful to record in a biography, as you have made this request so earnestly, I will write something brief right now. Although nothing is ever certain, as you are younger than me, once I've passed away, you must be the one to write my namtar."

Some time after this, during the year he left for central Tibet,[139] after giving the empowerment of one of his own mind treasures, Khyentse Chökyi Lodrö sat in his residence holding many scrolls of his own writings.

"These are the record of my obscured visions," he said. And then he looked at me. At that moment, the vivid memory of what he had previously told me flashed into my mind,[140] but I didn't dare ask him for the papers, which I now deeply regret.

Quite a large section of this namtar—the part that describes his perfect, profound, hidden qualities, free from exaggeration or understatement—

appears in the *Extraordinary Biography* at the end of this text, but I will also mention a few of those qualities here.

Not long after Khyentse Chökyi Lodrö arrived at Dzongsar, while he was practicing the *Heart Essence of the Mahasiddha's Wisdom Mind*, he saw the mahasiddha Thangtong Gyalpo in a dream. He was an arm's length[141] high and sat in the residence of the previous Khyentse. Filled with tremendous devotion, Chökyi Lodrö bowed before the mahasiddha, who placed a crystal in front of himself and said,

> Unstained by object,
> Unpolluted by grasping mind,
> Maintain inherent raw mind:
> This is the wisdom mind of all the buddhas.

With these vajra words, the same as those with which Guru Rinpoche had introduced Lord Khyentse Wangpo, Thangtong Gyalpo introduced Khyentse Chökyi Lodrö to the nature of his mind. Chökyi Lodrö said that this visionary experience had ignited his meditation practice, and he later made a statue of Thangtong Gyalpo from medicinal substances and clay and placed it in his residence.

From Khyentse Chökyi Lodrö's autobiography:

> In the year of the water ox,[142] the terrible news of the passing of
> The protector who, just by thinking of him, dispels the pain of
>   samsara and nirvana,
> The great omniscient Katok Situ Rinpoche,
> Reached the ears of this unfortunate one;
> I said prayers and made offerings to fulfill his aspirations.
> Throughout the years following his parinirvana,
> I have met my lama in most of my dreams.
> Although you, Protector, have entered into the dharmadhatu,
> I am confident you continue to care for me with kind solicitude.
> Sadness and joy are my constant companions.

As stated in his autobiography, Khyentse Chökyi Lodrö continuously had visions of the inseparable form of Jamyang Khyentse Wangpo and Katok Situ Rinpoche and received from them predictions about all that was to come, the good and the bad. Chökyi Lodrö's expression always melted with devotion when he spoke of Katok Situ's activities, his special care, and the kindness he showed him.

Immediately after returning to Dzongsar from central Tibet, Chökyi Lodrö sent an offering scarf to Kyabje Shechen Gyaltsab Rinpoche, who replied,

> Mahapandita Katok Situ has passed away, and
> This old man is also approaching death;
> The oil in the lamp of the Nyingma teachings is all but spent,
> So you must summon your courage
> And engage in the activities that benefit the teachings.

Shortly after sending this, his parting advice, Shechen Gyaltsab Rinpoche dissolved his mind into inner space. Chökyi Lodrö traveled to Shechen to see the kudung and pay his respects. For three consecutive nights, all the way from Pawog until he entered the presence of the kudung, Gyaltsab Rinpoche appeared to him in his dreams, telling him over and over again to spread the teachings of the *Treasury of Encyclopedic Knowledge*. Chökyi Lodrö said he understood this to mean that he should actively spread the lineage of the two Jamgön lamas. Later, when the new shedra had been established at Shechen Monastery, he specifically instructed the lamas and tulkus to introduce teachings on this text into the curriculum, which I believe was his way of fulfilling Gyaltsab Rinpoche's wishes.

In the year of the wood rooster (1945), after all the empowerments and oral transmissions of the *Precious Treasury of Terma Teachings* had been completed, during the consecration of the textual empowerment[143] of the *Embodiment of the Guru's Realization*, I requested that Khyentse Chökyi Lodrö confer blessings[144] for the entire entrustment seal of all the ocean-like Kama and Terma teachings of which Manjushri Guru Jamyang Khyentse Wangpo and his incarnation Khyentse Chökyi Lodrö had been the sovereign holders. Khyentse Chökyi Lodrö responded joyfully by relating one of his dreams to me, his ignorant student, as a way of inspiring me.

> Last night, in my dreams, I saw the precious tulku, Shechen Gyaltsab, sitting on a hillside by the white rock that looks like the Great Heruka, to the right of Dzamnang Pema Shelphuk (the Lotus Crystal Cave). He bestowed upon me all the empow-

erments and oral transmissions of Terdzö, culminating in the empowerment for the *Combined Practice of Vishuddhi and Vajrakilaya* from the oral lineage teachings of Khyentse Wangpo.

At the age of fifteen, when Chökyi Lodrö returned to Katok after his first brief visit to Dzongsar Labrang, his teacher, Khenpo Kunpal, asked him what Khyentse Rinpoche's residence was like. He replied that there was a statue of omniscient Longchenpa on the bed where Khyentse Rinpoche had dissolved his emanation body into the dharmadhatu. Later, finding no such statue there, Chökyi Lodrö declared that he had told Khenpo Kunpal a big lie! What must have happened, though, is that at that time he had had a visionary experience of omniscient Longchenpa.

Not long after he first arrived at Katok Monastery, he dreamt that the glorious wisdom mother, Ekazati, was constantly watching over him. He told Katok Situ Rinpoche, who instructed him to recite the offering prayers to Ekazati from Longsal Nyingpo's cycle of teachings. He asked me once, "Have you received any treasure boxes or yellow scrolls? This morning, I thought I saw Ekazati in the empowerment hall of Dzongsar Tashi Chime Drupe Gatsel, arrayed in rainbows and clouds. She left something that looked like a treasure box in front of the image of Vajradhara Khyentse that spoke."

In the year of the fire rat (1936), when Kham was threatened by foreign forces, Khyentse Chökyi Lodrö said, "This morning at dawn, Tseringma appeared before me, her body floating on the wind like a cloud and riding a lion. This is why I am performing the thread-cross ritual for the tenmas from the treasure teaching of Nyang."

It must have been during Khyentse Chökyi Lodrö's Hevajra recitation retreat at the glorious Katok Monastery that he dreamt of the goddess Remati[145] in the form of a young girl. At first, she seemed unable to walk as her legs were chained, but eventually she placed her secret door over our Lord Guru's mouth, at which he experienced a feeling of disgust. She then passed urine through her secret door and, starting with his mouth, showered his entire body. Finally, she miraculously flew into the sky. He had this dream for five consecutive nights, after which he composed an offering prayer to the goddess.

During the year[146] of numerous gatherings at the sacred place of Dzamnang Pema Shelphuk, while performing a hundred thousand recitations of tsok at the Vairochana meditation cave near that holy site, Khyentse Chökyi Lodrö mentioned privately that the goddess Düsolma had attended him and performed various activities.

When he conferred empowerments and instructions from the *Nyingma Kama* on the sublime incarnation of Katok Situ Rinpoche and myself, he said there existed an empowerment lineage for the sutra protector, Wrathful Turquoise Lekden, based on Tsang Shöpa's manual for the authorization blessing of the tantric protector Lekden. So we asked him to grant us this empowerment, and he gave it as a supplementary initiation. During the "commanding the obstacle makers" part of the protectors' practice, he had a vision of a glorious wisdom protector standing directly in front of him, who looked exactly like the tantric protector Lekden. (This incident is listed in his notes, which I myself have seen.)

On the same day, Khyentse Chökyi Lodrö said, "To fulfill the instructions of the previous Khyentse, Palyul Gyatrul Rinpoche instituted a drupchö based on the sacred texts of the *Nyingma Kama* at Palyul Monastery and disseminated empowerments and oral transmissions in all directions. He also published the Kama teachings in their entirety, including the ancient texts. The auspicious circumstances created by the vast amount of activities he undertook for the propagation of the Kama teachings are why it is still possible for us to receive and practice these transmissions today."

In the year of the wood monkey (1944), during the waxing moon of the third month, Khyentse Chökyi Lodrö bound the gods and spirits by oath through the *Heart Practice for Dispelling All Obstacles*, which he performed on the roof of the main temple at Dzongsar Monastery. At first a violent storm blew up, but when the sky cleared, he had a vision of an evil spirit being subjugated and offering him its life essence.

In the record of the dreams, and so on, that Khyentse Chökyi Lodrö experienced in his forty-second year, a similar account is given:

> At the site of the ruined temple near Neten Monastery known as Khawateng that was built during the time of the Dharma King Songtsen Gampo, as I performed the ritual for subjugating negative forces and invoking blessings, I experienced the presence of infinite three roots deities and numerous local deities and guardians. As I visualized a burial pit during the suppression dance, I had a vision of a demon with an extremely large body falling

headlong into the pit. On the following morning, while subjugating the land before building a temple there, I saw numerous vidyadhara gurus, including Guru Rinpoche, dancing in the sky, and my experience blazed. It made me want to dance too. But how can anyone trust the flickering, ephemeral experiences of mind?

This was written on the sixth day.

In the year of the wood dog (1934), when Khyentse Chökyi Lodrö was forty-two:

> During the early morning of the ninth day, as I began to recover from a stomach ailment, it occurred to me to work out to which of the Anuttara deities from the Sarma tradition I was most strongly connected. The moment I had this thought, I fell into a light sleep and in a vision[147] saw Nyen Lotsawa, middle-aged, quite short, and wearing a long scarf. His hair was slightly longer than I expected, his face was light brown, and he wore a sleeveless Tibetan garment. In front of him stood the mandala of *Guhyasamaja Manjuvajra*. At first the mandala looked as though it had been drawn in colored sand, then it instantly transformed into an immeasurable palace, inside which sat Jampe Dorje, about a hand span high, saffron-colored, and blazing with light. I saw myself sitting on the south side of the mandala and felt a strong aspiration to receive the empowerment, so Guru Jampe Dorje recited the following verse:
>
>> Immaculate self-awareness is itself ultimate joy;
>> Free from both the duality of grasping and fixation, and conceptual thought,
>> Pristine and completely uncompounded
>> Is the Great Bliss of all the buddhas.
>
> Once these words had been uttered, a blue consort emanated from the mandala and embraced my body, which had become translucent, and as a result, I experienced the bliss of coemergent wisdom. Then a multicolored syllable DHIH, surrounded by spheres of light, emerged from the heart of Jampe Dorje and

dissolved into me. Finally, Jampe Dorje also dissolved into me and my mind was free of concepts, like space. In that state, I awoke from the dream.

When I fell asleep again, a dark blue Lord Manjuvajra in monks' robes appeared in standing posture. Putting his hand on my head, he said, "Since you have been connected with Guhyasamaja Manjuvajra and Vajrabhairava throughout your many lives, practicing them will bring you the supreme accomplishment of Mahamudra." Then I woke up.

At the Trimön residence, I performed the tsok offering of the *Embodiment of the Three Jewels* with Khyungtrul Rinpoche. Our conversation was extremely profound, and I received the treasure phurba of Chöje Lingpa. At dawn the following morning, I dreamt that Khyungtrul Rinpoche introduced me to some people, saying, "Those men in the row to the right were born into the family lineage of Tibet and were heroes during the time of King Gesar; the girl in the row to the left comes from an extremely noble blood line and was born into the celestial family lineage of Dharma Kings." As she was being introduced by name, the other girls prostrated to her three times. After that I heard a voice say, "Protector Gur, the ultimate protector of the teachings," and "Avalokiteshvara from the Mitra tradition, whose activities to benefit beings are so numerous that they pervade the whole of space." At that moment, I woke up and dawn broke.

During his first visit to Samye, an extremely brilliant rainbow circled above the central tower of the temple and a gentle rain fell. On the middle tier of the temple, Khyentse Chökyi Lodrö performed more than one hundred thousand tsok offerings from the *Heart Practice for Dispelling All Obstacles* and other elaborate offerings and, as directed by the Tibetan government, performed the consecration, and so on. That night everyone saw fire blazing from a stupa for about an hour.

What's more,

> at Hepori on the fifteenth day of the third month, I performed a smoke offering, a ritual for purifying hills, a consecration, and a subjugation of negative forces. At the beginning of the invocation, my devotion prompted me to see Guru Rinpoche, Dorje

Drolö, and other deities perform vajra dances—so many that they filled the sky. I myself also spontaneously danced, without any referential thoughts.

During the main part of this ritual, I became aware of the presence of myriad beings from the eight classes of gods and rakshas, nagas and local deities, all bowing down to me. Appearing in the form of a wrathful deity, I took their life essence, dissolving it into the lotus seat and my heart, so it became inseparable from my own life's essence. At the moment the wrathful torma was thrown out, I had a vision of the destruction of a city of samaya-violating savages. I also performed an elaborate invocation of blessings.

In short, on that day, my state of mind was pristinely clear. I enjoyed performing the ritual, my awareness was sharpened, and I felt I was able to bring just a little benefit to sentient beings and the teachings.

In the year of the fire monkey (1956), during the night I spent near Sankasya in India where Lord Buddha descended from Tushita heaven, I had a dream. An old man with a magnificent topknot was carrying many black snakes of different sizes, tadpoles, black creatures resembling the thorny bushes that grow at Tso Pema, and a knot of five-colored snakes all rolled up in black cloth. When the man unrolled the wrapping, I had a feeling the snakes were in my residence at Dzongsar. At that very moment, the snakes scattered in different directions and slithered away—an indication it was necessary to perform a suppression ritual based on the *Wrathful Vijaya*, which, because of various inauspicious circumstances, couldn't be done while I was still in Tibet. In my dream, I felt that the creatures belonged to the Red Army. Then I remembered that only part of the *Wrathful Vijaya* sadhana had been deciphered by Jamyang Khyentse Wangpo and had not been included in the Kama and Terma teachings. I also remembered that the text contained rituals for ransom offerings and averting negativity.

By the sixth of the month, good circumstances had gathered spontaneously, just as they had in my dream. During the folding of the paper on which a demon is drawn, a black acharya with a topknot of matted hair uttered something. He was smiling and holding a vessel, the back of which was covered with drawings of different creatures. He also carried a leopard-skin mat. Although his words were incomprehensible, his appearance was a good sign.

At Sankasya, motivated by the sincere wish to benefit the teachings and all beings, I wanted to perform the suppression based on Vajrakilaya. But just before I began, great claps of thunder struck and a deluge of rain poured down. That night we had a massive storm, and it seemed to me that the storm was a display of turbulence. As it raged, I had a brilliantly distinct vision of myself visualizing, with utmost confidence, Vajrakumara and his retinue, and as a result, the turbulence died down.

At Darjeeling in the year of the earth dog (1958), on the fourth day of the seventh month, as we had a limited number of texts, only thirteen of us performed (mainly for the welfare of the government) the thread-cross ritual based on Yakchar's Tara sadhana. As a result, on the ninth day, at around four in the afternoon, as the thread-cross was sent towards the northeast, there was a gentle shower of rain. When the sky cleared a little, on the horizon where a white mist embraced the sunset, a clearly defined, circular double rainbow appeared. We all saw it, along with numerous other rainbows, and were amazed. Anyway, everything went well.

During the early part of the tenth day, this verse appeared in my exceptionally clear and vivid mind:

> If a temple—the residence of the Lord buddhas of the three times—
> That's not too big, and not too small,
> Is built on the peak of the eastern mountain
> (The one that looks like a majestic elephant),
> The teachings of the Buddha will be of widespread benefit,
> And in particular the country of Tibet will know happiness.

Although Khyentse Chökyi Lodrö always maintained he was not clairvoyant, where the welfare of the teachings was concerned, he sometimes said things spontaneously, and the snippets of prophecy that emerged during otherwise quite ordinary conversations would always prove to be true. When recognizing tulkus, and so on, Khyentse Chökyi Lodrö knew precisely the distance to the tulku's birthplace, the names of the parents, whether the household was wealthy or poor, the geography of the area, and what signs would be found around the house, such as the color of the earth, the shape of rocks, whether there was a stream or a lake nearby, and what kind of trees grew there. For instance, in an initial prediction, he said that the tulku of Kyabje Shechen Gyaltsab had been born in the vicinity of the small white stupa of Dowam Cholay. Then again, on the eighteenth night of the eleventh month in the year of the earth snake (1929), he made another prediction that matched the earlier one:

> Between Dowam stupa and Karma Gön, to a father called Pema or Dorje and a mother called Tsega or Lhamo, a son has been born under the birth sign of either the horse or the sheep, bearing the names Düpa and Da, into a household that's most probably nomadic, with a white guard dog and a prayer flag above a house by a pond.

The tulku found by following this prophecy was a boy. He was the son of Dorje Rabten, a descendant of Lingdong Chölu Dharphen, and his mother was Metok Lhadze. They lived near the small white stupa of Dowam, in front of the dwelling place of the great Kugyal Tsengö, in the region of Samdrupling. Spontaneously, on the same auspicious day they found the tulku, the eight thousand lines of a newly engraved *Perfection of Wisdom Sutra in Eight Thousand Lines* were placed on a table in the monastery at Karma Gön, and a new copper cauldron was installed. As a result, people developed great confidence in the accuracy of Khyentse Chökyi Lodrö's predictions.

In a dream, Chökyi Lodrö saw the protector Gur in person, so huge that he filled the earth and sky, living in the village of Meshö Hagda. He told me that this was without doubt a sign that Leda Tulku had been born there.

In his letter recognizing the supreme emanation of Mahasiddha Shakya Shri, he specifically mentioned the names of the parents; the exact number of body, speech, and mind representations and thangkas in the shrine room of the family home; and that one of the pillars had warped.

Although there were numerous other wonderful examples, I cannot record them all in detail because I do not have the relevant letters of recognition. There were so many such examples, though, that in terms of learning and realization, it was widely believed that Khyentse Chökyi Lodrö was endowed with inconceivable qualities worthy of the praise of the wise and those who cherish Rime. So most ordinary beings can forget about trying to conceive of the full magnitude of his authentic qualities, because it's impossible for them even to imagine a fraction of them. At the same time, by taking a sip of ocean water we can get an idea of what the whole ocean tastes like, and so there is no reason not to describe just a few of the qualities that my devoted mind could perceive.

5. How Jamyang Khyentse Chökyi Lodrö performed excellent activities for the benefit of the teachings and beings.

Since those who have mastered the ocean of activities of a bodhisattva quite naturally bring limitless benefit to all beings every time they use their body, speech, and mind, the glory of all that is desired, and peace and happiness are spontaneously granted. This section describes how Khyentse Chökyi Lodrö specifically promoted the peace and happiness of beings by giving many teachings and therefore actively turned the wheel of the profound and vast Dharma, which is the main practice of great masters who are sublime holders of the teachings. From the sutras:

> O monks! Two types of beings generate enormous merit, eradicate the root of negative actions, wage war against the maras, tear the banner of the maras to pieces, hoist the victory banner of Dharma, and turn the wheel of the teachings of the Tathagata. They are those who *teach* the Dharma with devotion, and those who *listen* to the Dharma with devotion. Therefore, with devotion, you must both teach the Dharma and receive teachings from the masters.

In this degenerate age, inconceivable merit is gained by giving teachings without guile, with the pure motivation of ensuring the longevity of the teachings for the benefit of beings to be tamed. The way such merit is accumulated is explained in the *Lion's Roar of Shrimaladevi Sutra*:

> Giving alms by filling with gold as many worlds as there are grains of sand in the Ganges
> Cannot match the merit gained by teaching a single verse of Dharma in this Dark Age.

From the verses of prophecy from *Avalokiteshvara Resting in the Nature of Mind*, one of Lord Khyentse's profound treasure teachings:

> In the future, countless emanations of the body, speech, mind, quality, and activity
> Of the emanation Dharma King Trisong Deutson
> Will protect beings in the Land of Snows,
> And rekindle the embers of the teachings, again and again.

Therefore, there follows an account of how Khyentse Chökyi Lodrö continuously and extensively taught and spread the gift of Dharma, inspired by his intention to benefit the teachings and beings.

Even at the age of ten, Chökyi Lodrö had an innate mastery over the secret treasury of the wisdom of two kinds of knowledge. So much so that he was able to guide others as their revision teacher from the moment he began his own grammar and vocabulary studies. He participated in the rains retreat at the glorious monastery of Katok and taught the Sangha. More specifically, while presiding over the *Amitabha Practice to Liberate Beings into the Realm of Great Bliss* in the great assembly hall, he gave a detailed explanation of the *Aspiration to Be Reborn in the Pure Realm of Sukhavati*. All those gathered there, noble and ordinary, were astounded.

Not long after Khyentse Chökyi Lodrö took his seat at Dzongsar Monastery, he taught *The Way of the Bodhisattva*, the *Ascertainment of the Three Types of Vow*, the *Verse Summary of the Prajnaparamita Sutra*, the *Treatise on the Sublime Continuum*, the *Prayer of Excellent Conduct*, and so on, to about twenty lamas and monks from Dzongsar Monastery, led by Ngari Tulku.

When the All-Pervasive Lord, Loter Wangpo, and his main student bestowed the great empowerments for the *Compendium of Tantras* at Lasey hermitage, Khenchen Shenga Rinpoche was the revision teacher for the *Seven Points of Mind Training* and the explanation of *Two Sections of the Hevajra Root Tantra*, and Khyentse Chökyi Lodrö was the second revision teacher for the teachings on the *General Commentary on the Tantras* by Lopön Sonam Tsemo and the first half of the *Great Wish-Fulfilling Tree*. Whenever necessary, he also taught the auxiliary sciences of Tibetan grammar, vocabulary, poetry, and so on; it was necessary several times.

At the age of thirty-three, Chökyi Lodrö was invited by Yutok Khenchung Wangdü Norbu of Horchi to give the empowerments and instructions for the *Four Parts of Nyingtik* and the *Heart Essence of the Vast Expanse* to an extremely large gathering. At the end of every academic year at Khamje Shedra, he would grant teachings and extensive empowerments, giving them freely to each and every devoted student who requested them, irrespective of their status.

Later in life, Khyentse Chökyi Lodrö continuously turned the wheel of Dharma. He gave teachings in Lhasa and for the two monasteries of Dorje Drak and Mindrolling in central Tibet; Nawochok, Kharchu, and Lhalung monasteries in Lhodrak; Taklung Monastery in Yardok; Lingbu Monastery in Tsang; Pema Yangtse, the main Sakya monastery in the capital of Sikkim;

Darjeeling; and so on—but most often at the seat of Dzongsar itself. However, he asked neither his patrons nor those who requested the teachings to organize teaching events. On the contrary, he tirelessly granted the gift of vast and profound Dharma, whatever was requested, in ways that suited each individual's disposition. He taught everyone impartially and without prejudice, from sublime masters who were holders of teachings to the humblest layperson, and always according to the practice tradition of the previous Khyentse. I will now list some of the major teachings he gave.

Up until he took a consort, Khyentse Chökyi Lodrö ordained a great many shramaneras and bhikshus in the Vinaya precepts, which are the foundation of Buddha's teachings. Throughout his life, he presided over the bodhisattva vow of the two traditions numerous times, using various manuals from the Sarma and Nyingma traditions.

In terms of the main turning of the wheel of Dharma of the Vajrayana, Khyentse Chökyi Lodrö gave extremely detailed empowerments, instructions, and oral transmissions for the ten huge volumes of the *Treasury of Precious Instructions*, which contain all the teachings on maturation and liberation, along with the oral transmissions of the eight great chariots of the practice lineage and minor associated instructions. The distinguishing feature of the *Treasury of Precious Instructions*, which he gave twice, was that Jamyang Khyentse Wangpo received all the distant lineage transmissions, practiced them individually, and received short lineage blessings directly in pure visions. He also gave

- the empowerments and oral transmissions for the fourteen volumes of the *Compendium of Sadhanas*, compiled by Lord Khyentse Wangpo—four times;
- the detailed transmission of the *Precious Words: The Explanation of Path and Fruition for Private Disciples*, the heart essence of Mahasiddha Virupa—three times;
- *Path and Fruition: The Explanation for Assemblies*—twice;
- extremely detailed explanations of *Two Sections of the Hevajra Root Tantra*, based on a combination of writings by the founding Sakyapa masters and lineage holders—four times;
- the explanation of the *Gur Tantras* and *Samputa Tantra*, which Khyentse Wangpo received directly in a pure vision—three times;
- all the great empowerments for the seven mandalas of the Ngor tradition—four times;

- the great empowerments for the two kinds of *Guhyasamaja Tantra* and the *Dakini Free of Self*—a few times;
- Sarvavid-Vairochana and Akshobhya;
- the nine Amitayus deities and the two immaculate deities (Tsuktor Drime and Özer Drime)—a number of times;
- the great empowerments for the twelve mandalas of the *Tantra of Purification*—three times;
- the exposition of *Two Sections of the Hevajra Root Tantra* from Marpa's tradition—a few times;
- *Treatise on the Sublime Continuum*—twice;
- the explanations for the *Profound Inner Meaning* and the *Two Minor Shastras*—many times;
- the instructions on Mahamudra by Karma Chagme and Kongtrul Lodrö Taye—many times;
- the blessing transmission of the deity and consort of coemergent Chakrasamvara from Rechungpa's tradition of oral transmission and the oral transmission of profound instructions from the manuals by Khyentse Wangpo—a few times;
- the blessing transmissions and explanations for the teachings of Shangpa Kagyü—a few times;
- the empowerments and instructions for Thangtong Gyalpo's chö—many times;
- the torma empowerment and oral transmissions for the ritual texts of chö from the Kamtsang[148] tradition—a few times;
- the great empowerment of the glorious Kalachakra of the two chariots, Jonang, and Shalu—eight times; and the supreme empowerment of Kalachakra and explanations of the six-branch practice of vajrayoga—a few times;
- the explanation of the tantra of Kalachakra based on the great commentary by Jamgön Mipham Rinpoche, of which Lord Khyentse Wangpo and Kongtrul Lodrö Taye were the lineage masters—once;
- the oral transmission for the *Perfection of Wisdom Sutra in Eight Thousand Lines*, which Mahasiddha Thangtong Gyalpo received directly from Arhat Angiraja (Neten Yenlak Jung) in a pure vision—three times;
- the explanations of the *Verse Summary of the Prajnaparamita Sutra*, *The Way of the Bodhisattva*, and other texts that omniscient Khyentse Wangpo had received from Acharya Manjushrimitra in a pure vision—many times;

- the oral transmissions of the precious texts of the Kadampa tradition, the biography and songs of Marpa, the explanatory transmission of Gampopa's *Jewel Ornament of Liberation* and the *Precious Garland of the Supreme Path*, and the oral transmissions of the collected writings of the five founding masters of Sakya and Ngorchen Dorje Chang—once each;
- the *Ascertainment of the Three Types of Vow*—many times;
- the oral transmissions of the collected writings of Ngulchu Thogme, the *Great Treatise on the Stages of the Path to Enlightenment* by Je Tsongkhapa, and the *Mountain Dharma* by noble Chagme—as many times as he could;
- the root text of the *Ornament of Clear Realization* and its great commentary by Rongtön—once;
- the *Flower Garland of the Vinaya*—a few times;
- the great empowerments of Chakrasamvara from Luipa, Nagpopa, and Drilbupa's traditions—many times;
- the explanation of the root tantra of Chakrasamvara—once;
- the oral transmission of the *Teachings on the Practice of Vajrayogini*—twice;
- Vajrayogini of Indrabodhi and Maitripa, the blessings for the *Direct Exposition of the Dharmata*, and the *Compendium of Mantras*—many times; and
- the ordinary and extraordinary authorization blessing for the Three Red Deities—three times each.

In addition, he often gave the great empowerments of the deities from the higher and lower tantras, such as the eleven-faced Avalokiteshvara (Tukchen Chuchig Zhal); Amoghapasha (Dönyö Shagpa); Sitatapatra; Grahamatrika (Za Yum); the forty-seven Medicine Buddhas; *Manjushri: Holder of Secrets*; Rechungpa's *Solitary Hero Vajrabhairava* from the Gelug tradition; the thirteen-deity Chakrasamvara from the Drukpa Kagyü tradition; and so on, but I cannot list them all here in detail:

- the great empowerment of Vajrabhairava from the Ngor and Tsar traditions—many times; and the explanation and textual transmission—once;
- the empowerment for Red Yamantaka—a few times; and the textual transmission—once;

- the empowerment and explanation of Gur—four times; and the textual transmission—twice;
- the empowerment and explanation of the Zhal protector—twice; and the textual transmission—once;
- all the detailed empowerments of the *Nyingma Kama*—three times;
- the empowerments of the *Mandala of the Peaceful and Wrathful Deities of the Magical Net, Avalokiteshvara Who Stirs the Depths of Samsara*, the *Great Assembly*, and *Vishuddhi and Vajrakilaya* from the Khön tradition—more than three times;
- the oral transmissions of the ancient Kama texts of about ten volumes—four times;
- the *Guhyagarbha*, the root tantra of the cycle called the *Net of Magical Illusion*; the (anuyoga) tantra called the *General Essentialization of All the Wisdom of the Buddhas*; and the *Fragment of the Root Tantra of Vajrakilaya*—four or five times;
- the oral transmissions of twenty-six volumes of texts, including the *Great Path of Buddhaguhya*, the extensive commentary by Nyima Senge, and the catalog of the *One Hundred Thousand Precious Tantras of the Nyingma*—once;
- the empowerments, explanations, and oral transmissions of the *Precious Treasury of Terma Teachings*—once;
- the empowerments of *Teachings with Restriction Seals from the Treasury of Terma Teachings*—three times;
- the empowerments of the seventeen tantras—a few times; and the oral transmission—twice;
- the great empowerments of the *Mandala of the Eight Great Deities: The Assembly of Sugatas*, the treasure revealed by Nyang Nyima Özer—three times; and the medium and abbreviated empowerments and explanations—a few times;
- the textual transmission of the *Wrathful Guru* and *Avalokiteshvara and the Great Dakini*—once each;
- the empowerments, instructions, and textual transmission of *Krodhikali*—once or twice each;
- the empowerments and textual transmission of Guru Chöwang's *Gathering of the Guru's Secrets, Avalokiteshvara: The Gathering of the Innermost Essence*, and *Vajrakilaya*—a number of times;
- the empowerment, instruction, and textual transmission of the *Innermost Essence of the Inseparable Union of Buddha*—once;

- the empowerments and instructions of the *Heart Essence of Yutok*—five times;
- the textual transmission and oral transmission of the *Four Medical Tantras*—once;
- the *Four Parts of Nyingtik*—five times;
- the empowerments and instructions for the two *Innermost Essences* (Lama Yangtik and Khandro Yangtik)—many times;
- the oral transmission of the *Seven Treasuries* by Longchenpa—twice;
- the root text and commentary on the *Trilogy of Finding Comfort and Ease*, along with the instructions;
- the root text and commentary on the *Wish-Fulfilling Treasury* and the *Treasury of Dharmadhatu*—many times;
- the accomplishment empowerment of the *Embodiment of the Guru's Realization* in detail—twice; and the essential empowerment—many times;
- the empowerment and oral transmission for the *Northern Treasures*—once;
- the detailed empowerments, instructions, and oral transmissions of the *Tantra That Directly Reveals Samantabhadra's Mind* and *Self-Existing, Self-Manifest Primordial Purity* from the *Northern Treasures*; *Wrathful Blue Vajrapani* from the *Tukdrup* teachings; Avalokiteshvara, *Razor-Edged Vajrakilaya* (*Phurpa Pudri*), and *Yamantaka: Lord of Life* from the lineages of Guru Padmasambhava and Nubchen Sangye Yeshe merged into one and revealed by Dumgya Shangtrom, and the empowerment texts—many times;
- *Pearl Garland of Yamantaka, Lord of Life* from the Nub tradition—once;
- the elaborate and abbreviated empowerments of the *Long-Life Practice of the Gathering of Secrets* and Vajrakilaya, Ratna Lingpa's treasure teachings—three or four times;
- the empowerments and instructions for Mahasiddha Thangtong Gyalpo's *Secret Conduct: The Oral Lineage of the Dakinis*—four times;
- the empowerment for Ngari Panchen's *Complete Gathering of Vidyadharas*—three times; and the textual transmission—once;
- the empowerments and oral transmissions of Dorje Lingpa's *Vast Expanse of the View*—once;
- the empowerments and instructions for the *Tantra of the*

Blazing Expanse of Luminosity and the *Heart Essence of the Hung Cycles*—twice;
- the elaborate and abbreviated empowerments of the *Mandala of Peaceful and Wrathful Deities* and the explanations of the six bardos from Karma Lingpa's treasure teachings—a few times;
- all the empowerments and oral transmissions of Jatsön Nyingpo's six volumes of treasure teachings—once;
- the empowerments, instructions, and textual transmission of the *Embodiment of the Three Jewels*—many times;
- the empowerments, instructions, and oral transmissions of Lhatsün Namkha Jigme's *Accomplishing the Life-Force of the Vidyadharas*, and the empowerments of *Vajra Essence*—many times;
- detailed empowerments and oral transmissions of *Twenty-Five Teachings with Restriction Seals* that the great Fifth Dalai Lama received in pure visions—four times;
- the complete cycle of Minling Terchen Rinpoche's treasure teachings—four times;
- the empowerments and instructions for the *Assembly of All the Sugatas*, particularly Vajrasattva—many times;
- the empowerments and oral transmissions of the sadhanas called the *Wish-Fulfilling Excellent Vase*—three times;
- the oral transmissions of the collected works of Minling Terchen and the scholar-siddha Tsele Pema Lekdrup—once each;
- the empowerments and oral transmissions of Terchen Dudul Dorje and Longsal Nyingpo's Dharma cycles—twice;
- the empowerments of Dudul's Vajrakilaya and Longsal's *Wrathful Guru*—many times;
- the explanations of *Wrathful Guru* and the cycle of the *Vajra Essence* teachings along with teachings on the supplementary texts—a number of times;
- the empowerments, instructions, and oral transmissions of the two root volumes of the *Heart Essence of the Vast Expanse*—many times; and *The Words of My Perfect Teacher*—also many times;
- the explanation of the commentary by Jigme Lingpa himself for his *Treasury of Precious Qualities* together with the commentary by Geshe Tendar of Mongolia—three times;
- the great empowerment of *Vajrakilaya: The Tradition of the King*—four times; and the textual transmission—twice;

- the empowerments, instructions, and oral transmissions of all the treasure teachings of omniscient Khyentse Wangpo and the oral transmission of his collected writings—twice;
- the rediscovered treasure *Avalokiteshvara: Ocean of Victorious Ones*, the *Ocean of Dharma That Combines All Teachings*, the *Gathering of the Dakini's Secrets*, the *Heart Essence of the Mahasiddha's Wisdom Mind*, the cycle of oral lineage teachings, the *Luminous Heart Essence of the Three Roots*, and others—many times;
- the empowerments and oral transmissions of all the treasure teachings of Terchen Chokling—three times; and
- the root verses and commentaries on the *Three Precepts* and the root verses and commentaries on the *Gradual Path Called the "Essence of Wisdom"*—many times.

The numbers of teachings and transmissions mentioned in this biography don't exactly tally with those mentioned in the autobiography, because I have counted only those teachings Khyentse Chökyi Lodrö gave in the latter part of his life, *after* he wrote his autobiography.

He also gave, as often as possible,

- Do Khyentse Yeshe Dorje's *Cutting Through: Self-Liberation from Fixation*;
- the mind treasures of Drodül Pawo Dorje, Adzom Drukpa;
- the empowerment of Mipham Jampal Gyepe Dorje's *Gyüluk Manjushri*;
- Lingtsang Gyalse's *Chandali, Long-Life Consort*; and
- Vajrakilaya from the Dharma cycle of Lerab Lingpa.

He also gave, a number of times,

- the great cause and path empowerments of the glorious Hevajra;
- the blessing transmission of *Naropa's Vajrayogini*;
- the instructions for *Naropa's Vajrayogini* from the Ngor and Tsar traditions;
- teachings on mind training (Lojong);
- the authorization blessing for Avalokiteshvara;
- instructions for the preliminary and main practices of the *Heart Essence of the Vast Expanse*;
- empowerments and instructions for the two kinds of *Heart Practice* and the *Heart Essence of Chetsün*, many times;

- authorization blessings for Hayagriva and White Tara from the Kyergang tradition and explanations of the long-life practices;
- *Vajrakilaya: The Oral Transmission Lineage*;
- the *Heart Essence of Deathless Arya Tara* and the *Combined Practice of the Three Roots*;
- the *Embodiment of the Three Roots*;
- *Vajrapani: Flame of Fire*;
- *Hayagriva: The Fiery Wheel of the Thunderbolt*;
- *Five Antidote Deities*;
- *Seven Deities* from the Shije tradition;
- *Avalokiteshvara Who Stirs the Depths of Samsara*;
- the Amitabha sadhana from the treasure teachings of Chokling;
- the three roots deities, the *Innermost Secret Guru Yoga Called the "Sealed Quintessence,"* and the authorization blessings for Hayagriva and Vajrapani from the *Heart Essence of the Vast Expanse*; and
- the elaborate and abbreviated long-life empowerments of Thangtong Gyalpo.

These are some of the teachings Khyentse Chökyi Lodrö gave to fulfill the wishes of the endless stream of people who came to him with requests. And although he could not give the transmissions of the entire *Compendium of Tantras* in one go, little by little he was able to give all the great empowerments of the higher and lower[149] tantras, except the *Kangyur*. It was as if there was no teaching Chökyi Lodrö received that he didn't then teach at least once.

His entire life was dedicated to listening to and teaching the Dharma, except when he was in strict retreat or traveling, and it was quite normal for him to give at least one empowerment or authorization blessing every day. Absolutely anyone could receive general Dharma teachings from him, such as the bodhisattva vow according to the Madhyamika tradition, an ordinary empowerment or authorization blessing for Avalokiteshvara, oral transmissions of the transference of consciousness, minor empowerments and authorization blessings for removing obstacles, long-life empowerments, and so on. But he never gave restricted teachings indiscriminately to the general public.

He taught laypeople how to practice virtuous activities by visualizing Avalokiteshvara and reciting the six-syllable mantra; applying the three noble principles (the root of the Mahayana path); and accumulating merit and purifying defilements.

He taught approach and accomplishment yidam practices individually to those bhikshus and shramaneras who had an interest in the profound teachings, giving each what they requested according to their discipline and tradition, but always tailored to their specific mental dispositions and enthusiasms.

To noble, learnèd, and disciplined people with honorable intentions who received, contemplated, upheld, propagated, and nurtured limitless teachings in the spirit of Rime, and who saw all the lineages of Buddhadharma purely and without bias, Khyentse Chökyi Lodrö gave vast and profound teachings freely and with great delight.

To those who focused on study, contemplation, and meditation and had already gained complete confidence in the teachings of all lineages, he explained each school's specific philosophical tenets and teachings on the ultimate establishment of the view. He also told the life stories of the lineage masters of each school and pointed out the extraordinary aspects of individual teaching lineages. He even explained in the minutest detail how to perform ceremonies and practices, including different chanting traditions and arrangements of music. He passed on his thorough knowledge of all these aspects of the teachings purely and authentically, and in this way completely fulfilled the wishes of practitioners, increasing their faith and confidence both in the teachings of the lineages they followed and in Khyentse Chökyi Lodrö himself.

He did not approve of those who tried to convert people from one tradition to another using deceit or personal charisma. Neither did he approve of those who deserted their own tradition or abandoned one teaching for another on the pretext of being open-minded but who were actually just fickle and careless. He particularly disapproved of those who held sectarian convictions, disturbed the minds of others, and encouraged divisiveness by finding fault with other traditions and their followers, and of those who privately wrote censorious letters that were circulated publicly and asked provocative questions.

In Chökyi Lodrö's own words, "These days, of all the five degenerations of the Kaliyuga, the degeneration of the view has become the most powerful. In fact, most Tibetans now seem to hold their *very own* 'view'!"

Quite apart from those who have stepped through the door of the teachings onto the path, even ordinary laypeople now hold a "view" and are more than eager to express their opinions about the authenticity or superficiality of various teaching traditions. But these empty mouthings are in no way comparable to the kind of authentic debate that those who hold Rime attitudes engage in to establish pure view and philosophical truth. Since the minds of such blatherers are possessed by demons, it is these people who cause the kind of factional disputes and divisive conflict among the schools that will eventually lead to the swift destruction of the teachings and the peace and happiness of all beings.

The authentic teachings are like the purest and most refined gold. They were established by the great founders who attained all the sublime bhumis and successive learnèd and accomplished lineage holders who examined the teachings using three kinds of valid cognition, actualized signs of having accomplished the path, and attained supreme realization through practice and meditation. To try to examine these pure teachings using just an ordinary, discursive mind can only result in the accomplishment of utter ruin! Therefore, it is best to put all your energy into establishing an absolute certainty in the view and in the philosophical tenets of the tradition you have entered, and to consider that your practice is the quintessence of all teachings.

At the same time, it is crucial that you abandon all negative, sectarian attitudes about other schools and, by perceiving them purely, train yourself to appreciate them. Not only that, if you can perceive the commentaries to the sutras and tantras purely, a close reading will show you that when understood in context, each teaching method and interpretation has its own unique characteristics.

Since all the teachings have the same ultimate meaning, the study of various commentaries will serve to clarify any doubts you might have about the particular view in which you have most confidence. The commentaries also provide the logic to prove that aspects of each teaching are unique. On top of which, they help improve our learning and contemplative skills, because understanding the reasoning that underpins a teaching naturally inspires devotion for all teachings. Therefore, to examine the teachings in this way is immensely important.

We live in degenerate times, and so to emphasize specific facets of a view—perhaps clarity or emptiness—or to highlight unimportant variations between lineages cannot possibly contribute to the kind of debate described in the teachings that is also an ornament to the Dharma. Chökyi Lodrö always emphasized the benefits of encouraging harmony between traditions.

I heard from Khyentse Chökyi Lodrö himself that in the verses of prophecy in the *Heart Practice That Fulfills All Wishes* revealed by Terchen Chokling, it says that when, at the end of this aeon, discord among teaching traditions is rife, an emanation of the Sovereign Lord, King Trisong Deutsen, will appear and bring harmony, thus benefiting both the teachings and beings. Chökyi Lodrö did just that, exactly as the prophecy predicted, and repeatedly advised the sublime holders and patrons of the teachings to do the same.

A flawed custom has grown up over the years that tolerates the performance of rituals by lamas who have little—or at best, partial—knowledge about how to do them. It was a custom that Khyentse Chökyi Lodrö never followed. When it came to the sequence of rituals and the traditional methods for bestowing empowerments of all schools and traditions, however difficult or easy they might be, he only ever followed specific instructions from the higher and lower tantras and the traditions of individual lineage masters. For most of the empowerments and drupchen rituals he performed, and even for authorization blessings and torma empowerments, he followed the traditional methods taught by the two Jamgön lords (Jamyang Khyentse Wangpo and Jamgön Kongtrul Lodrö Taye). Even later in life, in the fullness of his maturity when he had many students, he never lazily skipped sections in the practice, nor was he satisfied by merely going through the motions of a ritual.

In terms of the instructions he gave from the Sakyapa teachings, such as the *Path and Fruition: The Explanation for Assemblies and Private Disciples*, and so on, he would read each text three or four times in one session. He also said repeatedly how important it is to read the profound instructions contained in the *Treasury of Precious Instructions* (except those of the Nyingma tradition) combined with the *One Hundred Profound Commentaries* three times in one session, because this was the approach established by the two Jamgöns. He said that many gurus from various lineages had strongly emphasized the necessity of following this tradition.

The sacred texts state that to maintain the continuity of the explanatory oral transmissions for all the instructions of Sarma and Nyingma, it is enough to read the words at a speed that is comprehensible. Chökyi Lodrö himself followed this advice.

He always bestowed the gift of Dharma on those who requested it, but never taught just anyone without first checking whether or not they were genuinely interested and able to understand the essential points of the teachings, and so on. He did not treat the teachings carelessly, like scraps of leftover food to be scavenged by passing birds and dogs.

When he gave lineage holders and devoted students profound instructions as their heart practice, he commanded them to keep the relative commitments very strictly. As a result, his students developed confidence in the profound meaning of these unique teachings because they recognized how precious and rare they were.

However full his daily schedule, when a worthy student required a specific empowerment and instruction, Chökyi Lodrö would ignore all difficulties and teach throughout the night—even when holders of that particular Dharma lineage still existed (they were often extremely ignorant and rarely understood the teachings), and the lineage was in no danger of dying out.

No matter what you do, whether you teach, study, or practice meditation, the purity of your path depends entirely on your motivation. Therefore, every time he taught, whether elaborately or simply, Chökyi Lodrö always emphasized the methods for transforming motivation and expressly drew their vital importance to the attention of students he was preparing for the introduction to their true nature.

For all the teachings, empowerments, and so on, that he gave, although custom dictated that his students could not question the authenticity of his sources or even ask why they should receive a teaching, Chökyi Lodrö would explain everything in great detail, giving them all the information they could possibly want. This was how he fulfilled the wishes of his students, bringing benefit to the continuity of the teachings and arousing inspiration and great wonder in the minds of the wise.

When it was important to take into consideration the auspicious circumstances of a situation or to fulfill a specific purpose, Chökyi Lodrö would give his students books and inspire them by saying,

> I have received these teachings many times from many teachers, but not because I didn't believe what any one teacher had told me. All my teachers were endowed with excellent noble qualities. Those to whom the two Jamgöns gave special teachings about their personal practice and who elected to make those teachings their main practice were particularly fortunate, as they were recipients of a wonderful blessing lineage. Bearing this in mind, I received the teachings many times over. This was how I gathered most of the extraordinary transmissions.
>
> I have taught the profound instructions from this special lineage exhaustively, without omitting or adding anything, and

have remained faithful to the sacred texts and practice traditions of each lineage. My pure intention is to fulfill the enlightened wishes of the noble gurus and fortify the continuity of the teachings. Once you have received these teachings, whether they help you or not will depend entirely on how you put them into practice. Nevertheless, unlike the king who commands his subjects, I will not command you to keep any practice commitments.

As a rule, Chökyi Lodrö did not bind his students with practice obligations that would be hard for them to maintain. In an age when less and less importance is placed on the Dharma (an early sign of the degeneration of the teachings), he said that just to be able to teach and propagate Dharma with pure intention and without negative, selfish thoughts is excellent.

When he taught tantras and philosophical texts, he was at no time verbose. His explanations were neither overly complicated, intellectual extravaganzas that were empty of the key points of profound meaning, nor a miscellany of every scrap of information he knew, like a hunter clawing at both meat and fur. Instead, he would essentialize the profound teachings given in intricate commentaries and clearly explain in minute detail the most essential texts. This was how he directly and comprehensively taught the meaning of any text, sutra, or tantra in a way that would truly benefit the minds of his students, regardless of how intelligent they were.

When he clarified the meaning of a teaching, he only ever relied on the sacred texts and authentic explanation lineages from the Sarma and Nyingma traditions. He never engaged in or even alluded to either the establishment or refutation of different interpretations of the Buddha's teachings, and would not comment on whether or not those interpretations agreed with each other. Neither would he comment on their logic.

To virtuous beings with supreme intelligence, Chökyi Lodrö gave wonderfully detailed elucidations that radiated from the most profound meaning of the teachings. Even the simple rituals of commanding the spirits and giving blessings in order to drive away obstacles and negative forces or summon life-force, he performed meticulously, following authentic methods, complete with all the preliminary, main, and concluding rituals. He never did anything carelessly on the pretext that he could do as he liked because he was so highly realized. At the same time, he performed rituals in a relaxed way that inspired others. As he understood the essential points of Dharma and auspicious circumstance, his mind always remained free and open, unlike the ignorant and narrow-minded, whose minds are filled with foolish chatter and chained by their clinging to the idea that phenomena and its characteristics are truly existent.

No matter which ordinary or extraordinary, vast, and profound secret teaching he gave, he never had to prepare by reading the text. He knew all the teachings thoroughly, whether he had studied them or not. One of his most wonderful qualities was that however difficult a thorny point in the sutra or tantra texts might be, however complex an empowerment ritual or instruction, however mystifying the insertion of practices into rituals or the order of practice, his wisdom and intelligence would always increase to resolve the problem.

All these attributes were discernible signs that Manjuvajra, the All-Pervasive Lord of the Ocean of Mandalas, had manifested as the vajradhara who maintains the three vows, and were proof that our Lord Guru was a great pioneer of all the teachings of the Buddha, that he lived up to all his names, and that he even surpassed the qualities of the other sublime holders of the teachings.

These are a few illustrations of Khyentse Chökyi Lodrö's infinite good qualities.

Basically, were we to compare the enlightened activities of Khyentse Chökyi Lodrö with those of the previous incarnation of Manjushri, Khyentse Wangpo, we would not find the slightest discrepancy. However, as he had not one jot of pride either in being the tulku of Khyentse Wangpo or his own qualities, Chökyi Lodrö always took the lowest seat and endeavored to abandon pride completely. He also advised his students not to imagine that he actually was Khyentse Wangpo or that Khyentse Wangpo had been anything like him. Were they to do so, he said, there could be no greater wrong view. Jamyang Khyentse Wangpo, he said, had been the manifestation of Lord Buddha himself for this degenerate age and could never have been "an old man like me, a great jumble of faults, who misuses offerings and lacks even the least good quality."

When Chökyi Lodrö first arrived at Dzongsar, Kyabje Katok Situ Rinpoche put a thick cushion next to the previous Khyentse's seat, saying, "It would be good for you to sit here for the time being. If you were to sit on Khyentse Rinpoche's seat too early, it would be like a dog sleeping on the bed of a human being."

Chökyi Lodrö said that being young and arrogant, to him these words sounded like a scolding, and he didn't like it much. Later, once he understood the rationale behind what had been said, he developed a deep, unfailing confidence in Katok Situ Rinpoche's advice—a confidence that was reinforced continuously. He never thought of himself as Jamyang Khyentse Wangpo and told me that instead, he visualized Lord Khyentse Wangpo on the crown of his head and at the center of his heart, and continually and diligently prayed that the blessings of Khyentse Wangpo's three secrets would enter his mind so he could emulate his actions and behavior and fulfill all his wishes.

Even on a more ordinary level, Chökyi Lodrö's mind never wavered from meditating on the generation of renunciation for samsara. When he responded to requests for help, he usually added the caveat, "I can do as you ask if, in the meantime, the Lord of Death does not cut my life short." Throughout all his undertakings, he never once forgot about the inevitability of death. He never acted thoughtlessly as he worked to ensure the continuity of the study and practice of the teachings and the welfare of beings, and was always scrupulously mindful of cause and effect.

He personally saved prisoners condemned to death and every year saved the lives of many animals that would otherwise have fallen prey to butchers. He widely distributed blessed pills and protection cords to communities of nomads, and constantly inspired them to free tens of thousands of animals destined for slaughter. All animals offered to him were immediately freed and never sold or bartered. And although he initiated innumerable projects to build representations of body, speech, and mind, he never permitted animals to be butchered or accepted meat as a contribution towards those projects. His advice was always,

> The distinguishing characteristics of Buddhist practitioners are that we persist in undertaking positive activities and abandon those that are negative. Therefore, to pretend to practice virtue by personally or indirectly harming other beings will bring no benefit whatsoever. In fact, as all beings, irrespective of their status or stature, value nothing more highly than their own lives, it is very important to avoid taking the lives of others. A practitioner may be presumed to be very highly realized and might try to accumulate vast amounts of superficial merit, but if he mishandles the laws of karma, the only causes he will create are those

that result in rebirth in the lower realms. Such a person's actions will rarely be purely meritorious. Therefore, be extremely careful about what you do.

If Khyentse Chökyi Lodrö ever heard about someone being liberated through wrathful means, he would became very annoyed. He never indulged in reckless or irresponsible behavior, like drinking alcohol, singing, dancing, and so on, and his mind always remained stable, never for an instant wavering from the state of mindfulness and awareness.

Fearing the consequences of misusing offerings given out of devotion or for the dead, he would list the names of dead people for whom offerings had been made and perform purification rituals three times for each name. He also followed Jamyang Khyentse Wangpo's tradition of burning the list of names[150] at the end of each year, and would say prayers of dedication and aspiration at the end of Dzongsar Monastery's annual month-long Kunrik Drupchö (the intensive practice of Vairochana Buddha). There was a tradition, he said, of making tsa tsa from the ashes of the burnt lists. He also made offerings to the lamas who came from all over Tibet to visit him, and requested that they too say prayers for the dead and perform the liberation ritual.

He never forgot to perform weekly liberation rituals, and made burnt offerings again and again, saying, "Making burnt offerings with compassion brings immense benefit to all beings, irrespective of whether or not the person making the offering has attained confidence in creation and completion meditation, or how elaborate or simple the offerings and ritual might be." Thus, Khyentse Chökyi Lodrö often protected people who had died from the obstacles caused by malevolent, harmful spirits that might prevent them from taking a higher rebirth.

As he delighted in making offerings and giving charity, he constantly gave gifts of Dharma, material objects, medicine, and so on, to the terminally ill, needy old brothers from faraway places, the poor, the destitute, and those who were infirm. He continuously made elaborate tsok offerings on the auspicious days of the waxing and waning moon,[151] and on the special days associated with the Lord Buddha, and so on; and he always kept a huge amount of the substances required for ransom rituals to remove obstacles.

During empowerments, drupchens, and so on, he instructed his monks to make tormas and other offerings elaborately and carefully, and always stressed the importance of keeping the practice room clean and tidy. He maintained absolute cleanliness when filling statues and stupas with consecration mantras and substances and while preparing sacred substances (for example, amrita), cleansing water, vase water, and so on. Every morning, he washed and then dressed correctly in his robes.[152]

When he went on pilgrimage or to see representations of the Buddha's body, speech, and mind, he persevered one-pointedly in offering prostrations and circumambulating holy relics and sites, and never gave in to weariness or fatigue. In this he was very like the early Kadampa masters, whose practice tradition he admired enormously.

Khyentse Chökyi Lodrö did not make himself new or valuable secular material objects embellished with gold and silver, preferring to use the things he found in his residence. Likewise, he never owned new, modern machines or appliances from Tibet or India. At all times, he maintained the discipline of an ordinary hermit, just like the previous Lord, Khyentse Wangpo, and was inconspicuous and simple in all his activities—for example, in the way he dressed, the way he gave protection cords and amrita pills with his own hands, the food he ate, and the utensils he used.

He disliked the kind of exaggeration described in the story of the rabbit who frightened the rest of the animals in the forest by saying, "The sky is falling!" when a fruit had simply dropped into the lake with a loud splash. He also took exception to meaningless, threatening, or boastful behavior.

The radiance of his merit and the power of his inner meditation blazed, and not one of the great and powerful people who met him did so without feeling an overwhelming humility and devotion. His extraordinary character, his majesty, and the splendor of his great qualities had such a strong impact on the people around him that their devotion increased the closer and more intimate they became with him.

When he performed a ceremony for the welfare of the country or benefactors of the Dharma, it was usually either to pacify or to enrich. Whatever he did, it was always with the positive intention of benefiting others without attachment to self-interest. His activities to benefit the teachings and beings were extremely effective, and he made countless generous offerings and gifts. Yet he never exhibited pride in or attachment to his achievements or congratulated himself on having accomplished specific virtuous activities.

When asked for help with worldly and personal problems, he always gave straightforward, practical instructions and good long-term advice that was entirely in tune with the Dharma traditions of virtue and proper discipline, and that helped people in their daily lives. His advice, whether essential or elaborate, was always appropriate, suited each person's situation in life, and was based on his own experience.

Khyentse Chökyi Lodrö did not make prophecies as such, but depending on how much you trusted him, his advice often demonstrated incontrovertibly that he could see into the future.

Since it was hard for him to hear the least hint of something that might cause dissension among followers of the Buddha or damage, even destroy, the teachings (the kind of talk indulged in by those who are attached to their own unbending point of view and who have an antipathy to the opinions of others), no one dared to mention such things in front of him.

Whenever necessary, Khyentse Chökyi Lodrö exposed and corrected the faults and misbehavior of even great and powerful people, and set them on the right path.

To young beginners who came to him for instruction, he said, "At this stage, as you are young, it's likely you'll be distracted by desirable things. But if you do the preliminary practices of training the mind, study the texts analyzing cause and effect, and contemplate their meaning over and over again, you will be able to pacify and tame your mind." Beginners were very inspired by him, and he was always very relaxed with them. He would tell jokes lightheartedly as they talked together and was never abusive or contemptuous. So from examining how Khyentse Chökyi Lodrö related to others personally and indirectly,[153] we can clearly see that he had mastered renunciation and wondrous bodhichitta.

Khyentse Chökyi Lodrö had a genuinely great and compassionate mind, and so even people from foreign lands who spoke unfamiliar languages, irrespective of their beliefs or the teaching lineage they followed, developed a genuine devotion and respect for him that was even greater than the devotion they felt for their own lineage holders.

Therefore, as it is quite natural for sublime beings to be endowed with twelve qualities, Khyentse Chökyi Lodrö received in full the limitless stream of teachings based on countless sacred texts and instructions from the Sarma traditions and the Kama and Terma of the Nyingma. Throughout his entire life, he garnered profound and vast teachings without ever feeling he had collected enough. All teachings converged into him; he was like an ocean into which all the rivers of Dharma flowed.

Khyentse Chökyi Lodrö's contemplative mind was like the hold of a great merchant ship filled with the treasure of the ultimate understanding of the definitive view. He could therefore differentiate between the philosophical views of each school, and a wealth of the ultimate profound meaning arose spontaneously in his mind. Proof of this became evident when he questioned omniscient lama Jigme Tenpe Nyima, the Third Dodrupchen Rinpoche, about the teachings on ground, path, and fruition of Dzogpachenpo. Jigme Tenpe Nyima commended him for his matchless knowledge and specifically instructed him to hear and contemplate the teachings on ground, path, and fruition from the *Seven Treasuries* and the *Treasury of Precious Qualities*.

Khyentse Chökyi would always take each teaching he received beyond the level of mere words by practicing it one-pointedly, which was why all the excellent qualities of the paths and bhumis and the wish-fulfilling treasure of the two siddhis burst forth from him spontaneously.

His mind was naturally very sharp, and became incomparably sharp through training. His fame did not lie in his mastery of just one field of study, but in his command of all areas of learning, from the general sciences, Vinaya, Abhidharma, Madhyamika, Prajnaparamita, and the sacred texts of the secret tantras of Vajrayana, to the finest points of grammar. He told me that when he began to study philosophy, his understanding of the texts was less than profound because he found it hard to grasp their meaning. However, after he studied the *Treasury of Precious Qualities*, the door of his intelligence flew open. From then on, he said, he had no difficulty understanding any of the texts he studied. Which proves that the *Treasury of Precious Qualities* is a text imbued with great blessings.

One of Khyentse Chökyi Lodrö's innate virtues was that he never went beyond the prescribed limits of the rules of the *Three Precepts*, so his actions and behavior were completely pure and untainted. He was a most beautiful ornament to adorn the precious teachings of the Buddha.

His activities for the benefit of beings were unceasing and therefore extremely vast in number. All his enterprises began spontaneously; he never made any plans, prepared in any way, or made the decision to start with this, then in the middle do something else, and finally do that. This was how he was able, spontaneously and without obstacle, to accomplish effortlessly projects that were beyond the comprehension of even the great and the learnèd. And in the process, he always promoted the welfare of the teachings and beings.

Khyentse Chökyi Lodrö never had to prepare for a teaching, nor did he have to deliberate as he taught, yet he never mixed up the specific terminologies used by the different traditions and philosophies. He always knew how each tradition's philosophy was established and taught it without repetition or omission; and while his teachings were always profound, they could still easily be understood, and he explained the essential meanings very clearly.

In his autobiography, Khyentse Chökyi Lodrö wrote, "If I had studied elementary logical reasoning, I think I would have gained reasonable debating skills—not that such skills help much."

Khyentse Chökyi Lodrö really enjoyed logic and held the *Collected Topics of Logic* and other teachings on logic in high regard—it was as if he had an innate feeling for the subject, perhaps from his knowledge of it in previous lives. Whenever he met intelligent people, he would engage them in debate about the branch of philosophy with which they were most familiar and test their understanding by refuting their theses. However, when his opponent tried to test and refute his own thesis using logic and authentic quotations, Chökyi Lodrö's arguments would become even more profound. His power of reasoning was swift, sharp, and flawless. Sometimes he surprised everyone by unexpectedly quoting from sacred texts and commentaries in a continuous stream. The better his opponent was at coming up with authentic quotations and logical arguments, the better pleased he would be, and as he continued to debate, he would simultaneously commend his opponent's scholarly skills.

Now I'll turn to Khyentse Chökyi Lodrö's writing skills. When he was young he found writing difficult, but after reading the works of Kyabje Gyaltsab Rinpoche, the door of knowledge opened, and his writing ability was transformed. He showed some of his writings to omniscient Katok Situ Rinpoche and explained how his skills had been improved. Katok Situ responded by saying, "This is without doubt what is called the 'blessing of the Guru entering the mind of the student.'"

He wrote clearly, yet the meaning behind his words was vast. His turn of phrase did not obscure the meaning, nor was he verbose. He wrote neither too much nor too little, and each text was well structured. Usually he wrote so that his words could be easily understood, and his collections of praises, and so on, were beautifully adorned with glorious metaphorical expressions drawn from the poetry of Dandin. Scholars repeatedly admired and praised his spontaneous writings and, as they were written by one whose channel-knot of wisdom had been released, confirmed them to be authentic vajra songs.[154]

Having mastered the secret treasury of the two wisdoms merely by reading a Dharma book, he could pinpoint precisely in which texts the specific profound essential points had originally been explained. Therefore, Khyentse Chökyi Lodrö unquestionably had a brilliant memory and knew the contents of all Dharma texts from beginning to end.

He could remember the exact date he received each teaching from his sublime teachers, where they were at the time, and even the names of the Dharma friends with whom he received it. His memory was so good that whenever anyone was confused or skeptical, he could instantly recall and offer the appropriate information, completely banishing their confusion.

He could point out the location of any volume you cared to mention without having to refer to a catalog, even when the library was extremely large. Wherever a text fell open, he always appeared to have read that page before.

Khyentse Chökyi Lodrö's compassion was all-pervasive, and the moon of his enlightened mind and activity, like medicine, alleviated the degeneration of the teachings and the misfortunes of those living through this dark age of strife and conflict. He subdued harmful and malicious spirits by merely gazing at them with the power of his realization. And as clearly illustrated in the story of how he eliminated the blaze of invading barbaric forces, he had the unobstructed power to subjugate negative jungpo spirits and other demonic forces.

For this reason, in the words of the eulogy written by the great omniscient Fourteenth Dalai Lama, Ngawang Lobsang Tenzin Gyatso, sovereign holder of all the teachings of the Buddha in Jambudvipa, protector of the Land of Snows and supreme victor,

> Manjushrivajra himself sings in sixty separate tones
> A song of spring that upholds the infinite Dharma,
> And sows counsel in the hearts of countless wise beings.
> I pray to the glorious Guru, the protector of beings.

As His Holiness wrote, Khyentse Chökyi Lodrö's many distinguished students gathered in the Buddhadharma's great joyful grove of wish-fulfilling trees. They included renowned sublime masters who were lineage holders, and hidden yogis who had renounced all mundane affairs. Among them, Khyentse Chökyi Lodrö's main heart-sons were learnèd and accomplished masters who propagated the teachings and performed the activities of the previous Jamgön and root gurus of Chökyi Lodrö himself—Shechen Gyaltsab Rinpoche, Khenchen Kunzang Palden Chökyi Drakpa, and Jamgön Ngawang Lekpa. Most of his own teachers, including these masters, had received the nectar of profound Dharma from Khyentse Chökyi Lodrö and offered him praise in the form of long-life prayers, prayers of supplication, and so on. The example of Khyentse Chökyi Lodrö's life was equal to every word of their praise.[155]

> Holder of the lineages of the buddhas of the three times,
> Adept at celebrating the teachings of the three yanas,
> Sole guide of the beings of the three realms,
> I entreat noble Jamyang Chökyi Lodrö to live for a long time.

This prayer was offered by Manjushri Gatön (Ngawang Lekpa), who advised his students to recite it repeatedly. There were also numerous other fervent prayers of request.

Great and sublime masters who were Jamyang Khyentse Chökyi Lodrö's students included:

Khyentse Chökyi Lodrö's Sakya Students

- the present and previous trichens of the two palaces of Sakya, their brothers and sisters, and various relatives;
- Lhakhang Khenchen, and others;
- khenpos and shabdrungs of Ngor Ewam;
- Zimwog and Chögye Trichen of Nalendra;
- Yarlung Öntrul, and others from central Tibet;
- Khunu Lama Rinpoche Tenzin Gyatso from northern India;[156]
- Tsangsar Choktrul Rinpoche of Drakyab;
- Lama Jamyang Gyaltsen and his brother;
- the east and west Gyaltsen lamas of the Lhundrup Teng Dharma Centre, who were the spiritual masters of the king of Derge;
- Drakyab Khentrul;
- the two Dezhung Choktrul Rinpoches;
- Öntö Khenpo Khyenrab;
- the spiritual friend Chöphel Rabgye;
- Dosib Khenpo Thubten, the tulkus and chöjes, and so on, of Khardo

Monastery, who were the holders of the Tripitaka from the Derge region;
- Chöje of Deu Monastery in Amdo;
- and others.

These were the numerous vajradharas from the Sakya tradition who practiced the tantras and could teach and propagate them.

Khyentse Chökyi Lodrö's Kagyü Students

- the Venerable Palpung Situ Pema Wangchen and his heart-sons;
- Gyalse Jamgön Choktrul;
- Öngen Yangsi Rinpoche;
- the tulkus and lamas of numerous Kagyü monasteries in Gatö, Zurmang, Chidrok, Nangchen, and so on;
- Drukchen Rinpoche;
- Yongdzin Tulku;
- the Eighth Khamtrul Rinpoche;
- Chokdra Tulku of Dingche Monastery;
- and others.

These were the teachers of the four greater and eight lesser schools of Kagyü tradition.

Khyentse Chökyi Lodrö's Nyingma Students

- Minling Khen Rinpoche, Chung Rinpoche, Minling Dungsey Rinpoche, and his brothers and sisters;
- Rigdzin Chenmo of Dorje Drak;
- Namkhai Nyingpo Tulku of Lhodrak Kharchu;
- the Sixth Dzogchen Rinpoche of Dokham;
- Kushab Gemang Choktrul;
- Tulku Drime Özer;
- Dzogchen Khyentse, and others;
- the Sixth Shechen Rabjam Rinpoche;
- the Fourth Gyaltsab Rinpoche;
- Shechen Kongtrul Rinpoche;
- myself, Dilgo Khyentse Rinpoche;

- the supreme tulku of Katok Situ Rinpoche;
- Dralak Chaktsa and others—the tulkus of the golden thrones;[157]
- Palyul Zigak Choktrul;
- Ratrul Rinpoche;
- Muksang Tulku;
- the sons of Adzom Drukpa Rinpoche;
- the sons and tulkus of Tertön Lerab Lingpa, Tertön Drime Pema Lingpa and Drugu Togden (Shakya Shri);
- the two tulkus of Chokling;
- Drikung Tertön Ösel Dorje; and
- others from the Nyingma school.

The great scholar Geshe Jampal Rolpe Lodrö enthroned Khyentse Chökyi Lodrö as the Sovereign Lord of the teachings of the eight great chariots in Tibet at the Vajrabhairava temple in Chamdo and offered tenshuk and prayers for his long life. Geshe Jampal Rolpe Lodrö took him to be his teacher with deep devotion and praised him highly.

Khyentse Chökyi Lodrö's other students included

- Kunling Tatsak Jedrung Rinpoche;
- Minyak Kyile Kyabgön;
- Trehor Getak Choktrul;
- Gonjo Drodren Tulku; and
- others from the Gelug tradition.

He had many students from all traditions of Tibetan Buddhism capable of performing the two activities of benefiting self and others. These are just a few of the main ones.

Among the nobility of Tibet, most of the ministers, generals, and finance ministers were Khyentse Chökyi Lodrö's students:

- the great Dharma King of Derge;
- the king of Lingtsang;
- other kings, queens, princes, princesses, and the ministers of Gamde and Nangchen;
- the chieftains of Riche, Chamdo, Drakyab, Markham, Gonjo, Nyakrong, Treho, Minyak, Gyarong, Golok, and Amdo;

- the Dharma King of Sikkim; and
- senior monks and leading laypeople.

To put it briefly, countless students personally or indirectly received the grace of profound Dharma from Khyentse Chökyi Lodrö, including all the twentieth century's sublime holders of the teachings from Kham, central Tibet, India, and China; the devoted patrons of the teachings endowed with far-sighted generosity; and those who practiced in solitary places and continued to nurture the two activities of benefiting oneself and others.

6. How Jamyang Khyentse Chökyi Lodrö spontaneously accomplished the accumulation of vast merit during the course of his main activities.

The main focus of the sublime masters is to ensure the continuity of the study and practice of the teachings. Arya Nagarjuna, the second Buddha, extended the precious Buddhadharma's sphere of influence by building accommodation for the Sangha, new monasteries, and representations; making offerings to those representations; offering service and paying respect to noble objects of veneration; and giving charity to the destitute and disadvantaged. In the same way, our supreme Lord Guru spontaneously engaged in all aspects of meditation, study, and enlightened activity, without any one aspect overshadowing the others. How he taught and spread the teachings, which were the main aspects of his activity, has been mentioned above.

In terms of Khyentse Chökyi Lodrö's legacy of general activities, during the early part of his life, before his work had blossomed, it was not easy for him to accomplish everything that was necessary. Nevertheless, he had great strength of mind and never allowed himself to be discouraged. He simply got on with whatever it was he had to do without thinking about it too much.

After making tours to collect offerings during the summer and winter, as mentioned in the sacred texts:

> The sweet fragrance of a flower, or sandalwood, or even incense made from a hundred different herbs
> Can only travel on the wind, never against it;
> Whereas the fragrant qualities of noble beings do not depend upon the wind
> But pervade all directions.

As the news of his noble qualities spread throughout the land, borne on sweet Malayan[158] winds, Khyentse Chökyi Lodrö became famous. In addition to the offerings that accompanied requests for protection and prayers for the dead, countless devoted students (both the wealthy and powerful and the poor and insignificant) made unceasing cloud-like offerings of wealth and all the necessities. Khyentse Chökyi Lodrö never squandered or misused these offerings but rather put them towards building sacred images and stupas, printing texts, and making offerings and donations.

How he opened the door to the limitless sky treasury of generosity will be briefly explained here.

After Khyentse Chökyi Lodrö had been at Dzongsar for a few years, omniscient Katok Situ Rinpoche said, "The auspicious circumstance of having been recognized by Jamgön Kongtrul Rinpoche as the activity emanation of Khyentse Wangpo means that you were bound to benefit the teaching lineage of Katok in general, and that more specifically, you would help me nurture the shedra and build representations. But to comply with the dying request of Kalzang Dorje, I have had to leave you at Dzongsar. Unfortunately, though, gathering factions have divided those who like you from those who don't. So you must now return to Katok."

To which Chökyi Lodrö replied, "As I was chosen to remain at Dzongsar, it is my greatest wish to offer the monastery what little service I can. Without doubt, there is no one who can bring more benefit to the Katok lineage than you, Rinpoche, while you are alive. One day, I may be needed at Katok, so at that time I promise to serve the monastery by taking full responsibility for it for twelve years."

Situ Rinpoche looked at Chökyi Lodrö for a long time with wide, unblinking eyes, then said lovingly and with great joy, "Adsi! What more could I possibly ask? Do just that and you will fulfill all my wishes."

Katok Situ Rinpoche gave Chökyi Lodrö detailed instructions, which he followed to the letter. First, he renovated Thubten Norbu'i Lhünpo, the tantric shedra built by omniscient Situ Rinpoche at Katok Monastery, as its foundations had worn away completely. He also renovated the infrastructure and added three students, taking the total number of khenpos and students studying there to forty-five. Then, using mostly his own resources, he built and maintained a replica of the Copper-Colored Mountain buddhafield of Guru Rinpoche.

As if foreseeing how much it would help in the future, Khyentse Chökyi Lodrö appointed an administrator to run the monastery, thus instigating a new system that was very successful and much admired.

He personally supervised the construction of an extremely beautiful thirty-foot-high Buddha Shakyamuni temple in the shape of a stupa, which he also paid for, and an almost thirty-foot-high gilded copper statue of the Buddha as the main inner representation. The materials, proportions, design, and consecration substances used were of unrivaled quality. He also sculpted ten-foot-high statues in medicinal clay of each of the sixteen arhats and four guardian kings in Buddha Shakyamuni's retinue, had extraordinary murals painted on the walls, and so on, and put a gilded copper pinnacle on the roof. There were many temples and representations at his residence, Serkhang Dong, but I don't know the exact details of them all.

He also offered support—for example, money, materials, and advice—for building stupas and sacred images, and so on, as well as study and retreat centers at all the branches of this great monastery. This was how he took religious and secular responsibility for Katok Monastery for a total of fourteen years.

He found and enthroned the supreme tulku of omniscient Katok Situ Rinpoche, who was also recognized by the Fifth Dzogchen Rinpoche, Thubten Chökyi Dorje. He recognized and enthroned the reincarnations of Moktsa Tulku, Jewön Tulku, Drime Zhingkyong, and others, and entrusted them with the great treasury of teachings with two aspects[159] by giving empowerments, explanations, and profound oral instructions that were as vast and deep as the ocean. Basically, he ensured that Katok Monastery was cared for continuously, either by himself personally or by trusted students, until he passed away. In all these ways he was particularly gracious to the teaching lineage of Katok.

When the main temple of Rudam Dzogchen Monastery was destroyed by fire, Khyentse Chökyi Lodrö offered materials for its restoration, and many other things—for example, nine silk brocade thangkas of the eight manifestations of Guru Rinpoche that also depicted stories from the biography of Guru Padma entitled *Pema Kathang*,[160] cymbals, and other items.

At Shechen, when Gyaltsab Rinpoche printed Mipham Rinpoche's writings, and later when Shechen Kongtrul and Jewön Gelek Gyatso printed Gyaltsab Rinpoche's writings, Khyentse Chökyi Lodrö was first to offer his support for both projects, towards which he made many generous donations. He offered guidance when they established a new shedra, and he recognized and enthroned Gyaltsab Rinpoche's supreme tulku. This was how he benefited the Dharma seat of Shechen.

At the seat of Terchen Chokgyur Lingpa, Neten Monastery, Khyentse Chökyi Lodrö helped establish a new shedra for twenty-five new monks by sending letters to the feudal lords and nobility of Rinang[161] to ask for their support. He sent Katok Khenpo Tsultrim Nyima and the great scholar Khangmar Rinchen to teach at the new shedra (at different times) and also offered root texts and commentaries on the great treatises, and so on. By doing so, Khyentse Chökyi Lodrö cared for Neten Monastery fully. He recognized and enthroned the supreme precious tulku and conferred on him vast amounts of empowerments, explanations, and profound oral instructions.

Just as he cared for Neten Monastery, he took an enthusiastic interest in the seat of Tsikey.[162] The followers of this lineage were sustained solely by the grace and kindness of the incarnations of Lord Khyentse.[163]

He also sent khenpos to most of the Kagyüpa monasteries, large and small, in Derge, Chidrok, and Nangchen, and donated the materials necessary to establish new study and practice centers.

He renovated the retreat center at Dragang that had originally been built by the Dharma King of Derge but had fallen into disrepair. He established an extraordinary center primarily for the practice of the *Precious Words: Path and Fruition*—the orally transmitted teachings about the four valid factors of the glorious Sakya tradition—by instituting a fund of more than a hundred dri and thirty pieces of silver to provide stipends for fifty retreatants for as long as the teachings of the Buddha remained.

To fulfill Jamyang Khyentse Wangpo's enlightened wish to build a second glorious Samye Monastery as a source of benefit for the teachings and to bring peace to the beings of Tibet, on a site in Dzongsar village chosen by omniscient Lodrö Taye, Khyentse Chökyi Lodrö built Riksum Trulpa'i Tsuglhakhang Shedrup Dhargye Ling at Kham Jemathang. He then established an endowment sufficient to cover the food and offerings for fifty young monks and built them accommodation. Each shrine room was provided with a set of seven offering bowls and was beautifully decorated with images of Buddha Shakyamuni, the sixteen arhats, the four great guardian kings, Hva Shang, and murals of rocks, mountains, and valleys.

He established a framework of rules for the monks that ensured they would spend their time in study and contemplation and would fully apply and maintain the pure conduct stipulated by the Vinaya. They were to perform the *Three Daily Practices* in the mornings and brief torma offering to the Dharma protectors in the evenings. He also established the excellent and inspiring tradition of making outdoor offerings, including that of lining up rows of butter lamps around the outside of the temple during the evening of the four special days associated with the Buddha, and on the anniversaries of the main masters of the Sarma and Nyingma schools.

Following Katok Situ Rinpoche's instructions, Khyentse Chökyi Lodrö invited Khenchen Shenphen Jampe Gocha, who was learnèd, maintained pure discipline, and had a noble mind, to be the first abbot of Dzongsar Khamje Shedra. During the three years he spent in Dzongsar, Khenchen Shenga established the tradition of teaching the great treatises according to the Indian commentaries, including the Vinaya, the Abhidharma, the collection of Madhyamika treatises by Nagarjuna, *Four Hundred Verses on Madhyamaka*, the *Introduction to the Middle Way*, the *Five Dharmas of Lord Maitreya*, and *The Way of the Bodhisattva*. The activities of the great Khenchen Lama increased enormously, and in addition to these treatises, he also taught the *Commentary on Valid Cognition*, the *Treasury of Valid Logical Reasoning*, and so on. Khenchen Shenga and Khenchen Jamyang Gyaltsen[164] taught commentaries by the great scholar, omniscient Gorampa Sonam Senge entirely in accord with Gorampa's own interpretation.

More than a hundred monks from all lineages—mostly from the Sakya, Nyingma, Kagyü, and Gelug monasteries of central Tibet, Bhutan, and southeastern Dokham—were full-time students at the shedra, and many of them wanted to become masters of the Tripitaka, and to teach and propagate the teachings. As the shedra was so successful, many monasteries in upper and lower Dokham, both large and small, established similar colleges. And so Khamje Shedra became the model for the extensive development of study centers throughout the region of Kham and central Tibet.

Later, Khyentse Chökyi Lodrö constructed another temple at Khamje that was much bigger than the existing one. The main image in the temple was a fifty-foot-high gilded copper statue of Lord Maitreya. Its ornamentation and design were incomparably beautiful, and the sacred substances it contained included a large quantity of the four types of precious relics. The statue was supported by a lion throne and surrounded by an aureola adorned with six ornaments.[165] Exquisite paintings of the lineage masters of the *Three Precepts* of Sarma and Nyingma covered the walls, along with paintings of the twenty-five pioneering teachers in the Land of Snows, yidam deities, and dharmapalas. The inside of the temple was decorated with silk canopies, many pendants hung from the pillars, and a gilded copper pinnacle adorned the rooftop.

Acting on the wishes of the previous Khyentse, Chökyi Lodrö erected a statue of Manjushri as the main image on the lower floor of the central[166] temple at Dzongsar Monastery. It was made of gilded copper and sat on a magnificent throne amid an aureola adorned with many ornaments and elegant designs. It was surrounded by extremely beautiful Indian-style statues of Guru Rinpoche and gilded copper statues of Jowo Je (Atisha), the five founding masters of the Sakya tradition, and Ngorchen (Kunga Zangpo), each with a throne and aureola ornamented with jewels. He also built many other statues, such as the sixteen arhats and twenty-one Taras. The representations of speech were Tibetan translations of the precious *Kangyur* and *Tengyur* texts, and as the representation of mind, he built a lovely ornamented, ten-foot-high wisdom stupa of Kalachakra. To represent the dharmapalas, he commissioned a large, ten-foot-high thangka of Mahakala and his retinue, painted strictly according to authentic traditions and the painting ritual pith instructions. This was how the temple was filled with a great many representations of body, speech, and mind.

The pillars and throne were embellished with latticework, leaves, birds, dragons, and so on, beautifully carved in wood and superbly painted gold and many other colors. The temple was also adorned with gold-encrusted canopies and silk pendants. Later, Khyentse Chökyi Lodrö also built a four-story residence near the temple, with particularly elegant east and west sections, as a beautiful central area.

In the empowerment hall of Khyentse Chökyi Lodrö's residence, Tashi Chime Drupe Gatsel, he built a maroon-colored golden statue of the main deity of Phagma Nyingtik; gilded copper statues of the deities of the Phagma Nyingtik mandala and the three vidyadharas; an arrow's-length-high, maroon-colored golden statue of the glorious Kalachakra; gilded copper statues of the twenty-one Taras, the thirty-five Sugatas, and yidam deities such as Guhyasamaja, Chakrasamvara, Vajrabhairava, and Hevajra; and statues of the dharmapalas, such as the four-armed and six-armed Mahakalas, most of which were made of bronze. He also installed magnificent, carved wooden latticework in front of the statues.

On one side of the temple was an arm's-length-high bronze statue of the Black Foe Yamantaka, housed in a splendid Chinese-style structure. Khyentse Chökyi Lodrö also built a magnificent bronze statue of Buddha Amitabha and one of Buddha Shakyamuni made from East Indian bronze. Revealed treasure statues of Buddha Shakyamuni and Tara were placed in the temple, as were a kutsab of Guru Rinpoche revealed by Sangye Lingpa, a statue of the Vajrayogini from Naropa's tradition, and a statue of Vajrabhairava.[167] Each of these images was placed in its own gold and silver reliquary. Khyentse Chökyi Lodrö also built maroon-colored gold statues of Phagmo Drupa;[168] Je Rinpoche (Tsongkhapa), known as Tsongpon Gelek; and Minling Terchen Rinpoche. Behind the latticework were placed various statues of Vajradhara, Amitayus, Saraha, Virupa, and Guru Rinpoche in Heruka costumes, and so on. These are examples of the numerous representations of body, speech, and mind that Khyentse Chökyi Lodrö kept in his empowerment hall.

To the right of Chime Drupe Gatsel, he constructed a new residence with two shrine rooms and an assembly hall on the third floor. In the east shrine room, the main representation was a very fine bronze statue of Buddha Shakyamuni with a retinue of gilded copper statues of the sixteen arhats, each an arm's-length high, and the Derge edition of the precious *Kangyur* printed in vermillion ink on the best quality paper, with good-quality title tags, wooden endplates, and bindings.

In the western shrine room, Khyentse Chökyi Lodrö built statues and kept complete sets of the *Perfection of Wisdom Sutra in One Hundred Thousand Lines*, the *Treasury of Precious Instructions*, the *Compendium of Sadhanas*, and the *Compendium of Tantras*. He also included the collected works of Dagpo, Rongzompa, Je Tsongkhapa, Kunkhyen Gorampa, Shechen Gyaltsab, and Jamgön Mipham; Sazang's clear and concise commentary on *Kalapa*; Situ's (Chökyi Jungney) commentary on *Chandrapa*; Getse Pandita's commentary on Saraswati; commentaries on poetry written by Khamtrul (Tenzin Chökyi Nyima) and Bö Khepa (Mipham Gelek Namgyal); texts on the two types of astrology;[169] and texts on simile, poetic rhythm, and sound.

He made eight reliquaries ornamented with gold and silver; a clay statue of Terchen Chokling that bore an uncanny resemblance to the great tertön himself; and a special shrine representing the mandala of Nyenchen Thanglha, the personal guardian of both Jamyang Khyentse Wangpo and Jamyang Khyentse Chökyi Lodrö. Silk canopies were made for all these representations. The mandala of bestowing blessings upon a sacred place was placed on top of the residence, and a magnificent victory banner of gilded copper was erected as the appropriate ritual was performed.

At Rongme Karmo Tak Tsang, the sacred land that is the source of auspiciousness for the whole of Tibet, Khyentse Chökyi Lodrö established a retreat center for eight practitioners led by one retreat master. During their five-year retreat, they practiced the main three roots sadhanas from the profound treasures of Khyentse, Kongtrul, and Chokling, and to create spiritual links with them, they also practiced sadhanas from the eight great chariots of the practice lineage.

He extended the old retreat house that had been built onto the practice cave, adding an extremely beautiful assembly hall, a residence with a roof terrace above it, separate rooms for the retreatants, and adjacent to the temple, a dharmapala's hall and kitchen. He also made representations of body, speech, and mind and provided all the essentials, such as offering accoutrements, basic necessities, and texts for sadhana practice. He also provided an assistant for the retreatants, food, and the resources for making plenty of offerings.

At the sacred Garuda and Tiger[170] cave, Khyentse Chökyi Lodrö built an arrow's-length-high clay statue of Guru Nangsi Zilnön and an arm's-length-high statue of Guru Dewa Chenpo. The statues were beautifully painted and filled with extraordinary relics and holy consecration substances.

In the shrine room of the temple on the hilltop above the Utse temple, where smoke offerings were made, he built a number of statues of Guru Khepar Phakpe Rigdzin, each an arrow's length in height and surrounded by statues of Gesar, Thanglha, Machen Pomra, Ziltram, the five Tseringma sisters, and the twelve tenma goddessess. The statues were made of pure medicinal clay and were then painted and filled with consecration substances. These statues were commissioned by our supreme Lord Guru himself.

He also gave timely and detailed instructions for building new monasteries and renovating old ones at many of the Sarma and Nyingma lineage Dharma centers between Minyak in the east and Rekong in the north. He gave these centers representations of body, speech, and mind and all kinds of offerings and necessities, as well as help with fund-raising. The amount of times Chökyi Lodrö assisted monasteries and the extent of the offerings and help he gave are incalculable.

At the very least, he always praised and encouraged those who made new statues and shrines for the rooms of ordinary monks, provided support in the form of paint and consecration substances, and consecrated new statues. Whenever necessary, without waiting to be asked, he spontaneously gave pure gold paint and other offerings, which he presented with a traditional white scarf. This was how he continuously performed activities that increased devotion and joy in the minds of others.

In terms of his activities to increase the representations of speech, he put a great deal of effort into compiling all the miscellaneous writings of Jamyang Khyentse Wangpo that had not been included in the *Five Great Treasuries*, the *Compendium of Tantras*, or the *Compendium of Sadhanas*. He arranged them into more than thirteen large volumes, with a catalog written by Khewang Lama Tashi Chöphel, then made print blocks for many of the texts that the previous Khyentse had intended to publish, including

- three volumes of the collected root and supplementary teachings on Vajrayogini;
- the root treasure teaching and explanatory texts of the *Luminous Heart Essence of the Three Roots*, the *Gathering of the Dakini's Secrets*, the *Heart Essence of Deathless Arya Tara*, *Oral Transmission of Vajrakilaya Called "Vital Essence,"* and the *Heart Essence of Chetsün*;
- more than two volumes of Jamgön Mipham Rinpoche's writings, including the *Collection of Praises*, the *Collection of Advice*, and various instruction and sadhana texts, Dzogchen teachings, a commentary on the Seven-Line Prayer of Guru Rinpoche, and aspiration prayers and expressions of auspiciousness;
- the biography of Lord Khyentse Wangpo by Dodrupchen Tenpe Nyima;
- the biography of the Dharma Lord Patrul Rinpoche composed by Khenpo Kunpal;
- the *Vinaya Sutra*;
- and so on.

Using his own resources, he also made wooden print blocks of about twenty-five volumes of rare texts from both the Sarma and Nyingma traditions—for example, *Two Sections of the Hevajra Root Tantra*, the *Fragment of the Root Tantra of Vajrakilaya*, the *Immaculate Confession Tantra*, and supplication and aspiration prayers related to the daily practice texts; a commentary on the *General Essentialization of All the Wisdom of the Buddhas* that clarifies difficult points; and the commentary on *Guhyagarbha Tantra* called the *Words from Chimphu* by Nubchen Sangye Yeshe, and so on. All these texts were kept at Dzongsar Monastery except the commentary on *General Essentialization of All the Wisdom of the Buddhas*, the Katok version of the commentary on the *Guhyagarbha Tantra*, and some of Mipham Rinpoche's writings that were kept at Derge Lhundrup Teng as part of the complete set of his collected works.

Khyentse Chökyi Lodrö made print blocks for the *King of Samadhi Sutra*, Yakton's commentary on the *Ornament of Clear Realization*, Rongton's commentary on the *Introduction to the Middle Way*, and so on, by inspiring wealthy people to sponsor the project.

When thangkas of the mandala deities and tsagli for the *Precious Treasury of Terma Teachings* were painted, he checked and corrected the drawing of each painting and made resources available to pay for them.

He printed more than two hundred volumes of rare, essential philosophical teachings and instructions from the Sarma and Nyingma schools, the bulk of which were copies of the complete set of four volumes of the seventeen Dzogchen tantras, written in gold, and a volume of the root verses of the *Gradual Path Called the "Essence of Wisdom"* and its commentary. He also printed, from the existing print blocks, three sets of the precious *Kangyur* in vermillion ink, two sets of *Kangyur* in black, one set of *Tengyur*, and the most important collected works and commentaries on the philosophies of the sutras and tantras by numerous Sarma and Nyingma scholars and siddhas from central Tibet, Dokham, and Amdo. All together he printed more than fifteen hundred volumes of texts and always offered wooden endplates, bindings, and metal buckles for the books, and title tags and wrapping cloths of exemplary good quality.

In terms of his activities to increase mind representations, he built the wisdom stupa of Kalachakra that's already been mentioned; a Shakyamuni Buddha temple at Katok Monastery in the form of a stupa shaped like a house; a magnificent bodhi stupa at Dokhoma in the region of Zil; house-shaped stupas around the Khamje Shedra; and many other large and small Two Vimala stupas, constructed following traditional guidelines. He sponsored many such building projects himself and inspired others to do the same.

He made offerings daily and on auspicious days at temples that contained the three kinds of representations (mentioned above), and nothing he offered was ever included just for the sake of completeness. He would, for example, give detailed instructions to artists about how to draw and carve images with the correct proportions, based on his own artistic experience. He often inspected the works of art himself and richly rewarded those who produced splendid pieces. Through such efforts, he was able to create extraordinary and exemplary body, speech, and mind representations.

The thangkas Khyentse Chökyi Lodrö commissioned included twenty-one thangkas depicting the lives of the Buddha as described in the *Jataka* called the *Wish-Fulfilling Vine*, thirty-seven thangkas of the seven Dharma Kings, twenty-five Rigden kings, feudal lords, Butön, Dolpopa, noble Rangjung Dorje,[171] Situ Dharmakara,[172] and so on, all painted according to the Dharma history written by Jamgön Kongtrul and copied from the murals at Palpung Monastery. He sponsored many different sets of nine and five thangkas of the six ornaments and two supreme ones, the eight mahasiddhas, the eight manifestations of Guru Rinpoche, the twenty-one Taras, and the mother who protects from the eight fears (Green Tara), and so on; nineteen thangkas of the successive incarnations of Khyentse Wangpo; and thirty-five thangkas of the deities of all the treasure teachings of Khyentse Wangpo. In all, he made about three hundred good-quality thangkas of buddhas, bodhisattvas, three roots deities, and dharmapalas in various sizes, with borders, veils of gold silk brocade, and ornamental knobs that were often made of silver and gilded metals.

He sponsored numerous tsagli and mandalas of the Kama and Terma, including about 2,200 detailed empowerment tsagli and more than 350 thangkas of the mandala of the *Precious Treasury of Terma Teachings*, and he always provided funds for offering substances, particularly incense and butter lamps.

At Dzongsar Monastery, he also established the tradition of performing the elaborate drupchö of Vajrakilaya from the Khön tradition, its root dance, the dance of subjugation and liberation, and so on, to coincide with the auspicious day of Buddha's descent from the realm of the gods, and the anniversaries of Tsechen Kunga Nyingpo, Khedrup Khyungpo Naljor, and other great masters. He provided magnificent and well-crafted representations, offering substances, ritual materials, dance costumes, and so on, for this drupchö, as well as abundant resources for tsok offerings. He sometimes led the practice himself, supervising every aspect, including the methods used to perform rituals and maintain discipline.

At Khangmar Monastery in Terlung, he continually provided funds for the *Mindrolling Vajrasattva* drupchen.

Whenever necessary (which was quite often) Khyentse Chökyi Lodrö would perform one of about thirty drupchens, both elaborate and simple, from the Kama and Terma traditions, often in combination with the preparation and consecration of amrita. These drupchens were sponsored by Chökyi Lodrö himself and usually happened at the end of a retreat, on pilgrimage, as a special ceremony for the welfare of the teachings, or when specifically requested by devoted benefactors.

This is a rough list of everything I know, but I am unable to record precisely how many drupchens Khyentse Chökyi Lodrö performed during the earlier part of his life.

He also performed daylong sadhana practices for the consecration of amrita at several sacred places, including Yarlung Sheldrak, Bodh Gaya in the Noble Land of India, and Yangleshö in Nepal. These practices were even more beneficial than other group practices, thanks to the sacredness of the locations and because they were performed at the appropriate time.

Every monkey year during the monkey month,[173] he performed one hundred thousand tsok offerings and made more than one hundred kutsabs of Guru Rinpoche from sacred substances. He regularly performed dakini fire pujas, and so on, combined with one thousand, ten thousand, or one hundred thousand tsok offerings, or at the very least more than one hundred tsok offerings.

During his many visits to both famous and more obscure holy places in Dokham, central Tibet, and Sikkim, he made offerings and performed retreat practices, purification rituals[174] and consecrations, tsok and fulfillment offerings, fire pujas, smoke offerings, rituals to remind the gods and spirits of their commitments, and so on. The practices would be elaborate or essential, as appropriate, and were accompanied by tsok feasts and a large variety of the most excellent offerings.

At sacred places—most often at the three great holy sites in Tibet (Lhasa, Samye, and Tradruk); Bodh Gaya, Varanasi, and Shravasti in India; and the three stupas[175] in Nepal—he made ten thousand offerings of sensual delights many times, and offered gold to paint the faces of representations, magnificent robes, symbolic mandala offerings, ceremonial scarves, and so on. The elaborate offerings he made are clearly described in his pilgrimage travel journal.

He regularly performed elaborate tsok and fulfillment offerings on the tenth days of the waxing and waning moons, and he made elaborate cloudlike offerings on the four special days associated with the life of Lord Buddha, the full and new moon, the eighth days, the anniversaries of the great masters of the Sarma and Nyingma traditions, and those of his own sublime teachers, along with the relevant sadhana practices.

More specifically, Khyentse Chökyi Lodrö performed an elaborate *Gathering of the Dakini's Secrets* drupchö for seven days on the anniversary of his previous incarnation, Khyentse Wangpo, and annual one hundred tsok offerings based on the sadhana practice of the *Gathering of the Guru's Secrets* on the tenth day of the monkey month. He made tsok offerings on New Year's Day based on the sadhana *Practice for the Accomplishment of Activity Called "Precious Lamp,"* one of Nyang's treasure teachings, as New Year's

Day is also the anniversary of the Dharma King Trisong. In this way, he continued the tradition established by Jamyang Khyentse Wangpo.

He made butter lamp offerings continuously both inside and outside his residence, and a great number of offerings of water and tormas, and so on. At the same time every year, Khyentse Chökyi Lodrö made clean and pure offerings as elaborately as possible, without ever allowing the size of the offering tormas and tsok offerings to diminish in any way. He was single-minded in his practice of an inconceivable number of methods for accumulating merit.

In terms of the respect and reverence he offered to sublime masters, when Khyentse Chökyi Lodrö received the amrita of profound Dharma from gurus and spiritual friends, he always made long-life mandala offerings at the beginning, in the middle, and at the end of the teaching. The thanksgiving offerings he made always included holy representations of body, speech, and mind, followed by pure and authentic material offerings and all the necessities.

Khyentse Chökyi Lodrö also gave quantities of appropriate material offerings, food, monks' robes and begging bowls, vajras and bells, objects of support for practice, and so on—whatever was necessary—to the great lamas, khenpos, tulkus, and even the humble and ordinary practitioners who received empowerments and teachings from him.

Every year he made vast offerings to the study and practice centers of great monasteries and to Dharma centers affiliated with the different schools, and asked them to recite the *Kangyur*; he also made ten thousand, one hundred thousand, or more than one hundred million dharani mantras from the sutras and tantras that were important for that time, plus dedication and aspiration prayers, and so on. He also gave them timely advice. This was how he cultivated the extraordinary practice traditions of the masters of the past, graciously spreading the teachings and promoting the continuity of the teaching and practice traditions of the Buddhadharma.

Khyentse Chökyi Lodrö mentions in his travel journal that he made offerings to monks at the great prayer ceremony in Lhasa. On his way to holy places in central Tibet, with pure motivation, he offered tea and money to all the monasteries, large and small, on both sides of the Tsangpo River, from Radreng to Lhodrak and Sakya, regardless of their affiliation.

Consistent with the prophecy that Jamyang Khyentse Wangpo would bring peace to Tibet, Chökyi Lodrö sent many letters throughout Dokham saying that if the mani mantra of Avalokiteshvara were to be recited one hundred million times in all the regions of Amdo and Kham, the misfortunes of the times would be pacified and auspiciousness would increase. By doing so, he fulfilled one of Kyabje Katok Situ Rinpoche's wishes. This kind of group practice for accumulating mani mantras had not existed before Khyentse Chökyi Lodrö introduced it, and subsequently it spread throughout Tibet. Everyone connected with Chökyi Lodrö who took part in this practice found new meaning to their lives, which was how, both personally and through others, he brought peace and happiness to ordinary people.

Whenever necessary, Khyentse Chökyi Lodrö prepared and consecrated many hundreds of treasure vases[176] and distributed them to various villages. Some were dedicated to local deities known as "the heart of the owner of the earth," others to the nagas and wealth deities, and so on. During droughts, he would repeatedly scatter into lakes and springs the authentic naga medicine he had gathered, and perform rituals to summon rain.

Khyentse Chökyi Lodrö always gave the medicines he collected and carefully prepared to those who were sick and in need. He made large quantities of ngulchu tsotru chenmo, which is a medicine so difficult and expensive to make that most people can only dream of taking it.

He also made rinchen rilnag chenmo,[177] yangzab, mangjor, shelkar chorten,[178] ratna samphel,[179] wang ril nyernga,[180] and dashel chenmo.[181] The ingredients for these medicines were gathered and formulated precisely according to the medical texts. Khyentse Chökyi Lodrö also collected expensive ingredients such as giwang, wang ril, khache, and seru. He also often prepared tsotru dashel chenmo,[182] which contains large quantities of detoxified processed mercury. These pills helped a great many people and saved many lives. He also freely gave ritual substances used in amrita, rakta, torma, wealth and ransom rituals, fire pujas, and so on, to whoever asked for them.

He said repeatedly, "Since I have prepared these things because I want to help others, it's enough that they are used. I wish for nothing more." This was why he had no system for receiving payment for the medicine he distributed, either personally or through others.

He always gave blessed amrita or whatever was requested to all his visitors and made offerings for protection prayers and prayers for the dead, as well as generous material gifts. Khyentse Chökyi Lodrö consistently endeavored to fulfill the wishes of everyone he met, but his efforts never made him weary or sad.

He took special care of everyone with whom he had a spiritual bond, from those who had received a vast amount of empowerments and teachings from him, to those who had made only the simplest spiritual connection. Personally and indirectly, he always urged everyone to study and practice the Dharma. He helped the destitute, the poor, and the physically and mentally ill by giving them medicines to cure their illnesses, food, clothing, and so on. He even cared for animals like birds and dogs. And his eloquent conversation encouraged others to take an interest in the Dharma. This was how Khyentse Chökyi Lodrö inspired faith in the minds of beings with the four attractive qualities of a bodhisattva, and so on.

By the power of the immense amount of merit he had accumulated, he was able simultaneously to dispel all obstacles to worldly happiness and enlightenment by opening the door to the sky treasury of generosity.

From the *Jataka*:

> The nature of the moon is to delight,
> Of the sun to illuminate,
> Of fire to heat,
> Of wind to blow, and
> Of great beings, joyful with compassion,
> To benefit others.

7. How Jamyang Khyentse Chökyi Lodrö dissolved his body into the dharmadhatu after successfully completing his last activity, plus supplementary explanations.

Khyentse Chökyi Lodrö, the embodiment of nondual compassion and great protector of the teachings and beings, embraced an ocean of enlightened activities as he worked tirelessly in a multitude of ways for the welfare of all the teachings of the Buddha and all beings.

At the age of sixty-three, during the waxing moon in the fourth month of the wood sheep year (1955), he gave a teaching and some brief advice to a small group of students, then said,

> These days, those who practice Dharma in its pure and authentic form are as rare as stars in daylight. The minds of most people are possessed by demons! They think the good and ancient traditions connected with the precepts of the ten virtuous actions are flawed, and disparage the Noble Ones whose thoughts and actions are in perfect accord with the Dharma. Most of them follow a barbaric path of deceit that ruins both themselves and others. They ignore the truth of cause and effect, and children don't trust their parents.
>
> As far as teachers and monasteries are concerned, hearing, teaching, and meditation—the essence of Buddhadharma—are empty words. Teachers base their instructions on assumptions, and they gather students by force, and by tempting them with wealth. Yet they still claim to uphold the teachings.
>
> Not only ordinary people, but even those who consider themselves to be scholars, malign the Buddha's teachings and use the power of logic and quotations from sacred texts to support their own prejudices against other teaching traditions. This is how they steer their followers onto the wrong path. These so-called teachers only ever exert themselves to cheat and deceive—for example, by doing business and making loans for personal profit in the name of the welfare of the Dharma. They grab voraciously at black[183] offerings made for the benefit of the living and the dead, indulge in alcohol, smoke and gamble, slaughter living beings, engage in business, and revel in many other activities that cause laypeople to lose faith in them and in the Dharma.

They throw away their vows as carelessly as they throw stones. In fact, there are very few who even wear their robes properly, in spite of Buddha having said that, at the very least, it will always be possible to recognize his students by their robes. Far from upholding the teachings, the way today's teachers apply themselves personally and direct others is causing the teachings to degenerate as quickly as is possible. They imagine, for example, that laymen's dress, knives, weapons, and so on, are somehow terribly important.

Basically, everyone indulges almost exclusively in unvirtuous activities and therefore experiences unbearable sufferings in their present lives (disease, famine, warfare with deadly weapons, and so on). This is the nature of cause and effect, and it will never deceive you. People lose faith in the Triple Gem and rely instead on malicious demons for protection. In every respect, this kind of degenerate activity breaks my heart.

My purpose in saying this is not to remind you, rather ostentatiously, of how much you owe me for the teachings I have given. Quite unintentionally, this old monk has mumbled all this nonsense out of despair.

And our Lord Guru wept.

Not long after, turbulent visions and various other experiences prompted him to do a divination in the presence of Kutsab Rinpoche to determine whether it was more important for him to go into strict retreat or on pilgrimage. The result was that a very simple pilgrimage accompanied by few attendants would be best. And so he made his plans known to the monastery and local villagers.

In reality, it is certain the *cause* that compelled Khyentse Chökyi Lodrö to leave Dzongsar, and eventually Tibet, was the fact that he had completed the beneficial activities appropriate to that time. The *condition* was that he foresaw the imminent approach of unavoidable dangers that the future mayhem would bring. But he kept all this to himself, promised to return to the monastery soon, and fulfilled the wishes of his students by granting audiences and long-life empowerments, making aspiration prayers, and distributing amrita and material gifts, and so on.

He visited the temple and the dharmapalas' halls to make elaborate offerings and to offer traditional white scarves. He said prayers reminding the dharmapalas to carry out their activities, asked the jnanasattvas to remain in the representations, made aspirations, and recited prayers of auspiciousness. He also gave pertinent and exhaustive advice to the monastery, the villagers, the shedra, and the retreat center.

On the tenth day of the sixth (monkey) month,[184] he led elaborate sadhana practices and, on the twenty-third day, left Dzongsar to go on pilgrimage, accompanied by a small entourage. He camped in front of the cave of Pema Shelphuk, the king of sacred places and the most exalted of the holy places in the Land of Snows, where he performed one hundred tsok offerings based on the sadhana of the *Heart Practice That Spontaneously Fulfills All Wishes*. Many devoted students gathered, and he greeted them all personally.

The pilgrims traveled quite slowly, preferring to camp at holy places and sacred mountains, where they stayed for several days while Chökyi Lodrö performed tsok and fulfillment offerings, fire pujas, smoke offerings, purification rituals to revitalize the energy and sacredness of the mountains, powerful subjugation practices, invocation of blessings, and so on—whatever was appropriate to each place. As he made his way slowly through Kham, then Nakchukha and Radreng in the north, he fulfilled the wishes of everyone who came to see him before turning south towards the great holy sites of Lhasa, Samye, Tradruk, and so on, then to Tsang, Töd, Sakya, and the sacred hidden land of Sikkim. From Sikkim, he traveled twice to India to visit Bodh Gaya and various holy places, and once to Nepal. On his way, he made elaborate offerings and paid his respects to holy places and representations, and to all the Sarma and Nyingma monasteries. Countless beings, both high and low, were granted audiences by him, and he bestowed a vast amount of nectar-like teaching, always tailored to the needs of the students listening.

He settled in Sikkim temporarily, where he continued his vast activities for bringing meaning to the lives of those who sheltered beneath the grace of his immense nondual compassion. He did a mendrup drupchen of the *Three Roots Practice for Accomplishing the Life-Force of the Vidyadharas*. At Tashiding, he performed the practice of bestowing blessings upon a sacred place and constructed a dwelling for the local deities. He was also asked to do elaborate consecration ceremonies for the Tsuglhakhang, the Palace Monastery, and so on, which he did. At the request of devoted students, he gave regular teachings in Gangtok, Pema Yangtse (the main Dharma center of Sikkim), and Darjeeling. As a result of his own Dharma activities and teachings and those of his students,[185] he planted the seeds of ultimate happiness in the minds of many people from India and Europe.

Although a detailed written account about this time would be very valuable, I have only given a summary here because everything has been clearly described in Chökyi Lodrö's own travel journal.

During the New Year of the year of the earth pig (1959), when our Lord Guru was sixty-six years old, he began to show signs of ill health.

On the fifteenth day of the first month, he joyfully fulfilled a request to give teachings on the *Seven Points of Mind Training*. He said, "I have accumulated exceptional merit by reciting such a profound teaching on this auspicious day in the month of miracles, during such a degenerate time."

After this, his health gradually deteriorated. Nevertheless, he continued to give empowerments and teachings on the *Heart Essence of the Vast Expanse* three roots practices and the *Magical Net* from the treasure teachings of Chokgyur Lingpa to a group of students that included Kinnauris,[186] Bhutanese, Westerners devoted to the Dharma, and so on, saying, "Even though it is difficult to fulfill the wishes of all beings, it is essential always to try to satisfy the wishes of those who have wholeheartedly taken refuge in you." This was the last group of students to receive teachings from Khyentse Chökyi Lodrö before he passed away.

He was probably the only master whose enlightened aspirations and activity were inseparable from those of omniscient Jamyang Khyentse Wangpo, the great universal Dharma King, Sovereign Lord of all the teachings of the Buddha in the Land of Snows, whose Dharma activity was like that of a second Buddha in this degenerate age. This account of the example of his life, which was like dazzling light radiating multitudes of sparkling rays, is not just an expression of my wish to praise my teacher and exaggerate his qualities; it will be attested to by everyone who met him.

Khyentse Chökyi Lodrö completed all these inconceivable activities beyond compare. And then, as described in the *Magical Net*,

> In order to tame and mature ignorant beings,
> After taking birth, the Tathagatas demonstrate passing
>   into nirvana.

And from the *Sutra of Golden Light*:

> Furthermore, son of a noble family, the Tathagatas demonstrate passing into nirvana while sentient beings contemplate how rarely buddhas appear, how difficult it is to meet them, and the suffering and pain of samsara, and so on. Therefore, sentient beings never denigrate those who swiftly grasp, uphold, read, and understand all the meanings of the sutras taught by Bhagavan Buddha, then teach them perfectly and in detail to others. Thus, the Tathagatas demonstrate the brevity of life.
>
> [...] Therefore, son of a noble family, for these reasons and in these circumstances, the Tathagatas do not remain long in this world and quickly pass into nirvana. In this way, using excellent skillful methods, the Tathagatas completely mature sentient beings.

Even though the length of a Tathagata's life is not limited, as they are skilled in methods for taming beings, they make it appear as though they pass into nirvana. Similarly, as our supreme Lord Guru was ultimately the all-pervasive Bhagavan Manjuvajra, father of all the Tathagatas of past, present, and future, manifesting as the vajradhara endowed with the *Three Precepts*, had he thought it useful, he could have lived for aeons without aging or suffering illness. The display of death, life, old age, and sickness are the projections of ordinary people, and as those living in this degenerate age have little merit and even less good fortune, they were unable to receive Khyentse Chökyi Lodrö's compassion as reflected in his activities. He also saw that he could be more helpful in other realms and therefore indicated that he wouldn't live much longer. At the beginning of his illness, he said he was suffering from the same malady as that of the late Palpung Kyabgön, Tai Situ Pema Wangchok Gyalpo.

Here are some points extracted from what he had said the previous year when prayers were offered for his long life:

> Having been recognized by Jamgön Kongtrul Lodrö Taye Rinpoche as the tulku of Khyentse Wangpo, all the activities I have performed for the welfare of the teachings and beings were simply a continuation of the activities of Lord Khyentse Wangpo.

He went on to say,

> The divination I did in front of Kutsab Rinpoche at the age of sixty-three indicated that I should go on a pilgrimage to the holy places. I therefore visited all the holy places from Dokham to central Tibet, as well as those in both India and Nepal. I saw all the representations, prostrated, circumambulated, and made offerings to them and applied myself to all the virtuous activities that sow the seeds of enlightenment in the minds of numerous beings, regardless of their status. I always did my best to ensure that my aspirations and goals were virtuous, primarily so that the teachings of the Buddha would flourish and be secure, but also for the temporary[187] and ultimate[188] benefit of myself and others.

Then he said,

> I was even able to make a pilgrimage to India. Lord Khyentse Wangpo himself went on many pilgrimages to the holy places in Tibet but was never able to go to India. It was therefore my good fortune that going on pilgrimage to the holy sites in India fell to me, and at each of them, I offered prostrations and made offerings and good aspirations. I have always aspired to ensure that the efforts of those with whom I have a Dharma connection are worthwhile. Although I didn't do that much, I did my best and am satisfied. Everything I have accomplished was, I feel, an extension of the activity of the sublime lama, Khyentse Wangpo, and I did it all to fulfill his profound aspirations. It's difficult for an ordinary person to fully accomplish the noble intentions and activities of a sublime being. Nevertheless, I have accomplished everything possible within the limits of my mental capacity, using all means available to me.
>
> If I am ever able to return to Kham, there are still a few statues to gild and fill with consecration substances, which I'd like to do. It is also my heartfelt wish to recite *The King of Aspiration Prayers: Samantabhadra's "Aspiration to Good Actions"* one hundred thousand times. Apart from that, there's nothing much left unfinished. At the same time, I have no attachment to the activities I have accomplished because through them, I have accumulated merit perfectly.

I am now quite old. Taking into consideration my advanced illness, that I have moved to a different country, and this time of degeneration, it's quite obvious that I cannot escape death. But I lack the confidence not to fear it. However, once a person has been born, there is no escaping death; therefore, it's useless to feel regret. You request that I live for a long time, but it's extremely difficult to gain mastery over one's own life; I know myself well and cannot confidently promise that I'll be able to. Nonetheless, it would make me very happy if, by the blessings of the gurus and the Triple Gem, I were to survive another year, or even just a few more months. And I always pray as best I can that I will live for a long time.

In terms of long-life ceremonies, as I've already said, it is important that you perform them for the well-being of the teachings and sentient beings; by doing so, they will also quite naturally remove the obstacles to my life.

He then advised those attending him that after he had done some divinations he would tell them which ceremonies were appropriate for removing obstacles to his life.

Therefore, from the twenty-first day of the first month in the year of the earth pig (1959), Khyentse Chökyi Lodrö led the drupchö of the *Gathering of the Dakini's Secrets* for the anniversary of his previous incarnation. On the twenty-fifth day, he performed elaborate practices, like the praise and invocation of the dakinis, and made offerings that included a great tsok. And that evening, he began to display signs of serious illness.

At that time, monks led by the Ngor khenpos of Thartse and Luding performed *Drolma Yuldok*, a ritual for warding off invasions based on Tara; an offering ritual of one hundred tormas, one hundred butter lamps, one hundred effigies, and one hundred tsa tsas; the practice for repelling maras based on the *Heart Sutra*; burnt offerings and water torma offerings; the offering practice of the three long-life deities; the *Sixteen Arhats Practice*; a Tara sadhana practice; the *Fulfillment Offering to the Dharmapalas*; tsok and fulfillment offerings to the three roots deities; and a tenshuk.

Gyatön Lama performed numerous chö practices, rituals involving offering effigies to remove obstacles, long-life practices, and so on. Sogyal Tulku and Khyentse Chökyi Lodrö's close attendants continuously performed long-life ceremonies like tsok, and made fulfillment offerings to the dakinis, *Turning Back the Summons of the Dakinis*, and so on.

During the waxing moon of the second month, Khyentse Chökyi Lodrö displayed signs of a slight recovery. In Kalimpong, Dudjom Rinpoche specifically wrote long-life prayers for him, and Chökyi Lodrö reciprocated by writing long-life prayers for Dudjom Rinpoche.

For the auspicious tenth day, he performed elaborate tsok and fulfillment offerings. Around that time, the turmoil in Tibet began to escalate. The ultimate concern of most of the great masters who were holders of the teachings, and of Chökyi Lodrö in particular, was for the welfare of the teachings and beings. On several occasions, he said,

> These days we hear many stories about people from foreign countries taking an active interest in Buddhism, translating Dharma texts into their native languages and establishing Dharma centers. We should rejoice when we hear about such virtuous activities—they should not be repudiated! The activities of the buddhas are inconceivable.
>
> In our country, all the teachings of sutra and tantra have flourished for centuries thanks to the kindness of the emanation Dharma Kings, lotsawas, and panditas. The seeds of those teachings still exist, or at least haven't quite disappeared yet. It is therefore extremely important for everyone to persevere in protecting the teachings from degeneration and destruction by understanding their true value.

Khyentse Chökyi Lodrö said again and again that even if you can't see the true value of the teachings, by at least making aspirations with a good heart, you will bring great benefit. He was always very concerned about the future of the teachings and took responsibility for performing ceremonies to promote their welfare.

Although nobody could understand why, he constantly longed to return to Tibet. In all the letters I received from him while I was in Lhasa, and even in verses of aspiration, he never failed to mention going back to Tibet. But after he heard about the widespread destruction of the Buddha's teachings, apart from expressing his relief when the omniscient Lord Protector, His Holiness the Fourteenth Dalai Lama, escaped, he never again spoke about Tibetan issues with anyone, neither to those close to him, nor to strangers.

He said that although he would have liked to recite the *Wisdom Guru* for some students who had requested teachings, as they had not prepared adequately by doing the required purification practices thoroughly enough, they could not receive that teaching. Then he fell while getting out of bed, and as a result, his health deteriorated still further.

About thirty practitioners, including Neten Chokling Rinpoche and Gyatön Lama, performed the drupchen of the *Heart Essence of Deathless Arya Tara* for his long life. During the waxing moon of the third month, Gyatön Lama and Minyak Trulshik Rinpoche performed rituals for *Turning Back the Summons of the Dakinis* and offered Khyentse Chökyi Lodrö a long-life ceremony based on the sadhana practice of the *Embodiment of the Three Jewels,* sponsored by the Queen Mother of Sikkim. Another long-life ceremony was also offered during the receiving of the siddhis of the drupchen practice.

All possible traditional and modern medical treatments were offered to him, and although the pain caused by his fall slowly subsided, his illness remained serious, and it was difficult for him to stand up.

Sakya Dagchen Rinpoche, who was at Lachen, was invited to Gangtok. Dudjom Rinpoche, Dodrup Tulku, Chatral Sangye Dorje, and others were also asked to come to make prayers of aspiration for his long and healthy life. Venerable Khamtrul Rinpoche performed the ritual for averting obstacles and negative forces based on the practice of *Molten Metal Yamantaka*, tsok and fulfillment offerings, *Turning Back the Summons of the Dakinis*, and a long-life ceremony based on the sadhana of the *Embodiment of the Three Jewels*. Other long-life ceremonies were also performed continuously, during which, on the fifteenth day of the third month, enormous, elaborate offerings and a tsok feast were arranged according to Khyentse Chökyi Lodrö's instructions, and he himself did an elaborate tsok practice of Kalachakra. After that, he did no other ritual practices. From then on, besides having difficulty sitting or standing up, he did not appear to be seriously ill.

During the waxing moon of the fourth month, about twenty lamas, tulkus, khenpos, and lopöns—including the three khenpos from the Ngor tradition, Neten Chokling Rinpoche, Gyatön Lama, and others—performed tsok and fulfillment offerings, *Turning Back the Summons of the Dakinis*, and a long-life ceremony based on a three roots sadhana. With one voice, they requested that Khyentse Chökyi Lödro live for a long time, to which, for the sake of auspiciousness, he responded appropriately.

Again, they asked which ceremonies would be most apt and effective in ensuring his swift recovery from this display of illness. He responded by saying,

> Since my present illness isn't serious, I am sure I will recover quickly. I have no doubt that this is what you also wish. All the long-life ceremonies have already been elaborately performed, and there are no other important ones worth doing. But I would be grateful if the three Khen Rinpoches would perform the ritual for cleansing and purification.[189]

Sakya Dagchen Rinpoche (Kyabje Sakya Trizin Rinpoche) also came and performed ceremonies to stabilize Chökyi Lodrö's life, gave long-life empowerments equal to the years he had lived so far, and offered a long-life ceremony. Sakya Dagchen Rinpoche repeatedly requested that he give clear instructions as to which practices would remove the obstacles to his life. Khyentse Chökyi Lodrö considered his request and responded appropriately to create auspicious circumstances. Again, Dagchen Rinpoche performed purification rituals; offered long-life empowerments and the authorization blessing for *Manjushri Arapachana*, which Khyentse Chökyi Lodrö had wanted to receive; and repeatedly asked him to live for a long time.

Khyentse Chökyi Lodrö asked the Ngor khenpos to give him teachings, saying,

> As you are sublime beings who have ascended the throne of Lord Vajradhara, Kunga Zangpo, it is very important for me to establish spiritual links with you all.

Accordingly, they offered him authorization blessings and performed cleansing and purification rituals. Lamas, tulkus, devotees, and students did the offering practices of the three long-life deities and the barmas of the four directions, made one hundred thousand torma offerings to the dharmapalas, and practiced the sadhana of *Samaya Vajra* without interruption. Neten Chokling Rinpoche, Gyatön Lama, and other monks performed the ritual of *Yamantaka: Destroyer of Enemies* for averting obstacles and negative forces. Dodrup Rinpoche and his students did the tsok and fire puja of the *Consort Practice: The Queen of Great Bliss*. Other devoted students and benefactors also did elaborate ceremonies for his long life, such as one hundred thousand tsok offerings to the deities of the three roots.

Around this time, Khyentse Chökyi Lodrö spent several days reading his daily practices aloud, including practices like the brief *Prajnaparamita Sutra*. Then he gave the texts to his cook, saying, "Now, wrap them properly and put them on the shelf."

He mentioned that each night he dreamt about reciting the Marme Mönlam prayers at the conclusion of a drupchen ceremony. Then one night, he dreamt he was taking part in the Kagye drupchen. It was the end of the practice, and as he recited the prayer he noticed that the mandala had been completely dismantled and that the butter lamp offerings burnt rather dimly.

On the twenty-fifth day, as Khyentse Chökyi Lodrö had instructed, his attendants performed the tsok and fulfillment offerings from the *Consort Practice* from the *Heart Essence of the Vast Expanse*. That night, just after dusk, there was a violent earthquake. The following morning, with an extremely clear mind, our Lord Guru announced, "Today, I have recovered from my illness, and I feel like getting out of bed and going out." With these words he got up and, clasping a walking stick in his right hand, strolled around the palace for quite some time.

When His Holiness the Sixteenth Karmapa, Venerable Katok Situ Rinpoche, and others arrived from Bhutan, Khyentse Chökyi Lodrö granted an audience to Princess Wangmo of Bhutan and others, with whom he had a profound conversation. The following day, though, he again displayed signs that his illness was getting worse.

During the waxing moon of the fifth month, Sakya Dagchen Rinpoche and Gyalwang Karmapa repeatedly asked him to live longer, and he replied that he might recover if the Rinpoches prayed for his long life. Minyak Trulshik Rinpoche also urged him to live longer and performed purification rituals, and so on.

On the third day, various doctors from both Western and Tibetan medical traditions examined him with the help of the prince and Queen Mother of Sikkim. They said there was nothing wrong with his pulses. At this, our Lord Guru looked intently at the prince and Queen Mother, then smiled. About twenty lamas and monks then began to make one hundred thousand tsok offerings based on Vajrasattva for his long life.

On the fifth day, Gyalwang Rinpoche, the Sixteenth Karmapa, gave Khyentse Chökyi Lodrö the long-life empowerment of the *Embodiment of the Three Jewels*, after which they had a private conversation. Gyalwang Rinpoche then left for Rumtek.

Sakya Dagchen Rinpoche continuously performed ceremonies for him

—for example, the four types of suppression of samaya-violating demons based on Vajrakilaya—gave long-life empowerments, and performed purification rituals.

At one point, our Lord Guru, who appeared to be in a world of his own, mentioned to his consort that although all his other teachers were there, vajradhara Loter Wangpo still hadn't arrived. He then immediately snapped out of it, saying, "It was a dream. How could one not have dreams of confused illusory experience." After that he didn't speak much, but at times he made the summoning mudra with his right hand and placed it on his knee or heart, and at others, he would gaze into space for a long time and often looked towards the northeast.

On the sixth evening, his attendants offered him a little black tea, wine, milk, and so on. He took a little of each and for a while appeared to be free from the effects of illness, his mind relatively clear. After midnight, towards the end of ox time[190] (between 1 and 2 A.M.), as he recited the unborn letter (AH) several times, he demonstrated the act of becoming fully enlightened in the ground of the primordial expanse of inner luminosity. Immediately, a volume of posthumous teachings,[191] the most precious section of the Dzogchen teachings, and a chakra that liberates when worn were placed on Khyentse Chökyi Lodrö's body, which was now called a *kudung*, "sacred body." But the news of his death was kept secret for three days.

On the ninth day of the month, khenpos, lamas, and tulkus from the Sarma and Nyingma traditions, led by Sakya Dagchen Rinpoche, did the practices of making offerings to the guru and entreated him to come out of his meditation. And so the seal of secrecy was opened.

The kudung was thoroughly washed with saffron water and vase water blessed by the practices of Hevajra, Vajrasattva, Vajra Vidharana, Bhurkumkuta, and so on, and anointed with special substances, like amrita, camphor, and various medicines. The syllables for the different parts of the body were written in gold and placed at appropriate points on the kudung, along with chakras that liberate when worn and tantric texts, all in the correct order according to the Sarma and Nyingma tantras. The kudung was properly wrapped in white cloth anointed with saffron water, then yellow silk, and the space in between was filled with medicinal powders. It was adorned with sambhogakaya ornaments, and a vajra and bell were placed in the hands. With respect and reverence, it was placed on the throne in the Kangyur Temple,[192] and elaborate offerings were arranged in front of it.

First, lamas and tulkus led by Dagchen Rinpoche did the yidam practices of visualization, dissolution of jnanasattva, offerings and praise, prayers of supplication, and so on, as well as obstacle dispelling and purification rituals.[193] Then, those who had gathered were allowed to see the precious kudung. An unceasing stream of people from all walks of life were admitted, with the lamas and monastics going first. Sacred water that had been used for washing the precious kudung and other sacred substances were distributed to everyone, and in this way, they all made a spiritual connection with Khyentse Chökyi Lodrö, benefiting themselves tremendously.

From the tantra of the *Mirror of the Heart of Vajrasattva*:

> There are two kinds of nirvana: the attainment of perfect buddhahood, and the attainment of complete buddhahood. The attainment of perfect buddhahood is enlightenment without the residue of aggregates;[194] when one attains complete buddhahood, rays of light, sounds, relics, self-arising forms, and so on, appear, and the earth trembles.

And,

> Dakini!
> One who attains enlightenment
> In a mandala of light
> Is an emanation of a fortunate being;
> Such an emanation brings benefit quite naturally
> To the beings of the ten directions.

After dusk that night, just as described in the verse, an exceptionally brilliant, all-pervasive light—beside which the electric lights paled—blazed for a long time, and everyone was filled with great devotion. Even foreigners were known to have been amazed and to have said it must be a sign that a sublime being had passed away.

Then, from the Vinaya:

> Like creepers on the sal[195] tree,
> Those who rely on sublime beings
> Will be infused with excellent virtues.

Just as the branches of ordinary wood that fall in a sandalwood grove become infused with fragrance, it is natural for those close to the sublime, supreme guide of beings, including even the gods, to be infused with his excellent qualities.

Khyentse Chökyi Lodrö's treasurer, who was also his nephew, and other attendants, with pure and untainted minds, respectfully and with great determination, devotion, and diligence, made abundant and elaborate offerings to fulfill the aspirations of their Lord Guru. How they did so will now be explained.

As soon as the secret of Khyentse Chökyi Lodrö's passing was disclosed to his devoted students, his treasurer and attendants sent a telegram to inform His Holiness the Dalai Lama, who also replied by telegram. Even though Khyentse Chökyi Lodrö's passing was a great loss to the teachings and beings, His Holiness wrote, both for the world in general and specifically for his students, there was no doubt that Khyentse Chökyi Lodrö had foreseen that for him to leave this world for other realms would be extraordinarily beneficial. His Holiness also said he would make aspiration prayers that all Khyentse Chökyi Lodrö's wishes would be fulfilled. The treasurer and attendants sent His Holiness offerings of a bronze statue of Buddha Shakyamuni of exceptional quality and some money, with a request for prayers to be said. In return, His Holiness composed a wonderful prayer requesting the swift rebirth of Chökyi Lodrö's incarnation.

Gyalwang Karmapa's journey to Sikkim was delayed by the state of the roads, which had been blocked after heavy rain, so Khyentse Chökyi Lodrö's attendants sent him generous offerings with a request that he make aspiration prayers. Later, Gyalwang Rinpoche came to Gangtok specifically to perform ceremonies and make profound and vast aspirations before the precious kudung of Jamyang Khyentse Chökyi Lodrö. Offerings were also made to Dudjom Rinpoche and other lamas and tulkus whose monasteries were in and around Kalimpong and Darjeeling, with the request that they too say aspiration prayers.

For the first seven days, Kyabgön Sakya Dagtri Rinpoche of Dolma Phodrang and the khenpos and shabdrungs of Ngor and their monks performed the accomplishment practice of Vajrakilaya from the Khön tradition, preceded by rituals requesting permission to use the space for drupchen practice and preparation practices for the drupchen rituals, combined with the practice of making offerings to the sacred kudung. Venerable Tai Situ

Rinpoche, Gyatön Lama, and some monks did the sadhana practice of the *Wrathful and Peaceful Deities of Karma Lingpa*. Neten Chokling Rinpoche and his group did the *Confession and Restoration of Vajrayana Vows*. Khyentse Chökyi Lodrö's students recited eighteen hundred thousand mantras of the deity Samaya Vajra, and the moment they finished, between sixty and one hundred ordained monks (shramaneras and bhikshus) from the Sakya, Gelug, Kagyü, Nyingma, Shalu, and other traditions began one hundred thousand recitations of *The King of Aspiration Prayers: Samantabhadra's "Aspiration to Good Actions,"* which our Lord Guru had wanted to do himself in Tibet. They continued reciting this prayer every day and offered one thousand butter lamps and other magnificent and elaborate offerings.

For the tenth-day practice at his residence, Khyentse Chökyi Lodrö's consort led members of the inner circle of attendants as they offered a tsok based on the father practice of the Nyingtik, *Gathering of Vidyadharas*, and the fulfillment practice of the *Mandala of Peaceful and Wrathful Deities*. From then until the precious kudung was cremated, they offered tsok and recited the *Fulfillment and Confession Called "Stirring the Depths of Hell"* without interruption. The one hundred thousand tsok offerings based on Vajrasattva practice that I've already mentioned were sponsored by the government of Sikkim, which gave daily offerings of money, and so on, to the practitioners. It was decided that one offering practice from the Sarma tradition and one from the Nyingma tradition would be made to the sacred kudung.

In the second week, Thartse Khenpo and the supreme tulku of Ga Tharlam Monastery performed the drupchö of Hevajra, and the practice was led by the eldest Kyabgön Dungsey Rinpoche of Sakya Phuntsok Phodrang. Dodrup Rinpoche performed *Avalokiteshvara: Self-Liberation from Suffering*.

For the third week's practice, Sakya Jetsünma, Ngari Tulku, and others did the drupchö of Vajrayogini, and Gyatön Tulku performed the offering practice of Kalachakra from the Jonang tradition. As the occasion coincided with the twenty-fifth day, in the presence of the precious kudung, about forty lamas and monks—including the khenpos and shabdrungs of Ngor, led by Dagtri Rinpoche—performed the Vajrayogini drupchö, with elaborate offerings and a tsok. Many lamas and monks, led by Dodrupchen Rinpoche and Neten Chokling Rinpoche, performed the tsok and fulfillment offerings of the *Consort Practice: The Queen of Great Bliss*. Khyentse Chökyi Lodrö's consort paid her respects by making offerings of tea, food, and so on, as well as generous offerings of money to all the practitioners, including the assembly of monks who recited *The King of Aspiration Prayers: Samantabhadra's "Aspiration to Good Actions."* And at Khyentse Chökyi Lodrö's residence, the practice of *Vimalamitra's Guru Yoga Called the "Essence of Blessings"* was performed.

For the fourth week's practice, Ngor Khangsar Khenpo led the drupchö practice of *Sarvavidhi*, and the lamas and monks of Pema Yangtse Monastery performed the *Assembly of All the Sugatas*.

Offerings of money were made to the monks who recited *The King of Aspiration Prayers: Samantabhadra's "Aspiration to Good Actions."* As Khyentse Chökyi Lodrö had said it would be extremely auspicious for the shramaneras and bhikshus visiting that area of Gangtok to perform the ceremony for the restoration of vows, to comply with his wishes, about sixty ordained monks performed the *Restoration of Vows Ceremony for Auspiciousness*. Every day before they began to recite *The King of Aspiration Prayers: Samantabhadra's "Aspiration to Good Actions,"* the monks performed the ceremony for the restoration of vows and made one thousand of each of the five outer offerings. On the auspicious fourth day of the sixth month, one hundred thousand recitations of *The King of Aspiration Prayers: Samantabhadra's "Aspiration to Good Actions"* and all the supplementary recitations were completed perfectly by the lamas and monks who had been invited to participate. At Khyentse Chökyi Lodrö's residence, the Nyingtik and Tukdrup practices for making offerings to the guru were performed for several days.

For the fifth week's practice, Dzongsar Ngari Tulku led the drupchö of *Sarvavidhi*, and Lungtok Gomchen of Enchay Monastery led the practice of *Mindrolling Vajrasattva*. On the tenth day of the monkey month, one hundred tsok offerings based on the sadhana of the *Gathering of the Guru's Secrets* were offered at Khyentse Chökyi Lodrö's residence, and in front of the precious kudung, a group of practitioners presided over by Dodrupchen Rinpoche and another presided over by Chokling Rinpoche made one hundred tsok offerings based on the practices of the *Gathering of Vidyadharas* and the *Heart Practice for Dispelling All Obstacles*, respectively. These practices were sponsored by devoted students.

For the sixth week's practice, Khardo Khangsar Shabdrung led the practice of *Sarvavidhi*, and Yönru Tersey Lama and others performed the fulfillment practice of the *Peaceful and Wrathful Deities*.

For the last seven days, Thartse Rinpoche led the drupchö of *Sarvavidhi*, and Namtso Dochak Tulku and Neten Chokling Rinpoche led the practice of the *Peaceful and Wrathful Deities Who Stir the Pits of Hell* from the *New Treasures of Chokling*. On the twenty-fifth day, in addition to the two groups[196] of lamas and monks who were already performing ceremonies, all the other lamas and monks in the area from the Sarma and Nyingma traditions were invited to participate.

That night, in front of the precious kudung, they performed the elaborate practice of the *Gathering of the Dakini's Secrets*, including the individual fulfillment offerings and a thousandfold offering. On the twenty-sixth day, the two groups of lamas and monks each burnt a list of names of the dead and performed the liberation and purification rituals. Then for a few days, they all performed the practices for the flourishing of the teachings of Sarma and Nyingma, and aspiration prayers such as *The King of Aspiration Prayers: Samantabhadra's "Aspiration to Good Actions."*

This is a brief account of the practices performed.

People from all walks of life, including devoted students and sponsors, continuously made offerings and accumulated merit day and night with whatever wealth or ability they had. They spent all their time performing virtuous activities, or teaching, or listening to teachings, and reciting supplication and aspiration prayers. This was how elaborate tsok and other offerings were made and various practices performed throughout the forty-nine-day period.

Representations of body, speech, and mind were offered to Kyabgön Dagchen Rinpoche and the other lamas who had presided over the ceremonies. Large amounts of delicious food offerings were made to the khenpos, tulkus, and monks who had been part of the assembly, each offering appropriate to the recipient. Details about how their hosts' offerings delighted the lamas, khenpos, and tulkus have been recorded separately.

From the *Samvarodaya Tantra*:

> Completely cast aside all other kinds of offerings and
> Endeavor to make perfect offerings to the guru;
> By pleasing him, you will obtain
> The supreme wisdom of omniscience.

And from the *Guhyagarbha Tantra*:

> To make offerings of the five riches to the Sovereign Lord
> Is to make offerings to all mandalas;
> What need, then, to speak of their retinues?
> All negativity will be purified.

And from the *General Essentialization of All the Wisdom of the Buddhas*:

> Know your guru to be more precious
> Than the one thousand buddhas of this fortunate kalpa,
> Since all the buddhas of this aeon
> Manifest having relied on their guru.

And from the *Tantra of the Gathering of Precious Jewels*:

> Remembering your guru for one instant is far better than
> Visualizing one hundred thousand deities
> For one hundred thousand kalpas:
> The merit is limitless.

And from the *Sutra of Immaculate Space*:

> Ananda, sugatas cannot be perceived by all sentient beings. As a spiritual friend teaches the Dharma to whomever perceives him, thereby planting the seed of liberation, consider your spiritual friend to be greater than the sugatas.

The sutras and tantras include extensive teachings about how making offerings to the guru surpass those made to all the buddhas, and so exemplary virtuous activities for accumulating vast amounts of merit were undertaken to fulfill all Chökyi Lodrö's enlightened intentions.

During the waxing moon in the seventh month, the day the ceremonies concluded, Ngor Ewam Thartse Khen Rinpoche recited elaborate prayers to dedicate the merit. The following day, monks performed the *Restoration of Vows Ceremony for Auspiciousness*. From then until the precious kudung was cremated, vast and elaborate cloud-like offerings were made daily. Tsok offering practices were performed on the tenth and twenty-fifth days, and on full and new moon days, the ritual practice for the spread of the teachings (*Sixteen Arhats Practice*), aspirations, and so on, were performed, combined with ceremonies for the restoration of vows. The system of observing the ceremonies for the restoration of vows and rains retreats was established in Sikkim from that time on, thanks to the enlightened aspiration of Khyentse Chökyi Lodrö.

From the *Sutra of the Abundant Array of Ornaments*:

> Manjushri, by merely looking at where one who teaches Dharma dwells, or at his bones or his decayed body, inexpiable actions will be purified.

It is said that anyone seeing no more than the mortal remains of a sublime master makes a spiritual connection with him that will bring them tremendous blessings and give their lives meaning. So countless people from far away places, especially Kham and central Tibet, were offered the opportunity to pay their respects to the precious kudung and given a little of the water in which it had been washed. This is how the kudung became an object of veneration that generated vast merit for everyone who prostrated to it, made offerings and aspiration prayers, and accumulated virtuous actions and abandoned nonvirtuous actions in its presence. Its power to generate merit came, without doubt, from Khyentse Chökyi Lodrö's prodigious enlightened wish to help sentient beings.

I, too, upon hearing the news of the dissolution of our Lord Guru's mind into the dharmadhatu, applied myself to the best of my ability to making offerings and prayers. I arrived in Gangtok immediately after the forty-ninth-day practices had been completed and made whatever offerings I could afford, and so on. For a week, Khamtrul Rinpoche and I, with some monks, performed the *Mindrolling Vajrasattva* and an elaborate tsok and other offerings sponsored by Chökyi Lodrö's nephew, who was also his treasurer.

On the tenth day of the second monkey month, one hundred elaborate tsok offerings and the confession and fulfillment practices from the rediscovered treasure teaching called the *Combined Practice of the Three Roots* were performed. In addition, I was able to grant the empowerments for the *Two Vimalas*, and so on, to enthusiastic and devoted students.

After completing forty-nine days of ceremonies, preparations for building the memorial stupas began. In addition to the print blocks of consecration mantras from the Mindrolling tradition that were already in Sikkim, new blocks were carved for the mantras needed for the consecration of the stupa of the *Two Vimalas*. The mantras were printed on bark paper, anointed with precious substances, cut, joined together, and then rolled and wrapped in cloth. Great care was taken not to add anything, leave anything out, or make any errors. Also, as required, volumes of tantra and dharani sutra texts, and chakras that bring liberation when seen and worn, were copied out.

Specific preparations were necessary: life shafts were fashioned perfectly from bodhi trees, essential consecration mantras and prayers were written in pure gold, three pairs of yaksha chakras were etched on gilded copperplates and were then wrapped in exquisite silk, offering accoutrements were made, and substances were gathered for the mandalas of the *Two Vimalas*. Many treasure vases for nagas, local deities, wealth gods, and dispelling inauspiciousness were gathered, each filled with the appropriate prescribed substances, including the five sets of five substances common to all the vases, various medicines for smoke offering, grains, silk brocade, cloth, powdered precious substances, and the essence of the elements such as earth and water, and so on. As a result of great diligence, lavish spending, and overcoming many hardships, all these substances were assembled.

Lama Jamyang Lodrö Chokden, Khyentse Chökyi Lodrö's shrine master, instructed the pure bhikshus and shramaneras in the practice traditions of the two Jamgöns, and they prepared all the materials very carefully and without haste. When they were ready, Khardo Shabdrung, Gyatön Rinpoche, and I (with a few assistants) blessed the consecration mantras, life shafts, volumes of text, chakras, and treasure vases many times by practicing the individual sadhanas, preceded by dispelling obstacles and purification and consecration rituals, while four skilled craftsmen from Drakyab assembled and gilded the beautifully crafted, yellow-copper memorial stupa.

Both Jamyang Khyentse Wangpo and Khyentse Chökyi Lodrö said it was best to cremate a precious kudung. With that advice in mind, we discussed taking it to one of the holy places—Bodh Gaya, for example. But Trulshik Pawo Dorje insisted that it be cremated at Tashiding, the holiest place in Sikkim. He said that to have the cremation at Tashiding and to build a memorial stupa there would lay the foundation for the precious teachings of the Buddha to spread throughout the world, including the hidden land of Sikkim, and for the teachings to remain in this world for a long time. He also said it would bring vast benefit to all beings because of the inconceivable auspicious circumstances created by a combination of the enlightened aspirations of the great Lhatsün Namkha Jigme, one of the previous incarnations of Khyentse Chökyi Lodrö, and the aspirations of our Lord Guru himself. Also, when Chökyi Lodrö had visited Nenang, he mentioned that some time earlier, the image of where he would leave his mortal remains had appeared clearly in a dream and in his wisdom mind, and that the place he saw had definitely been Tashiding. So Trulshik Pawo Dorje's insistence concurred with our Lord Guru's dream.

The old wrapping cloths were taken off the precious kundung and it was anointed with liquid gold. New syllables for the different parts of the body were made, and the old ones replaced. Many chakras that liberate when worn, as well as mantras from the Sarma and Nyingma tantras, some written in gold and others printed from woodblocks, were placed on the kudung, which was once again elegantly wrapped in silk brocade anointed with saffron water. A sambhogakaya costume with precious ornaments was then offered to it.

Accompanied by offerings and music, the kudung was then taken to Tashiding, the holiest of holy places in Sikkim, on a day deemed auspicious by astrologers during the waxing moon of the eleventh month. The *Restoration of Vows Ceremony for Auspiciousness* was performed, and after the astrological event called "the movement of the serpent,"[197] Acharya Gyatön Rinpoche and Khardo Shabdrung—who had accomplished the approach practice for the *Two Vimalas* sadhana—performed, with their assistants, the blessing of the land ritual based on the sadhana called *Unstained Light*. During the ritual, they placed a treasure vase on each of the four sides and in the center of the base on which the cremation stupa would be built. The treasure vases contained substances to invoke the blessings of both Luchen Norgay (the great naga who increases wealth) and Sa-nying Tenma (the essence of the earth tenma).

The cremation stupa was built on a square, stepped base, on which stood a lion throne with hearth doors. A purkhang in the shape of a mahaparinivana stupa was erected on top.[198] The precious kudung was placed at the center of the vase-shaped dome facing east. The upper section of the stupa was beautifully adorned with a parasol, victory banners, pendants, and so on, and elaborate offerings were made. Ngor Thartse Khenpo, Khangsar Shabdrung, Khenpo Yönten Zangpo, and others performed Hevajra, while Neten Chokling Rinpoche and Gyatön Rinpoche led the *Mindrolling Vajrasattva*, and the supreme tulku of Dodrupchen, Katok Jewön, and I performed the *Shitro Tromtruk* from the *Heart Essence of the Vast Expanse* treasure teaching.

Dzongsar Ngari Tulku, Khenpo Lodrö Zangpo, and others performed

Vajrayogini from Naropa's tradition. Khachö Tulku of Pema Yangtse and Serdrup Dungdzin performed the *Three Roots Practice for Accomplishing the Life-Force of the Vidyadharas*. About sixty of those participating in the five Sarma and Nyingma ritual groups cremated the precious kudung by making fire offerings inseparable from the main deity of each mandala. They also burnt fragrant firewood like white and red sandalwood, and aloewood.[199] After the rituals had been completed, the doors of the purkhang were sealed with the symbols of the five buddha families, and there followed three days of offerings.

At sunrise on the fourth day, the purkhang was opened, and all the bones and ashes were carefully gathered following traditional practices so that nothing was lost, then preserved as objects of veneration. A tsok feast and other offerings based on Vajrasattva practice were made, after which the shramaneras and bhikshus daily performed the ceremony for the restoration of vows and self-visualization practice.

Following the traditional instructions found in the sacred texts, they ground the bones and ashes into a fine powder, mixed it with large amounts of powdered precious and medicinal substances, and made more than two hundred tsa tsas. All the tsa tsas were painted with gold and silver then consecrated by two groups of pracitioners led by those who had accomplished the approach practice.

During the construction of the memorial stupa, with devotion and joy all Khyentse Chökyi Lodrö's students, young and old, from the newest monk to the highest incarnate master, diligently transported building materials by hand. What fragments remained from the purkhang and tsa tsas were put into the memorial stupa, which was built on the original foundation of the cremation stupa so that nothing was left out. The principal contents of the stupa's lion throne were chakras, everything necessary for the yaksha deities, different treasure vases representing wealth deities, and a magnetizing vase for dispelling inauspiciousness. Each was visualized and stabilized through their individual sadhana practices. Four steps were built around the square base of the lion throne. On the fourth step, a *Tsuktor Drime* mandala was placed and consecrated with its sadhana practice.

On an auspicious day, having completed the *Restoration of Vows Ceremony for Auspiciousness*, the life shaft was placed on the mandala of *Unstained Light* inside the vase-shaped dome and consecrated with the elaborate ritual for erecting the life shaft, led by those who had accomplished the approach practice.

The main contents of the stupa were what are known as the four (sometimes five) types of sacred relics, or *ringsel*:

1. *Relics like mustard seeds*:[200] One authentic relic of our guide Buddha Shakyamuni from the sacred relic collection of Desi Rinpungpa, a relic of Buddha Kashyapa that was a treasure revealed by Jatsön Nyingpo, many relics from a stupa in Nepal,[201] a relic that appeared on a tooth of Guru Rinpoche, and so on.
2. *Dharma relics*:[202] More than seven hundred sets of the five types of dharani; a great many short mantras;[203] about fifteen sets of Nyingma dharanis; numerous mantras of the peaceful and wrathful gurus and other name mantras;[204] a few pages of sacred terma scrolls and Sanskrit texts; the authentic handwriting of the previous Khyentse, which formed the initial basis from which Vishuddhi's *Golden Lettered Scroll* from the *Seven Profound Cycles* was deciphered; and a few sections of Khyentse Chökyi Lodrö's writings.
3. *Body relics*:[205] The bones of many great masters of the Sarma and Nyingma traditions, the most significant being omniscient Longchenpa's brain relic, and the precious bones of Khyentse Chökyi Lodrö painted gold with mantras of the yidam deities written on them, which were wrapped with cloth and encased in a casket.
4. *Clothing, hair, and nail relics,*[206] *and so on*: Many fragments of robes and locks of hair from early Sarma and Nyingma masters, the most important of which were Guru Rinpoche's robe, the hair of Nubchen Sangye Yeshe and Nyang Nyima Öser, Khyentse Chökyi Lodrö's hair and nails, and a complete set of white inner garments that Chökyi Lodrö had worn for the sake of auspiciousness on various occasions.
5. *Dharmakaya relics*:[207] Relics such as a stupa from Kushinagar, holy tsa tsas handmade by great masters of the Sarma and Nyingma traditions, and more than three thousand perfect tsa tsas made from the bones and ashes of Chökyi Lodrö.

In addition:

- *Body representations*:[208] A holy gilded bronze statue of Guru Rinpoche, a wonderful clay terma statue of Vajrapani, and so on.

- *Speech representations:*[209] Volumes of the root tantras of the *Embodiment of the Guru's Realization* and *Intensely Blazing Wisdom Wrathful Guru*; a complete root terma text of the *Heart Practice for Dispelling All Obstacles*; some volumes of sutras, tantras, and shastras, such as the *Magical Net of Manjushri*, the *Verse Summary of the Prajnaparamita Sutra*, and the *Treatise on the Sublime Continuum*; a few faultlessly prepared chakras, such as the chakra for keeping the life shaft stable, discovered by Guru Chöwang, and the great chakra for gathering the Sangha from the Namchö cycle of teachings.
- *Mind representations:*[210] A sacred red-bronze vajra.
- *Quality representations:*[211] A casket containing amrita blessed during many drupchens by Khyentse, Kongtrul, and Chokling and also Khyentse Chökyi Lodrö; some amrita pills; and various long-life pills.
- *Activity representations:*[212] A meteorite phurba that was the terma of Ngadak Nyang, Nyima Özer.

The tip of the conical spire above the life shaft was filled to the top with chakras that liberate when worn and a volume of chakras wrapped in silk that contained, for example, Tenpa Buchik and chakras prepared and consecrated by Khyentse Chökyi Lodrö. Also included was the "resting in the nature of mind chakra that liberates when seen" from the *Stupa of Shakyamuni That Liberates When Remembered*, and a section from the *Heart Practice for Dispelling All Obstacles* cycle of teachings. It was then covered with a sandalwood board. In the alcove of the dome was placed a statue of Vajra Akshobhya that liberates when seen, as described in the *Tukdrup* itself, made with Katok Öntrul's own hands. The statue was of standard proportions and filled with consecration substances. The apex of the stupa was a gilded, ornamented crown, on top of which sat a sun, moon, and pinnacle. Inside the apex was placed a chakra of Sittatapatra, a volume of Gyaltsen Tsemo, and great dharanis and objects that liberate when seen. By arranging the consecration substances in this way, the stupa of great enlightenment was built using pure and authentic methods and complied perfectly with the dimensions used by the previous Lord Khyentse when he built the great stupa that liberates when seen at the great Dharma center of Lhundrup Teng. The details of that stupa have been given in a separate catalog.

After the stupa had been completed, khenpos and tulkus made sumptuous offerings and led the assembly of monks from all traditions in a daylong consecration based on the sadhana of the rediscovered treasure, the *Combined Practice of the Three Roots*, and the *Restoration of Vows Ceremony for Auspiciousness*.

The following day, a grand consecration ceremony was performed by Thartse Khen Rinpoche, Khangsar Shabdrung, Khenpo Yönten Zangpo, Khenpo Lodrö Zangpo, and others based on Hevajra practice. Katok Öntrul, myself, and some monks performed the ceremony—with tsok and fulfillment offerings, commanding the dharmapalas to fulfill their commitments, acknowledgement of patrons, and so on—based on the practice of *Mindrolling Vajrasattva*. Gyatön Choktrul and his assistants[213] performed the sadhana practice for the *Stupa of Shakyamuni That Liberates When Remembered* and the sadhana of the *Akshobhya Statue That Liberates upon Being Seen*. As a result of these practices, the jnanasattvas dissolved into the stupa and were requested to remain.

This was how the memorial stupa—the outer representation known as Chödong Rinpoche Tashi Drolwa Zhiden Chinlap Palbar (The Precious Stupa Endowed with the Auspicious Four Liberations, Blazing Splendor of Blessing)—was blessed and empowered as the paramount representation of the dharmakaya transcending samsara and nirvana and a field of merit for all sentient beings, including gods. It was built and blessed so it would remain for as long as samsara exists to bring auspicious glory to the teachings and countless beings, beginning with the sacred hidden land of Sikkim. Again, a preceptor, acharyas, and monks endowed with good qualities said prayers for the spread of the teachings and recited elaborate aspiration and auspiciousness prayers combined with the ceremony for the restoration of vows—activities that greatly increased the virtue of beings and the auspiciousness of the place.

The benefits of building such stupas and their purpose are as follows.

In the dharani sutras[214] and the sutras of the five great dharanis with descriptions of each, as well as the verses on circumambulating stupas, and so on, Buddha explained the good that comes from building or renovating a stupa that contains as its heart essence the four (or five) types of relic. He also explained the value of paying homage to it, making material offerings and offerings of respect and reverence. In particular, he explained the value of building a stupa using the correct procedures for installing the life shaft combined with the mandala of the *Two Vimalas*.

The contents of this stupa are exactly as Buddha had described them and included the chakras that liberate when worn, chakras that liberate when seen, the stupa that liberates when thought of, the statue of Akshobhya, the resting in the nature of mind chakra that liberates when seen, texts, and treasure vases. Everything that is customarily included had been correctly prepared as stipulated in the sacred texts and inserted into the stupa. Each item is said to bring great benefit. Therefore logically,[215] there is no doubt that the stupa is a sublime source of benefit for the teachings and beings, and that it is an unsurpassed field of merit that brings liberation through the four liberations. (Consult the individual texts for further details.)

In this case, as confirmed by the sacred texts, the place a great master attains nirvana is an unfabricated and spontaneously present buddhafield, an intrinsic display of wisdom. This truth inspired unwavering confidence in the mind of Khyentse Chökyi Lodrö's consort. She aspired to serve her glorious vajradhara master by both fulfilling his profound, enlightened wish and creating a field of merit for beings. She therefore also wanted to build a stupa the same height as Khyentse Chökyi Lodrö that would be placed in his residence as the inner representation. To honor her wish, a gilded bronze stupa of that height was made, along with a stupa a little taller than the length of an arrow, which was to be sent to Khyentse Chökyi Lodrö's seat in Tibet once the mayhem had died down.

During the waxing moon in the first month of the year of the iron rat (1960), consecration dharanis and substances were inserted into both stupas from the foundations up. A chakra of the *Two Vimalas* and a life shaft were put into the larger stupa during elaborate rituals, and the required number of tsa tsas made from clay mixed with Chökyi Lodrö's ground-up bones were also inserted.

The two principal contents of the smaller stupa were the chakra of *Unstained Light* that was specially drawn on the base and was the same as the chakra used for the *Stupa of Shakyamuni That Liberates When Remembered* and a consecrated life shaft. For the inner contents, apart from including fewer tsa tsas, most of the substances that filled the stupa at Tashiding (the outer representation) were also placed in the stupas made for the monastery and residence (the inner representations). An extraordinary, holy, gilded bronze statue of Vajradhara, about a hand-span high, was placed in the alcove of the larger stupa's dome, and a holy bronze statue of Avalokiteshvara was put into that of the smaller stupa. The dimensions of both these stupas had all the characteristics of the stupa of enlightenment at Tashiding and were painted with as much gold. They were beautifully adorned with all the excellent ornaments,[216] turquoise, coral, dzi, agate, amber, pearls, and diamonds, and with consecration mantras. Substances were also put into many other form representations.

Once the stupas were complete and other representations filled, on an auspicious day during the waxing moon in the second month, a gathering of practitioners, led by the Venerable Tai Situ Choktrul Rinpoche of Palpung, performed the consecration based on the sadhana of the *Profound Heart Essence of the Embodiment of the Three Jewels*. From the space of his wisdom mind, the great Gyalwang Karmapa also performed an extraordinary consecration of the representations.

During the waxing moon in the fifth month, on a day that coincided with the offering ceremony for the anniversary of the enlightenment of Khyentse Chökyi Lodrö, a one-day consecration ritual was again performed, led by Dagtri Rinpoche, the Supreme Protector and Lord of Refuge of the glorious Sakya tradition. The jnanasattvas were dissolved into the stupas and repeatedly requested to remain throughout numerous consecration practices.

The supreme and extraordinary field of merit for beings, including gods, was kept in the place where Khyentse Chökyi Lodrö had attained perfect enlightenment, on the ground floor of his residence at Tsuglakhang in Gangtok, Sikkim, the great Akanishta Palace of the array of vajras, the Dharma grove of the Rime teachings, and the center of our supreme Lord Guru's vast activities to benefit the teachings and beings.

Appreciation was shown to the masters, ordinary monks, craftsmen, and artisans involved in the cremation and funeral services through material offerings and money that pleased and gratified them. I haven't gone into detail about how much was offered and spent in order to accumulate this pure merit, uncontaminated by negative actions, as I shrink from committing the fault of boasting about virtuous activities. However, the cost of the materials used can be deduced from the abundant meritorious activities that resulted.

The daily offerings, offerings made on special occasions to the reliquary (the precious dharmakaya stupa, built following the procedures I've already mentioned), and those made inside Khyentse Chökyi Lodrö's residence included many water offerings, rows of lamps, several butter lamps that burned continuously, elaborate offerings made on full and new moon days and the eighth and sixth days of the month, and tsok and fulfillment offerings on the tenth and twenty-fifth days.

The *Vinaya Sutra* states,

Celebrate the special days!
Celebrate birthdays,
Haircutting ceremonies,
Ordination, and
The attainment of enlightenment.

Therefore, to celebrate the anniversary of our Venerable Lord Guru's mahaparinirvana, the following practices were performed for one week: the fulfillment practice of *Vimalamitra's Guru Yoga Called the "Essence of Blessings"* from the cycle of the *Heart Essence of Deathless Arya Tara* and the mind treasure teachings of the previous Lord, Khyentse Wangpo. The anniversary fell in the first monkey month, and one hundred elaborate tsok offerings were made based on the sadhana of the *Secret Practice of the Heart Essence of the Lotus-Born* and performed annually from then on.

In the winter of that year, to fulfill the enlightened wishes of Khyentse Chökyi Lodrö, the supreme consort traveled to the holy places in India to make the final offerings in his memory. She made elaborate offerings at Bodh Gaya, including ten thousand butter lamps, plus various supplementary offerings. Garlands of electric lights burnt throughout the night, both inside and outside the Gandola (the main stupa at Bodh Gaya), and so on. She also offered tea and money to the monks at the monastery, and offerings were made at the Tibetan monastery in Varanasi. She also made elaborate offerings at Tso Pema and all the other important holy places. She sponsored the whitewashing and anointing with fragrant perfumes of the three stupas in Nepal, offered clothes, and made one thousand elaborate butter lamp offerings at each. At Yangleshö (Pharping), she made tsok offerings, and so on, and the relevant practices, supplications, and aspiration prayers were performed over and over again.

In addition to the memorial services, embalming salts suffused with the sacred body's fluids were distributed to those devotees who wanted them, and a huge amount of salts were thrown into the river Ganges. Guru Rinpoche's biography states that the flesh of one who had taken birth as a Brahmin seven times is "great amrita," and Guru Rinpoche himself predicted that this kind of amrita would benefit beings immensely. He also said that the flesh of all the incarnations of Gyalse Lhaje[217] would retain the same kind of blessings, which Orgyen Lingpa explained later in his book about kudung, and which omniscient Jigme Lingpa[218] confirmed. Just as the flesh of a Brahmin (the great amrita that liberates when tasted) is immensely beneficial, the embalming salt used to preserve Khyentse Chökyi Lodrö's body brought inconceivable blessings to those beings who came into contact with it.

In short, everyone from all walks of life who relied on Khyentse Chökyi Lodrö practiced virtue commensurate with their mental capacity by one-pointedly persevering, in every way, to fulfill his enlightened wishes. To persist in fulfilling the enlightened wishes of the Guru brings inconceivable benefit and is the supreme kind of accumulation and purification. This is explained in the *Tantra on Recognizing the Qualities of the Guru*, which is part of the root tantra of Kalachakra:

> The result of any virtuous deed undertaken for the welfare of
>   the dead
> By relatives left behind
> Follows the dead person wherever they take rebirth,
> Like a calf follows behind its mother.
> Likewise, if devoted students make offerings with yearning devotion
> After the teacher passes into nirvana,
> His wishes will be completely fulfilled,
> And the students will attain the qualities of the master.
> Having recorded the exact day, month, and year of the master's
>   passing away,
> If offerings are made,
> Overwhelming negative actions accumulated throughout aeons will
>   be destroyed, and
> Liberation from the terrifying city of the Lord of Death will be
>   achieved.
> Even giving eyes to the blind of three thousand worlds,
> Or strengthening the life-force of those whose life-force has
>   degenerated,
> Or placing the same number of beings in the state of arhatship
> And making offerings to them for aeons does not equal the merit.
> Even negative actions committed throughout countless aeons
> Will be pacified without trace, just as the sun dispels darkness.

Therefore, as explained extensively in the vajra words of the tantras, making offerings to the guru brings vast benefits.

Throughout all these virtuous activities, the Sovereign Lord, the Dharma

King of Sikkim, Palden Döndrup Namgyal, and the Queen Mother, with unwavering devotion and pure samaya, offered their unequaled support. They also always cared for the students who had been left behind with great kindness. All their incomparable and generous support—sublime in nature and worthy of praise, offered with pure samaya to repay the kindness of the precious Manjushri Guru for having given them so many teachings—is truly a cause for rejoicing.

Part Two: The Special Explanation of the Extraordinary Biography

In two parts: the inner biography and the secret biography

The Inner Biography

*An Account of
Jamyang Khyentse Chökyi Lodrö's Inner Life*

The "inner biography," which is divided into three sections, tells of Khyentse Chökyi Lodrö's visionary experiences as he gained mastery over pure perception by practicing the profound yogas.

To begin with, I will show how Khyentse Chökyi Lodrö established himself as the true sovereign holder of the eight great chariots of the practice lineage, the master who illuminated the entire tradition of empowerment and instruction, and I will set out his experiences and visions as they relate to the different lineages.[219]

In the words of the great scholar and siddha Prajnarashmi (Sherab Özer):

> Passed down faultlessly from the glorious Vajradhara,
> The eight great traditions of the practice lineage in the Land
>   of Snows
> Are the legacy of the great siddhas of the past.
> Those who long for liberation must also follow this path.

And omniscient Gun Sagara (Kongtrul Yönten Gyatso) wrote,

> The eight great chariots of the practice lineage in the Land of
>   Tibet are
> Nyingma, Kadam, Lamdre (Sakya), Kagyü, Shangpa, Shije,
>   Jordruk, and Nyendrup.

With tremendous compassion and kindness, the noble lotsawas and panditas brought all the sacred texts, instructions, and pith instructions of the eight great chariots of the practice lineage to Tibet. By practicing them and attaining the fruition of supreme accomplishment, each of those sublime practitioners brought countless suffering beings to the state of supreme enlightenment.

Omniscient Jamyang Khyentse Wangpo zealously gathered all existing unbroken lineage transmissions by receiving them himself and then practicing them for a long time. Again and again, Khyentse Wangpo had visions of and received blessings from each of the great sovereign holders of the eight great practice lineages and of the yidam deities and dakinis. He was therefore able to receive in pure visions the extraordinary direct lineage transmissions of the oral instructions (empowerments, commentaries, and oral instructions), which he then gave to great masters of all lineages.

More specifically, Khyentse Wangpo gave the complete transmission of all the teachings of the eight great practice lineages to noble Jamgön Lodrö Taye, thereby ensuring the continuity of the teachings—it was like pouring water from one vase into another. Khyentse Chökyi Lodrö, in turn, received all these transmissions in their most detailed form, having first thoroughly examined their authenticity. He received the most important transmissions many times, practiced them, and transmitted them to other teachers. This was how he was able to leave a legacy that is, in every respect, without equal. And given everything I've told you here, it is clear that he was the true illuminator of the eight great practice lineages.

Here are a few examples of how our omniscient, Venerable Lord Guru received the authoritative transmissions in pure visions.

(a) How Jamyang Khyentse Chökyi Lodrö became a true holder of the teachings of the Nyingma school.

It was at Katok Dorje Den, a Nyingma Dharma center, that Khyentse Chökyi was first recognized as the supreme emanation of omniscient Khyentse Wangpo. It was also where he received the *Three Precepts*, perfected his studies, and contemplated the sutras, tantras, and minor sciences.

One of the distinguishing factors establishing noble Jamgön Khyentse Wangpo as the great sovereign of all the teachings of the Buddha in the Land of Snows was that he held the lineage of the secret treasury of the *Seven Transmissions* that emanated principally from the Kama and Terma traditions of the Nyingma school. Therefore, following Khyentse Wangpo's extraordinary example, Khyentse Chökyi Lodrö received the most precious essential teachings from masters like mahapandita Katok Situ, Shechen Gyaltsab Rinpoche, omniscient Dodrupchen Tenpe Nyima, Terchen Lerab Lingpa, and Drukpa Vajradhara Natsok Rangdrol—the teachings he received were those closest to the hearts of each of these great masters. They had all been students of the two Jamgöns and were great illuminators of the Nyingma teachings, endowed with the qualities of perfect learning and realization. All these masters empowered Khyentse Chökyi Lodrö as the holder of these teachings and transferred their wisdom minds to him.

Manjushri Mipham Rinpoche, who could see Khyentse Chökyi Lodrö's future, also expressed his admiration, saying, "The supreme emanation of my Guru Khyentse Rinpoche, who lives at Dzongsar Monastery, will become an extraordinary teacher." Khyentse Chökyi Lodrö lived up to this tribute by performing to perfection the approach, close approach, accomplishment, and great accomplishment practices for the infinite three roots deities of Kama and Terma. He also practiced the profound completion meditation and particularly the luminous Dzogpachenpo's samadhi of all-pervasive wisdom, from which he never wavered. He was a sky-like yogi of the great expanse.

Khyentse Chökyi Lodrö taught both greater and lesser tantras—for example, the *Two Vimalas of the Nyingma Kama*. Most notably he gave

- empowerments and explanations for each of the complete cycles of the three inner yoga tantras;
- the explanation of the *King of Tantras* (the *Guhyagarbha Tantra*), the *Magical Net of Manjushri*, and the *General Essentialization of All the Wisdom of the Buddhas*; and
- the transmissions for all the texts related to these tantras and for the *One Hundred Thousand Precious Tantras of the Nyingma*.

He gave empowerments and oral transmissions, as well as transmissions and explanations for all the existing undisputed treasure teachings of authentic treasure revealers, including the three supreme emanations, the twelve great lingpas, the three immaculate ones, the later tertöns such as the three powerful vidyadharas, Lerab Lingpa, and Drime Pema Lingpa and his sons.

He also gave the *Precious Treasury of Terma Teachings* continuously to teachers of the Nyingma school, exactly as each teacher wished. As a result of this continuous stream of transmission, the Fifth Shechen Rabjam Rinpoche gave the transmission of the *Rinchen Terdzö* at the great monastery of Ogmin Orgyen Mindrolling, and the transmission of Kama and Terma teachings of the Nyingma spread widely from Kham and the upper and lower regions of Tibet to Rekong in the north. It was also possible to print a complete set of tsagli for the mandalas of the *Rinchen Terdzö*.

Omniscient Khyentse Wangpo had deeply revered the Kama teachings, hailing them as the life-force of the Nyingma teachings. He had urged Terchen Chokling to receive the explanation of the *Guhyagarbha Tantra* in order to ignite his innate and acquired knowledge and had repeatedly told Palyul Gyatrül Do-ngak Tenzin and other teachers that the Kama were the most important teachings in the Nyingma school. And just as his predecessor had done before him, Khyentse Chökyi Lodrö also gave the transmission of the Kama a number of times during his life.

Through these activities, Khyentse Chökyi Lodrö provided exceptional support for the teaching lineages of Katok, Palyul, Shechen, Dzogchen, and the upper and lower seats of Chokling. In the shedras of these monasteries, he established the tradition of teaching and studying the writings of scholars and siddhas—like the masters of So, Zur, and Nub—and particularly the tradition of giving students a basic understanding of the writings of omniscient Rongzompa and Longchenpa, as clarified by the excellent works of Jamgön Mipham Rinpoche. He became the sole crown ornament of the boundless lineage holders of the Nyingma tradition, especially in those Dharma centers where he established the traditions I've already mentioned. His intention and activities were peerless in every respect and illuminated the Nyingma lineage in its authentic form. Thus, he was the great universal Lord of the Vidyadharas in the Nyingma lineage.

Khyentse Chökyi Lodrö continually had visions and received blessings from deities, vidyadharas, and dakinis who were the embodiment of luminous wisdom. Here are just a few of his infinite pure visionary experiences, exactly as he described them in his notebook:

> In the year of the fire monkey (1956), on the twenty-ninth day of the tenth month, I arrived at Tso Pema[220] and circumambulated the lake. After returning to the rest house, a strong feeling of devotion arose in my mind, and I saw Guru Rinpoche in a pure vision, his body transparent white light. Moved by this experience, a powerful urge to write a guru yoga sadhana arose in my mind, so I wrote one instantly.

In the same year, on the nineteenth day of the second ninth month, during the night I spent at Drulzhung Dzagak, I experienced pain in my upper torso and abdomen, which was cured by a special Tibetan medicine (*gitik*) and the blessings of Guru Rinpoche.

On the twentieth day, on my way down from Drulzhung Dzagak, I had a vision of Guru Tsokye Dorje Chang (the Lotus-Born Vajradhara Guru) in a form similar to the one described in the *Seven-Line Prayer Guru Yoga* by Mipham Rinpoche. As a result of this experience, Tsarchen Rinpoche's guru yoga appeared in my mind.

On the nineteenth day of the second ninth month, on my way down from Thangkhu, a gentle shower of rain fell as I passed through a dense forest. The sky was a brilliant blue, with clouds billowing right and left. Inspired by such beauty, I felt joyful and relaxed, and a mirage-like vision of Guru Rinpoche, wearing a hidden garment and brocade robe adorned with bone ornaments and dry skulls, appeared in the midst of the blue sky. In his raised right hand, he held a vajra; his other adornments were those usually worn by a Zahor-style Guru Rinpoche. Saraha, Shavaripa, Kukuripa, Maitripa and Marpa Lotsawa, and other masters also appeared.

> I say that I see with my eyes,
> Yet I must gaze with the eye that cannot see.
> It seems the experience of a false vision
> Has deceived this careless old man.

In the year of the fire rooster (1957), on the ninth day of the fifth month (as the tenth day was missing from the calendar), while performing the tsok practice from the *Heart Practice for Dispelling All Obstacles* sponsored by the Queen Mother of Sikkim, my devotion to Guru Rinpoche blazed. Feeling both joy and sadness, I experienced a hazy vision of Guru Rinpoche surrounded by a host of dakinis. They all kindly granted me great confidence so I wouldn't fear the turbulent times ahead . . . but self-created, deceptive experiences are not to be trusted.

Khyentse Chökyi Lodrö always said that in times of need, visions and prophecies were revealed to him whenever he prayed to Guru Rinpoche.

The sacred vajra places of central Tibet had been blessed by great learnèd and accomplished vidyadharas and were therefore inseparable from the primordially perfect holy places. Just by visiting them, Khyentse Wangpo experienced visions of yidam deities and dakinis who blessed him and entrusted him with the treasury of Dharma, and so on—accounts of which appear in his *Great Biography*. Khyentse Chökyi Lodrö had similar experiences and visions, as you will see if you compare Khyentse Wangpo's visions with the extraordinary pure visions recorded here:

> In the ninth month of the year of the fire rooster (1957) I went to Sengchen Namkyin in the mountains of Darjeeling to see the sunrise. As I gazed at the rising sun, I remembered that Mount Wutai Shan in China also lay in that direction, and tremendous faith in Vimalamitra arose in my mind. As a result, in a pure vision, I saw Vimalamitra descend slowly on rays of sunlight, then dissolve into me.
>
> While I was accumulating the *Guru Yoga of Vimalamitra*, I dreamt I read a few passages from a large, old volume of Dzogchen instructions. The first few pages were missing, and the book itself was ancient, with wide pages and closely written text that squeezed many lines onto each page—like a king's text of yellow parchment.
>
> One night, I dreamt I was in a temple giving the body, speech, and mind blessing empowerments for the *Guru Yoga of Vimalamitra* from the treasure teachings of Khyentse Wangpo to a crowd of monks and laypeople. I also dreamt I received tantra teachings from Jamgön Lekpa Rinpoche, who said he would come back and read the remainder of the text once I had reached the age of sixty-seven.
>
> During the night I spent in the lower part of Tro Dzong, I dreamt that two volumes of Vajrakilaya texts wrapped in black silk (one from the Rong tradition and the other from the Rok) appeared in the hands of Jamgön Lekpa Rinpoche. We read the *Commentary on Vajrakilaya Called the "Black Collected Words"* (*Phur Drel Bum Nak*) from them and talked a lot.
>
> At daybreak one day in the year of the earth dog (1958), I saw

in a vivid dream a luminous blue body about the size of an eight-year-old child. It might have been the main deity of the *Guhyasamaja Tantra*, or the *Magical Net*, or Akshobhya Buddha. I had this dream as I was about to complete one hundred thousand recitations of the *Do Gyü Ma*[221] prayer and while I was teaching the *Guhyagarbha Tantra*.

In the year of the fire rabbit (1927), on the twelfth day of the seventh month, while I was staying at Katok Monastery, I saw in a dream a great many ancient and modern texts stacked inside a house. I was sitting at a window, and in front of me sat an old man who looked like a nomad and was wearing a huge, greasy animal skin. He said he was Nubchen Sangye Yeshe. Intending to request teachings on the commentary to the *General Essentialization of All the Wisdom of the Buddhas,* I said, "It is said that before spreading the lineage transmission of these teachings, one should read them all first and only then give the transmission to others. As the number of volumes—said to be around four hundred—exceeds those of the *Kangyur*, that's impossible for me to do."

The old man replied, "Since these texts are the commentaries on the *General Essentialization of All the Wisdom of the Buddhas*, you may receive them all."

I think he said this because all the sutras and tantras of Sarma and Nyingma are contained in the *General Essentialization of All the Wisdom of the Buddhas*, which is the great secret treasury of all the teachings of the Buddha. He then appeared to authorize me to teach about forty volumes of ancient texts and placed a few others in my hands. After that, the old man transformed into the Sovereign Lord Marpa, russet-colored and with a large goiter in his neck. In my dream, I was convinced that he was Marpa, Hevajra in human form, and felt immense devotion for him. As a result, I had a vision of Hevajra, and the wish to receive an empowerment arose in my mind. Then the russet-colored man's lips moved as if he were reciting something, but I couldn't hear his voice. I woke up after many such dreams, but couldn't remember what had happened in detail—I forgot things because of obscurations caused by offerings I had misused.

In the year of the fire monkey (1956), on the fifteenth night of the twelfth month in Gangtok, Sikkim, I dreamt I entered a small temple inside which stood, in the midst of a pile of white offering scarves, a life-size statue with a round head—possibly the great early Nyingma vidyadhara, Nubchen (Sangye Yeshe). The statue then transformed into an actual person, and as he touched my forehead with his right hand, I felt his body shake and was filled with both joy and fear. Nubchen then recited a stanza of a prayer to Guru Rinpoche:

> Embodiment of the three roots, King of the Victorious Ones, Padmakara,
> I pray to you from the state of inseparability:
> May all diseases, malevolent spirits, and obstacles be pacified,
> The two benefits accomplished, and all our aspirations spontaneously fulfilled.

In a corner, a clay statue appeared, the height of a forearm. It resembled Phagmo Drupa, fat with a big belly and a broad, chubby face. He was wearing a meditation belt with his knees half raised. In his right hand, he held a horn trumpet into which he blew, and in his left hand, which was in meditation mudra, lay a skull cup. I felt he was one of my former incarnations. And in my dream, I also saw the Sanskrit word *samyaksam* ("perfect").

On the twenty-seventh night of the third month in the year of the fire rooster (1957), I dreamt I visited a Dharma library. The rooms had very high ceilings and contained countless stacks of texts, including some that were quite thick, with their pages edged in dark red. They looked a bit like the Narthang edition of the *Kangyur* and *Tengyur*, but when I examined them, I saw they were the *General Essentialization of All the Wisdom of the Buddhas* and other texts associated with that sutra. Chokden said the texts were the treasure teachings of Guru Chöwang. I replied I didn't know that these teachings were among those revealed by Chöwang. Then I opened a few volumes and found they were commentaries on various Nyingma tantras that had been revealed by Nyang (Nyima Özer). In my dream, I read them for a long time.

In the year of the fire monkey (1956), I visited Lhodrak Mrawochok. As I approached the monastery from below, I saw Lama

Ngadak Chenpo. He had a huge body and was dressed as an upasaka with a topknot of matted hair. He held a vajra in his right hand and a skull cup in his left. At the end of the vision, I experienced Lama Ngadak Chenpo dissolving into me.

Earlier, when Khyentse Chökyi Lodrö was living at Dzongsar, I made a request. "I've heard from Tulku Aben that an empowerment manual for Samten Lingpa's *Mandala of the Eight Great Deities: The Subduer of Haughty Spirits* still exists. If you ever find it, as neither the text nor the empowerment lineage exists in the *Precious Treasury of Terma Teachings*, I entreat you to bestow the empowerment upon me."

Chökyi Lodrö replied, "Last night I dreamt I received a text, which may be an indication that I will find it."

On the twenty-fifth night of the second month in the year of the fire monkey (1956), as I lay in a light sleep at Ogmin Orgyen Mindrolling, I saw omniscient Longchenpa in the form of an eight-year-old boy wearing a pandita hat and red robes. His hands were resting in the subjugating the earth mudra and five-colored lights streamed skywards from his upper torso. I experienced this vision for a long time.

Khyentse Chökyi Lodrö mentions other visions he experienced of that master in the colophon to the guru yoga of Longchenpa and of receiving his blessings. In his autobiography, he also wrote about receiving blessings from Longchen Rabjam in pure visions. I also heard Khyentse Chökyi Lodrö say that when he received the empowerments of the *Innermost Secret Guru Yoga Called the "Sealed Quintessence"* from the supreme Dodrup Tulku, Jigme Tenpe Nyima, he actually saw the guru as omniscient Longchenpa himself.

On the seventeenth day of the second month, while performing the consecration practice for the empowerments of Dorje Lingpa's cycle of teachings, *Luminous Expanse*, I had a brief vision of Minling Terchen. He transformed into the bodhisattva Dorje Lingpa, wearing blue clothes with long sleeves. His lower body was wrapped in a cloak, and he wore a blue lotus hat. Dorje Lingpa emanated many mandalas and gave me the empowerments for his treasure teachings. Finally, he gave me many volumes of texts.

Later, when Khyentse Chökyi Lodrö granted Khenchen Nüden of Katok Monastery and others the transmission of Vimalamitra's commentaries, like the *Reverberation of Sound*, from the seventeen tantra texts that had just been found, I asked our Lord Guru, almost jokingly, if it was appropriate to consider the oral transmission a direct lineage transmission. He replied, "Because these commentaries have almost the same meaning as that of the *Treasury of the Supreme Vehicle* and other texts in the *Seven Treasuries*, I have in effect received the *Seven Treasuries* many times. And as these texts are still available, I feel it would be good to give the transmission lineage a name.[222] So today, at the seat of Khyentse Wangpo, I have given the oral transmission to mark the auspicious beginning of the first propagation of this lineage of empowerments, instructions, and oral transmissions."

His words must have carried deep meaning.

(b) Jamyang Khyentse Chökyi Lodrö's visions and experiences related to the Kadam lineage.

Khyentse Chökyi Lodrö deeply revered and spoke highly of the activities and lives of the great kalyanamitras, the sovereign lineage holders of the precious Kadampa tradition. He also greatly admired associated teaching traditions characterized by the seven sublime Dharmas—like those of Jowo Je Atisha and his heart-sons, the Lord Lama Tsongkhapa, and so on—and always made elaborate offerings on their anniversaries. In this way, he opened wide the door of offering and generosity and tirelessly and unceasingly accumulated merit and purified obscurations.

I heard him acknowledge that, having perfected relative and absolute bodhichitta, by putting into practice all the teachings, advice, and oral instructions from the precious Kadampa tradition—specifically, teachings on the graduated path such as the *Lamp for the Path to Enlightenment* and the elaborate and essentialized teachings on training the mind—human and nonhuman obstacles to his life and activities could never defeat him, and his inner realization had been enhanced. He always stressed the great importance of training the mind in loving-kindness, compassion, and bodhichitta.

Khyentse Chökyi Lodrö established Thubten Shedrup Dargye Ling as a new center in the Dome[223] region, where the five volumes of philosophy expounded by the two great Indian pioneers, Nagarjuna and Asanga, would be taught and studied. He framed rules based on the Vinaya teachings for this Sangha of monks, who continually sounded the gong of Dharma by teaching and debating one thousand streams of excellent Dharma.

At various times, Khyentse Chökyi Lodrö made a point of receiving from sublime teachers the empowerments and instructions for Guhyasamaja, Chakrasamvara, Vajrabhairava, and so on.

The Sovereign Lord of all the teachings of the Buddha, the great Lord Protector, the Thirteenth Dalai Lama, Thubten Gyatso, and the Fourteenth Dalai Lama, Tenzin Gyatso, both cared for Khyentse Chökyi Lodrö with extraordinary kindness, filled his mind with the nectar of teachings, and empowered him by showering him with bouquets of praise. A great many masters of the old[224] and new[225] Kadampa schools personally received teachings from him or received them indirectly through one of the other lineage masters he taught. As such, he was truly a great upholder of the Kadampa lineage.

Khyentse Chökyi Lodrö's pure visions and experiences related to the Kadampa lineage were as follows.

In the colophon of the guru yoga of Jowo Je (Atisha), composed during his first visit to central Tibet, Khyentse Chökyi Lodrö mentions having visions of Jowo Je and his heart-son Dromtönpa and receiving blessings from them.

> On the nineteenth day of the ninth month, in the year of the wood sheep (1955), as I circumambulated the temple of Radreng, I saw in a vision a white, four-armed Avalokiteshvara with Jowo Je Atisha and Dromtönpa on either side of him, sitting with the three brothers[226] on the turquoise cypress tree of Shelding to the east. Moved by the experience, I recited prayers, received empowerments, and so on.
>
> In Dromtönpa's room, I had a clear vision of Lord Dromtönpa. At his heart in a sphere of light were many deities—Achala and others—from whom streamed tremendous rays of light. I made offerings, entreaties, and so on, with great faith and confidence. But could this illusory experience really have been a pure vision? It's far more likely to have been a deluded mental fabrication that sprang from overzealous devotion.
>
> On the twentieth day, I circumambulated the rock to the west on which the naturally arisen image of a horse could be seen, where I scattered my hair and nails. I rested under the

juniper tree behind the rock and saw a pure vision in the clear blue sky directly above the tree of the gurus of three Kadampa lineages, Jowo Je and his heart-son Dromtönpa, plus an inconceivable number of yidam deities and dharmapalas. From the gurus and deities, a thick cloud of countless spheres of rainbow light, adorned with a variety of hand implements, radiated like specks of dust in a shaft of sunlight and dissolved into me. Then everything gathered and dissolved into Jowo Je and Dromtönpa, and Dromtönpa dissolved into Jowo Je, at whose heart stood the great mother. Jowo Je then dissolved into the great mother who, in turn, dissolved into the bright yellow bindu at her heart. And finally, the bindu dissolved into me, sending a slight tremor through my body.

I received the direct lineage transmission of Guhyasamaja from the Venerable master Tsongkhapa in a pure vision. Later in the vision, I found a volume of vajra songs that included a *Calling the Guru from Afar*.[227] I showed the book to Venerable Tsongkhapa and requested the oral transmission and wisdom blessing[228] for the direct lineage of Guhyasamaja. In response to my request, Venerable master Tsongkhapa placed the text of *Four Combined Commentaries on the Guhyasamaja Tantra* (which had belonged to the previous Khyentse Wangpo) on my head and performed the wisdom blessing and aspiration prayer.

When I offered Khyentse Chökyi Lodrö the explanation of the *Four Combined Commentaries on the Guhyasamaja Tantra*, he said, "Although omniscient Khyentse Wangpo had a strong desire to teach the *Guhyasamaja Tantra*, his wish was never fulfilled. That today, at this great seat, we have been able to teach and study it is of tremendous significance."

He also said, "Although my imperfect perception cannot be trusted, I have seen the Venerable master Tsongkhapa on many occasions; at times his body was as large as Mount Meru, and at others it was the size of an average human being."

I heard this from Khyentse Chökyi Lodrö himself.

In the year of the earth snake (1929), as the moon waxed during the eleventh month, I dreamt that wearing a monk's red robe, I climbed a stone staircase to an assembly hall where I prostrated to a statue of the great Buddha Shakyamuni. Then, as I returned to the courtyard, having completed the recitation of the seven-branch prayer from the *Prayer of Excellent Conduct*, a tall lama appeared wearing a monk's red shawl and accompanied by an attendant I believed to be Tukwan Dorje Chang Lobsang Tenpe Wangchuk.

(c) Concerning the Lamdre, the precious words that have the four valid factors.

The previous omniscient Khyentse Wangpo was recognized and brought up as the tulku of Ngor Ewam Thartse Khenchen at Dzongsar Tashi Lhatse, the great Dharma center associated with the glorious Sakya lineage and the main seat of two successive incarnations of Khyentse Rinpoche. They both lived there for their entire lives. Khyentse Chökyi Lodrö was also the closest heart-son of numerous sublime lineage holders of the Sakya and Ngor traditions—primarily, vajradhara in human form, Sangdak Jamyang Loter Wangpo and Jamgön Ngawang Lekpa, who had been the principal students of the previous Lord (Khyentse Wangpo).

With great perseverance, Chökyi Lodrö received all the existing teachings transmitted through this tradition again and again. He continually practiced the yogas of visualizing deities, reciting mantras, and accomplishing the completion meditation associated with those teachings. He also received blessings from the gurus and yidam deities in pure visions, and acknowledged that he had attained the confidence to be able to command dharmapalas—including Gur Mahakala, Zhal, and others—to serve him and the teachings. He received blessings from Vajrayogini and attained the signs of having accomplished the three blazings and three gatherings. He performed the approach and accomplishment practices and ritual practices for empowerments and teachings precisely according to the specific practice traditions of Sakya, Ngor, and Tsar—proof that he was the supreme vajradhara. And he gave empowerments, blessings, and authorization blessings for the teachings of the outer and inner tantras that were included in the Sakya, Ngor, and Tsar lineages. These lineages hold the historical designation of "sovereign holders of all the teachings of the Buddha in the Land of Snows" and are known as the Sakyapa tradition.

Khyentse Chökyi Lodrö also often gave explanations for the completion meditation teachings and tantras, as well as oral transmissions for the collected writings of various Sakyapa masters. He helped disseminate the teachings of omniscient Gorampa Sonam Senge, who explained the points of view of the founding masters of the Sakya school according to the great Indian treatises, by establishing study centers where students were taught through reasoning and by reinforcing arguments with appropriate quotations from the sacred texts. He also established retreat centers where, through meditation and sadhana practice, the great secret oral lineage of instructions from *Path and Fruition: The Explanation for Private Disciples* were practiced. As a result, these study and practice lineages spread throughout Tibet, and Khyentse Chökyi Lodrö was hailed as the sovereign holder of the ocean of great secret tantras.

He built numerous magnificent temples and representations of body, speech, and mind—mostly at the great monastic seats—and established the elaborate drupchö of Vajrakilaya (the Dharma teachings from the Khön lineage handed down from father to son), the details of which have already been mentioned.

Basically, Khyentse Chökyi Lodrö was responsible for the propagation of the teaching, practice, and activity of all lineages of the Jamgön Sakyapas throughout the Himalayan region. He was also the root teacher of the great masters of Sakya and Ngor and the holders of those lineages; the principle masters were the noble Sakya Dagchens and Trizins of the Khön families, both active and retired. And throughout all these activities, he proved beyond doubt that he was the great illuminator of the teachings, the embodiment of the enlightened mind and activities of the great compassionate master Sachen Kunga Nyingpo, his students, and lineage holders.

Khyentse Chökyi Lodrö's pure visionary experiences of wisdom related to the Lamdre tradition were as follows.

> I recited the *Profound Path* at Mangkhar Kala cave where various texts were believed to have been translated, and as a result, I saw Drogmi Lotsawa in a pure vision. He was sitting in front of me wearing a pandita's hat and monk's robe with attributes similar to those of the statue inside the great cave, as he was holding a vajra and bell and his hands were in the crossed mudra. Drogmi Lotsawa was sometimes one with me and sometimes separate.
>
> In the seventh month of the year of the earth dog (1958), I was about to give teachings on the *Ascertainment of the Three Types of Vow* to Tsang Yangchö Tulku in Darjeeling, when I saw the Dharma Lord Sakya Pandita in a pure vision, sitting in half-

vajra posture, his two hands in teaching mudra, and dressed like
an Indian pandita. At his forehead was White Manjushri; at his
throat, the "lion of speech" (a form of Manjushri); at his heart,
Manjushri Jnanasattva; at his navel, White Saraswati; and at his
secret place, White Achali. My devotion for these deities induced
tremendous rays of light to stream from them and dissolve into
me. It was some time after I'd had these mirage-like visions that I
wrote them down, so I forgot about them.

One day in the tenth month, while I was in Gangtok, I saw
Dharma Lord Sakya Pandita in a pure vision, his right hand in
the teaching mudra, holding a sword and text supported by a
lotus, and his left hand in the mudra of equanimity, holding a
long-life vase. At Sakya Pandita's heart sat White Amitayus holding a long-life vase filled with amrita. Rays of light streamed out
of Amitayus's vase and converged into the vase held by Sakya
Pandita, then flowed into me.

I have also seen an account of a pure vision Khyentse Chökyi Lodrö had
when he was in his thirties, in which he received teachings on the *Treasury
of Valid Logical Reasoning* from the Dharma Lord Sakya Pandita.

One night in the year of the fire rooster (1957), I dreamt I saw a
faint image of vajradhara Kunga Zangpo at what was supposed to
be Ngor Monastery. The water in a round-bellied, silver pitcher
was said to be from his empowerment vase, so I drank some and
poured some on my head. As a result, I experienced great joy.

In the colophon of the prayer for making offerings to the glorious protector Zhal and requesting him to remove obstacles, and so on, Khyentse
Chökyi Lodrö signed his name as Kunga Thinlay Gyatso. When asked who
had given him this name, he replied that it had happened in a dream.

In my dream we were at Ngor Monastery and I received the
bhikshu vows from Ngorchen Dorje Chang, after which he gave
me this name.

He had tremendous respect for the Vinaya lineage transmitted through
Ngorchen.

In the year of the fire rooster (1957), on the twenty-fifth night of the fourth month, I dreamt I arrived at Ngor Monastery and stayed in one of the rooms there. I saw a clay statue of Mahakala Gur slowly entering the monastery through the lower main door, his huge face ten feet high. I also saw many other small statues of various Dharma protectors.

I can't remember when, but prior to this vision, I dreamt I was sitting on the middle throne of three in the assembly hall at Ngor Monastery, reciting prayers with the monks—but I have forgotten the details.

One day as the moon waxed in the eighth month, I received the Hevajra empowerment in a vision and an essential teaching on the *Triple Tantras* from the *Explanation of the Lamdre View* from an old lama wearing cotton robes, who was actually Palden Lama Dampa Sonam Gyaltsen.

One night in the eighth month of the year of the fire rooster (1957), I dreamt I was in the presence of the precious statue of vajradhara Tsarchen at Mangkhar Thubten Gephel Monastery and that I prayed with great devotion. As a result, I heard the syllable PHAT twice, and my mind was utterly free of concepts as my body quivered and shook.

On the twentieth day of the twelfth month in the year of the fire monkey (1956), while practicing the guru yoga of vajradhara Tsarchen, my devotion was such that I experienced a mirage-like vision of the vajradhara, almost life-size, whose color and form were the same as those of the precious statue at Thubten Gephel Monastery. Vajradhara Tsarchen made a prophecy; I received the four empowerments and then dissolved him into myself. As a result, I experienced being Hevajra with his retinue of fifteen goddesses free from self in my heart.

In the year of the wood sheep (1955), on the twentieth day of the eighth month, I passed through Dachen of Hor Yetha. On the nineteenth, as I gazed at the moon in the clear blue sky, I remembered Lord Loter Wangpo, and instantly a vision of him appeared before me, sitting with the moon behind him like an aureola. He then transformed into the wrathful Sangdak Vajrapani. I felt tremendous devotion and received empowerments from him. The guru dissolved into me, and I experienced vivid intrinsic awareness. That same day at the Yama Ngonpo'i Khuk encampment, the experience inspired me to write the guru yoga of Lord Loter Wangpo.

On the twenty-ninth night of a month[229] in the year of the fire rooster (1957), I dreamt I was in a monastery that I believed to be Tsetang Samten Ling in the Yarlung valley. There I paid my respects to a small fragment of what I believed to be one of Chögyal Phakpa's bones and two big pieces of what was said to have been Lama Dampa's (Sonam Gyaltsen) skull. An old monk gave me a few bone fragments the size of mustard seeds, and as I picked one up, a piece broke off, so I kept it. I also received a chunk of skull. I then saw a pile of old clothes said to have belonged to Lama Dampa, from which I wished to receive blessings. That was certainly my intention, but I can't remember whether I did or not.

Khyentse Chökyi Lodrö's autobiography contains accounts of him receiving blessings in pure visions from some of the Lamdre lineage masters.

After the colophon at the end of the *Supplication Prayer to Tsarchen* that includes "Thus, it was written by Kunga Trinle Gyatso Dhondrup Wangyi Gyalpo at Dar Drong Chen . . . ,'" and so on, he wrote,

I spent the seventh night of the second ninth month in the year of the fire monkey (1956) by the stupa, where I dreamt that I gave the speech empowerment of Manjushri Dharmadhatu. I also dreamt that in addition to my existing name, I was called Dondrup Wangyi Gyalpo. When Sakya Dagchen Ayu Vajra[230] gave me the empowerment for the wrathful activity of Vajrakilaya, I experienced the presence of Ngakchang Chenmo[231]—he was right in front of me. While praying to Jamyang Zi Ö Barwa and making aspirations, small signs of blessings appeared, but I cannot remember them.

This anecdote appeared in the colophon.

In Jamgön Lekpa Rinpoche's biography, it says that at the end of the cause empowerment of Hevajra and the *Path and Fruition: The Explanation for Private Disciples* that he gave to Khyentse Chökyi Lodrö, he had a vision of omniscient Khyentse Wangpo surrounded by the eight Gur deities. So, he wrote, "Khyentse Wangpo must have been pleased with the empowerments I offered to his tulku."

At that time, Khyentse Chökyi Lodrö also gained complete confidence that Lekpa Rinpoche was truly the emanation of Gorampa Kunga Lekpe Jungney. He said that when Lekpa Rinpoche gave the oral transmissions for the biographies of the masters of the Lamdre lineage, as he came to the end of Gorampa's biography, he said, "This kind of life story is beyond the understanding of ordinary childish beings." And with a piercing gaze, he looked at Khyentse Chökyi Lodrö for a long time. Chökyi Lodrö later said he felt his guru had recognized the confidence that had taken birth in his mind.

Lekpa Rinpoche said, "Since this Khyentse Tulku Rinpoche is my main student as well as my teacher, his image has been included on the thangka of the Lamdre lineage masters. I myself recite one verse of his long-life prayer daily, and all my students are also instructed to recite it diligently."

More significantly, Jamgön Lekpa Rinpoche instructed his main heartson, Dezhung Choktrul, to take Khyentse Chökyi Lodrö as his teacher, saying, "This Khyentse Tulku Rinpoche is an authentic, fully qualified vajra master, so there is no need to examine him." From then on, Dezhung Rinpoche considered Chökyi Lodrö to be his teacher. Later, even when he was very old, Dezhung Rinpoche would often make the long journey from Lithang to Dzongsar to receive empowerments from him.

Once, when Khyentse Chökyi Lodrö gave Dezhung Rinpoche the transmission for the *Magical Net of Manjushri* as a departing Dharma gift, Dezhung Rinpoche said he felt completely confident that Chökyi Lodrö was Manjushri in human form. And when he taught his students, Dezhung Rinpoche always said, as stated in the sacred texts, "The outer lama is the embodiment of the Buddhas . . ." and "an authentic master should be like Khyentse Tulku Rinpoche." They also had extraordinary and profound discussions about spiritual practice and meditation, the central point of which was the teaching on the *Nonduality of Samsara and Nirvana*. They were so close, it was as if their minds were one.

(d) Jamyang Khyentse Chökyi Lodrö's visions and experiences related to Marpa Kagyü.

As Khyentse Chökyi Lodrö had received and practiced all the major and minor instructions for the root and branch traditions of the Sovereign Lord

Marpa, the profound oral instructions of the four transmitted precepts in the Noble Land that are the direct path to attaining supreme accomplishment, he was always free from thoughts about the eight worldly preoccupations. As he had perfected the inner yoga of the view of luminous Mahamudra by diligently following the example of the early masters of the practice lineage and effortlessly discarding the unwholesome activities of distraction and indolence, the secret treasury of his experiences and realization overflowed. As he had the deepest devotion for and purest perception of the Sovereign Lords of the Buddha families, he developed the authority of devotion and realization.

It is obvious that Khyentse Chökyi Lodrö practiced the creation and completion meditations for tantras such as Chakrasamvara and Hevajra, the practice traditions of which have remained unbroken since the time of Marpa, Milarepa, and Dagpo (Gampopa). In particular, Khyentse Chökyi Lodrö considered special and practiced the blessing instructions[232] for the oral lineage of Rechungpa that was transmitted to Katok Situ Rinpoche by Lord Khyentse Wangpo; the six yogas and instructions on the Mahamudra of the Karma Kagyü and Drukpa Kagyü lineages that were transmitted to Gyaltsab Rinpoche by Khyentse Wangpo; and noble Karma Chagme's direct instructions on Mahamudra.

He gave the teachings listed above, along with the *Precious Garland of the Supreme Path*, the *Ornament of Liberation*, the *Profound Inner Meaning*, *Two Sections of the Hevajra Root Tantra*, *Treatise on the Sublime Continuum*, and so on, to enthusiastic students, thereby fulfilling their wishes. He also amazed everyone with his explanation of the *Single Intention* of Drikung combined with the profound essential points of sutra and tantra.

Khyentse Chökyi Lodrö's mind was inseparable from the minds of the exalted Sixteenth Gyalwang Karmapa Rangjung Khyabdak Rigpe Dorje, the great Maitreya Situ Pema Wangchok Gyalpo, the Tenth Surmang Trungpa Rinpoche Chokyi Nyinje, and Gyalse Jamgön Choktrul (the Second Kongtrul)—the fathers and sons whose enlightened intention and activity were as one.

Venerable Palpung Situ Rinpoche repeatedly told the king of Derge that, in those days, Khyentse Chökyi Lodrö was without doubt the only authentic master in Kham and Tibet whom people could trust and in whom they could take refuge. Chökyi Lodrö nurtured the lineage of Palpung in various ways and with great kindness, such as by overseeing the memorial services for the Venerable Situ Rinpoche after his parinirvana.

He became the crown jewel of the great masters of the Karma and Drukpa Kagyü lineages, and his enlightened aspiration and activity caused a system of study and practice to be established in the monasteries, large and small, that upheld the Karma and Drukpa Kagyü lineages. Therefore, Khyentse Chökyi Lodrö was a great mahasiddha and a learnèd and accomplished holder of the Kagyü teachings of the Sovereign Lord Marpa.

His pure visionary experiences related to this lineage were as follows.

> On the second day of the eleventh month in the year of the fire monkey (1956), as I sat inside Tilopa and Naropa's cave in Nepal, I saw Naropa in a pure vision, light blue in color, with a topknot of matted hair, and wearing bone ornaments. He was sitting in half-vajra posture with his knees raised, holding a skull cup in his right hand and sprinkling amrita with the ring finger of his left hand. Following this experience, I visualized myself receiving empowerments from him and dissolved the master into myself, and so on.
>
> As I traveled slowly down from Mandi town, the train came into alignment with the Kangra temple, which Gedun Chöphel says in his pilgrimage guide is the place that Mahasiddha Orgyenpa and Gotsangpa called Jalandara. At that moment, my mind rested in a state of peace from which a clear vision of many mahasiddhas, like Kukuripa, appeared in the sky before me.
>
> When I looked at the lifelike statue of Marpa in the red temple at Drowo Lung, I prayed with fervent devotion, received the Hevajra empowerment, and practiced the visualization of emanating and gathering in the mantra garland. As a result, in a pure vision, the statue stared at me intently and said,
>
>> Within the true nature of phenomena,
>> Path and fruition have never arisen.
>> This unfabricated natural mind
>> Is the spontaneously arisen wisdom of Mahamudra.
>
> I experienced pristine awareness unspoiled by contrived appearances and remained in that state for quite some time.
>
> As I gazed at the reliquary containing Marpa's remains at Ngok Trel Zhung, I had a vision of it transforming into the nine

deities of Hevajra, with the garland of the ashta mantra streaming towards me.

On the nineteenth night of the fifth month in the year of the fire rooster (1957), I dreamt of a man who looked like Lhodrak Marpa and wore similar clothes to him. He said, "It's been said that the transference of consciousness from one body to another is impossible, but Dharmadode managed it." Finally, I dreamt I held a white-bronze statue that was supposed to be a likeness of Dharmadode, but I don't remember any other details.

When I saw Namtso Lake for the first time, in a misty and confused experience brought on by devotion, I saw the palace of glorious Chakrasamvara, along with the mandalas of mind, speech, and body and many dancing dakas and dakinis. As a result of this experience, I recited the Chakrasamvara mantras I knew and repeatedly made prayers of aspiration that I might attain the same state as the deities.

In Darjeeling, during the nineteenth night of the seventh month in the year of the earth dog (1958), I dreamt I forgot which practice should happen on Lord Milarepa's anniversary at my Dzongsar residence and that the offerings that had been arranged were therefore put away. But then I had to do the practice the following day, and with one spin of the magic wheel, all five kinds of offerings appeared, one after another, without any effort. I was amazed. When I woke up, I recited with great devotion the prayer that includes the names of Jetsün Milarepa. As a result, in a mirage-like vision, I saw Jetsün in the form of Chakrasamvara, with face and arms as described in the elaborate sadhana, in what seemed to be a palace on the slopes of Mount Kailash. I prayed to Milarepa, wishing I could receive the oral transmission, and instantly, like an emanation mandala, I received the elaborate and essential empowerments, as well as the entrustment blessing for the text.

When I visited Tölung Tsurphu, I saw a hill behind the monastery that looked like Chakrasamvara, with face and limbs the size of the hill itself. A little way down the slope opposite the monastery was a cliff that looked to me like Karma Pakshi with a huge, dark red body.

In the year of the earth dog (1958), on the fifteenth day of the first month, while I was still ill with a stomach problem, I casually opened a volume from the library to the *General Commentary on the Tantras* by Karma Pakshi. Having read sections of the text at random for about two hours, in a pure vision that seemed to have been caused by what I'd read, I saw Pakshi in the sky before me, dark red with a black beard, a smiling, wrathful face, and staring eyes. His hands were in the subjugating the earth mudra, and there were a few short, fat dakinis in front of him. I prayed to them, asking that I might recover from my illness, and the dakinis and guru performed a few purification mudras. What looked and sounded like red flames then emanated from them, burning my body, and I transformed into the form of Guru Pakshi. As a result of this experience, a guru yoga appeared in my mind, and I wrote it down.

In the year of the earth dog (1958), during the waxing moon in the ninth month, I gave Chokden and others the oral transmission of the *Profound Inner Meaning*. During the second half of the tenth night, as I thought about Gyalwang Rangjung Dorje,[233] a life-size vision of him appeared before me, wearing the black hat and ceremonial robe, his hands in teaching mudra. It was my wish and intention to be entrusted with Rangjung Dorje's writings. At that moment, I saw a few volumes of text printed on white paper, and others that looked like gold printed on black paper. From time to time, many syllables appeared from Rangjung Dorje's mouth and dissolved into me.

On the thirteenth night of the month, I dreamt I met the Sixteenth Gyalwang Karmapa at Tsurphu. He wanted to give me a sacred relic, so he opened one of many treasure boxes, in which lay a few meteorite phurbas and antique bronze vajras wrapped in dharani cords with ribbons and tassels hanging from them. He asked me to choose one, but was too busy to look in my direction and moved away. I also dreamt I saw the previous Venerable Palpung Situ, but I've now forgotten that dream.

On the fifteenth day of the second month in the year of the fire rooster (1957), the day of the juncture of the sun and me zhi,[234] I gave an empowerment for the *Embodiment of the Three Roots*, the oral transmission for the long-life sadhana of Jatsön

Nyingpo, and other texts. That night I had numerous dreams about the monastery of Nedo Chagme Rinpoche, but I've forgotten the details.

I then fell into a light sleep and had a vision of Chagme Rinpoche. At first, he was wearing a meditation hat. After a while, I saw a young-looking, round-headed monk sitting some distance away from me in a large field. I wondered about receiving the oral transmission for his writings, because I had a feeling they would be the root text of the guru's written works. As I created the visualization for receiving the blessings, the guru gave me a page of lapis lazuli paper on which was written, in light blue ink, what appeared to be the source of his writings, and he entrusted me with it. Then he dissolved into light, and the text became a small stack of Dharma books. The books then transformed into a figure resembling the main deity of *Avalokiteshvara Who Stirs the Depths of Samsara*, his right hand in the mudra of granting supreme accomplishment and holding a vase of purification water that looked like a round-bottomed urn, his left hand at his heart in the mudra of granting protection and holding a garland of lotuses. As he dissolved into me, I transformed into the deity and woke up from the experience in that state.

(e) Jamyang Khyentse Chökyi Lodrö's visions and experiences related to the Shangpa Kagyü lineage, the Golden Dharma of the scholar-siddha Khyungpo Naljor.

Khyentse Chökyi Lodrö diligently received in great detail all the empowerments, explanations, and original sacred texts related to instructions given by Khewang Lama Tashi Chöphel, the heart-son of Jamgön Kongtrul Yönten Gyatso, who had received authorization for this path; from the retreat master Lama Karma Rangjung Künkhyab (Kalu Rinpoche); and others. And then he practiced them. He also undertook recitation retreats for the *Five Tantric Deities*, the *Combined Practice of the Four Deities*, the *Inseparable Unity of the Guru and the Protector*, and others. He included the practices and yogic exercises of this lineage in the curriculum for Karmo Tak Tsang's retreat center. With pure motivation, he engaged in the vast activity of giving empowerments and instructions to enthusiastic students, and this was how he established himself as the lineage master who upheld, nurtured, and propagated the Dharma of the seven great jewels of the Shangpa tradition.

About our Lord Guru's pure visionary experiences related to this tradition:

> In the year of the fire monkey (1956), during the tenth month, while reciting offering verses in Shavaripa's retreat cave at the Sitavana charnel ground, I saw Shavaripa in a pure vision with the carcass of a deer slung over his shoulder. He was holding an arrow in his right hand and a bow in his left. I had mirage-like visions of deities at the five centers of Shavaripa's body, and as my awareness was clear and vivid, I was able to experience the splendor of the blessings—at least to some extent. And my body trembled. Gönpo Tseten, who was in front of me, saw this happen. At that time, a guru yoga appeared in my mind, and I wrote it down in the temple outside the cave.
>
> Earlier, at Shechen, when I received the Shangpa teachings included in the *Treasury of Precious Instructions* from Gyaltsab Rinpoche, I had some wonderful dreams, but I've forgotten them now because I didn't write them down straightaway.

Khyentse Chökyi Lodrö told me that these dreams were tremendously significant, however there are no records of them.

The accounts of the visions of Mahasiddha Thangtong Gyalpo, one of the great pioneers of this lineage, and the blessings Khyentse Chökyi Lodrö received from him have been mentioned above.

(f) Jamyang Khyentse Chökyi Lodrö's visions and experiences related to Shije and Chö.

Having received in detail all the existing empowerments, instructions, and pith instructions for Shije, the profound instructions of Padampa Sangye, and the *Sublime Dharma of Cutting Through Demons* from the teaching tradition of Machik Labdrön, Khyentse Chökyi Lodrö perfected the required practices and constantly nurtured the activities of teaching, propagating, upholding, and sustaining them with great diligence. He received detailed empowerments, instructions, and oral transmissions for the cycles of the *Five Paths of Shije*, the profound teachings of Mahasiddha Padampa Sangye and Machik Labdrön's teachings on *Taking "Cutting Through" as the Path*. He then perfected the contemplation and meditation of these teachings and, by giving them appropriately, upheld and preserved this teaching lineage and prevented its power from diminishing.

More specifically, he practiced with the utmost respect and care the *Secret Conduct of the Great Oral Lineage*, an extraordinary lineage of blessings and practice that had been directly transmitted in a pure vision to the Lord Mahasiddha Thangtong Gyalpo by Machik Labdrön, inseparable from Vajrayogini. He wrote all the necessary practices and texts associated with this teaching and taught it to devoted and eager students as their personal practice, bestowing the teachings in full, including the entrustment seals, on those qualified to receive it. Therefore, Khyentse Chökyi Lodrö was truly the sovereign holder of the Shije and Chö traditions.

Khyentse Chökyi Lodrö mentioned the following in the colophon to the empowerment manual he wrote for the previous Lord's *Guru Yoga of the Heart Essence of the Oral Transmission Lineage* with Padampa Sangye as the main deity, having deciphered it as it had appeared in the expanse of his wisdom mind:

> At the age of sixty-five, I, Pema Yeshe Dorje, wrote this without any difficulty in a building near the great Tsuglakhang, the palace of the wisdom dakini, a wondrous and magical realm in Sikkim, on the twenty-second day of the twelfth month in the year of the fire rooster (1957). It is written exactly as it appeared in my mind as the result of a flickering vision I had of the form of Padampa Sangye. I assume it is an empowerment text for the Venerable Lama Pema Ösel Dongak Lingpa's guru yoga of Dampa Sangye, called the *Pure Vision and Oral Transmission Guru Yoga*.

And below that in his own hand, he wrote,

> In the same year, on about the twentieth day of the twelfth month, as I leafed through some biographies of the Shije masters in the *Blue Annals* of Gö Lotsawa, I saw Padampa Sangye very

briefly. He was maroon in color with black braids of matted hair, neither too long nor too short, and his two hands were either in the sky treasury mudra at his forehead or holding a damaru and skull cup.

Although there is no doubt that Khyentse Chökyi Lodrö would have had numerous wonderful visions during the day he practiced in front of the statue of Machik Labdrön at Zangri Kharmar, no written record is available.

(g) Jamyang Khyentse Chökyi Lodrö's experiences and visions related to the teachings on the six-branch practice of vajrayoga, the profound meaning of Kalachakra, the King of Nondual Tantras.

The great holders of the Kalachakra teachings in the Land of Snows, Jamgön Khyentse and Jamgön Kongtrul, received in full all the lineages of empowerments, instructions, and explanations for the two chariots of teachings, the tantras of the Jonang and Shalu traditions, and the practices of the glorious *Kalachakra Tantra*. All these teachings and transmissions converged into the ocean of our supreme Lord Guru's mind, and he taught and propagated them widely.

He made thirty-seven extraordinary new thangkas of the Buddha, the seven Dharma Kings, the twenty-five Rigdens, feudal lords, and lineage holders. Every year without exception, Khyentse Chökyi Lodrö performed elaborate offering practices in the third month on the auspicious day the wheel of the *Kalachakra Tantra* was first turned. He also explained to me the virtues of making offerings and practicing the Kalachakra sadhana on this special day. He never merely plagiarized the understanding of others when he taught and acknowledged that an extraordinary understanding of the profound meaning of this "king of tantras" had taken birth in his mind.

As his activities in this realm neared completion, the last practice he engaged in coincided with the auspicious day of the turning of the wheel of the *Kalachakra Tantra*. So he did an elaborate offering practice of Kalachakra. In the prayers he wrote, he mentioned again and again that in the future he would appear as the twenty-fifth Rigden king, Drakpo Khorlochen, and was therefore undoubtedly the lineage holder of the Kalachakra, the king of tantras.

Khyentse Chökyi Lodrö's pure visionary experiences relating to this lineage were as follows:

One day, in the eleventh month of the year of the fire monkey (1956), at Sankasya where Lord Buddha descended from the heaven of the thirty-three, I concluded a suppression ritual for the welfare of the teachings. That night I dreamt of the immeasurable three-dimensional palace of Kalachakra. As I entered it, offering goddesses sitting in the outer circle said that the body lying on her back among the inner circle of goddesses was one of their number. A drupchö was being performed at the center of the inner circle in front of me. Some monks were called upon to make the inner amrita offerings, and I woke up.

On the twentieth night of a month[235] in the year of the earth dog (1958), I dreamt that the base stone of the Kalachakra mandala at Vajrasana had once belonged to Sangye Yeshe. Some believed it had been flown there in an airplane, while others thought it had been carried there on various people's laps. In the dream, it was on this stone that I prepared to make fire offerings. I also dreamt I was about to make fire offerings on another small stone platform on which rested a dakini mandala.

On the twenty-third day of the ninth month in the year of the fire monkey (1956), I wrote,

> On the twenty-third of the twelfth month of that year, I thought about omniscient Dolpo Sangye. I prayed to him again and again and remember having a vision of his tiny form. Whenever I woke up, I prayed. In the second half of the night, I saw omniscient Dolpopa, life-size, wearing a bright yellow robe and sitting on a beautiful throne, and another vivid form that resembled this Lord's practice deity. I prayed and made aspirations for the obstacles to be pacified. Again, I dreamt that someone (who may have been Chinese) and I were marking the dimensions of a new temple with a kind of rope. I heard someone say that each side was to be thirty meters long.
>
> For a long time, as the moon waned during the night of the twenty-fourth, I had numerous dreams that are difficult to describe—for example, the praise to Manjushri *Gangloma* and the thirty-two commentaries valued so highly by Ngok Lotsawa manifested in the form of a book. The letters

transformed into firelight, and I sat in the middle of it. I also had a hazy vision of the three bodhisattvas abiding in the body of omniscient Dolpopa, and consequently wrote a guru yoga sadhana—my hand was guided by a demon!

There are also accounts of Khyentse Chökyi Lodrö's visions of receiving blessings from the omniscient master Dolpopa in the colophon of Dolpopa's guru yoga that he wrote during the early part of his life.

In an age when the transmission of empowerments and the creation and completion meditations for tantras such as the glorious *Kalachakra Tantra*, the *Vajra Peak*, and the *Vajradhatu Tantra* have become rare, Khyentse Chökyi Lodrö made a heartfelt commitment to teach, study, uphold, and spread these tantras. This is how he reinvigorated the teaching lineages of Butön, Dolpopa, Jonangpa, and Shaluwa.

(h) Jamyang Khyentse Chökyi Lodrö's visions and experiences related to Orgyen Nyendrup.[236]

Khyentse Chökyi Lodrö received in full all the existing transmissions for the sacred texts, instructions, and pith instructions for the *Approach and Accomplishment Practices of the Three Vajras*, which are the pith instruction teachings transmitted to Mahasiddha Orgyenpa by the vajra queen. He constantly aspired and acted to uphold, sustain, and spread these teachings and was therefore an authentic holder of the teachings of this lineage.[237] Although he undoubtedly had all kinds of visions and experiences that were signs he had accomplished these practices, I neither had the good fortune to hear about them personally, nor have I seen any records of them.

Not only that, Khyentse Chökyi Lodrö asked the holder of the Yungdrung Bön teachings, Dhome Shar Dza Togden, and his students to write new texts for the empowerments, instructions, and experiential instructions of their tradition. He inspired the followers of this lineage by always expressing his great admiration for them and never scorning them.

The spirit of Rime pervaded Khyentse Chökyi Lodrö's entire outlook, as he mentioned in the root verses of his autobiography:

> The previous Jamgön Guru loved all the teaching traditions like a mother. He could tell the difference between the tantras, transmissions, and pith instructions of each tradition and never con-

fused them or mixed them up. He gave teachings that suited each individual's capacity, and all the schools—Sakya, Gelug, Kagyü, and Nyingma—considered him to be one of their own lineage teachers. Although I lack the qualities of my predecessor, I look upon each of the eight great chariots of the Land of Snows with the purest perception. Unstained by the obscurations of wrong view, I have abandoned prejudice and the denigration of all traditions. I have endeavored, with great perseverance, to receive all the empowerments, explanations, pith instructions, and tantric oral transmissions for which lineages still exist and aspire to receive even more. Wishing, with the purest of intentions to preserve the teachings, in the spirit of Rime, everything I receive I also teach; I have also abandoned criticism, jealousy, and disdain of all beings, supreme and ordinary. I have generated bodhichitta and made aspirations, with the intention, as pure as the white of a conch shell or lotus root, to benefit all beings; and I have given meaning to the lives of everyone who has a connection with me. This is the essence of my biography.

The secret of the life of the previous Venerable Manjushri Guru, whose activities upheld, sustained, and propagated all the teachings of the Buddha in the Land of Snows is beyond all comparison, and in the words of omniscient Yönten Gyatso,[238]

> Honored for his innate and acquired knowledge—
> But never because that honor was solicited,
> Or because he was noble and wealthy—
> To the Buddhist tradition of Tibet,
> He is Lord of the Gathering, the Lord of All;
> In this respect alone, in this world
> He embodies the qualities of the second Buddha.
> He studied, contemplated, and practiced to perfection
> The essence of the sacred textual tradition;
> The empowerments, explanations, and oral instructions
> Of the ten pillars that support the study lineage;
> And the eight great chariots of the practice lineage
> That existed in the Land of Snows.

> Although he had completely abandoned obscuration and perfected realization,
> He appeared in order to tame beings with skillful means,
> Arising from the nonarisen state, and
> Transmigrating from the state of nontransmigration.

These words, Jamgön Kongtrul's praise of Jamyang Khyentse Wangpo, are the truth.

In addition to the visions and experiences I've just explained, which I compiled from Khyentse Chökyi Lodrö's personal notes, I have managed to collect accounts of various other visions and experiences he had. They are presented here exactly as they were originally written, with nothing changed.

> Dharma Lords, who teach the path of adopting virtue and rejecting nonvirtue
> And dispel the ignorance of beings,
> Glorious Supreme Guides,
> Please look upon me with compassion at all times.
> At the age of sixty-five, during the eleventh month,
> I, whose wisdom is enveloped
> By a net of conflicting emotion,
> Traveled to Vajrasana in the Noble Land of India.
> On the first of the two fifth days[239] of the twelfth month,
> While reciting prayers of supplication
> Under the great Bodhi tree,
> I experienced a shimmering vision.
> The Bodhi tree transformed into Buddha Shakyamuni,
> And at his heart sat a blue Vajradhara in sambhogakaya form,
> Without consort and holding a vajra and bell.
> At Vajradhara's heart sat Samantabhadra,
> Unadorned and in union with his consort.
> Countless buddhas surrounded Buddha Shakyamuni
> And were bathed in tremendous rays of light.
> I had the same kind of vision again on the second fifth day,
> So I wrote a guru yoga.

I aspired to offer tormas to four-armed Mahakala
But was unable to find the text.
That night, I saw the wisdom protector Mahakala
In the form of a black stone statue,
The lower body—his legs, and so on—immensely fat.
The next day I remembered the shrine master saying,
"The tantra called the *Source of Accomplishment* can be found
In the third volume of the *Collection of Tantras* in the
    Kangyur."
I felt that if I could find that text, I would be able
To base a practice I wanted to write on it,
And then recite it.
That night, I dreamt I performed a ritual
Based on that king of tantras;
It made me want to write an offering and fulfillment prayer,
And so I wrote a short one quite spontaneously.
As I made offerings in Shravasti,
A shimmering vision of a huge Tathagata,
Surrounded by a multitude of buddhas, and others,
Appeared in the blue sky above me.
After I returned to Gangtok,
I dreamt that in front of the Vulture's Peak,
I saw abundant offerings arranged on a beautiful shrine
That stood in front of a large stone statue of Buddha
    Shakyamuni.
Once when I was sick, I dreamt
I was in my old residence at Dzongsar, and
Trulshik visited me,
Touched me with his face and blew.
I saw a golden statue of Thangtong Gyalpo,
About an arm's length in height;
His right hand formed the mudra of subjugating the earth,
And his left the mudra of resting in equanimity.
Wine overflowed from the skull cup resting on a tripod of
    skulls,
And spurted high into the air, like a fountain,
Bearing a small long-life vase.

I placed the statue on an iron hearth.
Worried they might fall,
I grasped the skull and vase
And held them in my hands.

I had numerous such dreams, but have forgotten most of them.

As I made offerings and recited aspiration prayers near the Bodhi tree at Vajrasana in the Noble Land, I saw, in a pure vision, many buddhas and bodhisattvas surrounding the Gandola and in the sky above.

When I visited the holy sites in Shravasti, I felt the presence of numerous pale yellow buddhas in the sky; and during my visit to Sankasya, where Buddha descended from the god realm, I received empowerments from a vision of the Tathagata sitting in the sky before me, huge, with hands in teaching mudra. At the end of the vision, the Tathagata transformed into a yellow syllable DHIH and dissolved into me. So conceited!

In the year of the fire monkey (1956), on the second fifth day of the twelfth month, while I was doing an elaborate sixteen arhat sadhana practice on a terrace of the Boudhanath stupa, I felt the presence in the sky before me of many buddhas, bodhisattvas, sthaviras, and arhats. That evening, as I circumambulated the stupa, it suddenly appeared to become transparent, and inside I could clearly see the mandala of the *Eight Great Deities of the Peaceful and Wrathful Sugatas*. I therefore recited the *Fulfillment and Confession Called "Stirring the Depths of Hell"* and aspiration prayers as I offered prostrations. My mind was clear and my experience blissful.

Accounts of Khyentse Chökyi Lodrö being blessed by Arhat Angiraja (Yenlak Jung) in pure visions are mentioned in his autobiography.

Again, on the eleventh night, while sleeping on a train, I had a vision (triggered by a memory of Vasubhandu's reliquary stupa in Nepal) of Vasubandhu. He was wearing a pandita's clothing and hat, his right hand was at his heart in the mudra of granting protection, and his left in the supreme granting mudra. He was sitting in heroic posture with his legs folded in royal ease. Devotion arose in my mind, and I said prayers . . . which would have been good if my devotion had been genuine and not the kind created by demons!

One day, during the first month of the year of the earth dog (1958), in Gangtok, having been sick for some time with a stomach problem, I had a confused vision of a figure who was said to be Acharya Chandragomi. He was wearing the six ornaments I had seen at Katok on a mural by Phurbu and performed the Vajra Vidharana ritual of cleansing and purification. As a result, I recovered a little.

Again, on the twenty-seventh day of the second month, during the fulfillment ritual of the *Embodiment of the Guru's Realization*, the peaceful form of Shaza Khamoche (the ferocious meat-eating dakini) embraced me and sucked my vajra with her bhaga, which drew out blood, pus, and so on. I feel that this vision has helped me greatly to recover from my illness.

In the year of the fire rooster (1957), during the eleventh night of the ninth month, I dreamt an elderly lama was in the empowerment hall of my residence at Dzongsar—I think it was Mipham Rinpoche. The lama lightheartedly put forward a proposition challenging a statement made by a student who was also there. As I didn't understand whether or not the shravakas and pratyekabuddhas realized selflessness according to the Prasangika Madhyamika, as the sun set, I requested permission to debate with the lama and prostrated to him. I had intended to chant "The empty awareness Manjushri . . ."[240] prayer but couldn't remember how it began, so I chanted a different prayer. I lacked the confidence to chant the homage to Manjushri "The one, by wrong views, and so on . . . ," because I didn't think I could remember it, but the lama chanted it himself. He then responded to my arguments. I couldn't understand much of what he said, though, because his voice wasn't very clear.

On the twenty-third night, I received a one-page letter from Shechen Kongtrul Rinpoche. He wrote, "To avert my possible departure in the third month for the pure land, you should do a retreat at either Tsari, Enza, or Chongzhi cave." There were also a few lines of prophecy, but I can't remember them.

In the year of the earth dog (1958), on the twenty-sixth day of the seventh month, I had some wonderful dreams! My cook, shrine master, and I, along with a few others, arrived at the great temple of Derge Lhundrup Teng and sat inside it for a long time. The cremation stupa of the great Ngor Abbot Palden Chokyong was standing next to me, but its conical spire was missing, and the dome was covered with wooden planks. We cleared away the planks and woven bamboo covering because we wanted to see the whole kudung. Then I put my hand into the dome and found a huge amount of damp, rusty saffron powder and some round things. I took one out and saw it was a small, leafy radish. I put it to one side and again reached in. My hand touched what felt like bones and a heart. I then replaced the lid.

After a while, a person who looked like my shrine master, Chokden, pushed the sacred body down slightly and opened the dome of the stupa. The warm, wet saffron emitted a fragrant perfume. In the midst of the saffron lay an arm's-length-high kudung with an old-looking face, white hair that was not very thick and a little long, and legs with skin as soft and fresh as a baby's. It was nothing like a corpse and seemed to be an actual living person, with knees straight and feet pointing outward. Chokden took the body out, touched my back and head with it, then placed it in front of me. I prayed to it, making many fervent entreaties; received empowerments; and made aspirations. When I touched its body and face, I could feel it was breathing and warm. After I had paid my respects, the body was replaced in the dome of the stupa, a piece of cloth smeared with saffron taken from what looked like the shroud, and the dome resealed.

Again, I dreamt Tsewang Dorje gave me an antique gold statue of Guru Rinpoche Lama Norlha, about a hand-span high, holding a vajra-victory banner, a long object resembling a khatvanga, a *nehu-le* (an animal like a mongoose), and a treasure vase.

One night, during the year of the earth dog (1958), while accumulating the supplication prayer of Tsarchen Rinpoche, I had numerous ambiguous dreams. I dreamt I arrived at a place where many texts printed from Derge print blocks were stacked, and that it was necessary to do the deity practices of the *Heart Practice That Spontaneously Fulfills All Wishes* and the *Heart Practice of Tara*. I also had some indescribable dreams—for example, one in which I rather flamboyantly raised a few pages from what looked like a volume of *Gur Mahakala Called "Blazing One"* written on colored paper. Are these signs that such things are of great importance to me?

One night, I dreamt I saw two new thangkas of Vajrabhairava, one big and one small, hanging to one side of the temple. And at the end of the dream I saw an old thangka of Mipham's heart practice.

I visited the peak of Mount Kailash a few times, the second time to see if it would be a good spot to build a monastery. There weren't many people that day. It was a lonely place, and as I sat on a wooden platform, I saw a faint vision in the blue sky of insubstantial forms of wrathful Vajrapani, Vajrakilaya, and so on.

On the eleventh night of the second month in the year of the fire rooster (1957), I dreamt of two holy gilded statues of Green Tara, one after another, and although I couldn't see the actual statues as they were wrapped in yellow paper, I felt great devotion and joy.

On the thirtieth night, I dreamt a monkey attacked me. I whipped it, but it would not be subdued. Then I hit it with a vajra, and that helped a little.

In the year of the earth dog (1958), as I took a nap during the first day of the twelfth month, I dreamt of the Sukhavati buddhafield for quite some time. Beneath the blue sky, a vast mountain surrounded by rainbow light dominated the landscape, and two gigantic peacocks the size of small hills supported a throne. But the image was unclear, as if a mist had descended.

On the fourth night, I dreamt we reached a small monastery on a hill that was similar in shape to the hill on which Dzongsar Monastery stands but not as high. A few monks in robes offered me traditional white scarves, then sat on lower seats and told me I must live for a long time. They told me that this was Jowo Smritijnana's monastery, where all his representations were kept. When I asked the monks to which tradition the monastery belonged, they mumbled a lot, but I caught something like "Gelug monastery." We circumambulated the monastery and came to what appeared to be a protectors' hall. Inside were many representations, like a golden kutsab of Guru Rinpoche and a life-size statue of Damchen Chökyi Gyalpo with three wrathful faces, surrounded by many clay statues. I woke up having seen many such things.

One night, I dreamt that at dusk I went to meet someone thought to be the divine prince of Derge, Ngawang Jampal Rinchen. He was said to live in a grass hut with a very small door that stood inside an ordinary house in a hamlet at the foot of the mountain. He looked youthful, had a small topknot of dark matted hair, was clothed in green leaves, and sat gazing at the floor as I expressed my joy and devotion. The prince, who wore a red woolen robe, put a similar one around my shoulders, stood up, and went outside. I went with him, removed the robe, and offered it to him, having cut off a piece, saying I wanted it as an object of devotion. Then I stood naked before him. It was completely dark, and I couldn't see the whole vision properly, but I sensed there was a row of people and that he was beating them—Lakar Sogyal, for example. The prince was quite mad! He then lay on his back, naked, and said the boy might go crazy and cause internal strife. After many such dreams, I woke up.

I fell asleep once more and at first dreamt the same dream again. This time, the prince demonstrated various postures, saying that this was how he and Tsikey Chokling had received many empowerments and teachings from Khyentse Wangpo. After a while, playing a damaru and bell, he chanted, "At the very beginning of this age . . ."[241] He looked like a siddha to me. As I generated devotion for him, I felt the arrival of a jnanasattva, and great devotion arose in my mind. I also dreamt that the prince was known by the name Yeshe Gyatso.

The following day, I heard that Chakthak Drupchen had passed away. I'd always wanted to meet him and had never been able to. But that morning, I felt sure I had received his blessings.

Khyentse Chökyi Lodrö most probably wrote the following during his first visit to central Tibet:

> On the eighteenth day in the seventh month of the year of the wood ox (1925), during the night I spent below the Atsa Monastery, I dreamt of a high cloth cushion on a large throne inside a beautiful temple. I had a feeling the lama giving a great tantric empowerment was Jamyang Gyaltsen but wasn't sure. As he gave the blessing authorizing students to teach Dharma, which is the last of the vajracharya empowerments and comes after the five wisdom empowerments[242] that are part of the vase empowerment, I blew a large ritual conch, then climbed onto the throne and sat with my hands in teaching mudra. I felt a little scared because the throne was much higher than it needed to be. After Lama Jamyang Gyaltsen had performed the ritual of revealing the empowerment deity, and so on, I climbed down again. I dreamt I also received the three subsequent empowerments[243] with an authorization blessing at the end of each.
>
> Then at dawn, having paid my respects to the representations in a monastery on a rocky mountain, I saw Karmapa Khakhyab Dorje. He was sitting in a small house wearing his black hat, and in his lap lay an open relic box. I asked him to give me some of his holy objects. He showed me a golden box, saying, "This is a relic of the Buddha that once belonged to King Kanishka." Inside the box was an egg-size clay base that held just one relic. Once again, he showed me the golden box, saying, "The clay base was made by Nagarjuna." This time I saw three relics, and the base was embellished with imprints of what must have been other holy relics.
>
> I asked him to give me a relic, and with his own knife, he cut a large piece of brocade woven in a dark and wrathful human face pattern and gave it to me, saying it was a robe of Karmapa Düsum Khyenpa. As a result, the splendor of blessings and devotion blazed without limit. The Karmapa explained he couldn't give me that particular relic because it was priceless. He had another that he could give me, he said, but it wasn't a relic of Buddha Shakyamuni. After that, I woke up.

On the nineteenth night, which I spent with the Ludrup family at their home on top of the northern Lhari mountain, I dreamt I traveled through south Tibet to Yoru Tradruk. I saw an extremely beautiful temple that had not been there before, decorated with four styles of traditional brocades, including canopies, and so on, all gold and very new. I went to a place filled with many arm's-length golden statues of the peaceful and wrathful deities.

There was a temple that I'd not fully explored during my earlier visit, and a separate temple known as the Vairochana Temple. In the first temple, an extremely well-sculpted, fist-high Tara statue stood in the niche of the dome of what appeared to be the stupa that had been a support for Longchenpa's practice. Above the Tara was an Indian bronze statue of White Dzambala riding a dragon that had been the practice support of Bharo of Nepal. The artistry and form of the statues were so marvelous that it was difficult to take one's eyes from them. I picked them up and received blessings from them. I also often saw an eleven-faced Avalokiteshvara with another eleven-faced Avalokiteshvara at the crown of his head, which had been made from one of Longchenpa's bone relics and painted gold, with its eleven faces arranged on three heads, one on top of the other. I planned to offer pure liquid gold to the statues in each temple.

An assembly of monks in the Vairochana temple practiced the Hevajra sadhana according to the Ngorpa tradition and played the cymbals loudly as they left the temple. I recognized the beginning of a tune they played but can't remember what it was called. The only detail of this dream I remember is of entering the temple, but I was left with the impression that there was a protectors' hall inside it. Then a monk, who I thought must be the chief treasurer, said to me, "Last time you visited the monastery, I was not here." He then went through the representations one by one, asking, "Have you seen this?" But I don't remember precisely what was said. The treasurer held in the crook of his arm a clay hearth in which a charcoal fire blazed a brilliant red. He then threw the hearth to the ground, saying it had belonged to Nyen Lotsawa, and although it fell upside down, the fire continued to burn from top to bottom and did not spill out. In the end, the treasurer picked it up with the fire still burning, and I woke up.

At dawn on the tenth day of the seventh month, while camping at Juche Do in Kongpo, I dreamt of Gyaltsab Rinpoche. He was sitting on a high seat in a charming house where he was preparing to preside over a ceremony for taking the bodhisattva vow. He instructed a few of us gathered there to offer mandalas and recite prayers, which we did, and we also offered prostrations. After reciting prayers for bodhichitta to take birth in our minds from the preliminary verses of supplication of the *Heart Essence of Chetsün*, Rinpoche chanted what may have been the text of a purification ritual as he rang a bell. He alternately opened and closed his right and left eyes a few times, as if they were sore, and his face looked extremely radiant. Then, staring with wide-open eyes, he recited the vowels and consonants and the mantra of interdependent origination a number of times. Then I woke up.

At dawn after the twelfth night, I dreamt I was in a building that resembled a monastery with a man said to be Kyabje Vajradhara Katok Situ but who didn't look much like him. Although his hair was gray, his round face and body appeared youthful. Over four days, the lama bestowed the empowerments for the *Heart Essence of the Dakinis*, and on the last day, I dressed in my best clothes and went to the empowerment hall wearing a thönshu hat. As I walked in, the lama stood up and I took off my hat. He touched my forehead with his, then I sat on a high throne to the left of the lama's throne, and we chanted the empowerment text with those who had gathered to do the practice. We also chanted a chö practice—I think it was the *Songs of the Dakinis*.

I think a tummo fire empowerment was also bestowed at the end of the three awareness empowerments, although the *Heart Essence of the Dakinis* empowerment manual used wasn't the same as the one we'd used previously. Once the empowerments were complete, the lama asked me to bring him a bundle of rolled thangkas that included one depicting the empowerment mandala. Just as I was about to pick it up, I awoke. I wonder if this dream was a blessing of the holy site of Drakar Lhachu.

In the year of the iron horse (1930), on the twenty-seventh night of the ninth month, I dreamt I was at Phuma. An antique holy thangka of *Druptab Gyatsa* was on display in the shrine room, as was a new golden thangka with a standing Maitreya as the main image surrounded by a retinue of standing goddesses. I explained which goddess was Tara and which Chandan, and that the one wearing a peacock apron was Marichi and the one holding a jewel in her right hand was Vasudhara.

In the floor of the shrine's storeroom was a huge patched crack. I said it should be mended and enlarged the crack to a hole the size of four pillars with my knife. Then I said, "This could be a balcony!" and as I looked through to the floor below, I saw Sonam Wangyal pacing up and down, frowning. I also saw a thangka with what looked like embroidered borders. I can't remember the main image, but Longchenpa was at the front, Khyentse Wangpo to the left, Virupa to the right, and Khedrup Gyatso at the upper right—I've forgotten who was at the upper left. All the images were labeled, and Longchenpa and Virupa were blue with slightly wrathful expressions. I should examine the place I saw in my earlier dream that looked like Phuma.

In the year of the fire monkey (1956), on the fourteenth day of the eleventh month, during the night I spent at Raxaul,[244] I dreamt I was in a perfect painted house that was supposedly the residence of Öntö Khenpo Khyenrab. He was also there. Inside the house, which was the height of a human adult, stood a magnificent gilded bronze image of the Dudtsi Trokhar (Amritakundali) palace;[245] a magical wheel spinning in space; a life-size, white-bronze statue of nine-faced Vajrabhairava and consort; a slightly smaller, very majestic Vajrabhairava statue; and many other statues. Khenpo was about to give me one of them, but I don't think it would have been the large one. He asked me to pick up a flat stone statue about four fingers high. The statue was then washed to remove the dirt and was suddenly no longer a statue but a brick! Not only that, it was a brick of what seemed to be Indian cement. I wasn't at all satisfied.

When I examined the palace in detail, I found a statue of standing Avalokiteshvara with several arms (I forget how many) and one right hand in the mudra of supreme giving. Deities surrounded the statue, and several stood or sat on the crown of its head, but I couldn't say who they were. I asked Khenpo to give me the statue and he agreed I could take it. I went on to say that I would need to make a box in which to carry it. He said that if I couldn't take it immediately, it would be delivered during the eleventh month and that Khenpo would ... And that was all I dreamt.

The night before, I dreamt I gave all the empowerments for the *Precious Treasury of Terma Teachings* to a number of lamas and tulkus, including Shechen Rabjam—except for the *Twenty-Five Teachings with Restriction Seals*, which they said was not necessary. In the middle of reading the sadhanas of *Extracting the Pure Essence* and *Dorje Drolö* from the *Precious Treasury of Terma Teachings*, I woke up.

In the year of the fire monkey (1956), on the sixteenth day of the eleventh month at Birganj, I had a vision during the recitations of the protectress Marichi from the Shije tradition. Tselu[246] was ill at the time, and in my vision Ngari Rigdzin Lekden, Jangdak, and Chokgyur Lingpa were all huddled together directly above Tselu's head. I immediately wrote a prayer of supplication.

On the thirteenth night of the eighth month, I dreamt I circumambulated a huge structure in a strange, desolate valley but could not tell whether the structure was the dome of a stupa or a temple. As I walked from one side of the top step to the other, I was told a holy place was about to be opened on the upper south side. I opened the middle door and found a crowd of people. I walked through to the door on the southeast side, which I opened and found a passage leading to a spacious chamber. I also dreamt I heard people saying that many more could fit in and some other dreams, but I've forgotten most of them.

I woke up briefly, and when I nodded off again, it was as if I had reentered my previous dream, as two or three doors had opened and thirteen dakinis were singing together. Earlier that summer, I had visited the gardens in Darjeeling, so my dream was probably a memory of the songs and dances I enjoyed there. Nevertheless, I wonder if it was a sign that the sacred place of Pemakö should be opened.

On the twenty-ninth night of the eighth month, I dreamt a few attendants and I were climbing a narrow ledge on the left face of a white rocky mountain, and that we were on our way to open the hidden section of Ziltrom mountain. I also dreamt of walking through a stony valley behind the white mountain.

On the twenty-first night, I dreamt of Lopön Rinpoche (Guru Padmasambhava), an arm's length in height and wearing Zahor clothing. He sat on a lotus right in front of me, embraced by his consort, Tsogyal, and I asked him to grant me the supreme siddhi. I specifically made strong aspirations that the obstacles to my life would be dispelled, and experienced the amrita that flowed from the point of union of the guru and consort spilling onto the crown of my head.

One day in the year of the fire rooster (1957), while bestowing the empowerments and transmissions for the Dharma cycles of Jatsön Nyingpo at Gangtok in Sikkim, during the consecration of empowerment substances for the wrathful deity of the *Embodiment of the Three Jewels*, my awareness became sharp and my visualization of the deity's form pristinely clear and vast, filling the whole of space. I had a vision of numerous emanations radiating from the deity and subjugating all the gods and spirits, tearing out their hearts, and dissolving them into the deity's seat. Although it seemed it was necessary to perform the subjugation of gods and spirits, I didn't do it because I didn't think the vision was important.

On the first day of the eighth month in Darjeeling, I bestowed the empowerment for the *Wrathful Dark Blue Guru* from the *Northern Treasures* on more than ninety people, including tantra students, Thartse Khenpo Sonam Gyatso, the Queen Mother of Sikkim, and others. The night after I gave the preparatory initiation, I dreamt I was asked to subjugate a malevolent spirit living in the tearoom of my Dzongsar residence, which I did by visualizing a fire and maintaining complete confidence that I *was* Tukdrup Drakpo.[247]

On the fourth night of the tenth month in the year of the fire rooster (1957), I had a nightmare that frightened me. So I chanted out loud, "To Orgyen Rinpoche I pray . . ." and a few repetitions of the prayer that begins, "To the precious master, Padma Thotrengtsal, the Wrathful One whose Wisdom Blazes . . ." and generated fervent devotion. As a result, I dreamt I prayed to and received empowerments from the three-faced, six-armed wrathful one whose wisdom blazes, wrathful Guru Rinpoche, Yeshe Rab-bar, who was about the size of a five-year-old child. At first, he looked like a clay statue, then at times transparent like a deity, but I could see him clearly. Even after I woke up, I could not tell whether it had been a dream or reality.

One day, during the tenth month in the year of the earth dog (1958), I dreamt that we were climbing the steep ridge that comes after the peak that looks like the mountain at Rong called Sela. We had our donkeys and mules with us. Halfway up on the other side of the ridge stood a few yak-hair tents, and I had a feeling they belonged to the demon of the cliff. Tashi Namgyal and another monk were already far ahead of me when a raging tempest arose from the tents. The people in front of Tashi Namgyal and the monk were running fast, with others following behind them. When these people tried to hurt me, I clearly visualized myself as the Lord of Death, Yamantaka in his most powerful form, and offered the demons to his three mouths over and over again. As a result, the turbulence subsided.

On the first night of the tenth month, I dreamt I rode a horse to the top of a mountain, then, wearing a sertep hat, I ran down a steep slope like a young boy. When I reached the bottom, I saw a blue rock that was believed to be the torso of Rudra and also had a head. It was a ganachakra vessel belonging to the dakinis. I entered the hollow rock and told the people there what I had seen.

Not far from the rock were four steps made of something resembling blue earth, one side of which bore indicatations that treasure was hidden there. So I poked around with a stone and broke it open. Inside was a recess containing quite a few texts wrapped in green cloths, and as it grew bigger and bigger, I saw a bronze statue of Vajravarahi, a little more than an arm's length in height, and many other shrine objects. But I have forgotten the details.

When I visited the Gurkar cave, a rocky crag—believed to be the holy place of Mahottara—appeared to me as the mandala of the eight great deities with large, radiant faces, arms, and enormous, sky-like, transparent bodies.

In the practice cave of Guru Rinpoche at Lhodrak Sinmo Bar

Je, the treasure site of Nyang, during the *Consort Practice: The Queen of Great Bliss,* as I was about to invoke wisdom beings to the tsok, my experience ignited and I felt an urge to dance. But as there were people around, I stifled the impulse.

One day, in the third month of the year of the fire monkey (1956), as we approached Dorje Drak Monastery on a ferry made from animal skin, I had a vision. In the sky above the cliffs behind the monastery, the vidyadhara Lekden Je appeared in the form of a mantrika, with matted hair and holding a phurba and skull cup. Many other vidyadharas were also there, and clouds and rainbows filled the sky.

In the year of the fire rooster (1957), on the fourteenth day of the first month, I visited Drakar Tashiding in Sikkim. I had a number of audiences with the precious Sixteenth Gyalwang Karmapa and, on five occasions, saw directly in front of me but from quite a distance the precious hat that liberates when seen. I generated strong devotion and recited the seven-branch and mandala offering prayers. I also composed a prayer for the long life of Gyalwang Karmapa and had a visionary experience similar to one I had had during an audience with him in Tsurphu. I requested that an invocation of blessings treasure vase and a local deities treasure vase be consecrated with flowers and aspiration prayers. The Karmapa told me where to build a small palace for local deities, and on the sixteenth day, I inserted into it a local deities treasure vase.

On the seventeenth day, while making ritual preparations for the placing of a mandala and treasure vases, I composed some songs in the form of prayers of supplication. As I was about to write one to Lhatsün Chenpo, a devoted student from Lithang called Gema offered me a scarf, a silver top ornament engraved with the eight auspicious symbols, and a copper mandala plate engraved with the eight auspicious substances. I accepted the silver top ornament for the sake of auspiciousness and returned the rest. I wrapped the ornament in a white scarf and offered it to Gyalse Rinpoche with prayers of aspiration. After placing the treasure vases, we performed the invocation of blessings and requested that the deities remain by reciting the relevant practice from the *Embodiment of the Three Jewels.*

On the morning of the second seventeenth day, we hoisted flags and chanted praises and prayers of auspiciousness for the divine palace. I walked a little way into a fissure in the rock and reached a place where many small structures resembling stupas were arranged. There in the sky above me, I had a shimmering vision of the great Lhatsün in a heruka costume, holding a thigh-bone trumpet in his right hand and a skull cup filled with chang in his left. His body was huge, and he was surrounded by a retinue of many dancing dakinis.

On the twenty-fifth day, Khachö Rinpoche and about twenty other students performed an elaborate tenshuk ceremony based on the ritual for *Turning Back the Summons of the Dakinis* from the *Accomplishing the Life-Force of the Vidyadharas* at Pema Yangtse. I think it was during the invocation of blessings that the great Lhatsün Namkha Jigme—who was wearing a heruka costume and holding a long-life vase in his right hand in the mudra of supreme giving, and a skull cup filled with chang in his left— placed the long-life vase on my head. But as I was not able to note down the events until today, the thirtieth, I have forgotten the details.

During the twenty-fifth night, I dreamt of many stupas that were supposedly the reliquaries of omniscient Longchenpa. One or two of them were damaged and had pieces broken off. Inside one of them, I could see a naked kudung in sleeping posture. It looked as though a five-colored rainbow was shining from its spine. Sometimes the kudung appeared to be in scattered pieces, and at others it was whole. I repaired that stupa. On the twenty-sixth day, I was told about the naturally arisen rock on Shabje Gang (Footprint Hill) below Sangak Chöling, on the ridge above what were believed to be the ruins of Peling Monastery, and wondered whether my dream had been an indication that this would happen.

In the year of the fire monkey (1956), on the twentieth day of the second month, while bestowing the empowerment for the *Innermost Secret Guru Yoga Called the "Sealed Quintessence"* on Yönru Tersey Jamyang Sonam, during the mantra recitation, I thought of Vimalamitra with devotion. Consequently Lhatsün Namkha Jigme appeared to me, elderly and with long matted hair, but I couldn't see whether he was wearing long-sleeved clothes or monks' robes. His right hand formed the teaching mudra, while his left hand formed the mudra of equanimity and held a skull cup full of chang. Many light blue, transparent dakinis emanated from his body. I prayed to Lhatsün and received empowerments from him, and he joyfully uttered a few inspiring words, then dissolved into me.

As I slept, in the latter part of the thirtieth night of the tenth month, I had a visionary experience. The great treasure revealer Chokgyur Lingpa appeared, dressed as Guru Rinpoche. As it was necessary for him to perform a cleansing and purifying ritual and to bestow a long-life empowerment, he manifested as the mandala of White Amitayus from the *Magical Net*. First, he granted the empowerments of five vases, then the empowerment of the vase visualized as the deity, and finally the empowerments of body, speech, and mind. During the secret and prajna empowerments, a dancing, wrathful deity with consort appeared, slightly larger than a human being. Terchen Chokling gave the introduction for the fourth empowerment of sign and word with a mirror, a crystal, and a peacock feather. At the end, I heard a few verses that were prayers for auspiciousness. But I have forgotten everything now, unfortunate man, loaded down as I am with mountains of negative karma and obscurations.

The next night, which was the first day of the tenth month, about seventeen monks, led by Khachö Rinpoche of Pema Yangtse, performed a tenshuk based on the *Turning Back the Summons of the Dakinis* from *Accomplishing the Life-Force of the Vidyadharas*. During the practice, I had a vision. Initially it was a vision of a person dressed as a mantrika performing a wrathful dance, but then it wasn't so clear. As there were five vases, perhaps this vision was connected with the previous night's dream.

On the nineteenth night of the eleventh month, I dreamt I had an audience with Tertön Lerab Lingpa. I had gathered a few medicines, like arura, and so on, because I intended to perform a mendrup drupchen. As I was asleep in a house, the tertön, disguised as a tiger, leapt onto my chest and pressed me down with his forepaws. At first I was afraid, and I threw him off, much to his amusement. Then I stood up and visualized him as Vajrakumara, and he actually transformed from a tiger into Vajrakumara! I've had numerous strange dreams like this one. I think I had a vision of the tertön when I was accumulating one hundred thousand tsok offerings based on Lerab Lingpa's sadhana, the *Innermost Essence of the Razor-Edged Phurba*, but can't quite remember what happened because I didn't write it down.

On the seventeenth day of the tenth month, Dodrup Tulku performed a tenshuk for me based on the *Turning Back the Summons of the Dakinis* found in the *Consort Practice* from the *Heart Essence of the Vast Expanse*. During the practice, I had a pure vision of several masters in the sky before me, including Jigme Lingpa, whom I caught sight of through an open window. Also a mantrika with long, black matted hair, a round face, and a small beard, who I saw very clearly but didn't recognize.

One day during the third month, I had a vision of vajradhara Khyentse Wangpo. He was wearing monks' robes and held a long-life vase in his right hand. He gave me a long-life empowerment of Thangtong Gyalpo and assured me that I wouldn't face any obstacles for some years.

Earlier, when Khyentse Chökyi Lodrö was making thangkas depicting Khyentse Wangpo Rinpoche's garland of lives, he instructed the artists to paint Thangtong Gyalpo and Khyentse Wangpo holding long-life vases that overflowed into the long-life vase held by Khyentse Chökyi Lodrö. I have a feeling this thangka also depicted one of his pure visions.

During the fourteenth night of the ninth month, I dreamt I saw Jamgön Kongtrul Rinpoche holding a few pages of yellow parchment, from which the sadhana of *Vajrapani Holding a Vajra Cudgel* was deciphered. The pages weren't in Jamgön's handwriting, and I don't think they were from one of his treasure teachings but from those of another tertön. Again, as I received the sacred substance of worn yellow parchment, I felt joyful, and saw the great Kongtrul in different forms, sometimes his own and sometimes as Karma's heart-son.

In the year of the earth dog (1958), during the first night of the sixth month, I dreamt I bestowed an empowerment on a crowd of about three hundred monks and laypeople in the assembly hall of an unfamiliar monastery. I placed a small golden amulet on my head, and we performed a sadhana practice that was linked to the eighty mahasiddhas. For a long time during the tsok offering, I performed a tsok dance with a small vajra and bell in my hands. After that, I gave a very long explanation of the dance of auspiciousness called "The Gathering of Joy" but didn't get the chance to dance it myself or anything like that.

Khyentse Chökyi said that in the fourth month of the year of the wood monkey (1944), while performing an elaborate mendrup drupchen from the *Mandala of the Eight Great Deities: The Assembly of Sugatas*, he had a very clear vision of the eight vidyadharas (the authorized transmission holders of the Kagye) performing a vajra dance above the mandala shrine. I have also seen a note written on the *Twenty-Five Teachings with Restriction Seals* page of his practice text about how he had visions and received blessings from Chandali, the long-life mother. And a note stating that in the year of the water tiger,[248] when Khyentse Chökyi Lodrö was fifty-one, during the recitation practice for the preparation of extracting the elixir amrita pills based on the sadhana of *Manjushri from the Gyüluk Tradition*, he had a clear vision of Manjushri, his consort, and their retinue of four kinds of Saraswati above the mandala shrine. In the vision, he united with the four consorts one after another for a long time and each time experienced extraordinarily blissful wisdom. When he woke up, the attendants who were assisting him thought he was unwell and burnt purification incense.

How Khyentse Chökyi Lodrö received the transmission for *The Words of My Perfect Teacher* and the instructions for the preliminary practice of the *Heart Essence of the Vast Expanse* directly from the great bodhisattva Patrul Orgyen Jigme Chökyi Wangpo in a vision, and so on, is mentioned in his autobiography.

A Brief Explanation of How Jamyang Khyentse Chökyi Lodrö Received Authorizations for the Profound Terma Teachings—An Addition to the Main Biography.

It was obvious to everyone that our supreme Lord Guru lived his life and performed beneficial activities in a very similar way to his predecessor, omniscient Khyentse Wangpo. Although there is no doubt that Khyentse Chökyi Lodrö had authority over the extraordinary secret treasuries of Lord Khyentse, he put most of them aside, revealing very few, because beings lacked merit and the teachings had degenerated. However, to illustrate his infinite hidden qualities, I will explain here a small fraction of the treasure teachings that I myself witnessed him reveal, or that I heard about from others.

By merely looking at a yellow scroll of parchment of incomprehensible dakini writings, Khyentse Chökyi Lodrö immediately knew what the text contained and how to decipher the symbolic script elaborately, moderately, or simply, and when it would be auspicious to do so. Khyentse Chökyi Lodrö was therefore without doubt a great king of the profound treasure teachings.

Quite spontaneously or when he visited extraordinary holy places, he was able to see and recognize profound treasures hidden inside mountains, rocks, lakes, and so on, as well as the signs that indicated their presence. He wrote to his younger brother, Tulku Chime, telling him he should reveal a treasure hidden at the holy place of Dorje Drakmar in Meshö. He also wrote to tell me about a treasure hidden above the hill behind Dzongsar called Tashi Dil that should be revealed.

He told me, "A girl from Gonjo, a dakini, wrote many pages of dakini script and gave me a few. I wish I could give them to you, but I've already destroyed them." He also said that if he had any pure visions, he would give me the volume of terma script he had received from a master he believed to be Tertön Sogyal, indicating that I would be able to decipher them. However, I was not able to follow that up with him, and he didn't mention it again. Apart from this, Khyentse Chökyi Lodrö did not specifically reveal treasures that could be perceived by ordinary people.

He had countless pure visions and revealed countless mind treasures. I will now describe a few examples.

In the year of the fire monkey (1956), on the twenty-sixth day of the third month, a tsok offering based on the sadhana of the *Avalokiteshvara Resting in the Nature of Mind* was performed at Drakmar Drinzang. During the practice, in a shimmering pure vision, I received from Khyentse Wangpo Rinpoche, who had transformed into the mandala, the preparatory initiation with blessings for the ayatanas; the main empowerments, such as the outer and inner rituals for introducing the student into the mandala; and the awareness and vase empowerments. In an instant, Khyentse Wangpo Rinpoche bestowed the secret empowerment on me by uniting with four consorts. He also bestowed the prajna empowerment, the fourth empowerment, and the torma empowerment. But I cannot remember the vision precisely as I was not able to write it down until a few days later.

This tells us that although only the oral transmission lineage for the main earth treasure of Lord Khyentse existed (the sadhana of the *Avalokiteshvara Resting in the Nature of Mind*), Khyentse Chökyi Lodrö actually received the transmission of the empowerment lineage directly in a pure vision. Sadly, we were not fortunate enough to have been able to preserve the empowerment lineages of this practice—a deprivation I deeply regret.

Khenpo Tsultrim Nyima of Katok Monastery persistently requested that Khyentse Chökyi Lodrö write the sadhana of Guru Rinpoche's guru yoga combined with the three roots and the empowerment manual. Khyentse Chökyi Lodrö responded by writing the sadhana, saying it was a method for practicing the three roots by relying on indestructible inner skandas and dhatus, based on the relevant verses of the first vajra song by the previous Khyentse. In the colophon, he wrote,

> In order to nurture the devotion that springs from remembering the qualities of Orgyen Dorje Chang, the embodiment of the three roots, this guru yoga, known as the *Luminous Heart Essence*, manifested naturally from the blessings of Pema Ösel Dongak Lingpa, the Sovereign Lord of the infinite ocean of scholars and siddhas, through Jamyang Chökyi Lodrö, Vidyadhara Kunzang Ösel Nyingpo Tsal, who aspires to perform the activities of the Lord (Khyentse Wangpo) . . .

Among Khyentse Chökyi Lodrö's texts was a Manjushri tantra that had previously only been partially deciphered and which he himself completed. It was thought to be part of Manjushrimitra's Dharma cycle, the *Heart Essence of Seven Lights*. At the end of it, he wrote,

> Thus, every time I came across the *Essence of the Wisdom of Manjushri Tantra*, which was originally Pema Ösel Dongak Lingpa's mind treasure, I remembered that I wanted to finish deciphering the fifth section. But as I am lazy, it remained unfinished. When the text was found on the twenty-sixth day of the fifth month in the year of the earth ox (1949), my devoted student Chokden requested that I decipher it. So I wrote this text on the twenty-seventh of the fifth month, just as it appeared in my wisdom mind. May this be the perfect condition for the teachings on the ultimate meaning of Manjushri's Dzogchen teachings to spread and flourish.
> MANGALAM (auspiciousness).
> SHUBHAM (excellence).

This was how Khyentse Chökyi Lodrö completed various unfinished tantras and sadhanas, along with their empowerment manuals.
He also wrote

- a history of the practice of consecrating amrita from the rediscovered treasure, the *Gathering of the Dakini's Secrets*;
- the empowerment manual for Padampa Sangye's *Guru Yoga of the Heart Essence of the Oral Transmission Lineage*; and
- the vajra verses on the true meaning of the three neighs of the horse[249] from the oral lineage of Hayagriva.

In response to a request from Khenpo Namzang, who was learnèd in the five areas of knowledge, he devised

- the choreography for the ritual dance that was part of the *Profound Essence of Vishuddhi* from the oral lineage;
- the choreography for the liberation dance that was part of the oral lineage of Vajrakilaya; and
- the choreography for a brief offering dance.

He gave me

- the extraordinary instructions for completion meditation from the oral lineage of Vishuddhi and Vajrakilaya combined; and
- the long-life sadhana the *Queen of the Siddhas* belonging to the cycle of *Accomplishing the Vajra Life-Force of "Rainbow Body,"* a pure vision teaching by the previous Lord Khyentse.

More specifically, in a pure vision, Jamyang Khyentse Wangpo received directly from either King Indrabhuti or the great Brahmin Saraha an extraordinary and profound treasure teaching (in ten sections with four parts in each, making forty sections in all) about the profound and skillful path of the Vajrayana and the authorizations for the teachings. Today, we can only mention the names of these teachings because Khyentse Wangpo was unable to decipher them. However, Khyentse Chökyi Lodrö did manage to make sense of one section and wrote in the colophon,

> Ema! The extremely secret, vast instructions
> In forty sections;
> My secret words, the words of Saraha,
> I entrust to the vidyadhara, the emanated one.
> Although he lacks the merit to illuminate them,
> A fragment of one section of the entire cycle
> Will appear in the heart of Yeshe Dorje, and
> From the seed syllable in his heart will manifest
> The attainment of a vidyadhara.
> SAMAYA. GYA, GYA, GYA.

Thus I, Pema Yeshe Dorje, wrote this on the eighth day of the second month in the year of the water snake (1953) as it appeared in my wisdom mind during a recitation retreat of the *Heart Essence of Deathless Arya Tara* when I had an obscured vision of Saraha.

It is truly wonderful that Khyentse Chökyi Lodrö made these teachings available and that they arose, like all his other treasure teachings, from spontaneously arising auspicious circumstances. On the other hand, although there is no doubt that he had the ability to decipher the profound treasure teachings the previous Lord left unfinished, when reminded about them, Chökyi Lodrö would say, "Each cycle of Jamgön Khyentse Rinpoche's treasure teachings comprises creation and completion meditations and all related activity practices. They therefore contain the entire meaning of Buddha's teachings and are a complete path that can be practiced throughout your life—if only you would practice! While the conceptual thoughts of someone like me could, of course, be written down, who knows whether they would bring benefit or harm?" Basically, he had no interest in recording and propagating these treasure teachings.

At one time, Khyentse Chökyi Lodrö acquired a green-striped, jewel-shaped stone as a consecration substance for a statue of Guru Ratnasambhava (Lama Rinjung). He said he believed it to be the yaksha Gangwa Zangpo's life-stone,[250] which was one of Khyentse Wangpo's rediscovered treasures that had been given to Derge Lhundrup Teng Monastery as the inner support for the statue of the wealth deity, Lama Norlha. So, when the statue disintegrated, Khyentse Chökyi Lodrö retrieved the life-stone.

In his biography of Jamyang Khyentse Wangpo, Jamgön Kongtrul Rinpoche mentions a relic that sprang from one of Guru Rinpoche's teeth and had been offered to the previous incarnation (Khyentse Wangpo) by Nyenchen Thanglha, then reclaimed (therefore lost) by the treasure guardians a year before Khyentse Wangpo passed away. Nevertheless, Khyentse Wangpo gathered many other sacred relics at Dzongsar, and as he held his box of relics in his hands would say, playfully, that these were his termas. Although he gave relics to whoever asked for them, his collection was never exhausted, no doubt because the treasure guardians continually replenished it.

It was also clear that Khyentse Chökyi Lodrö had full authority over all Lord Khyentse Wangpo's profound treasure teachings and substances. When he revealed an extraordinary teaching through the blessings of Do Khyentse Yeshe Dorje, I asked him, skillfully, if it was appropriate to consider his guru yoga, *Bright Torch of the Innermost Essence*, to be like Do Khyentse Yeshe Dorje's guru yoga. I asked this because I felt it had all the characteristics of a mind treasure. He responded by asking, "What makes you ask?"

I replied, "Both the main deity of the guru yoga and Do Khyentse Yeshe Dorje wear the same heruka ornaments; they also share the name Yeshe Dorje."

Khyentse Chökyi Lodrö said, "Quite a number of teachings known as the *Heart Essence of Padma* appeared in my mind through the blessings of Do Khyentse Yeshe Dorje. And at around the same time, someone asked me for a guru yoga, so I wrote my *Bright Torch of the Innermost Essence*. But it's really just a slightly altered version of Do Khyentse's." Therefore, this guru yoga is definitely a mind treasure. The empowerment manual, texts of the tsok offering, and some notes also exist.

Khyentse Chökyi Lodrö considered his secret name, Pema Yeshe Dorje, to be an auspicious condition of great importance as it had been given to him by omniscient Dodrupchen when he received the empowerment of the *Gathering of Vidyadharas* from the *Heart Essence of the Vast Expanse*. He said that apart from *Cutting Through: Self-Liberation from Fixation*, the lineage for the words of Do Khyentse's other Dharma cycles no longer existed. However, some time ago, he had received authorization for all these teachings from Do Khyentse Yeshe Rinpoche himself, as well as the transmission of the essence of the teachings.

Later, he dreamt of a lake at the foot of a mountain in what appeared to be the Gyam Dothi valley from which a wide river flowed south. As Chökyi Lodrö and a few of his attendants (all on horseback) climbed up the hill near the lake, they met a mantrika on his way down. He had long, black, matted hair and was carrying many volumes of texts. This mantrika turned out to be Do Khyentse Yeshe Dorje, and he bestowed on Khyentse Chökyi Lodrö many empowerments, entrusted him with the associated teachings, and gave him texts. Khyentse Chökyi Lodrö said that in his dream, I was sitting on his left, and that he handed all those texts and teachings on to me. As I had been so favored in his dream, I asked our Lord Guru to bestow the blessings and entrustment of realization on me in the same way. He consented, and so I also had the great good fortune to receive all the blessings and entrustments of realization based on the three kinds of instruction texts for *Cutting Through: Self-Liberation from Fixation*. But I am not sure whether or not he deciphered and taught Do Khyentse Rinpoche's other treasure teachings.

I specifically asked Chökyi Lodrö to grant me the empowerment and oral transmission for the guru yoga of Guru Rinpoche, which was one of the treasure teachings he had revealed himself, and he kindly fulfilled my request. Before the empowerment began, as he described the origins of the teachings, he said, "I was overcome with grief at the dissolution of Situ Rinpoche's mind into the dharmadhatu, so I prayed to omniscient vajradhara Katok Situ again and again. As a result of his blessings, a cycle of teachings on guru practice appeared..."

He must therefore have posthumously received the *Combined Guru Yoga of Guru Rinpoche and the Three Bodhisattvas* from Situ Rinpoche, as well as the empowerment manual and instruction texts. And they all still exist.

After Tertön Drime Özer (Pema Lingpa) passed away, during the practices for making offerings to the sacred kudung, the cremation, and so on, Khyentse Chökyi Lodrö had visions of the tertön making his way to the Copper-Colored Mountain. He then revealed the root vajra verses that were Tertön Drime's posthumous teachings, the related guru yoga, and the empowerment manual, and he gave the empowerment and instructions to the tertön's two sons, Dechen Namgyal and his brother, along with a letter.

The guru yogas of Shavaripa and Tsarchen have already been mentioned.

Khyentse Chökyi Lodrö also revealed a detailed heart practice of Guru Rinpoche, a guru practice of Saraha, and the outer, inner, and secret guru practices of the Dharma Lord Sakya Pandita. But I am not sure if there are any historical records of these treasure teachings.

There is also a cycle of teachings on the practice of Guru Drakpo that Chökyi Lodrö deciphered from the symbolic script that appeared on the Guru Kutsab called "Den Me Ma," a terma revealed by Khyewo Rigdzin Chenpo and sacred practice support used by the sixth supreme Dzogchen Tulku. I have received this cycle myself, and it includes a sadhana, an empowerment manual, and activity practices.

In response to a request from Trulshik Pawo Dorje at the Boudhanath stupa in Nepal, Chökyi Lodrö wrote all the texts associated with the sadhana practice, empowerment, completion meditation, and activity practices of Simhamukha. He said that in it, all the blessings of the Kama and Terma teachings on Simhamukha are combined, particularly the oral transmissions of Vimalamitra. Therefore, a specific historical account of this treasure teaching should exist, but I haven't seen it written down.

Khyentse Chökyi Lodrö wrote,

> On the third day of the fourth month in the year of the earth dog (1958), I went to Darjeeling. We camped at the site of a king's palace, which had been razed by fire, and during the fifth night, I dreamt of a monastery that stood on top of a mountain. As I walked along the path towards the foot of that mountain, I heard a lama and many of his students—I thought it was Venerable Palpung Situ Rinpoche—chanting a visualization text in prose, not verse. They had gathered in one of the monks' rooms, and

after a while, I joined them. They told me they were performing the drupchö practice of White Simhamukha, but the lama was quite young and didn't look at all like Venerable Situ Rinpoche.

As I had the feeling I needed to receive the White Simhamukha empowerment, I asked the lama to give it to me. So he performed a short empowerment that I think came from the sadhana cycle of Simahamukha I had written earlier. It then occurred to me that a ritual for consecrating the mandala, a main sadhana practice, and elaborate empowerment texts for this sadhana cycle should also exist, and that the name of the main sadhana should be *Ocean of Accomplishment*.

In the same dream, I thought about the great sadhana of Simhamukha and its empowerment manual, the main deity of which had a retinue of nine wrathful dathvishvaris. Then I woke up.

Once I nodded off again, I continued my previous dreams. Someone said I should reveal the Simhamukha teachings that were hidden near a cluster of sewa[251] bushes at a charnel ground in southwest India called Dhurtö Ngampa Dradrok. I have forgotten the rest of the details.

Chökyi Lodrö was also responsible for quite a number of minor teachings that were related to revealed treasures, such as the authorization blessing manuals for teachings on the Four-Faced Glorious Protector and for Yudrönma, the protectress of the *Mother and Son Heart Essence*; the spontaneous vajra verses of *Lhamo*; the daily recitations of the kshetrapalas; and teachings on completion meditation, and so on.

Not only that, he also provided support for other treasure revealers. How he did so will now be explained.

As omniscient Khyentse Wangpo was one of the five king tertöns, all the tertöns of his time relied on him for advice and support, and as he wanted their activities to flourish, he always fulfilled their requests. Similarly, when Dechen Namgyal, the son of Tertön Drime Pema Lingpa, requested advice about the profound treasure he was destined to reveal, Chökyi Lodrö expressed absolute confidence that he was indeed an authentic tertön. He also told Dechen Namgyal that since, at that time, there was no greater tertön than Lerab Lingpa, and that he and Lerab Lingpa shared the same aspirations and karmic disposition, it would be auspicious for them to meet. Dechen Namgyal therefore met Lerab Lingpa and went on to receive vast treasuries of Dharma, wealth, and holy substances from him. As a result, the initial tendrel turned out to be both auspicious and excellent.

Khyentse Chökyi Lodrö instructed Drikung Tertön Ösel Dorje to perform rituals that would remove obstacles from his own life and received empowerments and instructions from Ösel Dorje's profound treasure teachings. He also offered the tertön his support and advised him about deciphering his Dharma cycles. As a result of this auspicious tendrel, Khyentse Chökyi Lodrö's gracious assistance was the direct cause for the teachings and activities of Tertön Ösel Dorje to spread and flourish.

He provided similar support for Tertön Tulku Dönkho, the brother of Shechen Rabjam Rinpoche, on whom he bestowed the empowerment for the *Heart Practice That Fulfills All Wishes* and blessed him with Kutsab Ngödrup Palbar. The tertön took refuge in Khyentse Chökyi Lodrö many times over the years, and when he made a tenshuk offering, he actually saw Chökyi Lodrö in the form of Guru Rinpoche inseparable from the kutsab for quite a while. During the Kalachakra empowerment, the deity known as Vajra Force manifested, and the tertön received numerous treasures of holy substances and teachings.

Thanks to Khyentse Chökyi Lodrö's support and aspirations, his younger brother, Tulku Chime, was able to open sacred hidden places, give empowerments, and propagate the teachings. Tulku Chime opened the holy place of Warti, one of the twenty-five most sacred places in Dokham. It was there that he established study and retreat centers, and the four activities for the welfare of the teachings and beings that he undertook increased considerably.

Khyentse Chökyi Lodrö wholeheartedly offered a long-life prayer of praise to the supreme emanation of Dudjom, Jigdral Yeshe Dorje, saying he was a great and authentic Sovereign Lord of extraordinary and profound secret treasures, thus creating exceptionally auspicious circumstances.

Ratri Tertön of Gonjo showed his cycle of teachings to Khyentse Chökyi Lodrö, who then explained how necessary it was to perform rituals for the welfare of the teachings and beings. Chökyi Lodrö also gave Ratri Tertön an aspiration prayer endorsed with his own seal that he had written for the tertön's long life and the spread of his profound teachings. And there are many other instances of our Lord Guru offering other tertöns all kinds of support.

Khyentse Chökyi Lodrö and a self-liberated yogini called Gyarong Khandro opened the sacred place of Gyagen Khyungtak on the hill above Dzongsar Monastery, and together they wrote a guidebook for that holy place. The treasure they then revealed in the retreat cave was an extraordinary maroon-gold phurba from which Khandro deciphered a short cycle of Vajrakilaya teachings. This dakini is believed to have spent a long time performing tsok and fire offerings for Khyentse Chökyi Lodrö's long life, during which she repeatedly had pure visions of him arriving at the tsok gathering in his wisdom form surrounded by dakas and dakinis.

Although I know myself to be a very ordinary person subject to all manner of faults, a stupid fellow who lacks the karmic disposition of a treasure revealer blessed by Guru Rinpoche, by the power of the compassionate blessings of both incarnations of the Venerable Manjushri Guru, I too have been able to note down the various bits and pieces that appeared in my mind, which turned out to be some kind of mind treasure that could only be revealed because the timing and circumstances were right.[252] The moment I showed my writings to Khyentse Chökyi Lodrö and explained their background, a profound confidence instantly took root in his mind, and he confirmed that they had arisen as a result of the auspicious condition of the transference of Jamyang Khyentse Wangpo's blessings from his mind into my own. He then received the transmissions for all the teachings I revealed.

On the tenth day of the monkey month in the year of the fire monkey (1956), Khyentse Chökyi Lodrö performed one hundred thousand tsok offerings for the three roots deities at Dzamnang Pema Shelphuk, the king of sacred practice places. Chimphu in central Tibet and Dzamnang Pema Shelphuk in Kham are the principal practice sites sacred to Guru Rinpoche. There is a naturally arisen mandala of the 725 Kagye deities in the meditation cave of Dzamnang Pema Shelphuk, and when the temple was built, omniscient Manjugosha himself marked where the pillars and beams should be, making it clear that the naturally arisen mandala should not be damaged. For this reason, Khyentse Chökyi Lodrö also performed a great mendrup drupchen there, based on the *Ocean of Dharma That Combines All Teachings*.

At his home, Tashi Chime Drupe Gatsel, he performed the mendrup drupchens from the *Heart Practice for Dispelling All Obstacles* and the *Oral Transmission Lineage of Vishuddhi*, several drupchö and mendrups from the *Gathering of the Dakini's Secrets*, several one hundred thousand tsok offerings, and so on. He personally presided over these practices, and through them created auspicious circumstances and gave the necessary support for my treasure teachings to flourish.

He bestowed on me the empowerments, instructions, and oral transmission for the whole of the *Precious Treasury of Terma Teachings* and the *Seven Transmissions* of the previous Lord Khyentse Wangpo, including the *Luminous Heart Essence of the Three Roots*, and the extraordinary blessings and entrustment of realization, again and again.

By the grace of Khyentse Chökyi Lodrö's great and absolute compassion, I deciphered a fraction of the previous omniscient guru Khyentse Wangpo's secret treasury, the symbolic scripts of which had first appeared to our Lord Guru in a pure vision. It was also he who told me which teachings would be revealed once the symbolic scripts were deciphered. Thus, his supervision and involvement dispelled my insecurities, giving me the confidence to decipher and compile these teachings in the hope that they would be of service to him. (This note is merely a small addition to the list.)

To put it briefly, I was at fault because my devotion is weak, and I am unable to deal with the display of awareness spontaneously. However, if the treasure revealer had been someone more fortunate than I, there is no doubt that the partnership between treasure revealer and guru would have been just like that of Terchen Chokling and Manjushri Guru, Khyentse Wangpo. This was how our supreme Vidyadhara Guru blessed my writings with a display of the abundant riches of his wisdom mind, just as the bodhisattvas who have gained mastery over the ten powers transform ordinary earth and rocks into gold. Having said that, I am not trying to suggest that I am a highly realized being or that I have authority over the profound teachings of supremely fortunate beings, and I ask that those who are wise and endowed with discriminating wisdom try to appreciate my reasons for mentioning anything at all.

An old mantrika from Rakchab showed Khyentse Chökyi a statue of the protector Gur that he had obtained from an animal-headed deity[253] he met on a farm. Chökyi Lodrö took the statue from the mantrika, saying that actually *he* should have received it, then replaced it with another representation and some other gifts.

One morning, when Chökyi Lodrö's secretary, Tsewang Paljor, went to make offerings in the innermost chamber of the guru's residence, he found an extraordinary maroon-bronze vajra on the doorstep. He showed it to Chökyi Lodrö, who made a joke and took it into his own care.

During his second visit to central Tibet, a man who looked like a businessman offered Chökyi Lodrö an extremely old bronze statue, a sword, a club, a bow, an arrow, a stick, and so on, all a little larger than a hand span.

At the time, Chökyi Lodrö showed no sign that the offerings pleased him. However, once the businessman had left, he said, "I have just received my semiwrathful Manjushri's hand implements." They were very precious to him.

This was how he revealed a great many statues and hand implements, either personally or through other people.

Khyentse Chökyi Lodrö instructed me to write a guidebook for the sacred place of Khyung Tak that he had opened himself, and one for the seat of Dzongsar Tashi Lhatse that he had previously seen in a pure vision and that was sacred to Manjushri Yamantaka.

He performed rituals to remind the gods and spirits of their commitments. He found new paths to holy places and wrote a guidebook for the path that leads to the hidden land of Trori Ziltrom in Derge through a rock that resembles a tent on a mandala. He also wrote guidebooks for the Wangchen Drak of Pawog; Shari Sangchen, which lies between Derge and Lhathok; Zegyal in Nangchen; Pugyal, the snow mountain in Khyungpo; Taklung in Yardok; some of the sacred places in Sikkim; and Yangleshö in Nepal.

These are just a few examples of our Lord Guru's revelations. Without doubt, he experienced the display of his wisdom mind in infinite pure visions and had complete mastery over the extraordinary *Seven Transmissions*, just like the previous omniscient Khyentse Wangpo. However, as Guru Rinpoche said, "Some tertöns do not reveal new termas, they uphold the old treasure teachings." This was true of Khyentse Chökyi Lodrö, who focused on teaching and propagating the infinite teachings of Sarma and the Kama and Terma of the Nyingma tradition according to the needs of individual students. Apart from that, he always refused to spread the writings and profound teachings he brought forth from the expanse of his realization, saying,

> How can you trust the experiences of someone who himself is so bewildered? We have no idea whether or not my writings will bring benefit or harm either to my mind or to the minds of others. For example, Khenchen Lama Tobden saw a written account of the visions of omniscient Katok Situ Dorje Chang, in which he was blessed by Katok Dampa Deshek and received directly in a pure vision the transmissions for numerous teachings from the Katok lineage. Khenchen Tobden repeatedly asked

omniscient Katok Situ Rinpoche to propagate those teachings and to finish writing descriptions of the pure visions. But Situ Rinpoche responded by saying, "There is no value in what my restless hand has written. If we all keep writing down our countless mystifying experiences, we will undermine the greatness of our root guru's direct lineage of pure visions. Even if we did try to emulate Khyentse Rinpoche, it would be like fireflies competing with the sun, and the result would not please the learnèd scholars and accomplished siddhas." Situ Rinpoche spoke the truth.

Khyentse Chökyi Lodrö simply ignored his own writings and terma revelations. And as it was extremely difficult for anyone to understand his mind, I couldn't summon the confidence necessary to ask him for specific details.

This is all for now, as there are not many other accounts that were either personally related by him or written down.

The Secret Biography

Now, a brief explanation of how Khyentse Chökyi Lodrö attained the extraordinary qualities that are signs he accomplished the path.

From the *Perfection of Wisdom Sutra in Eight Thousand Lines*:

> Furthermore, Subhuti, whatever the nonreturner bodhisattva mahasattva knows about the Dharma, he should know completely, and offer the generosity of Dharma to others.
> Grant my teachings for the sake of sentient beings and to bring benefit and happiness.
> May the teachings I give completely fulfill the good wishes of all sentient beings and make the gift of Dharma available to all.
> Subhuti, you must consider the bodhisattva mahasattva, fully endowed with all these qualities, to be one who will never return from unsurpassable, complete enlightenment.

Khyentse Chökyi Lodrö was graced with all the same qualities as those of the nonreturner bodhisattva described in the Mahayana sutras. He attained the results of the Vajrayana path, personally and indirectly, as explained in the accounts of his inner and secret lives, and all appearance and existence arose as the infinite pure mandala of the deities. Through the ultimate fruition of the activity that enhances realization, he attained the stage of no-more-learning.

Here, I will briefly explain how Khyentse Chökyi Lodrö adopted the activity that enhances realization and what that entails.

It is said in the completion meditation teachings of the great Sarma and Nyingma tantras, which are in complete agreement, that prior to attaining ultimate fruition, a practitioner must liberate himself and the mandala of all beings into the vajra family of the heruka. The method he should use is called the activity that enhances realization, and to practice it, he needs the help of a wisdom consort prophesied by yidam deities and gurus. Khyentse Chökyi Lodrö attained this stage; the verses prophesying that he would were written by the previous Lord in the form of a vajra song.

> Cuckoo[254] in the bamboo grove of Mon in the south,
> Singing the vina's melody from the east where dakinis linger,
> Come, be my partner in sorrow, help me extract the summer shoot.
> There is wonder in the blossoming lotus of joyful experience.

These are the actual words that predicted the previous Lord's future life.

To begin with, on the day Khyentse Chökyi Lodrö granted the transmission of the *Compendium of Sadhanas* to the Dagchen of Sakya Phuntsok Podrang and his sons, he wore a white lower robe as he bestowed the authorization blessings for the *Three White Deities*, and having just come out of retreat, he also had long hair.

I had told him that when he adopted the conduct of the Mantrayana, it would be more auspicious for him to wear a white robe. He responded to this stupid one by telling me about a pure vision that had appeared in his wisdom mind. In the vision, to express the kindness with which he cared for Chökyi Lodrö, Shri Heruka Namkha Jigme stroked his head again and again, saying that the time had come for him to travel as a wanderer to unfamiliar places and to conduct himself in the manner connected with the practice of awareness. On the same day, Khyentse Chökyi Lodrö had received two small bronze statues of Guru Rinpoche in the form of a heruka. All these elements, he said, had created the auspicious circumstances.

I also offered a song to inspire him to the realization and activities of a heruka, which would be extremely beneficial for him. Joyfully, he read the song again and again and indicated that Do Khyentse Yeshe Dorje had made the same prediction. This suggested that he could remember his life as Do Khyentse. And just like Do Khyentse, numerous visions and prophecies made by yidam deities and vidyadhara gurus had inspired him to adopt the activities of a mantrika.

As a sign of the dissolution of the elements—nadi, prana, and bindu—that signals the accomplishment of the inner path, from the age of about forty, Khyentse Chökyi Lodrö's body began to shake so violently that others could see it happen. Even when the shaking stopped, he was unable to speak, sometimes for a short period, sometimes for rather longer. He displayed these symptoms several times a day. What's more, when seriously ill, his feces and urine remained clear and pure, which was a sign he had attained the higher bhumis and paths. But when his feces and urine were abnormal, his health was good, as if the signs of wind, bile, phlegm, and so on, were at odds with each other. When the elements of his body were extremely disturbed, no matter which medicine or treatment was offered, it had no effect on his symptoms and did not improve his health. His precious body[255] would recover quite suddenly for short periods in the mornings and evenings, but his illness was beyond his doctors' understanding and confounded everyone.

Eventually, the doctors diagnosed the illness as *drib lung* ("obscuring winds") and offered him the appropriate medicine, while elaborate rituals were performed for his long life. Yet, as there was no sign of recovery or improvement, it became clear that the time had come for him to adopt the activity that enhances realization.

Khyentse Chökyi Lodrö said,

> How can my illness be a result of having practiced the path? As my mind is destitute of practical experience, there really is no reason for such a thing to happen. I don't know what kind of karmic residue I carry from my former lives, but to me, this illness looks like the dissolution of nadi, prana, and bindu.

By closely examining his words, our faith and confidence will deepen. However, he steadfastly hid his extraordinary qualities and ignored all the signs, saying,

> It's not necessary to do anything other than create auspicious circumstances for my life. And for me to set any other kind of example would be of no benefit whatsoever to the Buddhadharma.

At that time, all the students who understood the importance of and reasons for him adopting the activity that enhances realization wrote to Khyentse Chökyi Lodrö. The exalted Jamgön Tai Situ Pema Wangchok Gyalpo, the heart-son of the two Jamgön lamas and the great Sovereign Lord of the teachings of the practice lineage, wrote,

> The result of all the many divinations I have done at various times for the supreme Jamgön lama, Khyentse Chökyi Lodrö, has always been that the most important practice for his long

life is for him to accomplish his intentions without error. I was referring to this point.²⁵⁶ Although it may be a little late in his life, it is extremely important that we do everything we can to create auspicious and excellent circumstances.

Gyalse Jamgön Choktrul Rinpoche also told Khyentse Chökyi Lodrö that in terms of necessary auspicious circumstances, it was not too late for him to adopt secret conduct, and that the supreme Jamgön lama should always maintain the strong determination to live as the protector of the teachings and beings for a very long time. And he offered a tenshuk for Chökyi Lodrö's long life.

Everyone who understood how important this was for him—for example, the king, the prince, the queen, the ministers, and subjects of Derge—persistently begged him to adopt the activity that enhances realization. Drikung Tertön Ösel Dorje offered a letter of prophecy stating that Chökyi Lodrö needed to adopt secret conduct and take a consort as the support for his life. Khyentse Chökyi Lodrö's younger brother, Chime Pema Dorje, and I also offered prophecies. All these concurring prophecies eventually appeared to invoke the appropriate auspicious circumstances. However, our Lord Guru's primary reason for adopting secret conduct and taking a consort was a prophecy that arose clearly in his own wisdom mind. Until then, his behavior—how he dressed, drank tea, and so on—had always followed the principles of the Vinaya. For example, he only ever wore patched robes.

He wrote a section in his autobiography about having adopted secret conduct:

> I am now a little more than fifty-one years old.
> Although I have not even the tiniest attribute of a tertön or
>   a mahasiddha,
> If, for the time being, I survive,
> By trying to help myself, I may also be of some small benefit
>   to others.
> Therefore, in accordance with the verses of the secret prophecy
>   of the previous omniscient Lord,
> And the prophecies of sublime masters like the great Jamgön
>   Kongtrul,
> And to comply with the prophecy that appeared in my own mind,
> The auspicious circumstance for taking a consort as the support
>   for my life has been established,

> And I have renounced the vows of individual liberation of the
> sravakayana.
> Although by taking a consort I may not attain realization,
> I aspire always to maintain my virtuous intention.
> Although I cannot promise that this activity will bring benefit,
> As long as I am not overpowered by outer or inner circumstances,
> For now, I may live.

Enthralled by Khyentse Chökyi Lodrö's qualities and the signs of his accomplishments, the great scholar and siddha Dezhung Ajam Choktrul Rinpoche said, "There is no need for a great vajradhara like you to renounce your monk's vows," because this vajradhara had truly attained the higher stages of accomplishment.

From the tantras:

> Perfectly liberated from samayas and vows.

As we have already seen, Khyentse Chökyi Lodrö transformed all his precepts into all-accomplishing wisdom, so he had no need to keep his vows in the same way ordinary beings did. To ordinary beings, he always appeared as the great Sovereign Lord of experience and realization; therefore, it was appropriate for him to rely on the mudra of immediate cause, without forsaking the vows of both shramanera and bhikshu.

The foremost mahasiddha in the Noble Land, Saraha, for example, took the huntress as his consort. After doing so, he said,

> Until yesterday, I was a Brahmin,
> Until yesterday, I was no monk;
> From today onwards, I am a monk,
> The glorious Heruka is the supreme monk.

And having taken a consort, Saraha ordained Nagarjuna. There is no doubt that Khyentse Chökyi Lodrö was no different from Saraha. However, with the sole intention of benefiting tamable beings by means of concealing his good qualities, he observed all the precepts of the three authentic types of vow as stipulated in the relevant sacred texts, in the same way that ordinary beings practice the path in gradual stages.

Bearing in mind how necessary it was not to allow beings of this degenerate age to compromise their Vinaya discipline, which is the root of the sublime Dharma, at the time Khyentse Chökyi Lodrö changed the basis of his spiritual practice, he had already abandoned attachment to the eight worldly preoccupations and was primarily practicing the profound skillful method of the secret mantra (the true essence of the ocean of tantras and pith instructions). That is to say, however high his inner realization of view and experience, his behavior and appearance never denigrated the Vinaya precepts of the supreme guide, the Muni king.

People today undermine the greatness of the teachings. So many in this degenerate age compromise their precepts and vows for no reason yet lack true confidence in view or meditation. They even claim to have received terma prophecies and consequently adopt secret conduct. Therefore, to encourage others to be more careful, Khyentse Chökyi Lodrö set an example by both giving back his Vinaya vows and performing many services venerating the Sangha.

When the great Lhatsün Namkha Jigme adopted secret conduct, he offered his monks' robes and begging bowl to the statue of Buddha Shakyamuni and the monks at Vajrasana, and only then assumed the clothing of a heruka. Khyentse Chökyi Lodrö did the same by offering the things he had used as a renunciate to various monasteries—for example, the three types of robes that emit the pervasive fragrance of pure discipline, which he had always worn, and other possessions. Not only did he accompany his gifts with detailed instructions about how to display them as offerings on the special days when rituals were performed to support the spread of the teachings for as long as they remain in this world, but he also explained the purpose behind making such a display. This was how he demonstrated the act of giving back the shravakayana vows of individual liberation, which caused no harm and was of great benefit to the general well-being of the teachings.

He upheld secret conduct just like the great pioneers of the teachings in the Noble Land of India who, after adopting it, did not take on the role of abbot or preceptor of the Sangha. This aspect of Chökyi Lodrö's activity was a source of great inspiration for the wise.

Here are the essential points that explain Khyentse Chökyi Lodrö's purpose in adopting secret conduct in the vajra words of our Lord Guru himself.

Dispeller of the Darkness of Ignorance: A Letter to My Students

Homage to the Guru and Protector Manjushri!
OM SVASTI
With mind enthralled by the sublime Commander,
And trust in the ship of perfect virtue,
With its billowing white sails of devotion, diligence, and prajna,
I resolve to travel to the land of complete liberation.
This precious human body is favored with superb riches.
From the golden ground of supreme moral discipline
Springs the wish-fulfilling tree of incomparable samadhi
Bearing the exquisite fruit of peerless wisdom.
The seal confirms my commitment to single-mindedly trust
The teachings of omniscient Adityabhandu[257]
As if they were carved in stone, until the ultimate essence is attained
And they merge inseparably in one taste in the sphere of my mind.
Merely to be caressed in a whisper by the joyful Gentle Protector's
Sweet name gives meaning to our lives, and
Taking the great omniscient one as my crown ornament,
I spread his activities throughout the universe.
All those, high and low, who place a wish-fulfilling jewel
Atop a victory banner, then pray and make offerings,
Are granted the accomplishment of all they desire.
Thus have I been blessed by a tiny scrap of Khyentse Wangpo's wisdom mind.
By his grace, this precious human body with all its freedoms—
Although doubtless bereft of pure perception,
Dominated as it is by turbulent, stubborn, and discursive thoughts—
Is mostly infused with good intentions and actions.
Early signs that the sun of life
Will soon sink behind the western mountain are now clear,
And I must gather what is necessary

For one heading swiftly towards the Lord of Death.
The methods for averting death with magical incantations
Are as abundant as enchanted spring flowers
In the joyous grove of heaven;
Yet the true remedy—a drop of amrita, of life-force—is elusive.
For the vajradhara bound by the Ewam mudra,
To rely on four types of mudra is the great direct path
Taught in the unsurpassable great yoga,
The innermost essence of the ocean of tantras.
Ordinary beings with limited or mediocre intelligence
Who practice this path can stray onto the wrong track,
Just as the risks and profits from plucking jewels from the heads
    of poisonous snakes are high.
Yet those who are wise can benefit.
Completely concealed, wondrous magic,
The wisdom of great bliss arises as a dakini and
Unites with perfect formless wisdom
Through the form of the smiling lotus of bliss.
Therefore, although my confidence in taking this direct path,
So highly praised by our Guide, is as fragile as a cobweb,
I take the yoga of devotion as my path
And joyfully dance in perfect bliss and emptiness.
By the strength of the ferocity of this yoga,
Any idea of the Mara of Death is cast aside;
I intend and aspire to practice the supreme discipline
Of the great, fearless dancer of intrinsic deathlessness.
Like an illusory dance, dissolving chaotic existence into one taste,
Mind and appearance inseparable,
With fearless and almighty wisdom,
I will generate the wish, as pure as gold, to benefit all sentient
    beings.
But if I succumb to the influence of a negative mind,
Tightly bound by chains of selfishness and attachment,
The deities and my gurus will be displeased,
And the dharmapalas will crush my head.
If my mind does not dissemble,
And the fabric of the three doors encircles the thousand worlds
Entwined with strands of molten moon,

My pledge to spread
The teachings of my Lord, Jamgön Lama—
Whose only wish is to ensure the welfare of the Buddhadharma
 and all beings until the end of existence—
Will not be corrupted, and I will offer them all
As great cloud-like offerings to please the Buddha and his sons.
Although those in whom tempests of misconception rage
Criticize and, taking my behavior as their theme, berate me,
My mind is made up and I will not relent—
Not even the span of a kusha's tip.
Damaged eyes distort the pure phenomena they perceive;
Likewise, there are those who find fault
In the faultless Buddha who perfected all knowledge.
If this is so, what need is there to speak of one like me?
In the sutras and tantras we see that
Having taken a guru, we should make offerings with devotion,
Perceive his every move perfectly,
And respect him with three kinds of devotion,
Just as we respect the Buddha.
For such a student,
The treasure of supreme accomplishment
Lies in the palm of their hand.
Unable to bear the anguish of anxiety for
Those bound through me to the profound and vast teachings,
Who might develop wrong views and burn in the Great
 Central Place—hell—
I write candidly from compassion.
May cataracts from the eyes of liberation be cleared,
May a thousand sparkling eyes perceive reality perfectly,
May the blessings of the three secrets permeate the minds of all,
And may experience and realization increase further and
 further.
May my followers not be undisciplined
But diligently and virtuously shun transgression,
Practice the teaching of the Muni in its purest form,
And attain the state of omniscience.
May the power and blessings of the infinite three roots fill
 their minds,

And with sharp weapons, blazing chakras, and vajras,
May they destroy all haughty and belligerent forces, including demigods,
So nothing but their names remain.
May I, too, enjoy the splendor of indestructible deathlessness,
May the degenerations of this time be pacified throughout the world,
May celebrations of the new golden age reach their zenith, and
May the teachings and holders of the teachings flourish.
These verses were written sincerely by
A shabby old monk called Chökyi Lodrö,
Whose wispy hair was seized by Manjushri.
It was written at Tashi Chime Drupe Gatsel,
Where an ocean of scholars and siddhas gather,
At the propitious time, a hundred auspicious
And glorious qualities rained down.
May these words intensify pure perception.
SARVA DA MANGALAM.

This great secret vajra song was spontaneously written by Khyentse Chökyi Lodrö to dispel the doubts of the less fortunate and to inspire devoted students. The real intention and purpose behind the profound secret can only be realized through practice. However, if my words prove to be mere assumptions, I confess my error to the deities, gurus, and dakinis, and request their forgiveness.

Having written this vajra song, Chökyi Lodrö recovered from the illness that had so wracked his body. When he spoke with the khenpos and students of Khamje Shedra about his consort, he pointed out that in the Lamdre, the illness from which he had suffered for so long is said to occur during the initial dissolution of the elements. But to other devoted students, he said he had established the auspicious circumstance of secret conduct a little late.

If we take a closer look at this statement in consultation with the sacred texts, we can see that the essential point is that of the three stages of the dissolution of the elements, the final stage (the perfect fruition) is to meditate on vajra waves (the fourth path) with the help of the prophesied mudra endowed with a lotus. Butter must melt to separate the ghee from the solids before it can be burnt in butter lamp offerings, and so on. To melt butter, you need a fire, and to light a fire, you need fuel. Similarly, to attain the fruition of ultimate wisdom, you need illustrative wisdom, and to generate illustrative wisdom, you need a blissful sensation through which the subtle elements of the body must melt. To melt the subtle elements of the body, you need the fire of passion, and to feel that passion, you need the fuel of an authentic wisdom consort.

As it says in the *Root Tantra of Hevajra*,

> Perfect accomplishment of ultimate wisdom
> Can be attained by the yogi who practices the mudra.

And from the *Explanatory Tantra Gur*:

> The accomplishment of mudra, the great accomplishment,
> Cannot be attained by every being.

From *Sambhuti*:

> Without knowledge of the reality of the body,
> Even the practices of the eighty-four thousand Dharmas are fruitless.

And from the *Compendium of Vajra Wisdom*:

> Just as butter and sesame oil
> Cannot be obtained without processing milk and sesame seeds,
> It is impossible to realize the three consciousnesses
> Without mantra, mudra, and the union of vajra and padma.
> One who cannot perfectly unite bhaga and lingam
> Will not attain the samadhi of great bliss.
> By merely aspiring strongly for the samadhi of great bliss,
> You will relax at the first level
> And also train in the bhumi of no returning.

From the *Yogini Tantra of Conduct*:

> There is nothing that cannot be practiced
> By one endowed with a wisdom mind free from duality.

With a mind free of concepts,
One can enjoy all five sensual pleasures.

The tantras explain this in detail.

Similarly, since the key to realization taking birth in the mind swiftly is extraordinarily profound and supported by hitting the vital point of the vajra body complete with the four chakras (the basis of tendrel), the yogi must fully practice all five stages of the path: the view, creation and completion meditations, yogic discipline, and immediate cause.

From the *Glorious Tantra of Perfect Union*:

> . . . will attain Buddhahood or become Vajrasattva in this lifetime. Those who have attained such inconceivable qualities are sugatas—buddhas—and the example is perfect Vajrasattva.

And so, since the crucial point here is that the path of the causal yana and three lower tantras cannot remove the stains of the transformation of the three visions, it is not possible to progress to the level of a vajradhara, complete with all freedoms and attainments, by practicing these paths. Therefore, in the Vajrayana, the basis of the four chakras is matured into the four mandalas through the four empowerments. Having perfected abandoning and progressing within the body itself by hitting the essence through the practice of the four paths, during the ultimate fruition, the four modes of energy are dissolved by relying on the mudra of an authentic wisdom consort. Then the four chakras and the consort transform into the wisdom of the inseparable five kayas, and the siddhi of the wisdom being or Mahamudra is attained. Beings then benefit from unceasing, all-pervasive spontaneously accomplished activity.

From *Chakrasamvara: The Inseparable Union of Buddha*:

> Of all the magical illusions,
> The illusion of woman is the most extraordinary.

And from the *Wrathful Lone Hero*:

> There is no negative action other than detachment;
> There is no merit other than bliss;

Therefore, with this in mind,
Generate the bliss of passion.

As Chökyi Lodrö had practiced with great precision the true essence of the root tantra of Dzogpachenpo called *Reverberation of Sound*, as explained in the precious *Treasury of the Supreme Vehicle* and the root text and commentary on the *Wish-Fulfilling Treasury*, he had without doubt mastered view and discipline as described in the profound vajrayana tantras.

I have explained a tiny fraction of Khyentse Chökyi Lodrö's great hidden qualities in order to inspire confidence in those with impartial minds and have written down everything I have been able to fathom about how a practitioner should practice the view and discipline of the secret vajrayana path perfectly, as it's taught in the sacred texts. My sincere wish is to bring some benefit to the teachings, which these days are being destroyed from within by those who behave shamelessly while pretending to practice the secret mantra.

When Khyentse Chökyi Lodrö took his consort, the dawn of wondrous joy broke in the minds of all beings. Teachers and monks from monasteries of all traditions and lineages, and people from all walks of life—feudal lords, ministers, and the subjects of large and small kingdoms—came to see our Lord Guru to offer their joyful good wishes. A great gathering of gods and humans crowded into Dzongsar, filling it completely with the light of infinite virtue and auspiciousness.

Since he intended to wander aimlessly to practice the yogic discipline of all-victorious awareness (as predicted in the prophecy), Chökyi Lodrö adopted the activity that enhances realization and then gathered the accoutrements of a heruka, such as a vajra khatvanga that was as long as he was tall. But as his devoted students all begged him vehemently to remain at the seat of the previous Lord, it quickly became clear that by leaving he would cause them great distress. And so, because the only desire of a bodhisattva is to please sentient beings, he agreed to stay.

When Khyentse Chökyi Lodrö gave the Lamdre transmissions to the Dagchen of Sakya Phuntsok Phodrang and his sons, he told me that although he had adopted the Mantrayana path, he hadn't given up his monastic robes (the symbol of having taken the vows of individual liberation). He also said that he had worn both the ceremonial robes of a novice and those of a fully ordained monk during the teachings he had given during the empowerment. He did so, he said, to remind himself of their purpose, as the outer sign that marks the greatness of the Dharma of Buddha Shakyamuni.

He also said that having adopted the path of the Mantrayana, although it was improper for him to continue taking up space on the top floor of the monastery to keep up the pretense that it was still his seat, he had no alternative. The situation had been created by the auspicious circumstances that had arisen from various causes and conditions. Such auspicious circumstances, he said, can only be established naturally; they cannot be manipulated. So even if such circumstances appear to have been established temporarily, they do not necessarily bring about the desired result.

He also said that if he had adopted tantric discipline a little earlier in life, it might have brought more benefit, but having been bound by hope and fear, he hadn't paid much attention to it until this time. Nevertheless, since the initial auspicious circumstances had been faultless, the obstacles to his life at the age of fifty-six were definitely dispelled.

As far as his wish to wander throughout the land was concerned, since absolutely nobody could bear the thought of him leaving, he said he had no alternative but to stay where the blessings of the guru and Triple Gem had put him.

Khyentse Chökyi Lodrö also said that, where possible, he would serve the sacred seat of Lord Khyentse Wangpo by whatever means available, and if his wish to benefit the teachings and beings led him to propagate the teachings as best he could, the enlightened intentions of the sublime masters would be fulfilled, ensuring the continuity of the Buddhadharma. He said that to plant the seed of enlightenment in the minds of just one or two beings would bring great benefit, and that he would endeavor to continue doing so for the little time that was left to him.

Earlier, in the year of the earth rooster,[258] when I offered him a tenshuk at the end of the transmission of the *Precious Treasury of Terma Teachings*, he said, "Once I reach fifty or sixty years old, I will not live unless I become like you." He also mentioned that if he were given the opportunity to practice yogic discipline correctly, he had a feeling he would live longer and finally attain the vajra body of the great transference.[259] But he also said, "Is there any notion at all that cannot find its way into this mind of mine?"

If things had gone according to prophecy, he would have completed the activities left unfinished by the previous Lord, but the state of the teachings and the merit of beings at that time could not support such an undertaking.

As his only concern was for their welfare, he devoted himself to offering the relevant help to those living in this age. He therefore spent the majority of his life at the great Tashi Chime Drupe Gatsel—the Akanishta seat of the guru, the second Shri Nalanda, the secret Dharma treasury of Kama and Terma of the infinite ocean of teachings of all lineages—where he continuously turned the wheel of the profound and vast Dharma, maturing and liberating countless beings by all appropriate means.

> Entering both samsara and nirvana alike
> Through the magical display of vajra wisdom,
> Enriched with the precious jewel of freedom and realization
> In the infinite ocean of the infallible secret,
> The Supreme Protector gives life and
> All auspicious happiness and benefit to those connected with him.
> I pay homage once more to the Glorious Guru,
> The Sovereign Lord of the mandala and
> The crown ornament of samsara and nirvana.
> By remembering how your life and admirable teachings
> Make all phenomena virtuous—
> A treasure beyond price, praised in all sutras and tantras—
> I have written, without prejudice, all I know.
> Here, engulfed by the darkness of this degenerate age,
> The sun of immaculate transcendent wisdom
> Appears vivid and unobscured in the sky of Dharma and beings;
> Who would not praise such wondrousness!
> By perfectly arranging garlands of the Lord Buddha's starlike teachings
> In the sky-like space of the enlightened mind,
> From the thousand rays of light shed by the sun of sacred texts and realization,
> The celebration of the blossoming lotus of this fortunate aeon ensued.
> In the joyful grove of the heaven of scholars and siddhas of India and Tibet,
> Sounding the celestial gong, the extraordinary biography
> Multiplies the glorious wealth that delights and satisfies all
> And upholds the royal seat of supreme qualities.

Those who nurture the lotus grove of the supreme Dharma of the Muni king,
With its broad leaves of hearing, reflecting, and meditating,
Are constantly filled with the sound of profound and vast Dharma.
I hope that for you, this biography will serve as a celebration of the memory of our Supreme Guide.
My devotion, at its very root as pure and white as a conch shell,
My diligence, as profuse as leaves in a forest,
The life of Khyentse Chökyi Lodrö, the great ornament, the flowers and fruit,
Could become the glory of the teachings in the Land of Snows.
My deluded mind did not understand the secret meaning;
My wrongdoings, such as violating the bonds of secrecy,
I confess before my guru, the embodiment of nondual compassion.
Please purify my faults and grant your forgiveness right now!
Having seen the precious treasure of my guru's qualities
Through the immaculate eyes of precious devotion,
I have written this biography with confidence,
And aspire to follow in his footsteps throughout all my future lives.
Like sweet melodies played by learnèd and accomplished ones from the great centers of teaching and practice, on the flute of the three yana teachings,
Like bees dancing among abundant flowers, bringing great benefit and happiness, and
By the power of adorning this earth and all who live here with the four oceans of good actions,
The sufferings of samsara are instantaneously dispelled:
May this celebration be the glory of all beings!
By the power of the rising sun of enlightened aspiration,
May the light of the supreme tulku swiftly appear.
By nurturing the tamable beings who remain,
May he summon guests to the royal seat of Lord Buddha's teachings.
By glimpsing the extraordinary nature of Manjushri Guru's exemplary life and
By taking it as his crown jewel, never to be parted,
Lead me and all beings to liberation!
May I adorn all the teachings of the Buddha with words and realization,

May I uphold the sovereignty of the Dharma of the supreme vehicle,
free from degeneration,
May I be enriched with wonderful and excellent activity,
May I fulfill the wishes of the Buddha and his sons!
May infinite beings, spontaneously perfect
Within the all-pervasive dharmadhatu,
The great display of unchanging inexhaustible virtue and excellence,
Realize splendid and wondrously auspicious all-pervasive wisdom.

Thus, as specifically requested by Tsering Chödrön, the queen of dakinis and support for our Lord Guru's life, who offered an auspicious white scarf, and by his devoted students led by his nephew, the treasurer Tsewang Paljor, endowed with the glorious and immaculate moon of devotion and unbroken samaya, who said that I was the appropriate person to write a brief account of the life and liberation of the great omniscient Venerable Guru Jamyang Chökyi Lodrö Rinpoche, I—the worst of all students, called Gyurme Tekchok Tenpe Gyaltsen Rangjung Khyentse Özer, who was cared for by the supreme Dharma King of the three realms, Jamgön Yeshe Melong (Khyentse Chökyi Lodrö) with extraordinary kindness—wrote this biography. Taking his autobiography as the basis, I also referred to various notes about the visions he experienced during his second pilgrimage, with the permission of his shrine master, Lama Jamyang Lodrö Chokden.

I wrote this biography at Thubten Shedrup Gatsel, a place beautifully adorned with a replica of the Copper-Colored Mountain buddhafield, in the jewellike hills of Kalimpong near[260] the Noble Land of India. Later, after the necessary editing in consultation with my vajra brothers who had been attendants to our Venerable Lord Guru, the drafts were compiled into a single text at Sangzab Thekpa Chok Gi Chö Dzong[261] while I was in the southern country of Bhutan, a kingdom ruled by great Dharma Kings.

The scribes who wrote the text for the second edition were Khenpo Thubten Tsöndrü Phuntsok, a well-disciplined monk and holder of the Tripitaka, and Ngagpa Jigme Kalzang Palden, a yogi from Rekong.

May it be the cause for the glory of the Dharma and beings to soar and remain forever in all directions and times, and for infinite beings filling the whole of space to enjoy the secrets of the wisdom of the Venerable Sovereign Holder of Knowledge. This is my aspiration.

SARVADA KALAYANAM MANGALA BHAVATU

Notes

Throughout the notes section and the bibliography, "Tib." indicates the phonetic Tibetan transcription, whereas "Wyl." indicates the Wylie transliteration of the Tibetan—the formal orthography. The following abbreviations are used to indicate note sources:

Abbreviations

AP	Adam Pearcey
AZR	Alak Zenkar Rinpoche
DJKR	Dzongsar Jamyang Khyentse Rinpoche
DTR	Drubgyud Tenzin Rinpoche
JKR	Jigme Khyentse Rinpoche
KSP	Khenpo Sonam Phuntsok
KST	Khenpo Sonam Tashi
OTR	Orgyen Tobgyal Rinpoche

Remembering Rinpoche

1. Orgyen Tobgyal Rinpoche added, "Many of the stories they told me can also be found in the traditional biographies, like the *Great Biography* written by Dilgo Khyentse Rinpoche, the autobiography in verse written by Chökyi Lodrö at Dilgo Khyentse's request, the *Secret Biography*, and a short biography written by Rinpoche himself as a supplement to the biographies of the masters of Thangtong Gyalpo's oral lineage."
2. Tarthang Tulku went to Dzongsar in 1953 and remained there for about two years.
3. Near Katok Monastery.
4. Tsadra Rinchen Drak (Wyl. *tsa 'dra rin chen brag*), the sacred site above Palpung Monastery in Derge, Kham, where Jamgön Kongtrul Lodrö Taye founded his three-year retreat center and hermitage. It became Kongtrul Rinpoche's main residence.
5. Vajra Vidarana Dharani (Wyl. *rdor je rnam par 'joms pa zhes bya ba'i gzungs*).

6. This translation reflects information the translators learnt from Orgyen Tobgyal Rinpoche about this event.—DTR
7. Kalzang Dorje and Katok Situ Rinpoche were brothers and the nephews of Jamyang Khyentse Wangpo.—DJKR
8. Ekazati, Palden Lhamo, and Ber.—KSP
9. Gyurme Tsewang Chokdrup (Wyl. *'gyur med tshe dbang mchog grub*), also known as Katok Getse Mahapandita (1761–1829), was an important Nyingma scholar from Katok Monastery who famously wrote a catalog to the Nyingma Gyübum. Source: www.rigpawiki.org
10. Tharpatse Labrang at the main Ngor Monastery.—KSP
11. A nose-rope is threaded through the ring in the nose of an ox or yak as a way of tethering the animal. However, if the nose-rope is simply wound around the animal's head, it can go where it pleases because nothing is tying it down.—KSP
12. *Ornaments*, in this case, means tormas; banners; pendants; offerings; relics; representations of body, speech, and mind; and so forth.—KSP
13. Many great lamas used to address Chökyi Lodrö as Tulku Tsang.—KSP
14. Karse Kongtrul (1904–1952/53) was also known as Jamgön Palden Khyentse Özer. He was one of the Fifteenth Karmapa's sons.
15. Dilgo Khyentse Rinpoche names this lama as Drungnam Gyaltrul Rinpoche in the *Great Biography*.
16. Today, Khampa Gar Monastery sings the Trochu Tsok Lu called "The Vina of the Celestial Musicians" during the Trochu dance festival.—OTR
17. This is a different Yudrön than the Yudrön for whom Khyentse Chökyi Lodrö wrote the Pema Yeshe Dorje sadhana.
18. Jamyang Khyentse Wangpo had been a Tharpatse, as had his root gurus.
19. Dzongsar Khyentse Rinpoche explained that a migthur is quite small, and the ribbon had been tied to it for practical reasons, the same way a string might be tied to a key. But for Loter Wangpo, anything that had even been touched by Khyentse Wangpo should have been cherished and preserved, however old or tatty it became.
20. Khangmar Rinchen (Wyl. *khang dmar rin chen*), or Khangmarwa Rinchen Dorje, was the Sixth Khenpo of Dzongsar Shedra from 1940 to 1943. Although originally from the Nyingma monastery of Khangmar, in the eastern part of Derge, he was closely associated with Dzongsar Monastery. His teachers included Öntö Khyenrab Chökyi Özer, Drayab Lodrö, Katok Situ Chökyi Gyatso, and Jamyang Khyentse Chökyi Lodrö. For a large part of his life, he stayed in retreat. Source: www.rigpawiki.org
21. *rgya rto* pills that are sacred to the Sakya tradition.—KST, KSP
22. The chamberlain or chief of protocol.—KSP
23. Wyl. *Yang bum*.
24. The symbol used is a great elephant, one of the seven symbols of a great monarch.—KSP
25. Wyl. *gza' grib*.
26. This is an allusion to Khyentse Chökyi Lodrö taking a consort. Dilgo Khyen-

tse had already taken a consort, and Khyentse Chökyi Lodrö realized he now needed to do the same, to be "like you."—KSP
27. Wyl. *tshe 'gugs*.
28. The word that Khenpo used here to describe Khandro, who was in her teens at this time, was the Golok word *gemo*, which translates literally as "old woman." But the people from Golok call all women "old women," and even very young men talk about their wives as "my old woman."—OTR
29. Tib. *jong gyu*, Wyl. *sbyong rgyud*.
30. Lama Gyurdrak, who died in 1975, was chosen by Khyentse Chökyi Lodrö to be Sogyal Rinpoche's first tutor. The nephew of Lama Tseten and tutor of Khandro Tsering Chödrön, he was a great Dzogchen practitioner, and according to Trungpa Rinpoche, his father, Derge Yilungpa Sonam Namgyal, attained rainbow body in the early fifties.
31. Can be found in Khyentse Chökyi Lodrö's collected works.
32. It's a Tibetan belief that loads and saddles on a pilgrimage are good *tendrel*, meaning they help contribute to auspicious circumstances.
33. Wyl. *thur zhwa*.
34. The sixth Phakchok incarnation: Ngawang Jigme Drakpa Thubten Namgyal, the twenty-second throne holder of Riwoche, born into the same Sedor Bongkar family and then placed on the Dharma throne at Yang-gön Monastery.
35. The reincarnation of the great Dakini of Tshurphu, Khandro Orgyen Tsomo, who spent most of her life in retreat, was recognized by His Holiness the Sixteenth Gyalwang Karmapa as the present Mindrolling Jetsün Khandro Rinpoche.
36. In Jamyang Khyentse Wangpo's biography by Jamgön Kongtrul, she is mentioned as Samdhing Dorje Phagmo from the Jonang tradition.—KSP
37. The *Kunzang Gongdu* (Wyl. *kun bzang dgongs 'dus*), a terma revealed by Pema Lingpa at Samye Chimpu.
38. This is an honorific Tibetan way of saying that he cut a piece of flesh and bones away from the kudung.—KSP
39. Wyl. *nas ze*. In the bottom layer would be sand; in the middle layer, frankincense and mustard seeds; and in the top layer, barley or rice, when they had some (in India, it would have been flowers).—KSP
40. Jetsün Milarepa built this building for Dharmadoti, the son of his teacher Marpa. Translator Marpa instructed Milarepa to build this structure in order to purify the negative karma he had accumulated by killing twenty-one people with his sorcery. Only after accomplishing this task, Marpa initiated Milarepa into the mandala of Chakrasamvara and gave instructions on the Six Yogas of Naropa and Mahamudra.—KSP
41. The implication is that the white light represented Chökyi Lodrö's blessings.—KSP
42. An article about who Gerard Godet was and his tremendous contribution towards the establishment of Buddhadharma in the West can be

found on the Khyentse Foundation website at http://khyentsefoundation. org/?s=Gerard+Godet.
43. Jagö Tsang was the chief minister in the Derge government, and Jagö Namgyal Dorje was his nephew.—KSP
44. Tib. *tsen*, Wyl. *mtshan*. In this case, the triangle that represents the three liberations.—KSP
45. The practice for the moment of death.
46. Skt. *khakkara*; Wyl. *'khar-gsil*. The staff held by ordained Buddhist monks. Arhats and disciples of the Buddha are often depicted holding the staff in their right hands and an alms bowl in their left to symbolize renunciation and emptiness meditation.

A Wondrous Grove of Wish-Fulfilling Trees: The Biography of Jamyang Khyentse Chökyi Lodrö

1. In Tibetan poetry, the image of the lotus is often used to imply "playful and smiling."—DTR
2. According to the *Fortunate Aeon Sutra* (Skt. *Bhadrakalpikasūtra*; Wyl. *bskalpa bzang po'i mdo*), this aeon will see the appearance of 1,002 buddhas, the fourth of which was Buddha Shakyamuni.
3. In this case "qualities of liberation" (Wyl. *rnam thar*) means all the activities that sublime beings undertake to demonstrate to sentient beings how they can reach ultimate liberation successfully.—DTR
4. The path of accumulation, the path of application, the path of seeing, and the path of meditation. These are the first four of the "five paths" (Skt. *pañcamarga*; Wyl. *lam lnga*), and the fifth is the result, which is the path of no-more-learning.—KSP
5. Kyabje Dilgo Khyentse Rinpoche is referring to himself.—DJKR
6. Again, Kyabje Dilgo Khyentse Rinpoche is referring to himself.—DJKR
7. His name translates (roughly) as Gentle Melody, Intelligence of Dharma, Banner of the Unbiased Teachings, Glory, and Excellence (Wyl. *'jam dbyangs chos kyi blo gros ris med bstan pa'i rgyal mtshan gtsug lag lung rig smra ba'i seng ge dpal bzang po*).—KSP
8. According to the commentary by Jigme Yönten Gönpo, he is not only the holder of five eyes free of attachment, he is also completely unobstructed by any obstacle whatsoever.—DTR
9. "Great heart" here means the "essence from which the rupakaya emanates."
10. This is the "bodhichitta of action" (Wyl. *'jug pa sems bskyed*), which is to act on your wish to help or benefit others. It is one of the two subdivisions of relative bodhichitta.—DTR, KSP
11. On a relative level, names are important because giving something a name— *water*, for example—protects us from mistaking water for something else. Many spiritual traditions place a great deal of emphasis on names. In Hindu-

ism, for example, Shiva is the highest of all the gods and therefore has the most names. Ten thousand of his names appear in the form of a praise entitled the *Dashasahasranama*, which can be found in the Mahanyasa. Simply by repeating his names, praise is given to Shiva.

In Buddhism, too, names form the basis of many mantras—for example, OM VAGI SHWARI MUM for Manjushri, where VAGI SHWARI is one of Manjushri's names and means "Lord of Speech." One of the most famous tantras and an important basis of Manjushri practice is the *Manjushrinamasamgiti*, which is a long list of different praises using his many different names. The great masters of all Tibetan Buddhist traditions also tend to have several names, and Jamyang Khyentse Wangpo himself had many.—DJKR (with thanks to Dr. Robert Mayer)

12. Lord of the Naga Family, Lui Rigchok.
13. Meaning "omniscient protector" (Tib. *Gönpo Kuntu Zik*, Wyl. *mgon po kun tu gzigs*). —KSP
14. The Tathagata king of the mountain of precious jewels (Tib. *Deshinshekpa Norbu Tsekpe Gyalpo*, Wyl. *bde bzhin gshegs pa norbu brtsegs pa'i rgyal po*).
15. Shakyamuni Buddha, the historical Buddha.
16. Wyl. *'jam dpal grags pa*.
17. The formulation "good in the beginning, good in the middle, good at the end" is rooted in ancient Asian culture. It is considered to be a very auspicious thing to say. Here it is used honorifically, although even today Indians often ask, "What is your good name?" and say, "I've been blessed by your good presence."
18. The name that Dilgo Khyentse Rinpoche used here for Vimalakirti was Licchavi Drima Me Par Drakpa Lodrö Rabzhi.
19. Yangdak Heruka (Wyl. *yang dag heruka*).
20. 790–833 C.E.
21. Also known as Sakyapa Sonam Gyaltsen (Wyl. *sa skya pa bsod nams rgyal mtshan*) (1312–1375 C.E.).
22. Also known as Shonu Palwa.
23. There are three kinds of sons: a physical son, a teaching son, and a Dharma heir.—KSP
24. 1597–1659 C.E.
25. 1686–1718 C.E.
26. He was probably born in 1793.
27. Wyl. *rdor je rnam par 'joms pa zhes bya ba'i gzungs*.
28. This translation reflects information the translators learnt from Orgyen Tobgyal Rinpoche about this event.
29. Mongolian-style earrings that the Tibetan kings are often depicted wearing.—OTR
30. 1800–1866 C.E.
31. 1729–1798 C.E.

32. The first power is over life span, meaning he could live as long as he wanted to for the benefit of sentient beings.—DTR
33. "Lotus of nonattachment" (Wyl. *ma chags pad ma can*) refers to one who has attained the twelfth of sixteen bhumis described in the Dzogchen tradition.—DTR
34. When King Trisong Deutsen passed into nirvana, he attained buddhahood as Buddha Machak Pemachen (Lotus of Nonattachment). Buddha Machak Pemachen made a prophecy that Jigme Lingpa would live for 130 years, and his prophecy was fulfilled by Jamyang Khyentse Wangpo, who, according to Nyoshul Khyen Rinpoche's history of the Dzogchen tradition (*Marvelous Garland of Rare Gems: Biographies of Masters of Awareness in the Dzogchen Lineage*, Padma Publishing, 2006) had unofficially been recognized by Jigme Gyalwe Nyugu as the body tulku of Jigme Lingpa.—DTR, KSP
35. The vajra master.
36. Pema Yeshe Dorje is not a name that would ever be given to a monk or a celebate. By giving him such a name, the Third Dodrupchen Rinpoche confirmed the prophecy that Chökyi Lodrö would take a consort.—DJKR
37. These secrets included knowledge of Khyentse Chökyi Lodrö's past lives and that in those incarnations—for example, as Jigme Lingpa—Chökyi Lodrö had been Dodrupchen Rinpoche's teacher.—DTR
38. The source of Khyentse Chökyi Lodrö's discomfort was that Do Khyentse had the reputation of being a thug and a gangster, and the idea that they were inseparable, when Khyentse Chökyi Lodrö was himself a perfect monk, unsettled him.—DJKR
39. In this case, a sign that Chökyi Lodrö would get married.—DJKR
40. Buddha's representative in Tibet.
41. Tersey means "son of the Tertön."
42. Wyl. *bka' babs*.
43. Wyl. *rnam kun mchog ldan*.
44. Meaning that his preferences for certain lineages and teachings would have caused him to abandon or even reject others, had it not been for the spirit of Rime that Jamyang Khyentse Wangpo had instigated and instilled in him.—DJKR
45. Literally, "the channels of his throat were untied."
46. For a tertön, the authentication of the treasure teachings is of paramount importance. During Khyentse Wangpo's time, he and Kongtrul Rinpoche were the masters who had the authority to make such authentications. Authentication was considered to be so important that even though Jamgön Kongtrul Lodrö Taye was perfectly capable of deciphering *Tsasum Gongdü* himself, he didn't do it because Khyentse Wangpo had passed away and therefore could not authenticate his work. The highest honor for a tertön at that time was for his treasure teaching to be included in the *Rinchen Terdzö*.—DJKR
47. Many believed Mipham Rinpoche was the only Tibetan scholar to deserve

the title *mahapandita*. Here, Dilgo Khyentse Rinpoche is laying the credit for Mipham Rinpoche's great writing achievements at Jamyang Khyentse Wangpo's door, because it was he who gave Mipham Rinpoche the authority to write his commentaries. Therefore, thanks to Khyentse Wangpo's blessings and aspirations and their good connection, Mipham Rinpoche became the great master he is now known to be, whose fame has spread throughout the world.—DJKR

48. Not to be disciplined means they do not adhere to the rules of moral discipline that are the precepts of a monk.
49. The perfect qualities are to be learnèd, disciplined, and realized.
50. The translation given is very literal. A looser translation is
    Although the buddhas have transcended birth and death,
    By the power of the Buddha's compassion,
    His activity, a reflection of the karma and aspiration of beings to be tamed,
    Will remain for as long as samsara exists.
51. This is what the Tibetans call the part of the Yangtse River that flows through Kham.—KSP
52. Dilgo Khyentse Rinpoche isn't specific about which completion meditation Beru Khyentse received.
53. This means that Phakchok Dorje was Mahasiddha Shakya Shri's physical son (body son), as well as being his student (speech son) and main heir to his lineage (mind son).
54. He attained the state of *vajra dharma*, which is the royal seat of perfect realization.
55. The ultimate truth.
56. 1872–1935 C.E.
57. Jamyang Khyentse Wangpo.
58. Literally, "stretching between the eastern and western oceans."—DTR, KSP
59. Also known as the Eleventh Kenting Tai Situpa (1886–1952 C.E.).
60. Meaning through the part of Menshö where Dzongsar Monastery stands.
61. Articles that symbolize body (a statue), speech (a text), and mind (a stupa).
62. Refers to one of six emanations of Samantabhadra said to "tame the beings of the six realms."
63. Wrathful activity is liberation through skillful means and unconditional compassion.
64. Dakinis' seal of entrustment: historically, some tertöns, like Chokgyur Lingpa, were illiterate, yet they were able to write extraordinary texts. This was because the dakinis trusted them and therefore gave them a kind of gift for revealing treasure teachings.—DJKR
65. "Half a day" here means more than twelve hours.
66. Meaning "illuminating deathless vajra."
67. Vairotsana the Translator.
68. Literally "tied"; Khyentse Rinpoche said that when he was in Tibet, he actually saw statues of Dharma protectors tied to pillars.

69. The great tertön of Mindrolling Monastery, Minling Terchen Gyurme Dorje (Wyl. *smin gling gter chen 'gyur med rdo rje*), who was also known as Terdak Lingpa (Wyl. *gter bdag gling pa*) (1646–1714 C.E.).
70. Literally, "our Lord Guru manifested the mandala of his major and minor marks."
71. Literally, "dissolved his manifest body into the dharmadhatu."
72. Kalzang Dorje died almost immediately after writing the letter, which is why Situ Rinpoche was unable to negotiate Chökyi Lodrö's future.—DJKR
73. In this case, the activities were those of view, meditation, and action.
74. Lodrö means "knowledge" or "wisdom."
75. Literally "when the flower of his major and minor marks blossomed."
76. Wyl. *dgag*.
77. Wyl. *sgrub*.
78. Wyl. *gnang ba*.
79. Tibetans didn't celebrate individual birthdays, and many high- and lowborn Tibetans didn't know the exact date of their birth. Every Losar, all Tibetans became a year older, which means that, on paper, they look a year or sometimes two years older than they would be if they counted their birthdays.—DTR, KSP
80. The root mandala of the *Guhyagarbha Tantra*.—KSP
81. For example, amrita, images, crystal, and so on.
82. Wyl. *rnam rtog*.
83. Dilgo Khyentse Rinpoche is using Akanishtha—the highest heaven of great bliss—as the best of all honorific metaphors to emphasize just how exceptional Khyentse Chökyi Lodrö and his seat of Dzongsar Monastery were.
84. These empowerments are of water, the crown, the crown with added ornaments, vajra and bell, student, name, and authorization.
85. The four higher empowerments are the vase empowerment, the secret empowerment, the wisdom empowerment, and the relative worldly empowerment.
86. The four highest empowerments are the vase empowerment, the secret empowerment, the wisdom empowerment, and the ultimate beyond-worldly empowerment.
87. These two scripts are a kind of shorthand, and ordinary handwriting.
88. The common outer fields of knowledge include Sanskrit, grammar, logic, the arts, poetry, astrology, and medicine.
89. There are three approaches to Sanskrit grammar: Kalapa, Chandrapa, and Sarasvata.
90. A text that was appropriate to a specific time.
91. Also known as Vilasavajra or Lalitavajra, an eighth-century Indian master, perhaps from Oddiyana, who wrote commentaries on *Chanting the Names of Manjushri* and the *Guhyagarbha Tantra*.
92. Wyl. *phyogs bcu mun sel*.
93. Gendün Gyatso Palzangpo, the Second Dalai Lama (1475–1542).

94. This emanation of King Trisong Deutsen was called Lhase Tsangpa'i Metok.
95. This verse also appears in the *Verse Summary of the Prajnaparamita Sutra*.
96. Jamgön Kongtrul Rinpoche and Jamyang Khyentse Wangpo.
97. Wyl. *sku gsum bla ma'i rnal 'byor*. Other examples of three-kaya guru yogas are Tsasum Drildrup and Tukdrup Barche Kunsel.
98. Wyl. *ma ni bka' 'bum*. A collection of teachings and practices that focus on Avalokiteshvara.
99. In this case, the two traditions are the spiritual and the political.
100. The twenty-first day of the first Tibetan month.
101. Literally the "upper" and "lower" empowerments: the upper empowerment is for attaining complete enlightenment, and the lower is for specific activities, like exorcism.—KSP
102. Wyl. *srog shing*.
103. In Tibet, the monks and practitioners collect food to sustain them through their study and practice twice a year. In the summer, they collect mainly butter and cheese, and in the winter, they collect barley for tsampa.—KSP
104. A special empowerment that introduces a student to the nature of mind.
105. Wyl. *sgrub dbang chen mo*. The empowerment associated with a drupchen.
106. "Water ox" may be a typo in the Tibetan because Khyentse Chökyi Lodrö was thirty-three years old in the year of the wood ox (1925).—DTR
107. Wyl. *srog dbang*. Literally, "life essence" or "life-force." Basically, *srog dbang* is like introducing one person to another. More specifically, it's an introduction to someone with power, with a request that the person being introduced receive help from the more powerful person. It's called a life essence or life-force empowerment because not only are you introduced, but you are given a secret name, or seed syllable. It's like the connection between two people who then tell each other their secrets and become extremely close.—JKR
108. *Kathang* (Wyl. *bka' thang*) is an ancient Tibetan word that means "account." *Pema Kathang* is therefore an account of the life of Pema, or Guru Rinpoche. Many such biographies were written, but Dilgo Khyentse Rinpoche doesn't specify which one.—DJKR
109. Wyl. *srog gtad*.
110. Meaning Jamyang Khyentse Wangpo.
111. Wyl. *bden tshig grub pa*, meaning that everything he said was true.
112. Many lamas of the past combined the practices of Amitayus and Hayagriva, but in this list, Dilgo Khyentse Rinpoche doesn't specify which one.
113. Wyl. *rik pa'i rtsal dbang*.
114. Taksham was one of the Thirteenth Dalai Lama's gurus.
115. Wyl. *byad 'grol*.
116. Karse Kongtrul (1904–1952) was the immediate reincarnation of the First Jamgön Kongtrul, and Tsadra was Jamgön Kongtrul Lodrö Taye's retreat center.
117. Dilgo Khyentse Rinpoche's brother.

118. Jamyang Khyentse Chökyi Lodrö received as many of the teachings that Jamyang Khyentse Wangpo and Jamgön Kongtrul Lodrö Taye gave to their various heart-sons as their individual practices as he could.
119. Jamgön Kongtrul and Jamyang Khyentse Wangpo.
120. Not satisfied with receiving teachings through distant lineages, Khyentse Chökyi Lodrö would seek out more direct lineages of the same teachings and therefore received the same teachings again and again.
121. The heart-son of Atisha.
122. Zenkar Rinpoche explained this by saying that the reference to Chinese masks indicates how changeable things are and that they are not, in his words, "rigid or extreme." So the reference here is to understanding this changing quality and being flexible.—AZR, AP
123. Wyl. *dgongs srol dri ma med pa*.
124. Dilgo Khyentse Rinpoche didn't specify which one.
125. The tenth and twenty-fifth days of the Tibetan month.
126. The practice of dzogrim that requires effort, such as visualization.
127. Meaning by bestowing empowerments.—DTR
128. Meaning by offering instructions.—DTR
129. Literally, "fraction-like particles of dust."—DTR
130. Wyl. *thugs rje yas sprul*.
131. Literally, "through his continuous Dharma activity."—DTR
132. Wyl. *zhar byung*.
133. One way of looking at these miracle stories is that, according to the Nyingma teachings, all the qualities of enlightenment already exist within the space of the nature of mind, and all we have to do is realize them. The traditional examples used are if a sun exists, it always radiates rays of light; and if water exists, it's always wet. And so, if a being experiences emotion, she automatically also has wisdom. While the Sarma schools teach that beings who experience emotion have the *potential* for wisdom, which then needs to be nurtured and developed, the Nyingmapas teach that not only does the object of jealousy, etc., already have a buddha's body, but it is also already perfect, like the rays of the sun. Spontaneous accomplishment is therefore possible because the objects of wisdom are everywhere and perfect from beginningless time.—DJKR
134. The monastery is encircled by a courtyard with a ring of eight stupas standing around it.
135. Wyl. *bum chu*.
136. *La do* is difficult to translate directly as a noun. The connection between the *la do* (in this case, the stone) and Tseringma came about through ritual practices that link specific objects to various dharmapalas (in this case, Tseringma), and then it's as if the object becomes the dharmapala's favorite thing. Once that connection is made, the dharmapala will be attracted to wherever the object is kept. It works in a similar way to the attraction those associated with the Khyentse lineage feel for Tashiding. Khyentse Chökyi Lodrö's kudung is enshrined in

a stupa there, and therefore devotees of Chökyi Lodrö are attracted to that place.—Based on an explanation by JKR
137. Wyl. *grib btsan.*
138. Wyl. *srog snying.*
139. Ü-Tsang.
140. Dilgo Khyentse Rinpoche was upset when Khyentse Chökyi Lodrö told him Chökyi Lodrö would pass away first because he didn't want it to happen, and this is why he "didn't dare ask him." From a Tibetan cultural point of view, it would also have been inauspicious even to contemplate the death of his master, which was another reason for him not accepting the papers at that time.
141. About fifteen inches high; "arm's length" means the length of a man's forearm.
142. This may be a typo in the Tibetan text. Katok Situ Chökyi Gyatso passed away in the year of the wood ox, around 1925.—DTR
143. Wyl. *posti lung dbang.*
144. Wyl. *dgongs gtad byin rlabs.*
145. Palden Lhamo, consort of Mahakala.
146. These gatherings usually took place in a monkey year, which falls every twelve years.
147. Wyl. *gsal snang.*
148. A colloquial term for Karma Kagyü.
149. The higher are the inner Anuttarayoga tantras, and the lower are the outer tantras of kriya, upa, and yoga.—KSP
150. Symbolically liberating the dead as their names are burnt in purifying flames.
151. The tenth and twenty-fifth days of the Tibetan month.
152. He always wore all the items and colors necessary to be dressed properly as a monk. He never wore anything extra or inappropriate, and he never wore his clothing sloppily.—KSP
153. It is possible to examine a teacher *directly* by verifying his qualities for yourself—for example, by hearing him speak gently and give teachings appropriate to each individual, witnessing his kindness, and so on. *Indirectly* means, for example, that he didn't exhibit his own sadness about the sufferings of samsara but just gave advice to young students about how to train in renunciation.—KSP
154. Skt. *Doha.*
155. Wyl. *don la gnas.* He lived up to the meaning of his many names.—KSP
156. The Tibetan states "western India," probably because Kinnaur, where Khunu Lama was born, is west of Kham. However, Kinnaur is generally said to be in northern India.
157. Throne-holders of the main Nyingma monasteries.
158. The Land of Malaya is where sandalwood grows. Dilgo Khyentse Rinpoche uses the image of winds from Malaya sweetened with the perfume of sandalwood as the vehicle through which Khyentse Chökyi Lodrö's fame spreads.—KSP
159. These two aspects are the Dharma of the transmission of the sacred texts and the Dharma of realization.

160. Wyl. *pad ma bka' thang*.
161. Rinang is the region of Riche and Nangchen.—KSP
162. The other seat of Chokgyur Lingpa.
163. Namely, Jamyang Khyentse Wangpo and Khyentse Chökyi Lodrö.
164. Khenchen Jamyang Gyaltsen (1870–1940 C.E.) was the third khenpo of Dzongsar Shedra.
165. These six ornaments are the animals traditionally incorporated into a throne and aureola—for example, elephants, a garuda, and so on.
166. In a traditional Tibetan monastery, the central temple is called the *utse* (Wyl. *dbu rtse*).
167. A form of Yamantaka.
168. A student of Gampopa.
169. The two types of astrology are *kartsi*, based on the stars, and *naktsi*, which describes how to take out the dead, premonitions, and so on.
170. Wyl. *khyung stag gnas phug*.
171. The Third Karmapa.
172. The Ninth Tai Situ.
173. The seventh month of the year according to the Mongolian and Tibetan calendars.—DTR
174. Wyl. *khrus gsol*. A ritual for the purification of imperfections done by pouring or sprinkling water on icons, books, and stupas.—DTR
175. The Boudhanath, Swayambhunath, and Takmo Lüjin stupas. —DTR
176. Wyl. *gter bum*.
177. The great black precious pill.
178. The white crystal stupa pill.
179. The precious wish-fulfilling jewel pill.
180. The twenty-five empowerments pill.
181. The great moon crystal pill.
182. The precious purified moon crystal.
183. "Black" because if these offerings aren't used properly, they are poisonous.
184. Guru Rinpoche's birthday and a very auspicious date.
185. Literally, "directly and indirectly."
186. Kinnaur is in Himachal Pradesh, in the Lahul and Spiti region.—KSP
187. "Temporary benefit" means for long life, good health, etc.
188. *Ultimate benefit* means "enlightenment."
189. Wyl. *byabs khrus*.
190. Traditionally, the twenty-four-hour day is divided up, and each division is represented by one of the twelve Tibetan astrologocial signs.—KSP
191. Wyl. *'das rjes*. Posthumous teachings given by a master to his student after he has passed away, often described as pure vision teachings. For example, Garab Dorje gave Manjushrimitra the *Tsik Sum Ne Dek* (Wyl. *tshig gsum gnad brdegs*), *Hitting the Essence in Three Words*, or *Hitting the Vital Point in Three Words*.—KSP
192. The Palace Monastery at Gangtok.—KSP

193. Wyl. *byang khrus.*
194. Meaning the "body."
195. The Latin name of the sal tree is *shorea robusta.*
196. Sarma and Nyingma.
197. In Tibetan, *lto 'phye'i kha rgyu phyogs dang bstun,* which means "the direction in which the toche moves." *Toche* is a land-owning deity with a human torso and head and the tail of a snake instead of legs. It moves constantly, completing a full cycle of movement in 365 days, and changes direction every month.—KST
198. First the foundation is built, then the lion throne, on which is placed the *purkhang* (a vase-shaped dome), and suspended above the purkhang is a parasol. On a frame around the four sides of the stupa are hung pendants and banners. The cremation chamber is in the purkhang and is where the kudung is placed, facing east. Underneath the lion throne is the oven with four doors, through which wood is fed into the fire.—KSP
199. Skt. *agaru*; Latin *Aquilaria agallocha Roxb.*
200. Wyl. *yungs 'bru lta bu'i ring bsrel.*
201. Most probably the Swayambhunath stupa.
202. Wyl. *chos kyi ring bsrel.*
203. Wyl. *nye snying.*
204. Wyl. *mtshan sngags.*
205. Wyl. *sku gdung ring bsrel.*
206. Wyl. *sku bal ring bsrel.*
207. Wyl. *chos sku'i ring bsrel.*
208. Wyl. *sku rten.*
209. Wyl. *gsung rten.*
210. Wyl. *thugs rten.*
211. Wyl. *yon tan rten.*
212. Wyl. *phrin las rten.*
213. Gyatön Choktrul's assistants were not necessarily only monks; they were more likely to be all those performing the practice with him and would have included lay practitioners, the shrine master, the chant leader, musicians, and so on.—KSP
214. A *dharani sutra* contains dharani mantras, which in this case are the life-force of the stupa.
215. Traditionally, valid logic merely requires a reason supported by a quotation; therefore, the preceding paragraphs prove the benefits of the stupa.
216. In this case, ornaments that are *eye-amrita,* which means everything that is beautiful.—KSP
217. King Trisong Deutsen was the previous incarnation of Gyalse Lhaje.
218. This indirect prophecy is about the benefit Khyentse Chökyi Lodrö's remains will bring because he was an incarnation of Gyalse Lhaje.—DTR, KSP
219. Literally, "occasion." He will explain the pure visions according to the relevant time or lineage. For example, Khyentse Chökyi Lodrö's vision of Guru Rinpoche will be explained in the Nyingma section.—KSP

220. The Lotus Lake, locally known as Rewalsar Lake, can be found in the Mandi district of Himachal Pradesh, northern India.
221. A verse from a Sakya prayer by Ngorchen Dorje Chang Kunga Zangpo.—OTR
222. Khyentse Chökyi began a new direct transmission. He didn't hold the exact distant lineage for these commentaries, although the *Dzo Dun* texts he had received were very similar. As he didn't want to confuse people, he felt it was best to identify the lineage as being either direct or distant. This statement is as close as he comes to confirming that it is a direct lineage—as they had only just found the texts, there couldn't have been a distant lineage.—KSP
223. Another name for the region of Amdo.
224. The Kadampa tradition of Atisha.
225. The Kadampa tradition of Je Tsongkhapa.
226. The three brothers were the three main disciples of Dromtonpa: Potowa Rinchen Sal, Chengawa Tsultrim Bar, and Phuchungwa Shyönnu Gyaltsen.
227. A form of invocation and prayer of which there are many, but it is not clear which one Khyentse Chökyi Lodrö received in this vision.
228. Wyl. *thugs gtad*. Orgyen Tobgyal Rinpoche explains that this is a "transference of wisdom or realization to another." Wyl. *dgongs gtad* is an honorific way of saying *thugs gtad*. Jigme Khyentse Rinpoche clarified this further, saying it is a blessing from the wisdom mind of the master that gives the student permission to practice. It is the kind of blessing we ask very great masters to give us instead of forcing them to read a whole text.—OTR
229. The month is not specified in the text.
230. His Holiness Sakya Trizin.
231. Sakya Dagchen's grandfather.—OTR
232. When a tantra is enormously long, its essence is given as blessing instructions.
233. The Third Karmapa.
234. According to Tibetan astrology, *me-zhi* is the twelfth of twenty-eight stars. The juncture of the sun and the me-zhi star is very auspicious because it's the meeting of fire (sun) and wind (me-zhi) elements. It is called *tobden jorwa*, meaning "the powerful juncture."—KSP, Pema Buddha
235. The month is not specified in the text.
236. The teachings on the approach and accomplishment practice that Mahasiddha Orgyenpa received from Dorje Tsunmo (the vajra queen, Vajrayogini).
237. In many people's eyes, Khyentse Wangpo and Khyentse Chökyi Lodrö were Sakya lamas because Dzongsar was a Sakya monastery. However, here Dilgo Khyentse Rinpoche states that they were actually the holders of each and every lineage of Tibetan Buddhist teaching and received, practiced, disseminated, and cared for all these teachings.
238. Jamgön Kongtrul the Great.
239. According to Tibetan astrology, a day can appear twice in a month. In this case, the fifth day of the month appeared twice, and it is about the first of these two fifth days that Khyentse Chökyi Lodrö writes.

240. *The Empty Awareness Manjushri* (Tib. *Rik Tong Jampal Shönu*, Wyl. *rig stong jam dpal gzhon nu*) is a prayer by Mipham Rinpoche.
241. The first line of the *Invocation of Blessings* from the Rigdzin Düpa.
242. Wyl. *rig pa'i dbang lnga*.
243. The secret, prajna-jnana, and word empowerments.
244. Literally, "Raksor," but this is probably Raxaul, on the border between Nepal and Bihar.—DTR
245. This is a wrathful palace with consorts at the bottom and deities on the top. In some practices, there are eight such palaces to be visualized, and they must always be practiced during a mendrup.—OTR
246. Khandro Tsering Chödrön's sister, Tsering Wangmo.
247. A form of Guru Rinpoche.
248. There may be a typo in the Tibetan text because the water tiger year was 1902, and Chökyi Lodrö was only about nine years old. The translators believe "water tiger" should read either "water horse" (1942) or "water sheep" (1943).
249. Wyl. *rta mgrin gyi rta skad thengs gsum*.
250. A stone used as a consecration object for a statue.
251. Thorny plant with white flowers that resemble roses.
252. Could also be translated as "had ripened."
253. Tib. *tramen*, Wyl. *phra men*. Literally "hybrid"; in this case, refers to animal-headed deities.
254. In Tibet, the cuckoo is a magical creature and considered to be the king of the birds.
255. Wyl. *mtshan dkyil*.
256. Tai Situ Rinpoche's point is the advice he gave Khyentse Chökyi Lodrö about taking a consort.
257. Another name for Shakyamuni Buddha.—DTR
258. There may be a typo in the Tibetan text because the earth rooster year was 1909, and Dilgo Khyentse Rinpoche is believed to have been born in 1910.—KSP
259. Wyl. *'pho chen rdo rje sku*.
260. Kalimpong wasn't part of India at this time.—DTR
261. Semtokha Dzong, where Dilgo Khyentse Rinpoche was the first principal of the school of dialectics.—DTR, KSP

Bibliography

Abbreviated Five Tantric Deities, Wyl. *rgyud sde lha nga mdor bdus*

Abridged Kalachakra Tantra, Wyl. *dus 'khor bsdus rgyud*

Accomplishing the Life-Force of the Vidyadharas, Tib. *Rigdzin Sokdrup*, Wyl. *rig 'dzin srog sgrub*
   A cycle of teachings revealed by Lhatsün Namkha Jigme, which includes the famous practice of Riwo Sangchö.

Accomplishing the Vajra Life-Force of Rainbow Body, Tib. *Jalü Dorje Sokdrup*, Wyl. *'ja' lus rdo rje'i srog sgrub*

Activity Practice: A Garland of Jewels, Tib. *Trindrup Rinchen Trengwa*, Wyl. *'phrin sgrub rin chen phreng ba*
   A sadhana for making fulfillment offerings to the three roots deities and Dharma protectors revealed by Tertön Nyangrel Nyima Özer.

Akshobhya Statue That Liberates upon Being Seen, Tib. *Mitrukpa'i Chakgya Tongdrol*, Wyl. *mi 'krugs pa'i phyag rgya mthong grol*

Amitabha Practice to Liberate Beings into the Realm of Great Bliss, Tib. *Dechen Zhing Drub*, Wyl. *bde chen zhing sgrub*
   Popularly known as the *Sukhavati Sadhana*.

Anuttarayoga Tantra, "Highest Yoga Tantra," Wyl. *rnal 'byor bla na med pa'i rgyud*
   The highest of the four classes of tantra. According to the Sarma tradition, the highest yoga tantras are divided into mother tantras, father tantras, and nondual tantras. In the Nyingma tradition, the Anuttarayoga Tantra corresponds to the three inner tantras of Mahayoga, Anuyoga, and Atiyoga.

Approach and Accomplishment Practices of the Three Vajras, Tib. *Dorje Sum Gyi Nyendrup*, Wyl. *rdo rje gsum gyi bsnyen sgrub*

Ascertainment of the Three Types of Vow, Tib. *Dom Sum Nam Nge*, Wyl. *sdom gsum rnam nges*

Aspiration to Be Reborn in the Pure Realm of Sukhavati, Tib. *Dechen Mönlam* or *De Mön*, Wyl. *rnam dag bde chen zhing gi smon lam*

Assembled Realization of Dharma Protectors, Tib. *Chökyong Gongdü*, Wyl. *chos skyong dgongs 'dus*

Assembly of All the Sugatas, Tib. *Deshek Kundü*, Wyl. *bde gshegs kun 'dus*

Avalokiteshvara and the Great Dakini, Tib. *Tukchen dang Khandro Chenmo*, Wyl. *thugs chen dang mkha' 'gro chen mo*

Avalokiteshvara Resting in the Nature of Mind, Tib. *Tukchen Semnyi Ngalso*, Wyl. *thugs chen sems nyid ngal gso*
  One of Jamyang Khyentse Wangpo's best-known treasure revelations.

Avalokiteshvara Who Stirs the Depths of Samsara, Tib. *Khorwa Dongtruk*, Wyl. *'khor ba dong sprugs*

Avalokiteshvara with a Hundred Lotuses Who Stirs the Depths of Samsara, Tib. *Dongtruk Pema Gyaden*, Wyl. *dong sprugs padma brgya ldan*

Avalokiteshvara: Ocean of Victorious Ones, Tib. *Tukchen Gyalwa Gyatso*, Wyl. *thugs rje chen po rgyal ba rgya mtsho*

Avalokiteshvara: Self-Liberation from Suffering, Tib. *Tukchen Dugnyal Rangdrol*, Wyl. *thugs rje chen po sdug bsngal rang grol*

Avalokiteshvara: The Gathering of the Innermost Essence, Tib. *Tukchen Yang Nying Düpa*, Wyl. *thugs rje chen po yang snying 'dus pa*

Avalokiteshvara: The Lord of the Dance, Tib. *Pema Garwang*, Wyl. *padma gar dbang*
  A sadhana, the principal deity of which is Pema Garwang.

Bhurkumkuta, Tib. *Metsek*, Wyl. *sme brtsegs*

Black Dzambhala, Skt. *Jambhala*; Tib. *Dzambhala Nakpo*, Wyl. *dzam bha la nag po*
  An empowerment.

Black Garuda, Tib. *Khyung Nak*, Wyl. *khyung nag po*
  An empowerment.

Blazing Vajra Vajrapani, Tib. *Chakdor Dorje Mebar*, Wyl. *phyag rdor rdo rje me 'bar*
  A rediscovered treasure teaching.

Blue Annals, Tib. *Debter Ngönpo*, Wyl. *deb ther sngon po*
  Written by Gö Lotsawa Shönnu Pel, the Blue Annals are a historical survey of various sectarian spiritual traditions throughout Tibet.

Body Mandala of Chakrasamvara, Tib. *De Dril Lü Kyil*, Wyl. *bde dril lus dkyil*
  From the Drilbupa tradition. Drilbupa was one of the eighty mahasiddhas who

attained realization through the practice of Chakrasamvara. He is among the previous incarnations of Jamyang Khyentse Wangpo and Jamyang Khyentse Chökyi Lodrö.

Bright Torch of the Innermost Essence, Tib. *Nyingtik Saldrön*, Wyl. *snying thig gsal sgron*
A guru yoga practice that was a mind treasure revealed by Jamyang Khyentse Chökyi Lodrö in response to a request from the princess of Derge, Yudrön.

Category of the Bodhisattva Teachings, Skt. *Bodhisattvapiṭaka*; Tib. *Changchub Sempa'i Denö*, Wyl. *byang chub sems dpa'i sde snod*

Cause and Path Hevajra, Tib. *Ke Dor Gyu Lam*, Wyl. *kye rdo rgyu lam*

Chakrasamvara Called "One Who Illuminates the Hidden Meanings," Tib. *Bedön Kunsel*, Wyl. *sbas don kun gsal*

Chakrasamvara: The Inseparable Union of Buddha, Tib. *Demchok Sangye Nyamjor*, Wyl. *bde mchog sangs rgyas mnyam sbyor*

Chandali, Long-Life Consort, Tib. *Tseyum Tsendali*, Wyl. *tshe yum tsandali*
The long-life practice that focuses on Amitayus's consort, Chandali, revealed as a treasure by Lingtsang Gyalpo, the old king of Ling.

Clear Explanation of Kyerim and Dzogrim, Tib. *Kye Dzog Namshe*; Wyl. *bskyed rdzogs rnam bshad*
A teaching associated with the Kalachakra.

Collected Teachings on Vajrayogini, Tib. *Khachö Bebum*, Wyl. *mkha spyod be'u bum*

Collected Topics of Logic, Tib. *Dü Dra*, Wyl. *bsdus grwa*
A preliminary text about logic for beginners studied mainly in the Gelug scriptural colleges and study centers.

Collection of Tantras, Tib. *Gyü Bum*, Wyl. *rgyud 'bum*
The collected tantras of the Nyingma school.

Combined Guru Yoga of Guru Rinpoche and the Three Bodhisattvas, Tib. *Guru Rinpoche Rigsum Semapa Dang Drel Wai Ladrup*, Wyl. *guru rin po che rigs gsum sems dpa' dang 'brel ba'i bla sgrub*

Combined Practice of the Assembly of Kilaya Deities, Tib. *Phurba Düpa'i Drildrup*, Wyl. *phur pa bsdus pa'i dril sgrub*

Combined Practice of the Four Deities, Tib. *Lha Zhi Drildrup*, Wyl. *lha bzhi dril sgrub*
An elaborate guru yoga practice from the Shangpa Kagyü that focuses on the guru as Vajradhara.

Combined Practice of the Three Roots, Tib. *Tsasum Drildrup*, Wyl. *rtsa gsum dril sgrub*
One of Sangye Lama's treasure teachings, which was later rediscovered by Jamyang Khyentse Wangpo.

Combined Practice of Vishuddhi and Vajrakilaya, Tib. *Nyen Gyü Yang Phur Drakma*, Wyl. *snyan brgyud yang phur bsgrags ma*
One of the oral lineage teachings from the nyen gyü section of Jamyang Khyentse Wangpo's *Seven Transmissions*.

Commentary on the Root Verses of Vajrakilaya, Tib. *Dorje Phurba Tsadum*, Wyl. *rdo rje phur pa rtsa dum*
By Jamgön Kongtrul Lodrö Taye.

Commentary on Vajrakilaya Called the "Black Collected Words," Tib. *Phur Drel Bum Nak*, Wyl. *phur 'grel bum nag*
A famous commentary on Vajrakilaya written by Padmasambhava, Vimalamitra, and Shilamanju.

Compendium of Mantras, Tib. *Ngaktü*, Wyl. *sngags btus*

Compendium of Sadhanas, Tib. *Druptab Kuntü*, Wyl. *sgrub thabs kun btus*
A collection of major sadhanas and other practices from the Sakya tradition, compiled by Jamyang Khyentse Wangpo and his disciple Jamyang Loter Wangpo.

Compendium of Tantras, Tib. *Gyüde Kuntü*, Wyl. *rgyud sde kun btus*
A vast collection of teachings and lineages from all schools of Tibetan Buddhism, compiled by Jamyang Loter Wangpo.

Compendium of Vajra Wisdom, Tib. *Yeshe Dorje Künle Tüpa*, Wyl. *ye shes rdo rje kun las btus pa*

Commentary on Valid Cognition, Skt. *Pramāṇavārttika*; Tib. *Tsema Namdrel*, Wyl. *tshad ma rnam 'grel*
By Dharmakirti.

Complete Gathering of Terchen Lerab Lingpa, Tib. *Yongdzog Düpa*, Wyl. *yongs rdzogs 'dus pa*

Confession and Restoration of Vajrayana Vows, Tib. *Ngak Kyi Sojong*, Wyl. *sngags kyi gso sbyong*
A vajrayana sadhana for purifying broken vajrayana vows, generally practiced for the dead.

Confession of Downfalls, Tib. *Tung Shak*, Wyl. *ltung bshags*
A common name for the *Sutra of the Three Heaps* (Skt. *Triskhandhadharmasūtra*; Wyl. *phung po gsum pa'i mdo*).

Consort Practice, Tib. *Yumka*, Wyl. *yum ka*
An abbreviation of *Consort Practice: The Queen of Great Bliss*.

Consort Practice: The Queen of Great Bliss, Tib. *Yumka Dechen Gyalmo*, Wyl. *yum ka bde chen rgyal mo*
This peaceful dakini practice from the Longchen Nyingtik is one of Jigme Lingpa's treasure teachings.

Cutting One Liberates All, Tib. *Dzogchen Chik Chö Kundröl*, Wyl. *rdzogs chen chig chod kun grol*

Cutting Through: Self-Liberation from Fixation, Tib. *Chö Dzinpa Rangdrol*, Wyl. *gcod 'dzin pa rang grol*
From Do Khyentse Yeshe Dorje's cycle of Chö teachings.

Dakini Free of Self, Tib. *Dakmema*, Wyl. *bdag med ma*

Dakini's Oral Transmission Lineage of Chakrasamvara, Tib. *Dechok Khandro Nyengyü*, Wyl. *bde mchog mkha' 'gro snyan brgyud*

Dark Red Fierce Deity, Tib. *Tumdrak Marnak*, Wyl. *gtum drag dmar nag*
A Sarma practice.

Direct Exposition of the Dharmata, Tib. *Chönyi Ngöten*, Wyl. *chos nyid dngos bstan*

Dispelling the Faults of Samaya Defilements, Tib. *Damdrib Nyesel*, Wyl. *dam grib nyes sel*

Drolma Yuldok, Wyl. *sgrol ma g.yul zlog*
The Tara practice that wards off invasions.

Drolö from the Heart Practice, Tib. *Tukdrup Drolö*, Wyl. *thugs sgrub gro lod*

Drop That Embodies All Secrets, The, Tib. *Tigle Sangdzok*, Wyl. *thig le gsang rdzogs*

Drubgyal Tsepakme, Wyl. *grub rgyal tshe dpag med*
The practice of Amitayus by Thangtong Gyalpo.

Druptab Gyatsa, *One Hundred Sadhanas*, Wyl. *sgrub thabs brgya rtsa*
A collection of sadhanas found in *Druptab Kuntü*.

Eight Deities of Gur, Tib. *Gur Lha Gye*, Wyl. *gur lha brgyad*
The dharmapala deities who safeguard the teachings and practitioners of Hevajra, known as the Gur Mahakala deities.

Eight Great Deities of the Peaceful and Wrathful Sugatas, Tib. *Deshek Shitro Drupa De Gye*, Wyl. *bde gshegs zhi khro sgrub pa sde brgyad*

Embodied Realization of the Three Roots, Tib. *Tsasum Gongdü*, Wyl. *rtsa gsum dgongs 'dus*

Embodied Realization of the Yidam Deities, Tib. *Yidam Gongdü*, Wyl. *yi dam dgongs 'dus*

Embodiment of All the Buddha Families: Lotus Bud, Tib. *Rigdü Pema'i Nyugu*, Wyl. *rigs 'dus padma'i myu gu*

Embodiment of the Guru's Realization, Tib. *Lama Gongdü*, Wyl. *bla ma dgongs 'dus*

Embodiment of the Three Jewels, Tib. *Könchok Chidü*, Wyl. *dkon mchog spyi 'dus*
A treasure revealed by Rigdzin Jatsön Nyingpo.

Embodiment of the Three Kayas, Tib. *Kusum Rikdü*, Wyl. *sku gsum rigs 'dus*

Embodiment of the Three Roots, Tib. *Tsasum Chidü*, Wyl. *rtsa gsum spyi 'dus*

Essence of Liberation, Tib. *Droltik*, Wyl. *grol thig*
An abbreviation for Sherab Özer's *Self-Liberating Realization of the Essence of Liberation* cycle of treasure teachings.

Essence of the Definitive Meaning, Tib. *Ngedön Nyingpo*, Wyl. *nges don snying po*
A terma revealed by the Kagyüpa master Jatsön Nyingpo.

Essence of the Wisdom of Manjushri Tantra, Tib. *Jampal Yeshe Nyingpo'i Gyü*, Wyl. *'jam dpal ye shes snying po'i rgyud*
One of Pema Ösel Dongak Lingpa's mind treasures, rediscovered by Jamyang Khyentse Chökyi Lodrö.

Explanation of the Lamdre View, Tib. *Lamdre Ta Tri*, Wyl. *lam 'bras lta khrid*

Explanatory Tantra Gur, Tib. *Shegyü Gur*, Wyl. *bshad rgyud gur*
Often spoken of as the *Vajrapanjara Tantra* or the *Vajra Tent Tantra*, this is one of three basic tantras of the Hevajra cycle—*Hevajra*, *Vajrapanjara*, and *Sambhuti*.

Extracting the Pure Essence, Tib. *Dangma Chüdren*, Wyl. *dwang ma bcud 'dren*

Extremely Wrathful Hayagriva, Tib. *Tamdrin Yangtrö*, Wyl. *rta mgrin yang khros*

Eye-Opener, Tib. *Mikje*, Wyl. *mig 'byed*

Father and Mother Consorts of the Simultaneously Arising Chakrasamvara, Tib. *Dechok Lhenkye Yabka Yumka*, Wyl. *bde mchog lhan skyes yab bka' yum bka'*

Female Holder of Mantra, Tib. *Ngak Dakma*, Wyl. *sngags bdag ma*

Fierce and Blazing Wrathful Guru, Hayagriva, and Garuda, Tib. *Drakpo Takhyung Barwa*, Wyl. *drag po rta khyung 'bar ba*
The wrathful guru practice from the Longchen Nyingtik.

Fifteen Dakinis Free of Self, Tib. *Dagme Lhamo Cho Nga*, Wyl. *bdag med lha mo bco lnga*

Fifty-Verse Getsul Karika, Tib. *Getsul Gyi Karika Nga Chu Pa*, Wyl. *dge tshul ka ri ka lnga bcu pa*
Fifty verses of vows made by a novice monk or nun, which were written by Arya Nagarjuna.

Fire-Wheel of the Thunderbolt, Tib. *Namchak Mekhor*, Wyl. *gnam lcags me 'khor*

Five Antidote Deities, Tib. *Nyenpo Lha Nga*, Wyl. *gnyen po lha lnga*

Five Cycles of the Essence of Sadhana, Tib. *Druptab Nyingpo Kor Nga*, Wyl. *sgrub thabs snying po skor lnga*

Five Deities of Vajravarahi, Tib. *Dorje Phagmo*, Wyl. *rdo rje phag mo*
Dorje Phagmo is often translated as Diamond Sow or Vajra Sow but is better known as Vajrayogini, the main meditation deity in the Karma Kamtsang tradition.

Five Dharmas of Lord Maitreya, Tib. *Jam Chö De Nga*, Wyl. *byams chos sde lnga*
These are the root teachings that the next buddha, the bodhisattva Maitreya, transmitted to Asanga, who transcribed them—the *Abhisamayālaṃkāra*, *Māhayānasūtrālaṃkāra*, *Madhyāntavibhāga*, *Dharmadharmatāvibhāga* and the *Uttaratantra Shastra*.

Five Great Treasuries, Tib. *Dzöchen Nam Nga*, Wyl. *mdzod chen rnam lnga*
Jamgön Kongtrul synthesized the knowledge and experience of the many lineages of Buddhism in Tibet and recorded them in the *Five Great Treasuries*: *Treasury of Encyclopedic Knowledge*, *Treasury of Precious Instructions*, *Treasury of Kagyü Mantras*, *Treasury of Precious Termas*, and the *Uncommon Treasury and Treasury of Extensive Teachings*.

Five Paths of Shije, Tib. *Shije Lam Nga*, Wyl. *zhi byed lam lnga*

Five Tantric Deities, Tib. *Gyüde Lha Nga*, Wyl. *rgyud sde lha lnga*

Five Treatises on the Middle Way, Tib. *Uma Rik Tshok*, Wyl. *dbu ma rigs tshogs*
Five treatises on Madhyamika philosophy by Nagarjuna: *Mūlamadhyamaka-kārikā*, *Yuktiṣāṣṭikakārikā*, *Vaidalyaprakaraṇa*, *Śūnyatāsaptati*, and *Vigrahavyāvartanī*.

Flower Garland of the Vinaya, Skt. *Vinayapuṣpamālā*; Tib. *Dülwa Metok Treng Gyü*, Wyl. *'dul ba me tog phreng rgyud*
This text by Vishakadeva is also known as the *Vinaya Karika*.

Flower Garland Sutra, Skt. *Avataṃsakasūtra*; Wyl. *mdo phal po che*
One of the longest of all sutras—so long, in fact, that it includes chapters that have become known as sutras in their own right.

Four Combined Commentaries on the Guhyasamaja Tantra, Tib. *Drelpa Shidrak*, Wyl. *gsang 'dus 'brel ba bzhi sbrags*

Four Hundred Verses on Madhyamaka, Skt. *Madhyamakacatuḥśataka*; Wyl. *dbu ma bzhi brgya pa*
An important Madhyamika treatise by Aryadeva and one of the thirteen great texts that form the core of the curriculum in most shedras.

Four Medical Tantras, Tib. *Gyü Zhi*, Wyl. *rgyud bzhi*
Compiled by Yuthok Yönten Gönpo, these tantras were rediscovered by Drapa Ngönshe in the eleventh century.

Four Parts of Nyingtik, Tib. *Nyingtik Yabshyi*, Wyl. *snying thig ya bzhi*
The four parts are *Vima Nyingtik*, *Lama Yangtik*, *Khandro Nyingtik*, and *Khandro Yangtik*.

Four-Faced Treasure Protector, Tib. *Tergön Zhal Zhi*, Wyl. *gter mgon zhal bzhi*
A teaching from the Mindrolling tradition.

Fragment of the Root Tantra of Vajrakilaya, Tib. *Phurpa Tsadum*, Wyl. *phur pa rtsa dum*
Sakye Pandita found a small part of the original *Vajrakilaya Root Tantra* (Skt. *Vajrakīlayamūlatantrakhaṇḍa*; Wyl. *rdo rje phur pa rtsa ba'i rgyud kyi dum bu*) in Samye Monastery. Notes were written on it that suggested the text had belonged to Guru Rinpoche. It resolved many questions that had arisen about the authenticity of various Vajrakilaya practices. Sakya Pandita translated it into Tibetan, and the text is included in the *Nyingma Kama*.

Fruit of the Wish-Fulfilling Tree, Tib. *Paksam Nyema*, Wyl. *dpag bsam snye ma*
An abbreviation of *Commentary on the Three Vows Called "Fruits of the Wish-Fulfilling Tree"* by Lochen Dharmashri.

Fulfillment and Confession Called "Stirring the Depths of Hell," Tib. *Narak Kong Shak*, Wyl. *na rak skong bshags*
A famous practice of confession and fulfillment associated with the *Narak Dongtruk* tantra and compiled from the *Kagye Sangwa Yongdzok*.

Fulfillment Offering to the Dharmapalas, Tib. *Chö Kyong Kang So*, Wyl. *chos skyong bskang gso*

Gandavyuha Sutra, Skt. *Gaṇḍavyūhasūtra*; Tib. *Dongpo Koepa*, Wyl. *mdo sdong po bkod pa*
The final part of the *Flower Garland Sutra*.

Gangloma, Wyl. *gang blo ma*
A prayer to Manjushri that is believed to have been composed by five hundred Indian Panditas.

Garland of Jewels, Tib. *Chidön Rinchen Trengwa*, Wyl. *spyi don rin chen 'phreng ba*
A commentary on the *Guhyagarbha Tantra* by Minling Rabjampa Orgyen Chödrak.

Garland of Pearls, Tib. *Mutik Trengwa*, Wyl. *mu tig 'phreng ba*
An abbreviation of *Garland of Pearls of Yamantaka, the Lord of Life*.

Gathering of Precious Qualities, Tib. *Yönten Rinpoche Düpa*, Wyl. *yon tan rin po che sdud pa*

Gathering of the Dakini's Secrets, Tib. *Khandro Sangdü*, Wyl. *mkha' 'gro gsang 'dus*
A treasure revealed originally by Jomo Menmo, then rediscovered by Jamyang Khyentse Wangpo.

Gathering of the Glorious Ones, Tib. *Palchen Düpa*, Wyl. *dpal chen 'dus pa*
The wrathful blue yidam practice of the Longchen Nyingtik.

Gathering of the Guru's Secrets, Tib. *Lama Sangdü*, Wyl. *bla ma gsang 'dus*
The main lama practice in the *Rinchen Terdzö* and the *Döjo Bumzang* a treasure revealed by Guru Chöwang.

Gathering of the Innermost Essence of Deathlessness, Tib. *Chime Yang Nying Kundü*, Wyl. *'chi med yang snying kun 'dus*

Gathering of the Innermost Essence of Great Compassion, Tib. *Tukchen Yang Nying Düpa*, Wyl. *thugs rje chen po yang snying 'dus pa*

Gathering of the Innermost Essence: A Long-Life Practice, Tib. *Tsedrup Yang Nying Kundü*, Wyl. *tshe sgrub yang snying kun 'dus*

Gathering of the Sugatas of the Three Roots, Tib. *Tsasum Deshek Düpa*, Wyl. *rtsa gsum bde gshegs 'dus pa*

Gathering of Vidyadharas, Tib. *Rigdzin Düpa*, Wyl. *rig 'dzin 'dus pa*

General Commentary on the Tantras, Tib. *Gyüde Chinam*, Wyl. *rgyud sde spyi rnam*
Two *General Commentary on the Tantras* are mentioned in Khyentse Chökyi Lodrö's biography. One is by Karma Pakshi, the Second Gyalwa Karmapa, and the other is by Lopön Sonam Tsemo, who was the second of the five founding fathers of the Sakya tradition.

General Essentialization of All the Wisdom of the Buddhas, Tib. *Chido Gongpa Düpa*, Wyl. *spyi mdo dgongs pa 'dus pa*
Another translation for this, the principal text of the Anuyoga tantra, is the *Sutra which Gathers All Intentions*. Often spoken of simply as *Düpa Do*.

General Mandala of Three Families, Tib. *Riksum Chi Kyil*, Wyl. *rigs gsum spyi dkyil*
Part of the *Compendium of Sadhanas*.

Glorious Tantra of Perfect Union, Tib. *Pal Yangdak Par Jorwa'i Gyü*, Wyl. *dpal yang dag par sbyor ba'i rgyud*

Golden Dharmas, Tib. *Shangpa'i Serchö*, Wyl. *shangs pa'i gser chos bdun*
The seven golden Dharmas of the Shangpa Kagyü tradition.

Gradual Path, Tib. *Lam Rim Chechung*, Wyl. *lam rim che chung*
Texts by Buddhaguhaya related to the *Guhayagarbha Tantra*.

Gradual Path Called the "Essence of Wisdom," Tib. *Lam Rim Yeshe Nyingpo*, Wyl. *lam rim ye shes snying po*
A terma revealed by Chokgyur Dechen Lingpa and Jamyang Khyentse Wangpo, to which Jamgön Kongtrul wrote a famous commentary. Also translated as the *Gradual Path of the Wisdom Essence*.

Great Assembly, Tib. *Tsokchen Düpa*, Wyl. *tshogs chen 'dus pa*
A major anuyoga sadhana.

Great Biography
The common abbreviation for the principal biography of a master. So, in Dilgo Khyentse Rinpoche's biography of Jamyang Khyentse Chökyi Lodrö, *A Wondrous Grove of Wish-Fulfilling Trees*, the *Great Biography* is Jamyang Khyentse Wangpo's main biography, but in Orgyen Tobgyal Rinpoche's stories, the *Great Biography* is *A Wondrous Grove of Wish-Fulfilling Trees*.

Great Compassionate Avalokiteshvara, Tib. *Tukje Chenpo*, Wyl. *thugs rje chen po*
Tukje Chenpo is an abbreviated title that could apply to several texts, and in Khyentse Chökyi Lodrö's biography, Dilgo Khyentse Rinpoche doesn't always specify which it is.

Great Compassionate Peaceful and Wrathful Pema, Tib. *Tukje Chenpo Pema Shitro*, Wyl. *thugs rje chen po padma zhi khro*

Great Dakini
An abbreviation of *Avalokiteshvara and the Great Dakini*.

Great Liberation through Hearing in the Bardo, Tib. *Bardo Tödrol Chenmo*, Wyl. *bar do thos grol chen mo*
Still popularly known by its original English translation, *The Tibetan Book of the Dead*, the *Bardo Tödrol* is a terma revealed by Karma Lingpa and used to guide the dead after death.

Great Path of Buddhaguhya, Tib. *Sangye Sangwa'i Lamchen*, Wyl. *sangs rgyas gsang ba'i lam chen*

Great Peacock, Tib. *Mahjya Chenmo*, Wyl. *rma bya chen mo*

Great Secret Esoteric Oral Instructions, Tib. *Sangchen Lobshey*, Wyl. *gsang chen slob bshad*

Great Treatise on the Stages of the Path to Enlightenment, Tib. *Lam Rim Chenmo*, Wyl. *lam rim chen mo*
One of Tsongkhapa Lobsang Drakpa's most famous works.

Great Treatises, Tib. *Zhung Chen Kapo Nga*, Wyl. *gzhung chen bka' pod lnga*
In the Gelug tradition, all the root treatises on sutra written by the Indian masters are included in these five volumes of texts. In the Sakya tradition, they call it *Six Great Volumes of Treatises* and include the treatises written by Sakya Pandita. The Nyingmapas and Kagyüpas call it the *Thirteen Great Treatises*.

Great Wish-Fulfilling Tree, Tib. *Jönshing Chenmo*, Wyl. *ljon shing chen mo*
A text on tantra by Jetsün Drakpa Gyaltsen, the third founding master of the Sakya tradition.

Great Yellow Vaishravana, Tib. *Namsey Serchen*, Wyl. *rnam sras ser chen*
A wealth practice.

Green Tara
Two *Green Tara* practices are mentioned by Dilgo Khyentse Rinpoche. The *Green Tara* (Tib. *Droljang*, Wyl. *sgrol ljang*) of the Sarma schools is from the tradition of Nyima Bepa, and the Nyingma *Green Tara* is from Chokgyur Lingpa's *Tukdrup* teachings.

Guhyagarbha Tantra, Tib. *Sangwa Nyingpo*, Wyl. *rgyud gsang ba'i snying po*
Several translations are currently in use; for example, the *Essence of Secrets Tantra*, the *Tantra of the Magical Net of Vajrasattva*, and the *Tantra of Secret Quintessence*.

Guhyasamaja Manjuvajra, Tib. *Sangdü Jamdor*, Wyl. *gsang 'dus 'jam rdor*
A practice of Manjushri in the form of Manjuvajra from the *Guhyasamaja Tantra*.

Guhyasamaja Tantra, *Gathering of Secrets*, Tib. *Sangwa Düpa*, Wyl. *gsang ba 'dus pa*
The *Guhyasamaja Tantra* is a major tantra and yidam of the Sarma schools, and the main tantra of the "desire class" of father tantras.

Gur Mahakala Called "Blazing One," Tib. *Mebarma*, Wyl. *me 'bar ma*
A dharmapala practice.

Guru Dorje Drolö from the Teachings with Restriction Seals, Tib. *Gyachen Drolö*, Wyl. *rgya can gro lod*

Guru Yoga of the Heart Essence of the Oral Transmission Lineage, Tib. *Ladrup Nyengyü Nying gi Tigle*, Wyl. *bla sgrub snyan brgyud thig le*

Guru Yoga of the Six-Armed Blue Mahakala, Tib. *Chakdruk Tinga'i Lanam*, Wyl. *phyag drug mthing ga'i bla rnam*

Guru Yoga of Vimalamitra, Tib. *Vima'i Ladrup*, Wyl. *bi ma'i bla sgrub*

Guru Yoga That Pacifies Suffering, Tib. *Ladrup Dungwa Shije*, Wyl. *bla sgrub gdung ba zhi byed*

Guru's Blessings, Tib. *Lama'i Chinlap*, Wyl. *bla ma'i byin rlabs*

Hayagriva Who Liberates the Haughty Ones, Tib. *Tamdrin Drekdröl*, Wyl. *rta mgrin dregs sgrol*

Hayagriva Who Overpowers the Haughty Ones, Tib. *Tamdrin Drekpa Zilnön*, Wyl. *rta mgrin khams gsum zil gnon*

Hayagriva Who Overpowers the Three Realms, Tib. *Tamdrin Kamsum Zil Nön*, Wyl. *rta mgrin khams gsum zil gnon*

Hayagriva: The Fiery Wheel of the Thunderbolt, Tib. *Tamdrin Namchak Mekhor*, Wyl. *rta mgrin gnam lcags me 'khor*

Heart Essence of Chetsün, Tib. *Chetsün Nyingtik*, Wyl. *lce btsun snying thig*
One of the *Seven Authoritative Transmissions* of Khyentse Wangpo and one of the most important Dzogchen teachings of recent times.

Heart Essence of Deathless Arya Tara, Tib. *Chime Phagma'i Nyingtik*, Wyl. *'chi med 'phags ma'i snying thig*
Sometimes translated as the *Heart Essence of the Sublime Lady of Immortality* and the *Heart Essence of the Immortal Noble Tara*, this long-life practice is a treasure revealed by Jamyang Khyentse Wangpo.

Heart Essence of Garab, Tib. *Garab Nyingtik*, Wyl. *dga' rab snying thig*

Heart Essence of Manjushri, Tib. *Jampal Nyingtik*, Wyl. *'jam dpal snying thig*

Heart Essence of Padma, Tib. *Pema'i Nyingtik*, Wyl. *pad ma'i snying thig*

Heart Essence of Samantabhadra, Tib. *Kunzang Thuktik*, Wyl. *kun bzang thugs tik*
Dzogchen Desum and *Kunzang Thuktik* are the Dzogchen teachings discovered by Chokgyur Lingpa.

Heart Essence of Seven Lights, Tib. *Nyingtik Dönma Dünpa*, Wyl. *snying thig sgron ma bdun pa*

Heart Essence of the Dakinis, Tib. *Khandro Nyingtik*, Wyl. *mkha' 'gro snying thig*
A profound collection of Dzogchen treasure teachings transmitted through Padmasambhava to Princess Pema Sal and revealed by Pema Ledreltsal. One of the *Four Parts of Nyingtik*.

Heart Essence of the "Hung" Cycles, Tib. *Hung Kor Nyingtik*, Wyl. *hung skor snying thig*
One of Dorje Lingpa's treasures.

Heart Essence of the Immortal Lotus-Born, Tib. *Chime Tsokye Nyingtik*, Wyl. *'chi med mtsho skyes snying thig*
One of Jamyang Khyentse Wangpo's treasures.

Heart Essence of the Mahasiddha's Wisdom Mind, Tib. *Druptop Tuktik*, Wyl. *grub thob thugs tig, grub chen thugs tig*
Also translated as the *Essence of the Mahasiddha's Wisdom Mind*, this treasure was revealed by Khyentse Wangpo.

Heart Essence of the Pith Instructions of Dzogpachenpo, Tib. *Dzogchen Mengak Nyingtik*, Wyl. *rdzogs chen man ngag snying thig*

Heart Essence of the Three Bodhisattvas, Tib. *Riksum Nyingtik*, Wyl. *rigs gsum snying thig*
Sometimes translated as the *Heart Essence of the Three Families*.

Heart Essence of the Vast Expanse, Tib. *Longchen Nyingtik*, Wyl. *klong chen snying thig*
  A Nyingma cycle of teachings and practice discovered by Jigme Lingpa as a mind treasure.

Heart Essence of the Vidyadharas, Tib. *Rigdzin Tuktik*, Wyl. *rig 'dzin thugs thig*
  Terdag Lingpa's treasure cycle and one of the practices particularly associated with Mindrolling Monastery.

Heart Essence of Vimalamitra, Tib. *Vima Nyingtik*, Wyl. *bi ma snying thig*
  One of the *Four Parts of Nyingtik*.

Heart Essence of Yutok, Tib. *Yutok Nyingtik*, Wyl. *g.yu thog snying thig*

Heart Practice, Tib. *Tukdrup*, Wyl. *thugs sgrub*
  Heart Practice is shorthand for two practices mentioned in this book—the *Heart Practice That Fulfills All Wishes* and the *Heart Practice for Dispelling All Obstacles*—and can mean both or either one.

Heart Practice for Dispelling All Obstacles, Tib. *Tukdrup Barche Kunsel*, Wyl. *thugs sgrub bar chad kun sel*

Heart Practice of Tara, Tib. *Tukdrup Drolma*, Wyl. *thugs sgrub sgrol ma*

Heart Practice of Vajrasattva, Tib. *Dorsem Tukdrup*, Wyl. *rdor sems thugs sgrub*
  Also *Mindrolling Vajrasattva*. Dilgo Khyentse Rinpoche sometimes describes this practice as *Minling Dorsem* (Wyl. *smin gling rdor sems*).

Heart Practice That Fulfills All Wishes, Tib. *Tukdrup Yishin Norbu*, Wyl. *thugs sgrub yid bzhin nor bu*

Heart Practice That Spontaneously Fulfills All Wishes, Tib. *Tukdrup Sampa Lhundrup*, Wyl. *thugs sgrub bsam pa lhun grub*
  The cycle from which the famous prayer to Guru Rinpoche, *Sampa Lhundrupma*, has been extracted.

Heart Sutra, Skt. *Prajñāpāramitāhṛdaya*; Tib. *Sherab Nyingpo*, Wyl. *shes rab snying po*
  Also known as the *Twenty-Five Verses on the Perfection of Wisdom*, this is the most popular sutra of the Prajnaparamita collection.

Higher and Lower Abhidharmas, Tib. *Ngonpa Gong Og*, Wyl. *mngon pa gong 'og*
  The *Treasury of Abhidharma*, written by Vasubandhu, presents the lower system of Abhidharma, and the *Compendium of Abhidharma* written by Vasubandhu's elder brother, Asanga, explains the higher.

Highest Yoga Tantra, Skt. *Niruttara-yoga Tantra*; Wyl. *rnal 'byor bla na med pa'i rgyud*
  Popularly known as the Anuttarayoga Tantra, which is based on a slightly inaccurate back translation of the Tibetan into Sanskrit.

Immaculate Confession Tantra, Tib. *Drime Shag Gyü*, Wyl. *dri med bshags rgyud*

Immaculate Light, Tib. *Drime Ö*, Wyl. *dri med 'od*
Tai Situ Namgyel Drakpa's commentary on the *Kalachakra Tantra*.

Indestructible Deathless Gesar, Tib. *Gesar Dorje Tsegyal*, Wyl. *ge sar rdo rje tshe rgyal*
Lharig Dechen Rolpatsal's pure-vision teaching, transmitted through Mipham Rinpoche.

Indestructible Essence of Clear Light, Tib. *Ösel Dorje'i Nyingpo*, Wyl. *'od gsal rdo rje'i snying po*

Infinite Lord of Death, Tib. *Shinje Rabjam*, Wyl. *gshin rje rab 'byams*

Infinite Profound Instructions, Tib. *Zabtri Rabjam*, Wyl. *zab khrid rab 'byams*

Inner Practice That Spontaneously Fulfills All Wishes, Tib. *Sampa Lhundrup*, Wyl. *bsam pa lhun grub ma*
Also known as *The Prayer to Guru Rinpoche That Spontaneously Fulfills All Wishes*. This prayer forms the seventh chapter of the *Le'u Dünma* and is part of the treasure teaching *Tukdrup Yishin Norbu*.

Innermost Essence of the Dakini, Tib. *Khandro Yangtik*, Wyl. *mkha' 'gro yang thig*
Longchenpa's commentaries on the *Khandro Nyingtik*.

Innermost Essence of the Guru, Tib. *Lama Yangtik*, Wyl. *bla ma yang thig*
One of the *Four Parts of Nyingtik*, this text is Longchenpa's commentary on the *Heart Essence of Vimalamitra*.

Innermost Essence of the Inseparable Union of Buddha, Tib. *Yangti Sangye Nyamjor*, Wyl. *yang ti sangs rgyas mnyam sbyor*

Innermost Essence of the Razor-Edged Phurba, Tib. *Phurba Yang Nying Pudri*, Wyl. *phur pa yang snying spu gri*

Innermost Heart Drop of Profundity, Tib. *Zabmo Yangtik*, Wyl. *zab mo yang tig*
Longchenpa's essentialization of the important pith instructions from both *Vima Nyingtik* and *Khandro Nyingtik*.

Innermost Secret Guru Yoga Called the "Sealed Quintessence," Tib. *Yangsang Ladrup Tigle Gyachen*, Wyl. *yang gsang bla sgrub thig le'i rgya can*

Innermost Secret Razor-Edge Vajrakilaya, Tib. *Phurba Yang Sang Pudri*, Wyl. *yang gsang spu gri*
A sadhana revealed by Guru Chöwang.

Inseparable Union of the Buddhas of the Great Perfection, Tib. *Dzogchen Sangye Nyamjor*, Wyl. *rdzogs chen sangs rgyas mnyam sbyor*

Inseparable Unity of the Guru and the Protector, Tib. *La Gön Yer Me*, Wyl. *bla mgon dbyer med*

Intensely Blazing Wisdom Wrathful Guru, Tib. *Gurdrak Yeshe Rap Bar*, Wyl. *gur drag ye shes rab 'bar*
By Longsal Nyingpo.

Introduction to the Middle Way, Skt. *Madhyamakāvatāra*; Wyl. *dbu ma la 'jug pa*

Iron Scorpion Yamantaka, Tib. *Shinje Chakdik*, Wyl. *gshin rje lcags sdig*

Jataka, Skt. *Jātaka*; Tib. *Kyerab*, Wyl. *skyes rabs*
Accounts of the Buddha's former lives that form one part of the "twelve branches of the excellent teachings" (Wyl. *gsung rab yan lag bcu gnyis*).

Jewel Commentary, Tib. *Könchok Drel*, Wyl. *dkon mchog 'grel*
A commentary of the *Guhyagarbha Tantra* by Rongzom Chökyi Zangpo.

Jewel Ornament of Liberation, Tib. *Dakpo Targyen*, Wyl. *dwags po'i thar rgyan*
A famous survey of the ground, path, and fruition of the Buddhadharma, written by Gampopa.

Kalachakra Tantra, Skt. *Kālacakratantra*; Tib. *Dükyi Khorlo*, Wyl. *dus kyi 'khor lo*
One of the main tantras practiced by the Sarma or New Translation schools and famous for its unique presentation of cosmology.

Kangyur, Wyl. *bka' 'gyur*
Literally the "translated words" of the Buddha. The Kangyur is a collection of the Buddha's own teachings, both sutra and tantra, in Tibetan translation.

Key to the Precious Treasury, Tib. *Rinchen Dzökyi Demik*, Wyl. *rin chen mdzod kyi lde mig*
Dodrupchen Jigme Tenpe Nyima's famous commentary on the *Guhyagarbha Tantra*.

Khyentse Kabab *see* **Secret Treasury of the Seven Great Transmissions**

King of Aspiration Prayers: Samantabhadra's "Aspiration to Good Actions," The, Skt. *Āryabhadracaryapraṇidhānarāja*; Tib. *Zangchö Mönlam*, Wyl. *bzang spyod smon lam*

King of Samadhi Sutra, Skt. *Samādhirājasūtra*; Tib. *Do Tingzin Gyalpo*, Wyl. *ting nge 'dzin gyi rgyal po'i mdo*

Krodhikali, Skt. *Krodhikālī*; Tib. *Tröma Nagmo*, Wyl. *khros ma nag mo*

Lamp for the Path to Enlightenment, Skt. *Bodhipathapradīpa*; Tib. *Changchub Lam Drön*, Wyl. *byang chub lam sgron*
Perhaps Atisha's most famous work, in which he defined the three levels of spiritual capacity and laid the foundation for the lamrim tradition.

Life-Force Phurba, Tib. *Sok Phur*, Wyl. *srog phur*

Lineage of Vast Conduct, Tib. *Gya Chen Chö Gyü*, Wyl. *rgya chen spyod brgyud*
A lineage of the bodhisattva vow transmitted through Maitreya, Asanga, and Vasubandhu.

Lion's Roar Manjushri, Tib. *Ma Wai Sengye*, Wyl. *smra ba'i seng ge*

Lion's Roar of Shrimaladevi Sutra, Skt. *Śrīmālādevisiṃhanādasūtra*, Wyl. *dpal phreng seng ge'i nga ros zhus pa'i mdo*
Also known as the *Shrimaladevi Simhanada Sutra* or the *Shrimala Sutra*.

Long-Life Practice: A Garland of Vajras, Tib. *Tsedrup Dorje Trengwa*, Wyl. *tshe sgrub rdo rje phreng ba*
A long-life sadhana revealed by Chokgyur Lingpa at Tsegyal Drak.

Long-Life Practice "Iron Tree," Tib. *Tsedrup Chakdongma*, Wyl. *tshe sgrub lcags sdong ma*
A Nyingma tradition from the *Northern Treasures* for invoking the blessing of longevity.

Long-Life Practice of Extracting the Pure Essence, Tib. *Tsedrup Dangma Chüdren*, Wyl. *tshe sgrub dwangs ma bcud 'dren*

Long-Life Practice of the Gathering of Secrets, Tib. *Tsedrup Sangdü*, Wyl. *tshe sgrub gsang 'dus*

Long-Life Practice That Brings Complete Victory Over the Four Maras, Tib. *Tsedrup Dü Zhi Namgyal*, Wyl. *tshe sgrub bdud bzhi rnam rgyal*

Luminous Expanse, Tib. *Longsal*, Wyl. *klong gsal*
An abbreviation of *Tantra of the Blazing Expanse of Luminosity*.

Luminous Heart Essence, Tib. *Ösel Nyingtik*, Wyl. *'od gsal snying thig*

Luminous Heart Essence of the Three Roots, Tib. *Tsasum Ösel Nyingtik*, Wyl. *rtsa gsum 'od gsal snying thig*
One of Khyentse Wangpo's mind treasures.

Magical Net, Tib. *Gyutrül Drawa*, Wyl. *sgyu 'phrul drwa ba*
An abbreviation for the *Tantra of the Net of Magical Illusion*. Sometimes known as the *Extensive Magical Net*.

Magical Net of Manjushri, Skt. *Mañjuśrīnāmasaṃgīti*; Wyl. *'jam dpal sgyu 'phrul drwa ba*
The famous praise of Manjushri, sometimes translated as *Chanting the Names of Manjushri* or the *Litany of Names of Manjushri*.

Magical Net of the Three Roots, Tib. *Tsasum Gyutrül Drawa*, Wyl. *rtsa gsum sgyu 'phrul drwa ba*
A terma sadhana.

Mahamudra: The Ocean of Definitive Meaning, Tib. *Chagchen Ngedön Gyamtso*, Wyl. *phyag chen nges don rgya mtsho*

Mandala of Accomplishment, Tib. *Drub Kyil*, Wyl. *sgrub dkyil*
A teaching associated with the Kalachakra.

Mandala of Peaceful and Wrathful Deities, Tib. *Shyitro*, Wyl. *zhi khro*; see **Mandala of the Peaceful and Wrathful Deities of the Magical Net**

Mandala of the Eight Great Deities, Tib. *Dor Ling Kagye*, Wyl. *rdor gling bka' brgyad*
Revealed by Dorje Lingpa.

Mandala of the Eight Great Deities: The Assembly of Blood Drinkers, Tib. *Kagye Traktung Düpa*, Wyl. *bka' brgyad khrag 'thung 'dus pa*
This teaching is a part of *Druptob Thuktik*, one of Jamyang Khyentse Wangpo's mind treasures.

Mandala of the Eight Great Deities: The Assembly of Sugatas, Tib. *Kagye Deshek Düpa*, Wyl. *bka' brgyad bde gshegs 'dus pa*
A terma cycle revealed by Nyangrel Nyima Özer that focuses on the Kagye deities and is sometimes translated as the *Gathering of the Sugatas of Kagye*, *Eight Commands: Union of the Sugatas*, and *Assemblage of the Sugatas*. In Tibetan, the *Kagye Deshek Düpa* is sometimes abbreviated as *Kagye Derdü*.

Mandala of the Eight Great Deities: The Complete Gathering of Vidyadharas, Tib. *Kagye Rigdzin Yongdü*, Wyl. *bka' brgyad rig 'dzin yongs 'dus*
An earth treasure revealed by Ngari Panchen Pema Wangyal and based on the Kagye.

Mandala of the Eight Great Deities: The Complete Secret, Tib. *Kagye Sangwa Yongdzok*, Wyl. *bka' brgyad gsang ba yongs rdzogs*
A terma revealed by Guru Chöwang and deciphered with the help of his consort, Jomo Menmo.

Mandala of the Eight Great Deities: The Fortress and Precipice, Tib. *Kagye Dzong Trang*, Wyl. *bka' brgyad rdzong 'phrang*

Mandala of the Eight Great Deities: The Siddha, Tib. *Druptob Kagye*, Wyl. *grub thob bka' brgyad*

Mandala of the Eight Great Deities: The Subduer of Haughty Spirits, Tib. *Kagye Drekdül*, Wyl. *bka' brgyad dregs 'dul*

Mandala of the Peaceful and Wrathful Deities of the Magical Net, Skt. *Śāntikrodhamāyājāla*; Tib. *Gyutrül Shyitro*, Wyl. *sgyu 'phrul zhi khro*

Manjushri Arapachana, Tib. *Jampal Arapatsana*, Wyl. *'jam dpal ah ra pa tsa na*
A Sakya practice of Orange Manjushri.

Manjushri from the Gyüluk Tradition, Tib. *Jampal Gyüluk*, Wyl. *'jam dpal rgyud lugs*
A tantric practice of Manjushri.

Manjushri Who Overpowers the Lord of Death, Tib. *Jampal Chidak Zilnön*, Wyl. *'jam dpal gshin rje 'chi bdag zil gnon*

Manjushri: Holder of Secrets, Tib. *Jampal Sangden*, Wyk. *'jam dpal gsang ldan*
One of Marpa Lotsawa's tantric teachings.

Manjushri: Lion of Speech, Tib. *Mraseng*, Wyl. *smra ba'i seng ge*
From Padampa Sangye's tradition.

Manjushri: Lion of Speech from the Heart Practice, Tib. *Tukdrup Lama Maseng*, Wyl. *thugs sgrub bla ma smra seng*
Lama Maseng is one of the twelve aspects of Guru Rinpoche in the *Tukdrup Barche Kunsel*.

Mind Treasure: Guru of Great Bliss, Tib. *Gongter Guru Dewachenpo*, Wyl. *dgongs gter guru bde ba chen po*

Mindrolling Vajrasattva *see* **Heart Practice of Vajrasattva**

Mirror of the Heart of Vajrasattva, Tib. *Dorje Sempa Nying gi Melong gi Gyü*, Wyl. *rdo rje sems dpa' snying gi me long*
One of the seventeen tantras of Dzogchen mengakde teachings.

Molten Metal Yamantaka, Tib. *Shinje Trochu*, Wyl. *gshin rje khro chu*
Sometimes abbreviated as *Trochu*.

Mother and Son Heart Essence *see* **Four Parts of Nyingtik**

Mountain Dharma, Tib. *Richö*, Wyl. *ri chos*
By Yang Gönpa, a great yogi of the Drukpa Kagyü.

Mountain Dharma: Not Crossing the Threshold, Tib. *Richö Them-me*, Wyl. *ri chos thems med*
By Karma Chakme, who is also referred to as "Noble Chakme" by Dilgo Khyentse Rinpoche.

Nagaraksha, Wyl. *na ga raksha*
By Rinchen Lingpa of the Martsang Kagyü lineage.

Naropa Zhung Chung, Wyl. *na ro pa'i gzhung chung*
A minor treatise by Naropa.

Naropa's Vajrayogini, Tib. *Naro Khachö*, Wyl. *na ro mkha' spyod*

Net of Magical Illusion, Skt. *Māyājāla*; Tib. *Gyutrül Drawa*, Wyl. *sgyu 'phrul drwa ba*
A cycle of tantric texts that includes the *Guhyagarbha Tantra*.

New Treasures, Tib. *Tersar*, Wyl. *gter gsar*
An abbreviation of *New Treasures of Chokling*.

New Treasures of Chokling, Tib. *Chokling Tersar*, Wyl. *mchog gling gter gsar*
A collection of more than forty volumes of treasures revealed by Chokgyur Lingpa, as well as associated teachings, arrangement of texts, and commentaries primarily by Jamyang Khyentse Wangpo, Jamgön Kongtrul, Khakyab Dorje, Tsewang Norbu, Tersey Tulku, and Dilgo Khyentse Rinpoche.

Nine Deities of the Ocean of the Victorious Ones, Skt. *Jinasāgara*; Tib. *Gyalwa Gyamtso*, Wyl. *rgyal ba rgya mtsho*
Drime Kunga's Red Avalokiteshvara treasure.

Nonduality of Samsara and Nirvana, Tib. *Khorde Yerme*, Wyl. *'khor 'das dbyer med*
The teachings concerned with how to recognize and realize intrinsic awareness "as it is" are spoken of by the Nyingmapas as Dzogchen, by the Kagyüpas as Mahamudra, and by the Sakyapas as Khorde Yerme.

Northern Treasures, Tib. *Jang Ter*, Wyl. *byang gter*
The treasure teachings that were revealed by Rigdzin Gödem Ngödrup Gyaltsen in Tsang, western Tibet, an area considered to be in the north.

Nyingma Kama, Wyl. *nying ma bka' ma*
The canonical teachings of the Early Translation school.

Nyingtik, Wyl. *snying thig* or *snying tig*
The Nyingtik teachings are the heart essence of the Dzogchen teachings in the Nyingma tradition.

Obstacle-Averting Yamantaka, Tib. *Shinje Yangdok*, Wyl. *gshin rje yang zlog*

Ocean of Accomplishment, Tib. *Ngödrup Gyatso*, Wyl. *dngos grub rgya mtsho*
The main sadhana of a cycle of Simhamukha teachings and practices revealed to Khyentse Chökyi Lodrö in a pure vision.

Ocean of Dharma That Combines All Teachings, Tib. *Kadü Chökyi Gyatso*, Wyl. *bka' 'dus chos kyi rgya mtsho*
Ocean of Dharma, the Great Gathering of Transmitted Precepts was a treasure revealed by Yarje Orgyen Lingpa, who took it from a cliff at Yarlung Shedrak. It was later rediscovered as a yang ter by Jamyang Khyentse Wangpo.

Ocean of Sadhanas, Tib. *Druptab Gyatso*, Wyl. *sgrub thabs rgya mtsho*
A collection of sadhanas found in *Druptab Kundu*.

Ocean of the Victorious Ones, Skt. *Jinasāgara*; Tib. *Gyalwa Gyamtso*, Wyl. *rgyal ba rgya mtsho*
The practice of Red Avalokiteshvara from the Kamtsang tradition.

One Hundred Jewel Sources, Tib. *Jonang Rinjung*, Wyl. *jo nang rin 'byung*
From the Jonang tradition.

One Hundred Minor Dharmas, Tib. *Jo Wo'i Chöchung Gyatsa*, Wyl. *jo bo'i chos chung brgya rtsa*
By Atisha Dipamkara.

One Hundred Profound Commentaries, Tib. *Zabtri Gyatsa*, Wyl. *zab khrid brgya rtsa*
Jonang Kunga Drolchok's collection of one hundred instructions from all traditions.

One Hundred Sadhanas from the Narthang Tradition, Tib. *Narthang Gyatsa*, Wyl. *snar thang brgya rtsa*

One Hundred Sadhanas of Bari Lotsawa, Tib. *Bari Gyatsa*, Wyl. *ba ri brgya rtsa*
A collection of one hundred teachings or sadhanas made by Bari Lotsawa, the second throne holder of the Sakya school.

One Hundred Thousand Precious Tantras of the Nyingma, Tib. *Nyingma Gyübum*, Wyl. *rnying ma rgyud 'bum*
A collection of Nyingma tantras compiled by the great tertön Ratna Lingpa.

One Hundred Transmissions of Mitra, Tib. *Mitra Gyatsa*, Wyl. *mi tra brgya rtsa*
A collection of 108 tantric mandalas compiled by Mitrayogin.

Oral Transmission Endowed with the Four Valid Factors, Tib. *Nyengyü Tsema Zhiden*, Wyl. *snyan brgyud tshad ma bzhi ldan*
Another name for *Lamdre Lobshey*.

Oral Transmission Lineage of the Dakinis, Tib. *Khandro Nyengyü*, Wyl. *mkha' 'gro snyan brgyud*

Oral Transmission Lineage of Vishuddhi, Tib. *Nyengyü Yangdak*, Wyl. *snyan brgyud yang dag*

Oral Transmission Lineage Yamantaka, Tib. *Nyengyü Shinje*, Wyl. *snyan brgyud gshin rje*

Oral Transmission of Vajrakilaya Called "Vital Essence," Tib. *Nyengyü Netik Phurba*, Wyl. *snyan brgyud gnad tig phur pa*

Ornament of Clear Realization, Skt. *Abhisamayālaṃkāra*; Tib. *Ngöntok Gyen*, Wyl. *mngon rtogs rgyan*
One of the *Five Dharmas of Lord Maitreya*, the *Abhisamayalankara* is a commentary on the hidden meaning of the *Prajnaparamita Sutras*.

Ornament of Liberation, Tib. *Targyen*, Wyl. *thar rgyan*
An abbreviation of *Jewel Ornament of Liberation*.

Ornament of the Mahayana Sutras, Skt. *Mahāyānasūtrālaṃkāra*; Tib. *Thek Pa Chenpo Do De Gyen*, Wyl. *thegs pa chen po mdo sde'i rgyan*
One of the *Five Dharmas of Lord Maitreya*.

Ornament of the Middle Way, Skt. *Madhyamakālaṃkāra*; Tib. *Uma Gyen*, Wyl. *dbu ma rgyan*
  Written by Shantarakshita, this text is considered to be the quintessential root text of the *Yogacara Svatantrika Madhyamaka*.

Ornament of the Realization of Vajrapani, Tib. *Sangdak Gongyen*, Wyl. *gsang bdag dgongs rgyan*
  One of two commentaries on the *Guhyagarbha Tantra* by Lochen Dharmashri. The other is *Sangdak Shelung, Oral Instruction of Vajrapani*.

Outer Practice that Removes All Obstacles, Tib. *Chidrup Barche Kunsel*, Wyl. *phyi sgrub bar chad kun sel*

Padma Dakini, Tib. *Pema Khandro*, Wyl. *padma mkha' 'gro*
  One of Chokgyur Lingpa's treasures.

Parting from the Four Attachments, Tib. *Shenpa Zhi Dral*, Wyl. *zhen pa bzhi bral*
  A short teaching Manjushri gave to the Sakya patriarch, Sachen Kunga Nyingpo.

Path and Fruition, Tib. *Lamdre*, Wyl. *lam 'bras*
  "Path with the Result" instructions (related to the deity Hevajra) are the highest teachings within the Sakya school. They developed into two major lines of transmission: the general presentation known as *Lamdre Tsokshey* (the *Explanation for Assemblies*) and the secret presentation known as *Lamdre Lobshey* (the *Explanation for Private Disciples*).

Path and Fruition: The Explanation for Assemblies, Tib. *Lamdre Tsokshey*, Wyl. *lam 'bras tshogs bshad*

Path and Fruition: The Explanation for Assemblies and Private Disciples, Tib. *Lamdre Tsoklob*, Wyl. *lam 'bras tshogs slob*

Path and Fruition: The Explanation for Private Disciples, Tib. *Lamdre Lobshey*, Wyl. *lam 'bras slob bshad*

Peaceful and Wrathful Deities, Tib. *Shyitro*, Wyl. *zhi khro*
  Both the Kama and Terma traditions have a *Mandala of the Peaceful and Wrathful Deities*, but it's not clear to which Dilgo Khyentse Rinpoche refers in the *Great Biography*.

Peaceful and Wrathful Deities Who Stir the Pits of Hell, Tib. *Shitro Narak Dongtruk*, Wyl. *zhi khro narak dong sprugs*

Peaceful and Wrathful Gurus, Tib. *Lama Shyitro*, Wyl. *bla ma zhi khro*

Peaceful Form of the Mother Who Repels Negative Forces, Tib. *Makdzor Shiwa*, Wyl. *dmag zor zhi ba*

Peaceful Manjushri, Tib. *Gyüluk Jampal Shiwa*, Wyl. *rgyud lugs 'jam dpal zhi ba*

Pearl Garland of Yamantaka, Lord of Life, Tib. *Tsedak Nubluk Mutik Trengwa*, Wyl. *tshe bdag gnubs lugs mu tig phreng ba*
An empowerment manual.

Perfection of Wisdom Sutra in Eight Thousand Lines, Skt. *Aṣṭasāhasrikāprajñāpāramitā*; Tib, *Gyetongpa*, Wyl. *brgyad stong pa*

Perfection of Wisdom Sutra in One Hundred Thousand Lines, Skt. *Śatasāhasrikāprajñāpāramitā*
This the largest of the *Prajnaparamita Sutras* that's usually referred to in Tibetan as the *Hundred Thousand*.

Perfectly Accomplished Guru, Wyl. *yong rdzogs bla ma*
One of Khyentse Wangpo's treasure teachings.

Possessing Purity, Tib. *Dakden*, Wyl. *dag ldan*

Practice for the Accomplishment of Activity Called "Precious Lamp," Tib. *Trindrup Rinchen Dronme*, Wyl. *phrin sgrub rin chen sgron me*

Praise and Practice of Manjushri, Tib. *Jampal Tö Drub*, Wyl. *'jam dpal bstod sgrub*

Praise to Glorious Excellent Knowledge, Tib. *Pal Yeshe Yönten Zangpo La Tödpa*, Wyl. *dpal ye shes yon tan bzang po la bstod pa*

Praise to the Extraordinary Qualities of Buddha, Tib. *Thubpe Khyepar Phagtöd*, Wyl. *thub pa'i khyad par 'phags bstod*

Praise to the One Who Outshines the Gods, Tib. *Lhale Phul Jung Gi Tödpa*, Wyl. *lha las phul byung gi bstod pa*

Praise to Venerable Manjushri, Tib. *Jetsün Jampalyang La Tödpa*, Wyl. *rje btsun 'jam dpal dbyangs la bstod pa*

Pratimoksha Sutra, Skt. *Pratimokṣasūtra*; Tib. *Sor Do*, Wyl. *so sor thar pa'i mdo*
A list of rules governing the behavior of Buddhist monks and nuns.

Prayer of Excellent Conduct, Wyl. *bzang spyod*
Another name for *The King of Aspiration Prayers: Samantabhadra's "Aspiration to Good Actions."*

Precious Garland of the Supreme Path, Tib. *Lamchok Rinchen Trengwa*, Wyl. *lam mchog rin chen phreng ba*
By Gampopa.

Precious Lamp of the Accomplishment of Activity, Tib. *Trindrup Rinchen Drönme*, Wyl. *phrin sgrub rin chen sgron me*

Precious Treasury of Terma Teachings, Tib. *Rinchen Terdzö*, Wyl. *rin chen gter mdzod*
One of Jamgön Kongtrul's *Five Great Treasuries*, the *Rinchen Terdzö* is a com-

pilation of many of the termas that had been discovered, including Chokgyur Lingpas treasures.

Precious Words
An abbreviation of *Precious Words: Path and Fruition*.

Precious Words: Path and Fruition, Tib. *Sung Ngag Rinpoche Lamdre*, Wyl. *gsung ngag rin po che lam 'bras*

Precious Words: The Explanation of Path and Fruition for Private Disciples, Tib. *Sung Ngag Rinpoche Lamdre Lobshey* Wyl. *gsung ngag rin poche lam 'bras slob bshad*

Profound Essence of Vimalamitra, Tib. *Vimala'i Zabtik*, Wyl. *bi ma la'i zab tig*
Part of the *Heart Essence of Chetsün* cycle and one of Khyentse Wangpo's mind treasures.

Profound Essence of Vishuddhi, Tib. *Yangdak Zabtik*, Wyl. *yang dag zab tig*

Profound Heart Essence of the Embodiment of the Three Jewels, Tib. *Yangzab Könchok Chidü*, Wyl. *yang zab dkon mchog spyi 'dus*

Profound Inner Meaning, Tib. *Zabmo Nang Dön*, Wyl. *zab mo nang don*
Written by Rangjung Dorje, the Third Karmapa, who received the entire transmission of the Nyingma tradition as well as that of the Karma Kagyü.

Profound Meaning of Ati, Tib. *Ati Zab Dön*, Wyl. *ati zab don snying po*
The treasure teachings by Garab Dorje rediscovered by Chokgyur Lingpa.

Profound Path, Tib. *Lam Zab*, Wyl. *lam zab*

Profound Path in Seven Chapters, Tib. *Le'u Dunma*, Wyl. *le'u bdun ma*
The prayer to Padmakara in seven chapters that was revealed by Tulku Zangpo Drakpa in the fourteenth century.

Protector Ganapati, Tib. *Gönpo Tsokdak*, Wyl. *mgon po tshogs bdag*

Pure Vision and Oral Transmission Guru Yoga, Tib. *Ladrup Daknang Nyengyü*, Wyl. *bla sgrub dag snang snyan brgyud*

Purifying Perception, Tib. *Nangjong*, Wyl. *snang sbyong*

Queen of the Siddhas, Tib. *Drupa'i Gyalmo*, Wyl. *sgrub pa'i rgyal mo*

Radiant Pith Instructions, Tib. *Ösel Mengakde*, Wyl. *'od gsal man ngag sde*

Razor-Edged Vajrakilaya, Tib. *Phurpa Pudri*, Wyl. *phur pa spu gri*

Red Dzambhala, Tib. *Dzam Mar*, Wyl. *dzam dmar*
A manifestation of Vajrasattva as a wealth deity, known to Tibetans as Dzambhala Marpo.

Red Kingkara, Tib. *Kingmar*, Wyl. *king dmar*

Rediscovered Treasure: Guru Chakrasamvara, Tib. *Yangter Lama Dechok Khorlo*, Wyl. *yang gter bla ma bde mchog 'khor lo*

Rediscovered Treasure: Three Cycles of Lama Tennyi, Tib. *Yangter Lama Tennyi Korsum*, Wyl. *yang gter bla ma bstan gnyis skor gsum*

Removing Inauspicious Circumstances, Tib. *Tendrel Nyesel*, Wyl. *rten 'brel nyes sel*
Sometimes translated as *Dispelling Flaws in Interdependence*, these sadhanas are part of the terma revealed by Tertön Sogyal.

Restoration of Vows Ceremony for Auspiciousness, Tib. *Tashi Pa'i Sojong*, Wyl. *bkra shis pa'i gso sbyong*

Reverberation of Sound, Tib. *Dra Talgyur*, Wyl. *sgra thal 'gyur*

Root Explanation of Ashta, Tib. *Ashta Zhi Shäd*, Wyl. *ashta gzhi bshad*
Editor's Note: There's a typo in the Tibetan script that reads *gzhi* ("root") when it should read *bzhi* ("four").

Root Tantra of Hevajra, Tib. *Kyedor Tsa Gyü*, Wyl. *kye rdor rtsa rgyud*

Sadhana of the Lineage of Awareness Holders, Tib. *Rigdzin Dungdrup*, Wyl. *rig 'dzin gdung sgrub*
A practice of Guru Rinpoche from the *Northern Treasures* tradition revealed by Rigdzin Gödem.

Samaya Vajra, Tib. *Damtsik Dorje*, Wyl. *dam tshig rdo rje*
A sadhana for the purification of defilements caused by transgression of vajrayana vows, mainly practiced in the Sarma tradition.

Sambhogakaya Medicine Buddha, Tib. *Menla Longku*, Wyl. *sman bla longs sku*

Samputa Tantra, Skt. *Sampuṭanāmamahātantra*; Wyl. *yang dag par sbyor ba zhes bya ba'i rgyud chen po*
One of three basic tantras of the Hevajra cycle.

Samvarodaya Tantra, Skt. *Saṃvarodayatantra*; Tib. *Dom Jung*, Wyl. *sdom 'byung gi rgyud*
Sometimes known as the *Tantra of the Emergence of Chakrasamvara*, this tantra was requested and compiled by Vajrapani.

Secret Biography, Tib. *Sangwai Namtar*; Wyl. *gsang ba'i rnam thar*
Biography of Khyentse Chökyi Lodrö that was edited by Khenpo Kunga Wangchuk and published by Pewar Tulku based on Khyentse Chökyi Lodrö's private papers.

Secret Conduct of the Great Oral Lineage, Tib. *Sangchö Nyengyü Chenmo*, Wyl. *gsang spyod snyan brgyud chen mo*

Secret Conduct: The Oral Lineage of the Dakinis, Tib. *Sangchö Khandro Nyengyü*, Wyl. *gsang spyod mkha' gro snyan brgyud*
From Thangtong Gyalpo.

Secret Essence, Tib. *Sangtik*, Wyl. *gsang thig*
A cycle of treasure teachings and sadhanas revealed by Jamgön Kongtrul.

Secret Essence Guru Yoga, Tib. *Sangtik Ladrub*, Wyl. *gsang thig bla sgrub*

Secret Essence Vajrakilaya, Tib. *Sangtik Dorje Phurba*, Wyl. *gsang thig rdo rje phur pa*
One of three Vajrakilaya treasures revealed by Chokgyur Lingpa.

Secret Moon, Tib. *Dasang*, Wyl. *zla gsang*
Also translated as the *Secret Moon Essence*, this Mahayoga text appears in the Nyingma Gyübum and is sometimes counted among the Eighteen Mahayoga Tantras as the "tantra of enlightened speech."

Secret Practice of Dorje Drolö
An abbreviated form of *Secret Practice of Drolö Called "Taming All Malevolent Spirits."*

Secret Practice of Drolö Called "Taming All Malevolent Spirits," Tib. *Drolö Sangdrup Dukpa Kundül*, Wyl. *gro lod gsang sgrub gdug pa kun 'dul*
One of Jamgön Kongtrul Lodrö Taye's treasures.

Secret Practice of the Heart Essence of the Lotus-Born, Tib. *Sangdrup Tsokye Nyingtik*, Wyl. *gsang sgrub mtsho skyes snying thig*

Secret Practice of Vajrakilaya, Tib. *Phurba'i Sangdrub*, Wyl. *phur pa'i gsang sgrub*
There are many practices called *Secret Practice of Vajrakilaya* by different masters. The two mentioned in the biography are by Ratna Lingpa and Dudul Dorje.

Secret Practice Simhamukha, Tib. *Sangdrup Sengdongma*, Wyl. *gsang sgrub seng gdong ma*

Secret Treasury of the Seven Great Transmissions, Tib. *Kabab Chenpo Dün*, Wyl. *bka' babs chen po bdun*
Sometimes translated as the *Seven Authoritative Transmissions*, *Seven Special Transmissions*, *Seven Orders of Teaching*, or *Seven Successions of the Transmitted Precepts*. These seven kinds of transmission were received by Jamyang Khyentse Wangpo and Chokgyur Dechen Lingpa: the continuous transmission of sutra and tantra (*kama*), earth treasures (*sa ter*), rediscovered treasures (*yang ter*), mind treasures (*gong ter*), oral transmission (*nyen gyü*), visionary revelations or "pure visions" (*dak nang*), and revelations from memory (*je dren*).

Secret Wisdom, Tib. *Sangwa Yeshe*, Wyl. *gsang ba ye shes*

Self-Existing, Self-Manifest Primordial Purity, Tib. *Kadak Rangjung Rangshar*, Wyl. *ka dag rang byung rang shar*
A Dzogchen text from the *Northern Treasures*.

Self-Liberated Five Poisonous Conflicting Emotions, Tib. *Nyön Mong Duk Nga Rangdrol*, Wyl. *nyon mong dug lnga rang grol*

Self-Liberating Realization of the Essence of Liberation, Tib. *Droltik Gongpa Rangdrol*, Wyl. *grol thig dgongs pa rang grol*
A cycle of treasure teachings revealed by Sherab Özer, the Tertön of Trengpo (Trengpo Terchen), also known as Drodul Lingpa or Prajnarashmi.

Self-Liberation from Grasping, Tib. *Ati Dzinpa Rangdrol*, Wyl. *ati 'dzin pa rang grol*

Seven Deities, Tib. *Lha Dün*, Wyl. *lha bdun*

Seven Heart Essences, Tib. *Nyingtik Dün*, Wyl. *snying thig bdun*

Seven Points of Mind Training, Tib. *Lojong Dön Dünma*, Wyl. *blo sbyong don bdun ma*

Seven Profound Cycles of Chokling, Tib. *Chokling Zabdun*, Wyl. *mchog gling zab bdun*
Seven collections of practices revealed by Chokgyur Dechen Lingpa.

Seven Transmissions *see* **Secret Treasury of the Seven Great Transmissions**

Seven Treasuries, Tib. *Dzö Dün*, Wyl. *mdzod bdun*
Longchenpa's *Seven Treasuries* are the *Wish-Fulfilling Treasury*, the *Treasury of Pith Instructions*, the *Treasury of Dharmadhatu*, the *Treasury of Philosophical Tenets*, the *Treasury of the Supreme Vehicle*, the *Treasury of Word and Meaning*, and the *Treasury of the Natural State*.

Seven Verses, Tib. *Tsikdün*, Wyl. *tshig bdun*
Cycle of sadhana teachings discovered by Jamgön Kongtrul Rinpoche.

Seven-Line Prayer Guru Yoga, Tib. *Tsikdün Ladrup*, Wyl. *tshig bdun bla sgrub*
By Mipham Rinpoche, often referred to as the *Shower of Blessings*.

Seventh Lamp, Tib. *Drönma Dünpa*, Wyl. *sgron ma bdun pa*

Sharp Point: The Wrathful King in Whom All Power Is Gathered, Tib. *Trogyal Tobdü*, Wyl. *khro rgyal stobs 'dus*

Shitro Dongtruk, Wyl. *zhi khro dong sprugs*; *see* **Two Dongtruks**

Simhamukha of Vimalamitra, Tib. *Vimala'i Sengdong*, Wyl. *bi ma la'i seng gdong*

Single Intention, Tib. *Gong Chik*, Wyl. *dgongs gcig*
Jigten Sumgön was the founder of the Drikung Kagyü school, and this is his guide to Buddhist theory and practice.

Six Yogas of Naropa, Tib. *Naro Chödrug*, Wyl. *na ro chos drug*
Sometimes referred to simply as the *Six Yogas*, these six sets of teachings and practices form the basis of the inner yoga practices of Mahamudra, as practiced in the Kagyü and Gelug schools.

Six Yogas of Niguma, Tib. *Nigu Chödrug*, Wyl. *ni gu chos drug*
These six inner yoga practices originate from the Indian yogini Niguma, and although they have the same titles as the *Six Yogas of Naropa*, the way they are practiced is slightly different.

Sixteen Arhats Practice, Tib. *Ne Chok*, Wyl. *gnas brtan bcu drug gi cho ga*
The main verses of this practice are believed to have been written by the Kashmiri Pandita Shakyashri Bhadra, a teacher of Sakya Pandita. All traditions recite this prayer, but the sadhana is slightly different in each tradition. Dilgo Khyentse Rinpoche doesn't specify which version he means in his biography of Khyentse Chökyi Lodrö.

Sky Teachings, Tib. *Namchö*, Wyl. *gnam chos*
The treasure teachings of Namchö Mingyur Dorje.

Solitary Hero Vajrabhairava, Tib. *Jigje Pawo Chikpa*, Wyl. *'jigs byed dpa' bo gcig pa*

Songs of the Dakinis, Tib. *Chö Khandro'i Gyejang*, Wyl. *gcod mkha' 'gro'i gad rgyangs*

Source of Accomplishment, Tib. *Ngödrup Jungney*, Wyl. *dngos sgrub 'byung gnas*

Spear's-Length Sun Vajrapani, Tib. *Sangdak Nyima Dungang*, Wyl. *gsang bdag nyi ma mdung gang*
"Spear's-length sun" appears to refer to a time of day, but the implication is that this sadhana invokes blessings extremely quickly.

Stupa of Shakyamuni That Liberates When Remembered, Tib. *Shaktub Drendrol Chorten*, Wyl. *shak thub dran grol mchod rten*

Sublime Dharma of Cutting Through Demons, Tib. *Damchö Dü Chö Shije*, Wyl. *dam chos bdud gcod zhi byed*

Summary of the Gateway to the Perfection of Knowledge, Tib. *Khejuk Domjang*, Wyl. *mkhas 'jug sdom byang*
By Mipham Rinpoche.

Supplication Prayer to Tsarchen, Tib. *Tsarchen Dorje Chang Gi Sol Dep*, Wyl. *tshar chen rdo rje 'chang gi gsol 'debs*

Supreme Dharma, the Sublime Path to Great Bliss, Tib. *Damchö Dechen Lamchok*, Wyl. *dam chos bde chen lam mchog*
A terma revealed by the first Dodrupchen Rinpoche.

Supreme Emanation Hayagriva, Tib. *Tachok Rölpa*, Wyl. *rta mchog rol pa*

Sutra Completely Dear to Monks, Skt. *Bhikṣupriyasūtra*; Wyl. *dge slong la gces pa'i mdo*

Sutra of Golden Light, Skt. *Suvarṇaprabhāsottama*; Tib. *Serwö Dampa'i Do*, Wyl. *gser 'od dam pa'i mdo*
In Tibetan, there are three versions of this sutra: the twenty-one-, twenty-nine-, and thirty-one-chapter versions. The twenty-nine-chapter version was probably the most popular in Tibet and Tibetan Buddhist regions, but Dilgo Khyentse Rinpoche does not specify to which version he's referring in the text.

Sutra of Immaculate Space, Tib. *Namkha Drima Mepa'i Do*, Wyl. *nam mkha' dri ma med pa'i mdo*

Sutra of the Abundant Array of Ornaments, Skt. *Ghanavyūhasūtra*; Tib. *Gyen Tukpo Köpa'i Do*, Wyl. *rgyan stug po bkod pa'i mdo*

Sutra of the Torch of the Triple Gem, Wyl. *dkon mchog sgron me'i mdo*

Sutra Requested by the Noble Narayana, Skt. *Nārāyaṇṇāparipṛcchāsūtra*; Wyl. *sred med kyi bus zhus pa'i mdo*

Sutra which Precisely Explains Suchness, Tib. *Dekhonanyi Ngepar Tenpa'i Do*, Wyl. *de kho na nyid nges par bstan pa'i mdo*

Taking "Cutting Through" as the Path, Tib. *Chö Yul Lam Khyer*, Wyl. *gcod yul lam khyer*

Tantra of Purification, Tib. *Jong Gyü*, Wyl. *sbyong rgyud*

Tantra of the Blazing Expanse of Luminosity, Tib. *Longsal Barma*, Wyl. *klong gsal 'bar ma*

Tantra of the Gathering of Precious Jewels, Tib. *Kundü Rinpoche'i Gyü*, Wyl. *kun 'dus rin po che'i rgyud*

Tantra on Recognizing the Qualities of the Guru, Tib. *Lama'i Yönten Zung Wai Gyü*, Wyl. *bla ma'i yon tan bzung ba'i rgyud*

Tantra That Directly Reveals Samantabhadra's Mind, Tib. *Kunzang Gongpa Zangtal*, Wyl. *kun tu bzang po'i dgongs pa zang thal gyi rgyud*
A tantric treasure revealed by Rigdzin Gödem.

Tarayogini, Tib. *Drolma Naljorma*, Wyl. *sgrol ma rnal 'byor ma*
Tarayogini is a very wrathful, eight-armed form of Tara, who was introduced into Tibet by the great Indian mahasiddha Buddhaguptanatha.

Teachings on the Practice of Vajrayogini, Tib. *Khachö Bebum*, Wyl. *mkha' spyod be 'bum*

Teachings with Restriction Seals, Tib. *Gyachen*, Wyl. *rgya can*
An abbreviation of the *Twenty-Five Teachings with Restriction Seals*.

Teachings with Restriction Seals from the Treasury of Terma Teachings, Tib. *Terdzö Kagya*, Wyl. *gter mdzod bka' rgya*
Part of the *Rinchen Terdzo*.

Three Categories of Dzogchen, Tib. *Dzogchen Desum*, Wyl. *rdzogs chen sde gsum*
Dzogchen Desum and *Kunzang Thuktik* are the Dzogchen teachings discovered by Chokgyur Lingpa.

Three Cycles of the Secret Essence, Tib. *Sangtik Korsum*, Wyl. *gsang thig skor gsum*
One of Chokgyur Lingpa's profound treasures, containing a complete set of practices for Vajrakilaya, Vajrasattva, and Yangdak Heruka, the three principal yidams of Guru Rinpoche.

Three Daily Practices, Tib. *Gyun Chak Sumpa*, Wyl. *rgyun chags gsum pa*

Three Hundred-Verse Getsul Karika, Tib. *Getsul Gyi Karika Sum Gya Pa*, Wyl. *dge tshul karika sum brgya pa*
Three hundred verses of vows taken by a novice monk or nun.

Three Precepts *see* **Ascertainment of the Three Types of Vow**

Three Roots of Nyingtik, Tib. *Nyingtik Tsasum*, Wyl. *snying thig rtsa gsum*

Three Roots Practice for Accomplishing the Life-Force of the Vidyadharas, Tib. *Tsasum Rigdzin Sokdrup*, Wyl. *rtsa gsum rig 'dzin srog sgrub*
Part of the cycle of teachings revealed by Lhatsün Namkha Jigme that includes the *Riwo Sangchö*.

Three White Deities, Tib. *Karpo Lha Sum*, Wyl. *dkar po lha gsum*

Tiger Rider, Tib. *Tag Zhon*, Wyl. *stag zhon*
A Dharma protector.

Tilopa Zhung Chung, Wyl. *te lo pa'i gzhung chung*
A minor treatise.

Treasury of Abhidharma, Skt. *Abhidharmakośa*; Tib. *Ngön Pa Dzö*, Wyl. *chos mngon pa'i mdzod*
A complete account of the Abhidharma by Vasubandhu.

Treasury of Dharmadhatu, Tib. *Chöying Dzö*, Wyl. *chos dbyings mdzod*
One of Longchenpa's *Seven Treasuries*.

Treasury of Encyclopedic Knowledge, Tib. *Sheja Kunkhyab Dzö*, Wyl. *shes bya kun khyab mdzod*
One of Jamgön Kongtrul's *Five Great Treasuries*.

Treasury of Kagyü Tantras, Tib. *Kagyü Ngakdzö*, Wyl. *bka' brgyud sngags mdzod*

Treasury of Precious Instructions, Tib. *Dam Ngak Dzö*, Wyl. *gdams ngag mdzod*
Usually spoken of as the *Dam Ngak Dzö* but also described by Dilgo Khyentse

Rinpoche as the *Dam Ngak Rinpoche'i Dzö*, the *Treasury of Precious Instructions* is one of the *Five Great Treasuries* of Jamgön Kongtrul the Great.

Treasury of Precious Qualities, Tib. *Yönten Dzö*, Wyl. *yon tan mdzod*
A famous treatise by Jigme Linga describing the entire Buddhist path from the Shravakayana teachings up to Dzogchen. It is usually spoken of as the *Yönten Dzö* but is also referred to by Dilgo Khyentse Rinpoche as the *Yönten Rinpoche'i Dzö*.

Treasury of the Supreme Vehicle, Tib. *Tekchok Dzö*, Wyl. *theg mchog mdzod*
Usually spoken of as the *Tekchok Dzö* but also referred to by Dilgo Khyentse Rinpoche as *Tekchok Rinpoche'i Dzö*. It is one of Longchenpa's *Seven Treasuries*.

Treasury of Valid Logical Reasoning, Tib. *Tsema Rigter*, Wyl. *tshad ma rigs gter*
Sakya Pandita's classic work on logic and epistemology.

Treasury of Vast Teachings, Tib. *Gyachen Kadzö*, Wyl. *rgya chen bka' mdzod*
One of Jamgön Kongtrul's *Five Great Treasuries*, it contains his collected writings.

Treatise on the Sublime Continuum, Skt. *Mahāyānottaratantra Śāstra*; Tib. *Gyü Lama*, Wyl. *theg pa chen po rgyud bla ma'i bstan bcos*
One of the *Five Dharmas of Lord Maitreya*, the *Uttaratantra* is a commentary on the teachings of the third turning of the wheel of Dharma that explains buddha nature.

Trilogy of Finding Comfort and Ease, Tib. *Ngalso Korsum*, Wyl. *ngal gso skor gsum*
This trilogy of Dzogchen writings by Longchen Rabjam includes *Finding Comfort and Ease in the Nature of Mind*, *Finding Comfort and Ease in Meditation*, and *Finding Comfort and Ease in the Illusoriness of Things*.

Triple Tantras, Tib. *Gyü Sum*, Wyl. *brgyud gsum*
Sakya teachings.

Trönak, Tib. *Tröma Nagmo*, Wyl. *khros ma nag mo*
A Tibetan name for the treasure of *Krodhikali* revealed by Nyang Nyima Özer.

Turning Back the Summons of the Dakinis, Tib. *Sündok*, Wyl. *sun bzlog*
A long-life practice for turning back the summons of the dakinis, often performed in conjunction with a tenshuk.

Twenty-Five Teachings with Restriction Seals, Tib. *Dagnang Gyachen Nyer Nga*, Wyl. *dag snang rgya can nyer lnga*
Revealed by the great Fifth Dalai Lama.

Two Beautiful Ornaments
The two beautiful ornaments are *Ngontök Dzegen* and *Tsul Sum Dzegen*.

Two Dongtruks
The two dongtruks in the Kama tradition are *Shyitro Tromtruk* and *Shyitro Pema Gyaden*.

Two Kinds of Blessings of the Eighty Mahasiddhas, Tib. *Drubgyai Chinlap Rignyi*, Wyl. *grub brgya'i byin rlabs rigs gnyis*

Two Minor Shastras, Tib. *Shung Chung Nyi*, Wyl. *gzhung chung gnyis*
The oral instructions of Tilopa and Naropa.

Two Sections of the Hevajra Root Tantra, Tib. *Tsagyü Taknyi*, Wyl. *rtsa rgyud brtag gnyis*
Sometimes spoken of simply as the *Two Sections*.

Two Vimalas, Tib. *Drime Nam Nyi*, Wyl. *dri med rnam gnyis*
The *Two Vimalas* are the two immaculate deities, Tsuktor Drime and Özer Drime.

Two Vimalas from the Nyingma Kama, Tib. *Ngagyur Kama Drime Nam Nyi*, Wyl. *snga 'gyur bka' ma dri med rnam gnyis*

Ultimate Averter from the Essence of Liberation, Tib. *Droltik Yangdok*, Wyl. *grol tig yang zlog*

Unstained Light, Tib. *Özer Drime*, Wyl. *'od zer dri med*
A sadhana for consecrating stupas, etc.

Unsurpassable Innermost Secret Mother and Son Heart Essence of Vimalamitra, Tib. *Bima Nyingtik Mabu Yang Sang Lame*, Wyl. *bi ma snying thing ma bu yang gsang bla med*
The *Vima Nyingtik* (mother) and *Lama Yangtik* (son) from the *Four Parts of Nyingtik*.

Vajra Essence, Tib. *Dorje Nyingpo*, Wyl. *rdo rje snying po*

Vajra Peak, Tib. *Gyü Dorje Tsemo*, Wyl. *rgyud rdo rje rtse mo*

Vajrabhairava, Tib. *Tsarluk Jigje*, Wyl. *tshar lugs 'jigs byed*
Vajrabhairava is another name for *Yamantaka* and literally means "vajra terrifier." This practice is from the Tsarpa tradition.

Vajradhatu Tantra, *Tantra of Adamantine Space*, Tib. *Dorje Ying*, Wyl. *rdo rje dbyings*

Vajrakilaya from the Seven Profound Cycles, Tib. *Zabdün Phurba*, Wyl. *zab bdun phur pa*

Vajrakilaya of Nyak Lotsawa, Tib. *Nyak Phurba* or *Nyak Phur*, Wyl. *gnyags phur*
A terma revealed by Dilgo Khyentse at Karma Gon. According to Orgyen Tobgyal Rinpoche, Dilgo Khyentse Rinpoche saw a scroll emerge from the sleeve of a statue of Gönpo Bernakchen (Mahakala of the Kamtsang tradition), which contained the *Nyak Phur* teachings. Nyak Lotsawa, sometimes known as Nyak Jñanakumara, was one of the nine students closest to Guru Padmasambhava, who perfected the practice of Vajrakilaya.

Vajrakilaya: Overpowering the Forces of Mara, Tib. *Phurba Düpung Zil Nön*, Wyl. *phur pa bdud dpung zil gnon*

Vajrakilaya: The Display of Vajras, Tib. *Phurba Dorje Köpa*, Wyl. *phur pa rdo rje bkod pa*

Vajrakilaya: The Oral Transmission Lineage, Tib. *Nyengyü Phurba*, Wyl. *snyan brgyud phur pa*

Vajrakilaya: The Tradition of the King, Tib. *Gyüluk Phurba*, Wyl. *rgyud lugs phur pa*

Vajrakilaya: The Vast Display, Tib. *Gya Cher Rolpa*, Wyl. *phur pa rgya cher rol pa*

Vajrapani Dressed in Blue, Tib. *Gö Ngönchen*, Wyl. *gos sngon can*

Vajrapani Holding a Vajra Cudgel, Tib. *Chakdor Dorje Bedjön*, Wyl. *phyag rdor rdo rje be con*

Vajrapani: Flame of Fire, Tib. *Chakdor Mewal*, Wyl. *phyag rdor me dbal*

Vajrapani: Tamer of Spirits, Tib. *Chakdor Jungdül*, Wyl. *phyag rdor byung 'dul*

Vajrasattva of Manifest Joy, Tib. *Dorsem Ngönga*, Wyl. *rdor sems mngon dga'*
Sometimes known as *Abhirati Vajrasattva*, this sadhana is from the Mindrolling tradition.

Vajrasattva: Liberate into the Pure Realm of Manifest Joy, Tib. *Dorsem Ngönga Shingjong*, Wyl. *rdor sems mngon dga'*

Vast Expanse of the View, Tib. *Tawa Longyang*, Wyl. *lta ba klong yangs*
A treasure cycle revealed by Dorje Lingpa.

Verse Summary of the Prajnaparamita Sutra, Skt. *Saṃcayagāthāprajñāpāramitāsūtra*; Tib. *Sherchin Düpa*, Wyl. *sher phyin bsdus pa*

Very Wrathful, Tib. *Drak Trö*, Wyl. *drag khros*

Vidyadhara Heir of the Victorious Ones, Tib. *Rigdzin Gyalwa'i Dungdzin*, Wyl. *'rig 'dzin rgyal ba'i gdung 'dzin*

Vimalamitra's Guru Yoga Called the "Essence of Blessings," Tib. *Ladrup Chinlap Nyingpo*, Wyl. *bla sgrub byin brlabs snying po*

Vinaya Sutra, Skt. *Vinayasūtra*; Tib. *Dülwa'i Dotsa*, Wyl. *'dul ba'i mdo*
By Gunaprabha.

Way of the Bodhisattva, The, Skt. *Bodhisattvacaryāvatāra*; Wyl. *byang chub sems dpa'i spyod pa la 'jug pa*

White Amitayus, Tib. *Tsekar*, Wyl. *Tshe dkar*

White and Red Amitayus, Tib. *Tsepakme Karmar*, Wyl. *tshe dpag med dkar dmar*

White Enhancer of Life, Tib. *Karpo Tsephel*, Wyl. *dkar po tshe 'phel*
A white, four-armed protector practice for long life.

White Guardian, Tib. *Gönkar*, Wyl. *mgon dkar*

White Manjushri, Tib. *Jamkar*, Wyl. *'jam dkar*

White Six-Armed Protector, Tib. *Chakdruk Karpo*, Wyl. *phyag drug dkar po*

White Tara Radiating Six Rays of Light, Tib. *Drolkar Özer Drukdrak*, Wyl. *sgrol dkar 'od zer drug sbrags*

White Tara: Supreme Wish-Fulfilling Jewel, Tib. *Drolkar Yishin Norchok*, Wyl. *sgrol dkar yid bzhin nor mchog*

White Ushnishavijaya, Tib. *Namgyal Karmo*, Wyl. *rnam rgyal dkar mo*

White Varahi Who Kindles Prajna, Tib. *Phagkar Sherab Selje*, Wyl. *'phags dkar shes rab gsal byed*

Wisdom Guru, Tib. *Yeshe Lama*, Wyl. *ye shes bla ma*
A common abbreviation for *Wisdom Guru of the Great Perfection*.

Wisdom Guru of the Great Perfection, Tib. *Dzogpachenpo Yeshe Lama*, Wyl. *rdzogs pa chen po ye shes bla ma*

Wish-Fulfilling Excellent Vase, Tib. *Druptab Dodjo Bumzang*, Wyl. *sgrub thabs 'dod 'jo'i bum bzang*
A collection of Nyingmapa sadhanas written by Terdak Lingpa with the help of his brother, Minling Lochen.

Wish-Fulfilling Jewel Essence Manual of Oral Instruction, Tib. *Sheldam Nyingjang*, Wyl. *zhal gdams snying byang*
Sheldam Nyingjang is the abbreviated title of the *Sheldam Nyingjang Yishyin Norbu* (Wyl. *zhal gdams snying byang yid bzhin nor bu*), which is the root tantra of the *Tukdrup Barche Kunsel*.

Wish-Fulfilling Jewel That Spontaneously Fulfills All Wishes *see* **Inner Practice That Spontaneously Fulfills All Wishes**

Wish-Fulfilling Treasury, Tib. *Yishyin Dzö*, Wyl. *yid bzhin mdzod*
One of the *Seven Treasuries* composed by omniscient Longchenpa.

Wish-Fulfilling Vine, Tib. *Paksam Trishing*, Wyl. *dpag bsam 'khri shing*
Dzegya Paksam Trishing, literally "the wish-granting tree of hundred lives," tells the stories of the Buddha's former births, or *jatakas*.

Words from Chimphu, Tib. *Ka Chimphuma*, Wyl. *bka' chims phug ma*

Words of My Perfect Teacher, The, Tib. *Kunzang Lama'i Shelung*, Wyl. *kun bzang bla ma'i zhal lung*
By Patrul Rinpoche.

Words of Vajrapani, Tib. *Sangdak Shelung*, Wyl. *gsang bdag zhal lung*

Wrathful and Peaceful Deities of Karma Lingpa, Tib. *Karling Shitro*, Wyl. *kar gling zhi khro*
A terma revealed by Karma Lingpa.

Wrathful Blue Vajrapani, Tib. *Tukdrup Drakthing*, Wyl. *thugs sgrub drag mthing*
From the *Tukdrup* teachings.

Wrathful Dark Blue Guru, Tib. *Drakthing*, Wyl. *drag thing*

Wrathful Guru, Tib. *Gurdrak*, Wyl. *gur drag*

Wrathful Guru and the Great Compassionate One, Wyl. *gur drag dang thugs chen*

Wrathful Guru of the Assembly of Great and Glorious Herukas, Tib. *Lama Drakpo Palchen Düpa*, Wyl. *bla ma drag po dpal chen 'dus pa*

Wrathful Guru Rinpoche with Lower Part as a Phurba, Tib. *Namchö Gurdrak Phurshamchen*, Wyl. *gnam chos gur drag phur bsham chen*

Wrathful Guru Rinpoche: The Great Gathering of the Sugatas, Tib. *Gurdrak Deshek Düpa*, Wyl. *gur drag bde gshegs 'dus pa*

Wrathful Lone Hero, Tib. *Tumpo Pachik*, Wyl. *gtum po dpa' gcig*

Wrathful Red Guru Rinpoche, Tib. *Drakmar*, Wyl. *drag dmar*
A treasure revealed by Minling Terchen.

Wrathful Vaishravana Riding a Blue Horse, Tib. *Namse Ta Ngön Chen*, Wyl. *rnam sras rta sngon can*

Wrathful Vijaya, Tib. *Namgyel Drakmo*, Wyl. *rnam rgyal drag mo*

Yamantaka, Tib. *Zabdun Shinje*, Wyl. *zab bdun gshin rje*
One of the *Seven Profound Revelations of Chokling*.

Yamantaka, Tib. *Shinje Khathün*, Wyl. *gshin rje kha thun*
From the Nub lineage of the Nyingma Kama.

Yamantaka, Destroyer of Enemies, Tib. *Pharol Goljom*, Wyl. *pha rol rgol 'joms*
A new treasure revealed by Chokgyur Lingpa.

Yamantaka: Destroyer of Demons, Tib. *Shinje Drekjom*, Wyl. *gshin rje dregs 'joms*

Yamantaka: Lord of Life, Tib. *Shinje Tsedak*, Wyl. *gshin rje tshe bdag*
A terma revealed by Dumgya Shangtrom, therefore sometimes known as *Shangtrom Yamantaka*. It is practiced mainly in the *Northern Treasure* tradition.

Yogini Tantra of Conduct, Tib. *Naljorma'i Gyü Kunchö*, Wyl. *rnal 'byor ma'i rgyud kun spyod*

Zangchö *see* **The King of Aspiration Prayers: Samantabhadra's "Aspiration to Good Actions"**

INDEX

Note: Page numbers in italics refer to photographs. JKCL is an abbreviation for Jamyang Khyentse Chökyi Lodrö.

Abridged Kalachakra Tantra, 269, 370
Accomplishing the Life-Force of the Vidyadharas, 50, 233–34, 505, 506
Adeu Rinpoche, 62, 185
Adzom Drukpa, 21, 50, 72, 106, 113, 121
Akshobhya Statue That Liberates upon Being Seen, 453
all-accomplishing wisdom, 527, 534
Ani Pelu, *78*, 79, 232
Ani Rilu, 77–79, *78*, 232, 250
Appey Dorje, 8, *9*
Approach and Accomplishment Practices of the Three Vajras, 488
Ascertainment of the Three Types of Vow, 219, 474
Atisha (Jowo Je Atisha), 311, 470, 471–72, 554n224
Avalokiteshvara, 276, 292, 396, 471
Avalokiteshvara Resting in the Nature of Mind, 387, 510
Avalokiteshvara Who Stirs the Depths of Samsara, 483
Azhang Butse Lhaje, 150, 151, 152, 154

beginners, instructions for, 406
Benpa Chakdor, JKCL's visit to, 221
blessing instructions, 479, 554n232
Bodh Gaya, JKCL's visit to, 239–44, 425, 431
Bodhibhadra, 310, 338
bodhichitta, 359, 406
bodhisattva vows, 308–9, 396, 499
Bönpo masters, 117–18, 297, 488
Bright Torch of the Innermost Essence, 164, 513–14
Buddha Shakyamuni, 271, 340, 544n2
  enlightenment of, 269
  JKCL's representations of, 415–16, 417, 419, 420
Buddhadharma
  eight great practice lineages of, 461–62
  entering path of, 313–14
  JKCL on degeneration of, 397–98, 429–30, 436
  JKCL on restoration of, 235–36
  JKCL's contributions to, 350–52
  Khyentse Wangpo's contributions to, 278–88

Calling the Guru from Afar, 472
Category of the Bodhisattva Teachings, 308, 315
Chakdzö Tsewang Paljor, 7, 64, 69–71, 101, *240*, 519
  consort of, 167–69
  falling out with JKCL, 164
  Khyentse tulku controversy and, 34–36
  in Lhasa, 191–92, 193–94
  quarrel with Tsejor, 146–48

as relation of JKCL, 22
tertön's tooth and, 110
white dragon cup of, 187–88
Chakrasamvara: The Inseparable Union of Buddha, 534
Chamdo Monastery, 37–38
Chatral Sangye Dorje, 66, 116–17, *117*, 345–46, 437
Chime Pema Dorje (Tulku Chime), 346, 509, 517, 526
Chö tradition, 484–86
Chögyal Pakpa, 142, 276, 372, 477
Chögyam Trungpa (Surmang Trungpa), 101, *102*, 103
Chokden, *11*, *14*, *241*, 494
  as JKCL's attendant, 10–11, 62
  Khamtrul Rinpoche and, 100–1
  in Lhasa, 192
  at Mindrolling Monastery, 204
Chokgyur Dechen Lingpa, xiii, 87, 185, 190, 307
  JKCL's visions of, 501, 506
  Khyentse Wangpo and, 281–82, 283–84, 464
  seats of, 416–17, 552n162
  sons of, 276–77
  treasure teachings of, x, 186, 280–82, 326, 335, 398–99, 432
Chökyi Nangwa, 16–17
Chökyi Nyinje (Tenth Surmang Trungpa Rinpoche), 295, 346, 355, 479
Collected Topics of Logic, 408
Combined Practice of the Three Roots, 182, 453
Compendium of Sadhanas, 12–13, 132, 133, 136, 285, 326, 330, 371, 420, 421, 524
Compendium of Tantras, 140, 163, 284, 324, 326–27, 359, 388, 396, 420, 421
Compendium of Vajra Wisdom, 533
completion meditation, 279
  dissolution of elements, 524–25, 532–33
  of Dzogpachenpo, 463
  purification of prana of life-force, 370

wisdom consort and, 523–24, 525, 532–35
  with and without characteristics, 366
consecration ceremonies
  for Dzing Namgyal Gönkhang, 142, 372
  for great Maitreya statue, 139–40
  JKCL performing from afar, 135–36, 376
  for JKCL's memorial stupa, 452–53, 455
  at Tradruk temple, 370–71
Consort Practice: The Queen of Great Bliss, 56, 238, 373, 438, 443, 504
Cutting Through: Self-Liberation from Fixation, 514

Dagchen Ngawang Thutop Wangchuk, 295–96
Dagmo Kusho, 128, *129*, 130, 134
dakini fire pujas, 425
dakinis' seal of entrustment, 299, 547n64
Dalai Lama, Fifth, 17
Dalai Lama, Fourteenth, Tenzin Gyatso (Gyalwa Rinpoche), 97, 180, 436, 471
  JKCL's death and, 409, 442
  JKCL's divination for, 199–200
  JKCL's visits with, 201, 334
Dalai Lama, Sixth, Lobsang Tsangyang Gyatso, 272
Dalai Lama, Thirteenth, Thubten Gyatso, 105, 211, 334, 471
Dampa Dönpal, 337
Dechen Namgyal, 516–17
Dezhung Choktrul Rinpoches, 355, 356, 478, 527
Dezhung Tulku Ajam, 10, 63, 133, 167
  defense of JKCL's consort, 160
  Nyingma teachings and, 115–16
  teachings JKCL received from, 337–38
dharani sutras, 453, 553n214
dharma relics, 451
dharmakaya relics, 451
Dhongthog Tulku, 63

Dilgo Khyentse, *6*, 59, 62, 72, 77, *100*,
    101, 148, *257*, *259*
  birth of, xxv
  black scarf and, 254
  death of JKCL and, 256–58, 447
  enthronement of, 251–52
  gyalpo Shugden and, 84, 85
  JKCL's consort and, 162–64
  JKCL's illness and, 157
  JKCL's last conversation with,
    247–48
  JKCL's praise of, 235
  at Khampa Gar, 103
  Khenpo Nüden and, 122–23
  khenpos receiving teachings from,
    255–56
  at Lhari Ga, 87–89
  as Nak Ralma, 254–55
  Palpung Situ and, 92, 93
  Queen Mother of Sikkim and, 231
  Rinpoche's biography and, 3–4, 5,
    539
  rock footprint of, 175–76
  sacred hidden lands and, 171–72
  Sakya Gongma's visit and, 126–28
  teachings JKCL received from,
    349–50, 355
  treasure teachings of, 350, 518, 519
  vision at Tashiding, 258–59
Display of Awareness of Dzogpachenpo,
  360
Do Khyentse Yeshe Dorje, 274, 275,
  513–14, 524
Dodrupchen, Fourth, Jigme Trinle
  Palbar, 249, *249*
Dodrupchen, Third, Jigme Tenpe
  Nyima, 113, 121, 278
  empowerments to JKCL, 51, 275
  JKCL's visit to, 50–51
  teachings JKCL received from, 332,
    355, 360, 407, 463
Dogar Khenpo, 332–33
Doko Chulu, 98
Dolpo Sangye, 487–88
Dordrak Rigdzin Chenpo, 204–5
Dordzin Palden Jamyang, 339

Dorje Drak Monastery, 204–5, 504
Drak Yerpa, 191–92
Drakmar Drinzang, JKCL's visit to, 210
Drakyab Tsangsar Tulku, 339
Drikung Kyobpa Rinchen Pal, 272
Drikung Tertön Ösel Dorje, *107*
  prediction about consorts, 158–59,
    526
  teachings JKCL received from,
    345
  treasure teachings of, 517
  visits to Dzongsar, 106–10
Drime Pema Lingpa. *See* Tertön Drime
  Pema Lingpa
Drime Zhingkyong (Jewön Rinpoche),
  45, 46, 323–24, 416
Drogmi Lotsawa, 474
Dromtönpa, 354, 471–72
Drongsar Draknam, 208–9
Drop That Embodies All Secrets, The, 204
Drukpa Kagyü, 479–80
Drumo Wangchen, 63–64
Drungnam Gyaltrul Rinpoche
  (Drupwang Gyatrul), 97, 346–47,
  542n15
Drungyig Tsering, *14*, 86–87, 223–24
  as JKCL's attendant, 64–67, 83–84,
    101
Drupa Rigyal, 41
drupchens, drupchös, and mendrups,
  211, 233–34, 366, 370, 372, 424,
  425, 518
Drupwang Gyatrul. *See* Drungnam
  Gyaltrul Rinpoche
Dudjom Rinpoche (Dudjom Jikdral
  Yeshe Dorje), 66, 121, *196*, 255
  with JKCL in Lhasa, 192, 196, 197
  JKCL's death and, 436, 437, 442
  teachings JKCL received from, 345
  treasure teachings and, 517
Dudtsi Trokhar palace, 500, 555n245
Dudul Dorje, 20–21, 299
Dudul Rolpatsal, 299
Dungsey of Mindrolling, 83, 91
Dungsey Thinley Norbu, 244
Durtrö Lhamo, 200–1

Düsolma, 148, 380
Dzamnang Pema Shelphuk, 379–80, 518
Dzigag Choktrul Rinpoche, 344
Dzing Namgyal Gönkhang, 142, 372
Dzogchen Khen Rinpoche, Sonam Chöphel, 275, 341
Dzogchen Monastery, 160–61, 416
Dzogchen Pönlop, Sixth, 242–43, *243*
Dzogchen Rinpoche, Fifth, Thubten Chökyi Dorje, 161
  at Dzongsar Monastery, 83–84
  Khyentse tulkus and, 29, 32, 295
  teachings JKCL received from, 341, 360
Dzogchen Rinpoche, Fourth, Drubwang Mingyur Namkhai Dorje, 273
Dzogchen Rinpoche, Sixth, Jikdral Changchub Dorje, 91, 341
Dzogpachenpo, 118, 208, 228, 276, 359, 366, 407, 440, 463, 511, 535
Dzongsar Monastery
  criticisms of JKCL's consort, 160–61
  drupchö of Vajrakilaya at, 424
  Eighth Khamtrul's visit to, 99–103
  hardships on local villagers and, 141
  JKCL's benefitting activities for, 418–20
  JKCL's departure from, 223–25, 430–31
  JKCL's enthronement at, 29–30, 303, 307, 310
  Lhachen falling over at, 141
  masters who visited JKCL at, 91–121
  Palpung Situ's visit to, 91–93
  Sakya Gongma's first visit to, 126–30
  stories from, 135–43
  two bronze cauldrons of, 135–36
  See also Khyentse Labrang

eight great chariots of the practice lineage, xii, 319, 357, 367, 412, 420, 461–62, 489
Eight Great Deities of the Peaceful and Wrathful Sugatas, 492

eight worldly preoccupations, abandoning, 353, 359, 369
Ekazati
  JKCL's vision of, 379
  life-stone treasure of, 152–53
elements, signs of dissolution, 524–25, 532–33
Embodied Realization of the Three Roots, 282
Embodiment of the Guru's Realization, 292, 314, 378, 493
Embodiment of the Three Jewels, 50, 102, 437, 502, 504
Embodiment of the Three Kayas, 360
empowerments, 548nn84–86
  authorization blessings and, 497
  entering secret mantra mandala and, 309–11
  importance of tradition in, 399
  life-force, 334, 373, 549n107
Essence of the Wisdom of Manjushri Tantra, 511
Ewam Thartse Khenchen Jamyang Kunzang Tenpe Nyima, 337, 473
Explanatory Tantra Gur, 533

First Beru Khyentse Rinpoche, 293–95
Five Great Treasuries, 280, 421
Flower Garland Sutra, 267, 340
Four Parts of Nyingtik, 122, 203–4, 388

Gandavyuha Sutra, 308
Garuda and Tiger cave, 421
Gathering of Precious Qualities, 320–21
Gathering of the Dakini's Secrets, 56, 425, 435, 445, 511, 518
Gathering of the Guru's Secrets, 56, 425
Gathering of the Innermost Essence: A Long-Life Practice, 204
Gathering of the Innermost Essence of Deathlessness, 329
Gathering of Vidyadharas, 51, 56, 103, 275, 443, 514
Gatön Jampalyang, 355, 356
Gatön Ngawang Lekpa, *119*, 140, 477–78

Gatön Ngawang Lekpa (cont.)
    begging bowl of, 119–20
    JKCL's dream of, 466
    as JKCL's teacher, 309, 336–37, 410, 473
Gechak Monastery, 184
Gelug school, Khyentse emanation and, 296–97
General Essentialization of All the Wisdom of the Buddhas, 17, 24, 87–88, 446, 467, 468
Geshe Jampal Rolpe Lodrö, 334, 412
Glorious Tantra of Perfect Union, 534
Gö Lotsawa Yezang Tsepa, 272
Godet, Gerald, 227, 543n42
Godet, Robert, *226*, 227
Gongna Tulku, *14*, 91, *242*
    eavesdropping of, 115–16
    grave robbing and, 150
    Situ Rinpoche's belt and, 72–73
    stories told by, 14, 20, 41–42
    Tso Ziltrom and, 172–73
Gönpo Tseten, 9–10, *10*, 202–3, 239, 245
Gorampa Sonam Senge, xiv, 418, 474
Gradual Path Called the "Essence of Wisdom," 423
Great Yellow Vaishravana, 133, 371
Guhyagarbha Tantra, 255, 256, 317, 355, 445–46, 464, 467
Guhyasamaja Manjuvajra, 381–82
Guhyasamaja Tantra, 467, 472
Guru Jampe Dorje, 381–82
Guru Nangsi Zilnön, 199
Guru Rinpoche
    amrita and, 456
    guru yoga and, 465–66, 510, 514–15
    JKCL's representations of, 415, 416, 419, 424
    JKCL's visions of, 381, 382–83, 464–66, 502–3
    Khyentse Wangpo and, 282, 302, 377
    relics of, 451, 513
    sacred practice sites of, 518
    statue in Lhasa, 199–200
    statue in Tsang, 220

Guru Yoga of the Heart Essence of the Oral Transmission Lineage, 485
Gyagen Khyungtak, 173–75
gyalpo Shugden, 84–89, 374
Gyalse Jamgön Choktrul (Karse Kongtrul), 479, 542n14, 549n116
    death of, 96, 113–15
    Khyentse tulkus and, 295
    long-life of JKCL and, 526
    teachings JKCL received from, 348
Gyalse Kunzang Tenzin, 344
Gyalse Lhaje, 456, 553nn217–18
Gyalse Pema Namgyal, 299
Gyalse Pema Wangyal, 346
Gyalse Shenphen Taye, 117
Gyaltsab Kalzang Dorje, 110–11
Gyalwa Rinpoche. *See* Dalai Lama, Fourteenth, Tenzin Gyatso
Gyarong Khandro, 173–75, 517–18
Gyarong Namtrul, 173, 188, 190
Gyatön Lama, 435, 437, 438, 443, 448, 449
Gyurdrak, 174, 543n30
Gyurme Tenpe Gyaltsen, 336
Gyurme Tsewang Drakpa, 276–77
Gyurme Tsewang Gyatso (Gyurme Tsewang Chokdrup), 20–21, 24, 299–301, 326

Heart Essence of Chetsün, 204
Heart Essence of Deathless Arya Tara, 147, 158, 300, 437, 456, 512
Heart Essence of Seven Lights, 511
Heart Essence of the Dakinis, 332, 499
Heart Essence of the Vast Expanse, 26, 50, 300, 360, 373, 388, 432, 507, 508, 514
Heart Essence of Vimalamitra, 122, 178, 197
Heart Practice for Dispelling All Obstacles, 214, 380, 382, 452, 465, 518
Heart Practice of Tara, 495
Heart Practice That Fulfills All Wishes, 398–99, 517

*Heart Practice That Spontaneously
  Fulfills All Wishes*, 431, 495
Hevajra, 325, 467, 476, 479, 480, 481

Immaculate Light, 318–19, 370
India, JKCL's pilgrimage to, 237–46,
  431, 434
Infinite Profound Instructions, 280
*Innermost Essence of the Razor-Edged
  Phurba*, 333, 507
Innermost Heart Drop of Profundity,
  122, 197
*Innermost Secret Guru Yoga Called the
  "Sealed Quintessence,"* 469, 505

Jagö Namgyal Dorje, 85–86, *86*, 235
Jagö Tobden, 34–37, *35*, 85–87
Jamgön Amnye Zhab Kunga Sonam,
  272
Jamgön Kongtrul Lodrö Taye, ix, xi,
  xiii, 87, 204, 486
  accomplishments of, 280–81
  eight great practice lineages and,
    462
  Gyurme Tsewang Gyatso and, 300
  JKCL's vision of, 507
  Khyentse tulkus and, 23–24, 30, 32,
    33, 293
  praise of Khyentse Wangpo, 278,
    281, 286, 489–90
  prophecy for JKCL, 23–24, 30, 32,
    33, 37, 302
  sacred hidden lands and, 173
  treasure teachings of, 282–83,
    546n46
Jamgön Mipham. *See* Mipham
  Rinpoche
Jamgön Ngawang Lekpa. *See* Gatön
  Ngawang Lekpa
Jamgön Palden Khyentse. *See* Gyalse
  Jamgön Choktrul (Karse
  Kongtrul)
Jampal, 67–71, *68*
Jampal Zangpo, 340
Jamyang Chökyi Wangpo, x, 293
Jamyang Gyaltsen, xiv, 338, 497

Jamyang Khyenrab Taye, 311, 339
Jamyang Khyentse Chökyi Lodrö
  (JKCL), ii, *2, 14, 58, 137, 170,
  193, 226, 239, 240, 241, 242, 243,
  247*
  activities for benefitting teachings
    and beings, 387–413
  activities to increase representa-
    tions of body, speech, and mind,
    414–28
  on adopting secret conduct, 526–28
  attendants of, 59–71
  birthplace and forebears of, xxv,
    19–22, 298–301
  at Bodh Gaya, 239–44
  boiling skull cup and, 154–55
  ceremonies and practices performed
    after death of, 440–47, 455–57
  ceremonies and practices performed
    prior to death of, 435–40
  clairvoyance of, 141, 149–50,
    384–85, 406
  commanding spirits and averting
    negativities, 83–89, 173, 188–90,
    199–200, 372–75, 409
  compassion of, 358, 359, 368, 369,
    409
  consorts and, 92, 157–70, 525–28,
    535–36
  death and parinirvana of, 178,
    248–50, 256–58, 440–58
  on degeneration of Buddhadharma,
    397–98, 429–30, 436
  Dzongsar Monastery and, x, 29–38,
    303
  early life of, 25–27, 301, 302–5
  eight great practice lineages and, xii,
    319, 357, 367, 412, 461–62, 489
  enthronement of, 29–30, 303, 307,
    310
  excellent memory and intelligence
    of, 26, 407, 408, 409
  fears of, 73, 75–76
  founding of Khamje Shedra, xiii–
    xiv, 49–54, 418
  gyalpo Shugden and, 84–89, 374

Jamyang Khyentse Chökyi Lodrö (cont.)
  as holder of Nyingma teachings, 26, 462–67
  holy places of India and, 237–46, 431, 434
  illnesses of, 157–58, 231–32, 234–35, 432–40, 525, 532
  incident with mercury, 26–27, 371–72
  inconceivable hidden qualities of, 367–70, 376–77, 509, 535
  Indian and Tibetan texts studied by, 354–55
  introduction to nature of mind, 227–28, 377
  Jamgön Kongtrul's prophecy for, 23–24, 30, 32, 33, 37, 302
  Kadam lineage and, 470–73
  Kalachakra Tantra and, 486–88
  at Karmo Tak Tsang, 80–81
  at Katok Monastery, 23–27, 33–34, 39–47, 302–3, 388, 415–16
  at Khyentse Labrang, 55–73
  Khyentse Wangpo's seat and bed and, ix, 30–32, 402–3
  kudung of Orgyen Lingpa and, 210–12
  Lamdre tradition and, 473–78
  learning to read and write, 314–16
  letter to his students, 529–32
  life with Khandro, 169–70
  love of dancing, 77–79
  Marpa Kagyü and, 478–83
  marriage ceremony of, 163–64
  masters who visited, at Dzongsar Monastery, 91–121
  memorial and cremation stupas of, 236, 447–55
  miraculous stories about, 135–36, 371–76
  names of, 51, 266, 275, 303, 307, 309, 475, 477, 514, 544n7, 546n36
  Orgyen Nyendrup and, 488–508
  past incarnations of, 231, 271–88
  pilgrimages of (*see* pilgrimages)
  playing games and, 252
  porcelain cups of, 145–46, 187–88
  praises to, 278, 410, 463
  prostrating to women, 207–8
  reactions to taking a consort, 160–61, 164–67, 535
  recognition of tulkus, 331, 385, 416
  response to offerings of long-life prayers, 433–35, 438
  on restoration of Dharma in Tibet, 235–36
  restoring of Maitreya Hall, 137–40, 418
  retreats and retreat practices, 64, 171, 191–92, 227–28, 360–66, 388, 483
  right-swirling conch shell and, 192–94
  Rime movement and, xiii–xv, 350–52, 397–99, 488–89
  sacred hidden lands and, 171–76, 501–2, 517–18, 520
  at Sakya Monastery, 215–19
  Sangye Lingpa's bones and, 213–14
  Shangpa Kagyü lineage and, 483–84
  Shije and Chö traditions and, 484–86
  in Sikkim, 227–36, 247–50, 432–40
  sources of stories about, 3–17
  students of, 409–13
  sublime character of, 353–54, 359, 404–7
  summer camping and, 75–81
  swords and guns and, 148–49
  teaching style and methods, 366–67, 396–403, 407–8
  teachings and empowerments received by, 309–11, 316–57, 407
  teachings given by, 388–96
  training in three precepts, 306–12, 407, 462
  treasure teachings and, 292–93, 463, 509–21
  treasury of realization of, 358–86, 523–28, 532–39

at Tsadra Rinchen Drak, 113–15
as tulku of Khyentse Wangpo, ix,
  23–25, 29–30, 32–38, 278–88, 295,
  302–5, 402–3, 462
veneration and care for kudung of,
  440–41, 447, 449–50
visionary experiences of (see visionary experiences)
wrathful activities of, 21, 39, 372–73
writing skills of, 408
Jamyang Khyentse Wangpo
  accomplishments of, ix–x, 278–88
  Bönter Twewang Drakpa and, 118
  Chokgyur Lingpa and, 280–82
  consorts and, 162
  distribution of belongings of,
    110–11
  Do Khyentse and, 275
  at Dzongsar Monastery, 55
  eight great practice lineages and,
    462
  emanations of, x, 23–24, 25, 29–30,
    32–38, 251, 252, 293–98
  on future lives, 293
  Gab Balma and, 120
  gyalpo Shugden and, 87–88
  Gyurme Tsewang Gyatso and, 300
  Jamgön Kongtrul and, 280–81,
    489–90
  Jigme Lingpa and, 275, 546n34
  JKCL as tulku of, ix, 23–25, 29–30,
    32–38, 278–88, 295, 302–5, 402–3,
    462
  JKCL's compilation of writings of,
    421–22
  JKCL's visions of, 377, 507, 510
  Kalachakra teachings and, 311, 486
  Katok Monastery and, 23
  Loter Wangpo and, 284–85
  Mipham Rinpoche and, 283,
    547n47
  Orgyen Lingpa and, 211, 212
  praises to, 278, 281, 286–88
  realization of, 358
  sacred hidden lands and, 173
  seat and bed of, ix, 30–32, 402–3
  secretary to, 67
  self-depiction as a wanderer,
    105–6
  teachings received by, 319–20
  treasure teachings of, 67, 280–83,
    512–13, 516, 546n46
  vast Dharma treasuries and, 280–86
  visionary experiences of, 466
  wish to build a second Samye, 417
Jamyang Loter Wangpo. See Loter
  Wangpo
Jataka, 423, 428
Jigme Gyalwe Nyugu, 117, 546n34
Jigme Lingpa, 50, 274, 275–76, 456,
  546n34
Jigme Tenpe Nyima. See Dodrupchen,
  Third, Jigme Tenpe Nyima

Kadam lineage, 470–73
Kagyü school, 411, 417, 478–84
Kalachakra Tantra, 277, 285, 486
Kalachakra teachings, 318–19, 486
  empowerments, 101–2, 311
  JKCL's experiences and, 327,
    486–88
  root tantra of, 457
Kaliyuga, 397–98
Kalon Tripa Samdhong Rinpoche,
  196–97
Kalzang Dorje, x, 29, 32, 33, 303, 415
Kama and Terma teachings, 283–84,
  285, 301, 309–10, 321, 380,
  462–64, 520
Kangra, JKCL's pilgrimage and,
  245–46
Kangyur, 133–34, 339–40, 371, 419,
  420, 423
Karma Chagme, 479, 483
Karma Kagyü, 479–80
Karma Pakshi, 481–82
Karmapa, Fifteenth, Khakhyab Dorje,
  38, 207–8, 497
  Khyentse tulkus and, 293, 294, 295,
    296
Karmapa, Seventh, Chödrak Gyatso,
  207

Karmapa, Sixteenth, Rangjung Rigpe
    Dorje, *206*, 479
  at Bodh Gaya, 242–43, *243*
  death of JKCL and, 439, 442, 455
  at Drakar Tashiding with JKCL, 347
  JKCL's visions and, 482, 504
  JKCL's visit to Tsurphu and, 205–8,
    347
Karmapa, Third, Gyalwang Rangjung
    Dorje, 482
Karmo Tak Tsang Retreat Center, 53,
    54, 80–81, 111, 483
Karse Kongtrul (Jamgön Palden
    Khyentse). *See* Gyalse Jamgön
    Choktrul (Karse Kongtrul)
Katok Dorje Den Monastery, 302, 309,
    462
Katok Getse Mahapandita, 39, 40,
    542n9
Katok Monastery, 299
  expulsion of women from, 39–40
  JKCL as regent of, 39–47, 415–16
  JKCL's arrival at, 23–25, 302–3
  JKCL's pledge to serve, 33–34
  JKCL's teaching at, 388
  Khyentse tulku for, 23–27, 32
  response to JKCL's marriage, 165
  shedra at, 316–17, 355–57, 415
Katok Öntrul, 45–46, 173
Katok Situ Chökyi Gyatso, 13, *24*, 59,
    91, 113, 121
  cameras and, 112
  death of, 38
  JKCL's devotion for, 377–78
  JKCL's pledge to serve monastery
    of, 33–34, 415–16
  JKCL's precepts and, 306–7,
    309–10
  as JKCL's teacher, 292–93, 315,
    316–17, 318, 321–23, 355, 463
  Khyentse tulkus and, x, 23–25,
    29–30, 32–34, 302–3
  Khyentse Wangpo and, 296
  Khyentse Wangpo's seat and bed
    and, ix, 31, 402–3
  red belt of, 72–73

tulku of, 416
Katok Situ Dorje Chang, 520
Kela Chokling, 38, 120
Khamje Shedra, 12
  administration of, 53–54, 228–30
  destruction of, 230
  first abbot of, 51–53, 418
  founding of, xiii–xiv, 49–54, 418
  Gelugpa lama's visit to, 118–19
  great Maitreya Hall at, 137–40, 418
  JKCL's pilgrimage and, 181–82
  teaching tradition at, 388, 418
Khamtrul Dongyü Nyima, 99–104,
    100, 437
Khandro Chenmo (Khandro Orgyen
    Tsomo), 207–8, 543n35
Khandro Tsering Chödrön, *8*, *9*, *78*, 79,
    142, *170*, *239*, *258*, 539
  as consort, xiii, 92, 101, 159, 162–64,
    169–70
  dzi stones and, 232–33
  first visit to Dzongsar, 159–60
  Gyagen Khyungtak and, 174–75
  JKCL's death and, 250
  memorial stupa for JKCL and,
    454–55
  offerings to holy places of, 456
  past incarnations and, 160, 168
  Sakya Gongma and, 134
  singing of, 103
  as source of stories, 7–8, 45–46
Khangmar Monastery, 424
Khangmar Rinchen, 124–25, 416,
    542n20
Khardo Khangsar Shabdrung, 444,
    448, 449
Khargo Angkhar Tulku, 349
Khen Lop Chö Sum, 161
Khenchen Jamyang Gyaltsen, 52, 418,
    552n164
Khenchen Kunzang Palden. *See*
    Khenpo Kunpal
Khenchen Lama Gyaltsen Özer,
    342–43
Khenchen Ngawang Samten Lodrö,
    326

Khenchen Shenphen Jampe Gocha
  (Khenpo Shenga), xiii–xiv, 51–53,
  52, 418
Khenchen Thubten Rigdzin Gyatso, xi,
  307, 314–15
Khenpo Apal, 340
Khenpo Appey, 64, 124–25, *125*
Khenpo Dosib Thubten, 254–55, 349
Khenpo Jorden, 39, 40, 165–66
Khenpo Kunga Wangchuk, 4, *12*
  Compendium of Sadhanas and,
  12–13, 136–37
  stories told by, 12–13, 135–40
Khenpo Kunpal (Khenchen Kunzang
  Palden), 39, 379
  as JKCL's teacher, 124, 309, 316–17,
  319, 356–57, 410
Khenpo Lekshe Jorden, 345
Khenpo Namzang, 113–14, 511
Khenpo Ngakchung, 121–22, *121*, 168
Khenpo Nüden, 122–24, 470
  response to JKCL's marriage,
  166–67
  retreat of, 123–24, 167
Khenpo Öntö Khyenrab, 52
Khenpo Pedam, 124, 125
Khenpo Pema Losal, 307
Khenpo Rinchen, 13, 118, 178
  Dagchen Rinpoche and, 216–17
  Dilgo Khyentse and, 256
Khenpo Tsultrim Nyima, 41, 416, 510
Khewang Lama Tashi Chöphel, 318,
  483
Khyen Trukma (Galing Khyentse),
  32–37
Khyenrab Singye, 115, 136–37, 182
Khyentse Labrang
  administration of, 53–54
  attendants of, 59–71
  JKCL's early years at, 55–73
  Khyentse tulkus and, 33, 36
  men of business of, 68–71
  messengers of, 71
  pollutions of hearth at, 148
  regular rituals performed at, 56–59
  stories from, 145–55

See also Dzongsar Monastery
Khyewo Rigdzin Chenpo, 341, 515
Khyungtrul Rinpoche, 382
King of Aspiration Prayers: Samant-
  abhadra's "Aspiration to Good
  Actions," The, 172–73, 434, 443,
  444, 445
King Trisong Deutsen, 140, 161, 210,
  546n34
  emanations of, 319, 399, 549n94,
  553n217
  JKCL as incarnation of, 27, 273–74
  Khyentse Wangpo and, 281, 302
  Manjushri and, 292
Könchok Tenzin, 339
Kunga Palden, 346
Kutsab Ngödrup Palbar, 181, 430, 434
Kyabgön Dagchen Ngawang Kunga
  Sonam, 340

Lakar family
  dzi stones of, 232–33
  JKCL's consorts and, 158–59, 163
Lama Dampa Sonam Gyaltsen, 272,
  476, 477, 545n21
Lama Dzola, 139
Lama Godi, 194–96, *195*
Lama Gönpo Tseten. *See* Gönpo
  Tseten
Lama Ngadak Chenpo, 469
Lama Ngawang Tenpa, 339–40
Lama Norbu, 349
Lama Tashi Chöphel, 294, 327–28,
  355, 422
Lamdre tradition
  compilation of texts of, 284–85
  JKCL's practice and teaching of,
  278, 311, 338, 473–74
  JKCL's visions related to, 474–78
Lamp for the Path to Enlightenment,
  334, 470
Langdro Könchok Jungne, 271
Lerab Lingpa, 282, 333, 334, 463,
  506–7, 516
Lhalung Thuksey, tulku of, 219–20
Lhasa, JKCL's visit to, 192–202, 388

Lhatsün Namkha Jigme, 231, 233, 258–59, 448, 505–6, 528
Lhodrak Kharchu, JKCL's visit to, 219–20
Lhodrakpa Namkha Gyaltsen, 248
Lion's Roar of Shrimaladevi Sutra, 387
Lithang Shokdruk Kyabgön, 118–19
Lobsang Tenzin Gyatso, 296–97
Longchenpa, 16, 116, 464
    JKCL's visions of, 379, 469, 498, 500, 505
    skull of, 220, 451
long-life ceremonies
    JKCL's response to, 433–35, 438
    performed for JKCL, 435–40
Long-Life Practice: A Garland of Vajras, 186
Longsal Nyingpo, 272–73, 299, 302
Lopön Sonam Zangpo, 15, *15*
Losar celebrations, 57–59, 425–26
Loter Wangpo, 121, 251, 440
    clay statue of, 112
    compilation of tantras and, 284–85
    as JKCL's teacher, 228, 318, 324–25, 326, 360, 388
    JKCL's vision of, 476–77
    Khyentse tulkus and, 32, 33, 34, 297
    as Khyentse Wangpo's heart-son, 324, 473
    leather hat of, 71
    prophecies about JKCL, 230–31
    stories about, 110–13
    students of, 113
Lotsawa Sherab Rinchen, 272
lotus of nonattachment, 275, 546n33
Luding Gyalse Jampal Chökyi Nyima, 337
Luminous Heart Essence, 148, 276, 510
Luminous Heart Essence of the Three Roots, 285, 519

Machik Labdrön, 484–85, 486
Magical Net, 269–70, 432, 467, 506
Magical Net of Manjushri, 38, 266–68, 478

Mahabodhi Temple, 239–40
Mahakala, 42–43, 68, 112, 133, 142, 419, 476
Mahamudra, 366, 382, 479, 480, 534
Mahapandita Smritijnana, 271, 495
Maitreya, 315
    statue at Khamje Shedra, 137–40, 230, 418
Mandala of the Eight Great Deities: The Subduer of Haughty Spirits, 469
mani mantras, practice of accumulating, 426–27
Manjushri, *262*, 268, 276, 292, 350, 511
    names of, 267, 545n11
    short biography of, 269–70
    statue at Dzongsar Monastery, 418–19
Maratika, 173
Markham Gyalse Tulku, 76
Marpa, 272, 479, 480–81, 543n40
meals and eating habits, 59, 63–64
medicine, 71–72, 427
memorial and cremation stupas, 236, 447–55
Milarepa (Mila Shepa Dorje), 272, 274, 481, 543n40
Mindrolling Monastery, JKCL's visit to, 203–4, 388
Mindrolling Vajrasattva, 84, 424, 444, 447, 449, 453
Minling Chung Rinpoche, 203–4, *203*, 333–34
Minling Khenchen, Eighth, 203–4, *203*, 205, 210
Minling Lochen, 17, 197, 355
Minling Terchen, 301, 309, 330, 469, 548n69
Minling Trichen Rinpoche, 333
Minyak Trulshik Rinpoche, 437, 439
Mipham Rinpoche, xiii, xiv, 285, 416
    accomplishments of, 283, 546n47
    debate over viewpoint of, 124–25
    Dilgo Khyentse and, 298
    dislike of cameras, 112
    JKCL's dream of, 493
    Katok shedra and, 316

Khenpo Kunpal and, 356
praise of JKCL, 463
praise of Khyentse Wangpo, 278, 286–87
wooden house near Dzongsar, 106–7
Mirror of the Heart of Vajrasattva, 441
Mount Wutai Shan, 269, 466
movement of the serpent, 449, 553n197
Muchen Könchok Gyaltsen, 272
Muksang Tulku Kunzang, 375–76

Nagarjuna, 306, 352–53, 414, 470
Namgyal Dorje, 242–43
Namkhai Nyingpo, 212
namtar tradition, xi–xii, xv, xxiii–xxv
physical appearance and, 16–17
Nangchen, JKCL's visit to, 184–88
Naropa, 480
Natsok Rangdrol, 360, 463
Neten Chokling, Second, Ngedön Drupe Dorje, 20, 38
Neten Chokling, Third, Pema Gyurme Gyatso, 3, 4, 6, 7, 73, 76–77, *100*, 120, 145, 167
ceremony for averting sorcery, 188–90
grave robbing and, 150–52
JKCL's death and, 443
JKCL's illness and, 157–58, 437, 438
JKCL's protection blessing of, 153–54
spiritual treasure and, 152–53
wealth vase and, 154
Neten Monastery
JKCL's benefitting activities for, 416–17
JKCL's visit to, 185–87
New Treasures of Chokling, 329, 445
Ngawang Jampal Rinchen, 496
Ngawang Palzang, 344
Ngor Monastery, 172, 475–76
Ngorchen Dorje Chang (Ngorchen Kunga Zangpo), 276, 338, 340, 475
Nonduality of Samsara and Nirvana, 478
nonreturner bodhisattva, 523

Nub Namkhai Nyingpo, 271, 277, 302
Nubchen Sangye Yeshe, 467, 468
Nyen Lotsawa, 381
Nyenchen Tanglha, 111, 214, 420, 513
Nyingma school
JKCL as holder of teachings of, 26, 462–67
JKCL's students from, 411–12
Kama and Terma teachings of, 283–84, 285, 309–10, 321, 462–64
Katok shedra and, 316
masters who visited JKCL, 91
treasure teachings of, 280
Nyoshul Khenpo, 168

Ocean of Accomplishment, 516
Ocean of Dharma That Combines All Teachings, 211, 300, 370, 518
offerings
butter lamp, 217, 426
for the dead, 404
JKCL's making of, 425–27
JKCL's parinirvana and, 445–46
made at holy places, 425
made to JKCL, 219, 414–15, 455–56
summer collection of, 414
Öntö Khenpo Khyenrab, 318–19, 500–1
Orgyen Lingpa, kudung of, 210–12
Orgyen Nyendrup
JKCL's visions and, 488–508
JKCL's visions related to, 554n236
Ornament of Clear Realization, 87
Ornament of the Mahayana Sutras, 288, 303, 313, 358

Padampa Sangye, 484–86, 511
Palpung Öngen, 97
Palpung Situ, Eleventh, Pema Wangchok Gyalpo, 91–99, *92*, 138, 515
death of, 96–99, 113, 348
final visit to Dzongsar, 92–93
as JKCL's teacher, 309, 347–48, 433, 479
Khyentse Wangpo and, 296
last illness of, 94–96
on long-life of JKCL, 525–26

Palyul Gyatrul Dongak Tenzin,
    283–84, 380, 464
Panchen Lobsang Chogyan, 308
Pangkhar Gönpo, 84–86
Path and Fruition: The Explanation for Assemblies and Private Disciples, 399
Path and Fruition: The Explanation for Private Disciples, 132, 278, 325, 360, 474, 477
Patrul Rinpoche, 104, 275, 309, 508
Pema Gyurme Gyatso, 272
Pema Gyurme Tekchok Tenzin, 335
Pema Ösel Dongak Lingpa, 485, 510, 511
Pema Shepa Wangchen Tenzin Chögyal, 336
Pema Tukje Wangchuk, 343
Pema Yangtse Monastery, 233–34
Pema Yeshe Dorje, 51, 275, 546n36
Pemakö, 173, 188, 501
Perfection of Wisdom Sutra in Eight Thousand Lines, 44–45, 88, 313–14, 385, 523
Perfection of Wisdom Sutra in One Hundred Thousand Lines, 420
Pewar Tulku, 4, 12, 63, 108, 120
    death of Palpung Situ and, 96–98
    in Lhasa, 202
Phakchok Dorje, 295, 302, 343
Phalha Drönyer Chenmo, 146, 198, 199, 201
pilgrimages
    Benpa Chakdor and, 221
    at Bodh Gaya, 239–44
    departure from Dzongsar, 181–82
    from Derge to Sikkim, 181–221, 430–32
    Dorje Drak Monastery and, 204–5, 504
    Drak Yerpa and, 191–92
    Drakmar Drinzang and, 210
    to holy places of India, 237–46, 431, 434
    at Kangra, 245–46
    kudung of Orgyen Lingpa and, 210–12

    Lhasa and, 192–202
    Lhodrak Kharchu and, 219–20
    Mindrolling Monastery and, 203–4
    Namkhai Nyingpo and, 212
    Nangchen and, 184–88
    offerings made during, 425
    purpose of, 369, 430
    Sakya Monastery and, 215–19
    Sangphu and, 202–3
    Sangye Lingpa's bones and, 213–14
    Sankasya, 244–45
    Tsang and, 220
    Tsurphu Monastery and, 205–9
    Yarlung Zorthang and, 210
Pönlop Loter Wangpo. *See* Loter Wangpo
posthumous teachings, 440, 552n191
Prajnarashmi (Sherab Özer), 461
pratimoksha vows, 306–8
Prayer to the Garland of Rebirths, 271, 274
Precious Treasury of Terma Teachings, 13, 29, 34, 46, 84, 102, 161, 252, 280, 285, 300, 378, 423, 424, 463, 501, 519, 536
Precious Words: Path and Fruition, 366, 417
preliminary practices, 359, 360
Pure Vision and Oral Transmission Guru Yoga, 485

Queen Mother of Sikkim, 231, 233, 437

Rabjampa Orgyen Chödrak, 17
Rakong Sotra, 11, *11*
Ratna Lingpa, 272, 344, 347
Ratri Tertön, 517
Ratrul Thubten Gyaltsen, 344
Rekhe (Sa-ngen), 19–20, 299
relics like mustard seeds, 451
Remati (Palden Lhamo), JKCL's vision of, 379
Removing Inauspicious Circumstances, 333
renunciation, 359, 403, 406

Restoration of Vows Ceremony for Auspiciousness, 444, 446, 449, 450, 453
retreat centers, 53, 54, 80–81, 277, 374, 417, 420–21, 474, 517
Reverberation of Sound, 470, 535
Rigdzin Tsewang Norbu, 334–35
Riksum Trulpa'i Tsukglhakhang Shedrup Dhargye Ling, 417
Rime movement
  JKCL's contributions to, xiii–xv, 350–52, 397–99, 488–89
  Khyentse Wangpo and, ix–x, 278–86
Rinchen Terdzö, 463–64, 546n46
ringsel (sacred relics), 451
rituals, importance of tradition in, 399, 401
Rongme Karmo Tak Tsang, 420–21
Rongzompa, 464
Root Tantra of Hevajra, 533

Sachen Kunga Nyingpo, 276, 474
sacred hidden lands, 171–76, 501–2, 517–18, 520
Sakya Gongma of Dolma Phodrang (Sakya Trizin), 215, *215*, 216, 340, 442
Sakya Gongma of Phuntsok Phodrang (Sakya Dagchen Rinpoche), 91, *127*, *129*, 524, 535
  eldest son's birthday celebration, 130–31
  empowerments JKCL bestowed on, 132–34
  first visit to Dzongsar, 126–30, 145–46
  JKCL's death and, 437, 438, 439–40, 441
  JKCL's visit to, 215–17
  sacred dance of, 131–32
  second visit to Dzongsar, 134
Sakya Lama, 223–25
Sakya Lotsawa Jampe Dorje, 272
Sakya Monastery
  JKCL's vision of, 25, 273
  JKCL's visit to, 215–19
  protectors of, 218–19

Sakya Pandita, 135, 219, 276, 315, 372, 474–75, 515
Sakya school
  JKCL's students from, 410–11
  JKCL's teaching and activities in tradition of, 399, 473–74
  JKCL's visions related to, 474–78
  masters who visited JKCL, 91
Sambhuti, 533
Samten Dorje Phagmo, 208
Samvarodaya Tantra, 445
Samye Monastery, 382, 417
Sangphu, JKCL's visit to, 202–3
Sangye Lingpa, bones of, 213–14
Sangye Nyenpa Rinpoche, 72, *89*, 98, 99, 349
Sankasya, JKCL's visit to, 244–45, 383–84
Saraha, 245, 515, 527
Secret Biography, 4–5, 523–28
Secret Practice of the Heart Essence of the Lotus-Born, 456
Secret Treasury of the Seven Great Transmissions, 280
Seven Heart Essences, 282
Seven Points of Mind Training, 325, 388, 432
Seven Transmissions, 462, 519, 520
Seven Treasuries, 407, 470
Shabdrung Rinpoche Tashi Gyatso, 325–26, 359
Shakya Shri, 295, 302, 385
Shalu Losal Tenkyong, 277
Shangpa Kagyü, 483–84
Shardzapa Tashi Gyaltsen, 118
Shavaripa, JKCL's vision of, 245, 484
Shaza Khamoche, 21
Shechen Gyaltsab Gyurme Pema Namgyal, 5, 13, 91
  death of, 38, 331, 378
  Dilgo Khyentse and, 251–52, 297
  dislike of cameras, 112
  as JKCL's teacher, 307, 309, 329–31, 332, 360, 410, 463
  JKCL's vision of, 499
  Khyentse Wangpo's bed and, 31–32

Shechen Gyaltsab Gyurme Pema Namgyal (cont.)
  long-life ceremony for, 330
  tulku of, 385
Shechen Kongtrul Rinpoche, 331, 493–94
Shechen Monastery
  Dilgo Khyentse and, 251
  JKCL's benefitting activities for, 331, 378, 416
Shechen Rabjam, 46, 59, 66, 72, *253*
  at Dzongsar Monastery, 91, 141
  imprisonment of, 224
  JKCL's blunt knife and, 252–54
  JKCL's consort and, 161
  Rinchen Terdzö and, 463–64
  teachings JKCL received from, 331–32
Shedrup, 88–89, 161, 254
Shije tradition, 484–86
Sikkim, JKCL in, 227–36, 247–50, 432–40
Siliguri train station, feast offering at, 237–39
Simhamukha, 137, 515–16
Six Yogas of Niguma, 366
Sogyal Tulku, *241*, 435
Solpön Jamtra, 59–62
spiritual friend, relying on, 313–14
spiritual names, importance of, 544n11
spontaneous accomplishment, 370, 550n133
stage of no-more-learning, 523
Stupa of Shakyamuni That Liberates When Remembered, 452, 453, 454
Sukhavati buddhafield, 495
summer camping, 75–81
suppression rituals, 107–9, 380–81
at Sankasya, 244–45, 383–84
Sutra Completely Dear to Monks, 306
Sutra of Golden Light, 433
Sutra of Immaculate Space, 446
Sutra of the Abundant Array of Ornaments, 447
Sutra of the Torch of the Triple Gem, 268
Sutra Requested by the Noble Narayana, 313
Sutra which Precisely Explains Suchness, 358

Tai Situ Choktrul Rinpoche, 455
Tai Situ Orgyen Chökyi Gyatso. *See* Katok Situ Chökyi Gyatso
Tantra of the Gathering of Precious Jewels, 446
Tantra on Recognizing the Qualities of the Guru, 457
tantra teachings
  compilation of, 284–85
  JKCL's entering mandala of, 309–12
  taught by JKCL, 389–96, 463–64
  Vajrapani and, 271
Tara statues
  at Dzongsar Monastery, 72, 159
  JKCL's vision of, 495
  at Nangchen, 375
Tarthang Tulku, *12*, 13, 120
Tashi Chime Drupe Gatsel, 310, 419–20, 518, 537
Tashi Namgyal, 8, 9, *10*, *14*, 57, 71, 113–14, 142, 503
  at Drakmar Drinzang, 210
  as JKCL's attendant, 62–63
  JKCL's porcelain cup and, 146
  Khenpo Nüden and, 123–24
  in Lhasa, 192
  at Mindrolling Monastery, 204
  return to Kham, 228–30
Tashi Thongmon, 140
Tashi Tsering, 142–43
Tashiding (Sikkim)
  Dilgo Khyentse's vision at, 258–59
  JKCL's stupa at, 236, *258*, 448–49, 454
  JKCL's visit to, 347, 431, 454, 504
Tengyur, 419, 423
Tenphel, 338–39
Tenzin Phuntsok, 184
Terchen Rolpe Dorje, 348–49
Tersey Chime, 21, 70

Tertön Drime Pema Lingpa, 282,
    341–43, 463, 515, 516
Tertön Sogyal, 104–6, *105*
Tertön Tsewang Drakpa, 117–18
Tertön Tulku Dönkho, 517
thangkas, 423–24
Thangtong Gyalpo, 377, 484, 485, 507
Tharpatse Labrang, 110–11
thermos flasks, 79–80
Three Categories of Dzogchen, 248, 282
three precepts
    all-accomplishing wisdom and,
        527–28
    JKCL's training in, 306–12
Three Precepts, 306, 311, 407, 462
Three Red Deities, 133
*Three Roots Practice for Accomplishing
    the Life-Force of the Vidyadharas*,
    431, 450
Traleg Choktrul, 349
transference of consciousness, 396, 481
treasure (terma) teachings
    authentication of, 546n46
    of Chokgyur Lingpa, 281–82
    of deities of Kagye, 310
    of Dilgo Khyentse, 350, 518, 519
    JKCL and, 292–93, 463, 509–21
    Khyentse Wangpo's, x, 67, 280–83,
        512–13, 516
    relics and, 513
    treasure vases, 427, 448
Treasury of Encyclopedic Knowledge, 378
Treasury of Precious Instructions, 132, 251,
    280–81, 360, 389, 399, 420, 484
Treasury of Precious Qualities, 407
Treatise on the Sublime Continuum,
    287, 298
Trepa Tsang, 46–47, 72, 142–43
Trijang Lobsang Yeshe, 196–97
Tromge Bu Truk Truk, 183
Trulshik Ngawang Chökyi Lodrö,
    197–99, *198*
    Durtrö Lhamo thangka and,
        200–201
Trulshik Pawo Dorje, 448, 449, 515
Tsadra Rinchen Drak, 24, 113–15, 541n4

Tsang, JKCL's visit to, 220
Tsarchen Losal Gyatso, 278, 476, 494
Tsegyal Drak, 186, 187, 188
Tsejor, 39–40, 43
    as JKCL's attendant, 38, 55
    Loter Wangpo and, 110–12
    quarrel with Chakdzö, 146–48
    Tertön Ösel Dorje and, 109–10
    visit to Neten Monastery and,
        185–87
Tselu (Tsering Wangmo), *78*, 79, 501
    as consort, 159, 167–69, *168*, 238–39
    dzi stones and, 232
    past incarnations and, 168
    at Siliguri train station, 237, 238
Tsering Tashi, 67
Tsering Wangmo. *See* Tselu
Tseringma, 148, 373, 379, 550n136
Tsewang Dudul, 34, 51
Tsewang Paldrön, 3, *4*
Tsewang Paljor. *See* Chakdzö Tsewang
    Paljor
Tso Ziltrom, sacred hidden land of,
    171–73
tsok offerings, 366, 371, 382, 404, 425
    at Dzongsar Monastery, 56–57, 103
    on New Year's, 425–26
    at Pema Shelphuk, 431, 518
    at Siliguri train station, 237–39
Tsoknyi Monastery, 185
Tsongkhapa, xiv, 470, 472, 554n225
Tsultrim Tso, 301
Tsurphu Monastery, JKCL's visit to,
    205–9, 347
Tulku Urgyen, 205–9, *209*
*Turning Back the Summons of the
    Dakinis*, 435, 437, 505, 506, 507
Twenty-Fifth King of Shambhala, 277
Two Vimalas, 447, 448, 449, 453, 454

Uchen Phurbu Tsering, 138
Unstained Light, 449, 450, 454

Vairochana Temple, 498
Vajrabhairava, 141, 382
Vajrakilaya of Nyak Lotsawa, 103

Vajrakilaya practice, 131, 168–69, 384, 424
Vajrakumara, 244, 384, 507
Vajrapani, 221, 271, 276, 292
Vajrapani Holding a Vajra Cudgel, 157, 507
Vasubandhu, 492–93
Verse Summary of the Prajnaparamita Sutra, 292, 304–5, 308, 313, 314, 352, 369
Vidyadhara Tsewang Drakpa, 272
Vimalakirti the Licchavi, 271, 545n18
Vimalamitra, xii, 122, 273, 293, 466, 470
Vinaya precepts, 306–8, 389, 475
visionary experiences, of JKCL
　related to Kadam lineage, 470–73
　related to Kagyü lineage, 480–83, 484
　related to Lamdre tradition, 474–78
　related to Nyingma lineage, 464–69
　related to Orgyenpa, 488–508
　related to Shije and Chö traditions, 485–86
　of Shavaripa, 245
　treasure teachings and, 510–21
　various accounts of, 377–84
　vision from a previous life, 25, 273

Wara Monastery, 136, 140
wealth protection vases, 154
wisdom blessing, 472, 554n228

wisdom consort, 381–82, 523–24, 525, 532–35
Words of My Perfect Teacher, The, 508
wrathful activity, 547n63
Wrathful Dark Blue Guru, 502
Wrathful Lone Hero, 534–35
Wrathful Turquoise Lekden, JKCL's vision of, 380
Wrathful Vaishravana Riding a Blue Horse, 372
Wrathful Vijaya, 383

Yamantaka, 141, 342, 503
Yamantaka, Destroyer of Enemies, 94, 188, 438
Yamantaka: Lord of Life, 103
Yang-gön Phakchok, 190–91, 543n34
Yarchen Kyasu, 185
Yarlung Zorthang, JKCL's visit to, 210
Yegyal Namkha Dzö, 186, 187
Yenchokma, 224
Yidlhung Lhari Ga, 87–88
Yogini Tantra of Conduct, 533–34
Yongdzin Chöying Rangdrol, 213
Yönru, king of, 145, 177–80
Yudrön, 103, *104*
Yudrön (queen of Nangchen), 164, 185, 219, 375
Yutok Yönten Gönpo, 272

Zimwog Tulku, 91